WITHDRAWN
FROM
FORT HAYS STATE COLLEGE
LIBRARY COLLECTION

CHILD DEVELOPMENT

CHILD DEVELOPMENT

Concepts, Issues, and Readings

RICHARD A. HANSON

California State University, Chico

REBECCA REYNOLDS

WEST PUBLISHING COMPANY
St. Paul   New York   Los Angeles   San Francisco

A *Study Guide* has been developed to assist you in mastering concepts presented in this text. The *Study Guide* reinforces the learning of these concepts by presenting them in condensed and concise form. In addition, there are materials for self-study and self-evaluation. Answers to self-evaluation questions are included. This *Study Guide* is available from your local bookstore under the title, *Study Guide to Accompany Hanson and Reynolds' Child Development: Concepts, Issues, and Readings* prepared by Donalene M. Andreotti.

Acknowledgments

For permission to reproduce copyrighted material the authors are indebted to:

25, Copyright © 1978 Parents' Magazine Enterprises, Inc. Reprinted with permission of *Parents* magazine; **55,** Reprinted by permission from *Young Children,* vol. 31, no. 2 (January 1976), pp. 93–96. Copyright © 1976, National Association for the Education of Young Children, 1834 Connecticut Avenue, N.W., Washington, DC 20009; **82,** Reprinted with permission *Family Health* magazine October 1977 ©. All rights reserved; **112,** This article originally appeared in *Family Health* magazine as "The Nursery's Two Cruelest Words: Spina Bifida" in September 1978. John Grossmann, a senior writer with Feature Group, free-lances medical articles to many national publications. His article is reprinted by permission of the author; **136,** Reprinted from *Family and Community Health* 1:3, M. C. Doyle with the permission of Aspen Systems Corp., Germantown, MD; **169,** Copyright © 1977 Parents' Magazine Enterprises, Inc. Reprinted with permission of *Parents* magazine; **195** Reprinted by permission from *Young Children,* vol. 32, no. 2 (January 1977), pp. 71–81. Copyright © 1977, National Association for the Education of Young Children, 1834 Connecticut Avenue, N.W., Washington, DC 20009; **228,** Reprinted by permission from *Young Children,* vol. 33, no. 5 (July 1978), pp. 14–23. Copyright © 1978, National Association for the Education of Young Children, 1834 Connecticut Avenue, N.W., Washington, DC 20009; **262,** Copyright © 1978 Parents' Magazine Enterprises, Inc. Reprinted by permission of *Parents* magazine; **291** Copyright © 1978 Parents' Magazine Enterprises, Inc. Reprinted with the permission of *Parents* magazine; **341,** Copyrighted 1979 by the National Council on Family Relations. Reprinted by permission; **367,** Copyright © 1978 *Human Behavior* Magazine. Reprinted by permission; **390,** Reprinted by permission from *Young Children,* vol. 34, no. 2, (January 1979), pp. 37–45. Copy-

(Continued on facing page)

Copyright © 1980 by WEST PUBLISHING CO.
50 West Kellogg Boulevard
P.O. Box 3526
St. Paul, Minnesota 55165

All rights reserved

Printed in the United States of America

Library of Congress Cataloging in Publication Data

Hanson, Richard A
   Child development.

  Bibliography: p.
  Includes index.
  1. Child development. I. Reynolds, Rebecca, joint author. II. Title.
RJ131.H275   612'.65   79-26792
ISBN 0-8299-0336-4

right © 1979, National Association for the Education of Young Children, 1834 Connecticut Avenue, N.W., Washington, DC 20009; **419,** Reprinted with permission *Family Health* Magazine February 1978 ©. All rights reserved; **440,** From *A Child's Journey* by Julius Segal and Herbert Yahraes, copyright 1978 by McGraw-Hill Book Company. Reprinted by permission of the McGraw-Hill Book Company; **461,** Reprinted from *Today's Education,* vol. 68 (April-May 1979), pp. 62–65 with the permission of *Today's Education* and the author, Dr. Harold G. Shane; **489,** Reprinted by permission from *Young Children*, vol. 33, no. 4 (May 1978), pp. 25–32. Copyright © 1978, National Association for the Education of Young Children, 1834 Connecticut Avenue, N.W., Washington, DC 20009; **39,** Reproduced from *Childhood and Society*, 2nd Edition, Revised, by Erik Erikson, by permission of W. W. Norton & Company, Inc. Copyright 1950, © 1963 by W. W. Norton & Company, Inc.; **102,** Reproduced by permission of the International Anesthesia Research Society; **157,** Mary M. Shirley, *The First Two Years,* Vol. II, University of Minnesota Press, Minneapolis. Copyright 1933 by the University of Minnesota; **159,** Reproduced by permission of Dr. Nathan J. Smith, M.D.; **246,** Plate XVI "Crayon and Writing Behavior" from *The First Five Years of Life* by Arnold Gesell, M.D. et al. Copyright 1940 by Arnold Gesell. Reprinted by permission of Harper & Row, Publishers, Inc.; **304,** From *Good Little, Bad Little Girl* by Esther Wilkin. Copyright © 1965 by Western Publishing Company, Inc. Used by permission of the publisher; **327,** Adapted from Breland, H.M. "Birth Order, Family Configuration, and Verbal Achievement," *Psychological Bulletin*, 1974, 45, 1011–1119. Copyright 1974 by the American Psychological Association. Reprinted by permission; **358,** Copyright © 1968 by Newsweek, Inc. All rights reserved. Reprinted by permission; **337,** "The Development of Children's Orientations Toward a Moral Order I. Sequence in the Development of Moral Thought" by Lawrence Kohlberg. Reproduced from *Vita Humana*, 1963, *6*, 13–14 by permission of S. Karger AG, Basel; **404,** From *Developmental Tasks and Education*, third edition by Robert J. Havighurst. Copyright © 1972 by Longman, Inc. Reprinted with permission; **424,** J. P. Guilford, "Three Faces of Intellect," *American Psychologist* 1959, *14*, 469–479. Copyright 1959 by the American Psychological Association. Reprinted by permission; **433,** Reprinted by permission of the author from *Development and Adolescence*. Monterey, Calif.: Brooks/Cole, 1973; **450,** R. H. Monge, "Developmental Trends and Factors in Adolescents' Self Concept," *Developmental Psychology*, 1973, *8*, 382–383. Copyright 1973 by the American Psychological Association. Reprinted by permission; **458,** Reproduced by permission; **471,** Reuben Hill, "Social Stresses on the Family," *Social Casework*, 1958, *39*, 146. Reprinted by permission of the Family Service Association of America; **476,** Hetherington, E. M., Cox, M., and Cox, R. Beyond father absence: "Conceptualization of the Effects of Divorce." Paper presented at the Society for Research in Child Development in Denver, Colorado in 1975; **478,** Reprinted by permission of the authors; **407,** "Physical Growth" by J. M. Tanner. From P. H. Mussen, ed., *Carmichael's Manual of Child Psychology*, vol. I, p. 83. Copyright © 1970 by John Wiley, Inc. Reprinted by permission of John Wiley, Inc.

Cover photograph: *Baby at Play* (1876) by Thomas Eakins. Private Collection.

Preface

Children represent both the celebration of all that is joyous in our world, and the greatest single challenge for parents, teachers, students, and others who work with children. This book, which grown out of the attempt to understand this paradox, represents one small step in the quest for understanding.

One of the primary emphases of this book is looking at children in appropriate contexts. Children exist within a family network, and cannot be studied without paying close attention to this most basic of all social support networks. Children also exist within a society, which directly impinges upon the activities and potential of every child within its boundaries. Children are also part of a historical context—a legacy so rich and important that the study of child development is not complete without its inclusion. Because children are mainly chronological-developmental beings, this book is also largely developmental in approach. Within the developmental framework, however, the instructor and student will find considerable latitude for a topical investigation of children.

We have included features in this book that will not only enhance the student's breadth of exposure, but will also keep the reader interested in the study of children. For example, specific issues are highlighted within each chapter, including such topics as the baby-tender of B. F. Skinner, test-tube babies, the impact of television on sex-role development, the "hurried child," and many other interesting subjects. Each chapter also has a specific reading attached to it. These readings come from magazines, professional journals, and scholarly books related to the field of child development. Some readings are academically oriented, others more practical. Each reading discusses a very different aspect of the study of children, ranging from our society's attitudes toward children to the ways children react to the death of a parent. Taken together, these readings add a dimension that is slightly different from the standard text material. Thought questions are included at the end of each chapter, along with a small number of suggested readings.

Trying to come up with acknowledgments and thanks for a work like this is a major task. There are many friends and colleagues who are instrumental in the preparation of a book. In this regard, special thanks go to Dr. Jim Roberts, who in his infinite wisdom decided to hire an aspiring young teacher. We also wish to acknowledge and thank Donalene Andreotti of El Camino College, Lois Klezmer of Miami Dade Community College South, Stephen Salzman of Los Angeles Valley College, Phyllis Seabolt of Western Michigan University, Irma Galejs of Iowa State University, Gaston Walker of Tarrant County Junior College South, Cecile Mielenz of Northwestern State University, and Sherrill Richarz of Washington State University for their invaluable academic assistance.

We would like to thank the members of the editorial and production departments at West Publishing Company for the support and guidance that helped bring this project to fruition.

To the hundreds of college students who have been fundamental in determining the direction of this book, we extend a special thanks.

Contents

UNIT I   FOUNDATIONS OF CHILD DEVELOPMENT   1

Chapter 1   The Study of Children: Evolution of a Culture   3
Issue: The Economic Value of Children in America   13
Reading: The War Against Kids
John von Hartz   25

2   Theories of Development: Physiological Beginnings   31
Issue: Behaviorism Applied: The Case of the Baby Tender   44
Reading: Piaget in Action
Millie Almy   55

3   Genetics, Heredity, and Prenatal Development   59
Issue: Test Tube Babies   78
Reading: Healing Babies Before They're Born
Edwin Kiester, Jr.   82

4   Birthing and Neonatal Development   89
Issue: The Cesarean Delivery   107
Reading: The Nursery's Two Cruelest Words: Spina Bifida
John Grossmann   112

5   Social Implications   119
Issue: Men in the Delivery Room   122
Reading: Approaches to Childbirth
Mary C. Doyle   136

UNIT II INFANT DEVELOPMENT 143

6 Infancy: Physiological Development 145
   Issue: Infant Physical Development: The Use of Norms 157
   Reading: What Young Children Need Most In a Changing Society
      David Elkind 169

7 Infancy: Perceptive Skills and Learning 175
   Issue: Research with Young Children 183
   Reading: Stimulation in the First Year of Life? A Perspective on Infant Development
      Rose M. Bromwich 195

8 Infancy: Personality and Temperament 207
   Issue: The Infant and the Father 214
   Reading: Infant Day Care: Toward a More Human Environment
      Arminta Lee Jacobson 228

UNIT III THE YOUNG CHILD 235

9 The Young Child: Motor Abilities and Physical Development 237
   Issue: Hyperactivity in America 253
   Reading: Early Warning: Signs of Childhood Disease
      Peter Stoler 262

10 The Young Child: Cognition and Language Development 267
   Issue: I.Q.: A Valid Social Measure? 282
   Reading: Smart Kids Have Problems Too
      Gene Maeroff 291

11 The Young Child: Socialization and Early Education 297
   Issue: The Hidden Persuader: Television and Sex-Role Development 307

Contents

   Reading: Prosocial Television and Children's Behavior
       Paul Mussen and Nancy Eisenberg-Berg 318

 12 The Young Child: Families and Their Impact 323
   Issue: The Depletion of the Child's Family Resources 335
   Reading: Parents' Discipline of Children in Public Places
       Bruce W. Brown 341

UNIT IV THE MIDDLE YEARS 347

 13 Middle Childhood: Issues in Cognition 349
   Issue: Busing School Children to Achieve Racial Integration 364
   Reading: A Sense of Hope by Erika Duncan 367

 14 Middle Childhood: Games and Social Development 375
   Issue: The Hurried Child 383
   Reading: Old Games for Young Children: A Link to Our Heritage
       Ruth F. Bogdanoff and Elaine T. Dolch 390

UNIT V ADOLESCENCE 399

 15 Adolescence: A Period of Transitions 401
   Issue: The Secular Trend 409
   Reading: Epidemic: Teenage Pregnancy
       John C. Kelly 419

 16 Adolescence: Values and Egocentrism 423
   Issue: Adolescents and the Schools: A Crossroad 437
   Reading: Children Who Will Not Break
       Julius Segal and Herbert Yahraes 440

17 Adolescence: Social Realities 445
  Issue: Juvenile Delinquency 455
  Reading: Forecast for the 80's
     Harold G. Shane 461

UNIT VI   NEW DIRECTIONS   467

18 Children and Stress: A Contemporary Analysis 469
  Issue: Parents and Crisis: A Help or Hindrance? 485
  Reading: Helping Children Cope with Death
     Erna Furman 489

Epilogue   Children and the Future   497

Glossary   501

References   513

Index   533

UNIT I
FOUNDATIONS OF CHILD DEVELOPMENT

Courtesy of the National Gallery of Art, Washington, D.C.
Gift of Edgar William and Bernice Chrysler Garbisch.

The Sargeant Family, by an unknown artist.

1

The Study of Children: Evolution of a Culture

The study of children and childhood is an exciting one, combining biology, psychology, sociology, and anthropology. We approach the study of children from several distinct, though related, aspects: holistic development; idiosyncratic development; social-psychological development and psychobiological development.

HOLISTIC DEVELOPMENT

The term *holistic* implies a totality or wholeness: all of the organism. In much of the literature in child development there is a tendency to "slice up" the child into parts and to intensively study those respective parts. For example, those studying intellectual development find the things in the child's life that appear to be intellectual in nature, discover their development course, experiment with this development, and then flood the world with the information.

This may be very appropriate for some fields of study. It may allow us to feel like we have opened a window into the world of the unknown. However, through this piecemeal approach, we often lose the essence of the *contextual development* of children. Intellectual development does not stand separate from the whole child. It's quite possible that intellectual development may be a function of the child's temperament or perhaps his emotional feelings at the time; it is not just a separate dimension of the child's existence.

Children are very complex. The intellectual, social, emotional, and temperamental dimensions are interdependent; they interact with each other, they greatly influence the development of each other, and they develop their qualitative and quantitative aspects at different rates.

Context understanding: looking at children in their environment

Foundations of Child Development

How do you tell twins apart?
PHOTO BY TERRI WINTER.

In order to capture the essence of child development we need to remember this *reciprocal interaction* of the aspects of development, and to remember that each of these dimensions develops within the context of the *whole* child.

IDIOSYNCRATIC DEVELOPMENT

Nonexistent average:
there is no average age for many developmental stages because children vary so greatly

An idiosyncrasy is a behavior peculiar to the individual. By idiosyncratic development we mean that despite the fact that children develop basically the same, at the same rate and in the same sequence, the development of individual children can be and is different.

Some of the concerns of modern parents include questions like "Is my child developing normally?" "Will he walk on time?" "Will he talk on time?" and so on. Walking is a significant example. Many developmental charts indicate that the average time of walking is 11 months of age. This is a "nonexistent average" (Helms and Turner, 1975). The average age for walking is a misleading figure, because there is so much individual variation. Some children walk at 9 months, others at 14 months.

Another example of this is the appearance of the first teeth in the child's mouth. Parents agonize about when the first tooth is going to appear. In truth, the teeth will appear when they are ready, and not before. The timing of this appearance is different for each child.

Both of these examples point to the *idiosyncratic* nature of child development. Despite the fact that there are developmental norms for nearly every occurrence, most children will arrive at these developmental milestones at their own pace, and in their own time. If parents were somehow convinced of this fact, much of the early concern, particularly with the first child, would be lessened.

SOCIAL-PSYCHOLOGICAL MATRIX

There is a *synergistic* interaction between the social environment of the family and the psychological realities of each individual within the family. This combination produces a unique environmental network that qualitatively affects interactions and the learning of behavior. Handel (1972) described this phenomenon as the "psychosocial interior of the family."

In the *nature-nurture* argument of the day, this is the nurture side. We become what we are taught and what we are exposed to. A large part of child development has to do with imitative learning: observation of the behaviors of a "model," imitation of that behavior, and an internalization of that modeled behavior.

Nature-nurture: the controversy over biological determination vs. environmental influences

PSYCHO-BIOLOGICAL DEVELOPMENT

Psychobiological development represents the nature side of the nature-nurture argument. The nurture argument has been a very strong one during the last few years. The psychobiological argument, however, is making a comeback of sorts. Briefly, this philosophy states that much of the behavior that we had assumed as being learned, was in fact, more a result of genetic influences and some sort of biological plan for humans. This argument has been reinforced by recent research that states, for example, that some basic aspects of temperament and personality may be a function of genetics and biology, with socialization coming in later to either enhance or detract from this biological reality.

One final conceptual idea has to do with the course of a child's development. If development proceeds similarly for all children in a smooth, orderly fashion, it is said to be *continuous*. If we assume, however, that development actually consists of a series of significant "transitions" that are all different from each other, then we are assuming that development is discontinuous.

An example of a continuous theory is that proposed by Arnold Gesell: all children develop in a similar fashion, and advanced development is based on acquired experience. Discontinuous development is exemplified by the fact that some behaviors occur in an early form and then disappear: walking, object concepts, etc. (Bower, 1974a).

These factors interact in a dynamic fashion to produce the children we observe. To deny any of these dimensions is to take an unnecessarily narrow view of the world of the child.

THE CULTURE OF CHILDHOOD

Culture is learned through the process of socialization. The teachers in this process may be adults; they may be peers and/or siblings; they may even be television sets.

The culture of childhood is shared as children develop artifacts of their culture. This culture is transmitted through the games, the humor, and the activities of childhood. It may be transmitted through the hierarchy of a childhood group or gang, or through slang phrases. Children's games and language become a vehicle for the translation of the child's reality to the group situation. Within this setting, a great range of emotional and behavioral variation exists among children; in fact, children can and do thrive under conditions our culture would label inappropriate for humans in general (Goodman, 1970). Children share this process of development with each other and sometimes with significant adults. A culture of childhood may become so tight, so intact, that the participants may develop communication mechanisms and behavioral patterns that only they understand. Certain jokes, for example, are highly entertaining to children of a certain age for generation after generation. The jokes may be meaningless to smaller children or to adults.

Phenomena like these suggest that our understanding of children has been incomplete. We often do not understand that childhood is actually a culture, or subculture. Culture is defined as "... a set of ready made definitions of the situation which each participant retailors in his own idiomatic way" (Kluckhohn and Kelly, 1945, p. 91). There is a culture of childhood, which like all culture, is learned, shared, and transmitted.

Goodman (1970) has also suggested two basic misconceptions concerning the study of children. She is not convinced that age-stage progressions in child development are universal. For example, the American assumption that adolescence is a period of great stress and strain to all involved is not universal. In fact, adolescence may be quite the opposite, depending upon the cultural perspective. The "underestimation" phenomenon is the second major misconception. Goodman suggests that adults have great difficulty appreciating the quality of a child's perceptive abilities, cognitive

Underestimation phenomenon: tendency of adults to not fully appreciate children's abilities

abilities, and social understanding; we underestimate the abilities of children.

THE HISTORICAL PERSPECTIVE OF CHILDHOOD

In order to put the development of the child into the appropriate perspective, it is essential to understand the role of the child throughout the course of history.

Competency, both as an individual and as a participating member of society, has long been a very important factor. In earlier days, before industrialization, individual competency was a necessity; each person had to make a contribution to the maintenance of the society, or that person was a liability, a burden. In many preliterate cultures, adults were the able-bodied and competent members of society. They contributed to the maintenance of the society; children could not, and were therefore potential liabilities.

> Abortion and infanticide protected the society, unless its situation with respect to neighbors was such that war and pestilence kept down the numbers and made children valuable for war. Children add to the weight of the struggle for existence of their parents (Sumner, 1960, p. 308).

This quote exemplifies the need for competency in these societies, and points to the precarious position of children. It also points to the justification employed for these adult behaviors. Children and adults needed to be productive members of the society; if they were deemed to be unproductive, their position in the culture was a precarious one.

Some of the more "civilized" cultures also had interesting philosophies toward children and families. Plato felt that men over 55 and women over 40 should not have children; all offspring of such people should be taken care of by either abortion or infanticide (*The Republic*, V, 9). Aristotle also felt that imperfect children should be put to death. He advised that the numbers of children should be limited, and that if the set number of children were exceeded, abortion and similar life-ending techniques should be employed (*Politics*, VII, 16). These statements are probably reflective of the values and attitudes of a sizable segment of those populations. Even in an enlightened society such as Greece, these techniques were advocated by leading citizens.

The Jews of the early and mid-Roman times (approximately 100 B.C. to A.D. 1000) felt that abortion and infanticide were absolutely

Infanticide: practice of killing newborns or infants in some cultures

unacceptable. But examples of infanticide dot the history books. Early Australians practiced infanticide with regularity. In fact there was an early rule that a woman could not carry two children; if she had one child who could not keep up with the moving around and then had another, the younger child would be killed. Twins were also a real problem in early Australia, because of the same issue, and one or both of them were usually killed. Children of mixed racial heritage were subject to great cruelty and maltreatment, often resulting in death (Ratzel, *Völkerkunde,* II, 59, in Bremner, 1970).

In other parts of the world, sickly and "imperfect" children were often killed because they would require great care; sometimes firstborn children were killed because they were thought to be imperfect and not worth preserving. In some nomadic, subsistence-level cultures, after a child was killed, the mother proceeded to eat the remains so that she might recover the strength given to that child (Smyth, *Victoria,* I, 51; *Novara-Reise,* I, 32, in Bremner, 1970). The maximum number of children allowed in many of the cultures, particularly vulnerable ones, was four (Dawson, *West Victoria,* 39, in Bremner, 1970).

Obviously, children have not always occupied a positive place in society. If they were not productive, they were liabilities. The society did not have time to deal with anything unrelated or detrimental to the subsistence of the society. As McNall summarizes:

> The history of children and their play indicates that childhood itself is a variable concept. Children were expected to become non-children sooner in past stages of western history. And we know that the way in which other societies define the stages between childhood and adulthood is different from our own (McNall, 1968, p. 145).

And as Phillipe Aries, who wrote *Centuries of Childhood,* said:

> In medieval societies the idea of childhood did not exist. But the idea of childhood is not to be confused with affection for children (Aries, 1962, p. 128).

Children were not necessarily unloved. In fact, they probably were loved as we love children. It does appear, however, that environmental circumstances and other factors dictated some rather harsh procedures surrounding the arrival of children.

This is true for America as well. Children in this country have undergone large changes in status since the early days of this country, perhaps as massive as the evolution of childhood itself.

The Study of Children

Children in Colonial America

Many people think of the American nation as embodying the highest traditions of fairness and democracy. People within the United States have all the necessary freedoms for optimum development. We would expect that American children have also had an equally fertile environment for development.

In colonial America there was common agreement that the authority of the father was the most important factor in assuring the adequate development of children and the effective functioning of the family. The male had power over the female in most instances, and unquestioned obedience was expected of all family members. Many writers of the time equated the power of fathers to the power of kings—an interesting analogy, considering the early American patriots' lack of fondness for the English monarch!

The family performed a significant educational function for the children. Schools did exist in the colonial days but were definitely weaker in power than the family. This educational function involved teaching the basic skills of the time (which consisted of reading and enough writing skills to sign one's own name).

Two of the prevalent themes of child development during colonial times were *severity* (extremes of punishment and absoluteness of the punishment) and *absolute respect* for older people. The enforcement of this respect often bordered on repression. Children had their role assigned to them and absolute compliance was expected. The old adage "it is better to be seen than to be heard" was routinely adhered to.

Disobedience to parents brought severe punishment. For example, in the colonial days if a person 16 years of age and of "sufficient understanding" were to swear at or talk back to a parent, the penalty was death (Bremner, 1970). This rule was not absolute because an assessment was made of the parents' negligence; perhaps the parents had not trained the child adequately. If this were the case, allowances were made (*Massachusetts Records*, III, 1854; as cited in Bremner).

Families had distinct responsibilities to society. For example, in Massachusetts in the 1640s, parents were required to see that their children and other dependents were taught reading and a trade. There were legal officials in Massachusetts charged with the inspection of families to make sure that these responsibilities were being carried out (Bremner, 1970). Parents were brought before the proper authorities if they were found to be raising their children incorrectly.

The philosophy of rearing New England children during the colonial days is shown by the following quote from John Cotton:

QUESTION: What is the fifth commandment?
ANSWER: Honor thy father and thy mother that the days may be long on the land which the Lord thy God giveth thee.
QUESTION: Who are here meant by father and mother?
ANSWER: All our superiors whether in family, church, school or commonwealth.
QUESTION: What is the honor due to them?
ANSWER: Reverence, obedience, and when I am able recompense.
(John Cotton, *Spiritual Milk for Babes in Either England. Drawn out of the Breath of Both Testaments for Their Souls' Nourishment.* Cambridge, Mass., 1656, p. 4).

A generation gap may have existed, even in the colonial days.

I find the greatest trouble and grief about the rising generation. Young people are little stirred here; but they strengthen one another in evil by example and by counsel.

The young brood doth much aflict me. Even the children of the Godful make woeful proof (Ezekiel Rogers, talking to a minister of Charlestown, Mass., 1657 in Cotton Mather, *Magnalia Christi Americana*, London, 1702, III, 103–104).

Apparently, the people in the colonial times were not always sure of the fiber of the young people who were about to inherit the world that they built.

These examples also point to another dominating influence on children: religion. The authority of the father, the severity of punishment, the strictness and the structure of the family all had religious origins. Colonial society was a *sacred* one. The church maintained social order and *initiated* social change. Today the church often *reflects* social change; we live in a *secular* society.

Sacred society:
stable culture in which the church initiates social change

The Beginning of Change

The period of 1735 to 1820 has been called a period of enlightenment (Bremner, 1970). Radical positions such as *environmentalism* began to surface. Not all the actions of a child were motivated by some strange evil force inside the child; the environment of the child made a difference in the behavior of the child. This was a radical statement considering the beliefs of earlier times. Puritan parents had expected their children to passively accept the orders handed to them; later, children became active in seeking informa-

The Study of Children

tion and in their interactions with parents and other adults. Some of the traditional patriarchal assumptions came to be challenged during this first period of awakening (Bremner, 1970).

The American Revolution, like this period of change, tended to enhance the status of the young. Some of the leading figures in the American Revolution, such as Thomas Jefferson and Alexander Hamilton, were young men at the time of the Declaration of Independence. This swing to relatively young leaders represented a shift in the feelings toward younger people, but as we shall see, the situation surrounding children had not improved that much. As the economy of the country changed, the plight of children also changed and perhaps got even worse.

The Industrial Revolution and the accompanying upheaval in social and familial values and practices brought about unprecedented change; with it came child labor.

Industrial child labor began in America at the end of the eighteenth century (Bremner, 1971). Wool and cotton production was taken over by small shops in the late 1700s and these small shops, in many cases, became the forerunners of the factories that were to follow. The cloth-making industry was a significant one, especially in New England, and children played a vital role in this industry. Children were a plentiful, cheap source of labor for these endeavors.

Bremner has indicated that the number of employees in the cotton mills in 1809 was about at 4,000: 500 men and 3,500 women and children. The wages for children were calculated according to age (the younger the age, the lower the pay); children under 10 received about 50 cents per week, children ages 11 to 16 jumped to about $1.67 per week, with adult men sometimes earning up to $5 per week. A person just getting started in business was wise to employ as many children as possible. Adults thought many of the tasks were suited to children, because children lacked skill and could easily be made to do boring repetitive jobs (statistics from U.S. Bureau of Labor, *Report on Conditions of Women and Child Wage Earners*, VI, p. 62).

One of the important rules of child rearing of the day was that "idleness created evil," and wasted the minds of young people. Persuasive arguments were made for using children in the industries, even though the factory movement was getting away from the earliest system of apprenticeship. Very often, children were not being taught a specific trade or skill while working in the factory or sweatshop. Combined with the fact that there was no legal protection for the children in the factories, this made the work less than savory for these children.

Foundations of Child Development

A young girl, age ten, stands between the spinning machines she tends in a North Carolina cotton mill, photographed in 1909 by Lewis W. Hine.
INTERNATIONAL MUSEUM OF PHOTOGRAPHY, GEORGE EASTMAN HOUSE COLLECTION, ROCHESTER, NEW YORK.

Things slowly began to change. By 1820 America was starting to come out of its apathetic doldrums about the position of children in society. This slow process of change was a welcome relief, but the status of children was still vastly different from that of today and the rights of children were practically nonexistent.

The Study of Children

ISSUE

The Economic Value of Children in America

The three quotations below show the place of children in early American society. In No. 1, employers were urged to make use of people who were unemployable in agriculture. Two-thirds of the labor for the "manufactories" could be provided by women and children.
☐ Quotation No. 2 shows that young people should work. No older person of any worth was idle when he was young. Lastly, Quotation No. 3 is an actual newspaper want ad, designed to attract children to work in a factory.

I. There is an endless variety in the geniuses of men; and it would be to preclude the exertion of the faculties of the mind to confine them entirely to the simple arts of agriculture. Besides, if these manufactories were conducted as they ought to be, two thirds of the labor of them will be

A group of coal breaker boys, whose job was to pick out slate, photographed inside the breaker in 1911 by Lewis W. Hine.
INTERNATIONAL MUSEUM OF PHOTOGRAPHY, GEORGE EASTMAN HOUSE COLLECTION, ROCHESTER, NEW YORK.

carried on by those members of society who cannot be employed in agriculture, namely, women and children.

A second objection is that we cannot manufacture cloths so cheap here, as they can be imported from Britain . . . the expense of manufacturing cloth will be lessened from the great share of women and children will have in them; and I have the pleasure of informing you that the machine lately brought into this city for lessening the expense of time and hands in spinning, is likely to meet with encouragement from the legislature of Province (By Daniel Roberdeau, "A speech delivered in Carpenter's Hall, in the city of Philadelphia, 1775" in P. Force, ed., *American Archives* 4th ser., II [Washington, D.C., 1839] 143).

II. "We shall deliver them from the curse of idleness."

How long will it take us until we arrive at a sufficient age, and are fit to go to work? Surely, the time of youth is a very proper period to serve our apprenticeship. . . . We seldom find a person fond of labour in old age who has lived an idle life when young. . . . By manufacturing ourselves and employing our own people, we shall deliver them from the curse of idleness.

Idleness may be justly termed the bane of the mind, and the grand inlet to numerous vices. Nations that are remarkable for idleness and sloth, are for the most part prone to luxury, effeminacy, and extravagance (By A plain but real friend to America, "On Certain Manufactures," *American Museum* I [February 1787] 118–119).

III. Advertisement for child workers, eight to twelve years old, 1808:

Baltimore Cotton Manufactory

This manufactory will go into operation in all this month, where a number of boys and girls, from eight to twelve years of age, are wanted, to whom constant employment and encouraging wages will be given; also work will be given out to women in their homes, and widows will have the preference in all cases where work is given out, and satisfactory recommendations will be expected. This being the first essay of this kind in this city, it is hoped that those citizens having a knowledge of families, having children destitute of employment, will do an act of public benefit, by directing them to this institution. Applications will be received by Thomas White, at the Manufactory, near the Friends' Meetinghouse, Old Town, or by the subscriber (*Federal Gazette* [Baltimore], January 4, 1808).

☐ It is true that there are many adults today who feel that children do not do enough work and are not respectful toward older people. It is unlikely, however, that we would see today the type of writing exemplified in these quotations. It does not seem possible, for example, there would be many ads in the newspaper for children from the ages of eight to twelve to work in a cotton factory.

☐ What this issue points to is the significant change in the position of children in (1) the work force, (2) in society, and (3) in the family. Once children were sources of labor for the developing industries; today they are not. At one point in our history, children needed to pay a great deal of respect to older people; today this feeling appears to have declined to the point of nonexistence. In early times, the child's place was a subservient one; today it appears to have changed.

☐ Are these changes good for the child? Have they enhanced the child's place in society? There is a distinct possibility that all of the changes have not amounted to as much as they seem. America, despite some people's illusions, is not a child-centered society even today. As many observers have indicated, we have isolated, molded, pushed and shoved our children into becoming "thinking" and achieving beings. The question remains, however, *are* children in America better off today than they were when the quotations used in this section were written?

The Mid-1800s

Many of the questions being asked by parents of children in the early to mid-1800s are similar to the questions asked by parents today. How should discipline work? What is too much, and what is too little? What form of discipline will be best for my child for his or her future? After the 1820s, many manuals in child rearing began to appear. Some of them preached the necessity of returning to the ways of past generations, while others took rather radical positions advocating unheard-of levels of permissiveness.

The ideal child of this time was one who could be independent but still remain in agreement with parents over some of the essential points. Freedom of choice for children became possible, and families started to shift toward concern for the welfare of their children, rather than the concern for obedience and subservience of the earlier American families. But while children started to make gains within the environment of the family, there was still very little in the way of legal protection for children.

Alexis de Tocqueville, writing in *Democracy in America*, pointed out that there had been a change in the family patterns; the distance that had separated father and son had been lessened, and that the omnipotency of the father had been significantly altered. In 1835 he wrote:

> In America, the family, in the Roman and Aristocratic significance of the word, does not exist. All that remains of it are a few vestiges of it in the first years of childhood, when the father exercises . . . that absolute domestic authority. . . . In America there is . . . no adolescence; at the close of boyhood the man appears and begins to trace out his own path (de Tocqueville, *Democracy in America*, 1835, reprinted in Bremner, 1970, p. 347).

Observers of the American scene of the time were witnessing a change in the way the family had operated; de Tocqueville speaks of the firm hand of the father as necessary in the development of the child. The relaxation of paternal authority during this period signaled the beginning of a recognition of children's abilities and potential. And while fruition was some time away, this marked the beginning of the development of a concept of childhood and a recognition of children's place in their own maturation.

Occasional playfulness and facetiousness on the part of children were starting to be accepted and perhaps even encouraged (Wishy, 1968). Americans began to see that this sort of activity did not necessarily produce evil children or condemn these children to lives of idleness and nonproductivity. People began to suggest that children were not miniature adults, and that immaturity was the reason for their behavior. George Ackerley advised parents not to "fear noisy children." He went on:

> The noisy mirth of childhood ought never to be met with a frown, for it ought always be recollected, that it is not only natural to them, but actually necessary for the full development of every organ of the body . . . every effort to restrain them in their youthful gambols is as unnatural as it would be to confine the deer in the midst of the forest (G. Ackerley, *On the Management of Children*, New York, 1836, p. 61).

This suggestion to parents represented a radical departure from the traditional methods of child rearing. It challenged some of the basic assumptions concerning the reality of childhood and those concerning family operation and development. Children were now allowed, perhaps even expected, to make mistakes; their immaturity, not the devil's influence, accounted for this. The idea of children having fun growing up signaled the beginning of a new awareness of a child.

To show just how remarkable this change was, in 1847 a book was published called *The Evil Tendencies of Corporal Punishment*, by Lyman Cobb. While not abandoning corporal punishment, this

The Study of Children

book spoke of the need for children to learn from whatever form the punishment took. Meaningless beatings (meaningless to the immature child) made no sense; discipline was to be exercised giving consideration to the developmental maturity of the child and his ability to understand things like cause-and-effect relationships.

THE RIGHTS OF CHILDREN

Children have not always had rights commensurate with their position in society. During the nineteenth century, however, the rights of children in relation to parents and others steadily, but slowly, increased (Bremner, 1971).

Protecting children against physical abuse has been and still is a difficult task because of the difficulty in deciding where parental authority ends and state responsibility begins. Does the state have the right to interfere with the private dealings of families? While the answer to that question may be "yes" today, it has not always been so clear. Beating children for disobedience was not only practiced, it was endorsed as the proper way to deal with unruly children. Changing societal mores and values is a long and difficult task.

The movement to organize protective work for children had an interesting start. It developed as a direct outgrowth of protective work for animals (Society for the Prevention of Cruelty to Animals, SPCA). In 1874 in New York the Society for the Prevention of Cruelty to Children was formed, devoted exclusively to child protection. By 1900 the number of societies dedicated to the prevention of cruelty to children exceeded 250 (Bremner, 1971). The nature of these early agencies was largely "police-oriented," and it was not until a few years later that the social service philosophy (casework, family therapy, etc.) became popular.

The movement for children's rights has fluctuated over the years. All states and jurisdictions have laws that allow intervention into cases of child abuse and neglect and prosecution of the perpetrators of these acts. However, many people claim that children still do not have the same rights that adults do, nor the rights they deserve.

To deal with these issues, many states have adopted children's bills of rights. These documents declare children have the right to legal representation, a say in custody proceedings, and so on. Some say these changes are too little, and that change is not occurring fast enough. An outspoken supporter of children's rights,

Richard Farson, has indicated in his book *Birthrights* that children are entitled to far more than they are getting. He suggests:

> Our world is not a good place for children. Every institution in our society severely discriminates against them. We all come to feel that it is either natural or necessary to cooperate in that discrimination. Unconsciously we carry out the will of a society which holds a limited and demeaned view of children and which refuses to recognize their right to full humanity (R. Farson, *Birthrights*, 1974, p. 1).

Farson identifies the following rights of children:

1. the right to alternative home environments
2. the right to information; the right to educate oneself
3. the right to freedom from physical punishment
4. the right to sexual freedom
5. the right to economic power
6. the right to political power
7. the right to justice

We need a comprehensive approach to the problems of children's rights. This implies societal awareness and change, especially on the part of legal institutions and families.

PSYCHOGENIC THEORY AND EVOLUTION OF CHILDHOOD

Lloyd DeMause has studied the history of childhood and has come up with at least two major contributions to the literature. First is what DeMause calls the *psychogenic theory*. This theory explores the relationship between the adult and the child (a distance DeMause calls *psychic distance*). Psychogenic theory maintains that there are periods of assessment on the part of parents; they assess their own childhood and the relative position of their children. Change in the nature of parent-child relationships is dependent upon parents being able to realistically encounter, through their own children, some of the anxieties they had as children; work through them a second time; and qualitatively alter the status and place of their children. While lacking definitive empirical confirmation, this theory offers a fertile ground for the study of change within the parent-child relationship.

The Study of Children

Another major contribution by DeMause is his six-stage theory of the historical evolution of childhood, outlined below.

The first stage in the evolution of childhood was what DeMause calls the *infanticide mode*. Exact dates are hard to pinpoint, but De-Mause dates this stage from "antiquity" to the fourth century A.D. These were oppressive times; cultures were often in precarious situations, and were often ruled by bizarre religious rules and principles. Survival often dictated killing young babies; the burden they would bring would threaten the very existence of the group.

From about the fourth century to the fourteenth century, the *abandonment mode* was operational. The people of the day, not understanding the nature of children, were convinced that children were full of evil and that beatings were necessary to keep them in line. It is clear that expectations for the children exceeded the children's ability to meet those expectations.

The *ambivalent mode* (from the fourteenth to seventeenth centuries) had many different theories operating. The belief that children needed to be beaten into shape was still prevalent. On the other hand, there were flashes of change occurring: "environmentalism" appeared, the number of child-rearing manuals in print grew, and the content of these manuals varied considerably. This was indeed an ambivalent mode. Opinions about children varied considerably, depending on who was speaking.

The eighteenth century brought what DeMause calls the *intrusive mode*. Parents got closer to the child than ever before, attempting to control the child completely. But, probably as a result of the ambivalence of the previous period, the child was no longer considered to be full of evil. The humanity of the child was coming more into

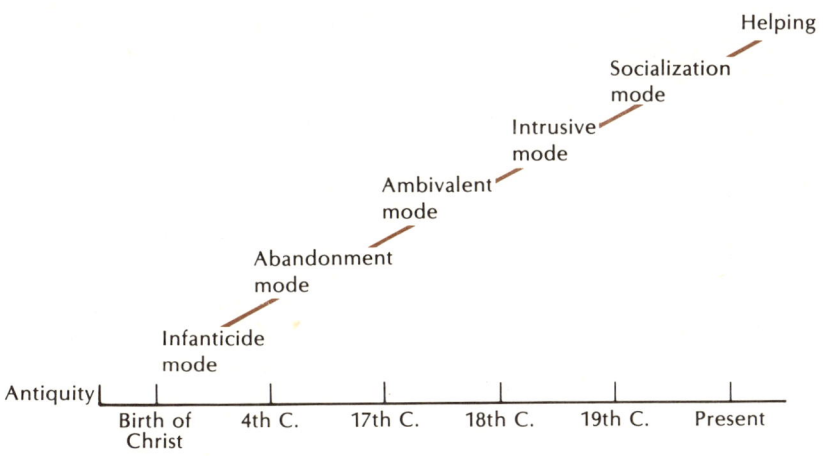

focus, and empathy between parent and child was a reality and even encouraged. Infant mortality rates dropped during this period as a more human understanding of children appeared.

The *socialization mode* (nineteenth to mid-twentieth centuries) saw child rearing change from a process of conquering the will of an inherently unruly child to a process of actually teaching the child. People began to be concerned with milestones of socialization, e.g., infancy, etc., and began to look for the environmental contingencies that made each milestone a reality for the child. This was a time when some very basic ways of thinking in child development started to take shape. Freud was working at this time, and the behaviorists were also setting a firm foundation in observation of children (see chapter 2).

The last mode of child rearing begins at the middle of the twentieth century and continues to the present. DeMause calls this the *helping mode*. During this period there is a specific concern for children's rights and the evolution of child therapy. This mode carries with it great promise for children. It also puts more explicit expectations on the shoulders of parents and alters these expectations. Parents are to guide, but *not as explicitly* as in the past; they are to be responsible, but possibly with less authority than they once had. It appears that this may be the most difficult parenting mode for parents; but as in the case with difficult tasks, the rewards in terms of relationships and outcome are much greater than they were in previous modes.

THE STUDY OF CHILD DEVELOPMENT IN THE UNITED STATES

The study of the child, academically and professionally, within the United States and other Western countries is an infant science. Given the status of children during the past, as we have indicated, it is little wonder that children and their development were not considered a topic for study. Besides, the study of children was not felt to contribute in any substantial way to the maintenance of the culture, as would, say, the study of ways to build roads and bridges; therefore, little time and energy was devoted to this study. That cannot be said today. There has been a proliferation of publications and research concerning the child, exemplifying the different place children are occupying in our society.

The study of the child is a multifaceted movement. The child development discipline actually has three distinct components and perhaps many more subcomponents. On one hand there is the tradition of developmental psychology; there is also the influence of pediatric medicine; and, lastly, there is child psychiatry (see chart below):

In the psychological realm, G. Stanley Hall is the so-called father of psychology. Hall approached development of the human from a basic, genetic framework and still stands as a pioneer in the study of human development (Senn, 1975).

John Dewey, an educator, had an interdisciplinary, psychocultural approach to the study of children. Lawrence K. Frank had an organizational and inspirational influence on the child development movement. An economist by trade, Frank started a child study center at Columbia University and then helped to start the child study center at the University of Minnesota. He was convinced that preschool education should be a part of home economics programs. This conviction led him to funnel foundation funds for nursery schools and child development programs to various colleges and departments of home economics. Among these were included the College of Home Economics at Cornell, the College of Home Economics at Georgia State and the College of Home Economics at Iowa State.

Robert Woodworth was probably "second only to Frank in contributing to the unification of the field . . ." (Senn, 1975). Woodworth helped in the organization that has now become the primary research and publication arm of child development: the Society for Research in Child Development.

John Watson was a behavioristic psychologist. He preached a rather rigid doctrine of behaviorism with respect to children, and

Study of Child Development*

Developmental Psychology	Child Psychiatry	Pediatrics
G. Stanley Hall	L. Eisenberg	K. Blackfan
J. Dewey	L. Kanner	H. Stuart
L. K. Frank	D. Levy	A. Washburn
R. S. Woodworth	D. Cohen	A. Gesell
J. B. Watson		C. A. Aldrich
A. Gesell		B. S. Polk
L. Terman		
S. Freud		
K. Lewin		
J. Piaget		

*For more information on these theorists, students should see Senn, 1975.

came off sounding restrictive and unpleasant. For instance, he spoke out strongly against any parent ever comforting a crying child or indulging in kissing a child.

> His (Watson's) attitude toward children, his attitude toward parents in the psychological care of the child is, it seems to me, pathological. . . . As far as he touched the raising of a child in America, I think it was totally a disaster (W. Kessen, quoted in Senn, 1975, p. 29).

There were other similar comments made about Watson and his emphasis on controlling behavior through the manipulation of reward contingencies and the environment of the child.

We will be discussing the other developmental theorists in the next chapter. It is clear that the field of child development is an eclectic science. The medical aspect is necessary, yet it does not provide the complete answer. Psychiatrists have also added immensely to the store of information in the field of child development. Yet, by itself, psychiatry cannot explain the totality of the development of the child.

One final model describes a very different way to look at the development of the child. Economic and political ideologies impinge upon the psychology of human development.

Capitalistic orientation: implies a continuous developmental model with single standard for all

MODEL I

Capitalistic Orientation (Anglo-American)

Primary proponents: Hobbes, Darwin, Hall
Implications: a continuous development model; all individuals are evaluated against single standards

Mercantilistic-socialistic orientation: implies emphasis on qualitative growth and multiple standards

MODEL II

Mercantilistic-socialistic (European)

Primary proponents: Rousseau, Piaget
Implications: qualitative growth models; encourages multigenerational and multicultural standards (adapted from Riegel, 1972).

The emphasis on sociocultural interaction is unique, yet highly relevant. By tying into the mainstream of the particular cultural mainstream, the theorist can reflect some of the very powerful influences within which children develop. This model also shows to the student of child development that there is a very strong need for theoretical integration; only through an adequate process of integration can the student hope to gain a firm grasp of the study of children within their cultural milieu.

The Study of Children

Melded together in a dynamic, developmental way, these separate yet related disciplines can explain the development of children. One discipline contributes to the other; they react to each other; this means an exciting and very meaningful adventure lies in wait for the student of child development. Perhaps the many facets —physical, emotional, and social—are why child development is so interesting. It is possible through the study of child development to gain a well-rounded insight into the reality of our own existences, thereby qualitatively improving ourselves.

Summary

1. The study of children should be broken down into several distinct types: the child as a whole being (holistic development), the child as an individual (idiosyncratic development), the child as a member of a society, a community, and a family (psychosocial development), and lastly, a comparison of the forces of biology to the forces of environment in the development of the child (nature-nurture debate).

2. Children need to be studied and appreciated within their context of development. There may be social class influences that affect development; there may be ethnic or traditional influences that affect behavior. Children cannot be studied outside of their world.

3. In many unique ways, children have a culture of their own. They have language, materials and traditions (like games) that seem to be fundamental to most groups of children. Observers of children need to be aware of some of the things that may be significantly affecting the culture of childhood, like television.

4. The history of childhood is a dismal one. It was not uncommon for children to be killed if they were excess baggage for the culture. Even in colonial America children were faced with high levels of physical punishment and excessive parental expectations for behavior, and were considered basically evil (the evil needed to be beaten out of the child). Only recently has the issue of children's rights begun to gain momentum and child abuse gained wide attention of parents and educators.

5. The psychogenic theory of Lloyd DeMause combines history with child development. In this theory we see the transition of child-rearing environments from infanticide all the way to a basic helping mode.

6. The study of child development in the United States is actually made up of three separate parts: developmental psychology, pediatrics and child psychiatry. The movement of the study of the child was discussed along with major contributors to the field in its early days.

Thought Questions

1. Why do we need to study the whole child? What is the nonexistent average? What does it have to do with overall child development?

2. What components make up the culture of childhood? How do you see childhood as a culture? Give some examples of how we overestimate and underestimate the child's development and abilities.

3. How has history changed in terms of acceptance of abortion? Compare the use of abortion today with that of centuries ago in terms of purpose and usefulness to society.

4. Discuss the history of children in terms of adult expectations for appropriate behavior. How do the themes "severity" and "absolute respect" relate to the child's place in the family and society today and years ago?

5. How far will American society carry the helping mode mentality in reference to children? What will the future bring in terms of the child's place in society?

Suggested Readings

Aries, P. *Centuries of Childhood*, New York: Knopf, 1962. *This book is one of the classics of the history of children around the world. The English translation is very readable for all students of child development.*

Bronfenbrenner, U. *Two Worlds of Childhood: U.S. and U.S.S.R.* New York: Basic Books, 1970. *Cross-cultural child development is discussed by one of the outstanding individuals in the field of child and family development.*

DeMause, L., ed. *The History of Childhood*. New York: Psychohistory Press, 1974. *This more recent discussion of the history of childhood is an anthology of works by historical and psychological scholars. Psychogenic theory is one of the major innovations found in this work.*

READING

Throughout history children have occupied different positions within their respective cultures. In this chapter we have discussed the prevalence of abortion and infanticide in earlier historical times and the role individual competency played in the ultimate survival of children.

Recently America has set itself up as the so-called bastion of childhood, a place where children are free to grow and develop unencumbered by the factors that made childhood somewhat unpleasant in the past. To demonstrate this belief in children, America has supported the United Nations proclamation of 1979 as the International Year of the Child.

John von Hartz sees things from a slightly different angle. In his essay, "The War Against Kids," he suggests that children are actually the forgotten members of our culture. The real feelings toward children in America are actually ones of negativism and disdain. The importance of this reading lies in pointing out that there is a great deal of everyday indifference toward children in America. Through this reading, perhaps a more realistic and appropriate perspective can be obtained on the greatest resource America possesses: its children.

The War Against Kids
John von Hartz

The letter from the irate businessman smoldered with indignation. During a supersonic jet transatlantic flight, he fumed to the editor of a major American newspaper, the cries of a babe-in-arms had distracted him from his paperwork. What's more, the man moaned, he had paid the full fare while the offending baby traveled for free.

The number of adults who nodded in agreement while reading the businessman's letter might shock the majority of American parents. After all, this country boasts that it is youth-oriented. Parents are motivated, even driven, by an urge to improve the lot and lifestyles of their kids. The quintessential advertisement for the American way of life is a gang of carefree, bronzed teenagers disporting themselves in some healthy pastime.

This admiration for youth has a dark side, however, one that is never apparent in the media blitzes aimed at well-off teenagers with their pockets full of disposable income. Taken as a class, America's children are the victims of a war waged on them by society—a conflict that many parents do not fully perceive.

Society's disdain for children is rooted in the nervous realities of today's attitudes toward life. In an age when existence often seems an unremitting series of hassles and high costs, kids symbolize two unwelcome entities: trouble and money. As every parent knows, kids complicate life. Supporting children in schools, playgrounds, libraries, and the array of public services that enrich growing bodies and minds costs dearly in public tax dollars. None of this is lost on self-aware Americans who have transformed the '70s into a decade aimed toward ego-gratification and self-fulfillment, and away from the responsibilities of child rearing and heading families.

Statistics confirm the swing away from kids. Some 60 percent of all American households have no children, according to figures based on the U.S. Statistical Abstract, 1977. Today the national birthrate is only 1.9 children per family, a figure below that rallying cry of the issue-oriented '60s, Zero Population Growth. (ZPG is achieved when the birth and death rates are equal in a given year.)

We should welcome the news that America is facing up to the catastrophic peril of overpopulation. And we do. Concern about the wisdom of bringing children into the world, however, is fostering the unwanted side effect of questioning the rights of kids in general. As the childless

JOHN R. MAHER, EKM-NEPENTHE

households determine national policies, views toward children are becoming frosted with antagonism.

This negativism toward youngsters reveals itself in dozens of obvious and subtle ways. Rental housing, particularly new complexes, is becoming the domain of adults without children—swinging singles, young marrieds, and older people. The basis of this exclusionary stance is rationally explained: younger and older people prefer to conduct their lives away from the noise and demands of kids. Children, however, constitute a significant portion of America's population; almost one third of the country is under 18 years of age. Segregating this large and lively percentage of Americans from housing is a loss for all of society. It is perilously close to self-destructive for men and women without children to isolate themselves from the questing, restless, and constantly curious personalities of the young.

Society also shows kids the back of its hand with its pernicious rejection of school budgets. This past summer, the voters of Ohio rejected more than half of the 200 community-tax-increase requests aimed at financing the public schools. Only with outside aid from state and federal coffers could some of these schools be opened in the fall. Nor does Ohio stand alone in this rebellion against the costs of public education. Across the country community school boards and taxpayers find themselves in pitched battle, with referendums for school monies more often going down to defeat than being approved.

The sharpest recent attack on children came with the passage of Proposition 13 in California. It may be years before the full effect of this limiting of property taxes can be assessed, but already one thing is certain—the kids aren't any better off because of it. Summer-school sessions were canceled across the state. After-school programs, including many sports activities, were slashed, and such disparate courses as drivers' education and Latin were lopped off the fall schedules. Library staffs and hours have been trimmed, and state-funded summer jobs—so critical to the budgets of working families—were eliminated.

The causes of this tax revolt are as complex and interwoven as the fabric of American life. Property-tax payers are bowed under the fiscal burden of community services, particularly the expense of running the schools. Anti-tax feeling reflects a disenchantment with busing and classroom desegregation, with an educational system that often turns out poorly educated kids, at ever-higher cost. Whatever the causes, the casualties are the kids. Lower budgets for local governments certainly won't produce better education or child-oriented services. The kids realize this and regard society's cutbacks as a series of frontal attacks.

Kids in trouble can expect little succor from states in these flint-hearted days. In Nebraska, for instance, foster homes which take in delinquent teenagers are granted only $4 per child per day. Unable to maintain children on this minimal payment, many foster homes in Nebraska must return their wards to reform school where the costs for caring for a child are twice that of sending him through college. And these children are not violent criminals; most of them are runaways from troubled homes, petty thieves, and incipient alcoholics. Since reform schools—like prisons—are little more than training grounds for crime, small wonder that our country's juvenile crime rates are streaking off the tops of most police graphs.

In daily life, the war against kids often consists of guerrilla skirmishes. Restaurateurs have been known to turn ghostly white when confronted by a mother and her young brood wanting a table. The supply of high chairs or comfortable seating for children is limited in most dining places, perhaps to restrict the number of child patrons. Department stores and other commercial operations make no accommodations for nursing mothers, who are relegated to crowded restrooms for periods of breast-feeding their babies. Parents must suffer if they wish to expose their children to the great artworks of man; museums either deny admittance to children or place a sanction on strollers, the one convenient method of transporting a child around the vast marble halls.

Kids even have a hard time finding clean and safe recreation areas in most urban communities. Playgrounds are commandeered by derelicts or gangs of toughs who drive the kids and mothers away. The playgrounds that are safe are regularly visited by untrained dogs who use the sandboxes as lavatories, exposing babies and young children to flagrant health hazards. Older kids must often stand by in despair while urban ball fields literally go to seed because park departments suffer retrenchments in maintenance personnel.

Even vacation trips with babies give no respite from the fray. A simple amenity like a diaper-changing table is a luxury no American air terminal seems able to afford (by contrast, many European airports provide them routinely). And passengers generally view young children boarding a train or plane with the affection cotton growers have traditionally accorded to an advancing boll weevil swarm.

America's ambivalence toward children is based in large part in a conflict between our myth of the family structure and its reality. This was one of the insights gleaned by a five-year study of the family by the Carnegie Council for Children, headed by Kenneth Keniston. Most Americans see the typical family as headed by a working father with a dutiful wife who remains at home with the kids and pets. Facts uncovered in the Census Abstract challenge this cozy concept. For the first time in America's history, more mothers work outside the home than stay in the kitchen and nursery. Only 40 percent of American households with kids are "typical," i.e., have a husband who serves as the sole wage-earner. (Even in this typical household, more than one-third of the wives plan to reenter the labor market.) In a larger percentage of American households with children—45 percent—both parents work. Some 14 percent of all American families are headed by a working woman.

The concept of a male-dominated family as the prime building block of American society refuses to perish. This nation grew and prospered on the belief that the individualistic male wage-earner held the family together. With his helpmate wife, he pushed aside the roadblocks that cluttered the path of the children.

This idealization of the family leads many taxpayers to refuse aid to families led by a male wage-winner. Yet many families, even those with two jobholders, require more help from the state than ever before. One reason for this is that families have grown smaller, and there are fewer people to share the load. In 1948, only one in 14 children under six years old was brought up in a single-parent family, according to the Carnegie study. By 1973 that proportion had doubled to one in seven children. Relatives who once aided in child raising are retiring from the family circle. And the number of children produced by each family is dwindling. At the peak of the post-World War II baby boom, the average child had almost three siblings while today he has less than one.

A composite picture of the modern family shows a small unit with one or two working parents, and few—if any—relatives, brothers, or sisters to lend a hand. While the parents are out working, the kids are left with babysitters who often do little more than plop themselves in front of that baleful eye that never sleeps: the TV. Or the kids are remitted to the daily custody of the state through public schools and day-care programs.

Since the 1960's, the government has created an outburst of services for children—Head Start, after-school programs, medical, counseling, and day-care services. Some of these programs, such as the model parent-child center reported in *Parents'*, July 1978, are exemplary. Other programs, however, have unfortunately fallen victim to misdirected goals and to the severe budget cuts of the '70s.

In spite of their deficiencies, these government programs for kids and their parents are a national priority. Ask any working mother to name the government service most useful to her and her reply is automatic: "Day-care programs." While government has taken the lead in this field, private industry could well follow suit. Any parent whose child is protected, nurtured, and well cared for during working hours is sure to be a better and more productive employee.

Similarly, working parents of both sexes would profit enormously from a more flexible work schedule that would free them to attend the needs of their kids. Far from being a utopian dream, flexible work time relieves the minds of the workers about their children, thus increasing their concentration and, ultimately, their effectiveness when on the job.

Attitude remains the most frightening weapon in the war against kids. Americans persist in making it difficult for parents to raise their young, then faulting them if they fail. Every funding reduction in programs for kids and every rigid rule that prevents a parent from giving his kid his undivided attention is a direct attack on the kids themselves. Parents must be responsible for the actions and behavior of their offspring. But it serves no discernible purpose to heap blame on a parent if a child is dragged through an indifferent society which is unwilling to open its wallet to supply the programs that add dignity to life.

Today, society has been entrusted with the task of helping to raise its children—this includes all the children from the littered streets of the ghetto to the sylvan glades of restricted suburbia. Without a thorough reexamination of the national attitude toward kids, the war will only escalate and worsen.

On reflection, any thoughtful American will realize that kids require support and understanding. Not only are these two commodities free, they restore the giver and receiver. Providing these precious human considerations is an undisguised gesture for peace. The next time a harried businessman is disturbed by a baby's cry, he might neglect his work for a moment and give the child his hand. It may not quiet the baby, but it will work wonders for the man.

PHILADELPHIA MUSEUM OF ART. GIVEN BY CARL ZIGROSSER.

Mother with Child in Arms (1916–'57–90–163) by Käthe Kollwitz.

2

Theories of Development: Physiological Beginnings

Students are sometimes frustrated by the theoretical framework of child development, the fact that there are many different ways of looking at the development of a child. People place emphasis on different potential molders of behavior. We will attempt to provide examples of this wide variety of theoretical orientations.

According to Webster's New World Dictionary, a theory is "a formulation of underlying principles of certain observed phenomena which has been verified to some degree." The observed phenomena in this case are the points of development in the human. Considering the complexity of the child, there are obviously many parts to a child development theory. Perhaps the intriguing aspect of theory in this area is that these facets are invariably interrelated, often in some complicated fashion.

For example, a child's language development might be explained by a relatively simple theory explaining each of five or six contributors to the development, which one happens first, and what occurrences, if any, might retard or accelerate this development. However, language development in children is highly complex. A child's temperamental boldness may prompt him or her to speak more and get more instructive feedback. Shyness or an intimidating adult may promote late speech in another child. What system will cover both variables? One theory says the development of language is the result of some internal, biological language generator; its development is merely the unfolding of a programmed response. It may happen early or late. Other theorists state firmly

A DEFINITION OF A THEORY

Theory: general principles offered to explain phenomena

that the primary operational factor in language development is some highly complex pattern of learning. Each theory tries to accommodate all the possible variables and still arrive at a system that seems true to life.

THEORY AND PRACTICE

Glaser and Strauss suggested several years ago that there are essentially five interrelated jobs of a theory:

1. to enable prediction and explanation of behavior;
2. to be useful in the theoretical advance of the discipline;
3. to be usable in practical applications . . . the practitioner should be able to learn from a theory;
4. to provide a perspective on behavior; and
5. to guide and provide a style for research on particular aspects of behavior.

(Glaser and Strauss, 1967, p. 3)

In child development we are often asked to explain the behavior of children. The problem with this is that it is very hard to explain the behavior of *all* children *all* of the time. When a parent asks "Why does my child bite other children?" it is possible to respond with a theoretical treatise on a significant fixation in the oral stage, where biting is the only way to adequately meet the oral needs of the child. If you respond to a parent in that way, however, you will probably alienate the parent.

Explaining and predicting the behavior of children is a formidable task. The difficulty of this task is the result of two very important aspects of child development research. The first is the complex interrelationship between the aspects of child development. There are many factors that can affect a given child in a given setting at a given time. This leads to the second major factor in child development research: control. Somehow, in order to effectively study children we must control as much bias as possible in the research. We must control for all outside influences that may be affecting behavior in the experimental setting, and we must somehow isolate the single behavior that we are trying to study.

Research control: the elimination of outside influences in experimental studies

Theories of Development

It is not possible to isolate the child, totally control his diet, feeding patterns, elimination patterns, and emotional phenomena and then subject the child to an experiment. However, unless we can *control* most or all of the variables, critics will question the validity of the findings. To be sure, there are statistical techniques that can help control some of these factors, but these may not be able to answer the question from the mother as to why her child was biting other children!

This is the dilemma we are faced with in the study of child development. As a result, there is sometimes a tendency to become completely immersed in the theoretical-research aspect of child development. Given technology (computers), available dollars, and the strong urge to make the study of child development a legitimate one, it is relatively easy to justify developing a consistent push toward research. This is a worthy goal; it helps us meet some of the goals of a theory. Unfortunately, some people lose sight of the human end of the spectrum and come to feel that child development is a study in research design, techniques, and explanation. If we lose the human perspective in research with children, we run the risk of developing a very narrow understanding of children.

On the other hand, the field of child development has a large practical, "hands-on" aspect. With child care centers, nursery schools and various forms of educational and intervention programs, there is a very significant practical aspect to child development. Because of this, it is possible to devalue research evidence and to rely on the feeling that nothing is equal to actual experience with children. The business of child development should be left to those people who work with children: the practitioners.

Both extremes are misleading. Complete allegiance to one pole denies the rich experiences and abundant information available in the other. Theory offers students a rich conceptual framework that will actually make the practical experience more worthwhile and effective. Practitioners need to be aware of all the available research in order to effectively understand what is happening with the children and to optimize their time with the children. Parent education, for example, is a highly useful blending of theory and practice. In order to help parents with education about children, the teacher must have experience working with parents; they can be a volatile audience. On the other hand, the teacher must be aware of the research concerning the developing child. One cannot exist without the other.

Arnold Gesell (1880–1961).
WIDE WORLD PHOTOS.

THE SYSTEMATIC THEORY AND METHODS OF ARNOLD GESELL

Norm:
a standard of development determined by observation of large numbers of subjects

Many people believe that systematic and objective data collection leads to a grounded theory. Arnold Gesell systematically and objectively studied the development of children, and his work truly meets the criteria we have set forth for the definition of a theory. Gesell's theory is important in its use of *developmental norms.* After observing children in settings designed to allow them to operate in a normal fashion, Gesell and his colleagues identified standard developmental norms of behavior. At any particular age certain behavior was considered normal and appropriate. A year later one could expect some behaviors to be dropped and other new ones to appear. Developmental theory comes to the conclusion that the development of the child is orderly and patterned (Gesell and Thompson, 1938).

Some people think that Gesell's theory of child development ignores the role of environmental change and learning. Gesell, however, states that he is very aware of other influences on development:

Theories of Development

> Our own concept of normative methods is colored by a keen appreciation of the abounding variety of individual differences. Indeed, the very richness of this variety creates the need for normative specifications. We need norms to detect and identify the numerous behavior characters. Without norms we could neither capture nor formulate the rich diversity of phenomena which nature provides . . . (Gesell and Thompson, 1938, p. 4).

In the 1938 work of Gesell and Thompson there are 40 tables of information containing norms for common things like waking patterns, sleeping patterns, vocalization, play, feeding habits, standing and walking behaviors. Gesell and his colleagues generated an immense amount of normative data on the development of children. This approach represented one of the first systematic studies of the development of the child. It added a rich perspective to a young science, and since these pioneering days, many normative studies have even gone beyond childhood to suggest a normative development picture of adulthood and aging (see for example, *Passages* by Gail Sheehy, or Daniel Levinson's *Stages in a Man's Life*).

PSYCHOANALYTIC THEORY AND FREUD

Freudian theory is one theoretical approach that has suffered over the years from misinterpretation. Freudian theory is quite rich, although there are significant portions of the theory that remain largely unsubstantiated. On the other hand, there are other important areas of the theory that are basically sound, and that have

Sigmund Freud (1856–1939).
WIDE WORLD PHOTOS.

significant implications for parents and other students of child development.

There are two major parts of Freudian theory. First of all, Freud suggested that there are four basic character structures of adults: oral, anal, phallic, and genital. (Freud also talked about another form of personality embodied in the phrases *id, ego* and *superego;* it does not appear that this typology was developed adequately, and the support for this form is nearly nonexistent.)

Secondly, Freud suggested that these personality types are the result of normal development, and that all children appear to go through a series of stages in a sequential and invariant way. In each stage a portion of the body becomes the primary source of satisfaction. For the infant the area of the body that predominates is the mouth. This part of the body is the infant's primary source of satisfaction: food is taken through the mouth, and exploration is through the mouth. Consequently, Freud felt that this region of the body was significant during the infant's life.

From the ages of one to three the area that receives the majority of the child's attention is the anal region. This is the time of toilet training and greater interest in excretory functions. From the ages of three to five, the genitals are the significant body region for the child. This is the phallic stage.

Age five to prepuberty is labeled the *latency phase,* which, in Freudian terminology, is a time of significant repression of the genital drives. With puberty there is a resurgence of interest in the genital region as the sexual urge begins to take hold.

Freud suggests that at each stage there is a concerted effort on the part of the individual to deal with and satisfy the dominant physical region. The demands of each of these regions, however, often run counter to the prevailing attitude of the socializing agent, e.g., the parent. What the child wishes to have happen perhaps cannot happen because of the strong wishes and behavior controls of the parents. One interesting example is the anal phase and the parents' firm wish to toilet-train the child. According to Freudian theory, the child would prefer to remain unencumbered, without the restrictions of toilet training. If the parents *control* this interest too firmly the child will never feel satisfied at having met his needs, and will carry this unresolved conflict forward through his life.

The mature person, according to Freud, is a person who gets his satisfaction from genital fulfillment. Genital excitement, rather than any other form of "fixation," is considered to be mature in style; sensations from other parts of the body serve to make the genital experience more complete.

As a psychoanalyst, Freud collected most of his information from patients in a clinical setting. Through retrospection and introspection, the patients showed Freud their problems and their feelings. Much of Freud's early theory is based on these sorts of data—clinical, and not systematically collected. The work of Freud and his colleagues, particularly early in the theory, is a classic example of an ungrounded theory (in the Glaser and Strauss definition). The data and theory were based upon fragile clinical settings, which do not always lend themselves to concrete theory building.

One of the keys to Freudian theory is the manner in which the individual deals with the particular drives unique to each stage of development. These mechanisms of "coping" determine the style of a person's life, his basic personality and the way of dealing with the world. Early styles of coping and early environment are very important in personality development. If the child cannot cope with the demands of a given stage, he may become *fixated* at that stage. Fixation implies stagnation within a particular stage, the inability to move on to a more mature way of interacting with the world. This fixation becomes a hindrance to the person, resulting in stereotypical behavior patterns, common mechanisms of defense and problems common in others who have been similarly fixated.

Freud and his colleagues emphasized the oral period and the importance of meeting the demands of this period. This means that there is a strong tendency in Freudian theory to state that what happens during infancy will affect all later personality development. Freud suggested that an infancy period that is either over-gratifying or frustrating to the infant in the realm of oral gratification can be the source of problems in the child and later in the adult. The undergratified may continually want more than they have. Those who have been highly gratified during the oral phase may assume that life will be bountiful and hence may be frequently disappointed.

Freudian theory has many characteristics that we cannot begin to go into here; it is important, however, to discuss the credibility of the theory in terms of its testability. Fisher and Greenberg (1977) have assessed the credibility of significant portions of Freudian theory and have reviewed 30 scholarly studies that examined the link between pertinent oral experiences in infancy and later attributes in adulthood. Overall, Fisher and Greenberg report that the evidence is fairly persuasive that there is a connection between the infancy period and later adult personality. There is not enough consistency in the evidence, however, to clear up the differences between undergratification compared to overgratification. There is very little information about how specific parental practices directly affect the formation of later oral characteristics.

Freud suggested that particularly frustrating experiences during the anal period (roughly ages one to three) would produce individuals who are more parsimonious and saving and inclined to a neat and orderly life; there may be a persistent insistence on neatness and orderliness. This is a time when parents are asking, perhaps demanding, that the child give up the freedom to eliminate at will.

Fisher and Greenberg reviewed 18 academic studies that attempted to link toilet training practices in childhood with personality attributes later in life. They found little support for the hypothesis that a child's toilet training determines whether he will exhibit orderliness, obstinancy and parsimony (Fisher and Greenberg, 1977). This suggests that there is sufficient complexity present in the developing human that simple, direct relationships are very hard to demonstrate.

THE PSYCHODYNAMIC THEORY OF ERIK ERIKSON

Erik Erikson's theory is a stage theory. At each stage the individual faces a set of demands, each of which has a positive and a negative outcome. Successful individual development means the accumulation of *positive* outcomes to each of these stages. Erikson's stage-dependent, psychodynamic theory is called the *eight stages of man*. These stages form an invariant sequence.

The first dilemma that the newborn child faces is whether or not his environment is capable of meeting the very basic needs of the

Erik Erikson (1902–   ).
WIDE WORLD PHOTOS.

Theories of Development

Eight Stages of Man*

stage 1	Basic Trust vs. Basic Mistrust
stage 2	Autonomy vs. Shame and Doubt
stage 3	Initiative vs. Guilt
stage 4	Industry vs. Inferiority
stage 5	Identity vs. Role Confusion
stage 6	Intimacy vs. Isolation
stage 7	Generativity vs. Stagnation
stage 8	Ego Integrity vs. Despair

*Adapted from E. Erikson, *Childhood and Society*, 1963.

child for food, warmth, security, and the like. If the environment does meet those needs, the first dilemma of the child's life will be resolved by the child's feeling he can trust his environment; he feels comfortable that his basic needs will be met.

Building upon this base, the child will reach out and interact with the world. He will actively demonstrate independence, which leads to confidence, which leads to becoming a more active participant in the world. All of these early resolutions form building blocks of character, and eventually these help the person live out the remainder of his life fulfilled, functional, comfortable, and capable. Without appropriately resolving these dilemmas, the individual is faced with a continuous process of meandering, not fully knowing himself, trusting neither himself nor the world around him.

Coping with the demands of life depends less on the strength of the demands and more on the consistency of character and internal "ego-strength." Effective resolution of these life dilemmas contributes to ego-strength, and ultimately to coping strength of the individual.

Basic trust: infants' feelings that their basic needs will be met

SOCIAL LEARNING THEORY

Learning is a term that often escapes definition. When we learn, we know we acquire some sort of knowledge or skill, which implies that there is a process going on. A consciousness is evident with information passing from some source and being internalized by the learner. Learning implies *activity on the part of the learner*. Taking the definition a step further, learning implies a *motivation* on the part of the learner; it implies paying attention to the world around us. Learning means doing something, and having a sufficient de-

Motivation: an influence that causes a person to act

Learning:
modification of behavior as a result of experience

velopmental readiness in order to learn. Learning theory is built on the factors that will accentuate or hamper learning.

Rotter (1954) has indicated that the two most important items in whether or not a behavior occurs are: (1) whether or not the behavior is reinforced; and (2) the value of the reinforcer to the subject. Bandura and Walters (1963) carry these assumptions further and say that the two points mentioned above do not adequately explain the acquisition of novel or unexpected responses on the part of the child. Social learning theory, as we know it today, encompasses the material mentioned above and more. Social learning theory encapsulates concepts such as:

imitation—the process of copying or trying to be the same

reinforcement (reward)—a strengthening or supportive agent

scheduling of reinforcement—a behavioristic term implying specific cycles of reward, designed to optimize the effect

observational learning—acquiring a knowledge or skill through paying attention to its performance; contrasted with learning by trial and error, or perhaps through coercion

Imitation can often strengthen the bonds between a parent and a child.
ROBERT V. ECKERT, JR., EKM-NEPENTHE.

vicarious reinforcement—a supportive agent or phenomenon experienced indirectly or through some other nondirect way

ADAPTIVE LEARNED BEHAVIOR

Social learning assumes that behaviors learned in an observation-reinforcement setting generalize to other situations. This is a very important assumption, for if behaviors learned did not generalize to other situations, the power of parents, among other things, would be in question. If a behavior appeared in only one setting, the stability of that behavior would be drastically reduced. The extent of behavioral generalization, however, is dependent upon elements of similarity between the new situation and the previous situation (Bandura and Walters, 1963).

In order for learning to be socially adaptable, it must be discriminated. Something in the process must indicate when a particular behavior is appropriate and when the same behavior is inappropriate. Aggression is an important example. In certain situations and with certain individuals, aggression may not only be acceptable, it may be desirable. A simple example is the athletic field. Here the aggressive behavior may be very appropriate. In the classroom, aggressive behavior is not appropriate. The child must be able to discriminate between settings where a behavior is appropriate and those where it is not.

REINFORCEMENTS

Reinforcements must be accurate and precise in order for some of these discriminations to be present. It is easier to socialize without discriminations, but the child (or person being socialized) is placed in a difficult position by this lack of flexibility in behavior.

Are all people equally susceptible to the effects of social learning? This question has been dealt with to some degree in the literature. It would appear that the answer is "no." In social learning terminology, Bandura and Walters state:

> . . . social behavior can be more easily elicited and more strongly reinforced in children in whom strong dependency habits have been built up (Bandura and Walters, 1963, p. 10).

Independent children may not learn as quickly or as well by this method.

Social learning theory also talks about three ways of inhibiting undesirable behavior. These three are:

removal of reinforcer—taking away a positive agent

aversive contingency—adding a negative agent to the situation such as physical punishment

nonreward—presenting neither a positive nor a negative agent to the learning situation; ignoring the behavior

Obviously, it is necessary to inhibit some of the behaviors of children. Both the removal of a reinforcer and an aversive contingency are forms of punishment; however, they each have different effects. The presentation of an aversive contingency (beatings, verbal abuse, etc.) focuses the attention of the child on the *disapproved* behavior, *not the appropriate behavior*. By focusing on the inappropriate behavior and directing the attention of the child to that behavior, the parent or teacher inadvertently is not extinguishing that behavior. In fact, the child has learned that there are specific behaviors that parents or teachers do not appreciate and find upsetting. The potential of this effect is impossible to calculate.

Aversive actions change behavior, as any parent can attest to; and the aversive actions are often swift, direct, and a great reliever of tension in the adult. But is this sort of change the ultimate goal and on what level is the change occurring? Most social learning theorists suggest that nonreward is more likely to result in the extinction of a particular behavior (Bandura and Walters, 1963). Nonreward may involve removing a previous reinforcer or merely ignoring a behavior that one does not wish to see again.

LEARNING IN SOCIAL SETTINGS

More recently Bandura has indicated that social learning plays a highly visible and thus highly important role in the development of language. As we shall see later, people believe that language may have its roots in a wide variety of things, e.g., the language generator, an entirely genetic origin, or some other combination of factors. Bandura has said:

> If children had no opportunity to hear the utterances of models, it would be virtually impossible to teach them the linguistic skills that constitute a language (Bandura, 1977, p. 12).

Theories of Development

The subject-model relationship is one of the keys to social learning theory. All of the factors that have a potential effect on the subject-model relationship are the focus of social learning theories. The sex of the model, the sex of the subject, the environment in which the interaction takes place, and countless other relationship-specific factors affect the nature of the modeling experience.

Many people think that social learning theory is a theory of manipulation; control is in the hands of some all-powerful reinforcing agent. The extremes of behavioral control and management have often been emphasized when discussing this theory: the individual is denied, has no power, and is completely at the will of manipulating agents. Bandura has attempted to deal with this argument in the following way:

> By arranging environmental inducements, generating cognitive supports, producing consequences for their own actions, people are able to exercise some measure of control over their own behavior.
>
> To be sure, the self-regulatory functions are created and occasionally supported by external influences. Having external origins, however, does not refute the fact that once established self-influence partly determines which actions one performs (Bandura, 1977, p. 13).

Direct and vicarious experience has an incredible and perhaps indelible influence on the developing child. The study of how these learning relationships work, develop, and eventually affect the developing child has been the focus of much research and discussion. The social learning theory acknowledges this kind of learning. Its broad scope offers many approaches to the study of children.

ISSUE

Behaviorism Applied: The Case of the Baby-Tender

The social learning theory deals with learned behaviors and their antecedents. It also deals with such fundamental things as reinforcement, schedules of reinforcement, and conditioning. One of the extreme applications of social learning principles is called *behaviorism*. We have already discussed the work of John Watson, who was a behaviorist.

☐ One of the more controversial applications of behavioristic principles was made by B. F. Skinner, when he proposed that all aspects of a growing child's environment should be controlled. He felt that if we could somehow control all of the environmental factors, we would have much greater success in child rearing. In order to apply efficient child-rearing techniques, Skinner built a contraption he called the baby-tender. In his own words:

> For our second child, Deborah, I built a crib-sized living space that we began to call the "baby-tender." It had sound absorbing walls and a large picture window. Air entered through filters at the bottom and, after being warmed and moistened, moved by convection upward through and around the edges of a tightly stretched canvas, which served as a mattress. (A small fan blew the air if it was hot.) A strip of sheeting 10 yards long passed over the canvas, a clean section of which could be cranked into place in a few seconds (B. F. Skinner, 1979, p. 30).

☐ Skinner's daughter was placed in this baby-tender as soon as she came home from the hospital. Wearing only a diaper, the controlled atmosphere in the

B. F. Skinner (1904–).
PHOTOGRAPH © 1979 BY JILL KREMENTZ

Theories of Development

baby-tender allowed the baby to stay warm and be free of some of the binding effects of small babies' clothing. Skinner felt that there were several specific benefits of raising his child in the baby-tender.

1. It was possible to control temperature and the invasion of other people's infections; Skinner claimed that Deborah did not have a cold for many years.
2. The baby-tender was a quieter environment than the regular crib situation. Skinner felt that this quietness contributed to regular sleeping patterns on the part of the child.
3. The baby-tender did not interfere with handling and touching of the child. She was removed for feeding and bathing, and Deborah never showed any sign of not wanting to go back into the baby-tender.

☐ Skinner decided that people should know about this project; perhaps they would also wish to get one (he was toying with the idea of getting the baby-tender mass-produced). He submitted an article to the *Ladies' Home Journal,* which was published in October 1945. The publication of the article, with editorial revisions, and the subsequent publicity raised a great deal of furor over the morality of the "baby-box," as it came to be called. People began to assume that Skinner was running psychological experiments with his daughter, using the baby-tender as the place for these experiments. The "heir conditioner," as it was to be called when and if it was mass-produced, prompted

The baby tender designed by B. F. Skinner. Note the sheet that can be pulled through the tender from the roll on the left and the window shade that can be pulled down from the top to darken the interior of the baby tender.
PHOTO COURTESY OF B. F. SKINNER.

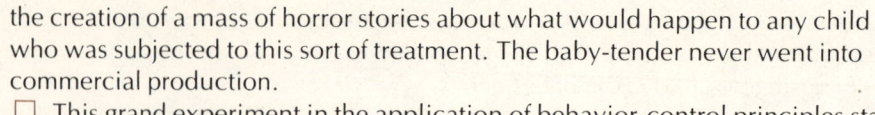

the creation of a mass of horror stories about what would happen to any child who was subjected to this sort of treatment. The baby-tender never went into commercial production.

☐ This grand experiment in the application of behavior-control principles startled many people. What is interesting is that this represents one of the few direct applications of theory to the practical world.

☐ Is the baby-tender a good idea? Would a child be deprived? Would there be too little contact with adults? Would there be too little contact with common "bugs," so that the child would never develop a system of immunities? There is not enough information to answer these questions absolutely. If we are to go by the effects that the baby-tender had on Deborah, the results are not horrible; in fact, things turned out quite well. As Skinner said:

> I have been asked if our daughter is suing me. Fortunately, none of this is true. Deborah is a very successful artist, and her colored etchings have been exhibited at private shows in the United States, Canada and London. She lives in London with her husband (B. F. Skinner, 1979, p. 40).

THE COGNITIVE THEORY OF JEAN PIAGET

Jean Piaget is a Swiss psychologist. His academic training was in the biological sciences, although most of his professional career has been involved with his theory of cognitive development in children. A prolific writer, he has been writing in the field of child development since the late 1920s. His approach is largely clinical, with his early observations of child development coming from observations of his own children.

Piaget's theory is an interactionist theory. While stressing a basic biological structure, Piaget emphasizes the importance of environmental contingencies, families, and other sources of social involvement. Phillips in discussing Piagetian theory has said:

> . . . the organism inherits a genetic program that gradually (through a process called maturation) provides the biological equipment necessary for constructing a stable internal structure out of its experiences with its environment (Phillips, 1975, p. 7).

Very simply, Piaget's cognitive theory distinguishes between immature and mature cognitive abilities. His theory suggests that there are several stages in the transition from a less-developed to a more-developed way of understanding. The first time a child tries

Theories of Development

Jean Piaget (1896–   ).
WIDE WORLD PHOTOS.

to walk, he usually fails; the first time he holds a pencil, he only scribbles. With time he walks with ease, and the scribbles become pictures and words. Intellectually the child does the same thing. What starts as reflexive, global, and egocentric becomes refined, sophisticated, and quite flexible.

The components of Piagetian theory are encapsulated in the following table:

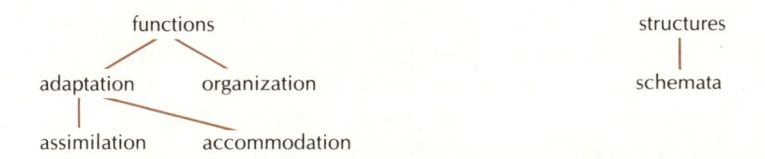

```
              functions                           structures
           /          \                               |
     adaptation    organization                    schemata
        |
   assimilation    accommodation
```

Piaget postulates that functions (or processes) are stable; they do not change with maturation and development. What changes during the course of a child's development are the internal structures (schemata) that the child possesses. Because of the operative processes, bits of information are processed by the child and incorporated into existing structures (assimilation) or into new structures created because of the characteristics of the information (accommodation). In addition to these processes, the child is continually organizing the information he possesses and receives and attempts to maintain homeostasis, or balance, in all the structures he has.

Cognitive structures are the agents that reflect developmental change in the child. If the structural components of the child's cognition did not change with differential exposure and learning, development could not occur. Everything would remain static. One example of the assimilation-accommodation process is when a child sees an object in his environment, for example, a butterfly. Upon perceiving this object the child may assimilate the image into an already existing category: the category for birds. When reminded that the object is not a bird but is a butterfly, the child will accommodate the new image or experience by creating a structural category in which the butterfly may be placed.

Piaget calls assimilation and accommodation *functional* invariants. These processes are characteristic of all children and are rooted in some innate mechanism. These processes remain the same throughout time, but they are not always in balance with one another. Assimilation may predominate in certain situations, while accommodation may predominate in other situations. Behavior is most adaptive when assimilation and accommodation are in balance (Phillips, 1975).

The human organism has a strong desire to keep the structure and internal workings of the system in balance. Piaget termed this process *equilibration*. Equilibration maintains balance through compensation within the person; when equilibrium is attained, the person is in a position to more effectively function and relate to the situations he finds himself in. One of the creative contributions of Piaget is his assertion that the balance is never static; it is continually occurring, adding a vital cognitive dimension to the reality of being human.

Equilibration:
maintaining a balance between assimilation and accommodation

In the earliest stages of development the structures (schemata) are probably reflexive. They are simple in nature and vital to the development of the child. As the child matures the schemata become more complex, more cognitive, more difficult to understand and appreciate. They also become interrelated and reciprocal in nature; i.e., they are dynamically related to each other, and things that happen to one structure directly and indirectly affect the other structures. The cognitive map of the child becomes a system of interrelated structures and sustaining processes.

Intellectual development is a continual *process* involving the input of information, the organization of that input, and ultimate reorganization of bits of information, depending upon experience and internal structure. Piaget has conceptualized this continuous process of organization-reorganization into four periods of cognitive growth. The child goes through four invariant periods in the development of cognitive maturation and sophistication. These periods of cognitive development are:

Cognition:
thinking and making judgments

the sensorimotor period

the preoperational period
the concrete operations period
the formal operations period

These stages are conceptualized as invariant, that is, the sequence remains the same. The periods are also conceptualized as being universal; all children go through them, although not necessarily at the same time nor at the same speed. In fact, not all people complete the cycle of development; some people do not develop all of the capabilities implied in the period of formal operations. Stage theories may seem overly simplistic. Don't be confused or fooled. These Piagetian periods represent sophisticated leaps in cognition for the child, and are qualitatively sound as well as being empirically derived.

The Sensorimotor Period

For the first four months of life the infant exercises the "wired-in" responses, the reflexive behaviors. Among these are sucking and related behaviors, hand grasp responses, and other similar behaviors. During the next four months, the child begins to pay a large amount of attention to his body, repeating behavior regularly. Gradually, the child's center of interest expands and moves toward environmental objects, and the child becomes very interested in interacting with the environment and seeing just what sort of an impact his actions can have. The behaviors are still highly repetitive but the infant takes a large measure of satisfaction (at least it appears so) in interacting with the environment and testing preliminary behavioral capabilities. A child with a noisy toy will shake the toy and wait for the noise; the infant repeats this pattern again and again until some other cue or need occupies his attention.

During the final three months of the first year of life the infant takes time to perfect the interactive behaviors he has developed and refines them into functional behavioral patterns. These refinements allow the infant to test out different behaviors during the second year of life. There is still a high degree of repetitiveness to the behaviors, but this really represents the first time the child is engaging his environment in an experimental way. Toward the end of this sensorimotor period the infant begins making the transition to the preoperational period. This transition involves considerably more intentional behavior on the part of the child as well as more active involvement and engagement with the world around him.

The Preoperational Period (ages 2 to 7, approximately)

Perhaps the biggest change that develops in the child during the preoperational period is the systematic use of symbols in the representation of an interaction with his environment. By *symbol*, we mean not only the use of words to represent objects, but also the use of mental images within the mind of the child. These mental images are used to organize experience and to relate to the world in some other way than just physical.

Entrance into the preoperational period is marked by increasing internalization of representational actions and increasing differentiation of signifiers from significates (Phillips, 1975, p. 63).

Going hand in hand with this symbolic usage is perhaps the most important developmental occurrence of early childhood: the development of language. The roots of language occur during earlier periods. However, the blossoming of language into a highly communicative act occurs during the preoperational period. The development of language signals a different way of putting thoughts together, a different way of conceptualizing the world. Language is a new, seemingly limitless, avenue of communication. Representational thought, keyed through the use of words, blossoms during the preoperational period. Not necessarily a sophisticated cognitive operation, this period nevertheless represents a significant departure from the form of reasoning present in the sensorimotor period.

The Period of Concrete Operations (years 7 through 11, approximately)

During the period of concrete operations the child, for perhaps the first time, is not totally impressed with his perceptions. What he sees or experiences or hears may now be contradicted in his mind. The period of concrete operations gives the child a great feeling of constancy, perhaps greater than he has ever had. There are finite dimensions to the world that the child understands. While not abstract or hypothetical, this reasoning can be highly accurate and very effective in helping the child relate to his world.

For the first time, the child is actively engaging in intellectual operations. Thought processes are internalized and problem solving begins to leave the overt trial-and-error process and becomes more cerebral and less action-oriented. Piaget refers to the processes present as representing mobility of thinking, flexibility, and ability to understand different though simultaneous perspectives.

The Period of Formal Operations (ages 11 to 15, approximately)

The most significant occurrence during the period of formal operations is the construction of abstract formulations of reality. These totally cognitive phenomena demonstrate the internalization of thought processes and the ability to manipulate real or imagined components of the world within the mind. The child is now in a position to ask "what if" questions. What if it had been this way? What if that had happened? What if we do this?

These propositions allow the child to consider future orientations to the world and to solve problems in abstract rather than concrete ways. These cognitive attributes bring about interesting personality changes.

Theories are tools to be used by students of child development to help them better understand the context the child is growing up in. Theories provide the framework for the study of children. It is important to keep in mind that they are theories, still being tested and added to, not completely salient separately; they combine to give the observer a rich contextual outlook on the developing child.

METHODOLOGY IN CHILD DEVELOPMENT

The collection of data on child development is crucial to substantiating theory and to the overall understanding of child development. How these data are collected is a separate field of study all its own.

The motivations for research vary; some individuals are interested in advancing the state of the art (science?), while others do research and publish solely to ensure their position on the faculty. This diversity in motivation produces a wide amount of diversity in the quality of research in the literature, although it is not safe to say which motivation produces the best research. Because of this situation, it is important for the student of child development to be cautious in reading about research and quite skeptical about how much one may safely generalize from the work. Items such as the size of the population studied, how that population was selected, the nature and quality of the instrument employed, and the skill of the experimenter all have to be considered by the careful reader.

Observation may be the most fundamental method of studying children. The skills developed in observation lay the groundwork for other methods of studying children. The goal of observation is: "to describe the natural habitats and behavior of children" (Wright,

1960, p. 78). Wright states there are four aims in the observational study of child development:

>the ecological aim: we see this as the contextual, natural environment argument
>the normative aim: this represents the need to find central behavior tendencies, common points of development
>the systematic aim: this represents the more controlled sort of study, as in a nursery school or a laboratory
>the idiosyncratic aim: smaller studies of individual children . . . more qualitative in nature, less quantitative

Looking at things the way Wright does, it appears that observation forms the basis for all research. Even in controlled (laboratory) experiments, observation is the basic tool of the student and researcher alike.

Using some of these basic techniques, the field of child development can be divided into several distinct areas: biological growth and development, the study of cognitive processes, personality development, social development, and the environment. Using one or more of the aims identified above, the researcher investigates a particular facet within a larger domain of child development.

Summary

1. Theories are often a source of anxiety among students of child development. Actually, theories are just tools for the student. They represent the underpinnings of the discipline and provide a perspective for the study of child development.

2. Child development possesses both a substantive theoretical aspect as well as a significant applied, or "hands-on" aspect. Extreme devotion to either end of the continuum is misleading to the student.

3. Gesell systematically and objectively studied children and developed norms for behavior and development. His theory states that the development of the child is orderly and patterned.

4. Freudian theory is one of the most misunderstood of all theories. It postulates a sequence of stages in child development. Evidence reviewed in the chapter suggests that parts of Freudian theory are quite accurate, parts are inaccurate, and parts are untested.

5. Effective resolution of the eight dilemmas postulated by Erikson contributes to ego-strength and coping abilities of the individual.

6. Social learning theory is based on the study of factors that aid and/or hinder learning. Some of the major terms seen in this theory include *motivation, imitation, reinforcement,* and *nonreward.*

7. Piaget's cognitive theory postulates an in-

variant sequence in the cognitive development of the child. Piaget also discussed the functional invariants (assimilation and accommodation) in terms of their specific contributions to childhood understanding.

8. Methodology in child development research is varied, partly because of differences in the motivation of the researcher. Observation of children is probably the most fundamental method of child study, and it forms the basis of all research.

Thought Questions

1. Give examples of how child development can be a field with both strong theoretical and applied dimensions.

2. What specific things should a theory do? How easy is it to explain the behavior of children?

3. Gesell and his colleagues developed norms for the development of the child. How did these researchers deal with the criticism of their work that said: "Your normative theory of child development ignores the role of environmental change and learning"?

4. Discuss briefly the source of the data for most of Freud's work. What effect might this have on the theory itself? What portions of the theory appear to be verified and what portions have literally no support (have not been verified)?

5. What is the importance of the establishment of basic trust in the infant? How important is the interaction of the child with his environment in the Erikson theory?

6. What happens to the learning process if the learner lacks motivation? Discuss the differences in effectiveness of a spanking after misbehavior versus nonreward after a misbehavior. Under which circumstances will each technique be effective? What do children learn in each situation?

7. According to Piaget, how is cognitive growth similar to other kinds of growth, like learning to walk or to write? What aspects of cognition reflect developmental change in the child? When does intellectual development stop?

8. In your own words, describe the basic aims of observational

study of children. How important is observation in the study of children? What is the relationship between observation and "real research"?

Suggested Readings

Elkind, D. *Children and Adolescents: Interpretive Essays on Jean Piaget.* 2nd ed. New York: Oxford University Press, 1974. *David Elkind is one of the significant researchers and writers in the field of child development. In this very clear and understandable book, Elkind describes even the most difficult aspects of Piagetian theory effectively.*

Gelfand, D., ed. *Social Learning in Childhood.* Monterey, Calif.: Books/Cole, 1975. *In this theoretical treatise, Gelfand deals with theoretical and research studies having to do with social learning and the child.*

Lerner, R. *Concepts and Theories of Human Development.* Reading, Mass.: Addison-Wesley, 1976. *Theory building and research issues are the primary directions of this work. It includes a good section on the nature-nurture issue.*

Skinner, B. F. *Beyond Freedom and Dignity.* New York: Knopf, 1971. *Skinner writes for laymen about the implications of behaviorism in dealing with the social problems of the day. Ideal for those students interested in the application of behaviorism.*

READING

Early in Chapter 2 we indicated that theory is often the hardest part of the study of child development for students. One of the most complex theories in the field is the one proposed by Jean Piaget. This theory has been subjected to a great deal of scientific scrutiny and testing, yet it remains one of the most difficult for the student to understand.

Millie Almy has taken essential elements of Piaget's theory and has put them into a more understandable form. Using very clear examples, Almy demonstrates the processes of equilibration and adaptation and shows the importance of being able to understand Piaget.

One of the keys to effective preschool and early childhood education is an understanding of the basic theoretical foundations of the field. Almy's explanation makes a marvelously rich theory applicable to the student of child development. As Almy noted, Piaget should not "be identified with the majority of psychologists who have influenced American education." Perhaps more explanations of the type Almy offers will make what Piaget has to say even clearer and more functional so that it may play a greater role in the education of American children.

Piaget in Action
Millie Almy

As word about Piaget has spread, psychologists, teachers, and others have tried to accommodate to ideas that often run counter to the behaviorist tradition in which most of us were brought up. Not surprisingly, we have assimilated Piaget's concepts to our own cognitive structures in ways that have often distorted and changed the concepts. It should also be noted that Piaget, although not altering the basic grand design of the theory that he began to sketch some fifty years ago, has explored new problems, made discoveries, modified some of his views, and strengthened others. Meanwhile investigators have conducted research, some of which is strongly supportive of the theory and expands on it, and some of which calls certain elements into question. Perhaps one can say that the theory is dynamic and does not stand still for the educator who wishes to put it to use in the classroom. Despite this, I think certain elements of the theory are basic and can provide some guidance to teachers.

Educators often identify Piaget as a learning theorist. This is an example of the way we tend to assimilate new ideas to old structures. Piaget's basic concern is not with learning (that is with changes in behavior that cannot be attributed to maturation) but rather with the development of knowledge. Accordingly, he cannot be identified with the majority of psychologists who have influenced American education.

Once the educator grasps the fact that Piaget's concern is with knowledge, or with knowing, and not with learning, the further distinctions that Piaget makes may only gradually be understood. For example, *physical knowledge*, knowledge that can be inferred directly from observation of the physical world, differs from *logico-mathematical knowledge*, knowledge that individuals construct from their own actions on the physical world. Again, it may be some time before the distinctions between *figurative* and *operative knowledge* become clear. *Figurative knowing* is static and tied to immediate perception. *Operative knowing* transcends the immediately given and can deal systematically and logically with transformations. It is the latter kind of knowing that, for Piaget, marks the mature intelligence, and in the long run enables the individual to deal more and more effectively not only with physical knowledge but with social and moral knowledge as well.

Whatever difficulty many educators have had with the different kinds of knowledge postulated by Piaget, most have, I think, had less trouble accommodating to the idea that the mature intelligence evolves through a series of stages, and that the thinking of the child differs from that of the adult, not merely in the quantity of concepts available but qualitatively as well. Even here, however, there is evidence that the theory has been assimilated to the traditional ways of schooling. Piaget's research has undoubtedly more often been used to determine the sequence in which concepts should be presented to children than to determine the nature of the classroom experience the children should have. In other words, educators have more often called on Piaget to determine *what* children should be taught rather than *how* they should be taught. It is the *how* that is most important if we are to see Piaget truly in action in the classroom.

Out of the hundreds of articles and books Piaget has written, only a few deal with matters of education. These suggest that the *how* is to be derived from an understanding of the factors that are involved in the child's transitions from the sensorimotor period of infancy to the concrete-operational thinking of childhood and finally to the formal operations that characterize the thinking of the mature adult.

Piaget identifies four factors that contribute to these transitions. The first three—maturation, action on the physical environment, and social interaction—are all involved in the fourth—the process of equilibration or self-regulation.

The fact that maturation is one factor influencing the way the child's knowledge develops does not imply, as many psychologists and educators have assumed, that Piaget espouses an emerging curriculum dictated only by the current interests and capabilities of the child. It does suggest, however, that certain kinds of curricular activities are more appropriate for certain ages than for others.

As Piaget has put it,

We must recognize the existence of a process of mental development; that all intellectual material is not invariably assimilable at all ages; that we should take into account the particular interests and needs of each stage. It also means . . . that environment can play a decisive role in the development of the mind; that the thought contents of the ages at which they occur are not immutably fixed; that sound method can therefore increase the students' efficiency and even accelerate their spiritual growth without making it any less sound.

Just as the recognition of the factor of maturation does not mean a curriculum that is tied to what the child can do today, so an emphasis on the child's action on the physical environment does not mean a curriculum that is only manipulative. The child grows in understanding of the world by testing the ways it responds to investigations and by observing the effects the child's own actions have. Such manipulation is essential in developing real comprehension. I am convinced that the reason most children are as intelligent as they are in the all too prevalent "look and say" curriculum found in most kindergartens and first grades and in too many preschools comes from the fact that they do actively explore their environment when they are outside the four walls of the classroom. On the other hand, children left entirely to their own devices miss many opportunities to derive fuller meaning from their experience. Social interaction is essential to move an ordinary experience with the physical environment to what Hans Furth calls "higher level" thinking.

The teacher who sees that the child who has just observed that "big" things float soon has an encounter with a big thing that sinks, contributes to the child's development, even if not a word is said. But words may also facilitate development, as when the teacher, having observed an older child arranging and rearranging a set of cubes in different patterns, inquires as to what the child found out through the manipulations. The teacher in the traditional classroom spends much time *telling* children about the world and then questioning them to see whether they have remembered what they have been told. Piagetian theory seems to call for a teacher who listens more than she or he tells and whose questions are designed to promote reflection and further inquiry on the part of the child.

Piagetian theory also emphasizes the importance of the child's interaction with other children. As children confront the beliefs of those who see things differently, as they adapt their

Theories of Development

wishes to others or vice versa in ongoing sociodramatic play, as they contest with each other in structured games, they become less egocentric and better able to take other viewpoints.

The influence on the child's development of maturation, of experiences with physical objects, peers, and adults, are all subsumed under the process of *equilibration* or *self-regulation*. This aspect of Piaget's theory has given both psychologists and educators difficulty. The process, Piaget maintains, is continuous with other organic functions. To American psychologists who have been trained to think more like physicists than biologists this concept has seemed incomprehensible. To the educator who has come to think of schooling as a process in which a competent teacher moves a group of children from one grade level to the next, proving the accomplishment by the results of achievement tests, the concept has been anathema.

Essentially, equilibration, from the viewpoint of the child, is a "do-it-yourself" process. A child may need much or little physical experience or confrontation with peers or questioning by teachers in order to accommodate existing cognitive structures to a new idea, and the way that idea is assimilated depends on what the child already knows or believes considering his or her own life history. Piaget does not suggest that because it is the child who is ultimately in control of his or her own cognitive development the teacher is thereby freed from responsibility. But he does caution with regard to logico-mathematical structures, "Children have real understanding only of that which they invent themselves, and each time that we try to teach them something too quickly we keep them from reinventing it themselves."

As I reflect on the complexities of Piaget's theory, I wonder not that so few teachers have tried to put it in action but rather that so many are doing so. When they do, they opt to focus not on behavior which is readily observable, but on development which can only be inferred. They choose to have classrooms that are filled with a variety of objects and for children who are actively engaged with them, rather than tidy classrooms where pencil, paper, and workbooks can be neatly stored and children sit quietly in their seats. Their classrooms will inevitably hum with conversation and discussion. The essential difference between their classroom and others, however, lies not so much in the ways they appear or sound as in the teacher's awareness of the ways each child thinks and the provisions made to support and facilitate that thinking. Such provision goes beyond the narrowly cognitive and takes into account each child's concerns and interests as well.

How do teachers who want to put Piaget's theory into action go about it? Furth says that teachers prefer to begin trying certain activities with children rather than getting into the theory. I suspect that is generally, although not always, true. But what activities? The answer to this, I presume, depends not only on the teacher's personal intellectual predilections, but also on which of the many interpreters of Piaget's theory he or she encounters. Some interpreters stay close to the theory and rely on it almost to the exclusion of other developmental theories. Others are more eclectic, calling, for example, on Erikson and Werner for further illumination of psychological processes and on Dewey and Whitehead for amplification of the pedagogical. Some interpreters believe that a good place for teachers to start is with the tasks that Piaget has posed children. Some have even incorporated such tasks into the curriculum. For others, as for some of my colleagues at the University of California, Berkeley, the tasks are a means of getting the teacher tuned in to the thought of children. In their program, student teachers, whether destined to teach at the early childhood, elementary, or secondary levels, conduct Piagetian interviews with children at all the levels.

To put Piagetian concepts into action requires, above all else, a thinking teacher. He or she looks beyond the child's verbalizations and manipulations and tries to understand what they mean to the child. This way of looking at and thinking about children is far from easy. It adds, however, a new and satisfying dimension to teaching.

USED WITH PERMISSION OF THE RIJKSMUSEUM, AMSTERDAM

Woman in Blue Reading a Letter, by Johannes Vermeer.

3

Genetics, Heredity, and Prenatal Development

The human being is first a biological creature. Chapter 1 discussed the importance of describing children in terms of their entire being, in all of the worlds children find themselves in. This chapter represents the first introduction to the biological reality. The beginnings of human life and the transmission of human characteristics represent a primary focus in human development, a vital link to our biological origins.

The transmission of human characteristics involves cellular biology. As such, the fundamental topics are inheritance, fertilization, and other vital processes that take place during the early, formative minutes, hours, and days of human existence.

Most cells in the human body are not directly involved in the conception and fertilization processes. *Somatic* cells form the muscle, bone, and organ tissue of the human body; they carry on the life-giving processes, carry the oxygen, rebuild the tissue, feed the cells, and do many other things. Another broad group of cells in the human body carry on the equally vital task of reproduction and transmission of human characteristics. These calls are called *gametes*.

THE GAMETES

Gametes: cells that carry on the human reproductive function

The egg (female gamete) is one of the largest cells in the human body. Some estimates have put its size at $1/175$ of an inch in diameter (Stern, 1973), still very small but large by cellular standards.

The eggs are produced through a process called *ovulation*, in which one (or possibly two) rudimentary ovum are "ripened" each month. These ovum are termed rudimentary because females are born with a lifetime's supply of these rudimentary eggs in the ovaries.

Foundations of Child Development

(Left) A human ovum in the follicle (a vascular body in the ovary). *(Right)* Human sperm cells. Both photographs taken at the Henry Ford Hospital, Department of Laboratories, Detroit, Michigan.
ARTHUR BOWDEN, R.B.P., PHOTOGRAPHER.

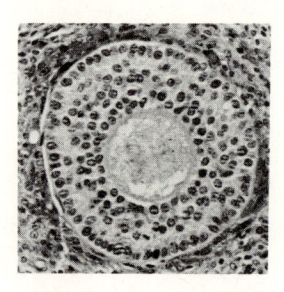

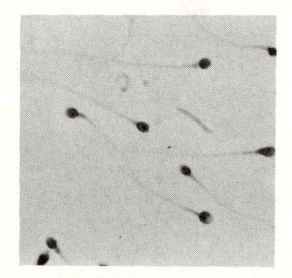

The male gamete, the sperm cell, is much smaller than the egg cell. The sperm cell has a head and a tail that is many times longer than the head; this tail aids the sperm cell in getting up to where the egg cell is. Spermatozoa are produced in the testes, and when combined with secretions from other internal organs, e.g., the prostate, form semen, which is ejaculated during intercourse. One ejaculation by a normal human male consists of approximately 200,000,000 spermatozoa (Stern, 1973).

The process by which gametes are formed is a different type of cell division process than that which the other cells go through. Somatic cells go through *mitosis*. Also called nuclear cell division, mitosis is a process in which an exact duplicate of the original cell is produced. Gametes are formed in the gonadal tissue (ovaries and testes) through a process called *meiosis*, or cell reduction. In meiosis, a cell with half the normal complement of chromosomes is formed. Gametes are different from somatic cells in that they have only 23 chromosomes (in anticipation of combining during fertilization and forming the full complement of 23 pairs, or 46 chromosomes).

Meiosis:
cell reduction process that forms gametes

CONCEPTION

Conception:
the process by which one sperm cell penetrates the wall of the egg cell, fertilizing the egg

After ovulation, the egg travels from the ovary through tubes called *Fallopian tubes*, or oviducts, which are approximately four inches long. These are connected to the *uterus*, or womb. Although the Fallopian tubes (named after Fallopins, who discovered them) are attached to the uterus, they apparently are not attached to the ovaries. They lie in very close proximity, however, and easily facilitate the egg transfer. If in its journey down the Fallopian tubes the egg encounters healthy, active spermatozoa, and *one* of the sperm cells manages to penetrate the wall of the egg cell, conception or fertilization has taken place. Typically, conception takes place in the Fallopian tubes, from which point the fertilized egg (zygote)

Genetics, Heredity, and Prenatal Development

travels down into the uterus and implants into the *endometrium* (lining of the uterus).

Endometrium: the lining of the uterus, where the fertilized egg implants

GENETIC MATERIALS

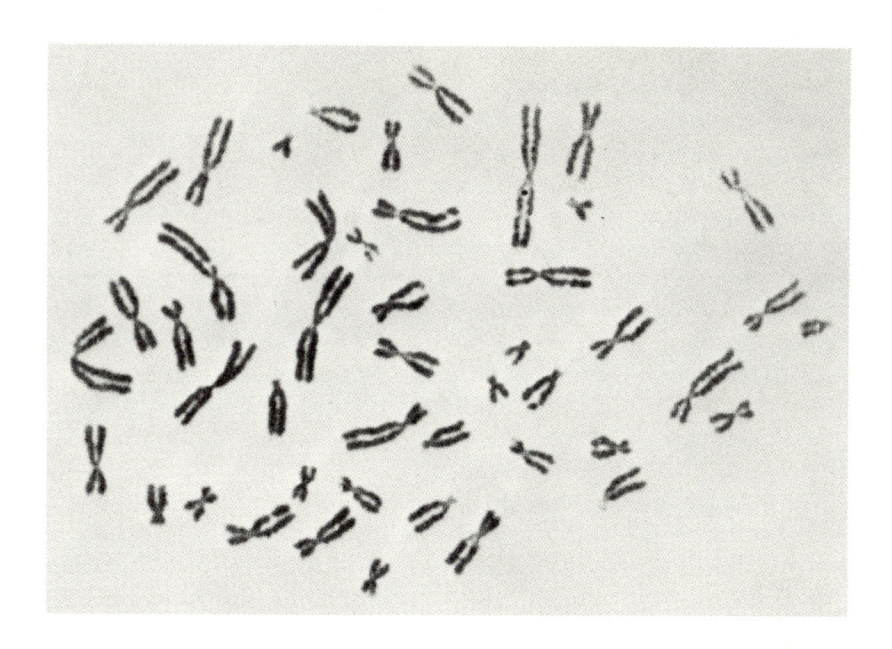

Within each cell of the human body there are many structures and facets, all of which play important roles in the processing of nutrients, maintaining body homeostasis, and, of course, dictating the course of development and heredity. The function of most of these items has been identified, but there are still parts of the human cell that function in unclear ways.

Among the components of the human cell are the *chromosomes*. In each cell (except as indicated earlier in gametes) there are 23 pairs of chromosomes, 46 in all. Chromosomes exist within the nucleus of the cell (that very small locus of control of the cell). The following figure shows the 23 pairs of chromosomes and their relative size.

As is evident from the figure, there are 23 pairs of chromosomes; 22 of these pairs are called *autosomes*. The 23rd pair is different from the rest; it is the pair thought to determine the sex of the person

A microscopic view of human chromosomes after homogeneous staining.

and is consequently called the sex chromosome. On the 23rd pair, the X and Y chromosomes are very different in size.

Other than during cell division, the chromosomes are long, very thin strands of material that are essentially invisible. During cell division they become tightly wound, commonly thought to be coils of material (Stern, 1973).

On each of the chromosomes in a somewhat linear arrangement are structures called *genes*. These entities represent hereditary properties, usually in combination with other genes. The paired chromosomes have the same genes; just as each chromosome has a "partner," so does each gene. These genes are paired in such a way that they occupy corresponding positions on the paired chromosomes; these two partner genes are called *alleles*. The word *allele* means literally "the other one" and in this sense is exactly that.

It is clear from genetic research that genes, singly, or in combination with several other genes, produce different effects. In the most simple of descriptions, alleles form genetic combinations (called the *genotype*). A person's apearance (the *phenotype*) depends on which alleles are in the genotype.

In certain situations, one allele is *dominant* over the other one. If placed in a combination with a recessive allele, the dominant allele has a greater impact in determining what traits a person will inherit. The influence of a recessive (nondominant) allele cannot be observed unless the person is *homozygous* for that trait (has two recessive genes paired at the right place on the chromosome). In other words, for a recessive characteristic to appear, the person must be homozygous for that trait. If the person is *heterozygous,* the influence of the dominant allele will take over. Obviously, if the person is homozygous for the dominant trait, there is no possibility that the phenotype will contain the recessive characteristic at all.

Perhaps the easiest way to explain this transmission effect is with an example, one of the most common being eye color. Let's begin by defining some symbols: B = the allele for brown eyes; b = the allele for blue eyes. The combination of genes (genotype) for eye color, using our terminology, could be one of three possibilities: BB or Bb or bb. Both the genotypes BB and bb are homozygous. Both alleles are the same. The Bb genotype is termed heterozygous because the alleles are different.

In the case of eye color, the allele for brown eyes is dominant to that for blue eyes, so B (the allele for brown eyes) is dominant over b (the allele for blue eyes). The chart on the facing page indicates what might happen with two parents who are heterozygous for brown eyes.

Here it appears that three out of four of the children will have

Gene:
smallest unit of genetic transmission

Dominance:
the ability of one allele in a pair to determine inherited characteristics

	B	b
B	BB 1	Bb 2
b	Bb 3	bb 4

Parent

Child 1 = BB
Child 2 = Bb
Child 3 = Bb
Child 4 = bb

brown eyes (BB—homozygous brown; Bb and Bb—heterozygous brown). Only one of the four children will have blue eyes, that child being homozygous for the recessive trait (blue eyes).

It is possible for two brown-eyed parents to have a blue-eyed child, but the odds are against it. If the brown-eyed parents are heterozygous, they each possess a gene for blue eyes although they do not manifest that characteristic. They could have a bb (blue-eyed) offspring. But blue-eyed parents can't have a brown-eyed child. Blue-eyed parents must be homozygous for that trait; their genotype would be bb. It would, therefore, be impossible, using this logic, for those parents to have a brown-eyed child. We all need to keep in mind, however, that this example is an oversimplification. Many families have had "throwbacks"—a child displaying a phenotype that seemed to have receded to extinction. There may be other alleles involved. And in the real world, eye color is often shaded. It is not always definitely one color; there may be shades of other colors. Eye color is probably affected by other modifying genes somewhere else on the chromosome.

Dominance does not mean that the trait is a good one and the recessive trait is a bad one. Dominance also does not mean that that characteristic is the one that will be transmitted. Dominance merely refers to the relationship between the alleles, not to the nature of the characteristic being transmitted. Most human characteristics are polygenic, i.e., they are produced as the result of complex interactions between many genes. Simplification is fine for example purposes, but human genetic transmission is a wonderfully complex operation, defying simplistic explanations of operation.

SEX DETERMINATION

As we have already indicated, there are 23 pairs of chromosomes in the human cell, but only one of these pairs determines the sexual identity of the person. On the 23rd chromosome, a female mammal has a pair of medium-sized chromosomes that are visually similar; these chromosomes have been termed the X chromosomes. The male of the species has one of these medium-sized X chromosomes, but has paired with that chromosome a smaller, Y chromosome (please refer to the chart showing the *karotype,* or arrangement of chromosomes, on page 61).

Half of the sperm produced in the male through the process of meiosis carry the Y chromosome; the other half carry the X chromosome. All of the eggs of the female that mature in the ovaries contain an X chromosome (she has no Y chromosome to give). Therefore, if an egg combines with an X-carrying sperm, a female will be conceived, and if an egg combines with a Y-carrying sperm, a male will be conceived.

These two different types of sperm cells appear to be different in more than just appearance. Landrum Shettles has indicated in some of his research that the two types of sperm are differentially affected by the pH of the vaginal environment, that they swim at different speeds and that they probably have different shapes (Shettles, in Rosenfeld, 1974). Shettles maintains that if certain practices are adhered to, the parents can greatly raise the odds of having a child who is the sex they wish.

Conditions Affecting Sex of Child*

Conditions that increase the chances of having a male	*Conditions that increase the chances of having a female*
1. Intercourse at ovulation	1. Intercourse prior to ovulation
2. Douche with base solution	2. Acidic vaginal environment
3. No female orgasm	3. Female orgasm desired

*Adapted from Rosenfeld, 1974.

Surveys have shown that both males and females tend to desire at least one boy baby, although many people do not have distinct preferences. A false assumption is that without help the baby is more likely to be a girl. Birth statistics do not support this. An egg has as much chance of combining with a Y as with an X sperm. It is interesting to note that it is the male component of conception that determines the gender of the child; the female offers eggs with X chromosomes only.

SEX LINKAGE

There are some traits that are related directly to the sex of the individual. Some characteristics link up on either the X chromosome or the Y chromosome. Y linkage is relatively unstudied, but it is a situation in which fathers pass a trait on to their sons but not to

Genetics, Heredity, and Prenatal Development

their daughters (because, of course, the daughters have no Y chromosome). It appears that only a few characteristics are transmitted in a Y linkage fashion (Stern, 1973).

X linkage, however, is famous because in history we have some notorious examples of X-linked traits being passed on. These situations (usually disorders) are produced by genes carried on the X chromosome. If a female has two genes, one a normal X and another X', which contains the recessive gene, she is protected from having the disorder by the fact that she has a normal gene on the homologous chromosome (she must be homozygous recessive for that trait to appear). However, if the male receives the X' chromosome from the female, he has no correcting gene on the other X chromosome, because he has a Y chromosome. Thus, the disorder appears in the male. Please refer to the chart below, illustrating what happens when a XX' mother and an XY' father produce children.

Sex linkage: the existence of characteristics directly related to a person's sex

	$\underline{X}$	$\underline{X'}$
X	XX a.	X'X c.
Y	XY b.	X'Y d.

Looking at these four possible genotypes, child *a* and child *b* will be unaffected by the disorder; child *c* carries the gene for the disorder but will not manifest it, and child *d*, a male, will be affected. In this mythical four-child family there are two males and two females. One of the two boys will be afflicted with the problem, and while neither of the two females will have the disorder, one of them will be a carrier of the gene.

If a normal mother and an affected father have children, there are different results:

	$\underline{X}$	$\underline{X}$
X'	XX' a.	XX' c.
Y	XY b.	XY

Here, all the male children are normal and all the female children are carriers of the disorder but do not manifest the disorder. From our examples it appears that with these X-linked disorders, male-to-male direct transmission never occurs (Hall, 1977).

Two of the commonest examples of these types of disorders are hemophilia and color blindness. Stern (1973) has indicated other sex-linked traits, including certain types of congenital night blindness, an X-linked type of muscular dystrophy, two types of diabetes, atrophy of the optic nerve, and so on.

GENETIC DISORDERS

Trisomy:
serious abnormality in which three chromosomes are paired instead of two

The term *congenital* means present at birth. The terms *genetic, inherited,* and *hereditary* have been assigned various meanings through the years. A trait may be a genetic trait, its occurrence owing to a genetic phenomenon, but it may not be hereditary, passed between generations.

Chromosomal disorders represent one category of genetic problems. A chromosal disorder may be an inappropriate number of chromosomes, such as 47 chromosomes, or it may represent the breaking off of a chromosome and its reattachment to another chromosome (translocation). A *trisomy* is three chromosomes paired at a given locus; most of the time this is fatal during early embryonic development (Hall, 1977). Swanson (1974) reported that about 20 percent of the embryos that are aborted spontaneously during the first months of pregnancy have trisomy or monosomy (one chromosome, no pair). The most familiar kind of trisomy is trisomy 21, which produces a child who is moderately to severely retarded and has several distinct traits: folded eyelids, dry furrowed palms, and a good disposition. This disorder is often termed *Down's syndrome*. Down's syndrome can also be produced by translocation of a gene.

Another class of disorders are the so-called sexual differentiation anomolies. Money and Erhardt (1972) have dealt extensively with these types of situations. One of these, Turner's syndrome, has a chromosomal genotype of XO. Females of this genotype have no ovaries, are very short in stature, have marked underdevelopment of primary and secondary sexual characteristics and have only 45 chromosomes: an X (female), but no corresponding chromosome. An XXY genotype is commonly termed Klinefelter's syndrome. This produces men who are disproportionately tall, are often below average in intelligence, and have 48, 49, and as many as 50 chromosomes (Stern, 1973; Swanson, 1974).

Sexual Differentiation Disorders*

Genotype	Frequency/Live Births	Name	Symptoms
XXY	1:1000	Klinefelter's syndrome	Sterile, feminized male; very tall; potential for retardation
XO	1:5000	Turner's syndrome	Sterile, underdeveloped female
XYY	1:1500	(no specific name)	Fertile male, taller than normal, potential for retardation; defect not transmittable
XXX	1:1000	(no specific name)	Infertile female; sometimes mentally deficient

*Adapted from Swanson, 1974; Hall, 1977.

Gene disorders are another source of genetic problems. A gene is thought to be a small piece of DNA (deoxyribonucleic acid) that controls the production of a single protein. An abnormal gene becomes manifest when it produces an abnormal trait or problem. Autosomal recessive disorders of this type include cystic fibrosis, PKU (phenylketonuria: the inability to metabolize phenylalanine hydroxilase), and sickle cell anemia. Parents are usually normal, but they are probably carriers. The trait is recessive, i.e., the genotype must be homozygous recessive, so that some of the children will be affected and some of them may be carriers. These problems are not sex linked and several children of the same generation can be affected (Hall, 1977).

A caution: the preceding has been an oversimplification of the genetic mechanisms. They are actually incredibly complex. Most characteristics of the human are polygenic, and we do not understand fully the genetic mechanisms involved in these conditions.

GENETIC COUNSELING

Genetic counseling is the process of obtaining as much information as possible relative to genetic concerns, so that intelligent decisions concerning children can be made. This process of education includes basic information about family history, phenotypical data, some intuitive "guessing" and even suggestions as to coping mechanisms should there be a problem. Hall (1977) has indicated that there are five specific areas of genetic counseling:

1. the diagnosis; what it is and how it was obtained

2. the natural history of the disorder
3. the recurrence risk
4. prevention (prenatal diagnosis; contraceptive information)
5. therapy

Genetic counseling gives to the client only the mathematical chances of a particular occurrence. It does not make the decision for the people involved, nor is it an infallible technique. Genetic counseling is important, however, because it obtains the information from families, which provides figures on the recurrence risk of a particular characteristic. This information could be vital in preventing the birth of children with severe problems, and could be instrumental in preparing parents with techniques and information related to the potential problem.

PRENATAL DEVELOPMENT

One of the most dynamic of the developmental periods of the human being is the prenatal period. This is the time when the organism develops from a microscopic entity of only one cell to the highly developed seven-to-nine-pound baby. The prenatal developmental period is not necessarily a period of continuous development. There are times of very rapid growth and there are times of consolidation; there are times for organ differentiation and there are times for organ expansion. Prenatal life can be roughly divided into three periods of unequal length and diverse function: the period of the zygote, the period of the embryo, and the period of the fetus.

The Period of the Zygote

As we mentioned earlier, conception usually takes place in the Fallopian tubes. The period of the zygote begins with conception and ends with implantation (the zygote literally fixing itself to the endometrium, the lining of the uterus). Estimates of how long this period lasts vary. It appears that the beginning of implantation takes place about seven days after conception, and secure implantation occurs anywhere from 12 to 14 days after conception (Shepard and Smith, 1977). Cell division, of course, has begun and is proceeding at a relatively fast rate.

Genetics, Heredity, and Prenatal Development

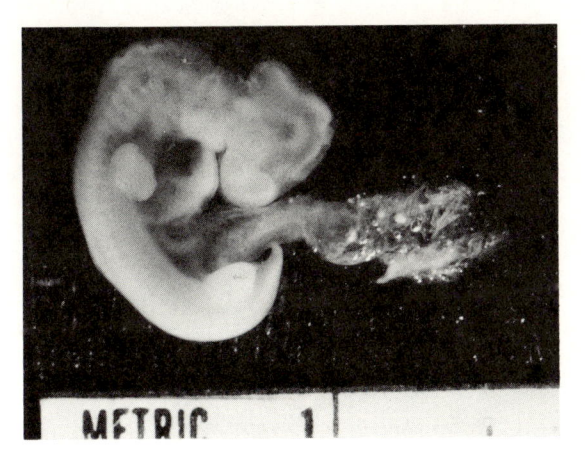

A 33-day-old human embryo measuring about 10.5 millimeters in length. Photograph taken at the Henry Ford Hospital, Department of Laboratories, Detroit, Michigan.
ARTHUR BOWDEN, R.B.P., PHOTOGRAPHER.

The Period of the Embryo

The period of the embryo lasts from the end of the zygote period (14 days after conception) to approximately 54 to 56 days after conception (Shepard and White, 1977). The predominant task during this period is the differentiation and development of the organs. By the end of the embryonic period organ development is not complete, but organ differentiation is. It would stand to reason, then, that any agent (drugs, radiation, etc.) that might interfere with organ differentiation could be exceedingly damaging. An agent that might not do any damage to the child in the other two periods could do large amounts of damage during the period of the embryo. The period of the embryo, then, is a "critical period" in the development of the human being (a critical period is a highly sensitive time when introduction of appropriate or inappropriate stimuli may significantly facilitate or hinder the development of the human).

By the end of the period of the embryo many bodily systems are operational. The primitive heart has started to beat and hormones are being produced. Both of these events demonstrate the fact that the brain is working to send electrical impulses to various body parts.

The Period of the Fetus

The final period in fetal development begins at the termination of the organ differentiation period mentioned above and lasts until the end of the pregnancy. The growth evident during this period is more expansive. It is the period when the fetus begins to move, and all the systems become more refined and operational (except, of course, for those being maintained by the mother, e.g., respiration). The final six to eight weeks of this period is primarily a time of adipose tissue (fat cells) development, so that a child who is born during this time may look rather lean.

The development of the fetus seems continuous; but within this continuous scheme, there are peaks and valleys of development. Different children, different genetic material, different intrauterine environments all reaffirm the possibility that the time distinctions we mentioned above are only general guidelines. Since we do not know exactly when these periods evolve, we must be careful in the administration of drugs, radiation, and other agents to pregnant women.

Not all embryos that are produced at fertilization actually implant, and not all that implant are carried to full term. There is some evidence that only about one-half of human conceptions make it all the way through a successful implantation in the uterine wall (Hertig et al., 1959).

The reason behind this relatively high failure rate is probably some sort of genetic coding problem with the fetus. The message necessary for survival is not present, and a natural process takes over; the zygote fails to implant and is lost in the normal menstrual cycle. In the cases of spontaneous abortions (after implantation), the percentage of these fetuses that have chromosomal oddities or damage present ranges from 25 to 60 percent (Boué, Boué, and Lazar, 1975). It looks as if this high mortality rate usually involves genetic problems of some degree.

OTHER FETAL SYSTEMS

Placenta:
membrane that supports the developing fetus

Of great importance to the developing fetus is the *placenta*, a vascular organ attached simultaneously to the uterine wall and the fetus (through a connecting system known as the umbilical cord). This organ is the liver, lung, and kidney for the fetus. The placenta carries to the fetus a supply of oxygen so that the cells may do their work, and carries away from the fetus the by-product of respiration, carbon dioxide. The umbilical cord carries to the placenta the waste material from the cells, and the placenta works to transfer this material to the mother's body so that it may be eliminated through her system. The umbilical cord contains three blood vessels (one vein and two arteries) packed in a jelly-like substance. Of course, the fetus, while *in utero,* does not take food through its

Genetics, Heredity, and Prenatal Development

mouth; the placenta provides the nutrients for the fetus without the baby needing to swallow food (however, babies do indeed swallow while they are in the uterus).

The placenta also produces hormones that help to sustain the pregnancy, including chorionic gonadotropin, progesterone, and estrogen. At the time of the baby's birth, the placenta weighs about 460 grams, which usually is about 14 percent of the fetal weight (Shepard and Smith, 1977). There is evidence that if for some reason the pregnancy goes well beyond the due date, there may be signs of malnutrition. It appears that the placenta has a certain

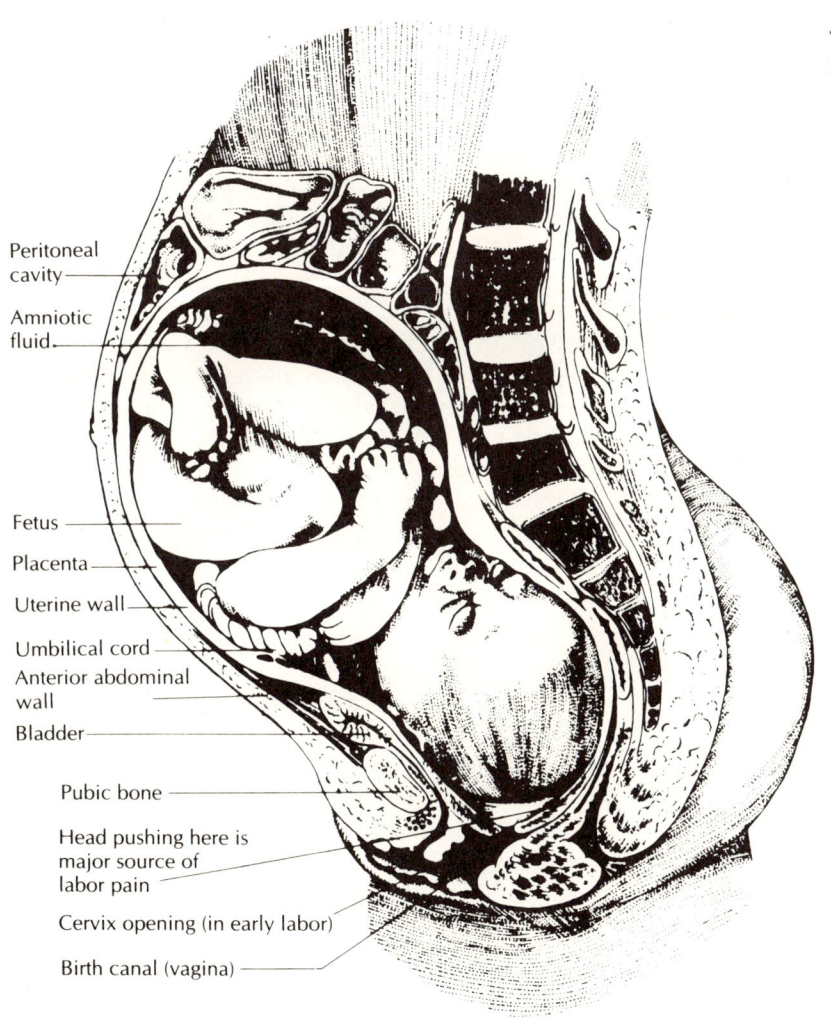

The position of the fetus prior to birth.

capacity at which it can work, and when that capacity is exceeded, the organism (in this case, the baby) begins to suffer.

For many years it was assumed that the placenta was a barrier, preventing substances from "crossing over" to reach the fetus. The protective shield theory is false. Most substances of smaller molecular weights will pass through the placenta. Anesthetic gas used during delivery, for example, will pass through the placenta and have a direct effect upon the fetus.

Recently Yvonne Brackbill has demonstrated that medication used during labor and delivery can have adverse effects on the baby (Brackbill, 1978, 1979). Four basic results have been demonstrated. First, in over 30 studies related to obstetric medicine, there is a consistent negative finding: obstetrical medication never improved normal infant functioning. Secondly, the effects of these drugs are not transient. The effects on the children were observable anywhere from one month to *seven years* after delivery. Thirdly, the effects of these drugs are related to dosage and potency of the drug. General anesthetics are stronger than local, and local anesthetics are stronger than no drugs. Lastly, the effects of drugs are not related to socioeconomic status, delivery style, or sex of the child.

The fetal nervous system—brain, spinal cord, ganglia (bundles of nerves)—all the way down to the nerve cell itself matures relatively quickly, as some neural activity is necessary for primary functioning. The basic functions of the nervous system develop early, but the more subtle and complex facets of neural functioning develop more slowly. By about the *26th day* of prenatal life the fusing of the neural tube into a primitive brain has occurred (Swanson, 1974; Hall, 1977; Stern, 1973).

FETAL ASSESSMENT

There are several distinct ways to assess the progress of the unborn fetus. Some of these techniques have been characterized as intrusions by the popular literature and have been branded as unnecessary by many people. However, these techniques represent significant advances in our ability to diagnose early problems and to deal with them. The technology of the day has advanced to the point where we can learn much about the unborn fetus. While the vast majority of all pregnancies are perfectly normal, it is good knowing that these methods are available for individuals who need them.

One of the more technical methods is called *amniocentesis*. In this technique a long needle is inserted through the woman's abdomen into the uterus. *Amniotic fluid* (the liquid that the baby floats in) is carefully removed and taken to the lab for analysis. This technique is possible from 13 to 14 weeks onward. The analyses can reveal the presence of any of 25 metabolic disorders that may be present (Dorfman, 1972). In addition, the sex of the child can be determined because the genotype is one of the results obtainable after laboratory work. This technique is not performed, however, for curious couples who wish to know the sex of their baby. Amniocentesis is performed when there are suspicions concerning the viability of the fetus. Any of a number of conditions may warrant this technique: genetic history; previous medical histories; known exposure to a variety of dangerous substances; and age of the mother.

Amniocentesis: extraction and analysis of amniotic fluid

Fetal monitoring is another way to assess the fetus's progress. One type of fetal monitor is strapped around the abdomen of the woman; another type has electrodes that are attached to the head of the fetus. Most often used during labor, both monitor fetal heart rate; heart rate can be a significant indicator of fetal distress, which may warrant further action.

Perhaps the most direct and poignant way of assessing the presence and activity of the fetus is the sensation of the baby moving within the mother's abdomen. This movement, which is sometimes called *quickening*, varies considerably in amount, type, and duration. Nevertheless, fetal movement is very conspicuous in its absence, and it is a concern to physicians and others monitoring fetal progress. Absence of movement might be indicative of a serious problem.

ENVIRONMENTAL IMPACT ON THE FETUS

As we have indicated earlier, the placenta does not prevent environmental agents from reaching the developing fetus. An agent is said to be *carcinogenic* if it has been shown to produce cancer; a substance is *teratogenic* if that substance is known to produce malformations in the developing organism.

As research continues into the impact of environmental agents upon the developing fetus, we are learning that there are many agents that inflict great damage to the fetus; it appears as if the list grows longer every day. Shepard (1976), in his book *A Catalog of Teratogenic Agents*, has indicated that there are literally hundreds of

Teratogen: agent that can produce fetal abnormalities

agents that, depending upon the situation and the animal involved, may be teratogenic.

The human fetus seems to be highly vulnerable to teratogenic agents during the second of the three fetal periods, the period of the embryo. As we know, this is the time of organ differentiation and development and also limb differentiation and development, obviously a very significant time. This period lasts anywhere from 14 to 60 gestational days, but due to the inability to directly measure the duration of this period, the mentioned limits have little meaning. Any time may be a bad time for these substances to be introduced to the human fetus. The first and third periods of fetal development are not necessarily immune to the effects of these substances.

The effects of these substances vary, depending upon the animal; not all substances have the same effect on all animals. For example, it appears that aspirin is highly teratogenic in rodents, but similar results have not yet been produced in humans. Thalidomide does not seem to cause problems in mice and rats although it is highly teratogenic in rabbits and humans (Shepard and Smith, 1977). Nearly anything, if administered in a high enough dosage and at the right time, will produce problems in humans, particularly the fetus.

There are four broad categories of known teratogenic agents: radiation sources, infections, maternal metabolic problems, and drugs and environmental chemicals (Shepard and Smith, 1977).

Radiation is a significant issue in this age of nuclear energy. On an everyday basis we are exposed to all sorts of radiation. The sun is a source of radiation; there is the massive network of microwave facilities; and there are microwave ovens. Exposure to X rays, particularly early in pregnancy, may be a source of problems. Even dental X rays, when there is no shielding provided, can cause problems in humans, particularly pregnant women.

As far as infections, rubella (German measles) can produce malformations in the fetus. A mother needs to be tested for rubella prior to and after becoming pregnant and to be aware of exposure to people who have German measles. Syphilis in the mother has the potential of producing deformities and congenital syphilis in the neonate.

Maternal metabolic problems are often subtle and complicated. Alcoholism on the part of the mother can alter the utilization of nutrients by the mother, but more importantly, alcoholic mothers eat poorly. They ingest insufficient amounts of protein and other vital nutrients. Babies born to alcoholic mothers often possess a set

Genetics, Heredity, and Prenatal Development

of characteristics called *fetal alcohol syndrome*. This very severe problem is exhibited in the baby as low birth weight, higher rates of stillbirth and miscarriage, and a general poor picture at birth. Many physicians feel fetal alcohol syndrome has become a national problem.

The following table shows a variety of agents (both chemical and other) and the potential effects each agent has:

Maternal Effects Causing Fetal Problems

Agent	Result
Maternal rubella	Cataracts; deafness; heart disease
Maternal emotional stress	Defects; abortions (spontaneous); prematurity
X rays; radiation	Physical deformities; stillbirth
Thalidomide (tranquilizer)	Physical deformities
Maternal smoking (tobacco; marijuana)	Low birth weight; prematurity; deformities
Maternal nutritional deficiency	Impaired intellectual function (protein deprivation); [effects of severe alcohol consumption probably fit here]
Maternal hepatitis	Potential fetal defects
Blood incompatibility	Rh factor (mother is Rh− and baby is Rh+); mother's body begins to produce antibodies to combat the Rh positive cells; this can result in severe damage to the fetus, particularly from the second child on.
Maternal age	Post-age 40 chances of Down's syndrome increase significantly

Smoking on the part of the mother is also dangerous. Babies of mothers who smoke heavily are often smaller and lighter in birth weight. There is also evidence that smoking produces an increase in fetal heart rate. Even household drugs like aspirin have been contraindicated in all trimesters of pregnancy by the Department of Health, Education and Welfare.

INFANT MORTALITY

Not all infants survive to birth, nor do all young babies survive for very long after birth. *Infant mortality* is the term describing the number of children who die at or very near birth. Infant mortality is affected significantly by three independent variables: education, income, and medical facilities. Obviously, all three of these are interrelated. The best medical facilities do not exist in the poorest part of our country. The better-educated individuals usually have more money, which allows them to live in cozy suburbs and pay for better medical treatment and facilities.

One of the popular myths in our culture is that America has no poverty. This myth is perpetuated by the people who live well within the system, who can afford to have the appropriate medical facilities and are educated enough to read a medical label or prescription and know when to see a doctor. However, there are significant portions of our population who live in situations where educational levels are low, poverty is rampant, and unfortunately, the medical facilities are understaffed and underequipped.

Does the United States have the lowest rate of infant mortality in the world? One might guess that it would, considering our wealth, influence, and ability to spend money in many different places. The following table, however, shows where the United States actually lies in comparison to other countries.

Selected Rates of Infant Mortality*

Country	Deaths per Infant/1000 Live Births
Chile	79
Austria	24
Israel	22
United States	17.6
Belgium	17
France	13
Japan	10
Sweden	10

*Adapted from U. N. Department of Economics and Social Affairs, United Nations, 1974.

To be sure, there are obstetric reasons for children dying at birth or shortly thereafter. Some of these problems include congenital malformations, malpresentations (see next chapter), anoxia (lack of oxygen), hyaline membrane disease (lungs unable to function), and so on. But there are environmental factors involved in these mortality figures, about which something could be done. The fact that we do not have the lowest mortality rates, given our technology and wealth, underlies the importance of some of these environmental factors. The World Health Organization, reporting in 1971, said that there is a significant need for greater health care services and much better planning in the delivery of health care. We sug-

Genetics, Heredity, and Prenatal Development

gest that the health delivery systems are *still* not adequate for all the American people.

This need for greater health care services has led to the adoption of national health services in several countries (England, Sweden, and others). These "socialized health programs" are set up to provide low-cost, highly effective health care to all members of society. In the United States these types of programs have been resisted for many years because they are supposedly inflationary and too socialistic. However, it is likely only a matter of time before the United States has a national program.

ISSUE

Test Tube Babies

The technology of childbirth has made some astounding advances in recent history. Perhaps the most significant and thought-provoking of these advances is the realization of a researcher's dream: the extrauterine conception of a human, implantation into a mother, and eventual birth of a normal, healthy baby. A feat that has been thought impossible for centuries is now bringing new hope to many couples who have been unable to conceive normally.

☐ The mechanics of *in vitro* (in glass) conception are relatively simple in theory, yet very difficult in application. The woman who cannot conceive normally is treated with hormones so that eggs within the ovary will mature. A laparoscope is used to locate the egg, which is then brought out through the abdominal wall via a needle. This egg is placed in a glass dish that contains blood serum and other nutrients; sperm from the father is then added to the dish.

☐ If the egg is fertilized by one of the spermatozoa present, the zygote is transferred to another dish containing more nutrients. The zygote is allowed to grow for approximately three to six days. At that time, the fertilized egg is ready to be transferred back to the uterus of the woman. In anticipation of this, the woman is again treated with hormones that prepare the uterus for the arrival of the zygote and eventual implantation. The zygote is then taken from the dish, inserted into the woman's uterus, and if everything goes as planned, normal embryological development proceeds.

☐ This process has been performed many times under laboratory conditions. During the summer of 1978, however, a healthy child conceived in this manner was born to a couple in England, and other such births have been reported since that first one.

☐ It is estimated that in the United States upwards of 10 percent of married women who want children cannot have them. Many times, this inability is due to blocked Fallopian tubes. In cases like these, the process described above may be the way for these people to have children. In addition, there is tremendous potential for genetic research present in this type of work; it may be possible to discover the cause of genetic diseases, and deal with problems before they become untreatable.

☐ In the United States, the movement for this sort of conception technique has taken off. Many infertile couples are taking advantage of techniques similar to those used in England. Doctors estimate the cost for the procedure at $1,500 to $4,000 (*Newsweek*, March 5, 1979).

☐ There are significant moral and legal questions yet to be answered about this technique. Some physicians feel that these sorts of efforts are Frankenstein-like

Genetics, Heredity, and Prenatal Development

techniques that toy with human nature. What is to be the end of such research? Will people use the techniques for other, less savory purposes?

☐ At the present time, it is not possible to get federal funds for use in research like this in the United States. There is a ban on *in vitro* research in this country. The future of this type of research is difficult to predict. Certainly there will be pressure on the government to release federal funds for this type of research. The debate over the morality and potential problems of children conceived in this way will continue; the ultimate resolution of the situation may one day rest in the hands of the United States Supreme Court.

The first test tube baby ever born was delivered by Caesarian section on July 25, 1978 to an English woman whose fallopian tubes had been blocked, preventing normal conception. The baby girl weighed 5 pounds 12 ounces and was normal.

Drs. Patrick Steptoe and Robert Edwards used the following procedure. They initially treated the woman with hormones (1) to stimulate maturation of the ova in the ovary. The ova were drawn out of the ovary (2) by a needle inserted into the woman through the abdomen. An ovum was placed in a dish which contained blood serum and nutrients (3) and sperm were added from the husband to fertilize the ovum. The fertilized ovum was placed in another dish of nutrients (4); there it divided a number of times for three to six days, creating a blastocyst. The woman was given additional hormones to stimulate the uterine lining for implanting the blastocyst. The blastocyst is placed in the uterus (5) and implants itself in the uterine wall and develops as it would in a natural conception.

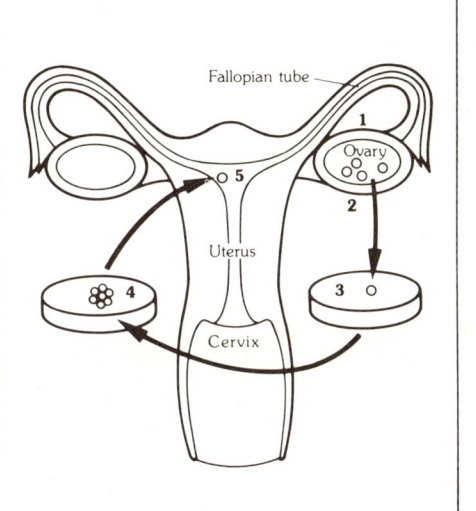

Summary

1. Humans are biological beings first. The most fundamental realization of this biological heritage is contained in the genetic and hereditary aspects of human development.

2. The female ovulates (produces an egg cell), which may be penetrated by a sperm cell (if one is present); this is called conception. The fertilized egg (zygote) will implant into the wall of the uterus in four to seven days.

3. The basic elements of genetic transmission are chromosomes, genes, dominance, recessiveness, DNA. The term *dominance* does not relate to the positiveness of a particular trait. It only refers to the relationship between paired chromosomes.

4. The male determines the child's sex. If the male contributes a Y chromosome, it will match with an X from the mother to produce a male offspring; if the male contributes an X chromosome, the result will be a female.

5. Some human characteristics are related to the sex of the individual. These characteristics

(baldness, hemophilia, etc.) are carried by the female, but are most often exhibited in the male.

6. Congenital (present at birth) birth defects have a wide variety of causes. Sometimes these conditions are produced because of environmental problems (drugs, radiation, etc.), sometimes they are produced because of the pairing of recessive genes, and sometimes there is no apparent reason for them.

7. Prenatal development is composed of three periods: the period of the zygote, the period of the embryo, and the period of the fetus. Very significant things happen at each of these stages. Some researchers state, however, that the second period may be the most crucial in the determination of problems for the baby because it is the period of organ differentiation.

8. It is possible to find out many things about the fetus before it is born, using fetal assessment techniques, including amniocentesis. Fetal assessment may be able to tell the doctor and the parents if there is a problem with the fetus.

9. Contrary to what we might expect, the United States does not have the lowest infant mortality rate. This surprising finding is in contradiction to the affluence of our culture, and points to the need for a comprehensive health program in the United States.

Thought Questions

1. Why is the study of genetics and heredity important to the study of children?

2. By what process are gametes formed? Describe the process of conception, implantation, and ovulation, citing locations, timing, and results.

3. Differentiate between the following terms: *chromosome, gene, dominant characteristic, recessive characteristic*. Is it true that all recessive traits are negative and all dominant traits are positive?

4. How can one trait be genetic but *not* hereditary? Give an example.

5. Why is it that women do not suffer from X-linked problems like men do? Can the Y chromosome also carry traits? What is a sex-linked characteristic?

6. How important is the prenatal environment in terms of the development of the fetus? Give examples of the effects of common, everyday materials that negatively affect the fetus.

7. Describe in detail at least one technique of fetal assessment. What can we find out through this technique?

8. What is the future of *in vitro* fertilization? What are the moral, legal and ethical principles involved in a technique like this? Should this technique be allowed to continue? Why?

9. From your point of view, why does the United States not have the lowest rates of infant mortality? Cite reasons why we perhaps *should* have the lowest rates. What can be done to improve the conditions for babies in the United States? Will the techniques you have indicated really work?

Suggested Readings

Dworkin, R.H.; B.W. Bourke; B.A. Maher; and I.I. Gottesman. "A Longitudinal Study of the Genetics of Personality," *Journal of Personality and Social Psychology*, 1976, 34(3), 510–518. *An intriguing research look at the interaction between personality and genetics.*

Nilsson, L. *A Child Is Born.* New York: Delacourte/Seymour Lawrence, 1977. *Perhaps the single most outstanding feature of this book is the truly outstanding photography of human reproduction. A lucid explanatory text accompanies the photos.*

Rugh, R. and L. Shettles. *From Conception to Birth: the Drama of Life's Beginning.* New York: Harper & Row, 1971. *The title of the book is indicative of the content. The great strength of this book is the excellent photo program concerning prenatal development.*

READING

Technology has played a fundamental role in the development of the American culture. The incredible mechanical and scientific advances that accompanied and followed the Industrial Revolution have brought new and seemingly always changing life-styles to Americans.

Interestingly, until recently there was very little medical science could do in the way of preventing and/or coping with high-risk pregnancies. Edwin Kiester, writing in *Family Health/Today's Health*, indicates that modern science has made some huge strides recently in the relatively new field within pediatrics called fetology.

Through a wide variety of sophisticated techniques, fetologists hope to lower infant mortality rates and deliver healthier babies. Kiester describes procedures like amniocentesis, fetoscopy, and sonography, which all contribute to improving prospects for normal fetal development. With these and other predicted technological advances, we may be soon treating disorders *in utero*, and cases that once meant disability or death for the infant may be treatable, assuring the child a normal life.

Healing Babies Before They're Born
Edwin Kiester Jr.

At the age of six months, Karen Spencer is the kind of alert baby that doting grandparents term "bright as a button." She has brown hair, shining dark eyes and she laughs with delight when her proud mother dandles her on a knee or scoops her from her playpen. Already, she can sit erect without propping, and when she smiles the faintest flash of white shows in the lower gums —the beginnings of her first teeth.

You'd never know to look at Karen that no one really expected her to be here at all. While she was still in her mother's womb, she was diagnosed as a victim of "Rh disease," or erythroblastosis, which systematically destroys red blood cells and dooms some babies before they are born.

But Karen was saved by a risky, exquisitely delicate procedure. Two months *prior* to birth, she was given a series of blood transfusions to bolster her ravaged supply and prepare her to face the outside world. By the time of birth, she had virtually healthy blood—and after intensive care, went on to a normal infancy.

Until a few years ago, trying to save the life of an endangered baby was often a frustrating experience. Even when a doctor recognized a threatening condition, there was little that could be done until the actual birth took place—by which time irredeemable damage might have occurred. Today, thanks to new equipment and daring techniques, doctors can literally treat babies in the womb. They can prevent some birth defects, minimize the impact of others and avert parental heartbreak and tragedy.

Fetology is the "frontier" of pediatric medicine, according to Dr. Michael M. Kaback of Harbor General Hospital in Los Angeles, one of the foremost practitioners of the specialty. "We have brought the maternal death rate to a new low, and now our emphasis is on lowering infant mortality and delivering healthier babies," he says. Dr. Kaback predicts that the number of conditions that can be corrected in the womb will increase sharply in coming years. The scope of current success was recently outlined in a study of 53,518 pregnancies in 12 hospitals by Dr. Richard L. Naeye of the Pennsylvania State University College of Medicine in Hershey. Between 1950 and 1975, Dr. Naeye reported, deaths between the twentieth week of pregnancy and four

Genetics, Heredity, and Prenatal Development

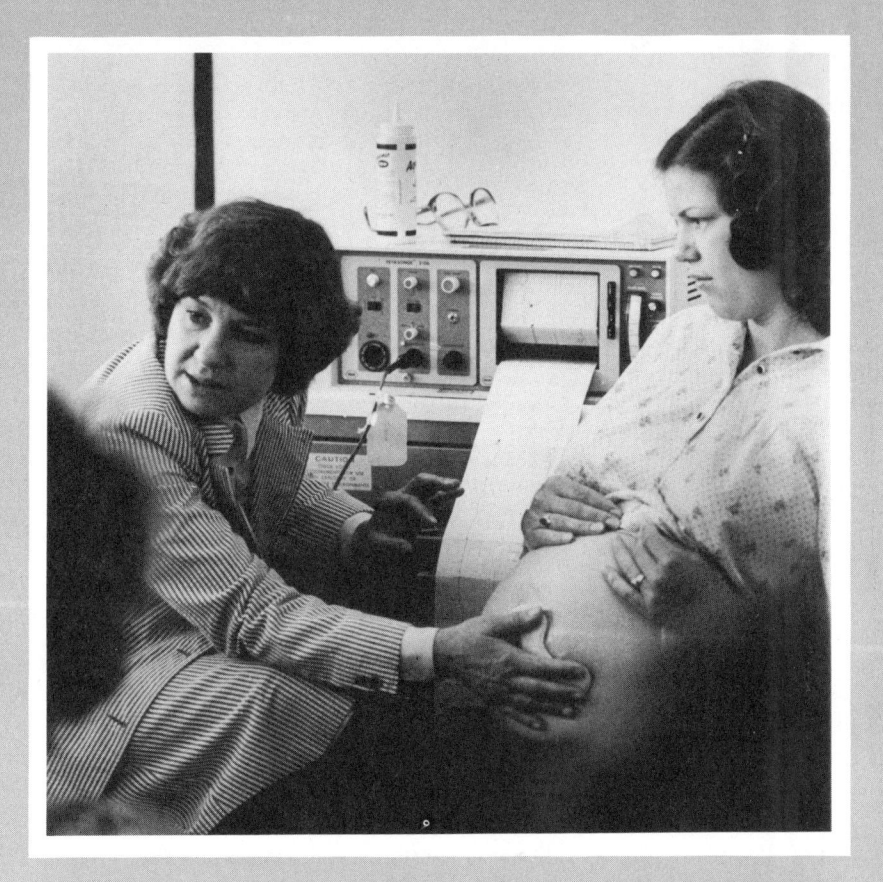

A nurse *(center)* explains how transducers fastened by a belt to the abdomen of this pregnant woman will record the heartbeats of her unborn child on the fetal monitor in the rear. By analyzing the heart rate of the fetus, the attending physician can study the exchange system between the mother's placenta and the fetus and the ability of the unborn child to withstand the stress of contractions during labor.
JEFFREY P. GROSSCUP.

weeks after birth fell from 29.2 per 1,000 live births to 16.1 per 1,000, a drop of 44.9 percent.

The prenatal blood transfusion that saved Karen has been used for more than five years, yet is still one of the rarest and most dramatic procedures performed by the fetal specialist.

Why was it necessary?

To begin with some common knowledge, the Rhesus, or Rh, blood factor is found in the majority of persons—the so-called Rh-positive. It is lacking in others, the Rh-negatives. When an Rh-negative mother conceives by an Rh-positive father, the child is likely to be Rh-positive, its blood incompatible with that of its mother.

The bloodstreams of mother and child are separate, but frequently some of the fetal blood will cross into the mother's system, which identifies it as an invader and triggers the production of antibodies to destroy it. This is seldom a threat during a first pregnancy. But the antibodies remain after delivery and, if the mother conceives again, may cross back from her system into the new baby's, destroying red blood cells and threatening the baby's life.

Fortunately, about ten years ago, it was discovered that injections of a substance called Rho-Gam, administered to the mother shortly after each delivery, could neutralize the antibodies and eliminate the peril. Rho-Gam is now given routinely to mothers known to be Rh-sensitive.

A few women with Rh-negative blood, however, are sensitive without being aware of it. They include those who have unknowingly received transfusions of Rh-positive blood, perhaps during surgery or after an injury, and those who have miscarried early without treatment, like Karen's mother, Joanne Spencer.

When Joanne, 35, became pregnant, she did not realize that her own body threatened the life of the baby she so desperately wanted. She had married in her early 30's but was not able to conceive at first. When she did become pregnant, she suffered a miscarriage even before she visited an obstetrician. She had never heard of Rho-Gam. But now that she was pregnant a second time her obstetrician explained the danger of Rh sensitization.

In her sixteenth week of pregnancy, Joanne's obstetrician sent her to Dr. Robert Creasy at the University of California, San Francisco. Dr. Creasy, a lean, blond man in his early 40's, is renowned for his skill in shepherding women through "high-risk" pregnancies. His first step was to perform amniocentesis: He inserted a long, thin needle into the pregnant uterus to extract a small amount of the amniotic fluid that surrounds the fetus and carries off its wastes. Cells from the sample were cultivated; they showed the baby's blood was indeed Rh-positive.

The impact of Rh-disease varies, depending on how many antibodies reach the fetal circulation. Some infants merely become somewhat anemic. In others, damage is severe, resulting in retarded growth or prenatal death. After the amniocentesis, Creasy began close surveillance, with ultrasonography, a technique that resembles marine sonar and bounces high-frequency sound waves off the fetal form to chart its growth and position.

At first, the effect of Rh-disease seemed minor, but then the baby's development slowed.

At 24 weeks, the threat seemed grave. "I knew the baby would die unless we intervened," Creasy recalls.

The problem in such cases is to maintain the infant life until the baby has matured enough to survive in the outside world. Creasy determined to transfuse O-negative blood (O is the universal donor blood) to replenish the baby's depleted supply. To do so required an operation as delicate as writing on the head of a pin while blindfolded. At 24 weeks, the fetus is less than 12 inches long and weighs only a pound and a half; the target area for the transfusion, the abdominal cavity, is smaller than a half dollar. The doctor, of course, cannot really "see" his patient but, as in amniocentesis, must insert a needle through the mother's abdomen into the uterus, through the amniotic sac and its fluids, which hold the baby, and into the tiny body. Each transfusion carries a 10 percent chance of inducing labor and producing a miscarriage.

Creasy carefully explained these risks to Joanne, who agreed to undergo the procedure. So he injected a dye into the amniotic sac, which the baby swallowed. By X ray, Creasy could then visualize the intestines. At 26 weeks, he administered the first transfusion, hitting the target dead center with 40 cubic centimeters (cc) of life-saving blood, about two thimblefuls. Almost immediately, the fetus became stronger.

But as the fetus continued to develop during this period of rapid growth, more blood was required. Thus, Creasy was obliged to repeat the exacting procedure twice more, at 29 weeks and at 32 weeks. The second transfusion was double the amount of the first; the third gave the baby an additional 110 cc. By now the baby's blood was almost completely O-negative, and development seemed normal. Therefore, rather than have her face further transfusions, Karen was delivered by cesarean section at 34 weeks. A pediatric emergency team stood by and rushed her to the intensive-care nursery. She remained there a month before her mother could bring home what she called "my little miracle."

Even more of a miracle baby is April Murphy, the three-year-old daughter of Paul and Teresa Murphy of Marshfield, Massachusetts, for she represents the first baby treated before birth for an inborn error of metabolism, which could have ended her life.

A sister April never knew, Heather, died in 1972 at the age of three months. Heather was a victim of methylmalonic acidemia, a congenital disorder so rare that only about two dozen cases have been reported since it was first identified 15 years ago. The condition results from the baby's lack of a certain enzyme needed to produce vitamin B_{12}, which is necessary to properly utilize methylmalonic acid (one of the substances produced when protein is broken down by the body). Lacking the vitamin, the acid accumulates and poisons the system, leading to mental retardation and eventual death.

Heather's death could not at first be explained. It took weeks of inspired laboratory detective work by Dr. Mary Ampola of Tufts-New England Medical Center in Boston, working with a tiny driblet of the girl's urine, to establish a diagnosis. Then came the task of breaking the news to the girl's parents. By ironic chance, each parent carried the defective gene for the rare condition. Odds were one in four a new child of theirs would develop the disease.

Like Joanne Spencer, Teresa Murphy yearned to have children. A Catholic, she flatly refused to consider abortion, even if a new baby showed the defect. Thus, when Teresa became pregnant again, and amniocentesis disclosed the presence of the fateful gene, Dr. Ampola decided on a radical step in the hope of producing a healthy child.

In other cases of methylmalonic acidemia, babies had been kept alive—though they were retarded—by a low-protein diet started at birth. How much brain damage preceded birth in this case was an unanswered question. But to forestall it, Ampola decided to treat the baby prenatally—by giving Teresa vitamin B_{12} in such great amounts that it might cross the placental barrier and offset the baby's deficiency.

"It was a gamble," Ampola admits. "We didn't know if either the mother or the baby could tolerate such saturation." But the Murphys agreed to try it. Every day for the final six weeks of pregnancy, Teresa received 5,000 times the normal adult requirement of vitamin B_{12}. Her thighs and arms were black and blue from the injections.

The gamble paid off. Early in December 1974, April was born, bouncy and normal. Placed on a special diet, she has grown satisfactorily in every way, and last summer a test measured her IQ at 118, well above average.

Methylmalonic acidemia may be only the first of 20 or more inborn errors of metabolism that doctors believe will eventually respond to prenatal treatment. Recently, Ampola has used the same methods against galactosemia—the inability to digest lactose, or milk sugar—a deficiency that, if undetected, can cause eye cataracts, mental retardation and fatal liver disease before the baby is a few months old. A milk-free diet started at birth has helped many victims to develop normally both physically and mentally. Overall, however, even treated galactosemics score below average in intelligence, indicating that brain damage sometimes occurs before birth.

David and Linda Fleming of Holyoke, Massachusetts, had one child who was galactosemic. So when Linda became pregnant again, she sought early diagnosis to allow for immediate treatment. Amniocentesis at 16 weeks showed positive results for galactosemia, and Linda was referred to Dr. Ampola.

Instead of injections, Ampola this time prescribed a special diet. Although expectant mothers normally drink a quart of milk daily, Ampola withdrew all milk and foods containing milk, which include many luncheon meats, margarine, bread and pastries, in addition to dairy products. She substituted calcium tablets to help build the baby's teeth and bones.

Gregory Wilhelm Fleming was delivered in May 1976. It was found at birth that he was just a carrier all along, rather than a victim, of galactosemia. Amniocentesis could not make that distinction. "We still don't know if a special diet will reduce the effects of galactosemia," says Ampola, "but we do know that it does not harm the baby. So in the future, probably all mothers who have had one galactosemic child will be placed on a milk-free diet."

Of course, the specialty of fetology is not necessarily limited to highly unusual cases. A whole array of advanced techniques and instruments now allows doctors to monitor more closely relatively uncomplicated pregnancies and thus to step in and prevent complications or danger to the baby.

Fetoscopy, for example, allows the obstetrician to peer directly into the womb and observe the baby. It is most commonly used to find out whether the baby is alive in the absence of a measurable heartbeat. A thin, lighted scope about the diameter of a pencil is inserted through an incision in the abdomen, and the doctor can then watch the baby's movements through the eyepiece. Fetoscopy is a delicate procedure; on rare occasions it may induce abortion, so extreme care must be taken.

Amniography involves injecting the amniotic fluid with a dye that the baby swallows and that shows up on an X ray—as was done prior to

Karen Spencer's transfusions. It helps detect whether certain soft tissues are growing properly.

Ultrasonography, which was used to monitor Karen's development, was experimental a few years ago, but now is widely employed to "visualize" the baby. Harmless, high-frequency sound waves are transmitted through the abdomen to the fetal form. Their "echoes" translate into a series of impulses that register on a screen, according to how far they have traveled, and provide an outline of the fetus. Ultrasound can check for malformations as well as a baby's position.

Something called the *challenge test* induces the hormone oxytocin into the mother-to-be in order to start mild uterine contractions like those of labor. Under this stress, the baby's heartbeat is monitored to judge whether it can withstand normal birth or should be delivered by cesarean section.

Other tests measure the amount of serum estriol cast off in the mother's urine during pregnancy; a rising amount indicates the baby is developing normally, while a decline may mean the baby is having difficulty.

Most pregnant women may never experience these methods. But they are standard practice when a woman is at high risk for both herself and the baby—diabetic, hypertensive, a cardiac case. By closely monitoring her condition and the baby's, the obstetrician can prescribe a change of diet, more bed rest, increased exercise, or necessary medication to produce a successful pregnancy. Recently, for example, Creasy delivered a four-pound, growth-retarded infant whose mother was diabetic, hypertensive and nearly 150 pounds overweight. With ultrasound and the challenge test, Dr. Creasy followed the pregnancy until the fetal growth slowed, then delivered the baby by cesarean section. Though small, the baby is thriving.

Amniocentesis, the sampling of amniotic fluid, dates back ten years, but doctors nevertheless feel it is still in its infancy. The procedure is most publicized as a means to learn the baby's sex in advance, or to determine if an over-37 mother carries the chromosome mutation that produces a Down's syndrome child. But its application goes much further.

According to Dr. Aubrey Milunsky of the Eunice Kennedy Shriver Center, Waltham, Massachusetts, more than 60 congenital conditions can be detected prenatally by amniocentesis. Dr. Milunsky says the test should always be used when family history points to possible chromosomal abnormalities, inborn errors of metabolism, gender-linked disorders, such as hemophilia, and congenital nervous-system malformations. A 1975 government study disclosed that the procedure does not increase the likelihood of miscarriage.

Recently, Dr. Mitchell Golbus of the University of California at San Francisco devised a method to sample fetal blood by taking a tiny droplet from the baby's scalp. This extract can be tested for such conditions as sickle-cell anemia, the blood disease that strikes blacks, and beta-thalassemia, common among persons of Mediterranean background.

Another discovery with profound implications for fetology is that genes producing birth defects often travel in company with other harmless genes. A British team has reported that six out of seven times, the young boys who are the exclusive prey of myotonic muscular dystrophy (MMD), a progressive fatal neuromuscular disease with a biochemistry that is unknown, manifest a particular, congenital pattern of saliva secretion. The gene for MMD cannot be detected, but the secretor gene can. Researchers say this kind of "gene mapping" may help determine prenatally the presence of many congenital conditions now undetectable.

Harbor General's Dr. Kaback sees the growing knowledge about life before birth as a definite step in the right direction. Speaking at a recent meeting of the American Society for Pediatric Research, Kaback predicted that medicine would soon be able to treat in utero such conditions as Tay-Sachs disease and sickle-cell anemia, whose biochemistry is known. In the future, Kaback said, the birth of a child like Karen Spencer will be a routine—not a dramatic—blessed event.

COURTESY OF THE SMITHSONIAN INSTITUTION, FREER GALLERY OF ART, WASHINGTON, D.C.

Childbirth (1329) by Yūzū Nembutsu Engi-Kuma Kura Period. Yamatoe School.

4

Birthing and Neonatal Development

Prenatal development is a very exciting, incredibly complex sequence of human growth. From conception through implantation and up to birth, the growth of the human fetus is truly a remarkable occurrence. It is true that the development of the fetus is normative and sequential, but it is also idiosyncratic. All fetuses do not develop at the same rate; some babies take more time to mature, and for some inexplicable reason, some babies decide to come a little earlier than expected.

The average length of the normal pregnancy, with both mother and baby progressing normally, is 266 days, which are counted from two weeks after the last menstrual period. A mother can expect about a 12-day amount of variation from that total. People often say that nine months is the typical length of the pregnancy. If we divide 266 days by 30.5 (average number of days per month), we get a figure of approximately 8.7 months, very close to the nine-month figure.

PRENATAL CARE

Prenatal care for expectant mothers begins, ideally, early in the pregnancy. It is recommended that prenatal care begin early, when many women need to have pregnancy confirmed through a pregnancy test. However, not everyone goes to be tested. Often the women who should probably be seeing a physician for prenatal care are not, and those who are perhaps less risk-prone are the ones who are seeing their doctors regularly. Everyone—the doctor, the mother, and the baby—are at significantly greater risk if the mother simply shows up at the emergency room to deliver the baby. The doctor, without a history or even a blood type to go by, is at a disadvantage. The baby is at greater risk when no one has prepared and taken responsibility for the birth.

There may be people who argue that regular prenatal visits are unnecessary for women who take care of themselves and are responsible for their health. A physician should know, however, the physical history of the mother, which may have a significant effect on the outcome of the pregnancy. Knowledge of maternal diseases, alcohol ingestion, and fetal movements, and an ongoing assessment and monitoring of maternal nutritional practices is also important.

It is important to enter pregnancy in the best of all possible health. No amount of prenatal care can totally alleviate the problems created by a severe nutritional deficit during the earlier years of the mother's life, for example. Prenatal care is of great importance to both mother and baby.

THE ONSET OF LABOR

Labor:
the process of contractions that push the baby out of the mother's body

The process of uterine contractions that literally expel the fetus from the mother's body is called *labor*. The factors that start the labor process vary considerably from one species to another. In human beings the precise cause of the start of labor is not known. Most researchers and doctors think that there are probably several separate occurrences operating together that trigger the uterine contractions. Among the possible occurrences are the release of certain hormones by the mother's body, the taking away of the hormones that maintain the pregnancy, perhaps fetal hormonal activity, and/or placental hormonal activity. A communication system is probably present that signals when the fetus is ready to be delivered. If we can learn how it works we may be able to prevent premature deliveries and perhaps increase infants' chances for survival.

THE COMPONENTS OF LABOR

Contractions are the muscular movements of the uterus during the expulsion process. These contractions work with other structural changes in the mother's body (discussed below) to push the baby out of the uterus and into the world.

Birthing and Neonatal Development

There are four functions of a contraction: (1) thinning out the cervix. This very important process is called *effacement*. (2) *dilatation* of the cervix. This is the process of expanding the cervical opening so that the baby may pass through it. The amount of dilatation is measured in centimeters; 10 centimeters is considered fully dilatated. (3) pushing the baby out of the uterus. This activity feels like a cramping or tightening sensation in the lower abdomen. (4) expulsion of the placenta, the organ that sustained the infant for the duration of the pregnancy. The detachment and ultimate delivery of the placenta is a crucial stage of the delivery process, and, as we will see later, can be a time of complications for the mother.

Uterine contractions are involuntary. The mother cannot initiate or control in any way the onset, regularity, or intensity of a contraction. Only during the last stages of the delivery process when the mother will push voluntarily, is there conscious muscular involvement on her part.

Contractions vary in intensity, duration, and separation, according to the stage of pregnancy and the particular individual. It has been said that no two pregnancies are alike. In the beginning, contractions may be 10 minutes apart and last only 30 seconds; as labor goes along they increase in duration and the time interval between them decreases. They are two minutes apart or less at the time of delivery, and last a minute or more in duration.

Effacement: thinning of the cervix during labor

Dilatation: expansion of the cervical opening during labor

THE LABOR PROCESS

Stage One: One of the signs that labor is beginning includes "showing"—the loss of the small mucous plug that had been in the cervix and the breaking of the amniotic sac. "Lightening" occurs, in which the baby moves down, engaging the pelvis. The mother has a changed lower profile, and her breathing may be easier because of less pressure on the abdomen.

The first stage of labor is the longest stage. It can last anywhere from 2 hours to 12 hours, or even longer. This stage is longer for mothers having their first baby than for those who are having their second, third, or fourth child.

This first stage lasts from the beginning of labor until the dilatation of the cervix is complete (about 8 to 10 centimeters). Dilatation does not necessarily occur before effacement; sometimes effacement occurs very rapidly, and dilatation has to catch up.

Stage Two: This stage begins when the cervix is dilatated about 10 centimeters and is completely effaced, and ends when the baby is

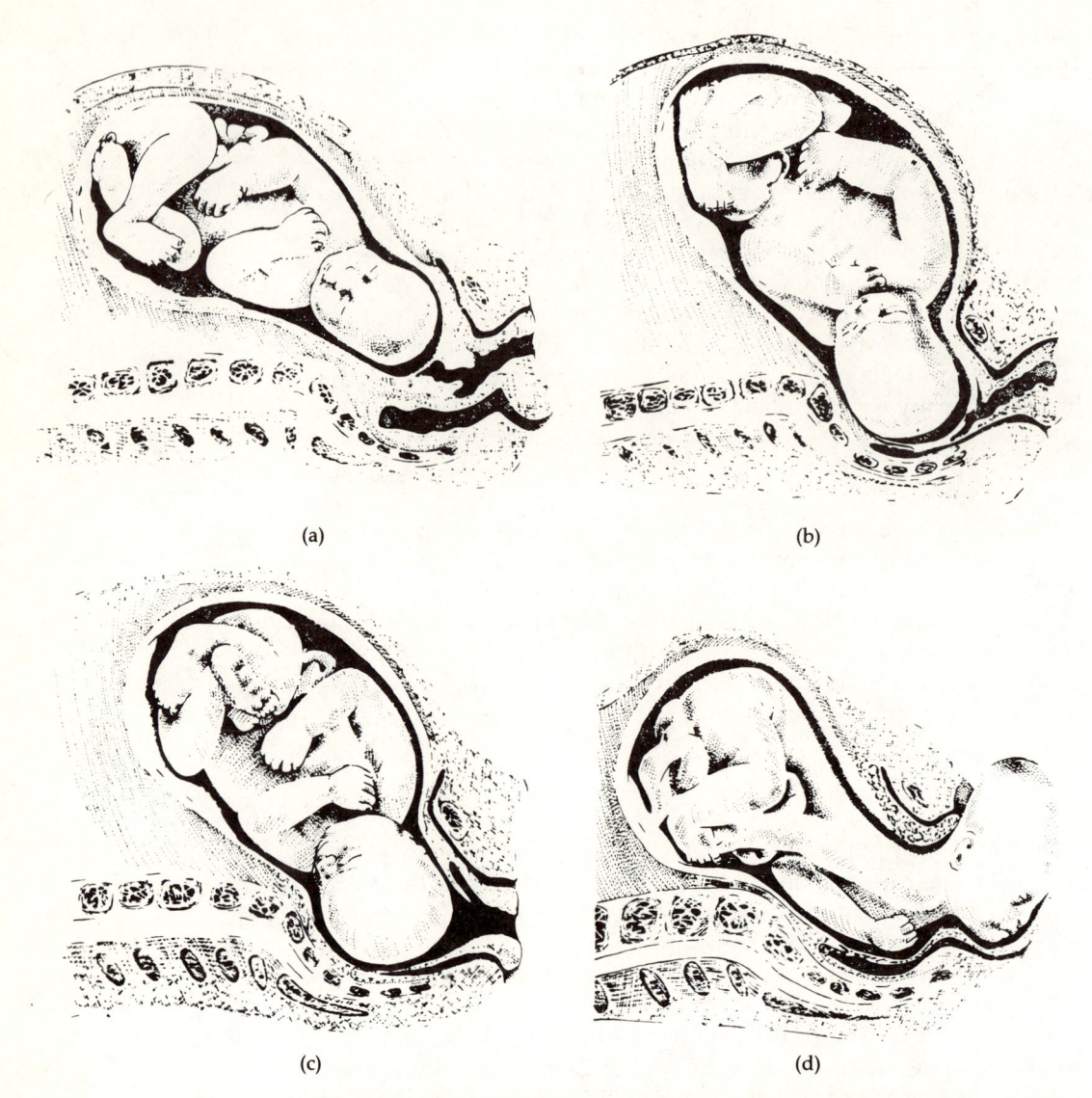

Events in the birth process. (a) Before labor begins; (b) early stages of labor, dilation of cervix begins; (c) cervix completely dilated; baby's head starts to turn; (d) late stage of labor; baby's head begins to emerge.

born. If the mother has never delivered before, this stage may last an hour or more; for mothers who have delivered before, this stage may last only a few minutes.

The contractions during this period are very strong. The baby is being pushed from the uterus into the vaginal canal. The baby's

Birthing and Neonatal Development

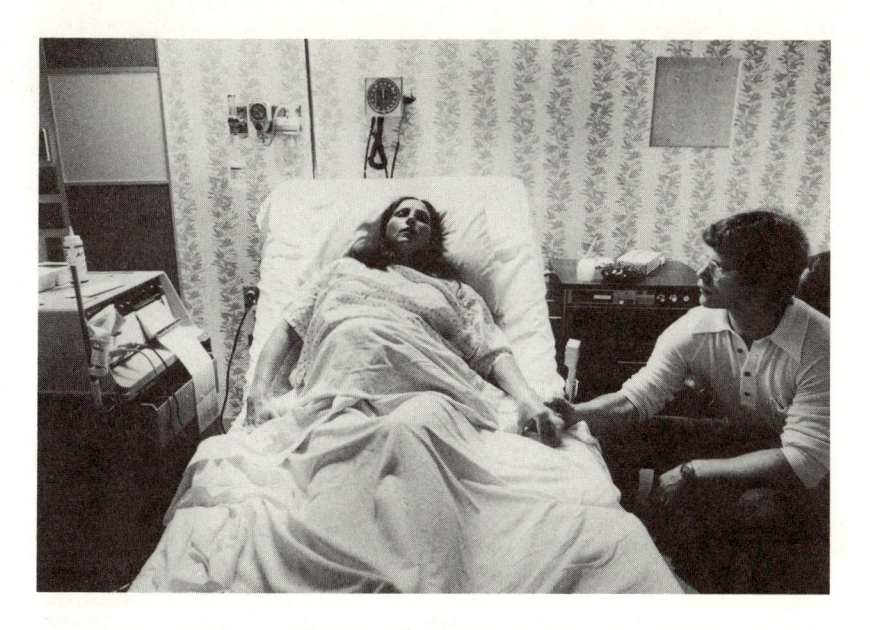

A couple in a labor room. Note the fetal monitor on the left.
JEFFREY P. GROSSCUP.

head is the largest part of the baby's body in terms of diameter; consequently, once the head is delivered, the birth usually goes quite fast.

About 95 percent of the time the baby is born in a vertex position, i.e., head first. Doctors use the term *presentation* to describe the part of the baby that "presents" itself first. A breech presentation is when the baby is presented buttocks first (which can take many forms, one leg turned under, feet first, and so on). These sorts of presentations probably represent only about 5 percent of all deliveries, but they can be very dangerous. The risk factor is several times that of head-first presentations, due to the fact that the mother is delivering successively larger portions of the baby's body. If it is known that there will be a breech presentation, a decision has to be made whether the delivery will be vaginal, or whether the baby will be taken by cesarean section (the surgical removal of the baby from the mother's abdomen).

In many deliveries the umbilical cord is looped once around the fetal neck. This is usually not a problem; the physician unwraps the cord when the head appears. In about 1 percent of the deliveries there is a serious problem with the cord and this tends to double the mortality rate.

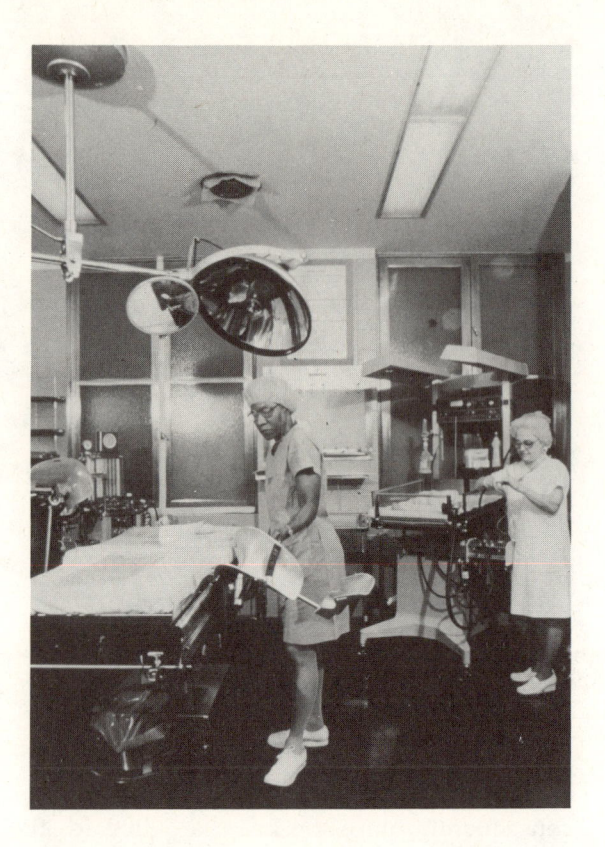

Nurses prepare the delivery room and its equipment. The Ohio Neonatal Intensive Care Center, right rear, is equipped with an emergency resuscitator. Courtesy of Henry Ford Hospital, Detroit, Michigan.
PHOTO BY RONN KAMM.

DELIVERY

The traditional hospital situation usually employs a labor room and a delivery room. The labor room is just what its name implies: a room where the labor process takes place until just before delivery. Labor rooms differ markedly in appearance and space, depending upon the hospital and its facilities. Some hospitals have private labor rooms, i.e., only one mother in labor in the room; but many hospitals have two beds per room. In addition to the beds and other materials you might find in any hospital room, there is also usually at least one form of fetal monitoring equipment.

In most labor rooms around the nation today, the husband and/or coach is encouraged to be in the labor room with the mother to offer support and encouragement. Labor is usually tiring work, and is also an important event to the woman, couple, or family involved. Having her husband or a friend present in the labor room for comfort and assistance is a great asset to a woman in labor. However, some hospitals object.

Birthing and Neonatal Development

Stage Three: This stage begins after the birth of the baby and ends with the delivery of the placenta. In about ten minutes the uterus will contract again and the disengaged placenta will be delivered. The uterine blood vessels that fed the placenta contract quickly and prevent abnormal bleeding from occurring.

Stage Four: The fourth stage of labor basically involves the post-delivery care of the mother. This includes watching for hemorrhaging, insuring rest for the mother, and giving important verbal and emotional support to the husband and/or other relatives and friends.

This final stage of labor and delivery is often not included in discussions of the delivery process. However, we include it here for two basic reasons. First, we need to keep our attention on the fact that birth is a process involving not only the baby but the mother. If we keep this fact in mind, the crucial hours immediately after birth are very important. Second, stage four is a time when the potential for complications is high, particularly a very common problem, maternal bleeding.

Often the doctor needs to perform an episiotomy. This surgical cut of the perineum (the tissue immediately below the vaginal opening) is designed to prevent stretching of the mother's tissues and eases the problem of tearing significantly. Not all women need episiotomies; doctors usually take into consideration the size of the mother, the size of the baby, the presentation, and so on, in deciding whether to perform an episiotomy. This procedure, if it is to take place, occurs during the second stage of labor. During the third stage, or immediately thereafter, the incision is repaired, and during the fourth stage of delivery the repaired incision is monitored for possible problems.

COMPLICATIONS OF BIRTH

Most of the time, the birth process is very normal and everything goes well. The mother and the baby go through the process and both are healthy after the delivery. There are occasions, however, when things do not go according to plan. These complications can be life threatening to both the baby and the mother.

Bleeding Excessively

For the mother, the period immediately following delivery may be the most dangerous. The reason is the risk of excessive bleeding, the leading cause of maternal deaths after delivery.

This excessive bleeding appears to be caused by two primary factors: (1) cuts and lacerations surrounding the cervix and vaginal areas, and (2) the possibility that pieces of the placenta are not detached from the uterus during stage three of delivery (McLennan and Sandberg, 1974; Hellman and Pritchard, 1971). Excessively large babies may be related to bleeding, due to the increased risk of tears and other structural damage. Some literature states that in cases of multiple pregnancies there is a higher than normal risk of excessive bleeding. This may also be related to greater potential damage to vaginal structures.

Prematurity

Prematurity: birth of a baby weighing less than 5 pounds or before 37th week of gestation

A baby that is born too early is typically termed a *premature* baby. A more precise definition of prematurity is necessary, however, because gestational age alone is not a sure indicator of the baby's viability. Generally, it is assumed that a baby with a body weight of less than 2,500 grams (about five pounds) or 37 weeks of gestation is premature. No infant has been known to survive below the weight of 400 grams (less than one pound), but realistically, a lower limit of 1,000 grams is a more accurate cutoff point for survival. The probability of survival of an infant weighing between 800 and 1,000 grams is quite low. It appears that 28 weeks is the lower limit of survival/viability.

Viability: ability of a fetus to survive outside the uterus

In the neonatal period, prematurity appears to be the principal cause of death. It accounts for about one-half of all neonatal deaths even though there are sophisticated infant care sections in many hospitals.

Why are babies born prematurely? One of the more obvious reasons is a multiple pregnancy. When there are two, three, or more infants, they simply run out of room in the uterus. In the case of quintuplets (five babies) birthweights in the range of 1,500 to 2,000 grams are common, if they are that high.

There are certain maternal diseases that contribute to premature births. In many of these cases, the doctor needs to terminate the pregnancy early due to the excessive risks involved if the pregnancy is carried to full term. In these situations an assessment of fetal development is made (through amniocentesis) and perhaps sonography (sound wave tracking of fetal position and development), and when a suitable level of maturity is attained, the baby is removed via cesarean section. It is also possible that abnormalities within the fetus will contribute to a premature delivery. But despite these factors mentioned, over one-half of all premature births are not explainable (McLennan and Sandberg, 1974).

There are extraneous variables that may predict prematurity. One of the more significant is the socioeconomic status (SES) of the parents. In low-income areas within the United States, the rates of prematurity are higher than in more affluent parts of the country. The same is true in overpopulated, poor countries; they have higher rates of prematurity than do countries where the SES is a little better. Nutritional inadequacy also may be related to prematurity.

Premature infants suffer from the lack of maturation of certain body systems. The most significant of these are the lungs. Respiratory distress (difficult breathing) is a very common problem in premature infants; the exchange of gases is inefficient or even nonexistent.

Another serious problem of premature infants is temperature regulation. It is in the last stages of gestation that subcutaneous fat is laid down in the fetus. This is a layer of fat that lies just under the skin and provides insulation. In a premature baby, this layer of fat is absent and temperature control is a greater problem than normal.

Of the premature infants who die, more than 80 percent die within the first 24 hours. If the baby makes it through the first 24 hours, the chances for survival are greatly increased (Hellman and Pritchard, 1971).

A paradoxical situation is often present: the baby needs oxygen, particularly if he is premature and in respiratory distress. The problem is that pure oxygen greatly increases the chances of retrolental fibroplasia, an opaque tissue forming behind the lens of the eye. This condition produces either partial or total blindness in the infant. High concentrations of oxygen (for resuscitation) appear to be better in short-term exposure.

The long-term effects of prematurity are not as clear as the immediate implications. A review of some of the literature, however, reveals that prematurity may be associated with problems in later development. For example, Taub et al. (1977) found that there was no difference between prematurely born and normally born children (ages 7 to 9½) in verbal intelligence, but the premature group was significantly lower in measures of motor performance. Wright (1972) followed up a group of prematurely born infants and matched controls ten years after their births. He found that prematurely born children exceeded their controls in mortality, mental retardation, poor school performance, and visual defects. Rubin et al. (1973) found low birth weight to be associated with psychological and educational impairment. Specifically, language development, school readiness, and general academic performance were impaired in the prematurely born children when compared to the full-term children. Lastly, there is some evidence of social problems in children who have been born prematurely. While they had more adjustment problems than full-term children, Berges et al. (1972; 1973) also indicates that the children who were premature outgrew some of the developmental problems that were apparent early in their lives.

Other Delivery Variations

As we have said, most deliveries are very normal and require no extra activities for normal and successful birth. In many delivery situations, however, certain devices are needed to aid the child (and mother) in the trip down through the birth canal. One of the more common are *forceps*. Obstetrical forceps are double-bladed instruments designed to aid the doctor in easing the child into the world. The blades of the forceps are placed around the head of the infant and are useful in helping the child down through the birth canal.

Forceps: double-bladed instruments used to aid delivery

Why use forceps? Sometimes medical complications demand a quicker delivery than would normally take place. Other times high dosages of anesthesia require the use of forceps. Fetal distress (excessively high or low fetal heart rate—less than 100 beats per minute or greater than 160 beats per minute) is another reason for using forceps during delivery. Caution is always necessary in the use of forceps, and their use is not dictated merely for expediency of the delivery or the convenience of the doctor.

Another variation from a normal delivery is called a *cesarean delivery*. This is the surgical removal of the fetus from the uterus. An incision is made in the lower abdomen of the mother, through the layers of skin and the uterine walls, and the baby is removed through the surgical opening.

Cesarean: surgical removal of the fetus

Cesarean sections are necessary for a variety of reasons. Perhaps there is weak (uterine) tissue due to a previous cesarean (although some recent writings have indicated that a second cesarean is not always necessary if the mother has had one). Prolonged labor or confirmed delivery complications, like a breech presentation, or a small pelvic area and a large baby, may require cesarean section. In some cases the placenta has developed over the cervical opening *(placental previa)*, and in this situation a cesarean is necessary. Six to seven percent of all births are cesarean (Hellman and Pritchard, 1971) and they are increasing in frequency. As you might expect, the infant mortality rate in these cases is several times higher than in vaginal deliveries, which is probably not the result of the

Birthing and Neonatal Development

method so much as the result of the problem the infant was having that called for the cesarean in the first place.

Other Perinatal Problems

There are other factors that contribute to death during the birth (perinatal) period. One of the more significant is deprivation of oxygen, or *anoxia*. The human body, whether a baby or an adult, requires oxygen to reach the cells. This vital gas is exchanged for one of the by-products of metabolism, carbon dioxide. If for any reason this exchange of gases is disturbed or stopped, the infant or adult is in immediate peril. It has been suggested that a human brain deprived of oxygen for only about a minute or two faces the risk of permanent brain damage and/or death.

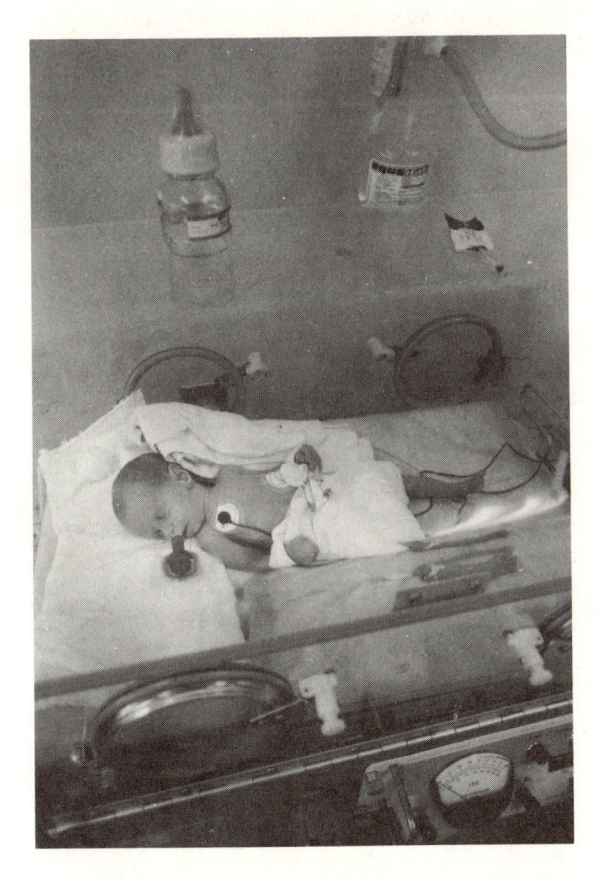

A newborn child in an isolette in the intensive care unit for neonates. The isolette is an incubator that is designed to provide controlled temperature, humidity and oxygen supply and to permit feeding and care of the newborn under aseptic conditions with a minimum of handling.
ROBERT V. ECKERT, JR., EKM-NEPENTHE.

Hyaline membrane disease is a problem produced by the immaturity of the lungs. Often a problem in prematurely born babies, hyaline membrane disease is life threatening and requires immediate attention on the part of the staff and extraordinary resuscitation procedures.

Infection can be a life-threatening situation to the baby. The delicate balance of antibiotic agents may not be sufficiently developed in the neonate or fetus. A maternal infection may produce a deformed child, or during the perinatal period, it may greatly increase the risk to the infant.

Drugs during Labor and Delivery

About 10 percent of maternal deaths are in some way directly attributable to the anesthetic agent used during delivery (McLennan and Sandberg, 1974). It is clear that there is a risk any time a drug is employed. In the case of delivery, there may be a maternal reaction to the drug that will produce these serious complications. In normal labor, anesthesia is probably not absolutely necessary. There are techniques that claim to greatly reduce the need for drugs during labor and delivery. These are discussed in the next chapter.

THE NEONATE

Neonate:
newborn baby

The term used to describe the newly delivered baby is *neonate*, meaning "new life," or "new person." Indeed, the neonate is a new person, although this person has been alive for some time.

Over 3 million infants are born in the United States every year. The problem is that not all of these infants survive to live one full day. About 17 out of every 1,000 live births do not make it through birth and the first day of their lives. This relatively high infant mortality rate contradicts the picture of affluence and effective health delivery systems in this nation, as we discussed earlier.

The neonate is a unique, complex creature. The human neonate may be the most vulnerable of all neonates during the first few days and weeks of life. There are many species of life who are walking and moving on their own a short time after birth. Human neonates are very dependent upon their caregivers because their behavioral response is very limited. They will not walk for many months, and will not even be able to turn over for a few months.

Neonates must adapt to a very different world from the one they were used to. The uterine environment had a consistent tempera-

Birthing and Neonatal Development

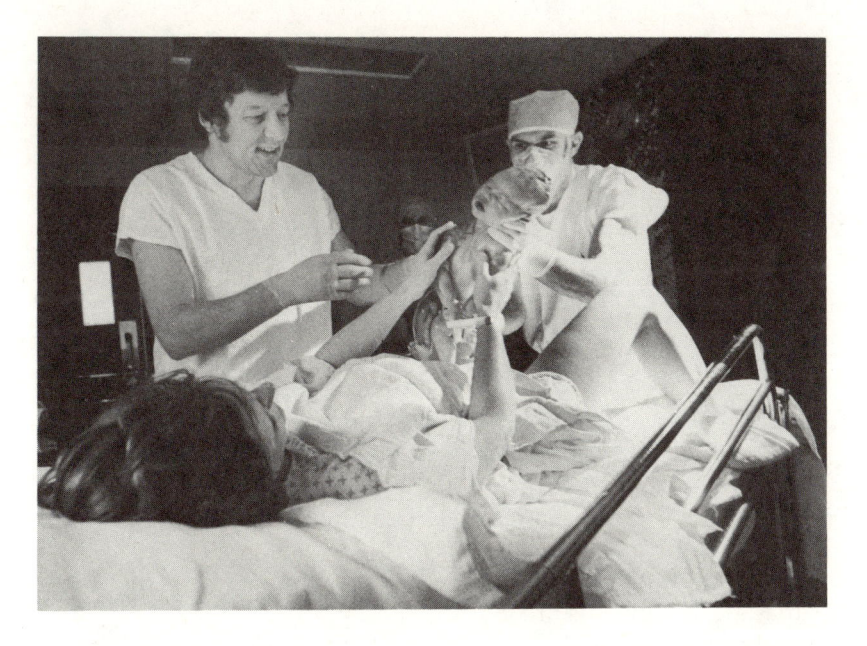

A neonate, parents, and the attending physician at the moment of birth.
JEFFREY P. GROSSCUP.

ture and humidity factor; it was an insulated environment, with the amniotic sac and fluid acting as cushions for the developing fetus. The new environment is much harsher, and although the sensory capacities of the neonate may be diffuse and generalized, the adjustment to this new world is of massive proportions. The dimensions of this adaptation are definitely physiological and probably also psychological.

Neonatal Assessment

At birth it is very important to immediately get a picture of just how the child is doing. This assessment will determine if extraordinary efforts are required and, if so, in which areas these efforts need be directed.

One of the more common assessment techniques is the *Apgar score*. Developed by Dr. Virginia Apgar, this technique utilizes five dimensions of neonatal activity in its assessment: heart rate, respiration, muscle tone, reflex irritability, and color of the skin. Each of these dimensions is rated on a three-point scale one minute after birth and about five minutes after birth.

Apgar Scoring*

	Heart Rate	Respiration	Muscle Tone	Reflexes	Color
0	Absent	Absent	Limp	No response	Blue
1	Less than 100/minute	Irregular, weak	Some movement in extremities	Some motion	Pink
2	More than 100 per minute	Regular, strong	Active, functional	Good movement	Pink all over

*Source: Apgar, 1953.

A score of 10 (two points for each of the five dimensions) is the best of all possible scores. Scores from 7 to 10 require only normal supportive measures. Scores from 3 to 6 indicate a depressed infant in one or more areas, and immediate attention is called for (and probably is already under way).

One of the criticisms of the Apgar scoring procedure is that some of the five dimensions are far more important than others; respiration, for example, is probably more important than reflex irritability, although they may be related.

BASIC LIFE PROCESSES AND TRANSITIONS

As we have indicated, there are some major transitions that need to take place as the infant is adapting to extrauterine life.

Respiration

Most infants breathe spontaneously at birth. Some cleaning and draining of the airways may be required, but babies are seldom slapped into consciousness as has been often portrayed in movies and other fictional accounts. The breathing passages are more than likely filled with water, at least partially. This fluid has a fetal origin; it is not amniotic fluid that has made its way into the breathing passages during the time the infant was in the mother's uterus. Prior to birth the lungs were not operating. The respiratory system has to make a significant transition from a nearly totally inactive system to one of life-sustaining importance.

Most pediatricians assume that prior to 28 weeks of gestation the lungs of a human fetus are not capable of exchanging gases. If birth occurs prior to this time, survival is unlikely because of the immaturity of the lungs.

Birthing and Neonatal Development

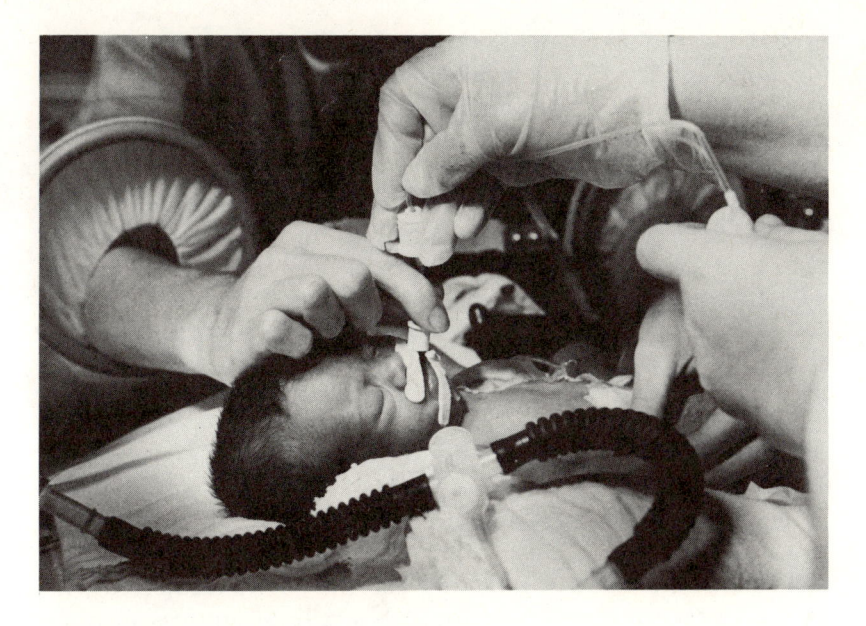

Shortly after birth, an infant's lungs are cleared of fluid.
JEFFREY P. GROSSCUP.

During delivery, part of the fluid that is in the lungs pushes out of the lungs and breathing passages as the chest-diaphragm (the muscle tissue that controls and operates breathing) passes through the birth canal. As the lungs are squeezed, the liquid is pushed out, and as the lungs recoil, air is taken in for the first time. This is why the majority of infants start to breathe within a few seconds of birth, and the initial stimulation for this first breath is the air entering the lungs itself. The neonate need take but a few breaths for the lungs to be completely expanded and working.

Circulation

Closely tied to respiration is the flow of blood in the system of veins and arteries called the circulatory system. The respiratory system and the circulatory system are closely related in that the blood carries the oxygen to the cells and carries the carbon dioxide back to the lungs for removal from the body. Unlike the respiratory system, however, the circulatory system has been in operation and working to spread nutrients to various parts of the fetal body for quite some time in the uterus. The heart, which is the primary organ of the circulatory system, has been beating since about the

In utero:
in the uterus

22nd day of the pregnancy and the circulatory system is essentially functional by day 26 (Swanson, 1974). Even though it is beating *in utero*, all of the features of the human heart, with its four chambers, etc., are not truly functional until birth.

At the time of birth the blood flow changes from placental to neonatal. This is a very important and significant transition. Blood vessels in the placenta begin to constrict, through a series of complex biochemical cues. Blood begins to flow into the fetal lungs where oxygenation begins for the first time. These steps seem to occur simultaneously or at least very close together as the neonate begins life outside of the uterus. There is a mechanism present in the fetal heart that keeps the blood from flowing into the dysfunctional lungs. This opening between the chambers of the heart closes at birth or very near birth and the heart begins its normal functioning.

Some of these changes are not as rapid as others. Sometimes the structure of the heart does not change immediately and the doctor will hear a "murmur" or a different sort of sound connected with the heartbeat. This sort of murmur typically disappears within a few days.

Ingestion-Digestion

Neonatal metabolism, or the activity surrounding the utilization of energy in the baby, is another system that undergoes a transition at birth. *In utero*, the baby did not ingest food through its mouth or eliminate through its own elimination system. At birth the ingestion-digestion system is untested but ready to perform its functions.

The neonate's metabolic system must now be able to (1) ingest food (mainly through sucking) and (2) absorb nutrients into its system through the structures it has available. The very complex cycles of energy transference and molecular breakdown must now work for the neonate. The liver must aid in digestion; the kidney must be ready to clean the blood; and the nervous system has to be ready to coordinate and direct all of these activities.

Normal infants will lose 5 to 7 percent of their body weight in the first three or four days of life. This weight is regained in about a week, although many people are still alarmed that babies will lose any weight after delivery.

Temperature Regulation

Temperature regulation is a very important aspect of neonatal survival. The neonate has a larger surface area to body weight

Birthing and Neonatal Development

ratio than the adult does. He is also born wet, often in an air-conditioned room. The baby's ability to generate heat is not able to compensate for the amount of heat lost during a typical delivery. Hence it is necessary to consciously plan for keeping the baby as warm as possible. This problem might be even more acute in premature infants, as we have stated.

Immune System

In utero, immunity agents from the mother protect the fetus by crossing the placenta and affording some measure of protection. At birth, the picture changes considerably. The baby moves from an environment that was virtually free from microbiological problems to a world that is full of them.

The neonate does have circulating white blood cells that have the ability to deal with infections. However, the baby's immunity system goes through a process of change in developing to its optimal degree. About two weeks after birth a more sophisticated immunity capability has been reached (Shepard and Smith, 1977). The early colostrum from the mother's breast also is rich in antibodies.

THE BEHAVIORAL CAPACITIES OF THE NEONATE

The most prevalent set of awake behaviors of human neonates is reflexive behavior. A reflex is a "primitive, unlearned and involuntary action that can be elicited by specific forms of stimulation" (Gardner, 1978, p. 568). Using this definition, perhaps even breathing is a reflex; and indeed, it is. Several specific reflexive behaviors have been observed in the neonate. We have used the term *awake behaviors* because actually the most prevalent behavior of any kind in the human neonate is sleeping. In addition to this, much of the waking behavior is spent in feeding and other caring activities by the caregiver(s). Burton White has stated: "In the first days, you can expect the baby to average about three minutes an hour of alertness during the day, and less at night. Such periods of wakefulness will lengthen rather slowly over the next month to an average of six or seven minutes an hour" (White, 1975, pp. 15–16).

White, in his discussion of the behavioral capacities of the newborn, speaks to several major issues: (1) the "piecemeal" nature of infant behavior, which implies a very short attention span; (2) the distinct and significant lack of mobility in the neonate; the baby cannot turn over, cannot crawl, and has little control of motor abilities; (3) the extreme sensitivity of the neonate, particularly to loud noises (noises adults may not think of as being loud) and bright lights.

Neonates can hear, and can determine the general location of the sound. Early in their development they can locate objects visually. Neonates can feel pain, although the babies may be unable to differentiate large amounts of any sort of stimulation. Also, while infants cannot interpret the smells that they experience, they can differentiate smells, particularly strong odors. There is evidence also that infants can differentiate tastes, particularly sweet and sour.

Reflex: involuntary response to a stimulus

Lastly, among the awake behaviors are the specific reflexes. The more primitive reflexes (sucking and swallowing) include the rooting reflex (infants turn their heads to stimulation applied to the lips and cheek); the Moro reflex (infants react to any change in head position by flinging their arms to the side and extending their fingers and returning their arms to an over-the-chest position); the grasp reflex (infants' fingers and toes automatically grasp an object that is placed in the "palm"); and the tonic neck reflex (head rotation causes extension of the extremities to the side the infant is looking, while flexion occurs in the opposite extremities). All of the primitive reflexes appear at or near birth and disappear within two to four months (Haslam, 1977).

Other reflexes include the Babinski (fanning of the toes in response to stroking of the sole of the foot), which may have neurological implications, particularly in the appearance-disappearance of the reflex. Often if the neonate is raised over the table by the abdomen, the arms and legs will show a "swimming" reflex of sorts. Similarly, if the baby is held upright perpendicular to the table, off the table, the feet and legs may engage in a rudimentary "walking" reflex.

Birthing and Neonatal Development

ISSUE

The Cesarean Delivery

If the baby is not born vaginally, the only other way to get the baby out is through a surgical incision; this procedure is called a cesarean section. There are several reasons to have a "section." Among them are a cessation in dilatation and/or contractions. For some reason, the labor process stops making any progress, and for the safety of the infant and the mother, the baby is taken surgically.

☐ It is possible that the baby may be too large for the structure of the mother to handle the baby. This is called *cephalopelvic disproportion,* and requires a cesarean section. Another reason may be a malpresentation. In situations where the presentation is anything other than vertex (head first), the doctor may elect to deliver the child via section. In fact, given the malpractice insurance problem, many doctors are not allowing any breech deliveries to occur vaginally. As soon as there is evidence of a breech presentation, they begin to head for the operating room.

As this fifteenth-century French manuscript illustration shows, the delivery of a baby by Cesarian section is an old surgical technique that had been performed successfully long before the invention of modern drugs, anesthesia, and monitoring devices.

REPRODUCED BY PERMISSION OF THE BIBLIOTHÈQUE NATIONALE, PARIS.

☐ There may be unusual bleeding in the mother. This may be a sign of placental previa (the placenta has covered the cervix); in these cases, a cesarean is necessary. One final possible reason to have a cesarean is the situation termed fetal distress. The progress of the fetus is monitored throughout labor, either through a fetal monitor or with a fetascope (the unicorn-like stethoscope that obstetricians and obstetrical nurses use). If the fetal heart rate becomes depressed and does not return to a normal rate (120–160 beats/minute), a cesarean is indicated.

☐ The operation itself is not like most major surgeries. It is important to have the mother awake, if at all possible. Consequently, the anesthesia used is termed a *spinal*. This technique deadens the lower half of the mother's body, but she is awake and alert and can answer questions, etc. The baby is removed surgically and is much wetter than the vaginally delivered baby. Many times the baby is shown to the mother, cleaned up, and given back to the mother, although these procedures vary considerably with the hospital. A cesarean is major surgery, so there will be some discomfort from the incision. Breast-feeding and most of the other activities between mother and child are possible and encouraged.

☐ Some women respond to a cesarean as if they did not give birth to the child. They get depressed and are concerned with their ability to deliver the child normally. This feeling of inadequacy and guilt is misplaced, but very real. Both husband and doctor need to be supportive in helping these women recover psychologically.

☐ Recently there has been a movement to have the husbands in the operating room for the section. Doctors have resisted this movement strongly. They maintained there is an increased risk of infection, and that the men serve no worthwhile purpose. In cases where the cesarean appears to be uncomplicated and the mother is awake, the father can provide a measure of support for the mother and share in the delivery of their child. In the cases of complicated and life-threatening cesarean sections, it is probably wise to not have the father present.

☐ The rate of cesarean sections has climbed from about 5 percent of all births (1968) to about 13 percent now; some doctors are estimating that in the not-too-distant future, the rate of sections will settle at about 25 percent of all deliveries (statistics cited in March 1979, *Good Housekeeping*, p. 233). This increase may be due to the malpractice insurance problem, which forces doctors to avoid difficult (or even potentially difficult) deliveries. Another reason for an increase in the number of sections is the adherence to the old idiom: Once a section, always a section. This practice is not necessary. Depending upon the situation, a mother may be able to deliver her second child vaginally, even though the first birth was by cesarean section. Lastly, we may have redefined what "fetal distress" is. Given the sophisticated techniques of monitoring, doctors may be more likely to use the cesarean section when signs of distress appear in the fetus. A few years ago, these signs would not have been picked up.

Birthing and Neonatal Development

☐ Hopefully, the increase in cesarean sections will not bring about an increase in the maternal mortality rate. Cesareans bring the risks of any surgery: infection, anesthetic reaction, respiration problems, and so on. It is too soon to state whether this will be the trend.

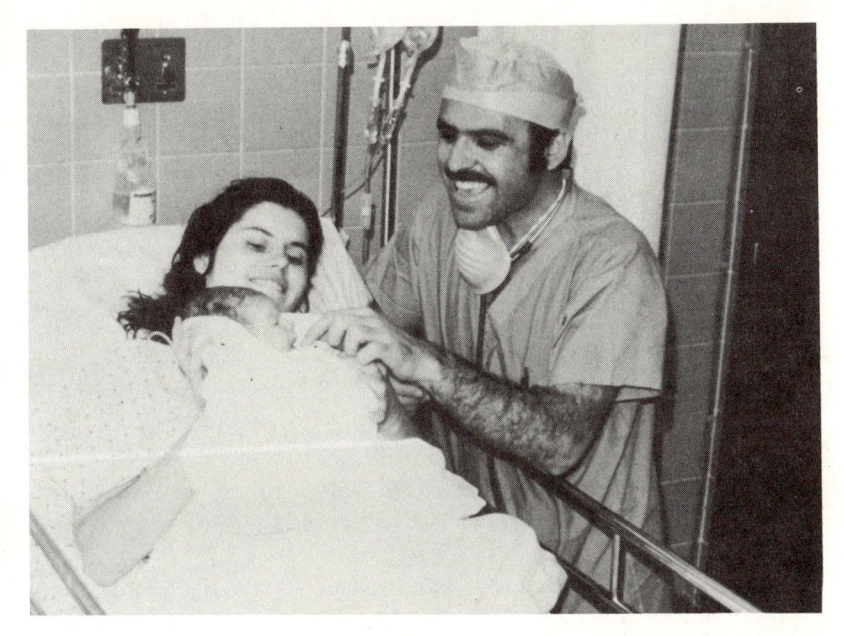

COURTESY HENRY FORD HOSPITAL, DETROIT, MICHIGAN.
PHOTO BY RONN KAMM

Summary

1. The average length of a normal pregnancy is 266 days. The prenatal care of the mother (and hence the fetus) begins immediately after determining that the woman is pregnant. Adequate and early prenatal care has been determined to be very important to the health of mother and infant.

2. Labor is the process of muscular contractions that push the baby out of the uterus. The exact trigger for labor is not known, but is probably a combination of hormonal signals from the mother and the baby. There are four basic stages of labor in the human, the fourth of which is the postdelivery care of the mother and baby.

3. There are a wide variety of birth complications. Most of the time, however, the birth process is normal and all goes well. Excessive bleeding is the most dangerous complication for the mother, and anoxia (lack of oxygen) is

the most dangerous condition for the fetus. Prematurity is a large category of birth irregularity that may have long-term effects for the child. Other irregularities include a malpresentation (breech) and the surgical removal of the fetus (cesarean section).

4. The neonate is a unique, incredibly complex creature. Possessed of functional yet inexperienced sensory abilities, the neonate is thrust into a cold, bright, very noisy world, quite unlike the warm, cushioned uterine environment. The Apgar score is one way to assess the viability of the neonate. In making the transition to extrauterine life, several bodily systems need to make big changes, including the respiratory, digestive, temperature, and circulatory systems.

Thought Questions

1. Why is the prenatal care of the mother important to the health of the baby? Is there any relationship between prenatal care and the viability of the neonate and the health of the mother? What is the relationship?

2. Just exactly what is labor? What starts labor? In what situations might there be danger for the mother or fetus? What are the specific functions of a contraction? Differentiate between dilatation and effacement. What is the fourth stage of labor?

3. Under what circumstances might it be necessary to surgically remove a fetus? Have C-sections been increasing or decreasing in frequency? Why? What is the most dangerous complication of birth for the mother? For the neonate?

4. What is the difference between a vertex presentation and a breech presentation?

5. What are the sensory capacities of the neonate? What are the behavioral possibilities found in the neonate? What bodily systems are operational? Describe each of these, stating their degree of operation.

Suggested Readings

Arms, S. *A Season to be Born*. New York: Harper & Row, 1972. *This very moving work chronicles the pregnancy of one woman. It is clearly presented and is accompanied by appropriate photos.*

Avery, G. *Neonatology*. Philadelphia: Lippincott, 1975. *Avery has compiled an anthology of medical literature. The book discusses care for the newborn as well as prenatal care. High-risk infants are given special attention.*

Osofsky, J.D., ed. *Handbook of Infant Development.* New York: Wiley, 1978. *Osofsky has compiled an important collection of readings relevant to neonatal as well as postnatal behavior. Of particular importance is the article by Yvonne Brackbill, "Obstetrical Medication and Infant Development." In the Osofsky handbook there are over 25 references to the effects of obstetrical medication on infant/child behavior.*

READING

The vast majority of babies born in the United States are healthy and normal in every respect. The magnitude of these normal births does not overshadow the tragedy of having a deformed or severely damaged baby. John Grossman, writing in *Family Health*, describes in a most lucid fashion one of the real tragedies of the nursery: Spina bifida. Surpisingly, two out of every thousand babies are born with this problem. Grossman describes the nature of the ailment and discusses how parents, teachers, and physicians have learned to cope with this very serious problem.

The Nursery's Two Cruelest Words: Spina Bifida
John Grossmann

Like most eager couples, Steve and Irmtraud Parrish had already decided upon names. David Stephen if a boy. Heidi if a girl. Shortly before midnight on January 17, 1975, Irmtraud went into labor and Steve drove his wife six miles to the hospital at Whiteman Air Force base near Knob Noster, Missouri. He stood close to his wife throughout the labor and delivery and at 3:30 A.M. watched David Stephen enter the world head first, face up, 20 inches long, weighing 7 pounds 5 ounces. The general surgeon who delivered the baby handed him to an Air Force corpsman who began to bathe the crying infant. The corpsman turned David Stephen over onto his stomach and then he stopped, curious about a silver-dollar-sized red spot on the baby's back. He called for the general surgeon. Irmtraud asked her husband what was wrong. "He's got a little scratch on his back," Steve told her.

A few moments later, Steve Parrish learned that the red spot on his son's back was more than just a scratch. "Your baby has spina bifida, a very serious birth defect," the surgeon told him. Taking Steve aside in the delivery room, the surgeon began to explain....

David Stephen was one of two in a thousand. Victim of a crippling birth defect, he was, like all children born with spina bifida, something of an ironic victim at that. Ironic because most Americans have never even heard of spina bifida, and yet each year upwards of 6,000 children are born with the defect. That makes it significantly commoner than mongolism, three times as common as cystic fibrosis—and a greater crippler of children than polio was at its peak. Spina bifida has remained virtually "unknown" and largely misunderstood because, until recently, most of its victims rarely lived longer than a few weeks or months.

"Spina bifida" literally means "cleft spine," a spine split in two because the vertebrae in the infant's back failed to come together during the first trimester of pregnancy. Figuratively, the words suggest even greater rifts within the medical, moral and legal communities.

To those familiar with the far-reaching implications of this unique birth defect, the words "spina bifida" fairly crackle with emotion. Understandably. They bring to the fore one of society's most torturous questions: Life or death in the nursery? And, especially in the past few years, they are at the center of a difficult debate: quality of life vs. sanctity of life. Spina bifida presents a staggering dilemma: Operate quickly and the child will *probably* live. But even doctors who have operated on scores of children born with spina bifida admit they cannot accurately predict how severe the inevitable physical handicaps will be. Nor can they rule out possible mental retardation. Withhold treatment and the child will *probably* soon die of an infection carried through the defective spine. But not always. Some 10 to 20 percent of those left untreated do not die, but usually deteriorate to little better than a vegetable existence.

In hospital waiting rooms across the country, over coffee and tears, this decision to operate or withhold treatment is made about 17 times each

Birthing and Neonatal Development

day. It is a decision no parent is prepared for, a decision many cannot make rationally. One of life's most blessed moments has turned to tragedy. And parents turn to the doctors for support, for information, for advice.

A neurosurgeon explains there are three types of spina bifida. The least severe is fortunately the commonest. Called *spina bifida occulta*, it involves an abnormal opening in the vertebrae, but no damage to the spinal cord or any visible signs of deformity, so most people never even discover they have the defect. Perhaps as many as 60 million Americans have this form of spina bifida.

A second kind of spina bifida is *meningocele*, so named because the meninges, the protective covering for the spinal cord, have pushed out through the opening in the vertebrae, inside a sac that protrudes from the back. The sac, or meningocele, can be as large as a small grapefruit, but since the spinal cord remains intact, the nerve pathways to the lower body are usually unaffected. After corrective surgery to reposition the meninges and remove the sac, the hole in the back is closed and the child will probably experience no further difficulty.

David Stephen Parrish was not so lucky. He entered the world with a third kind of spina bifida called *myelomeningocele*. With this condition, the spinal cord does not form properly, and it, too, protrudes from the back. In David Stephen's case, the malformed spinal cord was just beneath the bright red spot on his back. But usually, the spinal cord protrudes from the back inside a sac.

"The spinal cord is an extension cord for the brain. It's a conduit for carrying messages." The speaker is Donald Reigel, MD, chief of pediatric neurosurgery at Children's Hospital of Pittsburgh, and he is demonstrating how he counsels parents. "I immediately tell them it's nobody's fault. It isn't your fault, it's not my fault, it's not God's fault. It happened. You don't blame anybody because you got a cold. It's natural to get angry or upset."

As he speaks, Dr. Reigel reaches for a piece of paper and holds it out flat in front of him. "I tell them the central nervous system forms like a plate early in life and at about twelve to sixteen weeks it forms a tube." He rolls the paper into a cylinder. "And at one end of the tube is the brain and at the other end of the tube are the nerves that go to our legs and our bowel and our bladder. But when the tube came around, it didn't close. The nerves are there, but unfortunately they are, in effect, shorted out.

"That's a long way from what I really know [about spina bifida], technically and scientifically, but parents understand that. I avoid the word defective, because it has such a bad connotation, and I'm trying to prevent the negative image that their child is defective and that they are defective through something like guilt by heritage. And I explain that I can do an operation to cover the hole in the back."

The surgery, he explains, is only the beginning of an ongoing series of operations, examinations and therapy that will probably be necessary in the coming weeks, months and years. Most likely, the child will require brain surgery to implant a device called a shunt. The shunt is a thin plastic tube that runs from the brain to the abdomen to drain excess fluid and prevent or limit hydrocephalus. Hyprocephalus, or water on the brain, can enlarge the skull and exert tremendous pressure on the brain, causing mental retardation. Often children born with spina bifida also need foot or ankle surgery. Many will require additional spinal surgery around the age of ten to correct curvature of the spine. Because nearly all are incontinent, meaning they cannot control their bowels or bladder, urologic therapy is a necessity and urologic surgery a possibility. The child's paralyzed legs will require specially fitted braces. The list goes on. . . .

Because spina bifida ravages so many body systems, it demands a multisystem approach. At Children's Hospital of Pittsburgh, Reigel is but one member of a team that includes neurosurgeons, urologists, orthopedists, physical and occupational therapists, a neuropsychologist, orthotists (specialists who make and fit braces) and social workers. "We literally saturate both the child and the family with support," says Reigel. The care is coordinated, comprehensive and top-notch. The spina bifida clinic in Pittsburgh provides ongoing treatment for some 450 children—many from western Pennsylvania and others from eastern Ohio and northern West Virginia—making it one of the largest myelomeningocele clinics in the country.

Spina bifida clinics, of course, are a relatively recent development in health care. Only a generation ago, before doctors discovered a reliable method of closing the back, and before the perfection of a dependable shunt, there were few survivors and little need for clinics. Now there are perhaps several dozen spina bifida clinics throughout the nation. A poster on the door of the clinic coordinator pretty much sums up the collective philosophy. The poster reads: "When life gives you lemons, make lemonade."

Maureen Brower is eight years old. She is blonde, blue-eyed and has a cute, shy little smile that animates her entire face and reveals that the tooth fairy recently visited the Brower home in Glenwood, Illinois. Two years ago when Maureen wrote her name, it took up an entire page of a reporter's note pad, and the shaky letters had to make an impromptu right-hand turn to fit on the paper.

"Can I use your pen and paper?" Maureen asks. This time the lettering fits neatly in the upper left-hand corner of the page, leaving plenty of room below for a date: April 29. Her First Communion. A big day in her life, during which she made it all the way up the side aisle of the church by herself. Wearing a $2,000 steel brace that starts at her feet and continues upward, grasping her legs, supporting her back, until it fits collar-like around her neck, and with a crutch under each arm, Maureen pulled herself to the front of the church. It took her seven minutes. "My parents and grandparents said they were proud of me. And I'm proud, too. It just made me so happy."

Maureen now weighs about 35 pounds—45 if you count her braces. But when she was born nine weeks premature, she weighed only three pounds. "She's going to die anyway; why don't you have another baby?" a doctor suggested to Charlene Brower shortly after her daughter was born. Charlene was "traumatized." She asked a nurse to write the word "myelomeningocele" on a napkin. And for days, as Maureen clung to life, her mother clutched that napkin.

Maureen was transferred from a hospital about 30 miles south of Chicago to the University of Illinois Hospital, just west of downtown Chicago. When doctors there felt she was strong enough to survive surgery, they closed her back. Since then, Maureen has had nine more operations: plastic surgery on her back, five procedures connected with her shunt, two eye operations and surgery to cut both of her heel cords, to keep her feet from turning under.

Before her last operation Maureen asked her parents on the way to the hospital if it was all right for her to be scared. "She's been pushed through so much in teaching her to walk, in teaching her social situations," Charlene says, "that she isn't sure if it's all right for her to be afraid of things."

Maureen Brower is not a typical spina bifida child. There are no typical spina bifida children or adults. That, too, has contributed to misunderstanding about the defect. Spina bifida does not cripple its victims uniformly, because it can strike almost anywhere along the spine. Generally, the higher it strikes, the more severe the handicaps. A lower opening in the spine may mean less profound damage to the spinal cord. The lucky wear braces that stop at the knee. The unlucky never walk. The fortunate suffer no loss of mental functions. The unfortunate are mentally retarded.

And then there are the untreated. No one knows percisely how many, because the untreated are also the unmentioned. Years back, before doctors had the techniques and the technology to help babies born with spina bifida, a high percentage were reported stillborn. Too high a percentage. "Forty years ago my mother had a pact with our doctor before I was born," says one pediatric neurosurgeon who treats spina bifida. "My mother could run and play tennis. She wanted me to be able to do those things too." The pact this neurosurgeon doesn't mention by name involves, of course, euthanasia—the killing of a defective child, a child certain to be handicapped.

American statutes speak clearly on euthanasia. It is murder. Even so, many "mercy killings" and "right-to-die" cases, like the Karen Ann Quinlan controversy, seem anything but clear when debated by medical and legal experts. Many of these experts feel spina bifida further blurs the issue of euthanasia, because some say this unique birth defect prompts a qualifying adjective such as "passive" or "involuntary." Nontreatment of a baby born with spina bifida is not *active* euthanasia, the thinking goes, because no direct action brings about the death of the child. Withholding treatment usually leads to a fatal infection, and *that* kills the child.

It must be emphasized that spina bifida is usually treated in this country, so such instances of "passive" euthanasia are the exception. Also worth underscoring is the fact that, for an untreated spina bifida child, death often takes several weeks. Sometimes it comes in the high-risk nursery of a hospital. Sometimes, quietly, in a nursing home. "We have admitted quite a few infants where no surgery was performed," said an administrator of a Midwest nursing home. "What would be the quality of life? You can hold a flashlight to the head of some and see there's no brain tissue." In a recent stretch of months, three such children at the home died. "We want to serve the family, too. In some cases this has destroyed a family. We want the child comfortable here. We provide food, water and medication. Death is usually not long or painful."

Many nursing homes, however, simply won't accept a baby with an unclosed back. Administrators at these centers say they are dedicated to the treatment and development of individuals and refuse to offer what amounts to a deathbed. Therefore, death sometimes occurs at home. "One of our own nurses decided not to treat her baby," admitted a supervisor in the high-risk nursery of a Chicago area hospital. "She took the baby home and it did expire, after a month and a half." Not surprisingly, the mother declined to be interviewed, even on an anonymous basis.

The courts, too, have been silent on the issue of euthanasia in the nursery. With prosecutors looking the other way, this mind-wrenching question has been for the most part delegated to parents and their doctors. There are no easy answers. Few parents are even remotely prepared to make such a decision. They are uninformed or misinformed. Few have any idea, for example, that most of the March of Dimes and Easter Seal poster children have spina bifida.

Although doctors can now save the lives of nearly all children born with spina bifida, they still know relatively little about what causes it. "You're going to hear causes all the way from Irish potatoes to poisons in your drinking water," one neurosurgeon tells parents. There are indications, however, that genetic and environmental factors may play some causative role. Once parents have had one child with spina bifida, the odds of a second child with the defect rise from two per thousand to about one in twenty. Some studies point a finger at industrial pollution; doctors at certain spina bifida clinics have noticed a higher percentage of children from communities near industrial centers.

The defect pays little heed to social standing. It cuts across all economic levels. Some distinctions: It appears in girls slightly more frequently than boys; some ethnic groups, such as the Irish, Scots and British seem more likely victims; other groups, notably blacks, seem less likely to be affected.

Even though it's one of the commonest birth defects in American, very few researchers are presently looking for definitive causes of spina bifida. So there is very little chance, at the moment, of preventing it. Yet there is considerable effort being made, especially in England but also in this country, to perfect several promising methods of detecting the defect during pregnancy. Abortions would presumably follow. But it should be noted that abortions do not prevent the defect, they merely prevent the birth of a fetus believed to have the defect.

Methods of spotting spina bifida during the first trimester of pregnancy include ultrasound, amniocentesis and testing of the mother's blood. Ultrasound uses low-intensity sound pulses, in a manner not unlike sonar, to create a visual representation of fetal development. Amniocentesis (the analysis of amniotic fluid) and tests of maternal serum focus on a substance called alpha fetoprotein. High levels of alpha fetoprotein usually indicate the presence of a neural tube defect, such as spina bifida.

The defect is costly. It robs the child of mobility and perhaps mental ability. It wrenches at the very roots of the family structure and ends marriages (although many spina bifida clinics report a divorce rate much lower than the national average). And spina bifida costs money. "We used to estimate 'hard costs'—hospitalization, operations, braces, wheelchairs, etc.—for a child living at home until age eighteen at ninety thousand dollars," says Kent Smith, executive director of the Spina Bifida Association of America, a nonprofit group organized by parents of children with spina bifida. "That was five years ago. Now, I'd estimate those costs to be three, and possibly five, times as much." While insurance policies often cover most of these expenses, it is a rare family that doesn't wind up paying thousands of dollars to care for the child.

Then there are the so-called "soft costs," which strike family budgets less noticeably, but equally hard. Countless trips to the hospital and meals away from home. A larger car, usually a station wagon or a van, to facilitate use of a wheelchair. Maybe a relocation—from a two-story or split-level home to a ranch, or to a different school district with better educational and vocational programs for the handicapped. The list, like so many others concerning spina bifida, could go on and on.

Within the minority of Americans familiar with the defect—doctors, lawyers, parents and those affected by spina bifida—there is at least one consensus. All agree that the rest of us need to know more about this unique crippler of children, need to grasp its far-reaching implications and need to understand the kinds of difficulties faced by those who live each day with its handicaps.

Chances are, we could learn something about courage, love and determination from families like the Johnsons. Jennifer Johnson is 13. Her brother Dallas, 11. Both have spina bifida—and an outlook toward the future little different from that of other children their age. Jennifer wants to be a secretary, and Dallas, a wildlife photographer. They are, in a word, happy children, fully cognizant of their handicaps.

"Jennifer's got her problems with her back, and I've got my problems with my hips," says Dallas. Both lavish praise on their parents, a resolute and spirited couple who took it upon themselves to construct Jennifer's first leg braces after doctors at the Mayo Clinic told them "to come back in a couple of years when she's about five and ready to go to school." They also constructed what the children called "scooter boards" and "scooterbangers," so Jennifer and Dallas could move about at an early age. And they fashioned a family setting, with love and numerous "wrist spankings." A home where the word handicapped doesn't lodge in the throat —even of a visitor.

THE LOUVRE, PARIS. PHOTO BY PETER ADELBERG.

The Cradle, by Berthe Morisot.

5

Social Implications

There are many significant genetic and biological components of birth that are not significantly changed by anything society manages to do. Another part of the developing child seems to be entirely a function of its environment. This chapter begins the exploration of the interaction between the biological reality of being a neonate and the environmental realities that are often put upon the child.

Some technological innovations surrounding delivery have been developed over the years. *Fetal monitoring* is a standard procedure in some hospitals and with some doctors. This technique began as a diagnostic technique and was then incorporated into regular obstetrical practice. Application went from only certain high-risk situations to nearly all pregnancies, depending upon the place and situation. Other technical innovations include amniocentesis, and advanced and safer techniques of cesarean section. There have been advances in anesthesiology and drug therapy; all of these produce a birthing procedure very different from the past.

For the vast majority of time that humans have been on this earth, babies have not been delivered in hospitals. It was not too many years ago that most babies in the United States were delivered at home, with or without the aid of a midwife. With time and technological advancement, new techniques were developed. We do not wish to romanticize the past by saying that it was a better situation when most babies were born at home. We do have lower

Fetal monitoring: use of electronic devices for observation of the fetus *in utero*

maternal and infant mortality rates today than years ago, but some people are questioning the medical intrusion into the delivery process.

Some doctors even question the uses some of the technological innovations discussed earlier are being put to. Rattner (1977) has suggested that technological innovations developed to help with the unusual or abnormal cases have become over time the standard procedure. It appears that bottle feeding started this way, although there were and are many complex reasons for the popularity of formula feeding. The use and misuse of vitamins may be another example. Rattner notes that episiotomies have become standard procedure, perhaps inappropriately so.

The goal of the delivery process is ". . . a satisfied mother and infant" (Rattner, 1977). Both mother and infant need to be awake and alert, ready for early bonding. Modern delivery does not always allow this. There is the possibility that one or both participants (mother or infant) may be groggy from administration of drugs. It is possible that the mother (and father) may get only a glimpse of the baby before it is whisked away to the nursery. The parents may not be allowed to hold the infant at all for a period of several hours.

BIRTHING: CROSS-CULTURAL AND HISTORICAL PERSPECTIVES

Ethnocentrism:
an attitude that one's own group is superior

The belief of a culture that its way of doing something is the only right way of doing something is termed *ethnocentrism*. This view holds that "our" way of birthing children, if there is one way, is the only way, the right way; all other ways are foreign and probably less successful. This clearly is not true.

The patterns of a culture determine the way it structures major events, like rites of passage (adolescent to adult), or the birth of a child. These intercultural variations are paralleled by the possibility of intracultural differences (differences within a single culture). The variety in cultural practices is matched only by the number of cultures available for study.

In practically all cultures that have been labeled primitive (without written language) childbirth is an important event. It is a significant social event for the mother and family, and it is an important event for the society at large. Exceptions to this might be cultures that are essentially nomadic, in which more children can bring more problems of survival.

> In primitive culture, by far the most usual pattern is for the laboring woman to have two or more attendants for labor and

Social Implications

delivery. Often special huts are built for delivery and elaborate postnatal patterns developed (Mead and Newton, 1967, p. 169).

Unattended birth occurs in many cultures. By unattended we mean that when labor begins the woman goes off to be by herself for the birth of the baby; it is considered a private event. Cultures vary immensely in the amount of openness they allow concerning delivery. Some cultures are very open and frank, while other cultures insist on high levels of privacy. America would probably rank on the more private side when it comes to delivery; in fact, until recently, fathers have not been allowed into the delivery room as a matter of custom.

The role of the father, anthropologically, is as diverse as the various cultural patterns themselves. In some cultures the father is totally excluded; in others he is welcomed, in fact, he assists in the delivery. For the last 100 years or so, the American father's role has been interpreted as one of financial support, and not much else. The male was often pictured in the stereotypical position of pacing in the waiting room with an unlit cigarette hanging from his mouth.

ISSUE

Men in the Delivery Room

The delivery of children has undergone significant change in the United States. There was a time when all children were born at home with the assistance of a midwife. When doctors became more plentiful, the births were still at home; the doctor came to the home and aided with the delivery. During these times, the rates of maternal and infant mortality were high.

☐ The medical institution evolved from one of few doctors and even fewer hospitals. As hospitals became more and more plentiful, and as the doctors confined their practice to the hospitals, the location for the delivery of children changed from the home to the hospital. The mortality rates began to slowly decline during this process, reflecting greater understanding of the birth process, better and more efficient diagnostic and treatment techniques, and greater availability of medical services.

☐ During most of this time, there was one occurrence that remained relatively consistent: the conspicuous absence of fathers and men in general from the birth situation. This absence was due to several factors. Children, the behavior of children, and the birthing of children came to be considered womanly concerns. Men came to think of themselves solely in instrumental terms, convincing themselves that anything having to do with children was the responsibility of women. Perhaps the only exception to this was and is the handing out of discipline.

☐ As hospitals became more and more plentiful, the medical institution contributed to this conspiracy. They stated that men, with their unique set of germs, should not be with the mother during delivery; they would be in the way, and would probably pass out during the delivery, requiring medical care themselves. As a result of these historical and medical attitudes, the birthing world was faced with the creation of a new role: the nervous, chain-smoking father pacing the waiting room floor, anxiously awaiting word on the arrival of the child. This role was acted out to the hilt; men, being ignorant of the birth process, were very anxious. Most of them wanted to help, but were unable to do so, due to societal conditioning and their own insistence that there was little they could do.

☐ The LaMaze childbirth preparation movement brought about gradual but significant changes in this situation. For the first time, men were assigned a role: the coach. They were educated into the mechanisms of birth and labor, and they were given responsibilities. With these new roles, the level of confidence began to slowly increase, and childbirth became the responsibility of both parents.

Social Implications

☐ These new roles were met with resistance from the medical institution. Doctors still felt that there would be health risks for the mother and child having the father in the delivery room. There was still concern that the men would not be able to handle the physical aspect of delivery. Progress was slow in getting men into the delivery room.

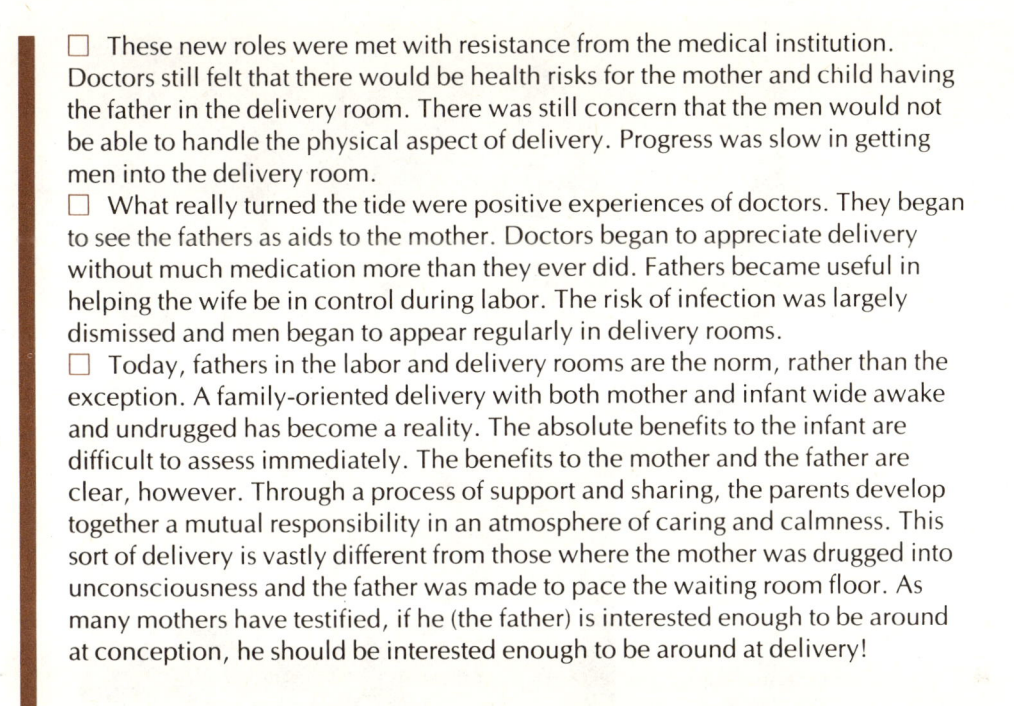

☐ What really turned the tide were positive experiences of doctors. They began to see the fathers as aids to the mother. Doctors began to appreciate delivery without much medication more than they ever did. Fathers became useful in helping the wife be in control during labor. The risk of infection was largely dismissed and men began to appear regularly in delivery rooms.

☐ Today, fathers in the labor and delivery rooms are the norm, rather than the exception. A family-oriented delivery with both mother and infant wide awake and undrugged has become a reality. The absolute benefits to the infant are difficult to assess immediately. The benefits to the mother and the father are clear, however. Through a process of support and sharing, the parents develop together a mutual responsibility in an atmosphere of caring and calmness. This sort of delivery is vastly different from those where the mother was drugged into unconsciousness and the father was made to pace the waiting room floor. As many mothers have testified, if he (the father) is interested enough to be around at conception, he should be interested enough to be around at delivery!

Even certain patterns of labor have an interesting anthropological perspective. For centuries, in many cultures, there have been attempts to speed up the process of labor. Sometimes people would stand around the female and push parts of her body in hopes of speeding up the delivery. There were primitive medications used to speed up labor and delivery; these drugs, usually herbal, had effects not unlike similar drugs used today for the same reasons. In some cultures, the cutting of the umbilical cord was delayed until the placenta was delivered; and in some cultures the cord was not tied off before it was cut. In ancient Rome it was suggested that immediately after delivery the hand be inserted into the uterus to pull the placenta out (Mead and Newton, 1967).

A very important aspect has been the use of the *midwife*, a person who assists at the delivery of a baby. Women, and occasionally men, have helped other women deliver their children for centuries. Prior to the development of hospitals, midwives were the ones who assisted in the delivery process.

In England the first formal and legal arrangements concerning the practice of midwifery occurred in A.D. 1512 (Donnison, 1977).

Midwife: a nonphysician who assists with a birth

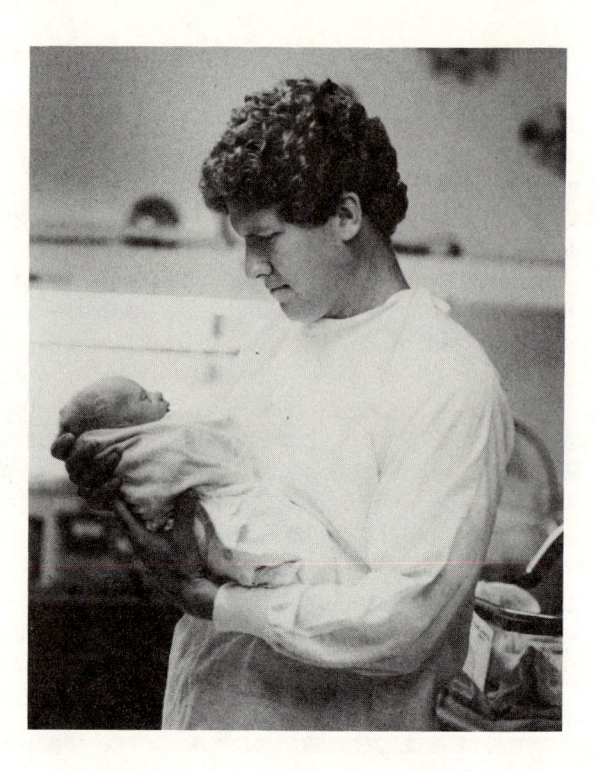

Father and daughter.
JEFFREY P. GROSSCUP.

Their legal status went through many transitions, and when the medical practice began to gain inroads, particularly in the United States, midwives found less and less work as the hospitals and the medical profession gained a foothold in the obstetrical care picture. In fact, in the United States midwifery has been illegal for a long period of time. However, it has been practiced illegally for many years in many parts of the country. Recently, some states have legalized the use of midwives, in one form or another (Oregon and California are examples).

NATURAL CHILDBIRTH

Natural childbirth: a birth that uses no mechanical or surgical intervention and no drugs

The term "natural childbirth" is an undefined and misleading term. We define a natural childbirth as one without the use of pain-relieving drugs, one without the use of mechanical intervention techniques, and one without electronic intervention and monitoring techniques. Under these terms, it is easy to see how a birth of this type could be considered dangerous by modern standards. This definition of a natural childbirth forsakes the technological

Social Implications

and medical advances that have been made. In most births, given the proper frame of mind for the parents and everyone else, this philosophy might be workable. For the minority of cases where there is a problem, this method is a potential disaster.

Prepared childbirth is quite another matter. The emphasis in prepared childbirth is educated, informed parents. Most prepared childbirth methods have evolved from the basic philosophy of Grantley Dick-Read. Dick-Read was convinced that much of women's fear and concern over labor is learned and/or a function of cultural influences. The ideas of pain and fear are enhanced through word of mouth and cultural expectations. Fear creates tension, and tension constricts muscles, creating more difficulty than necessary. Dick-Read felt that the fear produced as a result of ignorance was the type of fear that hindered the delivery process most.

According to Dick-Read, there are three basic elements in a prepared childbirth:

1. the education of the mother about anatomical and physical facts
2. physiological training of the mother, particularly in muscular relaxation and breathing techniques
3. psychological intervention techniques, including the creation of an air of confidence in the mother, and a good doctor-mother relationship (Dick-Read, 1954).

A more recent technique of prepared childbirth is the so-called psychoprophylactic method. This idea had its basis in Russia, in the late nineteenth and early twentieth centuries. This technique of prepared childbirth has to do with the technique of conditioned responses, and was based, in Russia at least, on the work of the Russian physiologist Ivan Pavlov.

The Russians were concerned with conditioning that would control the pain of childbirth. Ferdinand LaMaze, a French doctor, heard of the technique and traveled to Russia to learn how it worked. LaMaze was intrigued with the Russian claims of reduced length of labor, a decrease in certain stress-related problems on the part of mothers, and the diminished use of forceps in their deliveries.

LaMaze sought to expand the theoretical and practical aspects of psychoprophylactic technique in his own practice in France. As Dick-Read did, LaMaze suggested that it was possible to control the birth process more than it had been in the past.

Prepared childbirth: a birth for which both parents have prior training and in which both participate

Prenatal classes such as the one shown here help to prepare couples for pregnancy, birth, and parenthood.
JEFFREY P. GROSSCUP.

The Americanized version of the LaMaze technique, which has been widely incorporated into the fabric of American obstetrical practice, seems to emphasize several very important aspects:

1. As in some of the other prepared childbirth systems, the LaMaze method emphasizes *education.* This takes the form of classes for both mother and coach-father, which cover the rudimentary physiology and anatomy of the pregnancy process, including labor and delivery.

2. *Relaxation* is the second emphasis in the present LaMaze classes. Muscular relaxation has a two-fold effect. First, if the muscles engaged in the birth process can be relaxed when they are not working (labor), these muscles will perform more efficiently and not tire quite so quickly. Physiologically, the ability to relax will help the mother to rest and to make it through the delivery comfortably. Second, there are also psychological benefits to relaxation. Muscular tension often creates emotional tension, and vice versa. Through the education described above and the relaxation described here, the mother and coach-father will be able to deal with the emotional aspects of having a baby without unnecessary tension and debilitating anxiety.

3. The mother and father will come to have a feeling of *control* when undergoing this process. To feel in control of her own body will add an amazing air of confidence to the woman in labor. To be

Social Implications

able to help relax and provide comfort will provide the coach-father with his own feeling of control over the situation, freeing him to aid and assist in an even more positive way.

Implicit in this process is the cooperation between wife and husband or whoever else serves as coach. This may be the most significant aspect of the LaMaze technique. Literally pulling the male into a situation of responsibility and assistance, this technique represents the sort of cooperative relationship required for effective parenting; it makes sense to begin the process now. It is most appropriate to involve the male in the delivery of the baby. Our world today requires males who are expressive and capable of forming significant and meaningful interpersonal relations. Being present at the birth of the baby seems to implicitly and significantly commit both parents to the task at hand.

The theory of social support networks states that each human being sets up networks of people, friends, relatives and acquaintances for ongoing support and help with significant events. It makes sense to let the mother who is giving birth utilize the social support she has available to her. It is possible that this social support may make the event more meaningful and significant for her, the father, and the child. Not everyone desires this sort of situation, but facilities should be available for those who do.

Not everyone connected with the birthing process is convinced of the complete desirability of the so-called natural or prepared childbirth trend. For example, Fielding and Benjamin (1962) disagreed with the "movement" aspect of natural childbirth, apparently equating it with a fad. These authors declared that not all women can have a natural childbirth nor do all women want a natural childbirth. It is possible that much guilt and confusion is produced in women who cannot or do not wish to participate in the natural or prepared childbirth techniques.

It is true that some aspects of the natural or prepared childbirth phenomenon have assumed "cultlike" proportions. This unfortunate perspective has alienated some mothers and some physicians and created ill feelings within the birthing movement. It is ironic that an event so complex and unique and potentially so rewarding and fulfilling has been literally split into factions. Each of these factions sets up its own "right" way to have a baby. The group caught in the middle of all of this propaganda is the family that has not been indoctrinated either way. The result can be confusion and bitterness.

The natural-prepared childbirth techniques we have described do work within a contextual framework. The mother and father need to be accepting of these philosophies, as does the support network available (the doctor, nurse, and hospital, if that is the way the birth is going to happen). They do not work for all people, nor should they be forced upon any individual.

FEAR OF CHILDBIRTH AND DELIVERY

Despite the overwhelming "natural" component to childbirth, fear is often a common emotion in both the wife and husband. Fear has very traumatic implications. It can prolong labor, produce tension that can have physiological implications, and generally upset the situation of birthing.

Perhaps the primary cause of this fear is lack of knowledge. Not understanding basic physiological processes contributes to a general feeling of not knowing what is happening. The inevitable result of this is very real fear. Zac et al. (1975) have suggested that people who were involved in childbirth education classes scored significantly lower in anxiety and significantly higher in attitudes toward having a baby than those who did not take the classes. Of course, this produces a chicken-and-the-egg question: Are the people who take the classes already lower in anxiety (perhaps because they were better off socioeconomically, for example)? Huttel et al. (1972) found in their research that patients who had childbirth training and who had husbands present complained less of pain, appeared more relaxed, and were less likely to cry out than were patients without childbirth training.

Patients who have not had childbirth classes, have not read about childbirth, or have not been able to speak with someone knowledgeable about childbirth are the most susceptible to fears. Besides fear of the unknown, a reason for this is the way birth is portrayed on television and in movies. With no other models or information, our minds grab at what we do know, which is often gleaned from television and cinema. Unfortunately, they often portray birth scenes with an extra dose of panting, writhing, and screaming for dramatic purposes. When this is all a woman knows of birth, she may very well be anxious and tense.

It is not completely clear that childbirth training classes have anything to do with parenting anxiety at home after the birth of the child. Wente and Crockenburg (1976) found that lack of knowledge of parenting was predictive of high postdelivery adjustment problems in fathers. These authors did not find, however, that LaMaze training resulted in easier adjustment to fatherhood. Lastly, Meares et al. (1976) found an interesting correspondence between

Social Implications

postdelivery depression in mothers and the levels of anxiety exhibited during the pregnancy.

All of the needed evidence is not in. The studies mentioned do appear to be indicating that there is a relationship between training and fear. We are not sure how long this influence lasts or if it is effective for the father, but there is definitely something happening.

Closely aligned with education and prepared childbirth is another movement that is gaining increasing popularity in America. Termed "gentle birth" by its originator, Frederic LeBoyer, this is a technique of birthing the infant in such a way so as to avoid as much of the trauma of birth as possible.

GENTLE BIRTH

Gentle birth:
a delivery technique designed to avoid trauma for the newborn

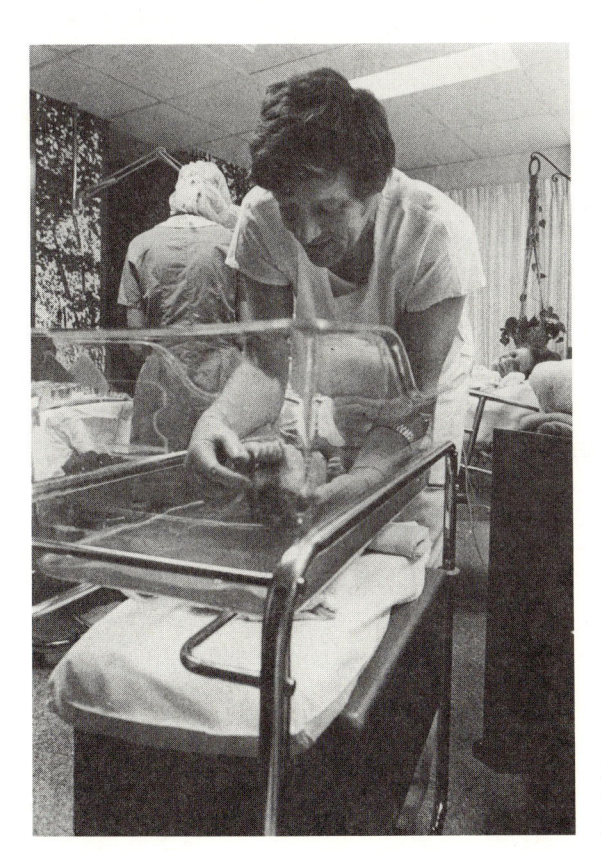

In the LeBoyer method of birthing, the father bathes the neonate just after delivery.
JEFFREY P. GROSSCUP.

As we have already discussed, there are significant technological influences in the hospital birth of a baby. The delivery room is kept cool on purpose, there are strong lights to allow for good vision, there may be drugs involved, and so on. LeBoyer maintains that these items can and should be avoided in the delivery of a baby.

The LeBoyer gentle birth method states that the baby should be born into a warm accepting environment, without bright edges of light, temperature contrasts, and a lot of noise. In order to create this womblike environment, LeBoyer suggests increasing the temperature of the delivery room so that the inefficient temperature regulation system of the neonate can adapt comfortably. He suggests turning off the bright lights and waiting a time before clamping and cutting the umbilical cord. During this waiting time, the baby is to be placed on the mother's abdomen and caressed. The baby is then removed and placed in a warm bath by the father, and after this gentle, warm bath, the baby is bundled and returned to the mother for early contact with the parents.

Using these techniques, birth becomes a less terrifying experience for the baby. This gradual and supportive transition to extrauterine life is deemed to be a positive first step in the child's life, which will carry long-term possibilities for life satisfaction. This is where the evidence begins to get a bit skimpy. A sufficiently controlled longitudinal study testing the viability of the LeBoyer technique has yet to be done. Until that study is completed, we may say that LeBoyer's method sounds pleasant and supportive. We do not know, however, what the long-term implications of the technique are.

THE SOCIAL CLASS ECOSYSTEM

Ecosystem:
a group of interrelated environmental influences

A child develops within the context of several simultaneously occurring "systems." There is the family, the educational system, the society, and the medical profession and its influence. A part of society that exerts a very significant influence is the social class milieu.

Social class refers to the ranking of individuals and groups of individuals into income- and prestige-dependent rankings. These subcultures begin to develop similar methods of socialization and child rearing and have different types and levels of social services available to them. As a result, children are very much a function of their social class.

Bee (1978) has indicated in a review of the literature that people's social class seems to be related to their mental health. There is a

Social Implications

The housing and other socioeconomic conditions in which a baby is raised can have a strong influence on that child's health and temperament.
BRUCE DAVIDSON, COPYRIGHT © MAGNUM PHOTOS, INC.

relatively consistent trend indicating that the highest rates of mental health problems are to be found in the lower social classes. However, it is not possible to answer the very important question as to whether these higher rates are the result of these people's social class, or if they merely reflect the filtering down of people who could not make a go of it in our competitive, rat race society.

Oftentimes poverty is accompanied by family disorganization. Family disorganization can take the form of poor parent-child contact, disorganization of family function, high levels of frustration, poor explanations and training, and so on.

It is also clear from the work of Kohn, Kagan, and others that there are differences in child-rearing techniques and philosophies that are dependent upon social class. These specific phenomena will be discussed later, but there is little doubt that social class plays a significant role in parenting.

Parents in lower social class situations have demonstrated higher levels of anxiety late in pregnancy, and interestingly, were more likely to have babies with difficult temperaments. Some scientists are saying that after maternal anxiety, social class is the most effective predictor of temperamental difficulties in children (Sameroff and Chandler, 1975).

The availability of health care services and accessibility of doctors vary according to social class. This fact explains much of the reason for the class-related differences in infant and maternal mortality in the United States. Of crucial interest here is the number of qualified doctors willing to practice medicine in less desirable areas. These phenomena make health maintenance very different for individuals of different social classes; preventive health care is a phenomenon of the upper classes, whereas health care in the lower social classes is very often on an acute basis.

THE NUTRITIONAL ECOSYSTEM

Another environment that totally envelops the developing child and may have profound long-term individual and species effects is the nutritional pattern of the child—a battery of behaviors, attitudes and substances. It is not possible to understate the importance and relevance of this particular situation.

Children's nutritional status is at first determined in terms of maternal nutrition during pregnancy and lactation (if the mother breast-feeds). Even as children mature and develop, their nutritional destiny is in the hands of the parents, or worse, in the "hands" of the "glowing blue box" (television), which exerts a profound and not completely understood effect upon children.

The relation of maternal nutrition to potential effects upon the fetus has been illustrated no more vividly than in some of the cases of malnutrition present during World War II. In Holland food rations were severely restricted after World War II. Pregnant women were down to less than 1,000 calories per day. The Food and Agriculture Organization/World Health Organization have suggested (1970) that the calorie intake of a moderately active pregnant adult female should be in the neighborhood of 2,550 calories per day. It appears that the babies conceived before the food shortage in Holland and born during the hunger period were shorter and had lower birth weights than those before this time. Researchers attribute this effect directly to the nutritional status of the mothers during this time period.

Children's nutritional environment can prevent them from realizing their full genetic potential in both physical and psychological ways. Nutritional deprivation, which is so subtle that it may be unknown to the parents and the child, can undermine nature's plan for bone development and muscular growth. It can hinder the development of endurance and put children in an inappropriately weak physiological position.

Nutritional deprivation, particularly the deprivation of key protein elements, has also been shown to hinder and retard children's intellectual development. While these effects are potentially remediable, they are also potentially permanent and put children in a most unenviable position in coping with the significant demands made by a very demanding social structure.

Weight gain during pregnancy is another aspect of the nutritional picture directly relevant to the child. Some interesting folklore has existed about the amount of weight to be gained during pregnancy. For example, at one time it was believed that if the mother was very careful and avoided gaining much weight, the baby would be smaller and the delivery would be easier. This is an unfortunate oversimplification of the growth process. The size of the baby *in utero* is of course somewhat dependent upon the nutritional status of the mother. But the size of the baby is much more dependent upon the genetic contributions of the mother and father, and birth complications are a function not only of the baby's size but also of the mother's size (which determines the size of infant she will be able to deliver). So this particular admonition easily fits into the section marked "folklore."

Another theory used to be that a healthy baby would be produced regardless of the mother's own nutritional history and nutritional practices during pregnancy. This idea is false. The mother's nutritional pattern both before and during the pregnancy are quite relevant to the health of the baby.

Pregnant women's weight gain is currently a topic of some debate among doctors. The weight gain itself is made up of the weight of the baby, an increase in the size of the uterus, the placenta, amniotic fluid, and an increase in breast tissue. It is currently being suggested that a weight gain in the neighborhood of 25 pounds is appropriate. The Committee on Maternal Nutrition (1970) has suggested that weight gain during the first trimester should be 1½ to 3 pounds, and approximately .8 pound weekly for the remainder of pregnancy. This would allow a weight gain of between 21.77 pounds to 23.27 pounds. Keeping in mind the principle of idiosyncratic development and the commonly spoken phrase "no two pregnancies are alike," these numbers represent reasonable estimates of weight gain during the course of the pregnancy. Both extremely rapid weight gain and very little weight gain may be signs of problems with the pregnancy.

There is a dynamic interrelationship between the nutritional system and other relevant "systems" children find themselves in. For example, there is an interrelationship between socioeconomic status and nutrition. The likelihood of nutritional problems is greater in the lower social classes.

Nutritional problems bear a significant relationship to low birth weight babies, and it has been shown that as many as 20 percent of low birth weight babies may develop some form of learning difficulty—some subtle, some obvious (Williams, 1974). Finally, it is quite possible that learning difficulties may be fundamentally related to the child's social class.

Summary

1. Technology plays a significant part in the birthing process in America. Fetal monitoring is one example of how technology has crept into the delivery room; drugs and other intervention techniques are other examples. Many people are questioning the medical intrusion into the birthing process.

2. The patterns of a culture determine how that culture will structure significant events, like childbirth. The variety in cultural practices related to birthing is matched only by the number of cultures available to study. In some cultures births are unattended; in others, births are attended by many members of the family.

3. In our culture, birthing has become unattended in terms of family members; births are attended by medical personnel. Recently there has been a significant reinvolvement in birth by family members, in the form of alternative birthing rooms or father-present LaMaze deliveries.

4. The natural childbirth movement is like most movements: it is actually several movements and there is a great deal of misinformation floating around about each of them. Prepared childbirth techniques, like LaMaze, have become very popular in American birthing patterns, yet these techniques do not suit all mothers nor all fathers. The husband and wife (and doctor) should work together to determine an acceptable birthing atmosphere, one that is right for all of the people (including the baby).

5. Prepared childbirth is made up of three factors: education of all participants about the nature of the birthing process; relaxation training of the mother, with the help and assistance of the coach (usually the husband); and control over each aspect of the birthing process.

6. Gentle birth (LeBoyer) is a relatively recent arrival to the American birthing scene. It is created in the belief that the traditional entry of the baby into the world is traumatic. This trauma may be eased through a warm delivery room, soft lights, quietness, and a warm, soothing postdelivery bath for the baby. This technique sounds fine, and there is some visual evidence that it works; there is little empirical evidence, however, that gentle birth has significant implications for the postneonatal life of the child.

7. There are many ecosystems that significantly affect the future of the baby. Discussed in this chapter were the social class ecosystem, which may have profound effects, and the nutritional ecosystem, which does have significant effects.

Social Implications

Thought Questions

1. How has technology altered the birthing process in America? What are the effects of this technological intrusion?

2. Is the American way of birthing the only way? Give some examples of how the birthing techniques differ across cultural and historical lines. Why have births been relatively unattended by family members during the last few decades? What has happened to birthing since the evolution of hospitals?

3. Differentiate between natural birthing and prepared birthing techniques. What are the fundamental elements of prepared childbirth? How do these techniques help mother and baby? Should everyone who is going to have a baby use LaMaze? What conditions dictate which technique to use?

4. What is gentle birth? How does it compare to prepared childbirth?

5. What are the influences of the social class and the nutritional ecosystems on the babies born into these systems? How do we control the impact of these ecosystems?

Suggested Readings

Arms, S. *Immaculate Deception*. Boston: Houghton-Mifflin, 1975. *This is a controversial work, to say the least. It discusses home birth from the perspective of a home birth advocate. A major emphasis in the book is the author's desire to devalue the clinical dimension of childbirth and advocate the human dimension.*

Fraiberg, S. *Every Child's Birthright: In Defense of Mothering*. New York: Basic Books, 1977. *Fraiberg discusses the importance of mother-infant bonding and the overall importance of infant caregivers. A moving book.*

LeBoyer, F. *Birth without Violence*. New York: Knopf, 1975. *In a moving, seemingly poetic way, LeBoyer describes the gentle birth procedure he so strongly advocates. Contained in the book are some heartwarming pictures of newborn children. A classic in the childbirth movement.*

READING

Childbirth in America used to occur at home, with the help of family and friends. The event was significant in its rich, supportive nature, yet potentially very dangerous—many mothers and babies died during delivery in the past.

Technology and the ensuing medical changes moved childbirth from a family-oriented event at home to a clinical event in a hospital delivery room. This change did bring lower infant and maternal mortality rates, but it also brought with it far more isolation for the mother and the lack of familial support during birth.

Mary Doyle, in her article entitled "Approaches to Childbirth," traces the history of childbirth and the many different options for delivery available today. The "illness model" of childbirth, requiring extended hospitalization, seems to be of limited utility today; there are so many more low-risk pregnancies. Among the current options are home birth, birthing rooms, and free-standing birthing centers.

The material described by Doyle represents the efforts of many nurses, physicians, and consumer groups to humanize the birthing process. As Doyle says, childbirth is not an illness. We have seen the beginning of the transition to a more educated and human birthing environment.

Approaches to Childbirth
Mary C. Doyle, R.N.

Traditional Childbirth

Prior to the 1900s, most births occurred in the home. Childbirth was a natural family and community event with traditions supportive of new parents. As medicine progressed and life-saving techniques advanced, more and more births took place in hospitals. This move, while reducing maternal and infant death rates, was not without drawbacks. Hospitals at the turn of the century were such a source of disease and infection that strict policies and procedures were needed to protect mothers and newborns. These policies focused on limiting contact between infants and "outsiders"—with outsiders including mothers, family members and friends. Hospital delivery rooms were modeled after operating rooms: functional and efficient from a hospital staff point of view, but impersonal and most unhomelike from the patient's. Childbirth was thus increasingly removed from its traditional context of family and community; it had become an "illness" requiring hospitalization.

Childbirth Today: Changing Knowledge, Attitudes and Expectations

Medicine since then has seen ever-increasing sophistication in saving and improving the quality of the lives of mothers and infants. Intensive care nurseries have been developed and entire new subspecialties—such as neonatology and perinatology—have come into being. Energies and efforts have centered on caring for ill or high-risk mothers and infants; until recently, the needs of the normal or low-risk family have been ignored. Childbearing families continue to be considered as ill persons in need of treatment, rather than as normal people experiencing a normal physiological process.

However, the needs of the low-risk family are now being examined as part of a broad new movement questioning conventional childbirth practices and seeking to develop various approaches to them. Professional as well as consumer journals are filled with articles on birth and its implications. The impetus for this "child-

Social Implications

birth movement" has come from a variety of sources.

Research has provided us with important new information on mothers, fathers and infants. The work of Klaus and Kennell on maternal-infant bonding raises serious questions about the wisdom of separating the infant from its family in the first hours and days of life. Brazelton's research on infant response suggests that early infant-parent interaction in a relaxed environment is needed and beneficial.

Research has also shown that the use of total anesthesia during childbirth decreases the mother's ability to respond and can also be harmful to the newborn. Consequently, current practice favors local or regional anesthesia instead. This means that most mothers are now awake and aware during delivery, a change that has provoked a critical look at the delivery environment. Is the impersonal, sterile "operating room" setting the best for the family, and is it really necessary for a safe and healthy birth?

Social factors are also influencing childbirth. The trend toward smaller families means that birth takes on greater significance to childbearing couples. There seems to be a feeling that "we're only going to do this once or twice, so let's do it right, let's experience it as fully as possible." This attitude is reflected in parents asking for more control over the birth process and in fathers wanting more involvement. The steady increase in childbirth education groups for parents is evidence of their desire for information and control. These classes emphasize the wellness model of childbirth, so more couples are approaching childbirth expecting to be treated as a healthy family and this expectation is in turn influencing childbirth practices.

Consumer groups are also concerned with the cost of traditional childbirth. Many insurance companies provide only limited coverage and new parents are faced with heavy expenses. Parents are questioning both whether they are getting what they paid for and whether they need what they got. Traditional centers thus need to examine their services and justify them to the consumer. Hospitals can no longer expect low-risk families to pay for high-risk equipment that they do not use or need.

Advances in perinatal medicine are another factor in the childbirth movement. Physicians can more accurately identify risk factors in mother or infant and apply preventative and curative treatment as appropriate. Sophisticated screening facilitates the individualization of care, thus leading away from the traditional model where everyone is treated in the same manner —as an ill person.

The illness model of childbirth has outlived its usefulness. The fact is that the majority of pregnancies and deliveries today are low-risk, and that many routine practices used in hospitals are no longer necessary. The operating room delivery setting, the heavy use of medication, banning fathers from the delivery room and maintaining closed nurseries—all of these are being examined and altered to meet the needs of the "normal" family, and new childbirth options are being developed. The childbearing family, particularly in larger metropolitan areas, now has a number of nontraditional choices available.

Childbirth Options

Home Birth

One of the more controversial childbirth options is home birth. This practice is more common in Europe but has recently resurfaced in the United States. Home delivery may be attended by a physician, nurse or midwife (professional or lay), depending on the practice and regulations in an area. The home birth allows parents to remain in a familiar and comfortable environment. The familiar setting reduces the mother's anxiety and assists her in maintaining control. The infant is not separated from the parents and birth is a family event that can be shared. The cost to the family varies depending on who assists the birth, but it is definitely lower than for a traditional delivery.

These benefits of home birth must be weighed against the potential dangers, however. When unexpected complications occur, lack of trained personnel and adequate equipment can have tragic outcomes. Few physicians or hospitals are willing to take the risk of becoming involved in home delivery. There are very few studies available on home birth in the United States, but European data indicate it has higher risk than hospital delivery.

The home birth movement seems to be a protest against the cold and restrictive environment

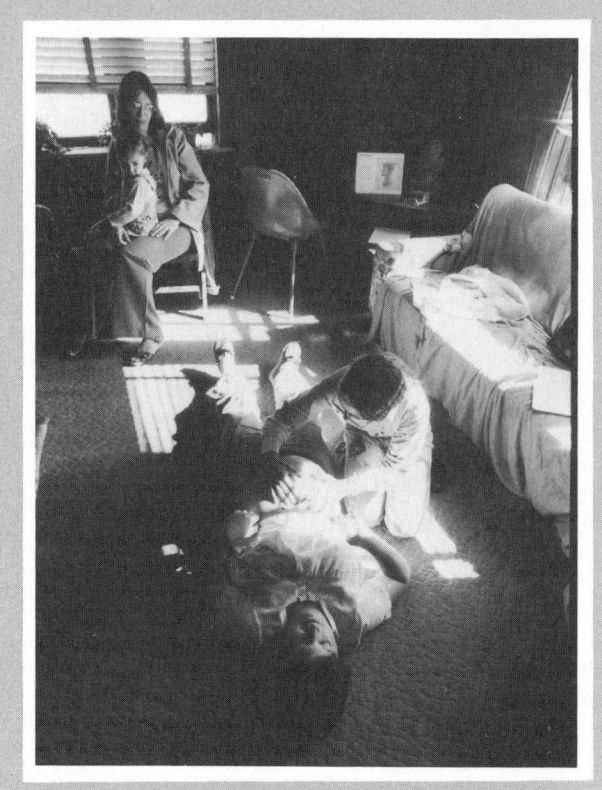

More women are choosing the home as an alternative birthing site. Here a midwife examines a woman in a late stage of pregnancy while others look on.
ROBERT V. ECKERT, JR., EKM-NEPENTHE.

surrounding hospital births. Consumers who are frustrated in attempts to humanize their hospitals or physicians in their area often see it as their only option. Due to the risks involved, this increase in home births has led consumers and professionals to work together on the development of other birth approaches.

Free-Standing Birth Centers

Another option available to parents is the birth center or birth clinic. The birth center is a separate facility but is usually located near a hospital or clinic and is often affiliated with a physician, group or hospital. It is staffed by physicians or midwives who have seen the family during the pregnancy to screen for risk factors. When a woman goes into labor she enters the birth center. Fathers, and often other family members, are welcome in birth centers. The delivery rooms are designed as comfortable bedrooms. Emergency equipment is usually nearby to handle unexpected complications, although transfer to the hospital is necessary when the trouble is severe. After the birth, the family stays together in the center from a few hours to 48 hours, depending on the center's policies. Restrictions on the use of the center, delivery procedures, use of medication and postnatal follow-up vary from center to center.

A birth center offers many of the advantages of home birth while providing emergency equipment and assistance not readily available in the home. Because of its physical location and separation from some hospital facilities, the free-standing birth center is somewhat restrictive in the population it serves, that is, it has stricter admission policies and screening criteria. There may also be some difficulty in getting insurance coverage for births in these centers, depending on the arrangements with physicians or hospitals. Costs are usually lower than traditional hospital births.

Social Implications

The homelike atmosphere in the Family Birthing Center at Providence Hospital in Southfield, Michigan encourages two older sisters to visit their family's newest member.
COURTESY OF PROVIDENCE HOSPITAL, SOUTHFIELD, MICHIGAN.

Birthing Rooms

Of the childbirth options currently available, the birthing room is the fastest growing choice. The birthing room is a combined labor-delivery-recovery room located in a hospital. It is decorated to resemble a bedroom, yet contains emergency equipment or has such equipment available right outside it. It is usually an option offered within a family-centered maternity unit. The birthing room is designed to insure medical safety while providing a more homelike environment. Having infant and parent stay together after delivery is an essential component of the birthing room. Other aspects, such as the style of delivery, procedures used, length of stay and use of medication, vary from hospital to hospital.

Birthing rooms have several advantages over traditional labor and delivery rooms. Labor and delivery in the same bed means that the mother can concentrate on using her energy in the birth process instead of moving from bed to cart to delivery table, which is distracting and painful. The homelike environment has a positive and supportive effect on the mother and enhances her feeling that she has control over what is going on. If a mother feels less helpless, she is better able to cooperate during delivery and may require less medication or anesthesia. Under these conditions, she may be more receptive to early interaction with her infant. The birthing room also provides a private, comfortable place for parents to become acquainted with their newborn. The fact that the birthing room is located in a hospital is often reassuring to families who want a less traditional birth but are more comfortable having the hospital's resources at hand.

A birthing room can be made out of a traditional delivery room, labor room or patient room. Remodeling involves painting or wallpapering with bright, washable material. Drapes, a colorful bedspread, plants and pictures enhance the room's comfortable aspect. Built-in cupboards or dressers hold supplies for labor and delivery as well as infant resuscitation equipment. Oxygen and suction outlets are located in the wall near the head of the bed. A lounge chair is available for the support person. Lighting for the delivery can be provided by a pull-down ceiling light or a portable floor spotlight. The type of bed used in the room will depend upon the procedures used in the room; it may be a regular single or double bed or one especially designed for labor and delivery.

Families using a birthing room enter the hospital in the early stages of labor. Couples may spend their time in the room itself or in a nearby early labor lounge. When delivery is imminent, the mother gets into bed and supplies for the delivery are wheeled into the room. The supplies are removed after delivery and the family is left together to get acquainted. An overhead radiant panel or a standard infant warmer is available to provide warmth for the newborn. Style of delivery, use of medication/anesthesia, delivery position and procedures are negotiated between the family and physician, but birthing rooms can be adapted to most styles and procedures.

Birthing Rooms: A Case Study

In April 1976, birthing rooms were introduced at Golden Valley Health Center in Minnesota, a hospital with a small maternity unit serving a low-risk population. Home births were not common in the area but most families were involved in prenatal education and were asking for an approach other than traditional delivery.

The first room was opened on a trial basis. The room was and continues to be an option offered to all families. We had planned to establish criteria for use of the room but this has not proved necessary. Use of the room and style of delivery is agreed between the mother and the physician. Physicians screen patients who are not good candidates for the room, although most procedures done in a delivery room can be done in a birthing room. Supplies and emergency equipment are kept in closets in the room.

When indicated, fetal monitoring, IVs and forceps are used in the birthing room. These procedures detract from the homelike atmosphere but are necessary in some cases. We prefer to offer these options in the birthing room rather than move families out of it at a critical moment in labor or delivery. Transfer to the operating room is necessary for cesarean section, however. Medications and anesthesia are available to the mother in the birthing room and an anesthetist is present to provide initial evaluation of the infant and emergency care if needed. Use of medication/anesthesia is determined by the mother and physician. Restricting use of the room to families planning totally "natural" births would screen out many families who can benefit from the calming atmosphere and early contact with their infants.

Unless an infant's condition is unstable, the infant remains with the parents after delivery. Parents share a meal and the mother's condition is closely monitored by a nurse. The nurse is available to assist with breastfeeding and usually weighs, measures and bathes the infant in the room. The mother is transferred to a regular room on the unit three to four hours after the birth. The infant may accompany her there or may go to the nursery—whichever the mother prefers. Total length of hospital stay is decided between family and physician. An increasing number of families return home within 48 hours of delivery.

High demand for the use of the birthing room resulted in our opening a second one in November 1977. There have now been more than 500 deliveries in our birthing room. In studying couples who use this option, we find they have usually attended some type of childbirth class, although this is not a requirement. They cite three major reasons for selection of the birthing room: (1) being able to stay in the same bed for labor and delivery, (2) the opportunity to interact with their infant after delivery and (3) the warm atmosphere. More than 50 percent of families served by the maternity unit use the birthing rooms; they are used by first time parents as frequently as by those already having children. Ninety-seven percent of mothers who select the birthing room are also planning to breastfeed. Parents perceive having a pleasant atmosphere and hospital safety as a major benefit of the birthing room.

Establishing a birthing room in a hospital may be opposed by nurses and physicians who are comfortable with the traditional delivery setting. Difficulties may also be posed by antiquated state regulations that impede liberalizing hospital policies. Consumer groups can be very helpful in overcoming such obstacles. As they become more vocal in expressing their needs, institutions and individuals will respond. Once the birthing room is in operation, nurses and physicians generally find their fears and misgivings about it are unfounded; many of them find their new sup-

Social Implications

portive and teaching roles to be very rewarding. A side benefit of a birthing room is that its operation usually leads to a reexamination of standard delivery room procedures. Many of the procedures used in the birthing room can be easily adapted to a delivery room or recovery room. This is particularly true of the provision for early contact between infant and mother.

Meeting the Needs of Childbearing Families

Childbearing couples do have various childbirth options to choose from in many parts of the country. Those interested in such options or in working with their physicians or hospitals in making changes should contact their local childbirth education group. These groups can provide educational materials on birth approaches as well as information on options available locally.

Childbirth is changing. It is not an illness, but an exhilarating experience and a turning point in the development of a family. It is the responsibility of consumers and health care professionals to insure that it is treated with safety and dignity. Traditional institutions must examine their practices in light of new research and consumer pressure which indicate that these practices are not in the best interests of the family. Only with consumers and professionals working together will there be an end to unneeded childbirth practices and a wide availability of options that truly meet the needs of families in the unique experience of birth.

UNIT II
INFANT DEVELOPMENT

SHELBURNE MUSEUM. SHELBURNE, VERMONT.

Mother Rose Nurses Her Child, Mary Cassatt.

6

Infancy: Physiological Development

Infancy has been defined as beginning at birth and ending when talking begins. Since children begin to speak at very different ages, this definition is quite loose. Our idea of who can "talk" has also changed over the years. Once children were considered to be infants until the age of seven, "because in this age *it* cannot talk well or form *its* words perfectly" (Aries, 1962). Now, many limit infancy to the first 12 months. Most children can speak at least one word intelligibly by then. Others feel that infancy can be extended to two and one-half years, when the child's vocabulary explodes to hundreds of words (Lenneberg, 1975). For our convenience, we will call infancy that period from birth to 18 months.

Perhaps no other time in our lives is as full of change and growth as infancy is. Newborn infants can hear extremely fine variations in sound, and they can see (somewhat), smell, taste, vocalize, and feel (Kagan, 1979). They are sensitive to the slightest changes. They are aware of and curious about their environment. Their bodies and minds are ready to begin the adventure of life outside the uterus.

But for all their presence and human characteristics they are pitifully small and weak. They cannot cope, and must be cared for. They are physically incompetent. They are totally inexperienced. In other words, the infant begins life entirely dependent on others.

Remarkably, in the space of a year and a half, these creatures will be able to stand up, walk around, move toys and furniture, feed themselves (in their own fashion), speak to others, and in general—though still dependent and in need of protection—they will be true human individuals. They will have definite personalities, and an amazing array of autonomous behaviors.

Part of this growth is physical—which will be the main subject of this chapter—but inseparably tied to physical growth is social and mental growth. Because infants are so dependent, they require constant nurturing from adults. The quantity and quality of this care affects children in many ways, including their physical development. In turn, physical developments stimulate social interaction and new learning opportunities.

Let us first look at what infants experience physically. What happens to their bodies? What changes take place?

HEIGHT AND WEIGHT

Growth is not steady or constant in all areas. Sometimes a child is growing up, sometimes out, and sometimes within. In the first year, a baby's average length (in the horizontal stage it cannot really be called height) usually increases by a third to a half, from around 20 inches to around 29 inches. Furthermore, the length is acquired more in certain areas than in others. The legs, for instance, grow more than the head.

Weight, on the other hand, almost triples in the first year, rising from around 8 pounds to around 20 pounds. The style and amount of the weight increase varies widely, depending on the child and on environmental influences. Each ethnic group has been found to have its own pattern of normal height and weight increases. For this reason, the traditional hospital height and weight charts, based on white middle-class American children, must be loosely interpreted. Individual heredity is another factor. One infant may have a tendency to accumulate fatty tissue. Another infant may have a tendency toward early muscle growth. This second infant could weigh more, though it might be smaller, because muscle tissue is heavier than fatty tissue.

Physical growth slows in the second and third year, then continues at a fairly stable rate until adolescence. The chart on the opposite page represents this pattern.

SKELETAL MATURATION

The original material from which our bones are made is a gelatinous protein tissue called *cartilage*. With the deposit of minerals, the cartilage becomes hard. Nerves enter the bone, and its struc-

Height and Weight Growth Chart*

	Birth	1st Year	2nd Year	To Adolescence	Adolescent Growth Spurt Age at Peak	Age When Growth Ends
Height	18–21"	7–10 more inches	5 more inches	2–2½ inches per year	Females = 12 Males = 14	Females = 18 Males = 20
Weight	Varies widely, usually under 13 pounds	Birth weight tripled	Birth weight quadrupled	5–6 pounds per year	*Total Gain During Adolescence* Females to 35 pounds Males to 45 pounds	Several years after adult height is reached Varies with individual

*Adapted from Tanner, 1970.

Ossification: gradual mineralizing of the bones

ture changes. This process of *ossification* begins before the baby is born, and continues after birth until late adolescence.

It is our bones that are the most reliable indicators of growth. All mature people do not look alike in terms of height, weight, body hair, or any other outward signs. There is no weight or height that determines adulthood. We can't say that a boy is a man because he weighs 150 pounds. But all mature bones do look alike. Regardless of length or width, all bones go through a specific sequence of development. They harden first in the middle, then at the ends.

All our bones are not hardening at the same time, however. There seems to be a sequential timetable for maturing among the different bones of the skeleton. Some of the bones of the hand ossify in the first year. Most bones ossify later (Grollman, 1964). The newborn's skull, for example, has six soft spots, called *fontanelles*, which ossify slowly. They can be detected until the child is about two years old.

The stage of ossification of any bone or bone group signals maturity. The skeleton with six ossified hand bones is more mature than the one with three ossified hand bones. When all the bones are completely ossified, physical growth is over.

The softness of infants' bones makes their skeletal structure pliable. The advantage of this is that children's bones are less likely to break. The disadvantage is that children are more susceptible to deformity. Muscular pulls, either from an odd habitually held position, or from a congenital muscular abnormality, can deform the shape of a bone. Caught early, problems of this sort can be corrected easily before the bone hardens.

MUSCULAR DEVELOPMENT

Newborn children have all the muscle fibers they will ever have. The fibers make up about 20 percent of an infant's weight, but they are small and undeveloped. A newborn is even too weak to combat the force of gravity, and will hang limp when lifted. In time, the fibers become longer and thicker. Usually the muscle groups near the head and neck develop first. During the second month, many children can lift their heads a little, and by the fifth month they can usually hold their heads erect without a supporting hand. This is no small feat, for their heads are very heavy.

Although the infant is capable of some rather refined muscular movements, like wrinkling the nose or curling the toes, these are reflexive, and not under voluntary control. Voluntary control over

Infancy: Physiological Development

the muscles comes slowly. During the first year, the large muscles function better than the small ones. General movements, like pounding or waving the hand, are easier for the child than precise movements like grasping a small object with the fingers. Infant boys tend to be more muscular than infant girls, a sex difference that continues throughout life.

GROWING NERVES

The main reason for an infant's increasingly more refined motor control is not simply that the muscles develop and grow, but that the nervous system controlling them improves. The nervous system is composed of the brain, the spinal cord, and the nerves. As with muscle fibers, all the nerve cells we will ever have are probably present at birth, but again, the cells are small, and not all of them are functioning. Nerve cells grow with body size to whatever length is necessary for their function. In an adult, some are several feet long. Regardless of length, however, a nerve cell, or *neuron*, is not considered mature until it is conveying impulses.

Neuron: nerve cell

Mature nerve fibers differ in appearance from undeveloped ones. They are sheathed with a fatty substance called *myelin*. The

Myelin: fatty substance that gradually coats nerve fibers

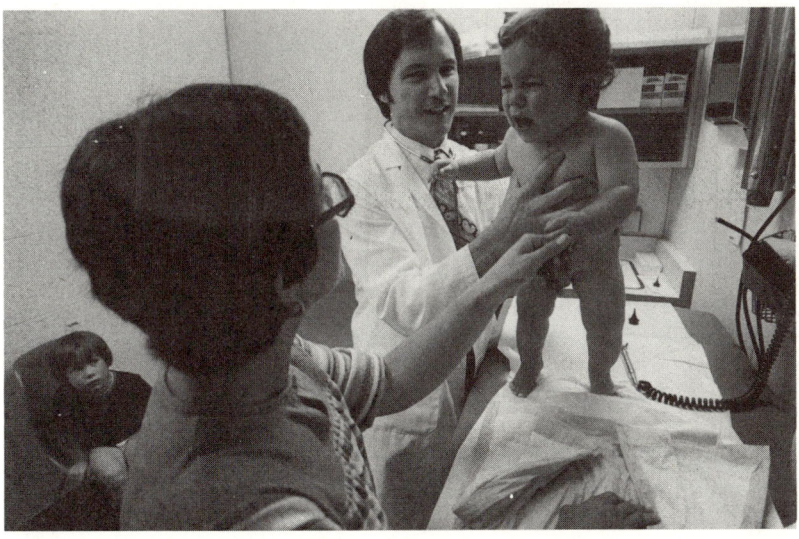

A pediatrician examines a baby boy while his older brother watches apprehensively from a chair nearby.
ROBERT V. ECKERT, JR., EKM-NEPENTHE.

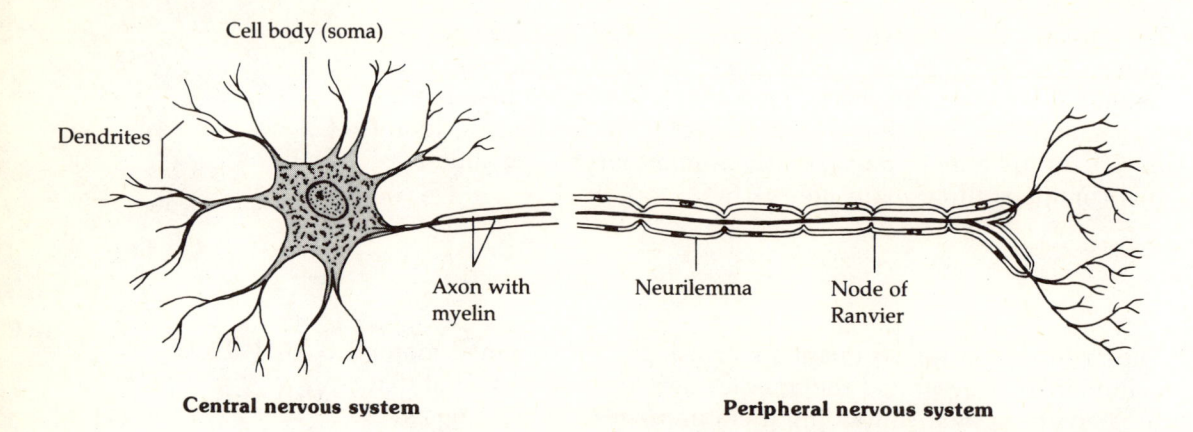

A "typical" neuron, or nerve cell, showing several of its important features. The nerve impulse usually travels from the dendrites to the branching ends of the axon. The neuron shown here is a motor neuron. Motor neurons originate in the brain or spinal cord and send their axons to the muscles of the body.

number of myelinated nerves is an indication of the development of the nervous system. Myelinization begins in the fetal stage and continues at least through adolescence (Tanner, 1970). Progress seems to be made in uneven spurts. For instance, sound nerves begin to myelinate in the sixth fetal month, and continue to develop slowly. Sight nerves, however, do not begin to myelinate until around the time of birth. They then complete the process rapidly. How much stimulation has to do with this process is unknown. A fetus could hear many noises, for example, but would not be in a position to see any images before birth.

The most developed parts of the newborn's system are the primitive nervous centers—the mid and hindbrains, and the spinal cord. These centers regulate heartbeat, breathing, body temperature, sucking and swallowing, and other instinctive reflexes. The larger outer *hemispheres* of the brain are relatively undeveloped at birth. The hemispheres are responsible for voluntary movements, memory, and intelligence. As these voluntary centers become more developed, children are able to control their bodies, learn from the environment, and modify instinctive reflexes. Some functions originally controlled by the primitive brain centers will be assumed by the voluntary centers. For instance, the function of walking first appears as a reflex in newborns. This reflex dies out around the eighth week unless it is "practiced" with the help of an adult (Bow-

Hemispheres: large outer portions of the brain

Infancy: Physiological Development

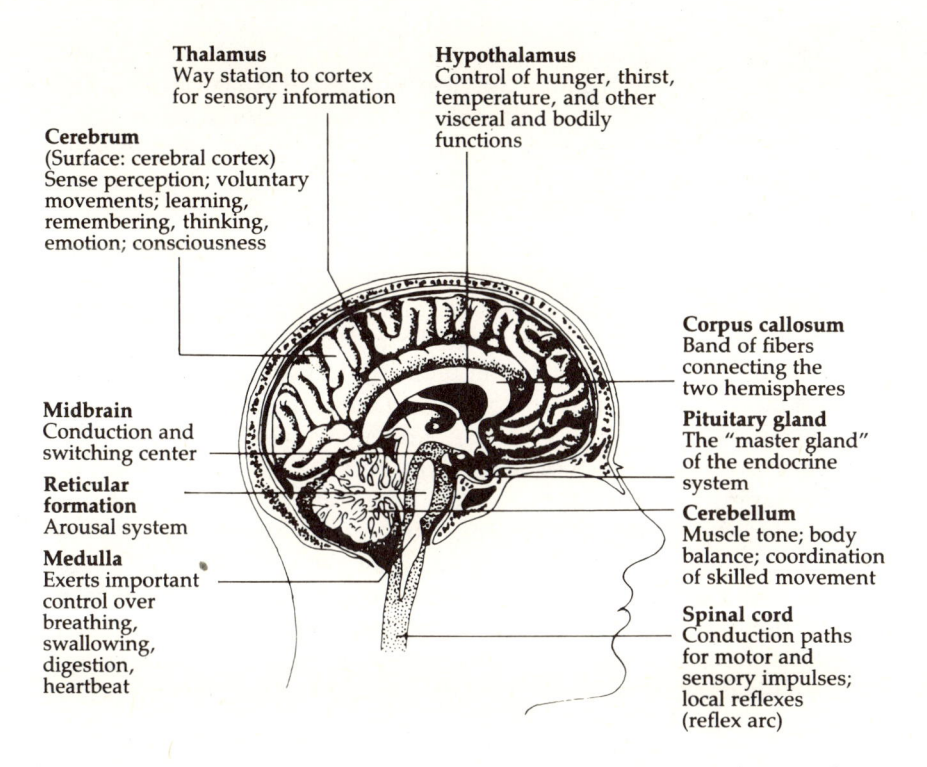

Thalamus
Way station to cortex for sensory information

Hypothalamus
Control of hunger, thirst, temperature, and other visceral and bodily functions

Cerebrum
(Surface: cerebral cortex) Sense perception; voluntary movements; learning, remembering, thinking, emotion; consciousness

Corpus callosum
Band of fibers connecting the two hemispheres

Midbrain
Conduction and switching center

Pituitary gland
The "master gland" of the endocrine system

Reticular formation
Arousal system

Cerebellum
Muscle tone; body balance; coordination of skilled movement

Medulla
Exerts important control over breathing, swallowing, digestion, heartbeat

Spinal cord
Conduction paths for motor and sensory impulses; local reflexes (reflex arc)

This simplified drawing shows the main structures of the human brain and describes some of their most important functions.

er, 1977). The infant is not yet strong enough to use this inherited behavior. Around one year of age, walking reappears as a voluntary activity, controlled by the outer brain. Swallowing is another example of an activity that is almost totally reflexive at birth, but almost totally voluntary later in life.

In the hemispheres, the first areas to develop are the primary motor centers, quickly followed by the primary sensory centers. By the end of the first month, the infant has some control over the upper trunk and arms. By the third month, all the infant's primary sensorimotor areas are relatively mature except for the areas controlling the lower limbs. The areas controlling eye movement develop especially rapidly up through the sixth month. From the sixth to the fifteenth month, there is proportionately more development in the associative/interpretive areas.

When children suffer brain damage at birth or in infancy, the damage is usually to the outer hemispheres. In such cases, the life support systems continue to operate normally and the child still lives. It is the sensorimotor and learning centers that are disturbed. Though there may be no change in behavior at the time of injury, the child will later fail to develop and learn in the area or areas that are damaged (Pines, 1973). These problems will not appear until late infancy or early childhood.

Interestingly, what happens to us on the right side of our bodies is recorded on the left side of our brains. If we hear a bell in our right ear, the left hemisphere ear area registers the sound. If our left hemisphere says "Raise your hand," it is the right hand that goes up. The two sides of the brain trade information through a bundle of fibers, called the *corpus callosum,* that connects the two hemispheres. The corpus callosum does not seem to be fully functional until age two, but from birth both halves of the brain are developing side by side. Slowly, however, certain activities are shuffled to one side of the brain. The left side of the brain specializes in speech. Spatial relationships are the specialty of the right side. This specialization becomes more definite, and less reversible, the older we get. A child of eight who suffers injury to his left hemisphere may lose the power of speech, but can relearn speech with his right brain. An adult in the same predicament will lose the power of speech forever (Pines, 1973).

THE ENDOCRINE SYSTEM

Endocrine system: glands and hormones that regulate body chemistry

The endocrine system regulates the infant's body chemistry. Without its help the child could not grow, digest food, retain salt, burn calories, or gain extra strength and alertness in times of danger. It also controls sex typing and the onset of puberty. Diabetes, hyperthyroidism, and other illnesses stemming from chemical imbalances are due to the malfunctioning of this system.

The pituitary gland is the main regulator of the system. By sending certain hormones it activates the other glands, like the adrenal glands, the pancreas, the thyroid, and the sex organs, to act. The pituitary also releases a growth hormone directly. Its peak activity occurs during the 23rd to 28th week of fetal development. After this the growth hormone's output declines, and it is secreted sporadically, rather than continuously, after birth. Because the endocrine system is responsible for growth, it is most active during periods of rapid body growth: that is, during prenatal development, the first two years of life, and adolescence.

Infancy: Physiological Development

INFLUENCES ON GROWTH RATES

Some children grow quickly; others not. Why? There is no single reason, of course, but rather a number of possible reasons. *Genetic inheritance* is one. Our physical stature and some of the ways we attain it are passed to us in our parents' genes. Tall children cannot be grown from short genes, nor early development eked out of average or late development genes. Genetic inheritance is racial as well as individual. A Tahitian child may be growing just as quickly as a Scandinavian child even though their final heights are radically different. Racially Tahitians are of short stature; Scandinavians, tall.

A related influence is *sex type*. Male and female children have different growth rates. Females develop sooner and in a more steady pattern than males at all ages from birth to adulthood. However, they develop fewer muscles and more fatty tissue, and, after childhood, they are generally shorter than males. Males are generally heavier at all ages because of their musculature. Their height, however, is about the same as females until puberty, when males tend to become much taller and heavier with longer limbs, larger hands and feet, and broader, deeper chests than women. All their development is slower and more susceptible to variation. Puberty for males arrives about two years later than in females, and attainment of final height and weight is also later than in females.

A third important influence on children's growth rates is the *environment* in which they are raised. Although infants are amazingly resistant to retardation of their growth cycles, physical development *is* affected by poor environmental conditions. Good nutrition is one essential part of a good environment. Malnourished infants use the nutrients they get to maintain the essential life support systems and nerve development first. Increasing their height and weight is of secondary importance. This is the first area in which growth slows or stops when children lack food. Without proper nourishment, their genetic inheritance may not be realized. A short period of deprivation will be made up with a compensatory growth spurt as soon as food is available, but a long period of deprivation will result in permanently stunted growth and an underdeveloped nervous system. The reverse is also true. Children who receive better nutrition than their parents did may grow taller and stronger than their genetic background would indicate.

Physical and psychological well-being is equally important. When children suffer extreme mental stress, growth-inhibiting chemicals suppress the growth hormones in the body (Tanner,

1970, 1973). Children who experience frequent or intense fear, anxiety, tension, or psychological abuse are known to develop more slowly. Height and weight increases fall behind normal patterns. Children may also react in this way when distressed by the bleak vistas, garbage, and broken glass of city ghettos, or other poor living conditions. Studies in Scotland showed that children of upper socioeconomic classes were taller and heavier than those of lower socioeconomic families. The quality and quantity of available food was not the only difference in these children's lives. Upper-class homes provided more living space, more pleasant surroundings, fewer siblings, and less family tension (Tanner, 1973).

A fourth influence on growth rates is *disease*. A child's body cannot afford to grow when it needs its resources to battle disease. Children prone to frequent illnesses do not grow as quickly or as much as children who rarely get sick.

The elimination of severe childhood diseases in many parts of the world has resulted in an evolutionary trend toward taller, heavier people. From ancient suits of armor we can deduce that men were not as tall once as they are now. Even records kept in the last 200 years show a significant increase in height and weight for both men and women. Records also show that the age of sexual maturity has been falling lower and lower every decade. In the 1840s, girls were 17 or older at menarche. Now most girls first menstruate around their 12th year. The age at which males experience the peak of their adolescent growth spurt has lowered through the last few centuries from age 25 (or older) to around age 14. The elimination of diseases is considered to be the major reason for these changes. (All of these occurrences have been lumped together and called the *secular trend*.)

This social reaction to physical development begins early. By the end of the first year, children show distinct differences in personality. Some traits, like passivity, may be partly or wholly genetic. But even between genetically identical twins there are noticeable differences (Bower, 1976). We suppose, therefore, that many differences arise from children's treatment by adults and older children. One early trait is sex identity. Even one-year-old children display some behaviors that cater to cultural attitudes toward their sex (Maccoby and Jacklin, 1974; Werner, 1979). We must assume that even these very young infants are sensitive to the expectations of others.

American culture stresses certain physical characteristics: height, a lean and muscular build, the regular features of media-determined "beauty," and advanced motor coordination. A more developed physical appearance will elicit a corresponding social

Infancy: Physiological Development

response. The infant's size, amount of hair, an early smile, or a tight grasp gain a baby extra attention from passersby. Such a child is offered more stimulation, more chances to become competent, and more positive social feedback.

Parents, though usually predisposed toward their children in any case, will also have personal expectations. "Hey! My little boxer. Get 'em, Sluggo." "She's a smart one. Look at her eyes!" But what if the child is disappointingly small or passive? The degree to which a child physically meets cultural and parental expectations will affect interpersonal relationships and self-esteem.

MEETING THE INFANT'S NEEDS

To maintain life, to grow, love, and learn, the infant must be cared for. Its basic needs must be met. Warmth, food, safety, and unregulated sleep are what the infant knew before and what it wants still. Slowly, as it becomes more accustomed to its new surroundings and interested in them, the needs will expand and change in importance.

Sleep: As it is almost impossible to keep infants awake when they want to sleep, most young infants get enough sleep—about 16–17 hours a day. A newborn's sleeping periods are shallow and short. They are usually no more than five hours long and frequently alternated with waking periods. After the first month, the total number of sleeping hours begins to drop and a pattern toward more sleep at night begins. By the third month, the baby sleeps about 15 hours a day, half of this at night. At the end of the first year, the baby will sleep long nights with two to three hours of daytime napping as well. The sleep pattern will be more like an adult's: deeper in general, with a rhythm of light periods every few hours.

One-year-olds are active creatures, which partly accounts for the changed sleep pattern. They literally wear themselves out. In fact, babies that are kept too inactive may become poor sleepers. But babies who are kept awake too much, or not provided a quiet time and place to sleep, may also be a problem. They will welcome sleep when it comes, but they can be fussy, cranky, and overwrought during the day (as any adult would be).

Warmth and Safety: Like many other animals, the human baby is born weak, helpless, and vulnerable—not even able to keep warm

The seat of a sofa is just the right height for sleeping.
ROBERT V. ECKERT, JR., EKM-NEPENTHE.

enough to sustain life in cold weather. Unlike most animals, the human baby will remain in this condition for several years. Adults must provide the warmth and protection that the baby needs.

One aspect of these needs is purely physical. An adult must provide the house, the heat, the clothes, the watchful eye, and the brawn that saves the baby from cold weather, dangerous falls, sharp knives and overeager or ill-tempered pets. The other aspect is psychological. The infant benefits from *knowing* it is safe. It is less anxious, more social, more open to experimenting and learning.

Infancy: Physiological Development

ISSUE

Infant Physical Development: The Use of Norms

A *norm* is an estimate of when a behavior appears. In the study of child development, norms are used extensively. Parents, teachers, doctors, and others want to know when a child took his first step, said his first word, used the toilet for the first time, and so on. For every developmental occurrence, there is a norm.

☐ To calculate a norm, we take a large number of children, observe them for whatever behavior we are trying to study, and note the times when these behaviors appear. We then calculate an average time for their arrival. Norms describe development; they do not explain development.

☐ To what use can norms be put? They can show us the progress of a particular child in relation to most children. Norms can show if the child is developing in a manner significantly different from the rest of the children of the same age. For example, if we have norms for the average weight gain of children, we may be able to determine if a particular child is gaining weight similarly or dissimilarly to other children. If there is an unaccounted-for increase in weight above the normative weight gain, the doctor may seek the parents' cooperation to reduce the caloric intake of the child.

Below we have indicated examples of norms that have been developed over the years for the development of locomotion in children.

The M. M. Shirley Sequence of Motor Development*

4 months	Baby sits with support
7 months	Baby sits with help
9 months	Baby stands with support (furniture, etc.)
10 months	Baby creeps
14 months	Baby stands alone
15 months	Baby walks alone

*Shirley, 1931.

☐ Bayley (1969) developed the Bayley Scale of Motor Development. According to those norms:

8.6 months	Baby can pull himself to standing position
9.9 months	Baby can walk with help
11.7 months	Baby can walk unassisted

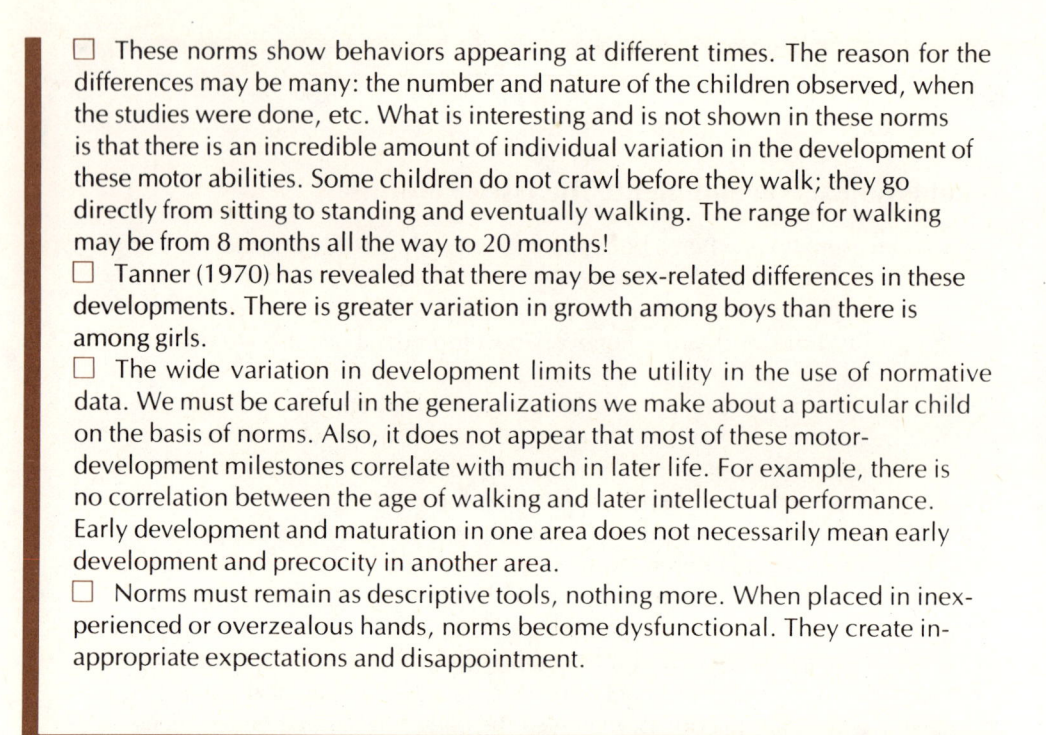

☐ These norms show behaviors appearing at different times. The reason for the differences may be many: the number and nature of the children observed, when the studies were done, etc. What is interesting and is not shown in these norms is that there is an incredible amount of individual variation in the development of these motor abilities. Some children do not crawl before they walk; they go directly from sitting to standing and eventually walking. The range for walking may be from 8 months all the way to 20 months!

☐ Tanner (1970) has revealed that there may be sex-related differences in these developments. There is greater variation in growth among boys than there is among girls.

☐ The wide variation in development limits the utility in the use of normative data. We must be careful in the generalizations we make about a particular child on the basis of norms. Also, it does not appear that most of these motor-development milestones correlate with much in later life. For example, there is no correlation between the age of walking and later intellectual performance. Early development and maturation in one area does not necessarily mean early development and precocity in another area.

☐ Norms must remain as descriptive tools, nothing more. When placed in inexperienced or overzealous hands, norms become dysfunctional. They create inappropriate expectations and disappointment.

Food: Now that the child is out of the womb, it must absorb its food in a totally new way, taking an active role. Fortunately, babies are born with reflexes that help them in this process. Instinctively they will search for food when touched near the mouth, suck (on anything), and swallow. The young infant spends a large part of its waking time eating.

The first food is usually milk, either breast milk or formula. Most babies' alimentary systems are too sensitive to ingest other types of foods. Their bodies are also geared for liquid foods. Anywhere between the second and sixth month some solids can be introduced, usually in the form of bland cereals and pureed fruits.

The first teeth may be present at birth, or they may not appear until the end of the first year. Whenever they appear the child usually shows some interest in chewy foods. Interest in solid foods increases when motor abilities develop enough so that the infant can sit up and pick up pieces of food with his or her fingers (usually somewhere between the fourth and seventh month), hence, their name, "finger foods." This increased ability also leads to a considerable amount of playing with the food.

Infancy: Physiological Development

The introduction of solid food may begin within the first few weeks of life. The exact timing of the introduction of solid foods depends upon the maturity and development of the child. This developmental posture needs to be accurately assessed before moving into new and/or exotic foods. Most pediatricians recommend the introduction of solid foods sometime between the third and sixth month. Smith (1977) has delineated five basic concepts relevant to the introduction of new foods into the infant's diet:

1. New foods should be introduced singly, and in small amounts; it is helpful to do this introducing when the child is hungry.
2. Foods introduced first should be those least likely to produce an allergic response; Smith suggests that some examples of this would be rice before wheat cereals, and vegetables before fruits.
3. Solids should be fed along with the milk (liquids) in order to prevent inappropriate caloric intake.
4. Use appropriate table family foods whenever possible, avoiding bland carbohydrates (bread, rice).
5. Schedules for eating food need to be developed; three meals per day is very appropriate for the one-year-old (Smith, 1977, p. 92).

The use of commercially prepared solid foods packaged under national brand names calls for caution and careful reading of the ingredients so as to avoid high levels of sugar, salt, and filler materials. People can grind their own baby food and ensure a better knowledge of the contents, utilizing natural fruits and vegetables that have essentially predictable ingredients and caloric levels.

Those who breast-feed their infants usually wean them between the ninth and twelfth months. By this time the child usually has some teeth. Cut-up pieces of almost any kind of food are of interest, and it is healthy and appropriate to offer a wide variety. Some children can manipulate a cup well enough by now to take liquids in this way. Others find a bottle less frustrating.

"I can do it by myself" is the attitude of children over a year old. Not only do older infants wield spoon and a cup with gusto, they may show decided preferences for some foods and dislike of others. It is still a good idea for parents to encourage a wide variety in the diet, but they should not be upset if the baby displays offbeat or lopsided tastes. It is a reflection of independence and is not harmful.

Meals are a time for getting attention and showing independence.
ROBERT V. ECKERT, JR., EKM-NEPENTHE.

Controversies about Infant Feeding

Breast vs. Bottle: The issues in this controversy are whether or not breast milk is nutritionally better for the baby than formula, and whether or not the psychological benefits of breast-feeding to mother and child are greater than those of bottle-feeding. Infants need about 117 calories and 150 milliliters of water per kilogram of weight every 24 hours to operate effectively.

Nutritionally, formulas have adequate amounts of the vitamins and minerals that infants need to grow. However, formulas are criticized for other ingredients. Often cows' or goats' milk is used in formulas. The fat content in these milks is higher than human breast milk, and greater than necessary for the human baby. Bottle-fed infants gain more weight in the first six months than breast-fed infants (Aitken & Hytten, 1960).

Breast milk, on the other hand, is perfectly designed for human babies. The milk itself changes through the first two weeks in ways that cater to the infants' needs. The infant receives from the

Infancy: Physiological Development

mother's first milk enzymes that aid in digestion and antibodies that provide temporary immunity to diseases. Other antibodies may be passed this way also. Breast-fed babies are less prone to develop allergies in childhood. For these reasons, breast milk does have a nutritional advantage over formulas. However, healthy children are raised on formulas. Bottle-feeding does not necessarily create problems.

Some people argue that the body contact that an infant experiences during breast-feeding is warmer and more natural. They say that the bond built between mother and child cannot be the same when a bottle is used. Certainly touching is important to the infant. In the nineteenth century many children, especially those raised in institutions, died of a disease called *marasmus* (from a Greek word meaning "to waste away"). The infants simply languished and died. Not until the beginning of this century was it discovered that cuddling, stroking, and touching the infants regularly cured the disease (Montague, 1971). It cannot be denied that the tactile quality of cheek on breast and mouth on nipple is unique and special to both mother and infant. Breast-feeding is the age-old natural method. But does the child suffer if not breast-fed?

Marasmus: progressive emaciation of neglected children

Harlow's well-known studies in the 1950s with baby monkeys and surrogate mothers came up with these results: all the baby monkeys preferred the (warmer) terry cloth mother, even when milk was supplied through the wire mother. Harlow remarked

> We were not surprised to discover that contact comfort was an important basic affectional or love variable, but we did not expect it to overshadow so completely the variable of nursing; indeed, the disparity is so great as to suggest that the primary function of nursing as an affectional variable is that of insuring frequent and intimate body contact of the infant and mother (Harlow, 1958, p. 676).

It seems then, that the object supplying food is less important to the infant's psychological health and welfare than the body contact that occurs during the feeding.

Harlow also observed that monkeys deprived of physical contact with adult or other infant monkeys showed emotional abnormalities later. Females failed to perform normally in their sex roles, and made inattentive or abusive mothers. This pattern of deprived childhoods leading to emotionally stunted adults has been observed in humans, too. "It appears probable that for human beings tactile stimulation is of fundamental consequence for the development of healthy emotional or affectional relationships. . . ." (Montague, 1971, p. 35). The infant is learning social and emotional cues from the body contact. The mother, father, older sibling, or any other caretaker could provide this essential physical attention to the infant. We can suppose that bottle feeding is detrimental to an infant's health only if the bottle is merely propped to drain and the infant not held.

In the matter of convenience, breast-feeding is undeniably superior. A long list of items must be on hand for preparing formula, including measuring devices, bottles, and materials to clean and sterilize everything.

Not only is breast-feeding simpler, but the mother benefits from it physically. When a child nurses, the woman's uterus contracts more quickly after birth. The baby's sucking stimulates hormones that suppress ovulation, and sometimes works as a natural contraceptive. Finally, lactation draws on the mother's physical resources, helping her to regain her former weight more easily (Montague, 1971).

However, it is not always reasonable for a woman to breast-feed her child. She may have tender or inverted nipples. Her milk flow may be insufficient or obstructed, or she may herself be ill. Some mothers work and cannot be with their babies at all the times they need to nurse. In such cases, it is better for both mother and infant if the child is bottle-fed.

Demand feeding: feeding a baby when it indicates hunger

Schedule vs. Self-Demand: The issue here is who decides when the baby eats. When the child is fed on schedule, the food is provided at certain intervals. When the child is fed on demand, food is provided when the child indicates a desire for it. Some people feel that infants are too young to be scheduled. Their hunger pains are the best clock. They will eat when and only when they need to. Others argue that babies will overeat on this plan. They also consider it an inconvenience.

The real issue here is one of power. It is also a matter that is culturally influenced. Parents who believe that children should respond to regulation prefer scheduling. Parents who believe that the parental role includes serving the child's needs tend to prefer demand feeding (Ainsworth and Bell, 1973).

Very young infants are the least amenable to scheduled feeding. As children get older, they will be able to tolerate schedules and will gradually fit into the eating patterns of the family.

Infants typically establish feeding patterns in the first ten days after birth. Infants' feeding by self-demand may begin with 10–14 feedings a day but soon drop to 5–6 (Kessen et al., 1970). This comes to one feeding approximately every four hours, which is the suggested interval when feedings are scheduled. Either way the infants' needs are met. There is no indication that self-demand feeders overeat.

MOTOR DEVELOPMENT

Motor development: maturation of physical skills

The well-cared-for infant grows at a tremendous pace. This tissue growth, combined with experience, allows the child to exhibit new physical capabilities every week. The muscles become stronger, and the child learns to coordinate various movements to achieve a desired result. Motor development is the most obvious display of the infant's overall growth. The patterns of progress are so regular among all children that some motor achievements are used as a yardstick for developmental normalcy. If a child is unusually late acquiring a particular skill, it sometimes indicates a physical disorder.

Children born before term lag behind term babies in their development. They do not have the same skills at four weeks that a term baby has. However, if their age is figured from conception, prematurely born infants have about the same skills at the same age as term babies. A six-week-old infant and a ten-week-old infant born four weeks before term will have the same conceptual age and will probably be at the same stage of motor development.

Although the term *motor skills* implies muscle coordination and focuses our attention on the muscles, early motor development is most closely related to development in the nervous system, and shares many characteristics with it. Development for both is *cephalocaudal* (head to foot) and *proximodistal* (center to periphery). As the nerves myelinate and become more efficient, the child can send messages to these areas and move them voluntarily. Slowly, with practice, the movements become smoother, more refined, and more complex.

Understandably, the infant is most interested in what is new and the first months are crowded with novel sensations. Since the child can just begin to move the muscles in the upper parts of the body, activities like locating sounds, tracking moving objects, grasping, and feeling or tasting objects are the most fascinating.

Early motor development is largely concerned with visually directed reaching and manipulation of objects. Newborns will grasp anything their palms touch. They may bring the object to the

Infant Development

Fetal posture	Chin up	Chest up	Reach and miss
0 mo.	1 mo.	2 mo.	3 mo.
Sit with support	Sit on lap Grasp object	Sit on high chair grasp dangling object	Sit alone
4 mo.	5 mo.	6 mo.	7 mo.
Stand with help	Stand holding furniture	Creep	Walk when led
8 mo.	9 mo.	10 mo.	11 mo.
Pull to stand by furniture	Climb stair steps	Stand alone	Walk alone
12 mo.	13 mo.	14 mo.	15 mo.

Infancy: Physiological Development

mouth, but they make no attempt to look at it. And though they stare with interest at objects around them, they do not reach to seize them. Three or four months later, they will grab at an object that appeals to them. They may become distracted by the sight of their own hand, however, and shift their attention to it, forgetting the original object altogether. As the sight of the hand becomes familiar, it is ignored, and the infant concentrates on reaching for the desired item. Once obtained, it will not only be tasted, but also pinched between thumb and fingers, pounded against the floor, passed to the other hand, pulled on (or apart), and in other ways explored.

In the middle of the first year, as the back muscles become stronger and under voluntary control, infants will enjoy sitting up, twisting around to watch a passing object, and pushing their bodies up from the floor. Locomotion—crawling, using a walker, pushing on chairs, and finally walking—absorbs the developing infant. At the same time, these older infants have more refined control of their hands and arms. By 12 months they can place one object on another, put small cups in larger ones, eat with a spoon, and drink from a cup.

These data support the popular opinion that motor development is primarily maturational. What part, if any, does experience play? It seems that as long as the child has some opportunity to explore and move about, development occurs "on schedule." In the case of walking, a classic study was made of Hopi Indian children. Traditionally raised Hopis spend most of their day for the first nine months strapped to a cradleboard. Their ability to move is severely restricted. Still, these infants began to walk at exactly the same age as unrestricted children (Dennis, 1940). Whatever experiences they gained in the mornings and evenings and between the ninth month and when they walked was adequate.

Can more practice hasten development? Probably not. The fundamental motor skills depend on body growth. Furthermore, whether the infant progresses quickly or slowly at first seems to have little to do with later motor development or intelligence (Bower, 1977). But environment does have some effect. When movements coordinating several actions have been tested, infants with more experience in the particular test situation did better than infants with no training in the task (Bower, 1976, White & Held, 1966).

The chart on the opposite page highlights an "average" infant's motor progress during the first 18 months.

Motor Developments*

By 3rd month	By 6th month	By 9th month	By 12th month	By 15th month	By 18th month
LARGE	**LARGE**	**LARGE**	**LARGE**	**LARGE**	**LARGE**
Reflexive movements which dominated in first month gradually fade	Reflexive movements gone	Creeps holding objects	Stands from squat without using props	Can stabilize stance by placing legs apart	Stable stance
	Can turn head easily	Crawls, climbs stairs			Toddles—longer, more certain steps
Baby can lift head to 45° angle for short time when on back or stomach	On stomach, or when lifted, extends arms and legs, arches back—like airplane	Assumes sitting position at will, can turn and reach for objects from sitting position	Can walk if hand is held—may walk alone (prefers to crawl)	Begins to walk alone—short erratic steps, uses whole sole of foot	Can push furniture and pull toys while walking
Can turn head		Pulls up on furniture, slides along it	May climb out of crib or playpen	May be able to throw ball—awkward, weak, release is ill-timed	Can walk up steps if hand is held (descends by crawling backwards)
Baby loses limpness—tenses body, holds it together compactly when lifted	Can push head and shoulder from floor		Can sit smoothly from standing position		
	Arches back, rocks on tummy, twists, rolls over	Can fall to sitting position from standing one		**SMALL**	Can turn around unsteadily
Can sit with support, but back is weak, head wobbles	Creeps on tummy	**SMALL**	**SMALL**	Object release exaggerated	May be able to sit in child's chair accurately
SMALL	Can sit supported for long time (back firm, head steady)	Can hold 2 objects at once, bang them together, place them beside one another	Can mark with crayon by banging or swiping	Marks crudely with crayon, holds it in primitive grasp	**SMALL**
Grasp is voluntary, uses whole hand			Shows hand preferences—holds with one, manipulates objects with other	Can build tower of two blocks	Can hold four blocks at once (holds objects to body with arm)
Swipes at objects (aim is poor)	Can sit alone for short time	Pinches with thumb and forefinger (can pick up string and small objects)	Places one object inside another		Can scribble with crayon
Reaches for objects with both arms	**SMALL**		Can take lids off containers		Can build tower of three blocks
	Interested in own hands	Can point, poke, hook and pull with index finger	Begins to master object release		Object release is improved, but still uncoordinated with other movements
	Grasps with thumb apposition		May be able to undress self		
	Rotates wrists, passes objects from hand to hand				

*From Caplan, 1973, and Gesell, 1940

Infancy: Physiological Development

Summary

1. Despite the presence of relatively sophisticated perceptive skills, human infants are very dependent upon the environment and their caregivers for sustenance and protection.

2. Height and weight develop relatively quickly in the human infant. These physical growth rates slow some in the second and third year, and remain relatively stable until the growth spurt in late childhood and early adolescence.

3. The skeleton of the infant develops through a process of ossification, which is the process of mineralization of the soft, cartilage-like bones of the neonate. Ossification is particularly noticeable in the skull of the infant and in the bones in the hand. The infant's muscles are very weak at birth; muscular development of the infant proceeds rapidly thereafter.

4. The nervous system of the infant develops rapidly both before birth and after birth. This developmental process does not end until some time in adolescence, when the brain is fully developed and all of the myelinization that will occur has occurred. The major components of the nervous system are the brain, the spinal cord, ganglion (bundles of nerves), and nerve cells. All of these components function to convey impulses throughout the system.

5. The brain appears to be arranged by hemispheres. One side of the brain appears to control voluntary function on one side of the body, and the other side of the brain appears to control voluntary function on the other side of the body. Hemispheric research, however, is far from conclusive, and much more research is going on.

6. There are several specific occurrences that significantly affect the course of physical development: genetic inheritance, sex of the child, environmental influences, and the type and amount of disease the child experiences. There is also a significant social aspect to physical development of the American child. Our culture defines what is a good body, what is a bad body; even the appearance of an infant will produce socially conditioned responses in adults.

7. The basic needs of infants include sleep, warmth and safety, and food. There are controversies over breast-feeding versus bottle feeding, and feeding babies on schedule or demand.

8. Motor development proceeds at a tremendous pace for the normal infant. There are specific directions of growth (e.g., cephalocaudal), and motor development appears to be directly related to nervous system maturation and practice.

Thought Questions

1. What can we do to protect the human infant as it begins to develop immediately after birth? Discuss the vulnerability of the human infant in comparison to infants of other species. What role does the caregiver play in all of this?

2. Describe the course of physical development in the human infant. What are some of the factors that significantly affect that development? Is the development of the child complete at the end of infancy? What dimensions of development continue into adolescence?

3. How does the skeleton of the infant develop? By what processes? Where can we most readily see the effects of these processes? How strong is the human infant at birth? Give some examples of the physical things the newborn can do, as well as the physical abilities the infant develops relatively quickly.

4. What are the components of the nervous system? How does the nervous system develop and when is this development complete? What is the function of the nervous system and what is the relationship between the maturation of the nervous system and motor development?

5. Discuss the specific occurrences that affect physical development. Give an example of each of these factors, and tell how each could hamper the development of the child. What role does our culture play in all of this?

Suggested Readings

Caplan, F. *The First 12 Months of Life.* New York: Grosset & Dunlap, 1973. *The early period of infancy is a vital and exciting time. Caplan's book accurately and completely describes the first year of life.*

Spock, B. *Baby and Child Care.* New York: Pocket Books, 1976. *There are few books that have sold as many copies as Spock's classic. It is a very readable and practical book designed to help the parent through practically every crisis with children. It remains one of the best child care manuals available.*

White, B.L. *The First Three Years of Life.* Englewood Cliffs, N.J.: Prentice-Hall, 1975. *Dr. White provides some of the clearest descriptions of early child development available today. One of the biggest advantages to this work is the very practical nature of the suggestions to parents and child care workers.*

READING

Outlining the basic needs of children is a basic task for the student of child development. These needs are of course physiological, but they go beyond that and become interactive with other aspects of the individual, including the environment and society. Identification of these biological and social factors is very important in assessing a child's status and progress. Our ever-changing society is a very demanding one, and each day it becomes harder to see just exactly what children need to satisfy society's demands.

One of the outstanding scholars in the field of child development, David Elkind, seeks to show us the complexity of the biological-sociological factors that make up the need schemes of children. He lucidly describes some of the basic needs of children in our society.

Elkind stresses the importance of understanding the developmental stages of a child's growth and being able to relate these changes to the way children learn and adapt to the environment. He suggests that parents today need to place more emphasis on the basic needs of their children.

Even though he lives in the city, this boy has found a place where he can have fun flying a kite.
BRUCE DAVIDSON, COPYRIGHT © MAGNUM PHOTOS, INC.

What Young Children Need Most in A Changing Society
David Elkind

Q. Dr. Elkind, you are well-known for relating child development theories to the actual practice of child rearing, and for putting these theories into useful perspective for parents and teachers. What, then, are the implications for parents and teachers of children's normal stages of development?

A. For one thing, we can relate developmental stages to changes in the way children learn at different age levels. Learning begins with observation and manipulation as in early childhood. Then labeling and classification follow in early and middle childhood. And finally, careful experiments and development of theories can be observed in adolescence. We shouldn't expect a child to function in a way more advanced than his age-related mental structures will permit.

Q. Does it seem to you that this runs counter to some current practices among parents and teachers?

A. It does. We often try to force children to learn things which are inappropriate to their stage of growth. In an article I wrote for *Parents' Magazine* some years ago, and in other articles, I've discussed the possible harm in putting too much stress on academic achievement in the preschool child.

Preschool children are often pushed into reading, although reading requires the use of complex concepts (like the fact that letters can have some elements of similarity and difference at the same time). But the average child only begins to understand that one thing can be like something else and different from it at the same time, at the age of six or seven. Only the brightest children comprehend this at age three or four.

Parents and educators should respect the child's intellectual limitations and not attempt to bypass them and push on to learning beyond his or her attained level. We shouldn't try to force the child to use mental structures that haven't developed in order to meet some outside standard of achievement. At each stage of development, the child has limits as to what he or she can learn that cannot be ignored.

Q. When do different mental abilities develop?

A. Rote memory develops and matures early; the structures for language and perception seem to be mature by the middle of childhood; and reasoning reaches its final form in adolescence. These periods are critical, and the child needs the appropriate stimulation during each stage. But the limits are flexible and it takes extreme and prolonged overstimulation or deprivation to seriously injure a child.

Q. How do children respond to stimulation in learning?

A. It depends upon the kind of learning. When children are acquiring new mental abilities, as opposed to acquiring skills or concepts, one can observe children actually seeking stimulation, which nourishes further growth. A child pulls a toy, it moves, and he or she wants to pull it again, because the movement is nourishing the abilities being developed. When the child finds something that nourishes his or her mental growth, and is enjoying it, other stimulations that might be distracting are tuned out. Once the child has acquired a new mental ability he or she reaches the stage of intellectual play, and tests the limits of the newfound ability.

Q. What are some of the major trends in child rearing today, or changes from the way parents felt in the fairly recent past?

A. Parents today seem more concerned about the child's intellectual abilities than they were a few years ago. They seem to think their own parents were too anxious about their "adjustment," or emotional well-being. Children today are under great pressure for academic achievement—to learn more, earlier. While this can lead to intellectual independence at a younger age, it can also result in more children who suffer from emotional problems because of school failure.

If a child thinks his worth is related to what he achieves, instead of who he is, failure in school can cause a serious emotional upheaval. This danger probably will grow in the United States because the trend toward smaller families puts even greater pressure on children, and means more competitive only children in the population. By the way, we are also pushing children into organized sports at earlier ages as well. It is part of the same syndrome.

Q. What other trends do you see in the United States today?

A. We are losing our predominantly child-centered approach to family life. Until a few years ago, the child's wants and needs took precedence over the parents'. Mothers, in particular, would sacrifice their own development for the sake of the children. Now the child is no longer viewed as the center of everything; his or her needs are more likely to be seen as equal to, but not greater than, those of the parents. This can lead to early emotional independence, with both good and bad possibilities.

The necessary separation from the family that begins in adolescence can become less harsh today because both parents and children already have interests outside of the family. When the young person is ready to leave home, the mother isn't as likely to feel that her world has collapsed—she may be deeply involved in a life apart from the children. This emotional independence also means that parents may get a divorce more readily if the marriage does not meet their needs; formerly they might have stayed in an unhappy marriage for the sake of the children.

Q. Statistics indicate that approximately eight million mothers in the United States are bringing up children in homes where the fathers are absent. What effect does this have on the child?

A. If one of the parents leaves home, the effect on the children depends on many factors. One of them is timing. If the father leaves when his children are quite young, it can be traumatic for the children, especially boys. At this age, boys see themselves as rivals to the father and have fantasies about getting rid of the father. If the father really leaves, the child may think that his fantasy created reality, and that he is responsible for the divorce. This could be a source of emotional problems related to guilt.

If a father dies, however, the child can deal with it more readily than if the father leaves home—there is a sense of grief with death, but that is a more positive feeling than rejection. The mother's sense of separation, rejection and anger can also be communicated to the children, and cause emotional difficulties. Our society should provide more counseling help for families struggling with the problems of death and divorce.

Q. Statistics also show that many more women with young children are now working than ever before. How does this influence child development?

A. The most significant factor is the quality of the substitute child care. This is important at any age, but it is most important in the first two years of the child's life, and crucial in the first year of life. There is no evidence that the mother must be the main caretaker; but the child does need mothering, and the ratio of children to caretaker should be no more than three to one, for children under two. As children grow older, quality care is still of great importance, but the ratio can be higher, say ten children to one adult. These ratios are rough estimates, and will vary with particular circumstances. With quality day care, there is no evidence that children are in any way harmed by being reared partially out of the home.

Q. When parents are thinking about a divorce, or if a mother is working, what kind of special help might be provided for the children?

A. When divorce is being considered, children as well as parents should be prepared for the forthcoming emotional trauma by counseling or at least by open discussion. Children need as much or more support during a divorce than the parents. If the mother of an intact family is working, or involved in interests outside the home, the father could spend more time with the children, although this may not be a realistic expectation—the increased pressure for outside achievement on women has not diminished the pressures on men.

Q. What do you see as a major need in families today?

A. Contemporary parents should be more concerned about the emotional needs of their children, and the quality of the time spent with them.

Q. What other trends do you see in family life?

A. The contemporary adults' loss of faith in reason, in science, in technology, even in the possibility of a better world, has had a profound effect on our children. We continue to be busy with our work, but our children pick up our loss of faith.

Young people today are searching for faith, something true, beautiful and abiding to believe in. This is a necessary framework within which to form a sense of personal identity. Since many adults have lost values, or so it seems to our children, they feel the lack of support in forming an identity. They feel they need an anchor to grasp—something like a religious crusade or the occult to make up for the moral weakness of adult society. Children need to know that we adults believe in something. We should share our faith and our values with them.

Q. In addition to your studies of preschool children, you've been engaged in clinical work with adolescents, and have written extensively about their needs. Is women's liberation causing great changes in interests among adolescent girls?

A. Despite women's lib, many adolescent girls are still mainly preoccupied with boys, with becoming mothers and having homes—although there is increasing consideration of other careers and of becoming persons in their own right. We still haven't resolved the problems women face in forming an identity apart from family roles. Social change has to fight the tremendous inertia of social habit.

Q. What are these problems?

A. Some of them develop from family dynamics. Men and women seem to arrive at a sense of identity in different ways. To begin to form your own identity, you have to differentiate, to see yourself as distinct from something or somebody else.

Initially, the child attaches himself or herself to the caretaker—usually the mother—and makes the primary identification with the mother. In the preschool years, when the boy begins to conceive of himself as a certain kind of self, a boy, he has to begin the process of breaking away and differentiating from his mother and gradually identifying with his father.

When the preschool girl realizes her femaleness, however, she doesn't have to differentiate or break away from the primary caretaker. She continues to identify with her mother, and maintain an unbroken history of identification with her. The kind of detachment and assertion of self that a boy first experiences when he breaks away from his mother, may not take place for women until they are married, perhaps not until after their own children have left home, when the woman must form a sense of herself as a person, and not as someone's daughter, wife or mother.

Changes in our culture are accelerating this process of differentiation and identity formation for women, however. Today, many women do not marry, and have to form identities apart from family roles at an earlier age, or women marry and have no children, or stop having children at a younger age. On the other hand, more women today do have a strong sense of themselves—an identity apart from family roles—and face difficulties in integrating their sense of self into family life.

Creating an identity is even more complex now because identity presupposes stable values. There are few social frameworks to help a woman build her own identity apart from family roles as yet, or to help a woman find a harmony between personal identity and family roles.

Q. How about your own family life; is your wife following a career outside the home?

A. Sally, my wife, recently completed a four-year program in music, and received a performing degree in piano. She now teaches at home and at school.

Q. How do you and your wife reconcile your careers and your children's needs?

A. We share in child-rearing tasks. I get the boys off to school in the morning. And we spend time with the children that is their time. The truism that the quality of time spent with the children matters more than its quantity is borne out by experience. Paying attention to a child when you're with him counts most.

Q. What is your attitude toward parenthood?

A. I think it's important that a parent *be* something to the child, because children learn by example. Be the kind of person you want your child to be, be honest about your feelings with your children and they will learn to be honest with you. And, when a child demonstrates responsibility, give him other freedom to do what he is able to do—we grow through the freedom to act responsibly. Good parenting is not easy, it means you have to work at it and to keep growing and learning along with your children.

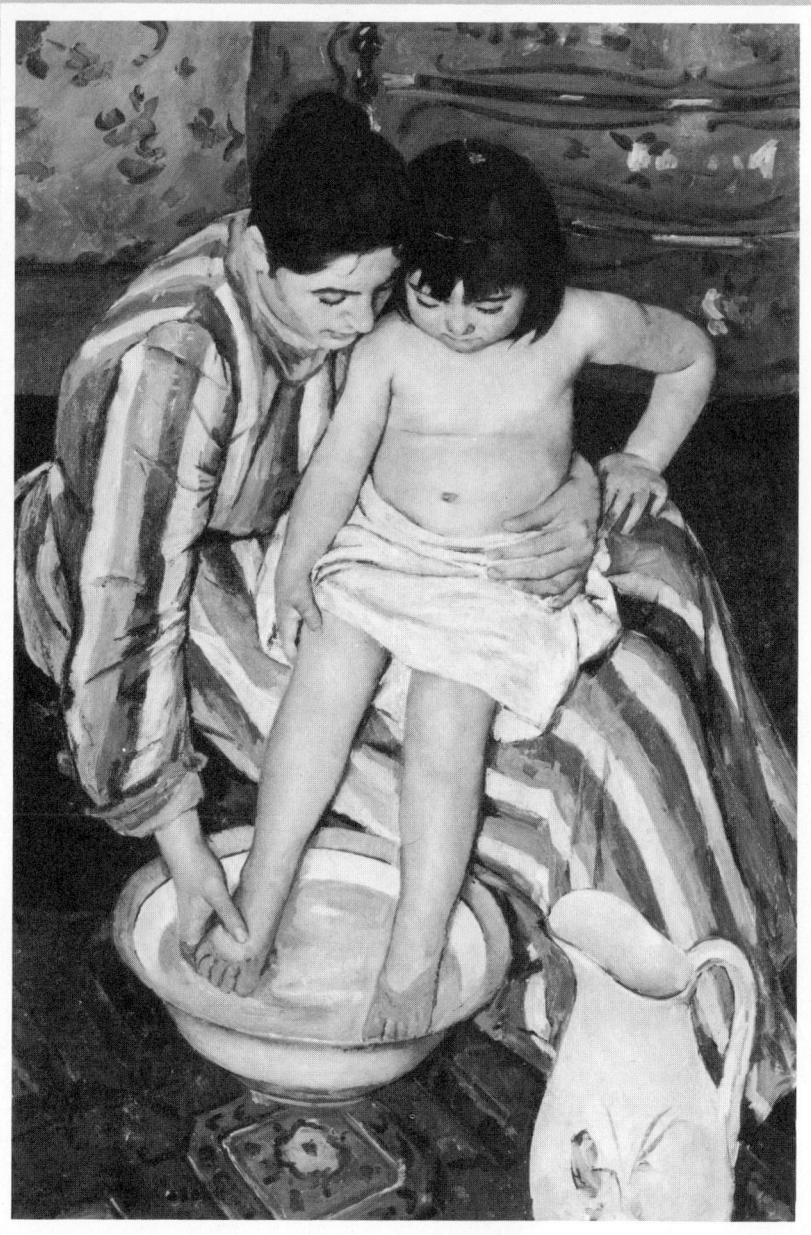

COLLECTION OF THE ART INSTITUTE OF CHICAGO.
REPRODUCED BY PERMISSION OF THE ART INSTITUTE OF CHICAGO, CHICAGO, ILLINOIS.

The Bath, by Mary Cassatt.

7

Infancy: Perceptive Skills and Learning

The period of infancy in the human is dynamic in terms of physical growth and development, as we indicated earlier. The infant is also developing rapidly in the area of perception. *Perception* is defined as the ability to take sensation (or stimuli from the environment) and translate it into information that the infant can use. Perception is the vehicle the infant uses to put the world in order.

Perception has a developmental nature to it; the processes of perception become more refined and sophisticated as time goes by. We should not assume, however, that young children do not have the ability to perceive stimuli in the environment. In fact, we probably underestimate the perceptive powers of infants. The problem in really understanding all that infants can perceive from their environment is that we have a problem communicating with infants. Young children cannot tell us specifically what they are seeing, feeling, or touching. Infants' perceptions may not be clearly visible to observers.

One way to see if the infant is perceiving a stimulus is to note whether the stimulus interrupts or stops the activity of the child. This *attention-disruption* technique gives us a crude indication that the child has been made aware of the stimulus. For example, if we

MEASURING INFANT PERCEPTION

Attention disruption:
a technique for measuring infants' perception

are trying to learn what types of sounds an infant will respond to, we may get the child involved in free play in a comfortable setting. As the child is playing, different sounds are introduced into the environment. If the child stops what he was doing at the introduction of a sound, we may assume that he has picked up the sound. Attention-disruption can also be used to observe visual stimuli. The problem with this technique is the lack of precision in terms of the perception; we cannot be sure of the accuracy of the perception.

Another commonly used technique in infant perceptual assessment is the heart rate. Using monitoring devices, the researcher can determine if there is a significant change in the heart rate (either faster or slower). This technique could be used to measure the infant's ability to perceive an approaching object. If the child is seated at the end of a long track and an object is slowly moved down the track toward the infant, we can determine if the approaching object produces a change in the heart rate. The way the heart rate changes, if it does, may tell us something about the child's perceptive skills.

One problem in the use of the heart rate technique is the variability of the infant heart rate. Sometimes the heart rate will slow down when an object approaches; other times it will speed up. It may be necessary to establish baseline information about the style of each individual child before deciding how and why that particular child is perceiving the object (for a discussion of this technique see Porges, 1974).

Another technique utilized to estimate the perceptive abilities of infants measures the electrical conductivity of the skin. During periods of stimulation it is thought that the amount of conductivity in the skin increases. Researchers may be able to detect perception by measuring the change in conductivity of the infant's skin. No current is introduced to the child in this technique; only monitoring occurs. Specific physiological differences between infants may make this technique less generalizable than it might have been.

Even with these techniques and others not mentioned, the measurement of infant perception is difficult. As we discuss specific perceptive abilities and the attempts to measure them, other unique ways of trying to understand infant perception will be demonstrated.

VISION

The eyes are not completely mature at birth. The eyeball is somewhat shorter in most infants than will be normal in later life. This results, technically, in a far-sighted condition in the human infant

Infancy: Perceptive Skills and Learning

(Spears and Hohle, 1967). Cell maturation is not complete in other components of the visual system. The optic nerve, for example, is not fully mature at birth. The baby's eyes will also have a puffy look to them at birth. This is due to the fluid retained in the baby's tissues, which will dissipate rather quickly (accounting for part of the weight babies tend to lose immediately after birth).

The physiological immaturities, along with the fluid mentioned above, mean that the neonate probably does not see very well. The pupillary reflex is often sluggish at birth, so that light is not accommodated as efficiently as it will be later. The focusing ability of the eye is also probably inefficient due to immaturity of the musculature surrounding the eye. There is a debate raging over whether infants can differentiate color early in their lives. The equipment necessary to perceive color is present at birth (Barnet et al., 1965). There is some evidence, however, that infants can discriminate the broad range of colors by the time they are four months of age (Bornstein, 1975).

Visual acuity is the term used to describe the preciseness of the infant's vision. Visual acuity includes the ability to perceive three-dimensional arrays, to make visual convergences, and to use tracking movements. All of these abilities require the use of muscles located around the eye as well as the eyeball and the optic nerve. Some researchers state that newborns have a fixed focal point about seven inches from their face (Stone and Church, 1979). For a baby to see the object clearly, it must be presented at about this distance. The eyeball cannot accommodate to other focal distances, as it will later.

Acuity: keenness of perception

As far as what infants prefer to look at, there is disagreement in the scientific literature. Scientists do agree that young infants prefer to look at a patterned stimulus rather than a plain one, but there is a variety of opinion concerning preferred visual patterns.

Fantz has designed several research projects designed to measure infant discrimination abilities. Seating the children in a comfortable position, Fantz exposes them to different visual arrays. In one study the children looked at a regular face, a distorted face, and a black-and-white oval. Each child was given a two-minute test of fixation, and the amount of fixation was measured. At virtually every age (he studied babies from birth to six months) the regular face elicited more fixation on the part of the infant (Fantz, 1961). In a later study Fantz used a face, plain circles, and circles of different colors. Once again the infants preferred the face pattern to any other pattern offered them (Fantz, 1965).

In a novel experiment concerning depth perception of infants, two researchers developed what they called the *visual cliff*. The

Visual cliff: an experiment to test infants' depth perception

Infant Development

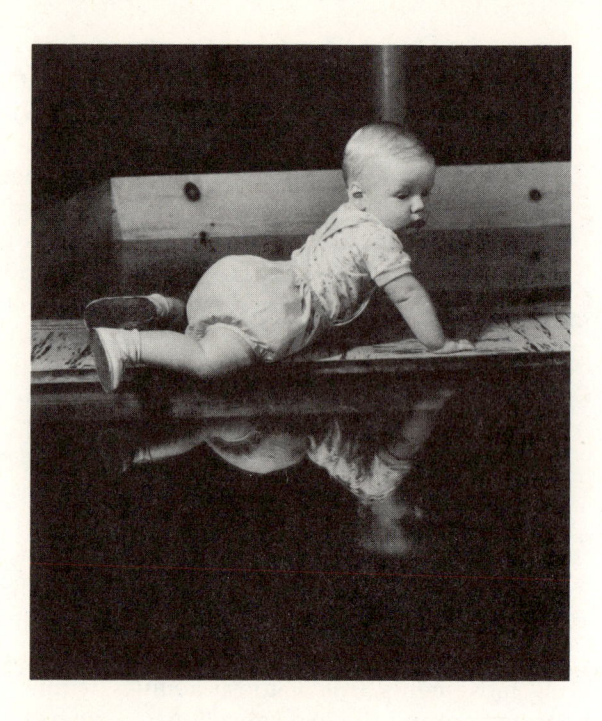

In an experiment, a young child refuses to go over the edge of the visual cliff.
PHOTO BY ALBERT FENN. LIFE MAGAZINE, © TIME, INC.

experimenters used a glass device that simulated the appearance of a drop-off (Gibson and Walk, 1960).

The infants were placed near what appeared to be a cliff. The researchers found that the depth perception of children who were able to crawl was advanced enough so that none of them would walk over the visual cliff. Other work with this apparatus has established that depth perception is related to developmental maturity. In most of the studies, infants of about seven months of age were able to perceive differences in depth. The earliest age at which infants were found to perceive these drastic differences is about two months (Scarr and Salapatek, 1970).

HEARING

In utero, the infant is suspended in amniotic fluid. This fluid often enters the ears of the fetus. The doctor suctions the fluid from the breathing passage of the neonate, but not from the ears. So, while all the equipment is present and in working order, this fluid may temporarily interfere with the hearing of the neonate.

Hearing in the human consists of sound waves vibrating the tiny bones in the middle ear. These vibrations are transformed into

Infancy: Perceptive Skills and Learning

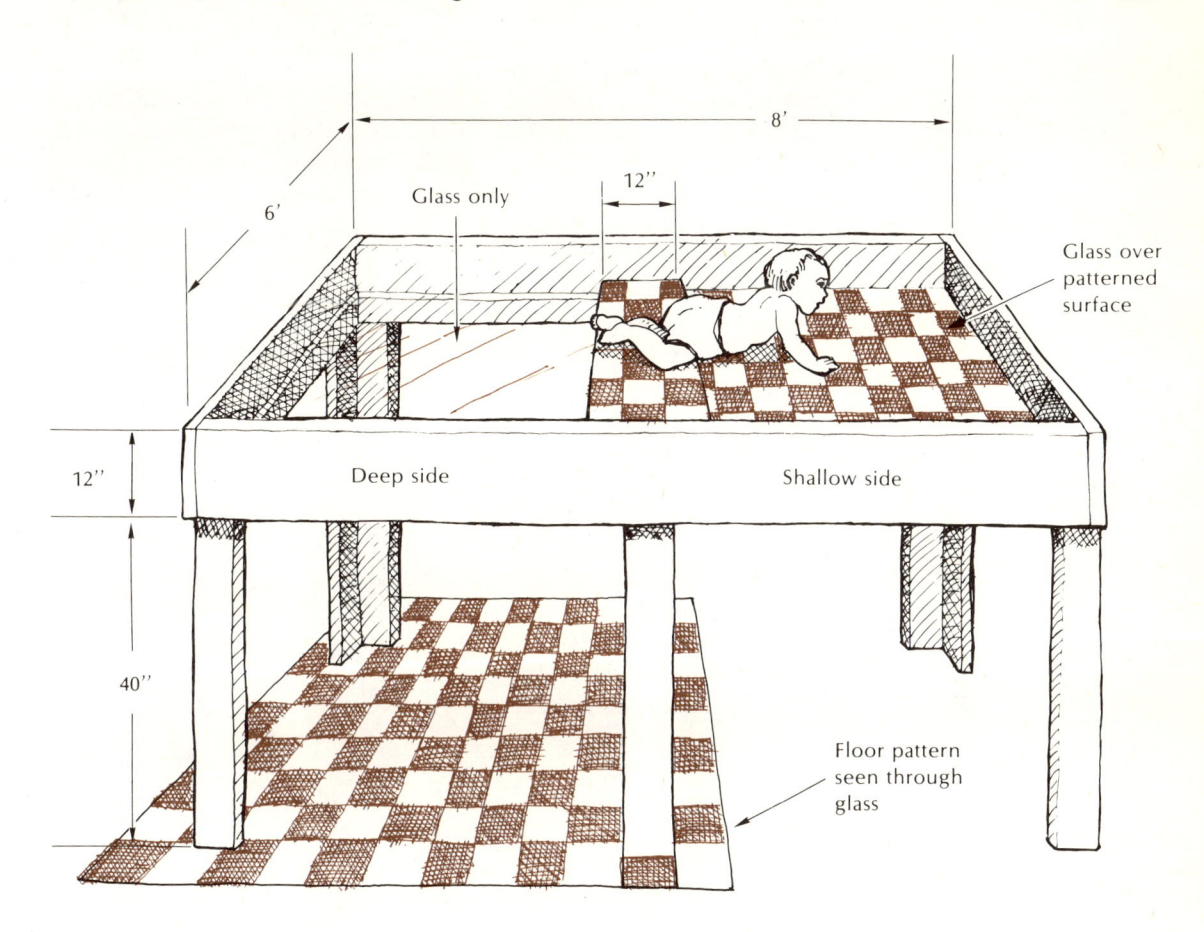

[Figure: Visual cliff apparatus. Dimensions: 8' long, 6' wide, table height 40", with 12" drop area marked. Labels: "Glass only", "Glass over patterned surface", "Deep side", "Shallow side", "Floor pattern seen through glass".]

nerve impulses and transmitted to the brain. Given the process and the equipment present, and despite the fluid that may be present, neonates can hear. They will respond to loud noises, throwing their arms back, grimacing and crying.

The infant, and the neonate in particular, respond to sound in a generalized way; they have not learned any specific behavioral responses to specific sounds. Infants are either soothed by a sound or distressed by it. As they mature they begin to differentiate sounds.

Some of the sounds that appear to be soothing to the infant are soft voices, the sound of a heartbeat or any other soft, rhythmic sound, and interestingly, the recorded internal sounds of the mother. There are indications from Japan and other places that these recorded sounds may soothe the baby.

The examples of research into infant hearing are varied. Horowitz has discovered that infants nine weeks of age are able to distinguish their mother's voice from that of another adult female (Horowitz, 1975). By the age of three months infants can discriminate specific sounds. In infant day care settings very young babies will respond to the crying of other infants in the center. The research in this area is varied and indicates clearly that young children can indeed hear (Simner, 1971; Eiman et al., 1971; Moffitt, 1971; and Horowitz, 1975).

Hearing may be one perceptive ability in children that we take for granted. Simply because an infant can differentiate types of sound and can localize sound, there is no guarantee that his auditory acuity will be sufficient for a classroom, for example. Hearing tests are appropriate for young children because there is often a complex relationship between hearing acuity and subtle learning disabilities. As Burton White has stated: ". . . it is considerably worse educationally for a child to have an undetected hearing deficit [worse than a visual problem]. Hearing is crudely tested at birth and at every regular pediatric examination. . . . Children can accurately localize sounds at three, four or five months, while at the same time having significant (educationally) deficits in discriminative power" (White, 1975, p. 245). White goes on to say that we have the power to accurately test children's hearing from the age of 3½.

TOUCH

One of the predominant ways of exploration for human infants is through the sense of touch. Touching is two-way: infants are touched by caregivers, and infants intentionally touch objects in their environment. As infants spend less time with their fists clenched, they begin to explore the environment by touch.

Neonates need to be touched. The skin stimulation produced by being touched provides children with physical and psychological warmth and a sense of reassurance concerning the meeting of basic needs. Changing diapers, bathing, feeding, and playing are all activities that give adults the opportunity to touch and talk to infants. This contact seems to soothe most babies.

As children mature, the small-muscle control in their hands also matures. Consequently, grasping (prehension) becomes a predominant avenue of sensory exploration. Touching objects allows children to discover different shapes and different textures, and it allows children the freedom to bring objects to their mouths. Mouthing objects is sometimes a continuous activity for young

Infancy: Perceptive Skills and Learning

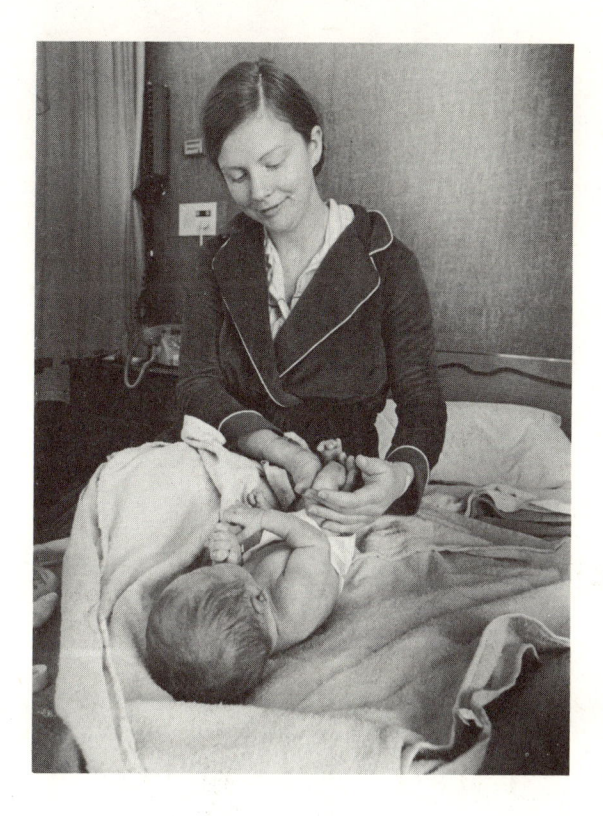

A mother massages her infant as a means of enhancing communication and bonding between the two.
JEFFREY P. GROSSCUP.

children. Also, many children develop a fondness for a particular blanket; this is usually because of the *feel* of the blanket. The smooth border material of the blanket is particularly attractive to children. This attachment to a blanket sometimes lasts until the blanket falls apart.

TASTE

Taste is facilitated by buds located predominantly on the tongue. These taste buds mature during prenatal life and are relatively well developed at birth. Some people have speculated that infants cannot discriminate taste at birth. People who have experience in a nursery or who have children of their own confirm the fact that it appears neonates can discriminate between plain water and sugar water. In fact, some writers are convinced that many children are given their first introduction to sugar at this age. This may somehow "set" that taste in children and they may have a preference for that taste later in life.

The research in this area is quick to affirm that infants quickly develop a taste for sugar. In a symposium on oral sensation in the infant, Maller and Dessor have reported that as sugar concentration is increased in solution, neonates are more likely to accept the solution. They are also likely to consume more of the sugar solution than plain water (Maller and Dessor, 1974). Another study has indicated that as the sugar concentration of the liquid increases, the baby will suck more slowly and experience an increase in the heart rate (Crook and Lipsitt, 1976). The researchers explain these effects as the infants savoring the sweetness of the liquid; they suck more slowly and their heart rate increases because of their excitement over the sweet treat!

For bottle-fed babies, most pediatricians currently recommend that the baby not go to bed with a bottle of milk or formula. The residual sugar from the milk or juice will build up in the baby's mouth. And even though the child may not now have teeth, this residual sugar becomes a precursor of later cavities. This "bottle-at-bedtime" routine is handled best by avoiding it in the beginning.

As infants get older, they will indicate their taste preferences in very obvious ways: they will spit a disliked food out, or perhaps throw it against the wall! Infancy is a good time to introduce children to a variety of foods, however. Infancy is also a time when mealtime needs to be established as a set time, without the obstructive presence of a newspaper or a TV set blaring. Mealtime, even for the infant, is an important time for the development of good habits and good relationships.

Infancy: Perceptive Skills and Learning

ISSUE

Research with Young Children

In this chapter, probably more than in any other, specific examples of research are cited so that we may better explain the process of perception and learning in young children. Research is the way to find the answer to many of the questions we have about child development. But just what are the purposes of research? What different types are there? And how do we protect the rights of children involved in research projects?

☐ The purposes of research in the beginning of a project, when the problem is being defined, are quite broad. First, social scientists seek to understand child behavior by describing the behavior (through observation), and then by attempting to explain the behavior. Secondly, researchers are interested in predicting the behavior, growth, and development of children. This information is particularly useful in the determination of developmental norms and the assessment of children's progress. Lastly, through the use of adequate information we may be better able to control the events that may significantly affect children's lives. If we know what factors lead to optimal development, we then can try to provide those conditions to parents and ultimately to children. If we can determine the effect of television on children's reading habits, for example, we may be able to control the amount of time children spend watching television and we may be able, ultimately, to change the quality of the TV programs being offered.

☐ The types of research are generally broken down into three broad categories: historical research, descriptive or survey research, and experimental research. Briefly, historical research involves the searching of literature and the finding of new sources of data for a particular problem. A primary example of the use of historical research is in the study of the family in American society. Important new sources of information are being discovered and a new picture of the American family of the past is being created.

☐ A second, very popular approach is called survey research, or descriptive research. Everyday examples of this type of research are, for example, the Gallup poll, the Harris poll, and other national opinion surveys that are done every day in this country.

☐ The third approach is called the experimental method. One of the "purest" of the research designs is called the pretest-posttest control group design (Campbell and Stanley, 1963). This design employs an observation for two groups, an experimental group and a control group. Some sort of experimental treatment is administered to the experimental group (not the control group), and then the two groups are observed again. Providing the two groups were similar before the

BRUCE DAVIDSON,
© MAGNUM PHOTOS, INC.

experimental treatment, the differences between the two groups after the experimental treatment will tell us if that treatment had any effect.

☐ An example of this would be using fluoride to protect against dental caries. In an experiment two groups would be matched, an experimental group and a control group. The experimental group would receive fluoride over a time period and the control group would not. At the end of the time period cavities in both groups would be measured.

☐ Of great importance in research that involves children is whether or not their individual rights are being protected during the research project. In order to ensure such protection, the Department of Health, Education and Welfare has required institutions at which research is performed on humans to approve and review all research proposals. This has been the case since 1966, with periodic revisions in the rules, at those institutions and/or projects that are federally supported. Most university campuses have initiated Human Subject Committees, which review each research proposal and check it thoroughly so that the rights of the subjects may be protected. Many universities have required

Infancy: Perceptive Skills and Learning 185

that all of the projects involving human subjects adhere to the HEW regulations, whatever their funding source.

☐ These regulations, which are designed to protect the children and adults involved in the research, include the right to privacy for the subject, the right to informed consent (which in the case of children requires the signature of one parent and in some cases the signature of both parents), the assurance of confidentiality of the data collected, and protection against physical, psychological, sociological, and legal risks.

☐ In the case of the research subjects, the risk-benefit ratio must be such that the benefits clearly outweigh any risk. As stated in the 1975 version of the Code of Federal Regulations:

> The risks to the subject are so outweighed by the sum of the benefit to the subject and the importance of the knowledge to be gained as to warrant a decision to allow the subject to accept (those) risks.

☐ The assessment of those risks is very difficult. But under the current regulations, it is safe to say that some of the research that has been conducted with children in the past may not be reproducible today. One of the important questions facing researchers in the field of child development today is the relevance of the proposed research and the risk/benefit ratio.

SMELL

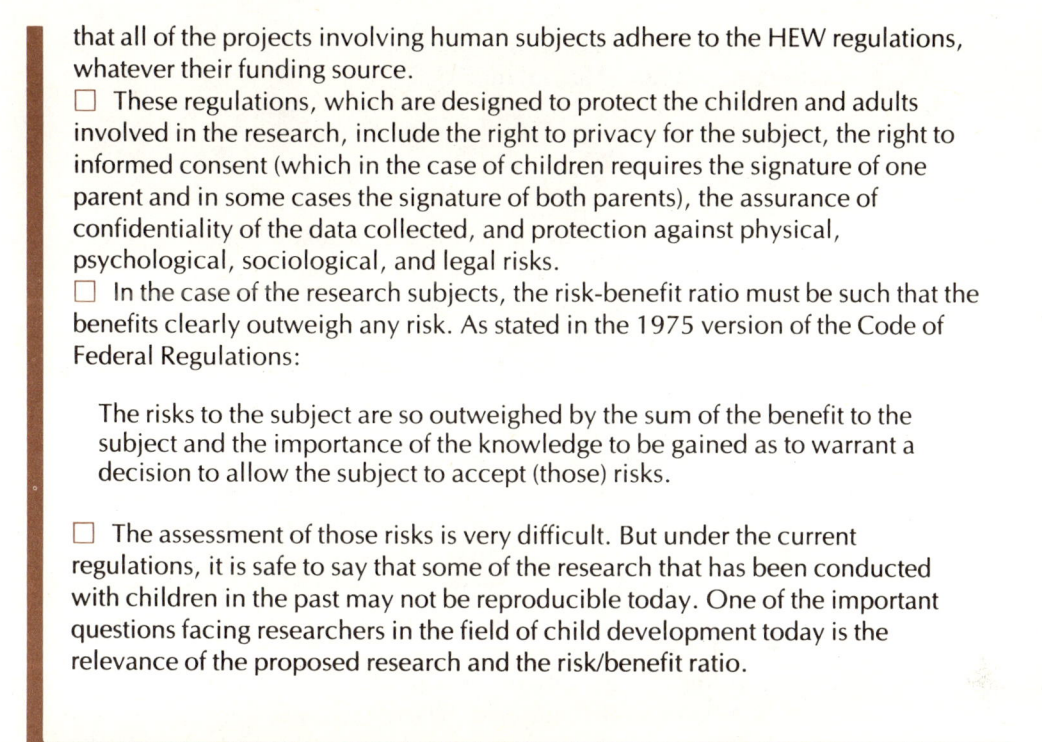

The sense of smell is also an innate sensory capacity in the human infant. Compared to other animals, the human sense of smell is inefficient. Humans rarely rely on their sense of smell for protection or to seek out game, whereas most other animals use their sense of smell for precisely these reasons.

Infants' sense of smell may be their most developed sensory capacity. Neonates react quickly to strong odors. They react by turning their heads; breathing patterns are also disrupted by a strong odor. Examples of smells that stimulate infants include ammonia, among other things.

The research in this area confirms these findings. In one experiment, a researcher suggested that infants could discriminate the smell of milk from their mother's breast. To test this hypothesis, the amount of time infants spent turned toward a breast pad soaked with mother's milk and a plain breast pad was measured. Babies spent significantly more time turned toward the pads scented with mother's milk. The babies were so good at this smelling task that they could differentiate the breast pad soaked with their own mother's milk from a breast pad soaked in the milk from a different woman (Macfarlane, 1977).

ATTENTION

Attention:
directing thought or senses to an object or task

In order for children to learn, they must focus their attention on the situation at hand. This focusing of attention allows children to take in the stimuli being offered by the environment; attention also maximizes children's integrative and cognitive skills. Attention is related to the perceptual processes we just mentioned. For some learning, visual attention is mandatory; for other learning, visual, auditory, and tactile attention are all required.

Attention implies the active engagement of the environment by the infant. Once engaged, the child takes in the information, processes it and eventually acts on it. Children will take in as much information as their maturational level allows.

Attention is supported by properly functioning perceptual systems. If there is a deficit in any one of the perceptive systems, the engagement with the environment through attention will be less firm. Learning will usually be disrupted; in fact, this sort of problem may be the beginning of a "learning disability." It has been suggested that if the environment is somewhat unstimulating, there will be less for the child to engage with in that environment, and this lack of attention efficiency may then generalize to other situations, like school.

On the other hand, some theorists insist that if the environment is *too* stimulating, other less exciting environments may not be able to grab the child's attention. A prime example of this has been related by teachers when they discuss TV programs like "Sesame Street." Many teachers say the average classroom cannot compete with the colorful, exciting images and events portrayed on TV. Consequently, school may be boring for some children.

INFANT LEARNING

Obviously, infants do not learn in quite the same way that older children do. An infant does not have the ability to pick up a book or listen to a news program or watch a movie to learn a variety of things. The actual mechanisms of learning may be the same, but the manifested behaviors are quite different.

Infancy: Perceptive Skills and Learning

The early behaviors of the infant are *reflexive*. Sucking is the most basic of these responses. Most of infant behavior, particularly the early behavior, has a reflexive behavior at its base.

Learning can be defined as relatively permanent changes in behavior that occur as a result of experience. In the infant, learning is most often discussed in terms of two occurrences: *classical conditioning* and *operant conditioning*. Classical conditioning is best illustrated through the experiment by the Russian scientist Pavlov with his dog. A neutral stimulus (a ringing bell) was paired with a reliable stimulus, one that repeatedly produced a response (in this case it was meat that caused the dog to salivate).

After repeatedly hearing the bell ring at the same time the meat was presented to him, the dog eventually learned to salivate at the ringing of the bell alone. This pairing of stimuli has come to be called classical conditioning.

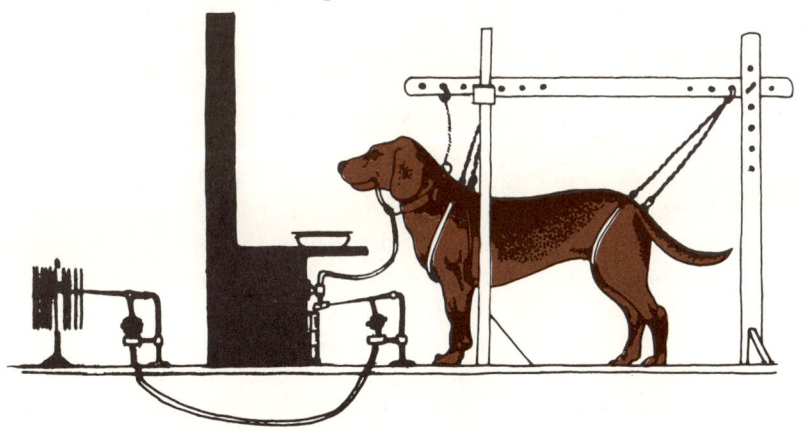

Classical conditioning: pairing of stimuli in a learning situation

Pavlov's conditioning apparatus. In Pavlov's early experiments, a tube carried saliva from the dog's mouth to a lever which activiated a recording device (far left). The placing of a dish of food in front of the dog was paired with various other stimuli for conditioning.

In the human classical conditioning often is seen during the feeding situation. The nipple in the baby's mouth is the reliable stimulus. Mother is the neutral stimulus. The nipple and the mother (paired stimuli) are repeatedly presented at the same time. After a time, with some infants, their mother's presence can elicit a sucking response, even though no nipple is presented (Fitzgerald and Porges, 1971; Lipsett et al., 1966).

The stability of responses learned in this way is related to the age and maturity of the child. There is some evidence that older infants

Operant conditioning: learning facilitated by reinforcement

are more consistent in their responses, and the behaviors tend to be more lasting (Papousek, 1967; Schell and Hall, 1979).

Operant conditioning is learning that is facilitated through the use of reinforcement. As we stated in an earlier chapter, a reinforcer is any occurrence that increases the likelihood of a response occurring. Infants learn quite readily through the use of reinforcing agents. Very novel experiments have been set up teaching infants to control an array of lights through the use of reinforcement.

Infant behavior, particularly the early behavior, is largely random and often without specific purpose. Once reinforcements start occurring, certain behaviors start reappearing. The most common example, one that parents learn about very early, has to do with the baby crying after bedtime. The first few times the baby cries after being put down may be for no specific reason, or to just see what might happen. As soon as the parent rushes in to the bedroom to aid the child, the crying behavior has been reinforced. It does not take too many reinforcements for the baby to realize that this behavior brings parents running. It is easy to get caught in this pattern. A variety of experiments done with operant conditioning have examined the relationship between adult smiling and infant vocalization, and have taught infants to start and stop a musical pattern by sucking the correct way (Lipsett et al., 1966; Butterfield and Siperstein, 1972; and Siqueland, 1968).

Infants develop the ability to discriminate objects and people very early in their lives. They also learn very quickly what behaviors will get their parents interested and what behaviors will not get them interested. Implicit in all of these abilities is the rapidly emerging ability of the infant to make decisions. It is true that these decisions are elementary. But when infants who perceive reinforcement coming from parents make a decision to use that behavior, they are operating at a surprisingly high level. Many times we underestimate the abilities of infants.

SENSORIMOTOR INTELLIGENCE

Piaget has speculated that the cognitive plan for humans unfolds as a series of sequential, invariant stages, discussed briefly in Chapter 2. The period unique to infancy is the period Piaget called "sensorimotor." The words he used to describe the stage are in themselves illuminating. The *senses* are fundamentally involved in infants' adaptation to the world. These innate mechanisms underscore the biological plan in child development. The term *motor* tells us that

Infancy: Perceptive Skills and Learning

children are going to do the bulk of their learning through manipulation of objects in their environment and by moving through that environment.

Piaget states that the sensorimotor period is a transition period (as are all the stages). The change here is from total dependence upon reflexive responses to rudimentary thought patterns. These rudimentary patterns are internalized and represent the beginnings of attempts at organizing the environment.

The theme of the sensorimotor period is that of balance between the sensorimotor patterns and the global, unrefined, cognitive structures (schemata). Cognition implies organization: putting objects into the appropriate category, labeling objects and people, and integrating all of these experiences into some logical order. As new perceptions are introduced to children, they reorganize their logical structure; this is an ongoing process.

The sensorimotor period lasts for about the first two years of the child's life. It is important to remember that this is an estimate of the age parameters; none of the stages occur at precise times.

There are several accomplishments of this period. One is a rudimentary understanding of cause-effect relations. This is primarily associational in nature. With time and repetition of a behavior, infants learn the associations between the act and the effects of that act. The learning is not completely efficient, but it is beginning to show. There is little pure thought, however, in causal terms.

When playing with an infant, if you remove an object from the infant's line of vision, he will begin to look for other things to do. It is as if the child considers that object to no longer exist; after all, he no longer sees it! As babies grow near the end of their first year, and definitely in their second year of life, they learn that an object may exist without being immediately visible to them. Piaget called this ability to understand that the object continues to exist without visual contact *object permanence*. This is a developmental milestone for the baby.

Object permanence: the realization that an object exists even when it can't be seen

Piaget and other theorists (Baldwin, 1967; Flavell, 1977) feel that significant strides are made toward the development of an identity during infancy. Before children are two, they can associate different parts of their body with words. When asked to touch their nose, they will be able to do so. All of these concepts have something to do with infants forming an image of themselves.

Some time around the age of 15 months, children begin asserting themselves. They begin to make specific demands on their parents, asserting their individuality at nearly every opportunity. If a child

A pleasant bike ride around town is usually a learning experience for children of any age.
ROBERT V. ECKERT, JR., EKM-NEPENTHE.

decides that he will go outside and play with the kitty rather than take his bath, he will indicate his wishes very clearly. If the parents insist, which they probably will, he will fight them, pulling, squirming, and falling to the floor. These behaviors reflect a growing sense of separate identity in the child and a desire to demonstrate independence.

The example above indicates that children under the age of two are capable of goal-directed behavior. Goal-directed behavior probably appears before the first birthday and is in full bloom during the second year. Children also develop vivid memories during these first two years, usually of things the parents would just as soon have the child forget. A preverbal child is quite capable of responding to a relatively complex command from the parents. There is one word that most children have a great deal of trouble learning: that word is "no." Children can comprehend very complicated verbal statements, but when a parent tells a child "no," it is as if the parent has suddenly switched to a foreign language. The

Infancy: Perceptive Skills and Learning

child may turn and give the parent a "who, me?" look, and continue with whatever behavior he was engaged in.

Egocentrism, which is discussed later in reference to other developmental periods, is clearly evident in early childhood and infancy. This is the child's feeling that he is the center of the world: "Everyone pays so much attention to me and everything I do makes a difference. I am really the center of the world." By the end of the second year, the child is beginning to appreciate the fact that he is just part of the larger world.

Egocentrism: a self-centered view of the world

The sensorimotor period is made up of six distinct developmental components. The table on page 192 shows these six with a brief description of each.

These stages are not hard and fast, as we have already indicated. Children pass through them at idiosyncratic rates, although there is some similarity between children. The behaviors of children are very repetitious, hence the word *circular*. Children find a behavior pattern that appears to work, and these behaviors are repeated over and over again. In time the number of behaviors increase as does the adaptability of children in relating to their environment.

Perhaps the most important element of infant cognition is *exploration*. This behavior is seen within the first month of life, and as soon as children become mobile, the exploration activity increases significantly. Infants explore with more than just their hands and arms. The first tool of exploration is vision; then there is touching as well as a great deal of mouthing behavior. Exploration in infants is made up of looking, feeling, gumming (mouth), and hearing (White, 1975).

Learning is the second major aspect of cognition in infancy. The basic types of learning have already been discussed. Through exploration and the resultant learning, infants adjust to this new and complex world. The emerging resources of children gradually enable them to organize their world and cope with increasing demands being placed on them.

Summary

1. There are several ways to attempt to measure the perceptive abilities of infants. Some of these ways include attention-disruption, heart-rate monitoring, and measuring the electrical conductivity of the skin.

2. The vision of infants is not as functional as it will be later, but it rapidly accommodates to the demands of their new world. The pupillary reflex develops rapidly and there is some evidence that infants can discriminate colors very early in their lives.

3. Infants appear to prefer to look at a patterned

Developmental Stages in the Sensorimotor Period

Name	Approximate age	Description
Reflexive stage	First month of life	Babies use only those skills that are innate; adaptation to the demands of life is through the use of these reflexes; the primary example used by Piaget is sucking
Primary circular reactions	About age 1–4 months	Babies practice behaviors; they become more purposeful and efficient; reflexes are put to other purposes; nonnutritive sucking makes its first appearance; some writers state that the first "habits" of the child appear during this stage of development
Secondary circular reactions	About 4–8 months	Babies explore and manipulate environmental objects. Piaget uses the example of a child in the crib accidentally kicking a suspended toy. Seeing what had happened, the baby began to kick the toy on purpose. This represents the beginning of intentional acts
Coordination-intentional stage	8–12 months of age	This stage represents the blossoming of intentionality; object-permanence is also an important part of this consolidation period
Tertiary circular reactions	1–1½ years of age	Infants manufacture novelty and experience rather than running; there is an understanding by children that their actions have effects
Beginnings of internal thought	Last half of the second year of life	For the first time, children can try things in their heads before actually doing them. Symbolism in play and other activities appears; children are no longer completely dependent upon overt trial-and-error methods of problem solving

stimulus rather than a plain one. Other than this conclusion, there is a great deal of disagreement in the literature over what infants prefer to look at. In the visual cliff experiments the development of depth perception appeared to coincide with the ability to crawl, indicating a possible connection between depth perception and overall maturation of the child.

4. *In utero*, the infant is suspended in amniotic fluid. This fluid may enter the ears of the infant and affect the acuity of the hearing for a short time after birth. Once this clears up, the infant's hearing ability is very good, although a neonate's response to sound is a very general one. There is some evidence that hearing deficits may be behind many of the learning problems children have.

5. Neonates and infants can discriminate tastes, and can develop a preference for sugar water over plain water rather quickly. As infants get older they will indicate their taste preferences more and more obviously, reacting to tastes not preferred and savoring tastes they prefer.

6. Learning in children is first dependent upon gaining their attention, so that they may deal with the situation. Infant learning comes in two broad categories: classical conditioning (pairing of stimuli) and operant conditioning (the use of reinforcement). Most learning is discriminative and based on the environmental contingencies present.

7. In Piagetian theory, the period of cognitive growth that most closely corresponds to infancy is the period of sensorimotor intelligence. This period is actually composed of several substages, all of which revolve around the manipulation and exploration of the environment along with repetition of behaviors.

Thought Questions

1. How do we measure the perceptive abilities of infants? How accurate are our measurements of infant perception?

2. What factors contribute to the effective visual skills of the infant? How sophisticated is infant vision? What is the pupillary reflex? What role do the muscles around the eye play in visual acuity?

3. What is the visual cliff? How might depth perception be related to motor abilities? How early can infants discriminate visual patterns? How effective is this early visual discrimination?

4. Is the following sentence true or false? Since the infant has no taste preferences or even the ability to discriminate taste at birth, it really does not make any difference if the neonate is given sugar water. What are the possible consequences of the

introduction of sugar water? Is there any relationship that you know of to dental caries? How do infants indicate their food preferences to parents?

5. Describe the basic differences between classical conditioning and operant conditioning. What is discriminative learning? Give an example of classical conditioning in the human baby. Do young babies respond to reinforcement? Do young babies ever train their parents? How?

6. Describe the different elements of sensorimotor intelligence. Why are some of the components labeled circular? What are the basic operations present in this stage?

Suggested Readings

Lewis, M., and L.A. Rosenblum, eds. *The Effect of the Infant on its Caregiver.* New York: Wiley, 1974. *Contrary to most works, this book explores the impact of the infant on the parents. Persuasive evidence is presented underlining the relevance of infants affecting the behavior of adults.*

Maccoby, E., and C. Jacklin. *The Psychology of Sex Differences.* Stanford: Stanford University Press, 1974. *Literally huge, this review of the literature of sex differences provides a fundamental framework for the study of sex differences. The work contains few startling discoveries but is immensely valuable in its comprehensiveness.*

Stone, L.J.; H.T. Smith, and L.B. Murphy, eds. *The Competent Infant.* New York: Basic Books, 1973. *This is perhaps the most comprehensive book published in terms of the literature surrounding infant development. There are over 200 selections covering an extensive array of topics.*

Tavris, C., and C. Offir. *The Longest War: Sex Differences in Perspective.* New York: Harcourt, Brace, Jovanovich, 1977. *This is a very good discussion of the nature of sex differences, whether the differences are real or imagined. Emphasis is on the learned dimensions of sex role behavior.*

READING

Can infants think? Do they learn? For many years scientists have not been able to accurately answer these questions. We certainly cannot subject babies to a series of verbal or written questions to measure their IQ, nor could they sit through a lecture and then take an examination over the material covered.

Infant learning is highly dependent upon perceptive ability and environmental support (food, warmth, and so on). Piaget has included infants in his cognitive plan, saying that the sensorimotor period marks the transition from complete dependence upon reflexive abilities and passive environmental support to basic thought patterns.

Educators are becoming more and more interested in the impact of basic environmental supports in the transition to basic thought processes. As a result, infant education programs are beginning to pop up around the country. In the following article, Rose Bromwich reviews research relevant to infant stimulation programs. The goal of these programs is basically to enhance optimal development for all children. Dr. Bromwich concludes, intriguingly, that infant stimulation per se may not be the most important ingredient for infant education programs. Her emphasis on parental education reinforces a fundamental contextual argument: the family of the infant is vital in terms of realization of appropriate educational experiences.

Stimulation in the First Year of Life? A Perspective on Infant Development
Rose M. Bromwich

Early education has recently been extended to include infancy, a trend preceded by a rising interest in research in infant development. Although there has been a considerable increase in the number of educational programs for infants, the demand still exceeds the supply. Knowledge available from recent research should be helpful in the formulation of high quality programs for infants and their families. This article will review recent research findings on certain aspects of infant development and discuss their implications for infant education.

Early Intervention

Early intervention programs have been geared primarily to two types of populations: the so-called "disadvantaged," and the handicapped and developmentally delayed. More recently it has been suggested that all infants would benefit from early education, the argument being that if early educational intervention makes even a slight difference in the intellectual functioning of the "disadvantaged" child, it should have a beneficial effect on all children. Furthermore, because the results of programs such as Head Start (in terms of the children's intellectual performance) have not been as impressive as anticipated, it has been argued that intervention should begin earlier. In fact, the term *early intervention* now often means beginning at birth.

The majority of intervention programs are for children from poverty families. Therefore, it is important to know when socioeconomic factors become significant in children's intellectual development. Evidence is abundant regarding the impact of socioeconomic status (SES) on development beginning at about the age of 18 months, especially in the areas of language and adaptive play. Bruner has succinctly stated the results of two studies of low and middle SES mothers' styles of teaching their preschool age children.

Reading aloud with an adult is an activity that young children can always enjoy and participate in.
ROBERT V. ECKERT, JR., EKM-NEPENTHE.

Middle-class mothers are more attentive to the continuous flow of goal-directed action. Second, they allow the child to set his own pace and make his own decisions more. Third, they intrude less often and less directly in the process of problem solving itself. Fourth, they structure the search task by questions that sharpen yet ease the search for means. Fifth, they are more oriented toward the overall structure of the task than responsive to component acts in isolation. Sixth, they react more to the child's successful efforts than to his errors.

These observations of difference in maternal styles have important implications for the ways in which the cognitive needs of young children might best be met.

Although the influence of the mother's teaching style is probably preceded by the earlier effects of her mothering style, there are as yet no data that clearly point to SES as a significant factor in the development of the "normal" and physically healthy infant during the first year of life. The findings of three studies indicate, at least as demonstrated by performance on developmental tests, that infant development is not significantly influenced by SES or ethnic factors before the age of about 15 months. Infant stimulation programs, however, have increasingly become part of "compensatory" education.

Infant Stimulation?

The newborn infant can respond to and discriminate between certain kinds of visual and auditory stimuli. These recently observed neonatal accomplishments give evidence of well-developed sensory functions resulting not from environmental learning but from biological maturation. It is often assumed that the young infant's sensory development could therefore be enhanced with increased visual and auditory stimulation. This assumption seems to be based on two currently unexamined and unconfirmed propositions: (1) that there is a positive correlation between intense early stimulation and rate of sensory development, and, *if* that correlation should exist, (2) that accelerating one aspect of infant development leads to overall optimal development. These are very shaky grounds on which to build early stimulation programs for infants. In fact, it may be unwise to assume that simply increasing the amount of sensory stimulation for infants will create more favorable conditions for their development. There seems to be mounting evidence that factors besides environmental ones play a very important role in the development of the infant.

Focus on Infant Attributes

The study of what infants bring to their interactions with others and with the physical world seems to have been overshadowed in the last twenty or thirty years by research on environmental influences on and socialization of the infant and young child. A balance needs to be restored—professionals working with infants and their parents must have the opportunity to know and understand both internal and environmental influences on the development of infants as well as the effects infants have on their "agents of socialization."

The four questions that will be discussed deal with aspects of neurological, affective, and cognitive development of infants that have implications for educational programs. This emphasis, intentionally one-sided, does not reflect a bias favoring "nature" over "nurture"; rather, it allows study of the infant—who and what each one is—in the context of and in interaction with the environment.

QUESTION #1: *What can be learned from certain neurological aspects of early development that has bearing on the relative roles of and the relationship between neurological maturation and environmental learning?*

The "doctrine of an infinite plasticity of the naive nervous system" of the newborn has been generally rejected. The research findings that follow indicate how prefunctional structures of infant behavior are "transformed by physiological maturation *and* interaction with the physical and social environment."

Studies of sleep and crying patterns show that dramatic changes take place during the first three to four months of life. These changes reflect rapid movement toward higher levels of neurological integration. The neural inhibitory processes seem to contribute much to that integration. Parmelee et al. state that there is a steady and rapid maturation of the infant's ability to sustain a prolonged period of [night] sleep in the first 16 weeks of life. . . . During this period, there is a similar but not so dramatic increase in the ability of the body to sustain a prolonged period of wakefulness associated with a dramatic qualitative change in behavior of the baby while awake.

Brazelton studied the crying patterns of newborn infants for whom environmental tension was estimated to be minimal. Crying increased from 1¾ hours per day during the second week of life to a peak of 2¾ hours at 6 weeks of age, followed by a decrease in crying, with a dramatic drop at 12 weeks of age. He inferred that the pattern is neurologically based; environmental factors increased or decreased the *amount* of crying without altering the general pattern. The study also revealed that increased crying tends to occur at the end of longer wakeful periods during the day (after the infant has established a diurnal sleep pattern). The infant who has progressed to an all-night sleep pattern thus has to deal with an accumulation of inner tensions due to an increase in daytime stimulation. This pattern coincides with a similar increase in tension at the end of the day in other family members (known as fatigue in adults). An infant may be reacting to what is experienced as overstimulation by increased crying, which functions as a release of tension.

In contrast with "normal" babies, some handicapped babies with neurological problems, who have not achieved neurological integration adequate to deal with internal and external stimulation, may cry almost continuously (except when asleep) for their first year of life or even longer. In these babies the low level of functioning of the neural inhibitors does not allow the babies to change their state from crying to noncrying.

Even among babies without neurological problems there is a wide range of response patterns to stimulation. Benjamin observed that infants with low sensory thresholds often avoid high levels of visual stimulation by turning away. Because this behavior and the onset of colic often coincide (at about 3 weeks of age), he speculated that overstimulation may contribute to colic. He suggested that when the infant seems to be experiencing overstimulation, the caregiver should intervene to reduce the stimulation which produced tension and therefore discomfort. The mother is usually able to determine the infant's tolerance threshold to sensory stimulation by reading the infant's reaction patterns.

An example of the young infant's reaction pattern to tension has been given by Brazelton, Koslowski, and Main. They observed that infants up to 16 weeks (especially between 12 and 16 weeks) exhibited a cycle of intense attention to an object and then withdrawal from it. The withdrawal, evidenced by a sudden turning away, and sometimes accompanied by rapid breathing, motor activity, or crying out, was interpreted as a necessary relief from the tension produced by "intense and rapt attention."

Maturational changes during early infancy, such as longer nighttime sleep and the diminishing of crying after a peak at 6 weeks, seem to indicate that as neural integration progresses, brain inhibitory mechanisms become more efficient. More effective neural integration can also be observed in increased respiratory regularity and a decrease in random body activity and eye movement during sleep. Parmelee and Stern found a similar decrease in body movements of premature babies during sleep. Movement-free sleep increased from 53 percent at 32 weeks conceptual age, to 60 percent at term, to 81 percent at 8 months of age. "These changes indicate a rapid growth in inhibition of body activity in sleep during this period." A similar pattern seems to occur during wakefulness and sleep: The infant's attentive behaviors when awake develop simultaneously with quiet and sustained sleep. This parallel development shows the increasing efficiency of "inhibitory and controlling feedback mechanisms made possible by the increasing complexity of the neural network and neurochemical development."

What is the relevance of these research findings to early stimulation? One of the important processes taking place in the first few months of life is that of neurological integration. This integration, occurring with neurological maturation, results in brain inhibitory mechanisms becoming more efficient in controlling random movements and in facilitating changes of state, i.e., from crying to noncrying. If maturation is evidenced by more efficient functioning of inhibitory mechanisms resulting in greater neurological control, then care must be taken that external stimulation does not interfere with this newly achieved level of neural integration. The quantity and type of stimulation appropriate for a six-month-old child may interfere with the maturation of neurological processes of a younger infant.

At birth, even among full-term infants, the state of neurological maturity varies. For example, long stretches of uninterrupted crying of some infants during the first 12 weeks of life, often labeled as colic and ascribed to digestive difficulties, may be due to an infant's inability to *inhibit* a behavior (crying) once begun. The ease with which an infant stops crying when comforted is probably a measure of the effectiveness of the neural inhibitory mechanisms. Another example of the functioning of these inhibitors is the increasing ability of infants to limit motor activity to those parts of their bodies that are needed to profitably act upon objects—e.g., when the interest of infants is focused on grasping objects (around the fourth month), they will be successful in doing so primarily to the degree to which they can eliminate random movement and therefore coordinate eye-hand action. Much later, the concentration needed to focus on one activity for a sufficient period of time to yield desirable results is also dependent on inhibitory mechanisms preventing distractibility.

The development of infants' increased control of their actions, made possible by their effective use of inhibitory mechanisms, is of primary importance in their ability to profitably utilize environmental stimuli. Both the complete absence of stimulation as well as excessive stimulation, when perceived as such by an infant, appear to have similarly detrimental effects on the functioning of these neural mechanisms.

The type, intensity, and timing of stimuli in the young infant's environment seem to bear significantly on whether the stimulation is beneficial or detrimental to development. Since infants vary greatly in their rate of neurological maturation, each infant must be observed and planned for on an individual basis. The neurophysiological functioning of *each* infant should direct the responses of the caregiver of that infant.

Individual differences among infants and young children have been highlighted by some longitudinal studies in the last few years. The consideration of such studies leads directly into the discussion of the second question.

QUESTION #2: *What are some of the individual differences between infants from birth on that cause them to respond differently to environmental stimuli?*

The evidence for differences in behavioral patterns of infants from birth is mounting. Thomas,

Chess, and Birch in their New York Longitudinal Study of Individuality in Behavioral Development have defined temperament as the behavioral style of the individual child which includes energy expenditure, focus, mood, rhythmicity, and tempo.

The authors emphasize that infants' patterns of response to environmental stimuli are, to a considerable degree, dependent on their "temperamental organization." The following nine categories of behavioral functioning emerged from content analysis of protocols of interviews with mothers of the first 22 children in the study:

Activity Level
Rhythmicity [in biological functions]
Approach or Withdrawal
Adaptability
Intensity of Reaction
Threshold of Responsiveness
Quality of Mood
Distractibility
Attention Span and Persistence

The investigators, in a later phase of the study, explain that behavior problems seem to result from the interaction of certain patterns of temperamental organization with environmental forces. The analysis of some of their data led them to identify, among others, two behavior patterns: that of the *difficult child* and the pattern of the *slow-to-warm-up child*. The difficult infant and child combines the temperamental attributes of low rhythmicity (in biological functions), withdrawal responses to new stimuli, low adaptability to change, frequent negative mood, and high intensity reactions. The pattern of the slow-to-warm-up child is characterized by withdrawal responses to the new but expressed in mild behavioral terms, low intensity of reaction, low activity level, and slow adaptability.

Throughout their writings, Chess, Thomas, and Birch stress that behavioral patterns develop from the interaction between the infant (with a particular temperamental organization) and a specific pattern of responses from the environment. For instance, the slow-to-warm-up infant needs time to respond and adapt to the new. If his or her tempo or reactivity is generally slow, the environmental stimuli must match the infant's tempo to prevent an eventual negative reaction to these stimuli. The accurate reading of the behavioral cues of the infant becomes a very important ingredient in decisions regarding the what, how, when, and where of the stimuli presented to the infant. The importance of accurately reading behavior is vividly reflected by further findings regarding several children who possessed temperamental qualities that would have predicted problems in environmental characteristics. When their parents received guidance in recognizing and responding to the children's behavioral cues, the children developed into "well functioning" individuals.

It is clear that behavioral individuality in newborn and developing infants must be a primary consideration in planning any type of early intervention program. Infants generally receive large amounts of environmental stimulation from birth on. The issue then is not one of increasing stimulation for babies but rather one of observing each infant and discovering what constitutes the optimal environmental match for that infant's individual make-up. A stimulation program that does not take into consideration neurological changes in early development and individual differences in patterns of behavior and response could interfere with, rather than aid, optimum development.

The mother or other primary caregiver undeniably plays the most important role in the infant's overall development. The next major question deals with the infant-mother relationship and affective interaction so critical in the child's early months and years.

QUESTION #3: *What impact do both mother and infant have on their affective interaction (attachment), and what is the role of that interaction in the infant's overall development?*

Ainsworth followed Bowlby's thinking that the infant's attachment behavior is instinctive: part of a behavioral system built into the organism. Specific infant behaviors such as crying and smiling (defined as attachment behaviors) are "released" by certain environmental stimuli. Crying, for instance, set off by the infant's perception of distance from the mother, which he wants to bridge, is categorized as a "signaling behavior" which, in turn, stimulates the mother "to come into closer proximity or contact with him."

The theoretical framework of attachment has yielded much research dealing with such subjects as mother-infant interaction during feeding, infant responses to separation from mother, individual differences in attachment behaviors, the relationships between cognitive development and attachment, and infant crying and maternal responsiveness. Studies in the latter two areas are discussed below.

Beckwith and Cohen found that at eight months of age, the frequency of *mutual visual regard* between mother and infant correlates significantly with test scores measuring cognitive development at nine months. These findings confirm the current view that reciprocity of interaction between mother and infant is a cornerstone of optimum infant development.

In another study, Bell showed that babies who displayed more desirable attachment behavior than other babies during a separation experiment gained the concept of person permanence before that of object permanence. According to Bell, "The most significant finding . . . is that the development of the object concept is intimately associated with the attachment of a baby with his mother." Bell relates her findings to those of two other attachment studies and emerges with the following conclusion:

A harmonious relationship between mother and infant seems to be the precondition for eliciting the type of "interest" in the baby which, Piaget hypothesized, so pervasively affects the development of sensorimotor intelligence. . . . Thus it is suggested here that there is an important dimension affecting the development of the object concept which transcends socioeconomic boundaries and often goes unexamined in studies aiming to isolate the essential features of "enrichment" or "deprivation." Specifically the findings of the present study lead us to the hypothesis that the quality of a baby's interaction with his mother is one of the crucial dimensions of "environmental influence" to affect this type of sensorimotor development.

The above statement eloquently addresses itself to issues of early intervention.

The rather dramatic findings of Bell's and Ainsworth's study, "Infant Crying and Maternal Responsiveness," have had an important influence on an intervention program with handicapped infants in which I have participated over the last four years. Focusing on the effects of the mother's "sensitive responsiveness" to her infant's crying, the findings reveal that the more the mother responded in a sensitive manner to the infant's crying during the first quarter of the first year, the less the baby cried in the fourth quarter of that year. "Sensitive responsiveness" means behaviorally that the mother not only picks up the crying infant but holds him or her affectionately for longer than a minute. It was found that infants whose mothers had given them relatively much tender and affectionate holding in the earliest months of life are content with surprisingly little physical contact by the end of the first year; although they enjoy being held, when put down they are happy to move off into independent exploratory play.

The results of this study contradict the behavioristic assumption that picking up a crying baby will reinforce the crying.

In a related study, Stayton, Hogan, and Ainsworth found that those infants whose signals had been promptly heard and sensitively responded to by their mothers were most easily controlled by their mothers from a distance. Bell and Ainsworth connect affective responsiveness of the mother to her infant's signals with the development of critical aspects of infant cognitive development:

Maternal responsiveness to signals fosters the development of communication. It does not interfere with the early development of increased competence, and through giving a child confidence, it positively encourages the later development of means-ends activities.

Infant intervention as practiced with handicapped and premature infants and their mothers in the UCLA Infant Studies Project has adopted a formulation for a progression of maternal behaviors with their infants deemed necessary for the developmental enhancement of the infant. This progression begins with two maternal attitudes-behaviors which were found to be essential in fostering the infant's cognitive development. Therefore the presence or establishment of these behaviors in the mother have taken priority over any direct behavioral goal for the infant. They are identified as (1) the mother's enjoyment of her infant, and (2) her sensitive responsiveness to the infant's cues and signals. After three years of clinical experience in infant intervention, the staff now operates on the assumption that lasting effects on the infant's cognitive development are possibly only when these primary conditions of mother-infant attachment exist.

The system of communication between the young infant and the mother is a very delicate one and the sooner the mother is able to read the behavioral cues of the infant, the more satisfying the mothering role becomes. Korner conjectures that infants whose cues are unclear and therefore difficult to read make it less easy for their mothers to satisfy them. The infant's poor communication interferes with the mother's feeling of adequacy in the mothering role.

Bell also emphasizes the impact the infant has on the caregiver. He distinguishes between (1) the life support and protection system and (2) the social interaction system that exist in mother-child interaction. In both these systems the infant plays a major part in the quality of the relationship. Bell stresses the importance of the mother's responsiveness to the cues of the infant and illustrates how the mother's appropriate stimulation of the infant is the result of her sensitive response. For example, many babies babble more when they are alone. This babbling functions as an attachment behavior by drawing the mother close to the infant. Reciprocal games between mother and infant result, games in which the babbling takes a different social form. In this manner, the mother and infant establish sequences of interaction that are mutually reinforcing.

Positive affect in mother-infant interaction is a basic requirement for optimum infant development. The importance of reciprocity and mutual satisfaction in the mother-infant relationship is being increasingly stressed in research findings and clinical experience. Not only does the mother have a clear effect on the infant's behavior, but the infant or young child significantly influences the mother's actions toward him or her.

Infant intervention should have as its primary goal the maintenance or encouragement of a positive attachment between mother and infant. Achieving the goal of mutually satisfying mother-infant interaction may do more to promote optimum development in the infant than any other focus. An infant intervention program must take care not to interfere with mother-infant attachment by either causing the mother to feel inadequate in the mothering role or dependent on the "specialist" for dealing with her baby. Such intervention would inadvertently interfere with the mother's enjoyment of her baby by creating doubts in her self-image as a mother, resulting in her lowered sensitivity to the baby's cues. The outcome could be detrimental to the infant's development and worse than no intervention at all. If the mother's sensitivity to the infant's behavioral cues is primary in her responses to the infant, to the relationship between them, and therefore to the overall development of the infant, the infant specialist must tune in to that relationship, support the mother's responsiveness, and help her find aspects of the infant's actions that she can enjoy and therefore build on. The mother's and child's behaviors will then be mutually reinforcing.

QUESTION #4: *How do infants develop sensorimotor skills to master their environments, and what kinds of experiences are most likely to enhance this process?*

In a series of articles, Bruner has formulated some theoretical propositions (based on behavioral observations) about the elements involved in the mastery of increasingly complex tasks in the early months of the infant's life. The material is summarized below.

1) Intention very early directs the infant's activity (Piaget's third stage of sensorimotor period).

2) Much of the infant's accomplishments in "skilled manipulatory activity" during the first year of life results from maturation rather than learning.

3) Before a goal-directed manipulatory skill is achieved, its components or "constituent acts" appear in rudimentary form. They are not yet "serially ordered" and coordinated with each other to make up the skill that will achieve the goal.

4) These individual acts are not learned but each appears when ready through the maturational process.

5) Each "constituent act," although not by itself able to achieve the goal, is oriented toward the goal.

6) These separate acts are eventually ordered and "orchestrated" to form the "manipulatory skilled act" of greater complexity in a manner that "reflects some internal principle of organiza-

tion triggered by the environment."

7) As soon as a goal is achieved through a newly learned skill, this skilled action, in turn, becomes a "subroutine" or "constituent act" of a not-yet-mastered higher-order skill.

8) Learning enters only as the skill must be *adapted* to the environmental situation or object.

The following observations of a four-month-old infant illustrate the above statements:

Goal: To grasp a cube and explore it orally.
Manipulatory skill needed: Visually guided reaching and grasping of object, then bringing it to the mouth. The infant is observed engaging in some form of each "constituent act" of the needed skill. All these now separate acts eventually become coordinated subroutines of the goal-directed skill. The acts are listed as observed in order of their appearance:

1. prolonged looking
2. activity of mouth, tongue, and jaws
3. raising action of arms and shoulders
4. clenching of fists in a grab pattern
5. movement of arms
6. outward flinging of clenched fist.

Gradually the infant learns to order and integrate the above acts into the manipulatory skill that will achieve the goal—get the desired object to the mouth. After accomplishing this task, the mastered skill is soon oriented to a different activity, i.e., bang an object on a surface or rotate it close to the eyes to examine it visually. Thus the mastered skilled action becomes a subroutine of a higher level activity.

The eight statements and the example above deal with goal-directed activity or acts where intention is discernible. This behavior illustrates Piaget's third stage (4 to 8 months) of the sensorimotor period.

Bruner also discusses play and the conditions of play which seem to favor optimal cognitive development. He asserts that much behavior can be observed "that seems to be without clearcut means-ends structure, where the activity seems more playful, where ends are changed to fit available means." He calls this "mastery play" and identifies it as "extending to new limits already achieved skills." Mastery play occurs in two directions:

1. Using a newly acquired object in as many different ways (engaging in as many different acts with that object) as are available in the infant's repertoire;

2. Using a newly acquired sensorimotor skill with as many objects as are accessible to the infant.

The child development orientation in early childhood education strongly values this type of spontaneous, autonomous play which fosters exploration and free experimentation in manipulatory, and later, symbolic play. Its importance is confirmed by observations of human infants as well as those of young primates. Bruner concludes that pressure-free play contributes immeasurably to the mastery of highly complex skills, i.e., the use of tools. He suggests that "in order for tool using to develop, it was essential to have a long period of optional, pressure-free opportunity for combinatorial activity." In a study of chimpanzee behavior it was found that the two conditions that *inhibited* experimental and exploratory (non-goal-directed) play with objects were: (a) providing an incentive or lure, and (b) reinforcing play behavior. "Play provides an excellent opportunity to try combinations of behavior that would, under functional pressure, never be tried."

Morris categorizes this type of non-goal-directed play in primates as "despecialized" or "opportunist" in contrast to "highly specialized." Those species that need greater variety and flexibility of behavior for optimum adaptation require this despecialized, playful, experimental activity which Morris identifies as the love of the new or "neophilia." Bruner stresses the importance of neophilia in the development of intelligence in the fullest sense.

The following propositions are related to the above discussion:

9) Autonomous play, in a relaxed setting that is not goal-directed but exploratory and experimental in nature, gives the infant opportunity to stretch his or her adaptive skills to the limits set by maturation.

10) Practice, although important, is generally most useful when nonspecific.

11) New achievements in both manipulatory activity and language are most likely to occur during spontaneous play—in situations where no demands are made on the infant either by the situation or by a person.

12) Such play is most likely to take place in an atmosphere that is not stressful, or, more positively stated, in the matrix of a satisfying, supportive affective relationship with the mother figure.

13) Skills closest to the upper developmental limits set by neurological maturation, those on which the infant has only a precarious hold, readily drop out under the pressure of adult expectation or demand.

Statements #12 and #13 apply equally to manipulatory skills and language—the two primary components of early intellectual development.

Bruner deals, at some length, with the concept of modeling. His and other investigators' observations of human infants and young primates can be summarized briefly as follows:

14) Modeling, which is an important source of social adaptation for the primate and human infant, can be described from the point of view of the young learner as "adult watching." The infant observes adult behaviors and incorporates them first into play.

15) In order for the young to profit from modeling, the child must have mastered some of the elements contained in the observed adult behavior pattern or constituent acts which may be complex or "high order actions."

Statements #14 and #15 apply to modeling, or even more direct demonstration, in the areas of manipulatory skills, language, and social behavior.

16) Symbolic play makes use of props as "pivots," that is, the prop becomes a pivot between the real and the imagined.

Although symbolic play, in which objects are given symbolic meanings (i.e., blocks become cars, a stick becomes a horse), does not usually occur in the first year of life, it seemed appropriate to include it here to give a fuller picture of the sequence and the potential of play.

In the statement below, Bruner makes explicit some of the implications of his work for infant education:

There is inherent in the description given of the growth of infant skill an emphasis on self-initiated, intentional behavior. Surely the chief practical recommendation one would have to make . . . is that the infant should be encouraged to venture, rewarded for venturing his own acts, and sustained against distraction or premature interferences in carrying them out. It is a point of view very alien from such ideas as preventing "deprivation" or providing "enrichment," both of which are very passive conceptions. . . . The controlling motif of skill acquisition as presented here is "opportunity to initiate and sustain action" in play and in carrying out intentions. . . .

The discussion of question #4 describes the infant as self-motivated or "internally programmed" to develop sensorimotor skills, but he or she must have a setting that provides an emotionally safe and pressure-free atmosphere and contains a physical environment with a variety of objects within reach which can be manipulated in a number of ways. Intervention, when it interveres with children's play, may obstruct rather-er than enhance the development of their skills for mastery of their environment.

The child's intellectual development during what Piaget calls the sensorimotor period has been discussed in this section; the child's play is the vehicle of that development. It has been stated that pressure-free play, play in which the child is not faced with expectations, is important for the child in learning to negotiate successfully with the physical world. There are other areas of infant and child behavior where some expectations are justifiably imposed, but those behaviors fall into the realm of social adaptation.

Summary: Infant Stimulation Reconsidered

In this article I have discussed aspects of the infant's early neurological maturation, individual differences of temperament and behavioral organization, mother-infant interaction and the impact of infants on their caregivers, and the development of sensorimotor skills.

The concept of "infant stimulation" was challenged because of the assumption that is usually associated with that concept, namely that increasing the infant's stimulation is a positive step toward enhancing overall development. Considerable psychological and medical research make it questionable whether the intent of infant education programs should be to increase the infant's stimulation. Rather, it is more in harmony with information presented here to work with the parents toward *increasing* their (1) awareness of their infant's sensory tolerance and temperamental organization, (2) enjoyment of their infant and their sensitive responsiveness to all his or her communications, and (3) ability to anticipate changes in behaviors likely to occur in the child's early development.

The term *infant stimulation* also suggests that the adult who provides the stimulation is the *active* one and the infant, who *receives it*, plays a passive role, i.e., the infant *reacts* to the adult's action. This type of process is not in agreement with the idea of mutuality of interaction between parent and infant (question #3) or with the type of play that fosters the development of sensorimotor skills (question #4).

To conclude, the term *infant stimulation* is misleading and should not be used in identifying educational programs appropriate for young infants and their parents. Why not speak instead of parent-infant education?

REPRODUCED BY PERMISSION OF THE SMITH COLLEGE MUSEUM OF ART, NORTHAMPTON, MASSACHUSETTS.

Boon Companions, by James Wells Champney.

8
Infancy: Personality and Temperament

Infant emotions are very difficult to assess adequately. If a child is placed into some sort of experimental environment where a researcher can control all of the related problems in measurement, it is likely that some of the essence of "humanness" will be lost. On the other hand, if observations concerning emotions in infancy are made only in naturalistic settings, it is difficult to see behaviors clearly because of the complicated milieu in which they occur.

Emotions in infancy are thought by some researchers to be broad, generalized sorts of reactions to a wide variety of situations the child may encounter in the course of an average day. Another point of view says that very young infants really do not have any intentionally occurring emotions; what we see as rage and happiness are merely broad behavioral classifications, really too broad to be indicative of anything. Still other people say that infants are capable of highly divergent, specific emotional states, and that with increasing age, these motivational and behavioral states are intentional and perhaps even predictable.

Infants do operate in different emotional frameworks. Generally, infants seem to have few emotional responses, which are generalized to a wide variety of situations. With advancing age the emotional repertoire expands; children articulate particular emotional reactions and tie them to specific occurrences. The *intensity* of the emotional behaviors, however, is very often great from the beginning of the child's life. The intensity of emotional behavior may be

EMOTIONS IN INFANCY

Intensity of emotions: degree of emotional involvement

intrinsically tied to the temperamental nature of the individual child. Depending upon temperament, social situation, and motivational factors, the range of emotional behavior can vary greatly between children raised in somewhat the same environment and can even vary considerably within the same child from moment to moment.

Preverbal infants confronted with a "no" from a parent will respond emotionally to that situation as they would to a physically painful situation (some would argue that pain is involved in both sorts of situations, except that the verbal reprimand produces psychic pain, which is no less real, however). As children mature, their responses to a parental "no" will change. Where once it brought about crying as an emotional response, later it may bring less overt emotionalism and more bargaining by the children, particularly after they are verbal. In some instances, children may express their emotional reaction to the verbal reprimand with absolute defiance and refusal.

SMILING

One emotional response in infancy that people are often very interested in is *smiling*. What is a smile? Where does it come from? What does it mean? All of these are important to ask when wondering about the nature of smiling in the human infant.

Some of the work of LeBoyer, cited earlier, has referred to the fact that in the delivery room, under the proper circumstances, newborn infants exhibited distinct smiles, as if they were quite pleased with what was happening to them. An important caution in interpreting pictures like these is the all too human tendency to project our own emotional states onto the child. We expect that a child should be happy. Our emotional response may influence our interpretation of the factual content of the picture.

Elkind and Weiner (1978) report on several research studies related to smiling in the human infant. For example, smiling develops in three rather distinct phases.

Reflective smiling: brief smiling by infants that is not social in nature

1. There is first of all, *reflective smiling*. These smiles are short in duration and probably do not mean much in the way of social interaction and contact. These reflective smiles could be indicative of some inner, physiological situation with the child. This particular type of smiling is the first to appear and lasts for a month or so.

2. At four to six weeks of life, the infant appears to enter into another distinct phase in smiling behavior. Elkind and Weiner call this the *unselective social smiling* stage. The duration of the smiles is

Infancy: Personality and Temperament

longer, and they really look like smiles. In this stage, the child could be smiling in response to specific environmental stimuli, such as a mobile placed over the crib, or a voice.

3. *Selective social smiling* does not occur until five or six months of life. As its title indicates, this is social smiling in response to cues and stimuli chosen by the child as being appropriate. A specific face or faces or specific voices are the stimuli that elicit selective social smiling. This occurrence, not surprisingly, seems to coincide with the child selecting particular people as favorites he wishes to be with most of the time (see Wolff, 1963; Ambrose, 1961; and Gewirtz, 1965 for detailed discussion). Smiling progresses from being completely unselective to being quite selective and with time it comes to be part of the contextual nature of social development, associated with particular people and particular settings.

Painting a strictly developmental picture in relation to smiling is a little misleading to the astute observer of children. The stages are not hard and fast. They appear to be sequentially invariant, but there may be exceptions and variations on that theme, depending

Social smiling: smiling in response to social stimuli

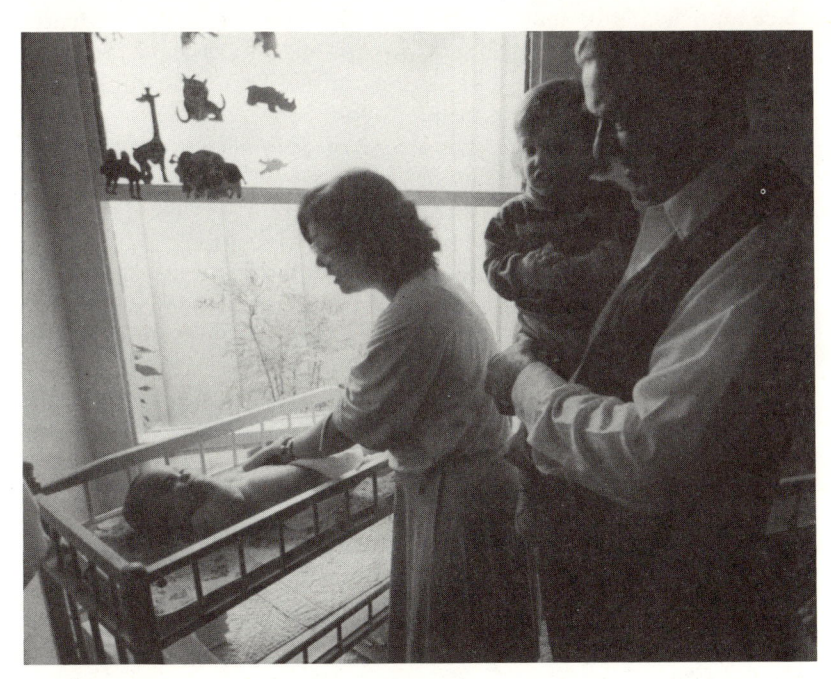

Changing a baby's diapers is another opportunity for a parent and a child to communicate with each other.
ROBERT V. ECKERT, JR., EKM-NEPENTHE.

upon the particular child. One should not assume that these different types of smiling behavior will automatically appear at the ages indicated.

Smiling and Perceptual Development

There seems to be a close relationship between smiling behavior and the child's perceptual abilities. Perceptual abilities are important in determining just what the visual field of the child is. Depending upon that visual field and the level of maturity, different sorts of stimuli will elicit smiling. For example, a voice will elicit a reaction before a smiling face, and a realistic face is more attractive than another drawing (Fantz, 1965).

FEAR

Fear:
unpleasant emotion caused by anticipation of danger

Fear in children is usually observable to parents and other adults in terms of facial expression and generalized crying behavior. Body posture, cowering, and other sorts of behavioral gestures may reflect high levels of fear in the child. Certain responses to fearful situations probably are genetic in origin. Babies have a fear of falling from early in their lives, for example. Loud, startling noises also frighten all of us, including babies.

Infants typically do not have fear of animals, of elevators, or even of the dark. These behaviors may come later in a child's life as the result of some simple form of association. As children grow older, these different sorts of fears begin to develop, and consistent adult mediation of them is often necessary.

Infants may react with a fear response to any sudden shift in the nature and intensity of stimulation (Gardner, 1978). If there is rapid movement, or a handing off to another person, or an intrusive noise or even a zooming face, fear could be produced. These instances all represent basic upsets of the infant's steady state. By the time children reach the age of two, fear has left the realm of simple response to divergent stimuli. Fear becomes a response integrated into the fabric of a child's personality and dependent upon the nature of the child's social environment. A most important added dimension as children leave infancy is that they will be interpreting the situations and placing their own framework on the situation.

As in smiling, there is probably some developmental aspect in fear in children. Bower (1976), in his study of kindergarten, second grade and sixth grade children, found significant developmental differences in the structure of fears over time. As grade level increased, there were decreases in fears that had imaginary themes, such as ghosts, monsters, and the like. With time there was an increase in the frequency of realistic fears, involving things like bodily injury and physical danger. The context of the child's development and the level of cognitive sophistication seem to play a significant role in the development of specific fear responses.

Fear, like the other aspects of emotional development, has a very significant idiosyncratic nature to it. The normative developmental pattern of fear responses may be a transition between imaginary sorts of motivations to motivations based in reality. Individual children, however, may exhibit fear responses unlike any developmental progression. It is quite possible that an older child will have fears rooted in the imagination.

Fear is not the same as separation-based anxiety. Anxiety produced because of separation from parents probably has its base in the development of a relationship between the child and caregiver. Fear has no such requirements. In fact, researchers are indicating that children in America today have more fears (numerically) than children in America used to have. There are more "things" in the world, real and imagined, that have the potential to take on fear-evoking characteristics. Even a child's lamp, decorated as a happy clown, can turn into a very fearful beast, preventing the child from sleeping in her room. Television, with its animated possibilities and all of its incredible occurrences, may be responsible for many of the fears of children.

Anxiety: apprehensive uneasiness

ANGER AND INDEPENDENCE

A behavioral response that is seen more and more often during early childhood is simple, outright anger on the part of the child. Anger is loosely defined as an emotional response to a feeling that things are not going well with respect to yourself.

Children can and do feel angry. Early in infancy, anger is probably not so visible. The very early months of the child's development are taken up developing the personality equipment necessary to feel the emotion of anger. Very quickly, this equipment develops and is quite functional.

As children are finishing the first year and moving into the second year, the reality of anger becomes quite clear. Most of the time infants' anger is an expression of emotion against any form of restraint being imposed on them. As we have stated earlier, the primary developmental crisis occurring in infancy, after the resolution of the basic trust–basic mistrust dilemma, is *autonomy* versus

Autonomy: a sense of independence

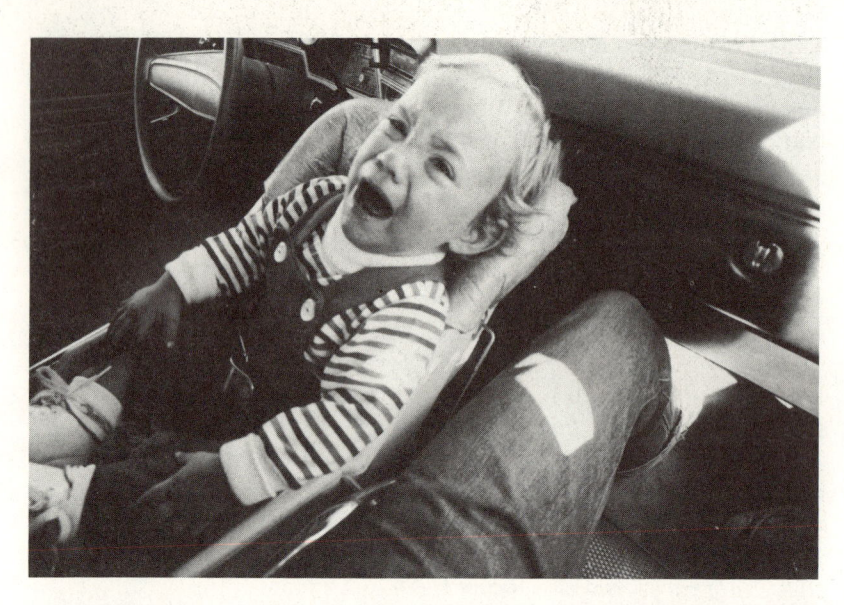

Perhaps this child's anger has resulted from the restraints imposed by the safety harness of a car seat.
ROBERT V. ECKERT, JR., EKM-NEPENTHE.

shame and self-doubt. A major developmental task of this part of children's life is to be able to balance the "no" messages with their own desire for autonomy. The successful resolution of this dilemma, provided the basic trust dilemma has been successfully dealt with, leaves the child with a comfortable sense of individuality and accomplishment. Unsuccessful resolution leaves the child in doubt, sometimes ashamed of his behavior.

Appropriate exercise of independence also needs to be integrated with appropriate demands for conformity from the social environment. However, in the process of articulating the relationships between autonomy and necessary conformity, anger is very likely a result. Anger may be conceptualized as a normative theme of the process of developing autonomy in the infant. Because this anger is an expected behavior, the adult world should be able to handle these quests for individuality in a sensitive and consistent manner.

Behavioral examples of children's anger in infancy include hitting at the adult, throwing things at the adult and around the room, squirming and wiggling away from the parent, and yelling and crying. A classic example is the infant who is mobile and walking and will protest and resist vigorously any effort to slow him down enough to get his clothes changed.

Infancy: Personality and Temperament

As the child develops language and other cognitive skills, the observable part of anger often changes form. It is expressed in more subtle, less overt fashions. There may be more verbal expressions of anger, and fewer physical expressions.

ISSUE

The Infant and the Father

Earlier, in another issue, we discussed the reintroduction of the father to the birthing process. We now turn to the role of the father with the infant. In America we have long assumed that children are *monotropically matricentric*. This is the assumption that infants will protest the departure of their mother, but not of their father. In fact, as Kotelchuck has indicated, "The influence of the father on the infant's early social development has been virtually ignored. . . . There have been virtually no studies directly observing fathers and their young children interacting" (Kotelchuck, 1976, p. 61).

☐ Given fathers' provider role outside of the home (which developed with the advent of industrialization) and the consequent elevated role of mothers in childrearing, it was commonly assumed in the first half of this century that fathers were actually unimportant in the development of infants. This feeling is inaccurate. An economic occurrence (industrialization) took fathers out of the home, their absence became traditional (it was not, earlier) and eventually, as so often happens, this tradition proliferated and became fact.

☐ However, fathers *are* important in the development of the infant. As early as 1964, evidence began to appear in the literature that the role of the father had been underestimated, and perhaps even ignored for far too long. In that year Carlsmith published a study attempting to discover the relationship between father absence and scholastic aptitude. Using a survey technique, Carlsmith found that the longer the father was absent, the greater effect on the children's ability, and the earlier the father left the home, the greater the effects on the children's aptitude.

☐ Hetherington, in a study published in 1972, has explored the relationship between father absence and behavior in teenage girls. In her study, father absence was manifested during the adolescent period, and the effects appear to be expressed as an inability to functionally interact with males. Hetherington goes on to state that it appears the father's absence during the first few years, say the first five, are the crucial ones in determining the effects of the absence.

☐ It appears that men are caught up in a myth that has enveloped our society. The myth states that fathers do not have much interest in babies, do not spend much time with them, and do not talk much to them. Studies of fathers' interactional styles seem to confirm this feeling. It could be argued, however, that these paternal behaviors are the result of the self-fulfilling prophecy: you do not have the ability nor the aptitude to interact with your infant; wait until the child can throw a ball or run before you interact with your baby.

☐ Men have been raised to be largely instrumental and inexpressive. This inexpressiveness generalizes to the interaction between father and infant. We have come to accept this tradition as fact, and continue to train our males to be inexpressive, especially in relation to children.

☐ One positive outcome of the human potential movement has been to open some previously closed doors to men. We are starting to see men involved in preschool education and day care; we find them teaching in the early elementary years; men appear to be more willing to adopt nontraditional roles, and to be expressive with their children.

☐ Interestingly, there is some evidence in the literature to support this sort of trend. Kotelchuck, in a study originally published in 1976 and later republished in 1978, indicates that many of our traditional stereotypes concerning infants and their fathers are inaccurate. For example, there is not only a mother-infant bond. When *bonding* became an attractive word, people started to assume that bonding took place only between the mother and the infant. The evidence indicates that there is not a unique mother-infant bond. Children are inherently interested in both parents; they protest the separation from both parents; and they love both parents in largely similar ways.

☐ This issue is an important one. Will these trends continue? Will we be able to expand even further to appreciate many of the human aspects of bonding and interpersonal relations? The stage has been set for a complete reexamination of the male's role in child development.

ROUTINES IN INFANCY

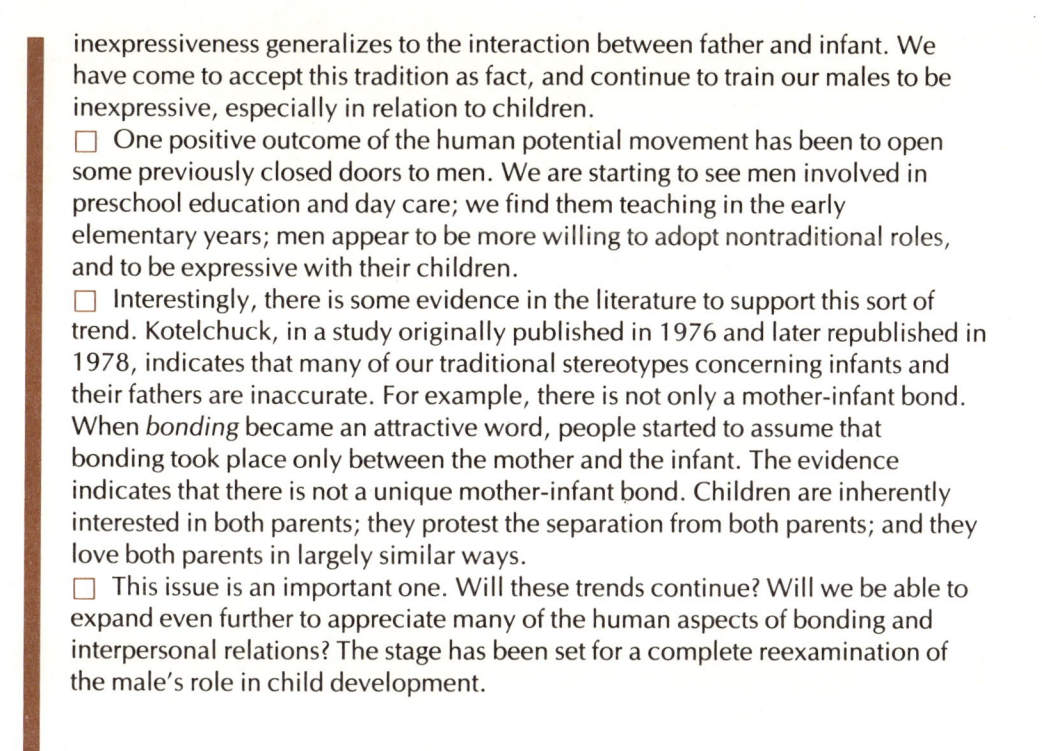

Much of infant care is made up of routine behaviors and interactions. Sometimes parents resent the use of the word *routine* because each behavior implies an interaction with the child. However, due to the frequency of these behaviors and the amount of time spent in these activities, it is quite safe to term them routines.

Feeding: The specific goals of infant feeding are: (1) to meet the nutritional demands of the infant as they relate to the child's developmental needs, and (2) to develop a healthy relationship between the infant and the caregivers. This relationship implies communication, affection, and attention directed by the adults toward the child (Smith, 1977).

Whether the child is fed by bottle or breast, it is vital to hold the baby close during feeding situations. This closeness should last as long as the infant does not sit in a chair at the table with the rest of the family. Fathers should play a significant role in this early feeding, even if the baby is being breast-fed. Fathers may hold children when they are being burped, among other things.

The actual feeding situation becomes an important matter for consideration. The use of utensils is inappropriate for pre-one-year-old children; but they can still be fed during the family mealtime, emphasizing the sociopsychological importance of the mealtime. Children need to have their own chair by this point (no sitting on parental lap), their own equipment (child-size), and a sense of fitting into the mealtime situation, both psychologically and socially.

The emotional atmosphere of mealtime is also quite important. For some reason, many family problems get aired at mealtime. The resultant tension is easily transmitted to the children, and may be translated into digestive difficulties and problems for the children.

Sleeping: Sleep is another routine of infancy that occupies a great deal of time in the child's life. Young infants sleep most of the time. It seems as though when they are not sleeping, they are eating.

The scientific study of sleep has been very intense. Kessen et al. (1970), in reviewing the research done on infant sleep patterns, have demonstrated that the duration of the longest single period of sleep increases from about 4½ hours in the first days of life to over 10 hours per day by the 25th week of life.

REM sleep:
rapid eye movement sleep, related to dreaming

Infant sleep occurs in cycles; there are many different levels of sleep in infants. Wagner (1939) found seven levels of infant sleep-waking activity: light sleep, deep sleep, REM sleep (rapid eye movement sleep, often associated with dreaming), and many others. The possibility for infants dreaming is certainly present. The specific nature of those dreams remains a matter of speculation.

Scheduling of infant sleep also becomes important toward the end of the first year and the beginning of the second year. Establishing rather firm guidelines, without exception, as to what is bedtime enhances the relationship between parent and child, provides structure for the child's life, and ensures, at least in theory, that the child will get enough sleep. Very soon children will attempt to see if they can modify the parents' behavior by calling for them or crying, just to see if their parents will come in and get them. This testing period is usually taken care of if parents ignore these plaintive cries, providing they have seen to it that all the basic needs—warmth, hunger, thirst, etc.—have been taken care of. Consistency is crucial in the management of sleep behavior.

PERSONALITY AND TEMPERAMENT

Personality has been defined as a collection of individual qualities that come together in a unique collection of emotions, values, and behavior. This set of values, attitudes, and ideals is a product of socialization, to be sure, as well as some genetic influences, many of which we do not as yet understand. Bower in his book on infant development says "personality refers to our repertoires for dealing with people" (Bower, 1977, p. 164).

The fundamental nature-nurture controversy is always a part of the discussion of personality. Just where does personality come from? The nature people say it is a product of genetically determined potential. The nurture people say personality is a function of socializing agents and environment. This controversy is very much like a pendulum: it keeps swinging back and forth along the continuum between the two extremes. When one piece of evidence is released, the pendulum swings one way; when another piece of evidence comes out, the pendulum swings the other way. Each faction of the argument insists that it is right, when in reality both are undoubtedly correct. Personality evolves from both dimensions: there is a real genetic component to personality and its correlates, such as intelligence; there is also very real societal and social input into our personalities that may overshadow the genetic input at times.

The oldest argument in favor of a genetic-based personality was probably the one fostered by Hippocrates in ancient Greece, who stated that the human is made up of four "humours" or bodily fluids: phlegm, blood, black bile, and yellow bile. The balance of these humours determined personality and temperament. John Locke, centuries later, insisted that each child was a *tabula rasa*, a blank slate that the environment would fill in.

Tabula rasa: the idea of the mind as an empty slate before receiving any outside impressions

A popular theme among social scientists today is that personality can be explained as basically genetic, with elaboration. The child is born with a significant basic genetic component. Personality is a function of genetics (modifiable and nonmodifiable) + environment + X. This model is probably not so simplistically additive; i.e., the components may come to be involved in varying degrees. But the important aspect about the model is that there is an unknown component, X. There is something intangible. It may be motivational; whatever it is, it is the key to solving the question as to what personality is.

Temperament in Infancy

Temperament in infants and children has been studied in depth by the research team of Thomas, Chess, and Birch. They have come up with some definitive findings.

Perhaps most fundamentally, it has been determined that temperament actually exists on eight or nine separate levels or dimensions. Temperament is not a single, unitary concept, but a multilevel, interactive phenomenon. Thomas, Chess, and Birch indicate that these levels include children's attention span (how long they will attend to a given situation or stimuli); their ease of distractibility; the nature and quality of their mood (belligerent, melancholy); the type and level of stimulation necessary to produce a reaction; the intensity of that reaction; flexibility and adaptability; rhythmicity; and level of activity (Thomas, Chess and Birch, 1968; Thomas and Chess, 1977).

A second major finding of the Thomas, Chess and Birch studies, which have been going on since about 1956, is that there appear to be three temperamental styles present in newborn infants. The three categories are called the easy baby, the slow-to-warm-up baby, and the difficult baby.

The easy babies eat and sleep quite regularly, in a fashion one would consider quite normal. These children are adaptable and display moods that are generally positive, very appropriate, and not disturbing to the parents. These children are, overall, very regular in their development and, put simply, mild babies.

The slow-to-warm-up children have difficulty in adapting to new people and new situations. These children are as the title of the group indicates: they may be a little more cautious in opening up to new people than are the easy babies. They are slower in opening up, but once they do, they are not distinguishable from the group discussed first. Obviously, patient parents are a necessity in the handling of these children. Time is the crucial variable in allowing these children to warm to the world.

The difficult babies are exactly the opposite of the easy babies. They are tyrants; they do not eat or sleep with any cooperation at all; they seem to be in a bad mood most of the time, throwing things and being very fussy. Temper tantrums are triggered at even the mildest of frustrations, and sometimes they occur without any motivation at all.

One problem with these categories is that the data are often reported incompletely, leaving out a few important points. In the Thomas, Chess, and Birch studies, the three categories of temperament we just discussed encompassed only 65 percent of the children studied. The remaining 35 percent was made up of children whose personality-temperament traits were too mixed for any sort of categorization. This is a very important point and points strongly to the idiosyncratic nature of child development.

Of the total number of children studied, those who fell into these three temperamental categories were divided into the following groups: 40 percent fell into the easy category, 10 percent fit into the difficult baby category, and 15 percent fit into the slow-to-warm-up category. There seems to be some indication in these data that there is a genetic component to temperament; for some children, at least, there are ingrained personality characteristics.

Thomas, Chess, and Birch used a longitudinal design and followed these children for a period of time. They found that about 30 percent of the total number of children develop some sort of behavior problems between infancy and adolescence. The group least likely to develop problems over time were the easy babies while the difficult babies were the most likely The researchers found that approximately 70 percent of the difficult babies needed some sort of psychiatric aid as they progressed through their childhood. These studies, while not definitive, are tantalizing and informative in their indications of firmly established personality characteristics that may be a constitutional part of all human beings.

To say that a personality characteristic is genetically based does not mean that the behavior is inevitable or that the child may be doomed to a particular personality or life-style. It does not mean that temperament cannot be changed (Thomas and Chess, 1977).

The Interactional Nature of Temperament

Temperament of children is definitely an interactive phenomenon. Although children's behavior has a genetic component, it is also affected by coming in contact with the environment. This contact creates a level of internal feedback to the individual, internally modifying that person's relationship to the world.

Temperament: disposition; characteristic emotional response

The genetic component appears to come first. It has two parts: one that is distinctly modifiable, and another that is resistant to change. A social being emerges quickly, and both elements of temperament are in relatively constant interaction with people, places, and things; the interaction produces feedback that returns to the modifiable portion of the genetic component, along with feedback that returns and modifies the social reality of each human being.

The interactional nature of temperament is frequently subtle and often overlooked. We often ask, "Now how did Billy come up with that behavior?" New behaviors are very often interactional and spontaneous. Factors such as socioeconomic status may be so significant that the form and shape of the behavior is typical and even predictable. Research is needed to determine whether different temperaments are "caused" by different social, personal, and familial situations.

Do environmental stresses push more children into difficult categories? The answers to these and other questions are not yet complete and may never be. A particularly interesting discussion of temperament in children is offered in the book *A Child's Journey*, by Julius Segal and Herbert Yahres (1978).

RELATIONSHIPS

Biological primacy:
the mother's prominent role in childbirth and infancy

Mother-Infant: The relationship between mother and infant is the one that is talked about the most. The mother plays an obvious role in the conception, gestation, delivery, and postnatal care (particularly feeding) of the human infant. This *biological primacy* has been typically followed in many, if not most, cultures by a *social primacy* in the area of child care as well.

Perhaps the most significant finding in the research on mother-infant relationships is the development of the infant's attachment to the primary caregiver, usually the mother. John Bowlby (1969) is a pioneer in the study of the development of attachment, as well as a pioneer in the study of separation and loss.

The infant makes a special emotional bond with the mother as the result of consistent and hopefully loving care and interaction between the two participants. This attachment typically occurs during the first year of life, probably between the ages of six and eight months. This relationship appears normative in development as well as cross-cultural. Bowlby maintains that this very special emotional relationship is established between the infant and the primary caregiver.

Attachment appears to be person-specific (the caregiver), time-specific (six to eight months of age) and place-specific, in that the infant desires proximity to the attached person. Bowlby states that this early attachment to a mother figure is crucial; if the child is deprived of this special emotional relationship, permanent damage may result. As an ethnologist, Bowlby saw that the infant's attachment to its mother provided the best chance for the infant's survival. Anthropologically, this appears to make sense. In cultures that were nomadic or relatively destitute, an infant that did not attach to the mother for protection, food, and all of the other essentials would surely perish. After this crucial first period, when the infant

Infancy: Personality and Temperament

grows into a mobile child, it is appropriate that he move away from the mother, establish a separate identity, and begin to care for himself.

It is abundantly clear that attachment does occur. It is not clear, however, what range of attachment behaviors is possible. Can attachments be multiple in nature? Can attachments be with the father? The answer to both questions appears to be "yes," but further research is needed to delineate the specifics.

A unique manifestation of the mother-child, or perhaps, the parent-child relationship, is the development of a theory about an exciting relationship between the parent and the child called *bonding*.

Marshall Klaus and John Kennel and their associates at Case Western University in Cleveland have been working to determine what effects, if any, there are from prolonged, early contact between the mother and the neonate. In their research, these people have identified the existence of a highly sensitive period in the neonate, occurring immediately after birth, which may appear to be related to functioning subsequent development. Their hypothesis is that during this sensitive period there needs to be close contact between the infant and mother in order to firmly root the child in the affectional and physical bond.

Mugging for the camera.
ROBERT V. ECKERT, JR., EKM-NEPENTHE.

Attachment behavior later on may be greatly enhanced through the facilitation of close mother-infant contact immediately after birth. During this sensitive period, the traditional hospital practice of separating the baby from the mother would have to be abandoned. The mother and child need time together immediately after birth to help form this most necessary relationship.

In the initial study by Klaus et al., 14 women gave birth in a traditional hospital manner, i.e., they were without any unusual amount of contact with their infants. There were 14 matched (for socioeconomic level, birth histories, and other important variables) women who were allowed an unusual amount of contact with their infants, far exceeding the typical delivery and postpartum procedure. The children who were born were then followed over time by the investigators.

The behavior of the mothers with extended contact was different: they appeared to be less trusting of leaving the baby with another person, there was more comforting behavior when the baby was crying, and they even engaged in more eye contact with their children than did the mothers in the traditional group. Klaus and Kennel found similar differences at one- and two-year intervals after the birth.

This unique relationship has come to be called *bonding*. It implies the existence of a sensitive period immediately after birth that may be crucial in the development of appropriate caregiving behaviors on the part of the mother and in the overall development of the affective and social relationship between the mother and the child. These data also imply that some of the customary hospital procedures may be inappropriate, at least for the people involved.

Father-Infant Relations: The relationship between fathers and infants is very often ignored. Due to anthropological, societal, and psychological reasons, the role of the father has been assumed to be one of instrumental support; he provides for the family, but is traditionally not a part of the expressive network created by the arrival of a new child. Because of this cultural bias, males have rarely been exposed to young children, they have had little contact with children as they themselves reached adulthood, and they are allowed to use this ignorance to avoid the affective responsibility of helping to raise the infant. In fact, we have institutionalized a vast ignorance of birthing and babies on the part of American males. Only recently have men been allowed to get involved; many still choose not to get involved in the birth and care of their own baby.

Infancy: Personality and Temperament

Bottle feeding is one way in which fathers can communicate very effectively with an infant.
ROBERT V. ECKERT, JR., EKM-NEPENTHE.

Contact between fathers and infants appears to be increasing, although we may be engaged in wishful thinking. There is increased involvement among some middle-class males; whether this is generalizing to the remainder of society is a matter of speculation.

The style of communication fathers have with their infants is different from the mothers' style of communication with the infants. Many studies have demonstrated that fathers play more with their infants and roughhouse with them more, leaving the changing and other routine work for the mother. This is unfortunate, because during some of the routine tasks, like changing, there is an important opportunity for communication between the parent and the child. It is not unusual for the infant to prefer to interact with the father precisely because he may be more fun, while the mother may be the only one to slow the child down for changing and other tasks.

It is apparent that when fathers are given the opportunity, supported in the activity, and prepared for it, they can be very effective contributors to the infant's life. If this is the case, the child can grow to understand both parents, and can see both parents in all of their respective roles. Early contact with the father may improve the child's ability to deal with male strangers in his early life and will surely give the child a fuller picture of the real world.

STRANGER ANXIETY

One social behavior on the part of the child that is a direct function of the child's development of relationships with the parents is the gradual development of mistrust of strangers. This wariness is manifested in crying, withdrawal, and seeking the protection and solace of the parent.

The development of stranger anxiety varies across different children. While highly idiosyncratic, stranger anxiety usually begins to appear between the ages of five to eight months. It is possible that it may peak around the end of the first year and begin to decline thereafter, but this is not always the case.

In order to ease the impact of stranger anxiety, children need to see their parents leave, stay with a baby sitter, and then see the parents return. Gradually, through a process like this, children are capable of separating themselves from their parents. Often the first day at nursery school is very difficult because children cannot cope with their parents leaving. In serious cases, it takes months to overcome this fear.

This fear of separation from parent and the fear of strangers are both very real fears. The fear needs to be respected, and it need not become destructive and damaging to the child. Paying attention to the child's situation, using techniques of gradual introduction to new and different situations, and offering consistently high levels of love and affection all aid in dealing with this situation.

A most ironic offshoot of this situation is that sometimes when a young child or infant is separated from the parent, the child protests vigorously. But when the parent returns to pick up the child, the child rejects the parent; it is as if the child is saying, "You left me, now I am angry with you." This is quite possibly true. The child may feel a bit angry at being left and may reject the parent. This creates a strong potential for increased levels of personal parental guilt.

RELATIONSHIP CORRELATES IN INFANCY

There appear to be two very important elements in infants' relationships with people that have much to do with the success of the relationships.

As we mentioned earlier, Erikson has postulated eight stages of man. These stages are actually each a crisis, the resolution of which determines the course of development for the child or adult. Trust-versus-mistrust is the first major dilemma for infants. Adequate resolution of this dilemma implies that children will develop a high degree of trust in their environment; basic needs are being met. An unfavorable outcome would imply the development of fear, mistrust of environmental support, and so on.

While this correlate may be theoretical and speculative, trust in the environment *is* important for the development of infants. The first year of life is important, and it centers around a relationship with significant adults. If these relationships are unsatisfactory, it is unlikely the child's basic underpinnings will be weaker than if there had been a more adequate affectional-effective relationship.

A second major correlate during this period is the second stage of Erikson's developmental paradigm: the major dilemma during the second year of life surrounds the issue of autonomy versus shame and doubt. A favorable outcome here is an adequate level of independence in children. Children not allowed this sort of freedom have doubt in their ability to make independent decisions.

Autonomy and independence need to be balanced with appropriate direction for infants from adults. As is commonly understood, children will frequently take as much rope as they can, whether they can handle it or not.

Summary

1. The emotional makeup of infants is difficult to assess. Infant emotions are probably broad and undifferentiated early, and with time gain focus and purpose. Infants vary widely in the intensity of their emotions and the ways in which they express their emotional feelings.

2. One emotional response that gets much attention from caregivers is smiling. It appears that smiling actually develops in stages, and the initial stage is reflexive, not particularly social or intentional. Very quickly, however, the smile becomes a significant mechanism of communication for the child.

3. Fears are present in children. It was suggested that children in America today may have more fears than their earlier counterparts. This may be due to a more scary society and the influence of intrusive devices like television. Fear has an idiosyncratic base to it, and may be based on real or imaginary occurrences; children may fear people, places, or things, or all three.

4. The development of autonomy is a major developmental task of this period. A major task of this time is to balance all of the "no" messages with an internal sense of independence.

Anger on the part of the child is often a result of the expression of independence. It is expressed by children in a number of ways; e.g., hitting, verbal assault, and so on.

5. There are several important routines present in the infant years, including feeding and sleeping.

6. Personality and temperament were discussed in some detail. Personality obviously has some environmental determination. However, the research of Thomas et al. is indicating that there may be a significant genetic contribution to temperament as well. It appears clear that temperament is an interactional phenomenon.

7. This chapter concluded with a discussion of relationships between mother and infant and father and infant. Biological primacy and social primacy are key cultural issues that determine the role the respective parents will play in the development of their children. Attachment and bonding were the primary dimensions discussed. The result of the formation of relationships appears to be one form or another of stranger anxiety.

Thought Questions

1. Why is the emotional makeup of infants difficult to assess? How do emotions in infancy develop? When we say childhood emotions are idiosyncratic in development and intensity, what do we mean?

2. Trace the developmental nature of the phenomenon of smiling. When does the child appear able to socially smile in a selective fashion? How is smiling a technique of communication for the child? Give examples.

3. Why might children be more fearful in America today than 100 years ago?

4. How might the expression of autonomy on the part of the child be interpreted as a problem by the parent? Of what importance is autonomy to the development of the child?

5. What appear to be the origins of childhood temperament? What implications do your answers to this question have for parenting?

6. Differentiate between attachment and bonding. Can infants bond to their fathers?

Suggested Readings

Brazelton, T. *Infants and Mothers: Differences in Development.* New York: Delacourte Press/Seymour Lawrence, 1969. *One of many books by Brazelton, this work deals with motor development in detail. It concentrates on the first year of life and is directed primarily toward parents. Very readable.*

Klaus, M., and J. Kennel. *Maternal-Infant Bonding.* St. Louis, Mo.: Mosby, 1976. *This is the definitive work in the area of bonding. Klaus and Kennel present a thorough review of the bonding literature.*

Lynn, D. *The Father: His Role in Child Development.* Monterey, Calif.: Brooks/Cole, 1974. *The role of the father is getting more attention in the literature. Lynn's book reviews the father-related literature extensively and presents a refreshing look at the role of the father in child development, in our culture as well as around the world.*

READING

One of the realities of the 1980s relevant to children is the rapidly increasing demand for day care facilities. More and more women are choosing to work, so day care is becoming a reality for more and more children in the United States.

This chapter discussed some of the vital aspects within the parent-child relationship. The importance of these dimensions is greatly underscored when one considers that more and more children are spending a significant portion of their day away from their parents in the presence of other caregivers.

Because of these facts, social scientists have started to do research designed to determine the general and specific effects of day care on children. Arminta Lee Jacobson, writing in *Young Children*, examines the literature on mother-infant interaction. As a result of her research, an illuminating collection of characteristics of competent infant caregivers is presented; this model may serve as a guide for infant day care programs across the country. As more and more young children become involved in day care programs, parents and professionals alike need to be aware of the conditions necessary for the optimal development of children in a healthy and safe environment.

Infant Day Care: Toward a More Human Environment
Arminta Lee Jacobson

What implications for infant caregiving in day care can be drawn from mother-infant interaction research? Few studies have been done on interpersonal caregiving competencies or the effect of discrete caregiving variables on infant development in day care settings. Yet the spiraling increase of out-of-home care for infants demands research attention, both for professionals concerned with infant day care and for parents needing such services. The following discussion examines mother-infant interaction research in order to delineate current areas of exploration and to synthesize findings into a helpful format for administrators, educators, researchers, and others interested in upgrading the quality of infant day care.

Importance of the Primary Caregiver

The importance of the primary caregiver in an infant's development is often overlooked, although several research studies have given evidence of the relationship between early caregiving experiences and competencies in later childhood. In a longitudinal study of environmental determinants related to human competency upon entering school, White and Watts found that ratings of competency of children at age six varied very little from ratings of competency of those children at age three. Further investigation pinpointed the period of 10 to 18 months as the most crucial in determining a child's later competency, especially in the areas of social skills and attitudes.

Yarrow et al. studied the relationship between mothering experiences during the first six months of life and selected intellectual and personal-social characteristics at 10 years of age. For boys, the Wechsler Intelligence Scale for Children IQ and several aspects of a child's relationship to others at 10 years of age were related to variables of maternal behavior at six months of age. In another study, the social environment was shown to be highly significant in influencing infant functioning, independent of dimensions of the inanimate environment.

In a report by Bayley and Schaefer, results of an analysis of data collected in the Berkeley Growth Study between 1928 and 1954 showed maternal and child behaviors to be intercorrelated over an 18-year span of growth. The relationship to maternal behaviors was more significant for boys. Coping capacities of older children were found to be significantly related to early mother-infant interactions in a study by Murphy of 31 children and mothers. These studies and others contribute to the growing recognition of the impact of human relations in the earliest years of development.

Research studies of mother-infant interaction have varied in the type of interrelationships studied as well as in research design, data collection, and analysis. Categories of maternal and infant variables chosen to enter into relationship models have only gross similarities among investigations. Study of interpersonal behavior by its very nature requires direct observation of behavior and is susceptible to subjectivity in measurement. Behavior patterns are often quite complex, and interrelationships not included in the research model are often overlooked. Although infants have a limited repertoire of relationship responses, adult transactions are practically unlimited in variety and complexity. Nevertheless, important information discerned from such studies helps to identify those interrelationship variables which effect optimal development in the early formative years.

Although the mother-infant dyad has been the focus of most research seeking to explain social determinants of infant behavior and development, findings from such research can easily be generalized in terms of appropriate behavior for any adult serving as a primary caregiver of an infant, even for a limited part of the day, as in a day care setting. What is conducive to optimal development in one setting could logically be conceived as appropriate in another setting.

An exception which must be made in generalizing research findings of mother-infant interaction to day care is the area of attachment of infant to caregiver. In a series of ongoing studies of mother-infant relations, Ainsworth and Bell have pinpointed quality of attachment between mother and infant as being related to other aspects of infant and maternal behavior. Mutual attachment of infant and caregiver cannot be assumed in a day care setting. Nature and degree of attachment of primary caregivers and infants in day care have not been investigated and would be difficult to study due to the common instability of such relationships over time and the confounding effects of other adults and infants.

Areas of Adult Influence

Given the limitations of research methodology and generalizations, what evidence from recent research can serve as guidelines for infant day care personnel in providing an optimal human environment for infants?

Infants' physical, emotional, social, and cognitive development is shaped to a great extent by the behaviors of the primary caregivers in relation to the children. Primary caregivers can be conceived of not only as determinants of infants' physical survival but also as social agents against which infants test their growing competencies and conceptions of self and the world. The extent to which adults initiate interactions with or respond to infants, the affective nature of those behaviors, their content and context, all have an influence on infants' developing responses and behaviors and the context within which different facets of their development emerge.

Infant Competence

Personality characteristics, control, involvement, responsiveness, and attachment are some of the many types of maternal influences found to be related to infant development. In a study of the mother-infant dyad, a sequence of relationships between personality characteristics of mother, modes of maternal behavior, and responses and development of the infant was defined. The nine factors resulting from this composite appear to be distributed along a continuum ranging from child-centered to mother-centered maternal functioning. Effective mothers were defined as those whose infants were lovingly responsive to them and accelerated in development. The characteristics these mothers seemed to have in common were: (1) attentive, loving involvement with their infants; (2) high levels of visual and vocal contact; and (3) play involvement. The mothers producing the more accelerated infants were characterized as self-confident and skilled in their caregiving and individualistic in style.

White and Watts found that infants assessed in their study as highly competent had mothers who differed significantly from mothers of infants judged less competent. Mothers of the more competent infants involved themselves in more mother-infant interactions. Even when their infants were as young as 12 to 15 months, these mothers spent more time with "highly intellectual" activities and used interaction techniques which taught or were facilitative in nature. These mothers decreased their use of restrictive techniques as children grew older while mothers of the less competent infants increased their use. From the analysis of attitudes and values of mothers in the study, characteristics related to optimal development of children included a positive attitude toward life in general; enjoyment of infants in the one-to-three-year age range; an acceptance of the incompatibility of infant needs and preservation of possessions and household order; and the willingness to take risks for the sake of infants' curiosity and development.

Ainsworth and Bell studied infants' competence in direct dealing with the physical environment as measured by developmental competence on the Griffiths Scale. Positive relationships were shown between infant competence and maternal factors of sensitivity, acceptance, cooperation, and the amount of floor freedom allowed the infant. Amount of playing with the baby by the mother was also positively correlated with developmental scores of the infant. Frequency of punishment was negatively related to infant competence.

Level and variety of social stimulation provided by a primary caregiver in the home have been found to be positively related to functioning of five-month-old infants. Infant functioning which related significantly to social stimulation included goal-directed behaviors, reaching and grasping, and secondary circular reactions. Adult responses, contingent upon infant distress, were found to be significantly related to goal-directed behavior in the infant.

Other studies exemplify findings which support an optimal level of interaction, reporting a curvilinear relationship between development and degree of attention. In studying the development of coping ability in young children, Murphy found that optimal early mother-infant interactions were characteristized by a balance of attention and autonomy, of interaction and letting the infant alone part of the time. Too much or too little attention, body contact, and talking to infants were found to be not good for infant development. These findings concur with findings which characterize mothers of slow-developing infants as exhibitionist, vigilant, and including both high and low levels of physical contact. Murphy also found that patterns of mothering were related to individual infant temperaments in different ways, indicating the need for flexibility in interaction patterns.

Infant Vocalization

Mother responsiveness and infant vocalization have been examined in several studies. Clarke-Stewart reported a high relation of responsive maternal speech and children's competence in a longitudinal study of infants from 9 to 18 months of age.

Responsive mothers—those who ignore few episodes and respond with little delay—have infants with more variety, subtlety, and clarity of noncrying communication. During the second, third, and fourth quarters of the first year, infants of responsive mothers cried significantly less than infants of unresponsive mothers. Beckwith also reported a positive relationship between mothers' ignoring of infants and frequency of infant crying. Infants who cried little had a wider range of differentiated modes of communication than did infants who cried often. Amount of maternal play behavior has also been found to be positively related to amount of infant vocalization.

Perceptual-Cognitive Development

In the last decade, perceptual-cognitive development of very young children has interested researchers and parents. A study of perceptual-cognitive development in infants 12 weeks of age also stressed the importance of maternal responses which are contingent upon the infant's behavior. Perceptual-cognitive development was found to be moderately related to the overall response of mother to infant's crying and vocalization and the amount of touching, holding, and smiling exhibited by the mother, and highly related to the amount of looking by the mother.

These findings concur with other studies which characterize effective mothers as being very responsive to and involved with their infants.

An investigation of the relationships between maternal behaviors, infant behaviors, and individual differences in infant IQ was made with the same infants at two interviews, during age ranges from 7.2 to 9.7 months and 8.5 to 11.3 months. This study revealed that low maternal verbal and physical contact within the home were significantly related to lower IQ on the Cattell Infant Intelligence Scale. Maternal restriction of infant exploration was found to be related to decreased interest in attaining speech during the last quarter of the first year and was significantly related to lowering of IQ scores.

Clarke-Stewart also reported maternal restrictiveness to be negatively related to scores on the Bayley Scale of Mental Development at 18 months. In this study the Bayley measure was highly correlated with the mother's nonphysical stimulation—looking and talking. Responsiveness of the mother was also related to the child's Bayley score and to the child's speed of processing information, schema development, language, and social and emotional competence. Stimulation by mother to promote achievement has also been found to be related to Cattell IQ scores at six months of age.

Ainsworth and Bell have studied cognitive development in White middle socioeconomic status (SES) infants and Black lower SES infants in terms of development of the concept of object permanence and scores on the Griffiths Development Scale. Infants who had harmonious interactions with mothers sensitive to their signals and who had developed attachment relationships of normal quality tended to develop the concept of person permanence in advance of object permanence. At 8 to 11 months these infants were also advanced in the level of object permanence achieved. Harmonious attachment relationship, as well as floor freedom, were highly related to development scores.

Infant Play Behavior

Another area of consideration is the development of infant play behavior. According to findings by Clarke-Stewart, the best single predictor of play behavior in infants was the amount of stimulation with toys and objects received from the mother at home.

Other researchers have studied quality of investigative behavior and exploratory play and its relation both to maternal behavior and to the quality of infant-mother attachment relationships. They found a significant relationship during the last quarter of the first year between frequent harmonious transactions with the mother, mother responsiveness to infant-initiated interaction, and the infant's greater exploration of toys and advanced behavioral schemata in play.

Social Development

Social development and play appear to be enhanced by some of the same maternal behaviors. In studying relations between the mother's behavior and the quality of the child's attachment, Clarke-Stewart found a number of nonlinear relationships. Optimally securely attached children —those able to use mother as a secure base from which to explore the environment and to which to return periodically at times of stress or for reassurance—were associated with homes where there was not constant exposure to a great number of people and where mothers were socially stimulating, responsive, and affectionate. In particular, the children's attachment was highly related to frequency of maternal social behavior.

In studying the use of mother as a secure base from which to explore, Ainsworth and Bell studied quality of infant attachment in relation to maternal ratings. Infants rated as highest in actively seeking proximity and interaction with mothers all had mothers above the median in sensitivity to infant signals, acceptance, cooperation, and accessibility.

The early manifestation of infant obedience indicates progress in social development. In a study by Stayton, Hogan, and Ainsworth, maternal variables of sensitivity, acceptance, and cooperation were all highly intercorrelated with infants' compliance with commands during the last quarter of the first year. Frequency of verbal commands, frequency of physical intervention, and amount of floor freedom permitted the infant were not found to be related to compliance with commands.

Happiness

An obvious measure of effectiveness in interpersonal relations with infants is the degree to which positive affect or happiness is observed in the infant. Smiling and vocalization and the absence of crying and fretting are seen as evidence of happiness. An infant's expression of happiness has been found to be most closely related to the mother's expression of positive emotions. Mothers who vocalize and smile frequently have been found to have infants who vocalize and smile frequently. The more positive the maternal behaviors, the less frequently the infants fret and cry. Infant fretfulness has been observed to be related to maternal rejection and self-control. Lower levels of infant fretfulness are associated with maternal effectiveness in physical, social, and instrumental behaviors.

Implications for Infant Day Care Workers

Despite the inconsistency of focus and the nebulous nature of desirable maternal behaviors, mother-child interaction studies provide a sound research base for determining desirable caregiving attributes. In view of the empirical evidence on the importance of human interactions to infant development, it is clear that infant day care workers must be highly competent in interpersonal skills for quality caregiving. It is imperative that day care administrators hire and train infant caregivers on the basis of their attitudes and behaviors in interpersonal relations with infants.

Table 1 represents a synthesis of characteristics which provide an optimal human environment for infant caregiving, as generalized from the research findings. The categorization of caregiving behaviors can be used for further development of competency profiles for infant caregivers. Administrators of infant care centers will be most interested in those items helpful to selecting and evaluating infant caregivers; characteristics reflected in Table 1 provide possibilities for structuring interview or evaluation schedules. More specific attention to developmental levels of competence within behavior indexes could lead toward individualized training experiences for infant day care staff.

Further research, directed toward specification, assessment, and integration of infant caregiving behaviors, is needed, since only through delineation of these important human behaviors can child care personnel plan knowledgeably for the optimal care of infants.

Other implications for the placement of caregivers in day care settings come from research findings which highlight cultural, racial, and SES differences in maternal expectations for infants and in mother-infant interaction behaviors. Developmental differences in infants have been associated with caregiver differences. Consideration should be given to placing caregivers in day care settings where their cultural and SES values and expectations are similar to those of the families served.

Recognition of wide variations in caregivers' attitudes, sensitivities, and behaviors should also prompt day care professionals to work cooperatively with parents in setting caregiving goals for infants. Parents can help caregivers define the infant's nature and needs and the kind of environmental variables most effective in maximizing the infant's potential.

The crucial importance of the earliest experiences of life need continual emphasis and investigation. It is hoped that persons responsible for planning day care experiences for infants will be creatively sensitive to ways in which the quality of life for infants can be improved.

Table 1. Characteristics of Competent Infant Caregivers.

Desired Caregiver Characteristics	Cues to Desirable Caregiver Characteristics
I. Personality Factors	
A. Child-centered	1. Attentive and loving to infants. 2. Meets infants' needs before own.
B. Self-confident	1. Relaxed and anxiety free. 2. Skilled in physical care of infants. 3. Individualistic caregiving style.
C. Flexible	1. Uses different styles of caregiving to meet individual needs of infants. 2. Spontaneous and open behavior. 3. Permits increasing freedom of infant with development.
D. Sensitive	1. Understands infants' cues readily. 2. Shows empathy for infants. 3. Acts purposefully in interactions with infants.
II. Attitudes and Values	
A. Displays positive outlook on life	1. Expresses positive affect. 2. No evidence of anger, unhappiness, or depression.
B. Enjoys infants	1. Affectionate to infants. 2. Shows obvious pleasure in involvement with infants.
C. Values infants more than possessions or immaculate appearance	1. Dresses practically and appropriately. 2. Places items not for infants' use out of reach. 3. Reacts to infant destruction or messiness with equanimity. 4. Takes risks with property in order to enhance infant development.
III. Behavior	
A. Interacts appropriately with infants	1. Frequent interactions with infants. 2. Balances interaction with leaving infants alone. 3. Optimum amounts of touching, holding, smiling, and looking. 4. Responds consistently and without delay to infants; is always accessible. 5. Speaks in positive tone of voice. 6. Shows clearly that infants are loved and accepted.
B. Facilitates development	1. Does not punish infants. 2. Plays with infants. 3. Provides stimulation with toys and objects. 4. Permits freedom to explore, including floor freedom. 5. Cooperates with infant-initiated activities and explorations. 6. Provides activities which stimulate achievement or goal orientation. 7. Acts purposefully in an educational role to teach and facilitate learning and development.

UNIT III
THE YOUNG CHILD

© S.P.A.D.E.M., PARIS/V.A.G.A., NEW YORK   PICASSO MUSEUM, BARCELONA, SPAIN.

The Sick Child, by Pablo Picasso.

9

The Young Child: Motor Abilities and Physical Development

Great changes have taken place in the child's body during infancy. Yet at 18 or even 24 months, the child still has the appearance of a baby. The body is short and chubby; the proportions of infancy still dominate. In the next four to five years the child's body changes even more drastically. The arms and legs elongate, the belly flattens, and most of the "baby fat" is shed. The child takes on the appearance of a small adult.

With the increase in size and sturdiness comes more physical strength. The child's mobility increases. This leads to new experiences, first-hand opportunities to manipulate what was formerly forbidden or out of reach. A tremendous amount of practical knowledge about the physical world is acquired, not to mention the social learning that occurs. Now children are allowed, or even sent, out of the parents' sight. Independently, they can investigate things and people of the world. Many pieces of information are gathered purely accidentally; others are discovered through absorbing repetitive experiments.

The first growth spurt is essentially over by age two, but in relation to the child's diminutive size, the growth that occurs is significant. From age two to age seven a child is growing about 2–2½ inches per year, and gaining 5–6 pounds a year. This means that the child

THE COURSE OF PHYSICAL DEVELOPMENT

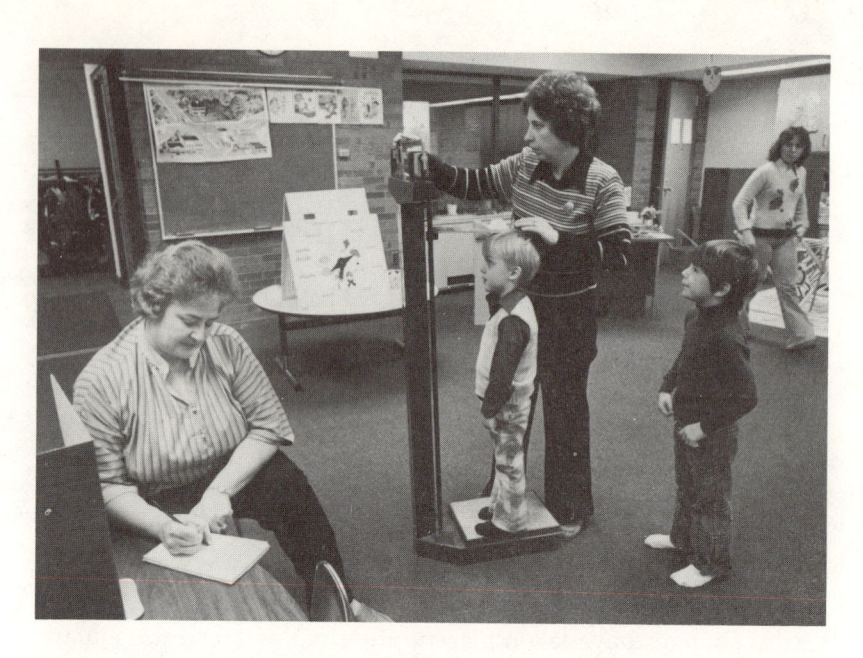

Frequent checks of a child's weight and height help to chart the individual's growth pattern and relate it to broader growth norms.
ROBERT V. ECKERT, JR., EKM-NEPENTHE.

increases in height from about 36 inches to about 48 inches, which is probably two-thirds or more of his total adult height. The seven-year-old measures to midchest on many adults. and is tall enough to see over countertops. In this time, the child's weight will approximately double, from 25–35 to 55–65 pounds. Depending on whether the child is a boy or a girl, this will be one-half to one-third the eventual adult weight. More significant to the child is the fact that adults will carry 30 pounds without complaint, but 60 pounds are usually made to walk.

Most of the increase in weight is due to muscle growth. This is true for boys and girls—with boys tending to be heavier because they have more musculature. Other tissues and skeletal growth make up the rest. For instance, by age six the brain has acquired 90 percent of its total weight. Except for the brain, however, nervous tissue has little weight. This does not mean it is not growing. It is going through an important stage in these years. The nerves are myelinating, a process that is mostly complete by age six, although it continues through adolescence.

Skeletal growth at this time has several aspects. Some bones, like those in the skull, which began as several bones, merge to make

The Young Child: Motor Abilities and Physical Development

one solid bone. In other places, such as in the hand, new cartilage appears and begins to ossify, creating a new bone where none was before. All through the body the bones are lengthening and ossifying, although at six or seven the skeleton still has remarkable elasticity. An active area of skeletal change is the mouth. By three, most children have all 20 of their baby teeth. These serve for several years. Then, usually between ages six and seven, they begin falling out. The permanent teeth that formed in the gums during the first two years and have been waiting there since begin to erupt, taking the place of the baby teeth.

Elasticity: flexibility

Total growth increases are less dramatic than the effect of the changing proportions. The head began very large—one-third the child's total length at birth. By two, the skull's growth is relatively slow. The arms and legs, however, greatly increase in length. By age seven they are 2½ to 3 times their length at birth. The legs will make half the body height. This is also the adult leg-to-height proportion. When we measure the head and trunk, however, the head is still relatively large. Another aspect of physical appearance is that two- and three-year-old children are often knock-kneed. This situation usually corrects itself by age five.

Of course, there is variation among children. Boys tend to be slightly larger and heavier, but only slightly so. Children who are larger than average at age three usually remain larger than average through childhood and into adulthood. When the histories of early adolescent maturers have been examined, researchers have found that they were children who matured early all along the sequence (Tanner, 1970).

To reach such universal statistics researchers must gather information from as wide a sampling as possible. Individual studies are usually from rather small and often narrowly selected groups. They are often conducted with children within a limited age range as well. For instance, one study may be on 106 eight- to ten-year-old black, urban children in Pittsburgh. Another study may be on 48 rural Scottish children between the ages of seven and nine. Some studies do follow the same group of children in their development for several years. Each child's growth is observed from age 3 to 15, for example. Because of the difficulty of keeping track of large numbers of children in our mobile society, these studies usually have a relatively small number of complete histories. People assessing overall growth patterns rework this type of data in several different ways to sort out environmental influences and other variables. After comparing hundreds of cross-cultural examples, they attempt to find general trends in growth that apply to all children.

MORE MOTOR SKILLS

For the infant, just learning to grasp an object successfully was a great achievement. Many months were spent learning to hold the body upright and learning to walk a few steps. These skills are barely mastered at a year and a half. In the years of early childhood that follow, all the basic skills are refined and expanded, so that by six or seven most children move with considerable agility. The improvements in coordination fall into three giant categories: balance, locomotion, and prehension.

Balancing the body is not only a feat in itself, but also affects the way children perform other movements. Visual cues and body sensations must be processed so that children can compensate for the uneven environment. Very young children attempting to walk on a cushion that lies on the floor may find themselves falling over backwards. Older children will know that to step upon the cushion they must bend their knee and lean forward. This control of body posture, which is built intuitively in children through trial and

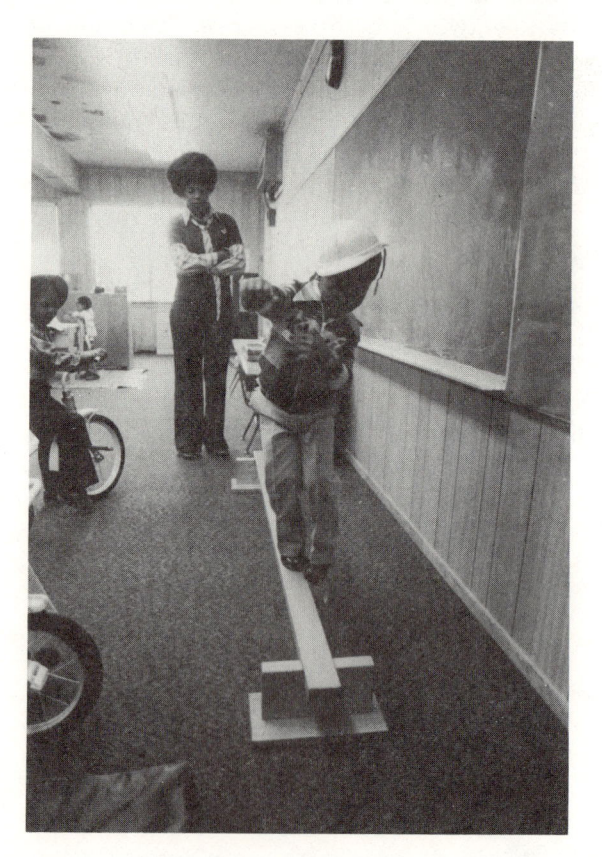

This simple test helps determine a child's balance and muscular coordination.
ROBERT V. ECKERT, JR., EKM-NEPENTHE.

The Young Child: Motor Abilities and Physical Development

error, enables them to perform old skills more gracefully as well as add new ones to their repertoire. Infants usually throw their entire body in the direction of an object they want to grasp. Older children merely reach with one arm. They can do this because they have more strength in their torsos, and also because they have learned that the total body movement is unnecessary.

Infants balance when standing by spreading their legs apart, but young children use pressure from toe and heel. This difference explains why infants cannot stand alone on one foot, much less kick a ball with the other one. However, by age three children can land from a jump on both feet and hold balance through toe pressure and body posture. And by four or five they can both stand on one foot and kick a ball with success.

A child's means of *locomotion* include crawling, walking, climbing up and down steps, hopping, skipping, and running with speed. At 18 months children crawl well, but walk in a stiff-jointed fashion, using the whole sole of their feet. Their balancing technique of shifting their weight from side to side produces the characteristic toddle of toddlerhood. During the second year they begin to flex their knees more and move from heel to toe when they step. They also begin to run now, and climb steps, standing on each one before attempting the next. By age three they will ascend stairs taking steps with alternate feet if they have a railing for support, and by age four they can descend them the same way. Four-year-olds are quite steady at a walk or a run, can turn in midstride, and perform other movements (like carrying a large toy) at the same time. By five children can skip on alternate feet, run with speed, stop quickly, and turn and maneuver adroitly. All the basic body movements are automatic and under voluntary control. Children are now ready to begin combining locomotion with other movements to accomplish such tricks as catching a Frisbee, or kicking a soccer ball on the run (see, for example, Cratty, 1970; Espenschade and Eckert, 1967; Gesell et al., 1974).

Locomotion: methods of moving from place to place

In the area of *prehension* children are already fairly adept, in a general way, by age two. They can feed themselves, undress themselves, open containers, poke objects into small openings, and begin to draw. They still wait to contact objects before they grasp, however. During the third year this visual-grasping coordination improves so that children anticipate the object, and adjust their fingers to a suitable position for grasping the object on contact. They can also release objects smoothly now. Releasing is more difficult than grasping. Most children cannot release beans or marbles with enough control to drop them through the neck of a bottle until they are 2½–3, even though they can pick them up before

Prehension: the act of taking hold and letting go

they are a year old. In practical terms, this causes children to commit clumsy mistakes like spilling a cup of juice immediately after safely setting it on the table. By five, this type of problem is greatly reduced. Five-year-olds can grasp and release quickly and accurately.

In the years between age two and age seven, the trend in motor activities of the hand is simply toward refinement and complexity. Below are some accomplishments of young children during these years, listed roughly in chronological order.

2–3 Picks up blocks easily
     Releases by pressing held object against surface
     Strings beads with large needle
     Can turn pages of book
     Holds crayon with fingers only
     Can unbutton, but not button
     Releases freely, but often inaccurately
     Throws ball with forward thrust of arms and body

4–5 Grasps from side instead of from top
     Holds with thumb and middle finger
     Can brush teeth
     Can tie shoe laces with difficulty
     Builds tall towers of blocks
     Throws ball awkwardly using shoulder and elbow thrust, rotates body
     Begins to form letters for writing
     Can cut with scissors

6–7 Ties shoe laces easily
     Aligns cubes when building tower
     Throws ball with wrist and finger release
     Can form letters for writing
     Can sew with needle and thread
     May be able to jump rope
     May be able to hit ball with bat, paddle, or racket

(Gesell et al., 1946; Gesell et al., 1970)

Young children spend large amounts of time exercising their muscles in physical play. Older children do too, but older children can become absorbed in stationary activities just as often. They have the motor skills to execute intricate tasks that require stillness. Children find this competence around their sixth year. Seven-year-olds are noticeably less impulsive, and more interested in mastery, than five- or six-year-olds.

The Young Child: Motor Abilities and Physical Development

Learning to tie your own shoes is always harder to learn than learning to untie them.
ROBERT V. ECKERT, JR., EKM-NEPENTHE.

SEX DIFFERENCES IN MOTOR DEVELOPMENT

Girls build houses for their dolls and project personal situations, whereas boys build roads, tracks, bridges, tunnels, and use their houses for tanks, airplanes, army trucks and fire engines . . . boys prefer war games to the milder forms of house play (Gesell et al., 1946, p. 82).

Gesell's profile of five-year-old children at play is not as outdated as one might think. It is widely accepted that boys and girls display differences in motor activities. Boys tend to engage in more physical activities, and are slower in acquiring small motor skills. Girls, it is said, develop small motor coordination earlier, leaving gross motor activities behind. They are characteristically more passive, more hesitant to engage in physical interaction. Despite the liberation movements of the seventies, the opinion that these differences are natural to each sex is popularly held today.

The question is, "Are there really sex-related differences in motor development?" and if so, "Why?" The answer to the first question does seem to be "Yes." Young boys and girls often may be found engaging in different motor activities. "Why?" is a more complicated question to answer.

There are biological differences in males and females that may contribute to diverse styles and pace in motor development. Males tend to be more muscular from birth to old age. This has led to the idea that males need more time to exercise these muscles and release the tension in them through aggressive rough-and-tumble play. We expect this type of play from them. However, Roger Brown noted (1965) that physical types overlap considerably between the sexes. There should be just as many muscular girls who would enjoy active play as nonmuscular boys who would prefer more passive games. These girls and boys tend to be ignored in child profiles.

A second biological distinction may be that females are physically more advanced at birth than males, and continue to mature more quickly and steadily. For this reason, they are supposed to be interested in more intricate and innately passive motor activities at an earlier age than boys. One observer proposes that female timidity is the result of earlier development. When infant girls were suddenly placed in a strange setting, "some froze" or began to cry, while "some boys" distracted themselves (and avoided fear) with irrelevant activity. The infant girls' reactions were ascribed to better perception of, and greater sensitivity to, their environment (Kagan, 1971). The author's use of the words "some girls" and "some boys" implies that there may have been little difference overall in the boys' and girls' reactions. When all the major studies of perceptual and physical performance are listed together, more than half show no sex-related variance at all (Maccoby and Jacklin, 1974). As with the muscle argument, early physical maturation may influence motor development, but here too there is undoubtedly considerable diversity between and within the sexes.

Struggling to dress dolls and shoving a truck across the floor utilize distinctly different motor skills. Dressing the doll requires more small motor achievement than truck-pushing, which can be accomplished with gross motor movements. However, children do not choose these pastimes for motor difficulty. They choose them because of their social context. Doll dressing is approved and encouraged feminine behavior. Imitation truck driving is approved masculine behavior. Perhaps boys would engage in passive or more refined motor activities at an earlier age if social expectations encouraged them to do so. Society urges children to improve in motor skills that are appropriate to their sex-role identity. An important reason for differences in motor development, then, is that they are tied more closely to masculinity and femininity (sex roles) than to femaleness or maleness (sex type).

Sex role:
image of certain behaviors being appropriate to each sex

Today, many parents and day care staffs try to create environments that are free of stereotyped sex roles.

> One objective to help reach this goal is "to present both boys and girls in active and quiet play." The image of young children that is commonly portrayed in children's books, toys, and television programs is rigidly defined according to the sex of the child (Langenbach and Neskora, 1977, p. 181).

And recognizing the strong influence that imitation has on sex-role acquisition (Bandura and Walters, 1963, and others), more attention is given to offering children a wider range of acceptable models.

> Another objective . . . is "to present men and women performing a variety of jobs outside the home." It is no wonder that 90 percent of preschool girls say they want to be a teacher, a nurse, or a mommy when they grow up. These are the only roles they see women performing (Langenbach and Neskora, 1977, p. 183).

CHILDREN'S ART

All young children are artists. As soon as children can hold a marker they begin to make pictures. The first efforts are scribbles to the adult world, but immensely satisfying to children. Given an ample supply of paper, they will draw prolifically. Sometimes the page has only one mark across it. No matter. The work is complete; the desired image made. The children work to their own requirements, which seem to follow definite patterns.

There is a characteristic sequence to children's drawing. The first efforts are simply marks. They can be crossed lines, or lines that curve in loops. Then come wild repetitive scribbles. Next come combinations of loops and lines, and finally combined forms like circles under a rectangle to represent a car. At age 2½–3 children begin working on a basic circle form. Spokes or rays are added to make "sun" shapes. Children will represent almost everything with this shape. It can be a face with arms and legs attached, a hand with fingers, a cat, or simply a design with no representational meaning. Rhoda Kellogg (1970) calls this shape the mandala form, and shows with numerous illustrations how children make the world conform to it. She suggests that children work by their own aesthetic principles. They are not trying to represent a person or tree or cat in its individuality, but rather they are fitting the world into a predetermined shape for aesthetic balance.

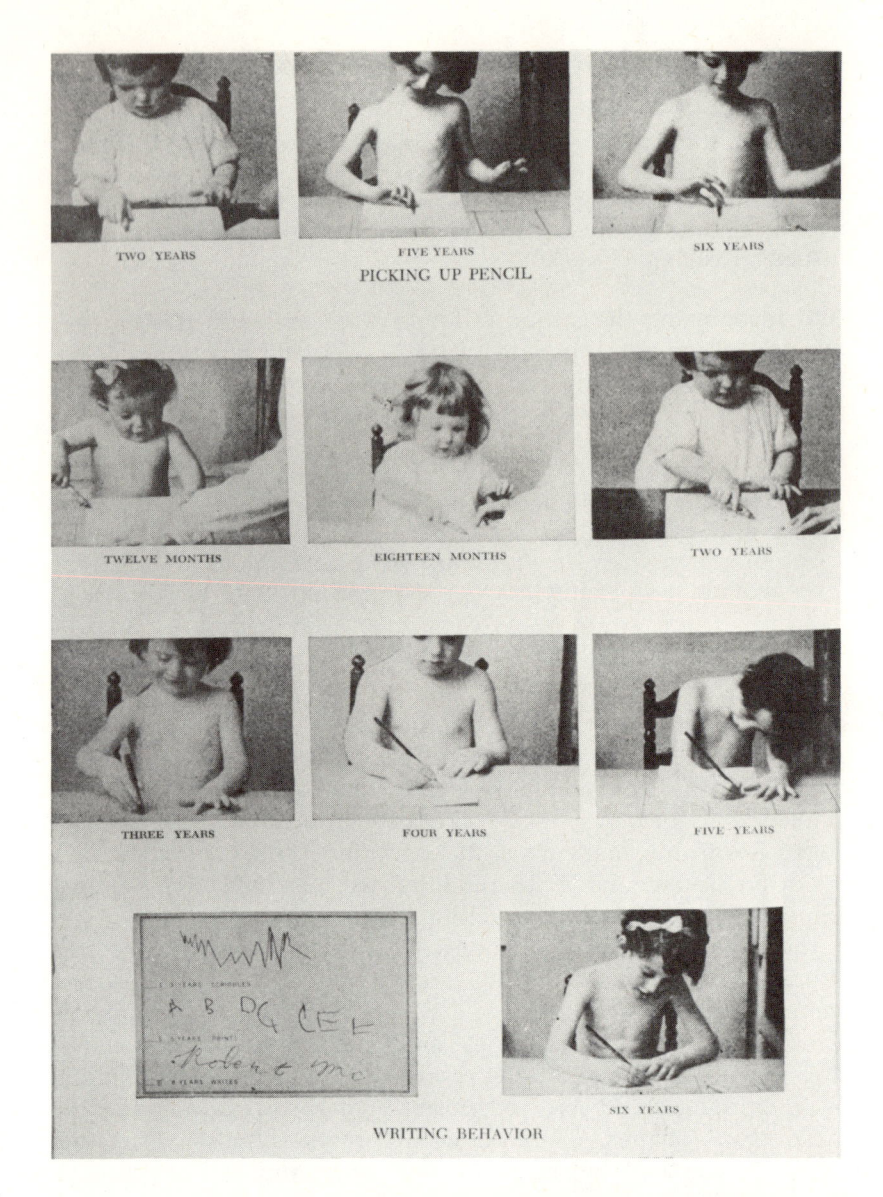

Children's drawing and writing skills at various ages as studied by Arnold Gesell. Plate XVI "Crayon and Writing Behavior" from *The First Five Years of Life* by Arnold Gesell, M.D., et al.
COPYRIGHT © 1940 BY ARNOLD GESELL. REPRINTED BY PERMISSION OF HARPER & ROW, PUBLISHERS, INC.

Unfortunately we do not know what turn children's art would take without outside influences. Inevitably, around age three or four, peers and adults comment on the children's work. This sets adult standards before them. Very early children begin trying to reproduce the world according to cues given by others. Serious efforts toward representation may begin as early as age three. The ability to draw controlled straight lines opens the door to box forms like houses, windows, chairs, and cars. Although at three, models are still imaginary rather than concrete, some representational art is learned simply by imitation. At one day care facility a four-year-old girl drew a highly praised rainbow. At the end of the day each child was bringing home his or her own replica of it.

The child of three or four draws with meager regard for proportion or completeness. People may tower over trees. And often people will be missing an arm or both feet. This usually causes the child no concern. The next person may have four limbs but no mouth. The idea that children "forget" to draw on hands or a mouth because they feel impotent or shy is not consistently supported by any body of evidence. All children forget some features sometimes. By six or seven, however, children are more self-conscious about the accuracy of their pictures. They are aware of the effects of point of view and the distortions of perspective, although they cannot always properly show them.

Drawing serves many functions. It helps develop the small motor movements necessary for forming letter and number symbols. It also seems to help children think about sequences of events, cause and effect, movement, form, and color. Grappling with the solutions for representing three-dimensional forms on a two-dimensional surface is undeniably stimulating to children. Over and over again they work on this intellectual problem. Lastly, it provides a visual accompaniment to innumerable stories, day dreams, and child monologues (Kellogg and O'Dell, 1967; McFee and Degee, 1977; Kellogg, 1970).

PERCEPTION

By their second year, children are quite adept at locating the source of a sound or following a moving object. They have caught the rhythms of their native language, and are wise to the effects of gravity. They can distinguish an approaching object from a receding one. In short, their basic perception skills are fairly developed. They still lack experience, however. They can be tricked easily with illusions, which seem bursting with magic. But all too soon, this wonderful age ends. Five-year-olds are not so gullible, and seven-year-olds enjoy performing the magic tricks that amazed them when they were three and four.

Interacting with the real world increases children's accuracy about perceived phenomena. Children learn to judge distances and speed and what is solid. They learn that balls will come back to you if you throw them against a wall; waterfalls can't be grabbed in your fist. Cognitive changes also affect perception skills. When children begin to think symbolically about a moving object, they can imagine its course of movement. In this way, they develop a sense of sequence and continuity for moving objects. They can anticipate a ball's reappearance after it has rolled behind a chair. And when children begin categorizing, they can organize perceptions, too. Trees are several feet tall; grass only inches high. Studies of children's perception skills show that with each passing year, young children can decipher confusing phenomena more quickly and more accurately.

The most confusing perception problems for children between three and seven are figure rotations, reversals, and mirror images. Four-year-olds seem to be unaware of the change in position, and see each version as a separate image (Gibson, 1969). This is so even though they can easily recognize that a book or a realistic figure (a stuffed animal, toy, or chair) is "upside down." Skills like reading or writing depend on the mastery of figure-change problems. "Ns" can't be placed on their sides or they will be "Zs." A "b" and a "d" and a "p" do not read alike. And a "c" on its side is no letter at all. Children must learn to recognize the letter shape in any position, know which is its "proper" position, and know which letters *are* reversals of others, and how to identify them from contextual clues.

Loss of Sight

The perceptual abilities of children who have lost their vision early in life must come from tactile and aural experience instead. Although at first blind infants explore more timidly than sighted babies, they seem to perceive the world after some physical experience with it very much in the same way. In their drawings, blind children between the ages of five and eight represented chairs, tables, and people with an awareness of spatial orientation, point of view, and perspective that was similar to the awareness of sighted children (Greenburg, 1978). For instance, several children depicted a plate as round when seen from above, but as a squashed ellipse when seen from a side view. When fingers crossed, one "covered" the other. Their sense of rounded shapes is quite accurate. Angular shapes are more difficult for them to draw from tilted

The Young Child: Motor Abilities and Physical Development

points of view, which may or may not mean that they are harder to "see." Drawing a cube poses problems for sighted children, too. Interestingly, blind children do not seem to be confused about reversals, mirror images, and rotation. Unhampered by the changing visual image, they can more easily identify an object in any orientation (McKinney, 1964).

Loss of Hearing

The blind have some sense of "seeing" through their other senses, but the deaf have no similar means to recapture the realm of sound. Except for the vibrations of deep sounds like drums or a large bell, deaf children have no way to know sound. Though other perception skills may be normal or even acute, this area is lost to them. The aspects of life that depend on it are affected, too. The rhythm of language and the social interaction born of talk are lost. Most deaf children are behind in language skills and never reach more than a fourth-grade reading level. The deaf communicate well through sign language, but because so few people know how to use it, deaf children must usually attend special schools and remain apart from the mainstream of society. It is important to remember that deaf children sometimes give the appearance of being slower or less intelligent. This unfortunate mistake has meant a very restricted future for these children. They are not necessarily slower; in fact, they may be very intelligent.

TOILET TRAINING

An important achievement of early childhood is control over the bowels and bladder. All children pass this milestone eventually, but some with more ease than others. It is a stage of physical development like any other—holding a rattle or drawing a circle—but because our society considers elimination a private and unclean activity, this aspect of development attracts more attention. Parents involve themselves, which complicates the child's situation. Also, the child's self-image during this period has long-reaching effects on later behavior and personality. Children who cannot control themselves until late in childhood often face embarrassment and self-recrimination. Freud believed that the "anal" personality resulted from stressful elimination experiences. Such children become unduly interested in neatness, cleanliness, and timing, and overly concerned about controlling situations and exposing the body (see the discussion of Freud's theory in chapter 2).

Toilet training can be a source of parent-child conflict.
ROBERT V. ECKERT, JR., EKM-NEPENTHE.

The age at which children develop voluntary control over the anus and bladder varies. Awareness of the bowels precedes bladder control. Bowel movements tend to be regular before the end of the first year. Children frequently indicate that a movement is about to occur by their behavior or facial expressions, even before they can talk. Bladder control is usually not voluntary until 15–18 months. Full control comes even later. About 75 percent of all three-year-olds stay dry through the day, but 10 percent of all children will wet themselves occasionally (usually at night) throughout childhood (Tanner, 1970).

Though children cannot control themselves in the early years, they can be trained to perform when placed over a pot. One method is to place children on the pot or toilet when it seems they may need to eliminate. After this activity has been repeated successfully several times, children may become conditioned to the event and try to eliminate when on the pot. At the same time they are being conditioned to wearing dry clothes, and learning to avoid the unfamiliar and disagreeable sensation of wetting oneself.

Toilet training follows cultural attitudes toward elimination. The Chinese train their children by the conditioning method. The child is not punished for failure to perform or for mishaps during the day. It is assumed that the parents are responsible for providing the opportunity at the right time. Nor is hurrying the process important (Mead, 1955). American training stems from old European attitudes of cleanliness. Nineteenth-century child-rearing literature warns against retaining the "poisonous matter" in the bowels too long, lest it would be reabsorbed by the body and cause illness. To avoid this, developing habits of cleanliness early in life was stressed. The attitude in American culture has been to train children as early as possible, using disciplinary measures if necessary. One method has been to set children on a pot and make them sit there until something comes out. Failure to perform and accidents are punished with spankings or withdrawal of affection or a privilege. Another method is to have children act out the situation with a doll, talk about keeping dry, and reward successful experiences with treats (Azrin and Foxx, 1974). This method still implies that accidents deserve punishment.

One implication of the American method is that the parents are responsible for when and how well the child is trained. Some parents feel personal pride or failure in their child's performance. Since voluntary sphincter control is maturational, early training tends to take longer than later efforts. It is also frequently less successful. Parents who attempt to train the child early and become anxious or dissatisfied with their child's progress complicate the training with parent-child conflict. Studies have shown that parents using strict, coercive, or punitive methods are less successful than those who are mild and affectionate during the training (Sears, Maccoby, and Levin, 1957).

More people today are toilet training their children at an older age. In 1957 the average age at which toilet training was completed was 18 months (Sears, Maccoby, and Levin, 1957). In 1966 it was 22 months (Heinstein, 1966). Recent literature advises parents to wait until the child is 2–2½ years old before beginning training (Langenbach and Neskora, 1977).

INTERACTIONS BETWEEN PERSONALITY AND MOTOR DEVELOPMENT

We see that motor development does not occur independently of the rest of a child's life. Parental involvement is one kind of influence. Temperament is another. The easygoing child will attempt less than a child driven to mastery, but good-humored children will also be less intimidated by particular task failures. Aggressive children engage in more physical contact, but in ways that cause adults to impose restrictions. Most of these personality influences simply create variety in a universal sequence of development. Sometimes, however, personality developments deeply affect motor activity. Two extremes are autism and hyperactivity.

Child *autism* is a mysterious disorder that is usually considered to be a form of mental illness. Autistic children are extremely withdrawn and passive. They talk little, if at all. They barely relate to any adults or other children, and do not show affection, even to parents. They will focus on inanimate objects and spend long periods of time in tracelike states or performing repetitive movements like rocking back and forth on the floor.

Autistic children are always slow to develop both language and motor skills. Some are considered intelligent; others, retarded. Initially, there does not seem to be any physical reason for this. Their bodies are healthy, but they choose not to use them actively. About one-third of these children can function in society by adulthood. The other two-thirds remain handicapped for life, and must be cared for by others. Some research links autistic behavior to a failure in language acquisition (Rutter, 1975). Other research seems to indicate a connection with neurological imbalances. Psychological profiles on parents are inconsistent. They have found both warm and cold personalities. The only definite statistic on parents is that their average education level is high.

On the other extreme is *hyperactivity*. This behavior disorder is characterized by "... a consistently high level of activity that is manifested in situations where it is clearly inappropriate, and is coupled with an inability to inhibit activity on command" (Ross and Ross, 1976, p. 288).

ISSUE

Hyperactivity in America

The term *hyperactivity* or *hyperkinesis* has become a trade word during the recent past. As late as the middle sixties the word was largely unheard. During the last 10 to 15 years, however, more and more people have become familiar with the phrase.

☐ Basically, hyperactivity refers to uncontrolled or uncontrollable motor activity on the part of children. This sort of behavior is very conspicuous in the elementary classroom, from where most referrals come. An attention span of only a few seconds is accompanied by almost constant motion on the part of the child. Obviously the learning of these children is impaired, as is the classroom atmosphere. Consequently, there is considerable concern over these children, and much time has been spent in trying to understand and control the problem.

☐ There are three common treatment modalities employed:

☐ (1) *Behavior modification*—in this treatment, appropriate behavior on the part of the child is rewarded. Inappropriate behavior is not rewarded or is punished. Elaborate schedules of reinforcement are used in an attempt to get the child to operate in a more normal manner. There have been reports of significant success in the application of this psychological technique.

☐ (2) *Drug therapy*—in many cases, the first thing that is tried is the administration of amphetamine-like drugs to the child. In the case of the hyperactive child, these drugs have a paradoxical effect: they slow the child down. The reasons for this are unknown, but people have offered many possibilities. Perhaps the introduction of methylphenidate (ritalin, the most commonly used drug) stimulates the inhibitory centers of the child; perhaps it stimulates the production of a specific neurotransmitter (norepinephrine) and allows the chemical balance between the neurons to normalize, facilitating normal neural function. Whatever the reason, these drugs work on some children. Children do develop tolerances to these drugs, and larger dosages are required to maintain the same effect.

☐ (3) *Diet therapy*—Dr. Ben Feingold insists that hyperactivity is a form of allergic reaction to certain foods, specifically artificial food colorings and flavors. He has developed a diet to control for these factors. Interestingly, people who have tried the diet report significant levels of success. Apparently, some children respond quite nicely to diet therapy.

☐ It is possible that hyperactive behavior is a normal variant of personality. We as parents, teachers, and doctors may be overreacting to the situation and artificially creating a problem and then treating the problem. It may be that we have become more sophisticated in our perceptive and diagnostic techniques

> and are simply finding more of these problems. Some people insist that hyperactivity among children is a myth (see Shrag and Divoky, for example) while teachers who have had hyperactive children in their classrooms insist that this is a real problem and that the treatment really does make a difference.

PROBLEMS FOR THE YOUNG

Disease

Our society is plagued with several ills that afflict children generation after generation, even though some diseases that were common in the beginning of the twentieth century are almost unknown now. Among these were diphtheria, whooping cough, typhoid fever, scarlet fever, tetanus (lockjaw), polio, and smallpox. Smallpox has been so nearly eradicated on a worldwide basis that doctors do not even vaccinate children against it any more. The chances of dying as a reaction to the vaccine are greater than the chances of contracting the disease during one's life.

Children still "catch" measles and mumps, however, although not as frequently as they did 25 years ago. Mumps is a contagious viral disease that children usually catch between the ages of five and ten years. It brings a fever, headache, earache, and painfully swollen glands in the neck and face. Usually recovery is rapid and complete. Fairly frequently it causes inflammation of the brain (encephalitis) or of the brain membrane (meningitis), but there is usually no permanent damage. Severe cases can cause deafness or sterility in males, but this is rare. Today it can be prevented if a child is vaccinated against it. The vaccine, which has been used since 1967, is usually given to children around 15 months of age.

There are several forms of measles. Rubella (the German measles) is a highly contagious but otherwise mild disease with a rash and low 24-hour fever. Rubella is the same disease discussed earlier that has disastrous implications for pregnant women. Since 1969 there has been a vaccine for it, which is usually given to children around 15 months of age.

The true measles, rubeola, is a more serious illness that lasts about two weeks. Also highly contagious, the disease starts with symptoms similar to those of a bad cold, and a high fever (up to 104°F.). A blotchy rash develops all over the body in a few days. Over the next week and a half the rash fades. The danger of this disease is that complications may arise. About three of every ten cases results in pneumonia. Occasionally encephalitis or death occur. The youngest children are hit the hardest. Since 1963 there has been a vaccine for rubeola, which at first had a significant impact. Until the 1974 the incidence of measles steadily declined, but since then the disease has been coming back.

Why is this happening? Mainly because many children today have not been immunized. Since the incidence of disease declined, many parents and doctors became more casual about immunizing infants and young children. In 1977 about one-third of all children under age fourteen had not been immunized. This exposed them to epidemic situations. Severe cases of measles can cause deafness or blindness, so allowing children to go unprotected is risky. Today the trend of doctors and others in the medical profession is toward stricter observance of immunization schedules (all data taken from DHEW Publication No. (OS) 77-50058, 1977).

Accidents

Accidents have probably always been a major health hazard for children. They seem more important in our modern American society partly because other hazards have been reduced, and partly because our attitudes toward children have changed. Two hundred years ago illness claimed many more young lives.

> The general feeling was, and for a long time remained, that one had several children in order to keep a few . . . People could not allow themselves to become too attached to something that was regarded as a probable loss (Aries, 1962, p. 38).

Today there are many people who have fewer than three children. They trust medical science and social protections. They expect all their children to grow up. Accidents are the only unforeseen catastrophe.

Accidents are primary causes of childhood death in the United States. For children under the age of one, accidents represent the seventh leading cause of death and account for approximately 2.64 percent of the deaths.

Between the ages of 1 and 24, accidents are the most common cause of death. For children one to four years of age, 39.86 percent of all deaths are accident-caused (motor vehicles account for 37.54 percent of those). For children 5 to 14 years, accidents cause 48.9 percent of all deaths (slightly over one-half of them are vehicle related). For young people aged 15 to 24, accidents account for about 52 percent of the deaths, and nearly 70 percent of these are related to motor vehicles. It is interesting to note that the accident death rate for boys is about 2.49 times higher than the accident death rate for girls.

Young children tend to be accident-prone. They need constant supervision for their own safety. Two-year-olds will climb slides and jump off walls, trusting that your arms will catch them (even if you are several yards away). Four-year-olds will run pell-mell without watching the ground before them. In their egocentric exuberance young children forget to look both ways before dashing into a street or out a door. They have no sense of caution, or even of what is dangerous. Imaginary fears convey more danger than fire or motors, which are intrinsically fascinating. Young children are curious and impulsive, and lacking experience. Adults must be the ones to take the responsibility for hiding poisons and sharp implements, for children cannot judge the destructive potential of such items. They are simply exploring the world.

Child Abuse

What could be worse than to be small, weak, and helpless, and caught in a violent environment over which you have no control? This is the plight of the abused child. Child abuse has undoubtedly always existed, but children had no legal rights that protected them until very recently. The problem of battered and neglected children was "discovered" in the 1950s by the press. Since then more and more studies have been made and more and more cases reported every year. In 1962 there were 662 cases reported; in 1968 there were 13,000; in 1975 there were an estimated 60,000 cases; and in 1977 an estimated 1.5 million (Sage, 1975). The truth is that we do not know how many children are severely mistreated by their parents. The difference between corporal punishment, which our society condones, and a beating is sometimes slim. Many cases go unreported. And many children cannot or will not speak out to save themselves.

Who abuses? It can be anyone, for a variety of reasons. A study in Chicago found the highest percentage of abusers reported to them fell in these categories:

Caucasian
female
about 30 years old
husband about 30

Protestant
high school or college graduate
two children (probably boys)
secretary, housewife, or teacher
husband is factory or office worker

(Collins, 1978, p. 44).

But fathers have been the cause of injury, too. And sometimes both parents are responsible. Although it is not necessarily true that people who abuse children are impoverished, stress is a factor. Poverty, marital discord, loneliness, or job anxieties can increase stress.

> My husband and I are separated, and I went to live with my father. . . . I had an abortion during the time I was gone. . . . I found out I was pregnant, and we just decided there was no sense in having a baby. I kind of flipped out and . . . because of my own personal problems with the abortion and the marriage, I was taking it out on Robbie. . . . (Collins, 1978, p. 35, Interview #28).

Another common feature among child abusers is that they themselves were raised in similar conditions. This is especially true of parents who chronically subject their children to severe abuse or neglect. Unhappily, the cycle repeats itself.

Parents sometimes feel the sadness of their situation as much as the children do. They see themselves involving their children in their own problems.

> Making them feel less than nothing because I felt less than nothing. It was like a chain reaction, you know. When I recognized what I was doing, I did feel horrible about it (Collins, p. 35, Interview #7).

These parents can try to help themselves. Others are beyond help. They want to kill their children, or ignore them, because they cannot stand the children acting as children—the yelling, the needs. They feel no affection for their child, only disgust.

> If only they wouldn't fight so much. Then I get sick of them. They never pay any attention to me. I have a headache, they yell just the same (Young, 1964, p. 12).

Who is abused? Again it can be any child, but more often it is a boy. And the most severely injured (including fatalities) are children under four. Children this young are too underdeveloped, weak, or slow to escape beatings or resist adult strength. Broken bones, burns, split lips, welts, deep bruises, internal injuries, lost teeth, concussions, and head injuries are the frequent result of their encounters with adult violence (American Humane Society, 1962).

Sometimes one particular child in a family is singled out for abuse. The other children are treated well, while one child is made the scapegoat for parental resentments.

The long-term effects of abuse on children depend on the type and duration of their abuse. Children who are not fed are labeled *severely neglected*. Their growth may be stunted and they may become mentally retarded from lack of nutrition. *Severely abused* children are those who are badly beaten or otherwise physically tortured. They may develop physical deformities, or disorders that result from head injuries. Both types of experience, neglect and abuse, if endured for very long, usually make it difficult for the

The first recorded case in which the courts were used in the United States to protect a child, Mary Ellen, from physical abuse occurred in 1874 when Henry Bugh and Etta Angell Wheeler convinced a New York court to take the child away from its mother. Mary Ellen at age 9 *(left)* when she appeared in court displayed bruises from a whipping and several gashes from a pair of scissors. The photograph on the right shows her a year later.
AMERICAN HUMANE ASSOCIATION.

child to develop normal social ties or behavior later in life. The chance that they will have behavior problems or abuse their own children is high.

Remedies: What can we do for abused children? In some cases counseling individually or in groups, like Parents Anonymous, provides the insights and support that parents need to control themselves. Sometimes providing financial aid or a job can vastly alter the parent-child relationship. These avenues of help are probably not used enough.

The most common course of action taken when schools, neighbors, or social workers report severe abuse is to remove the child or children from their home and place them with a foster family. This alternative sometimes improves the child's lot, and sometimes it does not. The negative aspect of this remedy is that the experience is dislocating and confusing for the children. They are left in limbo awaiting court hearings and placement. They may be wrenched from their neighborhoods, friends, siblings, relatives, and even social class. Occasionally a foster parent is worse than the original one. In any case, the children must adjust to new surroundings, which is rarely an easy task for anyone. They may wonder for years about what kind of parents could have wanted to hurt or abandon them, and what they did to deserve such treatment. Intellectual and emotional adjustment to foster homes seems to be best when the children receive periodic visits from their biological parents. Because the visits can be tense, they used to be discouraged. However, evidence now shows that in the long run children benefit from these visits psychologically (*Science News*, 1978, p. 101).

Summary

1. The course of physical development in the young child is one of slower rates and less dramatic changes than were present earlier. There are three significant motor abilities that develop during this period: balance, locomotion, and prehension.

2. There are sex differences in motor development. While there are some basic differences between boys and girls, there appears to be a very strong social influence in the determination of the activities children perform. Sometimes these social influences are interpreted as actual physical differences in behavior and development.

3. All young children are artists. Children begin to make marks as soon as they can hold a marker. Drawing serves to improve small muscle coordination and helps children think about sequences of events, shape, form and color.

4. The loss of certain perceptive skills, like vision

and hearing, is crucial to all children, but particularly young children. It is important to make no assumptions concerning the intellectual ability of children who have certain perceptual deficits until adequate ways of assessing their abilities are developed.

5. Some important results of interaction between personality and motor development (and possibly other things) are autism and hyperactivity. Hyperactivity is more common, but both are very important and significant occurrences in today's society. Unfortunately, there are no simple answers to either of the dilemmas.

6. Children's problems include disease (which can usually be controlled, but often is not), accidents (the leading killer of children), and abuse (an epidemic in our society).

Thought Questions

1. Compare the physical development of the young child to the physical development of the infant. What are the differences, if any? Discuss any possible implications for parenting.

2. How does our society condition sex differences into children? Are any of these socialized differences reflected in motor development?

3. What are the advantages of mainstreaming a perceptually disadvantaged child into a regular classroom? How do we underestimate the ability of these children?

4. How do adults shape children's art? Is this necessarily a good thing? How?

5. How do we control child abuse? Why would parents abuse their children?

6. Why don't parents immunize their children? What has happened to many childhood diseases as a result of this indifference?

Suggested Readings

Baker, B.; A. Brightman; L. Heifetz; and D. Murphy. *Steps to Independence: A Skills Training Series for Children with Special Needs.* Champaign, Ill.: Research Press, 1976. *Special need children often present a huge problem for parents and teachers. This book is basically a how-to in terms of dealing with special need children.*

Fontana, V. *Somewhere a Child Is Crying.* New

York: Mentor, 1976. *Child abuse is the topic of this moving and articulate account. This book is a must for students of child development.*

Mussen, P., and N. Eisenberg-Berg. Roots of Caring, Sharing and Helping. San Francisco: W.H. Freeman, 1977. *A section of this book appears as a reading. The book concerns itself with the development of prosocial behavior in children. The biological and cultural dimensions as well as the rule of the mass media are all discussed in terms of children's prosocial behavior.*

READING

As we have stated, our society is plagued with many ills that afflict children generation after generation. Some of the diseases that were common at the beginning of this century are nearly invisible today; other childhood problems have been with us since antiquity and are still present.

Writing in *Parents' Magazine*, Peter Stoler describes the situation of childhood illness in our country today. Stoler devotes considerable time to the issue of avoidable illness in children, as well as providing us with a discussion of the many diseases that strike children.

Early Warning: Signs of Childhood Disease
Peter Stoler

As any parent can attest, childhood is a time of illnesses. "I worry all the time," is a typical parent's confession. "There are so many diseases, so much that can happen to a child."

This attitude is understandable. But it is not always medically sound. Though childhood is not without its risks, it is not the minefield that nervous parents imagine it to be. Many, indeed most, children not only survive it, but thrive. And even more can make the passage from birth to adulthood safely if they—and their parents—would use good sense and take precautions. "Most childhood diseases are either preventable or treatable," says a pediatrician at Columbia Presbyterian Medical Center in New York. "We have the means to deal with most child health problems."

His point is well taken. Before World War II, the so-called "childhood diseases" still posed serious threats to the survival of many American children. Today, the dangers of these diseases have been greatly diminished. Diphtheria, for example, is so rare that some doctors can now go through a lifetime of practice without seeing a single case. Isolation of the organism that causes the disease and the development of a safe, effective vaccine have made this ailment into a medical anachronism.

Other childhood diseases have succumbed to better treatments and increased understanding. Mumps, a viral infection of the salivary glands, still afflicts children (as well as adults), but causes few problems if recognized and treated promptly. Any parent who spots the characteristic chipmunklike cheek swelling produced by the disease need only call a doctor to learn that mumps is easily treated with fluids and aspirin, or acetaminophen. It is only when treatment is delayed that such complications as kidney disease, deafness, involvement of the testicles or ovaries, and, in rare cases, encephalitis can result.

Chicken pox, with characteristic pustules, is even easier to recognize and treat. The disease, while uncomfortable, generally produces no lasting effects. It may, however, make an individual who has had it more susceptible to shingles—a painful nerve inflammation—later in life. Both chicken pox and shingles are caused by the same virus, a still incompletely understood organism called herpes zoster.

Streptococcal infections, illnesses caused by bacteria of the streptococcus family, are another controllable threat. These diseases (such as scarlet fever and the upper-respiratory-tract infection known as "strep throat") can be successfully treated with such antibiotics as penicillin or erythromycin, and usually run their courses without complications. But under no circumstances should these ailments—which can be recognized by, among other signs, the high fevers they produce—be dismissed or taken lightly. Any streptococcal infection can, if untreated, lead to rheumatic fever, a complication that may leave its young victim with permanent heart damage.

The Avoidable Illnesses

Other common diseases that can permanently afflict children are, fortunately, preventable. Measles, for example, is an entirely avoidable disease. Yet today, some fourteen years after the development of a good, effective measles vaccine, thousands of children still contract this ailment. Some of these children suffer permanent damage; the disease can even be fatal. Aspirin, fluids, and rest are usually all that is needed to treat an uncomplicated case of measles, which can be recognized by its characteristic spots and fever; complicated cases may require hospitalization. Penumonia is a major risk associated with measles. Measles encephalitis is another major complication, which can trigger seizures, and can leave a child with permanent brain damage, deafness, and mental retardation.

An equally avoidable disease is German measles or rubella, a mild viral infection that does little damage to those who contract it, but which can have a profound effect on the unborn child of any woman who develops this ailment while pregnant. If rubella occurs during the first month of pregnancy, there is a 50-percent chance that the fetus will have an abnormality such as cataracts, congenital heart disease, deafness, or mental retardation.

A similarly escapable malady is poliomyelitis, which crippled and killed thousands of American children during a 1955 epidemic. The product of a virus that infects nerve fibers and destroys the anterior horn cell (the last cell in the chain of neurons connecting the brain and a particular muscle), polio was once the most justifiably feared of all childhood ailments. But the development, first of a killed-virus vaccine, then of an even more effective vaccine made from live, but attenuated, viruses, has robbed polio of much of its terror. Immunization is almost 100-percent effective against this disease.

But despite the availability of immunization, polio remains a threat. Public-health officials report that many parents now no longer bother to have their children immunized against polio because they believe the disease to have been eliminated. Their misunderstanding could prove fatal. "Polio vaccine is like a life jacket," says an official at the United States Public Health Service's Center for Disease Control (CDC) in Atlanta, Georgia. "Just as a lot of people drown because they have life jackets but don't wear them, a lot of people could still get polio because they haven't bothered to get the vaccines."

His warning is well given and not merely where polio is concerned. According to doctors, there are thousands of children across the country who have never been immunized against polio, measles, or rubella. Reservoirs of the viruses that produce all of these diseases still exist. So, as a result, does the possibility that an epidemic of any—or all—of these ailments could erupt and afflict the unimmunized. "Vaccines exist to prevent some of the most debilitating diseases of childhood," says the man from the CDC. "Any parent whose child gets one of these ailments has no one but himself to blame."

Perils of Infancy

Infectious diseases, however, are not the only threats to a healthy childhood or obstacles to development into a healthy adult. One of the greatest obstacles to a sound childhood is infancy. For nearly 30 years, a small but growing group of doctors has been studying the ways of helping children through their first perilous days and weeks of life. Now their field, called perinatology, has become a recognized medical specialty, and physicians at major medical centers around the country have expanded their old premature nurseries into what amount to fullfledged intensive-care units for the newborn.

Their interest is important, for no period of childhood is as fraught with dangers as its beginning. "The worst time to be alive in your whole life is the first 24 hours," says Dr. Alfred N. Krauss, associate director of the perinatology unit at the New York Hospital–Cornell Medical Center in Manhattan. "The mortality rate for newborns is about twenty per thousand. You don't get a mortality rate like that again until you get into your 60s."

The major problem confronting perinatologists is respiratory-distress syndrome (RDS), or, as it is sometimes called, hyaline membrane disease, a breathing problem that affects premature infants and accounts for half of all neonatal mortality. Krauss and his colleagues deal with this problem by placing the infants whose lungs have not yet fully developed in respirators, to help them breathe until they are able to breathe on their own.

But RDS is not the only problem that perinatologists must deal with to help their tiny patients make it to childhood. Practitioners of this new specialty are also studying and, to the extent possible, treating a wide variety of congenital and genetic problems, many of which can slow or even prevent development. The first thing perinatologists do with their young patients is look for any gross anatomical problems that might be life threatening, such as congenital heart disease or intestinal blockages. They also run a series of tests to identify certain genetic problems, such as phenylketonuria (PKU), a condition that can, if untreated, cause mental and physical retardation. In addition, they run an Apgar test, scoring the newborn infant on such things as motor reactions and muscle tone. "The Apgar score isn't all-revealing," explains Krauss. "But it's a good way of identifying those babies who are having trouble adjusting to being born."

Doctors can, of course, identify many such babies before birth; they are the ones whose mothers have been exposed to diseases, drugs, or other problem-causing conditions during pregnancy. Many other babies are recognized at birth as candidates for perinatology's special treatment. Those who get it benefit enormously. As recently as a decade ago, the mortality rate for babies like those currently under intensive care at Cornell's modern center was as high as 70 percent. Today, it is below 20 percent.

Control and Conquer

For those who make it through infancy, other inborn ailments can still present problems. Little can be done for the child with a serious genetic disease: doctors have yet to learn how to replace the missing genes that cause the production of vital hormones or enzymes. Some children with genetic disease, unfortunately, show no symptoms of their conditions until late in life. But in some children, a common disease—which can cause blindness, kidney problems, and fatal heart and circulatory problems—begins and can be recognized early.

The disease is diabetes—an inability to properly metabolize sugars—which can be traced, scientists believe, to the absence or malfunction of a single gene. Diabetes is incurable, but it can be successfully managed and treated, and the earlier this treatment begins, the better the victim's chances of escaping diabetes' complications. Diabetes cannot be home diagnosed by most parents, but doctors can and should recognize it when they perform the blood-chemistry portion of a child's regular physical examination. And treatment should be begun promptly. Many juvenile diabetics not only learn to take care of themselves, but given an early chance to develop some self-sufficiency, they manage, despite their disease, to lead relatively normal lives.

So do epileptics, who were once shunned and, in some states, even forbidden to marry. This disease—with its characteristic seizures ranging from the brief staring spells of *petit mal* epilepsy to the "falling sickness" of classic *grand mal* epilepsy—can be managed rather well by anticonvulsant drugs. Indeed, there is even some evidence that if treatment is begun early enough, some epileptics will actually outgrow their seizures, while most of those who do not can carry on normal activities as long as they remain on anticonvulsants.

Stalking the "Silent Killer"

Parents whose children are known to suffer from diseases like diabetes and epilepsy may, despite the nature of the ailments themselves, be ironically fortunate. These diseases can be recognized early enough for effective treatment. But there are some children whose life-threatening disease may not be recognized for years. These are the victims of the "silent disease" hypertension, which is not a nervous disorder but a medical term for high blood pressure.

Adult hypertension is one of the most common of all diseases; doctors estimate that in the U.S. alone, somewhere between 23 and 26 million people suffer from it. Many die from it, too. Hypertension is the major cause of the strokes that cripple and kill thousands of Americans each year. It is the major cause of kidney disease, which afflicts thousands more. And it is a contributing factor in most cases of heart disease.

But hypertension is not unique to adults. Doctors increasingly believe that hypertension is in large part hereditary and that it begins, in most of its victims, in childhood. In fact, says Dr.

Maria I. New, program director of Cornell's Pediatric Clinical Research Center, anywhere from 1 to 11 percent of all children may be hypertensive, some dangerously so.

Doctors are still searching for the causes of juvenile hypertension and studying the best drugs for treating this condition, which can be medically controlled in adults. But they do have some ideas. Given the well-established link between hypertension and obesity in adults, doctors are helping overweight hypertensive children to reduce both their weight and their risks. Meanwhile, they are pleading for better recognition of this pervasive problem and urging pediatricians not only to check children's blood pressure, but to do so regularly. "Hypertension is manageable," says Dr. New. "But only if we detect it and begin treating it early enough."

Dr. New's statement can be applied to all childhood ailments. Most childhood ailments do not—or need not—cause problems in later life. But many will if they are not recognized and dealt with early. Pediatricians and the great pediatric centers that are being developed around the country can manage and treat these diseases, and they have been doing so with increasing success, even with such old killers as cancer. But they can't do the job alone. They need help from parents. Parents can help their pediatricians—and their children—by bringing their youngsters in for examinations regularly. They can help even more by bringing their children in quickly. A child who has been acting out of sorts may be suffering from nothing worse than growing pains. But he may also be showing the first signs of something far more serious. Parents without medical training cannot always tell the difference. A good pediatrician can.

The Country School, by Winslow Homer.

10

The Young Child: Cognition and Language Development

As children grow older, we are aware that they *know* more. We can see this from their speech and actions. What we see inspires us to say things like, "Paul isn't a baby any more. He really seems like a *child* now." What is the difference between the way a child seemed two months ago and the way that same child seems to us now? And how did that change come about? Why is the child "older"? Speech and actions are only the outward signs. They reflect what is going on inside. It is how children change inside, how they "think better," that makes them seem older.

Strictly speaking, the word *cognition* means "knowing." Knowing can be as simple as identification (that is a tree), or it can involve evaluation and judgment (I know why he won't let us go). The study of cognition includes these aspects and several more, including problem-solving ability, memory, symbolic representations, and manipulation of symbols. Actual content is not as important as the process of thought, or how we organize bits of information we already possess. The study of cognitive development can be defined as the study of how people acquire knowledge and how they use it.

COGNITIVE DEVELOPMENT: WHAT DOES IT MEAN?

By the end of the sensorimotor period, children recognize that objects have their own existence. The car still exists out in the garage even though you have shut the door. However, children do

PREOPERATIONAL THOUGHT

not seem to think about objects unless they are present or have just disappeared. When they do think about them, they always have their own identity—a car is always a car, a door is always a door.

Symbolism: using an image to represent a real object

An important development during the second year, and usually evident by age two, is the use of *symbolic imagery*. One day it occurs to children that they can use a substitute (a symbol) to represent something *that is not there*. The red plastic car that sits on the rug is not only a red plastic toy, it also *stands for* a real car that runs on real roads. It is a symbol. Even the word *car* may be sufficient to transform a wooden block into a car. This use of language is different from the child's former use of it because the word *car* is not being used to identify a real car or to identify the toy, which also may have been called *car*. Here, the word *car* is being used to stand for the car. If you attach the word to an object, that object is also a car. The use of symbolic imagery marks the beginning of *preoperational thought*.

There are a variety of possible symbolic images. They can be visual or auditory. They can be words or remembered sequences of behavior. They can be conscious or unconscious. A famous example of a behavioral image is Piaget's observation of his daughter Jacqueline at 16 months, 3 days (Piaget's background as a biologist resulted in the precise recordings of a true naturalist). One day his daughter witnessed a boy throwing a tantrum.

> He screamed as he tried to get out of a play-pen and pushed it backward, stamping his feet. J. stood watching him in amazement, never having witnessed such a scene before. The next day she herself screamed in her play-pen and tried to move it, stamping her foot lightly several times in succession (Piaget, 1951).

Because Jacqueline's tantrum so closely resembled the boy's, it was clear that she had retained a mental image of it, and reproduced it. She may not have been conscious that she was copying the boy, but she obviously was. Somehow she remembered the event and could apply the memory. This ability is called *deferred imitation*. It is an important feature of preoperational thought.

A second feature based on this ability is *symbolic play*. Now that children have begun to retain symbolic images of all sorts, they can manipulate them. They are no longer limited by their immediate surroundings. They can pretend that a block is really something else—an apple. They can also pretend that they are doing something with it—cutting it with a knife (a stick)—based on a behavior sequence retained from some earlier situation. At first this sort of

The Young Child: Cognition and Language Development

play is related directly to concrete objects in hand. Later it becomes internalized. It is not unusual to find a young girl (or boy) of five or six sitting alone at some time during the day talking to herself and motioning in the air with her hands and arms. If you listen, you may discover that the "game" or "story" is quite complex. Still, it does not need objects or other people to start it, or to keep it going. This fantasy play does not exclude the more concrete version. Both types of play may continue side by side indefinitely. The appearance of each, however, marks a progression in the development of preoperational thought.

Why does a young child, especially from two to four, engage in so much symbolic play? Piaget felt that there were two reasons. One is that through imitative play children can explore situations mentally and gain information about things that are not present. Unconsciously, they are learning the use and the usefulness of symbols. Later mental development will build on this knowledge. Secondly, children use symbolic play to maintain emotional stability. At this time in their lives adults are pressuring children to conform to social norms. They also encounter many new objects and situations every day. How should they act? And why aren't they allowed to do as they want? Life is confusing and frustrating, but through symbolic play children can arrange the world to suit their wishes. Frustrating situations can be enacted, or relived, with children coming out on top as the winner, and by their own means. A boy might say to himself, "Mom won't let me go out so I will just put her in the closet and fly out the window on my trike." He does it all, in play, and in this way balances emotional reactions to inadequacy with feelings of success. It helps him adjust to reality (Ginsburg and Opper, 1969).

A third feature of preoperational thought is that children can now consciously create *novel responses* to people, objects, and problems. In the sensorimotor period children could only react directly to a stimulus. When responses differed, it was at random or by accident. With the advent of symbolic imagery, children can consider and reflect. Their scope is wider than the immediate surroundings, so they can deal intellectually with numbers, colors, size, shapes, or entire events as they could not do before. They can imagine different possibilities before they act, and then choose among them. Maybe a child at a family party wishes to have some crackers from a bowl. He remembers that the last time he took the whole bowl into his bedroom and was scolded. He sees adults taking just one at a time and going back for more, but this seems an unsatisfyingly slow method. He decides to try taking two or three at a time and coming back for more. This child is not responding automatically, nor is he imitating the adults. His response is considered and new.

These developments, it must be remembered, do not appear suddenly. A child may seem to use an object symbolically one day, and then behave entirely in sensorimotor patterns for the rest of the week. The process is gradual and continues gradually. In fact, the preoperational stage itself is divided into two phases: the *preconceptual phase* (about two to four years), in which the child tends to rely on objects to represent other objects, and the *intuitive phase* (about four to seven years), in which many symbols are internalized, and thought processes involve a wider range of associations and are more complex.

Preconceptual phase: nonsymbolic stage in children's development

Intuitive phase: a stage in which children use symbols to represent objects

Unique Characteristics of Preoperational Thought

The use of symbolic representation greatly advances preoperational children's thinking abilities over what they were before. Their thinking is more flexible. But it is still noticeably different from an adult's. Not only lack of experience makes a young child's view of the world "simplistic." Other characteristics of preoperational thought contribute to this, as well.

Egocentrism: This term means that children see the world from their point of view. They cannot put themselves in another's place. They sincerely believe that what is true for them must be true for others as well. They also relate all things to their own experience. Piaget asked a five-year-old, "Who invented the game of marbles?" The child replied, "My Daddy did" (Piaget, 1926). If you told that same child that you had learned the game from your father too, he would assume that his father had taught yours.

This characteristic is the most important one to keep in mind when considering or dealing with young children. The other characteristics named below are all related to it in some way.

Young children think that the world revolves around them. It is a shock when they realize that the more they know, the more they are expected to take care of themselves. Fortunately, this revelation comes slowly, and adults, if not peers, are indulgent for several more years.

Growing older is a slow process of decentering. Young children are still near the beginning of this process and filled with a sense of their own importance. Their egocentrism affects their perceptions, their reasoning, and their judgments. They believe that many things exist or happen because of them, that decisions by others

The Young Child: Cognition and Language Development

depend on them, and that their desires cause or can change events. Young children are great believers in magic, especially their own magical powers. Many five-year-olds are convinced that traffic lights turn green because, and only because, they use their magic on them.

Centration: Preoperational children often err in their judgments because they tend to center their attention on one aspect of a situation or object; this is called *centration*. Piaget demonstrated this feature through experiments on conservation, which will be discussed later. Anyone who has worked with young children has certainly witnessed it. A girl may think that she is older than her playmate because she is taller. Or she may think that her friend has more cookies to eat because they are more loosely arranged on her plate and take up more room, or that she herself has more because hers are stacked and look higher. In all cases the child fails to consider all the possibilities. Instead she concentrates on one aspect, and bases her judgment on that.

Irreversibility: This trait is closely related to the two already mentioned. Young children have difficulty understanding that certain

Centration: concentration on one aspect of a situation or object and ignoring of other characteristics

Concentration and hand-eye coordination take time to develop in a young child.
ROBERT V. ECKERT, JR., EKM-NEPENTHE.

situations can be reversed and still be the same, or true. For instance, most five- and six-year-olds learning addition consider 2 + 3 and 3 + 2 to be completely different problems. They do not recognize that one is the reverse of the other.

Focusing on States: In preoperational thought, imagery is usually static. When considering a dynamic process, children will focus on states during the process, but will have great difficulty conceptualizing or explaining the transformational stages. If you push over a tower of blocks, and ask a preoperational thinker to draw what happened to the blocks when they fell, he will probably show only a picture of the tower and a picture of the blocks on the ground. He does not seem to retain the visual image of the blocks tumbling through the air as they fell. He would be incapable of explaining, "The tower leaned over further and further until the blocks slipped free and fell to the floor individually, some bouncing and rolling before they came to rest." He has concentrated on the beginning and ending *states,* rather than the *transformation.*

Transductive reasoning: children's thinking in terms of a relationship between two dissimilar, separate items

Transductive Reasoning: If you have never had the pleasure of a leisurely chat with a three- or four-year-old, you should try it. They have a memorable style for explaining the world, backed by a zany logic, that is totally intriguing. Their reasoning, like their language, is somewhat abbreviated, but this is the charm of it. And they consider it quite adequate.

A mature thinker in our culture usually arrives at a conclusion through either *inductive* or *deductive* reasoning. Inductive reasoning starts with a particular item and generalizes (this plant needs water to live, so all plants must need water to live). Deductive reasoning works in the reverse, taking a general statement and applying it to a particular (all plants need water to live, so this plant must need water to live). Furthermore, the mature thinker's thoughts are influenced by accumulated knowledge and a belief in causal relationships.

Piaget found that preoperational thinkers use neither method. Instead they use what he called *transductive* reasoning. They jump from particular to particular, creating a relationship between two separate items. Their conception of causal relations is quite broad. Furthermore, their conclusions are strongly influenced by past routines and immediate desires. Piaget's daughter Lucienne explained one day, "I haven't had my nap, so it isn't afternoon." Naptime is determined (caused) by family routines. Afternoons are a portion of a time sequence. Since they often happened at the same time, Lucienne reasoned that one caused the other.

Effects Upon Basic Concepts

These then are the outstanding characteristics of preoperational thought: symbolic imagery and its uses, egocentrism, centration, irreversibility, static thought, and transductive reasoning. These features are not exclusive to preoperational thought. They may also appear later. They do appear together, however, in young children's minds, and their combined effect produces the norm for preoperational thought. They also affect young children's understanding of certain basic concepts. We have notions about our physical world that are accepted and shared by all in our culture. These are ideas about time, space, quantities, series, and classes (what things group together). Older children and adults utilize these basic concepts every day. Young children, however, struggle to grasp their meaning.

Time is a very difficult concept for young children. Their attention to the immediate present is so absorbing that future prospects and memories of the past both fade into the realm of time-that-is-not-now. Having no foundation, labels for time like an hour ago, yesterday, tomorrow, the other day, next week, and so forth are not clearly understood. Children can remember an event (a state), but have no sense of how long ago it happened. Similarly, children can understand that a pleasurable or feared event will take place in the future, but have no sense of when. A sense of the past precedes a grasp of the future, but even six- and seven-year-olds have trouble placing events that are more than a few days away. Judging a unit of time is also very difficult to impossible. In a book of children's recipes, cooking times were reported as follows:

Popcorn: "It takes about ten hours to get going."
Lemon Pie: "It goes ten hours in the oven and ten in the refrigerator."
Steak: ". . . put it on the stove at 8 degrees or 10 degrees and cook it for four hours."
Apple Pie: "Put it in the oven at 9 degrees for five minutes" (Martel, 1974).

Time is quickly expanded by hunger!

Some aspects of spatial relationships come much more quickly than time, while others seem to be obscured by concepts of time. A sense of immediate *space* and its labels (up, down, over, under, inside, outside, here, there) seems to come quite early. However, even older preoperational children have trouble with relative and comparative space. Left and right is a difficult concept. Imagining the appearance of the room from a different vantage point is difficult. And if it takes longer to walk around Mary Lee's house (because you stop to talk and look at things) than around John's, the child assumes that Mary Lee's is more spacious regardless of the true amount of physical space. Labels for large areas such as towns or states cannot be understood in terms of space. Nor will the preoperational child recognize that you have exactly the same amount of space in your house if you changed or added some walls. The child will tend to focus on immediate stimulation, such as the number or size of the rooms, rather than the total amount of space. However, this last example is more a concern of quantity than of space.

The ability to compare *quantities* relies on two other abilities: the ability to recognize a one-to-one correspondence, and the ability to conserve. A *one-to-one correspondence* is achieved by matching items from each collection that is being compared. If you have five cups and five saucers, you can prove that you have the same number of each by matching one cup with each saucer. If you had six cups, one would be left over and you would know that you had more cups than saucers. You do not need to know how to count to recognize this relationship. If something is left over in one group, there is more of that item. Very young children, however, do not recognize a one-to-one correspondence. They are likely to say that there are more saucers because the saucers are bigger, or prettier, or arranged in a long line. In other words, they center on appearance rather than on amounts. Even older preoperational thinkers, who do recognize the one-to-one correspondence, may judge on appearance. Even after they have told you that there are five saucers and six cups they may say "There are more saucers, because you can see it." They do recognize a one-to-one correspondence, but they don't know what it means. They cannot conserve.

The ability to *conserve* is the ability to recognize that despite changes in form or placement the total amount of whatever you are dealing with remains the same. Piaget devised several experiments using water, clay, wire, counting tokens, weights, and other objects to probe children's understanding of conservation at different ages. In one experiment he filled two identical glasses with the same amounts of water. The child watched as he poured the water from one glass into a taller, narrower glass. Then he asked the child if the amount of water in both glasses was the same. A preoperational child would say there was more in the tall, narrow glass. Then he would pour the water from that glass back into its original glass. Now the preoperational child would say that there was again the same amount of water in both glasses. The child believed that the *amount* of water could change depending on its *shape* (commercial advertisements and packaging techniques try to convince us of the same thing daily). The child responded in the same way when Piaget changed the shape of a ball of clay, bent or snipped a wire, or rearranged tokens on a board. Piaget concluded that preoperational children cannot conserve. Their judgments are distorted because they center on some apparent trait like height or length, and because they cannot reverse processes.

Of course, children are always "practicing" conservation without being aware of it—at tea parties, or in sand boxes with beach buckets. Around the age of six or seven, children usually master conservation of quantity. Curiously, they cannot apply this knowledge to other properties. The ability to conserve weight is not developed until age nine or ten, and children do not understand conservation of volume until eleven or twelve. A typical seven-year-old will have concrete ideas about filling juice glasses, but preoperational ideas about how much the filled glasses weigh. When children have mastered conservation we usually think of them as having left the stage of preoperational thought in that area.

Seriation is an important concept, for it helps us put our world in order. Many decisions depend on our being able to recognize shades of difference—big to little, loud to soft, light to dark. To do this we need to know how to construct a series.

From infancy we are conscious of degree. Babies can differentiate between cooing and loud noises or bright and dark rooms. But these are gross comparisons. It takes many years to develop a sense for fine distinctions. Preoperational children do not yet have a developed sense of progression, but older ones show some awareness of order. In an experiment preoperational children were given a set of sticks and asked to put them in order from shortest to longest. The youngest children tested (four and five years) set them at random. Slightly more developed thinkers put some in order, but finished with random placements. And some children made a staircase arrangement with the tops of the sticks, but disregarded the bottoms (Ginsburg and Opper, 1969).

As you can see, these results are in keeping with preoperational characteristics. The children did not see the transformation between big and little, only single separate sticks. Those who built staircases were working toward a goal (make the sticks go higher), but they centered on tops rather than the entire image. It is evident that preoperational children do not understand the concept of a series.

Another important ability we need for organizing our lives is *classification*. In order to manage all the incoming data we receive daily, we must identify it and sort it. We are glorified mailrooms.

Classification: categorization of objects on the basis of similar characteristics

Here two young children work with their teacher on a problem in classification.
ROBERT V. ECKERT, JR., EKM-NEPENTHE.

What information is necessary today? What is threatening? What is unwanted? What is boring but must be remembered because our brother asked us to find out? We probably classify information from the day we are born, through the functions of organization and adaption. However, it is clear that we can make strange associations in our preoperational years. When asked to group colored chips, a five-year-old might put three reds, two blues, and one yellow in a single pile because "red is my favorite, and there is some blue in my bedroom too, and a little yellow—right here." The child centers on red, but then includes other colors that come to mind through egocentric imaginings unrelated to the task. Mixed assortments are typical with preoperational children.

To the adult mind, classes have certain properties. They are defined either by what is in them *(intension),* or by what should be in them *(extension).* The first property must determine the second. That is, if the class is made up of red objects, that tells you what should be in it (red objects). Classes can be mutually exclusive (no reds with blues). They can also have subclasses (within the red group there may be red triangles and red squares).

By the end of the preoperational period, children can usually classify objects at least by shape and color. They also recognize simple subdivisions. They do not truly comprehend the nature of classes, however, and cannot sort objects if class definitions are too complex.

WHAT TO EXPECT

We cannot overstress how important it is to recognize the numerous variations in development. Equally important is that the development will happen in a particular sequence. Piaget's experiments with Swiss children encouraged him to suggest age norms, but there were many variations in his own data. In similar experiments in Martinique, children made the same progressions, but reached each stage about four years later (Ginsburg and Opper, 1969).

Piaget considered four elements to be responsible for development: *physical maturation, physical experience, social transmissions,* and *equilibration.* Without certain physical developments, children cannot acquire certain experiences. Until your eyes focus you can't be expected to accumulate detailed visual images. Though many physical experiences are shared (chewing food), each person has a unique repertoire. Furthermore, social situations are different in each culture, subculture, and even family. If you come from a culture (or family) that glorifies magic, you may remain in a preoperational stage longer than if you come from a science-oriented culture that encourages you to learn the laws of physics. Lastly, each person struggles to stay sane. This is what Piaget meant by equilibration. You always try to coordinate all you know. You absorb what you can, but ideas or scenes that do not fit your world are "sorted out." You cannot properly assimilate them. You can probably remember learning a new word and then seeing and hearing it everywhere. Probably you had been exposed to it many times, but since it held no meaning, it was "sorted out."

Many people have the impression that at two or at seven children *should* be showing certain behavior, or that with tutoring they can always become smarter. Piaget's only "should" is that children should have explored thoroughly the preoperational realm of any topic before they should show concrete behavior there. "How can we accelerate development?" is what Piaget calls "the American question" (Elkind, 1976). He believes that children can develop only as fast as they will adapt and organize. "Pushing" children does not work. They cannot accommodate information that is too complex. It is sorted out, or they learn the forms by rote but do not and cannot understand until they have reached a proper stage of development.

Social attitudes are very important. Providing specific social and physical experiences gives children the opportunity to experiment and make advances in that field. Certainly children learn skills that are necessary in their culture before they learn others. If operating a calculator is a familiar experience in your culture but rowing a boat is not, you may learn to operate the calculator at age 6 and to row at 20. In another culture this would be an eccentric or even disastrous development. At age six you would be a misfit—adept in an unnecessary skill (at least for your age) and retarded in rowing. Or, closer to home, if conning your friends out of 25 cents is more important than knowing that $1.00 \div 4 = .25$ (decimals and all), you may do better at the candy counter than in school.

In dealing with children who seem deficient in their cognitive development, it is wise to observe carefully. Children are mobile and curious creatures. A deficiency in one area may mean a wealth of knowledge elsewhere. Different or inaccurate information may have set the child behind standards of our culture. This problem can often be overcome in time. Some simply develop more slowly than others although they are just as competent in the end.

ACCURATE PERCEPTIONS

Preoperational children will tend to make many inaccurate judgments. Their perceptions are often distorted by personal interest and lack of experience. They have difficulty separating fantasy from reality. They can also easily arrive at false conclusions because the material is too complex to assimilate or accommodate, but too stimulating to ignore. Instead it is organized in a distorted form. Children with many inaccurate or unrealistic perceptions will be slowed down in their development as they try to keep their equilibrium. They are living off balance.

How do children acquire an overload of inaccurate perceptions? They may be exposed too often to complex situations. They may be too restricted, and discouraged from experimenting. They may have no one to explain peculiar experiences they encounter or see on television. They may be given false social cues (parents who smile at inappropriate moments—during a fight or when the child is in danger). There are children who seem to accumulate an unusual number of false conceptions. Unless they are provided with experiences that build accurate perceptions, these children will always have difficulty functioning.

WATCHING CHILDREN

Piaget's theories stem from his early work in Paris, where he developed standardized tests on reasoning abilities. Piaget found himself interested in the children who made wrong responses. What were they thinking? Piaget's observations, experiments, and theories are popular, in part, because they reflect such common sense. His work also reflects personal interests. His experiments are oriented toward mathematical principles and physical laws. There are many topics he did not explore. Why *do* some children develop more quickly than others? Who most influences a child's development: the child? parent? society? Why do children think concretely about one thing and preoperationally about another? How can you know whether a child is a mature thinker or merely a well-socialized rote learner? How does an original thinker respond on these experiments? What about Mozart, who composed a symphony at age four? We, like Piaget, might do best to question, "Why doesn't this child fit the theory?"

ASSESSMENT OF INTELLIGENCE

Young children in America today receive more attention than they ever have had before. Not the least of parental concerns is the question, "Is my child smart?" By this most parents mean, "Am I raising an intelligent child?" It is interesting that the question is not usually raised until children enter school. Now, with the rise of another institution, day care, and the prevailing attitude that the young child's environment will influence later achievement, children are under scrutiny at earlier and earlier ages.

Intelligence:
the ability to learn or understand

Testing Young Children

Children display memory and intelligent behavior from infancy. But how do we test it? The Stanford-Binet test covers ages 2 to 20. There are several other intelligence tests, usually covering only a specific age group, that are widely used. Especially well known are Bayley's test for infants, the Merrill-Palmer and the Minnesota Scales for young children, and the Weschler Intelligence Scale for Children (WISC) for the older range. There are also Weschler tests for 4–6½ year olds and for adults.

Infant tests depend on sensorimotor developments. In the first year, blinking at shadows, following an object with the eyes, seizing objects, and showing exploring activity are some of the items tested. In the second year, children are tested on items such as imitating adult activities, using a stick to obtain a toy placed out of

Testing in an elementary school.
ROBERT V. ECKERT, JR., EKM-NEPENTHE.

reach, imitating words, naming objects, and building block formations (Bayley, 1969).

The tests become more verbally oriented as the children grow older. They also include more and more items that require logical reasoning and good memory. Besides motor tasks like throwing a ball, 3–6½-year-olds are asked to name objects, parts of the body, colors, and missing items in a picture (like a man with no nose). They must draw lines, circles, and other shapes, assemble puzzles, and fold paper (Anastasi, 1968). Many children begin taking the more formal intelligence tests at age five, six, or seven. Although the WISC and some other tests include performance tasks, the tests for older children are predominantly paper and pencil affairs that rely heavily on verbal abilities, especially reading skills. The Binet test, for instance, is primarily verbal in character.

Predicting Intelligence

The original Binet test, called the Binet-Simon test, was never meant to be a yardstick for intelligence. Its purpose was to separate subnormal children from those who would be likely to perform with average ability or better in French schools. The test does do this (Escalona, 1954). Children with physical or social disabilities can be identified at an early age. Beyond this useful task, intelligence tests of young children do not prove helpful in predicting later intelligence or school performance. Children's short attention spans, fatigue, and lack of motivation for completing the tests are major reasons why young children produce inconsistent scores. A child's IQ may fluctuate 15–25 points between three and seven years of age. Between the ages of 3 and 12 a child's score may change as much as 60 points.

ISSUE

IQ: A Valid Social Measure?

An IQ is a ratio between a child's mental age (determined by some test) and the child's chronological age. This ratio yields a number; the average IQ in America is said to be 100. People over 130–140 are considered geniuses and those whose IQs are below 60–70 are predicted to have trouble in school and in life in general.

☐ The tests to determine maturational age vary considerably. Some tests are mainly verbal, yielding a verbal intelligence score. Other tests try to measure specific skills like spatial or mathematical. It has been indicated that if IQ tests are given to children over the age of five, they are quite predictive of children's success in school. Perhaps the safest thing we can say is that there is considerable debate over IQ tests and what intelligence is and where it comes from.

☐ Some people have assumed that an IQ test is as accurate and specific as tests of physical skills. This could not be further from the truth. IQ tests were designed so that people could make simple comparisons between a particular child and a group of children of similar age and background on whom the test was standardized. This basic purpose has been ignored in some of the applications of the tests.

☐ Is IQ a result of heredity (nature) or environment (nurture)? Arthur Jensen, in a classic piece in the *Harvard Educational Review* (1969), stated that about 80 percent of the differences in IQ performance can be traced to differences in genetic background. This was interpreted in some interesting ways. Since blacks invariably score lower on certain IQ tests, it was assumed according to Jensen's logic that blacks are genetically inferior. To counter this assumption, Adrian Dove created the Dove Counterbalance General Intelligence Test, which was made up of questions relevant to the social milieu of blacks. White respondents have a great deal of difficulty with the test. With this and other similar attempts, people have tried to show the cultural bias inherent in tests of this type.

☐ IQ tests are not necessarily tests of creativity; nor are they tests of productive thinking. They appear to be tests of experience. In this sense, they are somewhat counterproductive.

☐ Segal and Yahraes (1978) advise considerable caution when attempting to use IQ tests. In fact, they state that some people's interpretations of IQ scores have led to a perpetuation of racism in this country. We must consider the following factors:

(1) There are differences between people on the basis of social surroundings, some of which may contribute to IQ differences.

(2) There are significant shortcomings and cultural bias in IQ tests.

(3) There are significant individual differences in motivation and behavior while taking tests.

(4) What are the residual effects of prejudice? Can we estimate them? (pp. 277–278).

☐ There appear to be several important issues. First, IQ, intelligence, or whatever the term used, is a function of the complex interaction of several factors: genetic makeup, environmental opportunities, family environment, school encouragement, and so on. Secondly, there is a great amount of variability in the IQ measure. It can change from testing situation to testing situation.

☐ On the basis of these factors, we must be wary of making important life-span decisions on the basis of an IQ score. It may be nonpredictive, inaccurate, and very misleading.

LANGUAGE DEVELOPMENT

In the period of young childhood, roughly two to seven, children's language blooms from basic abbreviated statements to complicated expressions. Their vocabulary increases from 200–300 words to several thousand words, and sentence structure develops from simple utterances of a few words to complete, well-conceived sentences. The progression of development, with numerous variations, is fairly regular, as many well-documented studies show. How children come to understand language elements and communicate with them is a mystery that may never be unraveled.

Before the mid-1950s theories of language development were usually based on personal observations of one or two children (usually the author's own), or more objective surveys of a cross section of the population. The theories were behavioral and proposed that children learn language by copying adults, responding to reinforcements (like smiles or attention), associating words with objects, and rote learning. The study of language development centered around the number and type of words children were likely to understand or use at any particular age, and the length of the sentences they spoke.

In 1957 Noam Chomsky published an influential book, *Syntactic Structures*, in which he proposed that all children have a sense of grammar from birth. A child will not make sentences like "I dogged," or "See swims." All children recognize "dog" as a noun, and "see" as a verb. According to his theory, all people have a mental faculty called a language acquisition device—LAD. Working automatically, like an instinct, this faculty allows children to process the language they hear, internalize the linguistic rules of their culture, and construct appropriate communications. All statements begin with a *kernel sentence* that is formed into the eventual spoken sentence by making several grammatical *transformations*. Examples of grammatical transformations would be replacing a noun with a pronoun, changing the tense of a verb, or adding modifying words or phrases. The kernel sentence "Jenny find ball," might become "Yesterday, I was finding golf balls near the back fence." The *deep structure* of every sentence is the kernel sentence. The meaning of ambiguous sentences like "John is wonderful to teach," or "Visiting relatives can be difficult," depends on the deep structure of the sentence.

Chomsky's theory significantly changed the focus of language studies. Rather than concentrating on overt characteristics like production and performance, more recent studies have explored what children mean by their one-, two-, or three-word statements, and how they use grammar to create sentences they have never heard before.

Vocabulary Growth

The number of words a child knows at any age is a unique feature of that child. It is certain that all children can understand more words than they use in everyday speech. The ability to speak intelligibly words they know is subject to the rate of their physical development—especially of the auditory system and motor control of the lips and tongue—and to social stimulation. Most studies work with expressive vocabulary, partly because it is almost impossible to gauge the extent of a child's receptive vocabulary.

Estimates vary, but according to Eric Lenneburg (1967) the average expressive vocabulary of a one-year-old is three words; of a two-year-old, 272 words; and of a three-year-old, 896 words. Roger Brown (1973) suggests that a two-year-old understands around 250 words but spontaneously uses only 40 words or so most of the time, which are combined into a huge variety of utterances. It has been noted that growth is erratic. Children will use a new word for a few days or weeks and then retire it for several months before reintegrating it into their working vocabulary (Bloom, 1970). Average growth is indicated on the charts opposite.

MLU—Mean Length of Utterance

By age two, most children are making two-word statements. At first these may sound like two one-word statements, each word having equal emphasis. "Car. Ride." Later the two words are uttered as a phrase and are given intonation to denote questions, surprise, interest, etc. Sometimes a third word is added to a two-word phrase—"This sock. Dirty."—as the child works to expand the statement (Bloom, 1970).

By three years of age, most children have moved into three-word expressions, at least, if not much longer ones. Even late bloomers, who may never have spoken a word until age three, will often start with three-word sentences. And a verbal three-year-old is quite capable of generating a sentence like, "Why do you have a apple dere?" Sentence length increases each year. By age six, most children can express themselves in complete, and sometimes long and complicated, sentences.

Grammar, Syntax, and Semantics

As soon as children use two words together, it is apparent that they are aware of grammar and that they use syntax. A regularity of word order appears. It is not necessarily adult word order, but it places words so that they make sense. This orderliness has been observed in children of every language that has been studied.

Pivotal Grammar: In the early 1960s Martin Braine (1963) suggested that children in the two-word stage used what he called *pivotal grammar*. Instead of thing words (nouns) or action words (verbs), children used pivot words and open words. All words were either pivots or open words. The two constructions a child might use were:

Pivotal grammar: a theory about children's language at the two-word stage

See doggie		Baby go
See man	or	Man go
See boat		Horsie go

Some pivots were verbs, some were adjectives *(big)*, some were adverbs *(more)*. Some pivots appeared only in the first position: "That man," "That horsie"—never "Man that." However, pivot words were not supposed to appear together or as open words. Braine's theory did not explain words that children can and do place in both positions, as in "More book" and "Want more."

Semantic Grammar: The Grammar of Meaning: Roger Brown (1973) criticized this narrow but popular explanation, noting that children do use a pivotal strategy, but also use other constructions. Pivotal grammar did not consider children's intentions as they spoke. Brown and others included the psychosocial aspects of speech. Observing the setting and what the child was trying to communicate gave new insights on how the child was using language.

Ann Bloom noticed that children used the same two-word statement to express different ideas. Her subject, Kathryn, said, "Mommy sock," once to indicate *possession*—"That's Mommy's sock," and another time to indicate an *agent-object* relationship—"Mommy, put on my sock." Bloom identified three more relationships in two-word expressions:

> Location—"Sweater chair." (The sweater is on the chair.)
> Attribute-object—"Party hat." (This is a party hat.)
> Object-object—"Umbrella boot." (Mommy is carrying an umbrella and a pair of boots.) (Bloom, 1970).

Bloom felt that there were even more possible relationships since some expressions, though perfectly sensible, did not fit these categories conveniently (Bloom, 1970). When we consider what children are trying to say, and what they mean by what they say, it seems that it is impossible to pin down the exact number of possible constructions they can form.

Eric Lenneburg, an advocate of semantic grammar, theorized that the semantic field of a word is "very large and coarse" when children first begin to speak. As they learn new words and how to use them, they can make more precise statements. The semantic field of each word shrinks in proportion to children's ability to use many words together.

> No longer does the word *mommy* cover in a vague way every aspect of the family provider, nor the word *sock* the entire realm of sock topics (Lenneburg, 1975).

So we can suppose that as children practice with language, the intended meaning of each communication becomes more specific. Furthermore, their usage seems to be based on adult grammar and syntax, even though these first statements are generalized and imperfect.

Three Words, and More

Children make a quantum leap with language when they begin speaking in three-word sentences. Though the statements are still abbreviated (this is sometimes called telegraphic speech), it is clear that children understand how to make a grammatical relationship between two elements—"Jenny get cup," "Jenny under Daddy," "This big tree."

At first children center on the words that convey the main ideas of the sentence: the subject, main verb, and object. Slowly they expand on these ideas with modifiers. Many functional words like articles *(a, an, the)*, prepositions *(in, on, at)*, or auxiliary verbs *(would go, will go, might go)* are ignored by children in their early speech, but are added in time. This is probably because they are not necessary for communication at first. When an adult says, "That sure is a big dog under Dave's couch," a three-year-old needs to hear only "Dog couch," or "Big dog under couch," to grasp the situation. If that child speaks those short sentences, others nearby usually understand him. But, as children grow, adults spend less effort guessing meanings, and expert more clarity from the child.

Grammatical Errors: The clearest indication that children are not simply copying adults, but are acting upon internalized rules of some sort, as Chomsky proposed, is in their use of past tense verbs. Many irregular verbs, like *to be, to have, to see,* or *to feel,* are used often and heard frequently in everyday speech. At first children *do* copy adult usage. Later, they drop this correct usage and substitute regular past tense formations—"we goed," for "we went," or "we seed," for "we saw." Almost all children go through a stage of using these incorrect forms of speech despite the fact that they do not hear adults using them. After some time, they again recognize and use the correct forms.

Overgeneralization: incorrect application of grammatical rules

LANGUAGE AND SOCIAL SETTINGS

Because people from different social classes have different attitudes toward child rearing and personal interactions, social background affects language learning. It has been found that lower-class adults do not speak to their children as often or with as large a vocabulary as middle-class adults (Tulkin and Kagan, 1972). The middle-class mother uses more complex language. As she goes about her daily tasks talking aloud, explaining phenomena, reading signs, she is modeling language skills for her child. As the child grows older, the mother uses more advanced constructions (Reichle, Longhurst, and Stepanich, 1976). Without any special schooling, her child will be more familiar with a wider range of verbal skills than the lower-class child.

In an experiment, lower-class mothers were asked to read to their children for ten minutes every day. When compared to a control group, the children in this experiment showed improved verbal skills as a result of this direct verbal attention. Other studies have also indicated that children whose parents read or talk to them frequently have better language skills than other children. Older children and "caretakers" also provide modeling and stimulation.

Language is affected by social class and reflects social class. Children will learn the language patterns they hear in their immediate community. Contrary to many people's beliefs, nonstandard English is not deficient in expressiveness, but is simply different. It has its own well-kept rules, and although vocabulary and speech forms are sometimes more limited, both children and adults can convey their ideas fully to those who speak their language (Labov et al., 1967). Nevertheless, standard English is the yardstick of respectability. Many children from ghettos or rural areas with strong dialects are pressured by parents or schools to learn it. For them the effort must be a conscious one, like learning a foreign language.

LANGUAGE AND COGNITION

Do we need language to learn to think? Or is language just a means of expressing our thoughts? Piaget took the second view, suggesting that language is not necessary for thinking. It is true that deaf children show regular cognitive development even though language abilities develop late (Furth, 1966). Piaget also thought that words can facilitate thinking. If you know the word *yogurt* you can think about it in many ways without having the yogurt itself in front of you. Many psychologists believe that language plays a large role in the process of thinking, especially in abstract thought. With an abstract vocabulary we can think about a large number of ideas conveniently.

Another question is: how does language control thought? If we call a tyrant and yogurt by the same name, how does this affect our conception of what a tyrant is or what yogurt is? Some people believe that language shapes mental activity, and that people who speak different languages also think differently. Eskimos have over a dozen names for snow—ones for fresh snow, half-melted snow, dry snow, sticky snow, wet snow. Eskimo children will have many more ideas, and more precise ones, about snow than children from Los Angeles who may never have seen any. And if Californians have not learned the word for snow, can they think about it? How do we think about things for which we have no name?

Summary

1. The Piagetian stage that characterizes this point in child development is called preoperational thought. It is characterized by symbolic imagery, egocentrism, centration, and transductive reasoning, among other things.

2. Some of the basic operations present in this stage include conservation, seriation and classification. Piaget feels that cognitive development is a function of physical maturation, physical experience, social transmissions, and equilibration.

3. Assessing the intelligence of children is a formidable task. If intelligence is defined as the ability to learn, few tests of intelligence assess that ability. They measure what has been learned, and of course, they say little about the creativity of the child.

4. Language development goes through a developmental sequence, like most things in child development. The first stage is crying, then babbling, one-word, two-word, three-word and eventually complete sentences. There are many theories of the development and use of grammar and syntax by young children. The development of language is dependent upon the familial and social setting the child matures in.

Thought Questions

1. What is the importance of the development of symbolic thought? What are the other elements of preoperational thought?

2. What is the utility of intelligence tests? How might we be able to make better tests of intelligence? How do *you* define intelligence?

3. How is language development affected by the environment of the child? How can we enhance the language development of the child?

Suggested Readings

Anastasi, A. *Psychological Testing.* New York: Macmillan, 1976. *Comprehensive review of psychological testing and children. While not a book for everyone, it provides a broad overview for the student with special interests.*

Block, N.J., and G. Dworkin, eds. *The I.Q. Controversy.* New York: Pantheon, 1976. *The title of this book is self-explanatory. The social and political implications of IQ testing are discussed in detail. IQ and race are stressed by the authors.*

Dale, P.S. *Language Development: Structure and Function.* 2nd ed. Hinsdale, Ill.: Dryden Press, 1976. *Dale gives to us a good overview of language development. It is distinctive in its comprehensiveness.*

Lowenfeld, V., and W. Brittain. *Creative and Mental Growth.* 6th ed. New York: Macmillan, 1975. *Children's art is the focal point of this work. In this description of the nature of children's art, the authors point to a more sophisticated readership.*

READING

Cognitive development in children occurs within several contexts in our society. Among the predominant sources of intellectual development of the child are the family, the peer group, and the school. These are all in addition to the genetic potential of the individual child.

Recently the educational system has come under close scrutiny. Many people are very concerned about children not possessing basic skills when they leave the school system. This accountab lity argument has resulted in a "back to basics" movement within most school districts within the United States. The school system has attempted to respond to a perceived need.

A need that the school system seems to have trouble responding to is serving gifted children. It is one thing to create a curriculum that will teach all of the fundamentals to children; it is quite another to create a curriculum that will educate and challenge the gifted child. These very intelligent children are often caught in an inflexible system that cannot possibly meet their needs.

Gene Maeroff indicates in the following reading that gifted children are "the stepchildren" of the school systems. Gifted children are qualitatively different from other children, and need to have their special needs met just as any other group of unique children does, like the retarded, the learning disabled, and so on. Maeroff's article paints a graphic picture of the situation and serves as a call for action for all of the gifted children stuck in inflexible schools across the country.

Smart Kids Have Problems Too
Gene Maeroff

Dorothy A. Sisk, the director of the federal government's Office of the Gifted and Talented, was going through her mail one day recently when a pile of report cards and test results tumbled out of one of the envelopes. The mass of data was accompanied by a letter from a mother pleading that Dr. Sisk try to save other children from a fate similar to that spelled out in her son's grim school records.

It seems that the boy began school as an exceptionally bright and promising pupil with high grades and superior test scores. Gradually, however, his performance deteriorated, and the child resigned himself to low achievement, leaving his potential grossly unfulfilled. Now, his mother wrote, he was a school dropout, lying on a bed in the next room, peering into a television screen.

Dr. Sisk gets 500 letters a day, and few are so depressing. But almost all of them—from students, parents, teachers, counselors, principals, and school board members—ask what can be done to improve the education of gifted children in the United States. These are the two percent to four percent of all students for whom the ordinary classroom can be fraught with the frustration of a prison cell. They are youngsters whose curiosity and creativity know no bounds. In the worst of circumstances, in situations devoid of intellectual stimulation, they can be transformed into listless and frustrated dropouts like the boy whose mother wrote to Dr. Sisk.

Gifted students are the stepchildren of our nation's schools. Most of them seldom receive the extra attention and enriched assignments that they should have to thrive and grow. They don't have the benefit of teachers with special training or courses that are properly challenging. And most school districts don't have enough money to provide the high-powered attention that gifted children need.

Preference in federal aid for elementary and secondary students is given elsewhere. The paltry $2.5 million budget of Dr. Sisk's office pales by comparison with the $500 million that Washington provides for students who are mentally or physically handicapped, or the $2 billion it spends on pupils from economically disadvantaged families.

The pity is that a child's intelligence, improperly handled, can fail to blossom to its fullest; like an unwatered flower, it can wither. "We are increasingly being stripped of the comfortable notion that a bright mind will make it on its own," Sidney P. Marland, Jr., the former United States Commissioner of Education, wrote in a 1972 report to Congress on the gifted child that has become a classic document.

From the outset, the gifted are not like other children. What will suffice for their peers will not be enough for them. Their attention span is longer, their learning rate is faster, their potential for abstraction is greater, their sensitivity is keener, and their need for exploration in depth is consuming.

Parents of the gifted must be careful not to mistake the signals. Misbehavior or disinterest can mask boredom in a student who finds the work too easy. The extent to which intelligence goes unrecognized was demonstrated in a study in Pennsylvania last year; it found that more than half of the youngsters referred to a program for emotional disorders had I.Q.'s of more than 130, which is the beginning of the gifted range. Their disorderly behavior could easily have been the result of having to sit in classrooms where they were bored to tears.

Parents who suspect that their children are gifted must be prepared to act as advocates for them. If there were a manual to help mothers and fathers spot the signs of brilliance in their youngsters, these are some of the characteristics that might be highlighted during the preschool years:

—Early use of advanced vocabulary. Gifted children pick up language facility quickly. While other youngsters are still using one-syllable words and simple sentences, the gifted are already speaking in multi-syllable words and more complex sentences.

—Ability to grasp cause-and-effect relationships. Gifted children understand abstract ideas easily. They can figure out what makes things happen and they can sense the consequences of various actions.

—Periods of intense concentration. When other children's minds wander, the gifted are still paying attention to the task at hand. They can become totally absorbed in activities that quickly tire other children.

Parents who think that the school may have failed to acknowlege their children's intelligence should not hesitate to ask that an intelligence test, and perhaps a creativity test as well, be given to their youngsters. If the school is uncooperative, they should seek testing by an outside psychologist. But parents should make every attempt to work with the school if it is at all possible. Alienated school officials can make life difficult for a child if they see the parents as "the enemy."

The worst cases in which intelligence is overlooked involve girls and minority students of both sexes. Too many teachers are simply biased in their expectations and pay little attention to the traits of these children. Furthermore, cultural prejudices tend to keep girls and minority students from reaching their full intellectual growth, making it that much more of a problem to discern the exceptional promise that may be buried deep within such a child.

A background paper on gifted children that was circulated recently within the U.S. Office of Education stated that "With the heavy emphasis on remedial education for inner-city youngsters and budget problems that appear insurmountable, it is rare that inner-city school officials expend effort on either identifying disadvantaged inner-city gifted or establishing programs for these children."

It took an alert teacher, for example, to realize that a girl in her class in a Maryland school was gifted. The child's own parents weren't aware of her great ability. The teacher noticed on test paper after test paper that the youngster left doodles on the margins. She was also getting good scores. Upon further observation, it became apparent to the teacher that the work wasn't challenging the child. The marginalia was the result of her having to use up idle time after racing through the tests, which were too easy for her.

The problem of insufficient challenge was demonstrated last spring when a group of more than 100 high school seniors gathered in Washington. They had been chosen by the federal government as Presidential Scholars, the cream of the intellectual crop in the 50 states. One of the speakers who addressed them, Ernest L. Boyer, the U.S. Commissioner of Education, asked how many of the students had homework to do every weeknight. Only half raised their hands; the other half said they found high school so easy that they could get top grades with a minimum of effort. They didn't have to take work home.

One difficulty in getting schools to pay heed to the needs of the gifted is a widespread feeling that such children should be the last to get anything extra, especially in this era of limited resources. After all, they are already blessed with extraordinary talents. Egalitarianism is the order of the day, and even in the best of circumstances there is little sympathy for the most able children.

"One of the problems in stimulating support for education of the gifted," Dr. Sisk says, "is inherent feelings of parents that it is not quite appropriate to demand programs for their children. If those same parents had children with defects, they would be willing to seek every bit of professional and educational help for their children."

Nancy Page, 18, the daughter of a county agricultural agent, has seen the problem up close. She just graduated from public high school in Bennington, Vt., and is entering Harvard University this fall. She wants to study literature and philosophy.

"Some people say the gifted ought to make it on their own, but that's incredible," says Miss Page, who was selected as a Presidential Scholar for her outstanding achievement in high school. "The whole idea of equal opportunity should mean that the gifted are helped to reach their full potential. We don't put someone with a learning disability in a regular class: we shouldn't put the gifted in regular classes. They should get their own special work. Some people resent talent, though, and they think egalitarianism means equal treatment for all. Too often, people tend to equate democracy with mediocrity.

"A lot of teachers are afraid of intelligent students. They give the best marks to the students who comfort the teacher in the teacher's assertions. These teachers don't reward creative thinking. I acknowledge we can't expect endless resources to be made available for the gifted, but the people in the school can at least have a good attitude toward the gifted. That doesn't cost money. Right now, some members of the Bennington School Board are trying to get rid of the calculus course at the high school to save money. They think that since calculus is taught in college, a high school shouldn't bother offering it. That's preposterous."

Even when an agreement can finally be extracted to do something for the gifted there is the problem of deciding who the gifted really are. Traditionally, most parents have assumed that gifted children are those of unusually high intelligence. But today, for purposes of funding programs, officials have expanded the definition; the phrase "gifted and talented" is used. Programs have been extended beyond the intellectually gifted to include students whose exceptional performance or potential is in a single academic field, in creative or productive thinking, in the visual or performing arts, in "psychosocial" skills (group leadership) or in "kinesthetic" ability (dance and athletics).

If you think this means that money for the gifted and talented goes to student council presidents, basketball players, and kids who like to act in school plays, you are right. This is undoubtedly part of the egalitarian influence, and the effect is to allot the intellectually gifted only a small part of an already tiny appropriation.

There are, of course, some school systems that try to provide special programs for bright kids. One model: The Pine View School in Sarasota, Fla., with about 500 pupils from the fourth through the 12th grade. The pupils are admitted on the basis of tests and recommendations. Once inside Pine View, they are given a great deal of flexibility so they can work faster and in much greater depth than they could if they were in other schools in the county.

Teachers at Pine View have developed an approach they call "Advex"—Advance and Explore. The time a child spends on a subject is not necessarily squeezed into traditional periods; this also promotes individualization in the curriculum. Pine View works in tandem with other schools in the county system. The students maintain a cross registration at their regular neighborhood schools to participate in varsity sports, extracurricular activities and courses that might not be available at Pine View.

For the parents of the intellectually gifted, regardless of how little or how much is done to aid their children, there is a series of difficult decisions to be made. Mary Haneman of Wilmington, N.C., for example, just saw her son William graduate from high school at age 16. He skipped two grades and Mrs. Haneman is still wondering whether it was the best thing for him even though he seems well-adjusted. "Maybe he has been hurried into adulthood," she says.

Bill Haneman was ahead of other youngsters from the very beginning. His teachers started giving him extra books to read as early as the first grade and by the third grade he was pursuing an independent study project on prehistoric life. The school didn't quite know how to deal with him. "He was bored a lot and we tried to supplement his school work with things we gave him to do at home," Mrs. Haneman recalls.

As their son entered fifth grade, the Hanemans asked the school to run a special evaluation of him. They were prepared to take the money they were saving for his college education and spend it on a private school if that was the only way of getting him into the proper learning environment. The evaluation was performed in the fall and a report was sent to school headquarters. By spring, nothing had been done for their child.

Mrs. Haneman asked about the lack of action. She was told by the evaluator that it didn't make any difference because no matter what was done for Bill, he would just have to sit and be bored until he reached high school.

"We didn't think that was much of an answer," says Mrs. Haneman, who beseeched school officials to find other children like her son and put them together in one class. The officials didn't do that, but they finally allowed Bill to advance directly from the fifth grade to the seventh grade; he skipped again before completing junior high. As a result, he had to attend a school seven miles from home—and the school district refused to provide transportation. The Hanemans were responsible for transporting him back and forth each day.

"Even with moving him up," says Mrs. Haneman, "I don't think he was sufficiently challenged. It would have been nice if he had been able to go over to the college nearby to take math courses, but that wasn't permitted because he would've missed some of his other high school courses."

Bill Haneman is now entering Duke University to study engineering. Meanwhile, another young man—the one whose mother wrote to Dr. Sisk—is languishing in front of the boob tube. Being gifted in America can be a liability. And until the country wakes up to this fact and decides to do something about it, the minds—and futures—of many young people will continue to be squandered.

REPRINTED BY PERMISSION OF THE SOUTH DAKOTA MEMORIAL ART CENTER, BROOKINGS, SOUTH DAKOTA.

The Prairie Is My Garden, by Harvey Dunn.

11

The Young Child: Socialization and Early Education

Socialization is the process of transmitting culturally relevant materials. How to behave at the dinner table, the names of famous historical people or events, the rules for baseball—all these exemplify some types of cultural materials that are transmitted to members of a society. The transmission is made up of the values, attitudes, and norms for that particular society. Because modern America is complex, the items that we transmit via socialization are complex, and the process is complex. Society provides no easy answers for how some of our cultural materials are passed along. We only know that they *are* transmitted and that the specific agents of socialization include parents, peers, school, and various other mechanical and human transmitters (television, for example).

Sex-Role Socialization

The development of sex roles is a very "hot" topic of discussion today. Classrooms at nearly every level of education discuss aspects of sex-appropriate behavior. The women's movement has become a conversation piece in legal, social, and recreational circles.

A sex role is a belief about the gender appropriateness of a particular behavior or attitude. In every society on earth, children learn over time behaviors or attitudes defined by their culture as being appropriate for a particular sex.

THE PROCESS OF SOCIALIZATION

Socialization: transmittal of a society's values, attitudes, and norms

Origins of Sex Roles: The Biological Perspective

At least a part of what we observe as sex-appropriate behavior can be explained in terms of biological development. Biologically, men and women, boys and girls, are not alike. There are obvious physical differences: average body size, musculature, genital development, etc.

If we look at animal studies, there is conclusive evidence that there is a distinct biological influence in the development of sex-appropriate behavior. With human beings, however, the relationship is much less clear. After all, there is seldom anything perfectly straightforward when studying the development of the human.

With humans, there is evidence that there are behaviors that are related specifically to the sex of the individual. Maccoby and Jacklin (1974), in their review of research about psychology of sex differences, have indicated that there are at least three specific sex differences in behavior: (a) females frequently excel in verbal skills and abilities; (b) males do better in tasks requiring quantitative/spatial abilities; and (c) males are more aggressive than females. The researchers found these differences crossed cultural lines consistently.

Prenatal sex hormones, which are secreted by the endocrine glands, have a great deal to do with the physiological differentiation between the sexes. These very powerful hormones also have something to do with the basic sex differences in the behavior of young children. Of particular importance is the secretion of *testosterone*, or the male hormone. At the sixth or seventh week after conception, there appears to be a critical period for the secretion of this hormone. If the hormone is present (due to the combination of X and Y chromosomes), the undifferentiated genitals to the fetus will develop into a penis and a scrotum. If the hormone is not present, the undifferentiated genitals will develop into female genitalia. Primary sexual characteristics of the female apparently develop without specific hormonal stimulation during this critical period.

Are these prenatal hormones related to the findings of Maccoby and Jacklin, as suggested above? As we will discuss below in the case of aggression, probably yes. The development of sex-appropriate behavior is very complicated, however, and more research is needed.

The biological effects are primary effects; however, the specific biological effects may not be as numerous as those generated by social-psychological variables. The primacy of this biological determination can be questioned. For example, there are cases on record where a normal infant boy is injured, is transformed through surgery, and is raised as a normal infant girl. This very rare occur-

The Young Child: Socialization and Early Education

rence implies some radical sorts of intervention, but it does demonstrate what can be done if necessary.

A Special Case: Aggression: There is evidence that suggests that levels of aggression may be biologically determined. Human sex differences in aggression are basically taken for granted: the male of the species is consistently more aggressive than the female, in almost every culture. Some graphic examples of this are that men usually make war, not women; violent crime is most often committed by male criminals, not female.

Aggression:
forceful action intended to dominate

In terms of the origin of sex differences in aggression, Weitz (1977) discusses three possible biological sources of sex differences in aggression: brain structure, hormones, and chromosomal structure.

The human brain does not appear to contain an "aggression center." Aggression is a very complex behavioral response to a sequence of interrelated actions. In research with habitually violent criminals, abnormal EEG patterns *(electroencephalograph)* appear in certain parts of the brain that do not appear in the EEGs of nonviolent criminals. Also, there have been many experiments in altering the structure of the brain of criminals, which have produced "success" in some cases; the results are largely inconclusive in terms of what is the exact origin of the aggressive behavior.

Hormones are almost always a part of the discussion of aggression. One theory of the effects of hormones states that the hypothalamus (which is part of the brain) becomes "indelibly sex-typed through the action of sex hormones thereby permanently disposing the animal to male or female physiological and behavioral responses. . . . In most animals this critical period of hormonal action is thought to occur prenatally just before the genitalia are formed and thereafter is immutable" (Weitz, p. 16). When testosterone is present, a male "mind" develops; if not, a female mind develops. Weitz says:

> In most species male sexual behavior involves more aggression than does the female, therefore, effects on the sexual system are often intertwined with changes in aggressive behavior. . . . The fact the sex hormones seem to have a direct effect on aggression in all species and that they have an early and pervasive influence on the nervous system, seems to be a strong factor in explaining the sex differences in human aggression (Weitz, pp. 17–18).

One other biological explanation of aggression in humans is chromosome effects. For example, a certain group of very aggressive males have the sex chromosome configuration of XYY, rather than just XY. The XYY male finds ". . . an androgen bath at a critical point in embryological time, leading to male development" (Weitz, p. 19). These males are uncontrollably aggressive.

There is then a biological basis for aspects of sex-role behavior. The utility of these findings for students of child development or for people who are working with children is somewhat limited. In most instances, these biological differences are unchangeable, but on the other hand, they may be not as significant as the sorts of influences we will discuss below.

The Learned Aspects of Sex Role

Two ways we learn our sex roles are by *identification* and *imitation*. Identification has to do with the internalization of the values of other people. It comes from classical Freudian theory, which states that children identify with significant adults, usually parents. "Freud's theory of psychosexual development is an identification theory par excellence, and it was Freud who first introduced the term. Freud believed that children incorporate large chunks of the same-sexed parent's personality into their own, mainly as a way of reducing the anxiety and conflict caused by Oedipal desires. Today most theories do not give such a central place to sexual motivation; instead they emphasize the child's desire to be similar to someone of the same sex; to be like someone who is powerful; to enjoy vicariously the position of someone who has status" (Tavris and Offir, 1977, p. 168).

The figure opposite demonstrates three ways to look at the identification process. In A we have what is called *same-sex identification*. The girl can directly identify with and imitate the behaviors and attitudes of the mother; the boy can do the same with the father. This is a very normative developmental sequence.

B is termed *cross-sex identification*. We feel cross-sex identification has been underestimated in terms of its importance; it may be as important as same-sex identification. It is vital that children learn of their androgynous natures; men, women, boys, and girls all share some of the same characteristics. Masculine and feminine may be more similar than dissimilar. The cross-sex identification relationship is very important in the total development of children of both sexes.

Interaction pattern C shows a very common pattern in America: parent absence (usually the father). In this father-absent identification model the same-sex identification relationship is available for the girl and the cross-sex identification relationship is available for

Cross-sex identification: a child's identification with the parent of the opposite sex

The Young Child: Socialization and Early Education 301

the boy. Half of the relationships are missing, however. The boy is lacking the same-sex relationship and the girl is lacking the cross-sex relationship.

This absence would be produced by a divorce, a death, or some similar removal of the father. Even when the father is present, he may be effectively absent due to the nature of his job outside of the home or his decision that child rearing is best left to the woman. To make up for this absence, an image of the masculine model is created (by the mother and other women, teachers, for example), and the children are encouraged to identify with this image of what a man is. This vicarious identification is probably a weaker form of relationship. It is quite possible that these disturbed identification patterns cause problems; that is, they may prevent the child from developing in a normative fashion, free of significant gaps in sex-role socialization.

The other word we hear much about in sex-role development is *imitation*. This term comes from a social-learning tradition and it says that sex-typed behaviors are learned through a process of mimicking the behavior. There is some sort of adult reaction (positive or negative reinforcement) and then there is the internalization of the behavior. Imitation, or modeling, has been the subject of a great deal of research into questions about types of models and their effectiveness. It appears that ". . . parents are the most nurturant and powerful people in the child's world . . . they are assumed to be very effective models" (Tavris and Offir, p. 165).

Another way of explaining the development of sex roles has to do with the cognitive development of the child. As children mature

A. Same-Sex Identification

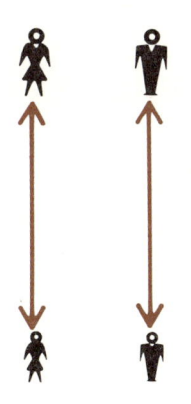

B. Cross-Sex Identification

C. Father-Absent Identification

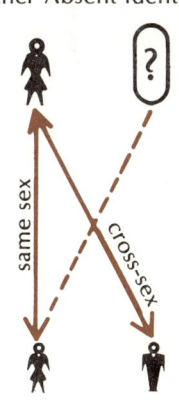

Children like to dress up in adults' clothes and act out adult roles.
ROBERT V. ECKERT, JR., EKM-NEPENTHE.

cognitively, they learn that gender is important and prominent in the attitudes of people and groups. As children seek to become competent individuals, certain behaviors become more rewarding than others and children are very aware of what these behaviors are. Many of these rewarding behaviors just happen to be sex typed. Part of the development of sex roles is initiated by children; they are not passive receptacles of the messages of society. There is an active involvement in the process, which is a function of the growing cognitive awareness of children.

The figure on the opposite page looks at the process of identification. This theoretical statement synthesizes the processes apparently involved in sex-role development. There are many factors that make up input into children's awareness. This input comes in the form of the influences at home, the age of the child, the sex of the model, age of the model, the type of television advertisements the child watches, and so on. These factors become part of chil-

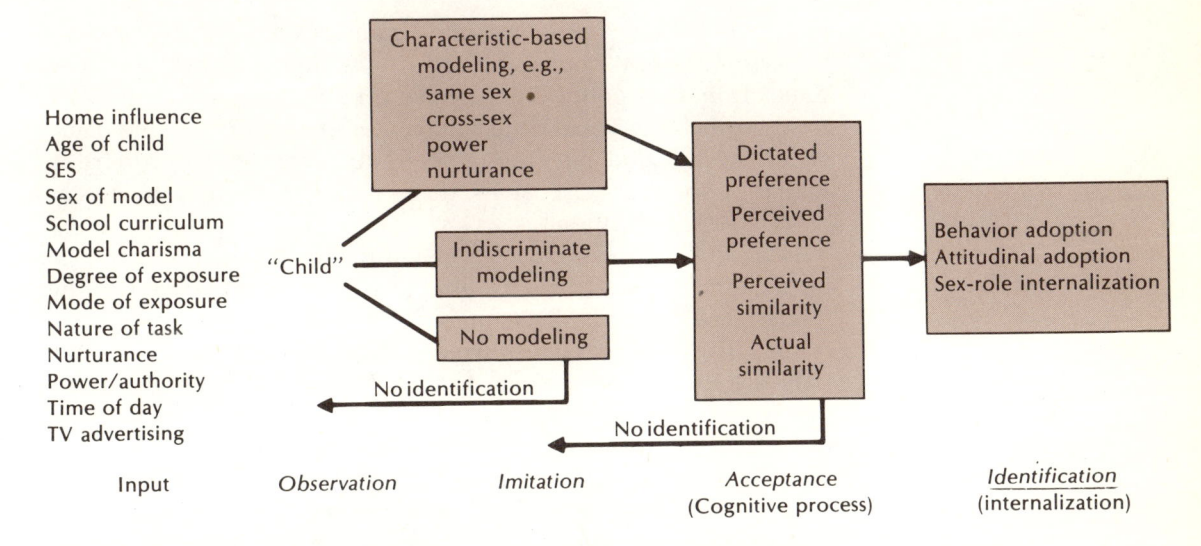

The Young Child: Socialization and Early Education

| Input | Observation | Imitation | Acceptance (Cognitive process) | Identification (internalization) |

Input:
Home influence
Age of child
SES
Sex of model
School curriculum
Model charisma
Degree of exposure
Mode of exposure
Nature of task
Nurturance
Power/authority
Time of day
TV advertising

Observation/Imitation: "Child" → Characteristic-based modeling, e.g., same sex, cross-sex, power, nurturance / Indiscriminate modeling / No modeling

Acceptance: Dictated preference, Perceived preference, Perceived similarity, Actual similarity

Identification: Behavior adoption, Attitudinal adoption, Sex-role internalization

No identification

dren's observation process. These factors will sometimes be modeled by children; they are trying out the behavior to see if it fits. But before the behavior becomes a part of children's behavior repertoire, there is a cognitive process of acceptance that must first take place.

What we are saying is that not everything children see and/or are exposed to, nor every behavior that children model (imitate) will become internalized parts of their behavior. There is more to identification than simply imitating the behavior or being exposed to the influence. There are many examples in which the parents will be exemplary models, the child will watch no aggressive television programs, and the child will be enrolled in the best of schools, yet the child will exhibit unacceptable behavior. The parents will wonder where the behavior came from.

On the other hand, as this example indicates, the child may be exposed to a subtle form of advertising, for example, yet not model the behavior. The behavior may still end up as part of the child's internalized behavior patterns. There is an observation on the part of the child, there may be imitation of those behaviors, there is a cognitive reaction that mediates the process, and there is eventual behavior internalization.

Timing of Sex-Role Development

Sex-role development begins before birth. There is significant biological input during embryological development that appears to influence the development of gender and sex role. The sociological impact of sex-role immersion apparently occurs at birth and continues from that point. Adults have certain stereotyped images of what boy babies should be like and other images of what girl babies should be like, and even though boy babies are more *like* girl babies than they are *unlike* girl babies, these stereotypes begin the process of sex-role socialization.

This early process may begin with things like different color blankets for babies (pink for little girls because they are soft and fragile, and blue blankets for boys because they need "harder" colors). The differential way we decorate the rooms of our children indicates that we are convinced that boys and girls have different needs in terms of color and, ultimately, treatment. As children grow, we begin to make behavioral generalizations according to sex. If a boy is active, rough and tumble, and maybe a bit aggressive, he is "all boy." We like to reinforce in girls a very different set of behaviors and attitudes. One example of the attitudes we have for children is taken from the book *Good Little, Bad Little Girl:*

> The good little girl would jump out of bed the minute she heard mommy call.
> The bad little girl would cover her head and pretend she heard nothing at all.
> The good little girl always dressed by herself.
> She put on her own socks and shoes.
> The bad little girl cried, "My socks are too small! And my shoelace is all tied in knots!"
>
> The good little girl ate her dinner quite slowly and washed her hands and face before.
> The bad little girl gobbled hers in a hurry and then looked around for more.
> The good little girl said her prayers in the morning, and she said her prayers at night.
> The bad little girl forgot.
> The good little girl said "please" and "thank you."
> The bad little girl did not.
>
> When mommy had guests, the good little girl would stand quietly by. In a nice little way, "Excuse me," she'd say, "May I go out to play?"
> The bad little girl wouldn't wait for a lull. She burst right into the talking.
> She'd whine and she'd cry, "I want to go out!" You never heard such a squawking!
>
> (from E. Wilkin, *Good Little, Bad Little Girl*, Racine, Wisc.: Golden Press, 1972)

The Young Child: Socialization and Early Education

The book finishes by showing the reader that the good little girl and the bad little girl are one and the same. How many attitudes do you see being suggested in this story for children? This sort of literature demonstrates the types of expectations we have for children based on sex, in this case. This book is designed for the young child; obviously the process is well on its way by this time.

In terms of when specific sex differences can be seen in children's behavior and when children start acting very sex appropriately, there is some evidence that children consistently operate in a sex-typed way by age three (Thompson, 1975; Flerx et al., 1976).

What is interesting are the behavioral limits we attach to boys and girls as they are growing up. The figure below demonstrates the funnel approach to understanding these behavioral expectations over time. We suggest that early in children's life the behavioral limits for boys are much narrower than the behavioral limits for girls. People in America expect boys to be *boys* sooner than we expect girls to be *girls*.

As time passes for boys, the behavior limits imposed upon them gradually expand. By the time they are adolescents, their behavioral limits have expanded considerably. For girls, the reverse occurs. Girls in America have relatively wide behavioral limits in early life, which constrict over time. By the time girls are adolescents, their behavioral limits have been constricted considerably.

This is exemplified by the labels we attach to individual children who go beyond the normative behavioral limits assigned to them. Girls, because of relatively wide limits, and no big hurry on the part of society to make sure that they become and stay "all girl," can occupy the role of tomboy with a large amount of assurance that no one will really mind. Society's perception of the term *tomboy* is not particularly negative. In fact, in one study it was shown

Tomboy: name used for a girl who behaves like a boy

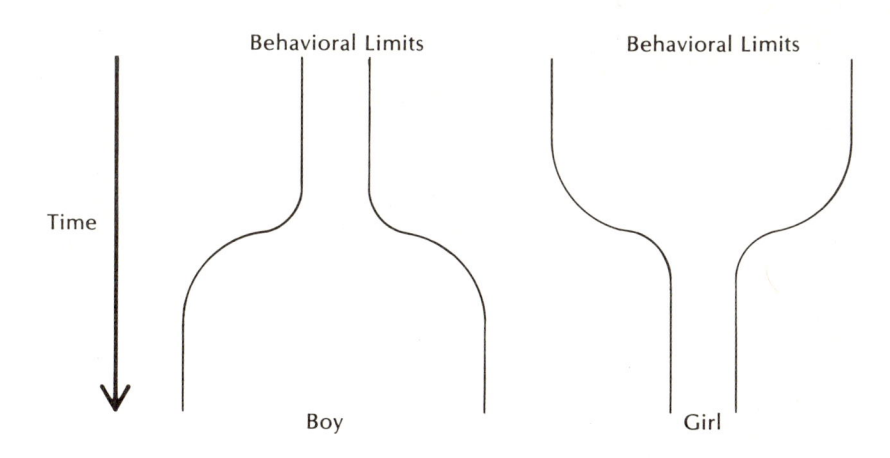

Sissy:
name used for a boy who behaves like a girl

that among junior high girls, 63 percent of them reported that they were tomboys. Fifty percent of a sample of adult women interviewed for the same study also reported that they had been tomboys in childhood (Hyde et al., 1977).

The English language really does not have a term for boys that is similar to that of *tomboy*. The closest thing we have for a boy who goes outside the normative sex-typed behavioral limits is the term *sissy*. Contrary to the acceptability of being a tomboy, being a sissy is a shameful thing that boys try to avoid at all costs. You will not find too many boys admitting to the fact that they are sissies. In fact, if you call them that, you had better be prepared to defend yourself. Very few men, in reflecting back on their childhoods, will admit to having been a sissy.

Inappropriate gender behavior for girls does not appear to carry with it the social stigma that inappropriate gender behavior of boys does. Why? It could be that because we are a patriarchal society, we want to see a pure symbol of strength as the foundation of our society. It may be because women historically have been expected to do physical labor in the fields or around the house that required strength and stamina. Besides looking sweet, women were always expected to have inner reserves of strength. It could be that in our focus on males and inattention to females we have made stricter standards for males.

Symbolic Sex Role Socialization

There are several symbolic agents of sex-role socialization present in modern America. The agents include books (as we have already demonstrated), toys, television, and the heroes of children. Children's toys characterize boys differently than girls. The action toys are boys' toys; the dolls and the play stoves are toys for girls (even though most boys really enjoy playing house and preparing meals). Chemistry sets and erector sets are characteristically designed for and given to boys; yet there is nothing innate about boys' or girls' desires to play with these different toys.

The effects of these symbolic sex-role socialization phenomena tend to be overwhelming. The suggestions to children concerning what is and what is not sex-appropriate behavior are very strong. These symbolic sources of reinforcement go a long way in perpetuating the sex-role differences we see in our society today.

The Young Child: Socialization and Early Education 307

ISSUE

The Hidden Persuader: Television and Sex-Role Development

ROBERT V. ECKERT, JR., EKM-NEPENTHE.

One of the more obvious, if unintentional, effects of television is its persuasion in terms of boy-girl, man-woman behavior. On television, there are usually clear sex roles and they are presented in very convincing, effective ways. Society is mirrored in its television programs; or at least it is mirrored in the minds of the writers and producers. Because most of television is financed through commercial advertising, the writers and producers of television alter their mirrors so that the program is assured of selling. In this regard television is not accurate; the persuasiveness of TV is not affected at all by its accuracy, however.

☐ Children's television shows, and adult shows, for that matter (studies show that millions of children are up at 10:00 P.M. watching television), have many sex biases in them. The little racing sets are advertised by boys; the dolls are advertised by girls (except if the "doll" is action-oriented, like GI Joe). Except for the recent emergence of shows like "Police Woman," "The Bionic Woman," "Charlie's Angels," and "Wonder Woman," men are the heroes and the ones who right the wrongs of the world and save women from their plights. Even in a show like "The Bionic Woman" (who had extraordinary abilities), all too often the superior skills of the bionic woman were not enough. A strong, brave man would have to think of a way to save her.

☐ In most of the series that have lasted, sex roles are depicted in largely traditional ways. Usually, the woman are depicted as more passive, dependent, and unable or unwilling to take care of themselves. The women do most of the work seen in TV households, and the women are most likely to be the predominant child care agents.

☐ Men, on the other hand, are typically cast in the adventurous roles. The male is usually more assertive than the female, more active, successful, and reliable. These characteristics are particularly true if the male we are looking at is a "good guy." Bad guys, while still aggressive, display some traditional female characteristics. They are undependable, weak, and lacking intestinal fortitude.

☐ Two researchers have attempted to determine the types of behavior seen on television (Sternglanz and Serbin, 1974). Males are much more likely to display aggression and constructive levels of activity than females. Females on TV are more likely to be giving in to males and more likely to try to avoid harm. Interestingly, the children's TV programs that were observed showed nearly an identical incidence of nurturance between males and females.

☐ The inferior position of woman is even more obvious when individuals of different races are involved. The image of black females on TV is perhaps worse than white females. Only recently have the networks realized this discrepancy and taken steps to improve it.

☐ Given the presence of television (over 95 percent of American homes possess sets) and the amount of time children spend watching it (more time than they spend in school), television must be considered a very real persuader of children. Much of the attitudes children have concerning what boys do and what girls do come directly from the television set. One interesting example has been the effect of the exploits of stuntman Evel Knievel, a man who risked life and limb driving his motorcycles over rows of buses, trucks, or anything that could be lined up. He became incredibly popular with male children. Boys began setting up ramps in the street and driving their bikes over them; even the structure of bicycles changed to that of a motocrosslike bicycle (short stature, larger tires, and big spokes).

☐ Television has the ability to influence nearly every child. The play behavior of children becomes saturated with whatever they are seeing on TV, and the children carry the same attitudes that are exemplified on the screen. Boys are more likely to adopt aggressive roles, to mimic violent fights, and to generally speak in terms of winning and losing (which, by the way, is a concept usually presented very simplistically on TV).

☐ Only the future will tell us what effect these sex-stereotypes will have on our children. There is little doubt that the behaviors change; do the internal attitudes also change?

The Young Child: Socialization and Early Education

Just what is play to children? It is the language of child development. Play is the child's work. Kaplan and Kaplan (1973) have provided us with some specific sorts of things that are characteristic of children's play:

1. Playtime aids growth—both physically and psychologically.
2. Play is a voluntary activity that is intensely personal. Children can use their ideas and put them into action in the way they desire.
3. Play offers children certain freedom of action. In play, children are masters of their world; they need not worry about failure or ridicule.
4. Play can be a basis for the development of language. Even when children are playing by themselves, they often carry on a running conversation; the practice in solitary and group play aids language development.
5. Play has the ability to enhance interpersonal relations. Children in group play interact with each other, defining relations.
6. Play is a way of learning adult roles—dramatic play, in particular, allows children to try on the world of the adult; again, there is no fear of rejection or recrimination.

In short, play is vitalizing for children. It is a dynamic interaction with the world, both the real world and the symbolic world. It has important physical and psychological outcomes.

Ages and Stages of Play

Play is a function of interaction: interaction with the environment, interaction with materials, and interaction with other people. It is a compilation of learned behaviors, discovery behaviors, and projected behaviors, and involves the development of rudimentary social skills. Cognitive development plays a role in the ages and stages of play, as does the nature of the social and educational experience of the child. This produces different types of play, and also a sequential nature to the development of play.

Infant Play

The primary aspect of infant play is exploration of the environment, of the parents' faces, of anything reachable and/or visible. Human babies engage their environment almost immediately. As

PLAY

Play:
spontaneous activity of children

their physical and perceptual abilities develop, the nature of the environmental engagement becomes more sophisticated.

Exploration evolves into the first major stage of play, called *solitary play*. This is the child playing alone, with materials perhaps, perhaps without materials. Solitary play is very concrete early in the child's life, but as the child matures, it can and does take on symbolic proportions. Most of the play during the early years is solitary play; but there may be interactive aspects to play even when children are very young. For example, it is not uncommon for a 12- to 15-month-old child to insist that the parent play with him.

Parallel play: children playing beside each other but not interacting

Children gradually move into a play form termed *parallel*. Two children play side by side, perhaps even using the same material. However, the children do not interact; they just play alongside of each other. There is no common goal to the play; the children play in a solitary fashion, but they do so in conjunction with another child.

Group play represents a more advanced stage of social interchange. Here the children play together. Spontaneously, they begin interacting with a common goal. The children may even define some basic rules for their interaction. The rules, however, are loose and changeable. Dramatic play is one example of group play. The children set up a household, for example, define who is the mother, father, and baby, and proceed to act out a typical day. These kinds of situations are fascinating to observe: the similarities between the dramatic play and the adult world are interesting, as are the novel approaches to life that appear.

These stages of play are not entirely sequential, and certainly they are not fixed into a rigid schedule. Very few young children will engage in group play; but older children will engage in solitary play. Parallel play activities can occur at nearly any age. At each stage of play there may be a certain degree of fantasy or symbolism displayed by the child. Toddlers use fantasy, although it is very rudimentary, and as children mature, their use of fantasy matures and becomes more complex.

EARLY CHILDHOOD EDUCATION

Early childhood education is made up of two distinct movements: the day nursery or day care aspect, and the nursery school aspect. The differences between the two are probably less significant than the similarities, especially in terms of program content. Day care centers are designed to serve a group of parents who need ex-

In the People's Republic of China, these five-year-old youngsters are developing their hand-eye coordination by playing a game that uses fishing poles, hooks, and paper fish.
PHOTO BY ROBERT W. ROMIG.

tended care for their children. Day care centers are open for longer periods of time than nursery schools and concentrate more on the care of the children from all angles, and less on a strictly educational function (which is characteristic of nursery schools). Nursery schools have more of an educational function and attempt to supplement children's environment (Moore and Kilmer, 1973).

History

The first nursery school in the United States is believed to have opened in New Harmony, Indiana, in the 1920s (Moore and Kilmer, 1973). The program has grown erratically since then. The rate of growth of child care centers has been dependent upon what is happening in the society. For example, during times of war, child care centers make a comeback; there is a real need for child care services when women are fully employed. But in the 1950s, when the "cult of the housewife" really flourished, day care centers and nursery schools did not get the societal support that they had received earlier. Presently there is an increasing need for child care services in the United States, but there is not significant political governmental support for expansion of quality child care facilities.

Today, even though there are perhaps 20,000 child care centers in the United States, there is demand for many more than that.

Under the Great Society programs of Lyndon Johnson, a new and innovative child care movement was started in 1965. This program, called Head Start, is a compensatory educational program. It is designed to aid children from low-income situations who, according to theory, are deprived of appropriate stimulation and opportunity. It was designed to augment the environments of these young children and to provide them with at least one hot meal during the day.

The Head Start movement was revolutionary in some aspects. It brought with it increased attention on the young child in America. It fostered training programs for child care workers and it inspired many local and state laws concerning the operation and maintenance of child care centers.

More recently, another government program has had an impact in the area of early childhood education. The Child Development Associate program is a training and certification program for child care workers. It provides minimum standards for child care workers and enhances the professional nature of the child care business.

Types of Programs

Todd and Heffernan (1977) have identified several types of early childhood programs. One type is termed day nurseries, or *day care centers.* Day care serves a wide range of children, with flexible hours and flexible ages for the children. Some centers have "drop-in" capabilities, which means that children can be left at the center without advance registration or preparation. Other day care centers do not allow this. Day care centers serve children from infancy through the age of six, and sometimes there are after-school day care programs for even older children. Day care centers are designed to meet the needs of working parents, student parents, and other special-need parents who require extended child care services.

Compensatory education: education aimed at overcoming deficits in children's development or background

Head Start Centers Head Start compensatory preschools operate on school-like schedules, with only certain children qualifying to enroll there. A distinct advantage to parents is that Head Start provides transportation for the children. These programs are academically oriented and also concerned with the health and nutrition of the children.

School-Affiliated Preschool Groups School-affiliated preschool groups can be one of several forms. One very common form is a university

The Young Child: Socialization and Early Education

child development laboratory. These centers are nursery schools in the largest sense. They have limited enrollments, limited times for the children, and usually specified male-female ratios. Child development laboratories train child care workers and provide students of child development the opportunity to observe the behavior of preschool children. Recently, school-affiliated preschool groups have started appearing in high school settings. These unique groups allow younger individuals some practical insight into the behavior of young children as preparation for either parenthood or a career in child care or education.

Industry-Based Preschool Groups Once in a while, private industries will provide child care for their employees. This is not yet a common practice in America, but it is hoped that industry people will see the advantages of providing this type of service in terms of employee satisfaction and regularity of attendance. As more and more families find that they need the income from both the father and the mother, this need for child care will increase substantially.

The Private Sector There is a variety of privately based child care services available across the country. Often church based, these centers may be day care centers or nursery schools. They often reflect specific programmatic and value orientations. These centers

Preschoolers enjoy learning together.
ROBERT V. ECKERT, JR., EKM-NEPENTHE.

are supported by parent fees, and tend to be higher in cost; low-income people often cannot afford centers of this type. In some cases, the centers are parent cooperatives; i.e., parents are responsible for their own center in terms of work time and commitment. All of these programs have parental involvement of one type or another.

Early Childhood Education Philosophies

1. The *Head Start* philosophy is essentially compensatory, attempting to make up for past deficits, and also to make sure that these children are at no disadvantage when they enter regular school. Cognitive development is emphasized in these centers, and it is hoped that the enriching experiences of Head Start will allow the children to begin school at the same developmental level as other children.

2. The *Montessori* preschool philosophy is somewhat different. Here, the environment is recognized as being very important. There are specific activities and exercises that the children do every day in order to prepare them for educational experiences. There is a great deal of work done in the area of sensory development, in terms of shapes, colors, puzzles, and other manipulative materials. The children are allowed to proceed along a mostly individual course, moving at their own pace.

3. Another model is the so-called *Bereiter-Engleman* program. This is a remedial program, but it deals with academic skills and has a defined teaching methodology. The curriculum is defined, and is presented to the students in small groups with close proximity to the teacher. The teacher states the concept she wishes them to learn, and through a process of student repetition and oral involvement, the children learn the basic concepts. If the lesson has to do with what an equal sign means, the equation $4 = 4$ is placed on the board. Each aspect of the equation is highlighted, repeated orally, and shown graphically so that children may learn that what is on one side of an equal sign must equal what is on the other side.

4. The *traditional program* is a relatively free program in terms of overt curriculum and specific instruction. The children have a choice as to what they wish to do and the teacher's role is that of facilitator. Some of these programs may not even have a "circle time" or a "story time," except when these groups evolve more or less naturally. University child development laboratories are often structured in this way.

Evaluation of Preschool Programs

Generally, early childhood programs are effective in terms of children's growth and development. They can at least partially help to solve certain life problems for children and they can greatly enhance their social development. These findings are particularly true if the family is closely involved in the program (Bronfenbrenner, 1974; Miller and Dyer, 1975). Not all the comment concerning early childhood education has been positive. Lilian Katz, writing in 1973, has indicated that

> if we teach our children to expect thrills each day we seriously handicap them. In early childhood programs and in other segments of our society we have become accustomed to settling for cheap thrills and quick success, which may in fact be hollow success.
>
> In the recent years of rapid expansion in early childhood education, we exaggerated its power to overcome long standing social, psychological, and economic problems. We now need to take stock of what we have learned and settle down to the long labor ahead of us.

It seems clear that with young children, elaboration of basic concepts is preferable to acceleration of the cognitive domain of the child. Elaboration grounds children in common sense and sensible interaction with their environment; in the long range, it is clearly preferable.

In a 1979 symposium on the persistence of preschool effects at the Society for Research in Child Development in San Francisco, a thorough review of many preschool programs was presented. Preschool education presents many advantages, according to the information presented. Nine years after the preschool experience, the children reported improved attitudes toward school, they were more likely to be going to college, and on the basis of self-reported data, people who had preschool experience appeared to have less frequent adjustment problems through childhood.

Summary

1. Socialization is the process of transmitting culturally relevant materials. Sex-role socialization is the transmission of information relevant to the gender-specific behavior acceptable in a culture. There appear to be behaviors in humans that are specifically sex related. Sex differences, like many aspects of child development, have both a biological base and an environmental base.

2. The learned aspects of sex role are dependent upon the processes of identification and imitation. Cross-sex identification may be as important for the developing child as same-sex identification. Sex-role development probably begins at (or before) birth. The influence of society, and in particular the media of television, is great, perhaps unmeasurable.

3. Play represents the work of children. Play aids growth, allows children a measure of freedom and independence, helps in the development of language, and is a prominent means for learning adult roles. The play of children goes through a series of stages, from solitary to parallel to group play.

4. Early childhood education is made up of two distinct aspects: the day care dimension and the nursery school dimension. The history of the early child education movement is revealing; this is a recent movement, and still does not have the complete support of American society. The types of programs include Head Start centers, child development labs, and private cooperative day care centers. Most of the evidence indicates that preschool experience is an advantage for the child.

Thought Questions

1. How is the process of socialization related to the culture in which it exists? What is the influence of sex-role socialization in American society?

2. What are the functions of play for the child?

3. Describe the sequence in the development of children's play. How important is this sequence?

4. What is the difference between a day care center and a nursery school?

5. What are the advantages of a parent-cooperative child-care center? Disadvantages?

6. Why does American society discount the importance of preschool education? How would you convince a layman of the importance of a preschool experience?

Suggested Readings

Becker, W. *Parents Are Teachers: A Child Management Program.* Champaign, Ill.: Research Press, 1976. *A very practical guide for parents that gives ways to turn the home into a very supportive environment for child development.*

Bettelheim, B. *The Children of the Dream.* New York: Macmillan, 1969. *Bettelheim presents in this work a detailed analysis of the communal* child-rearing system in Israel. He describes both the strengths and weaknesses of the kibbutz situation.

Bossard, J., and E. Boll. *The Sociology of Child Development*. 4th ed. New York: Harper & Row, 1966. *A less recent book, it maintains significant value in its lucid discussion of the socialization process and the dynamic influence of the family.*

Elkin, F., and G. Handel. *The Child and Society: The Process of Socialization*. New York: Random House, 1972. *A definitive discussion on the process of childhood socialization. Particular attention is given to the agents of socialization such as the family and the school.*

Moore, S., and S. Kilmer. *Contemporary Preschool Education: A Program for Young Children*. New York: Wiley, 1973. *The philosophy of different preschool programs is presented. Moore and Kilmer provide a very useful and complete description of specific aspects of preschool education.*

Provence, S.; A. Naylor; and J. Patterson. *The Challenge of Day Care*. New Haven: Yale University Press, 1977. *This recent work on day care is based on an extensive research project. It provides a good perspective on ideal day care settings.*

Read, K. *The Nursery School: A Human Relations Laboratory*. 6th ed. Philadelphia: W.B. Saunders, 1976. *Katherine Read is one of the true giants in preschool education. This book is a must for students of child development, particularly those interested in early childhood educational programs.*

READING

The issue presented in this chapter dealt with television as the hidden persuader. In that discussion the power of TV as an influence in the development of sex roles was presented. There is little doubt that TV presents some very formidable stereotypes to children.

Television is also criticized for dealing with violence in a much too realistic fashion (almost surrealistic) and for manipulating children with sophisticated advertising and promotion of commercial products. Television is not all negative, however. In the reading that follows, the potentially positive aspects of television are presented.

Paul Mussen and Nancy Eisenberg-Berg present evidence, which was taken from their book, *Roots of Caring, Sharing, and Helping,* that television characters who perform positive actions are emulated by the children who watch the behaviors. The authors imply that if children would and/or could be exposed to programming that presented positive and prosocial behavior, they would model that behavior. There is no way of telling how long the modeled behavior would last nor the extent of the modeling that is possible. It is very important to note, however, that the evidence seems to indicate that children can learn positive behaviors from watching them on television.

Given the amount of TV the typical American child watches, this sort of information is vital. The impact of TV on American children is profound. Provided the content of the programs is controlled, there is a chance that this impact can be very positive.

Prosocial Television and Children's Behavior
Paul Mussen
Nancy Eisenberg-Berg

Television characters who perform (model) prosocial actions (helping others, offering nurturance and sympathy, sharing) are emulated by children-viewers. Some of the most extensive and salient research on this subject was conducted by Friedrich and Stein. They examined the effects of various types of prosocial television programs on preschool pupils between the ages of three and five. Children were shown one of three types of television programs each day for four weeks: aggressive cartoons (Batman and Superman); prosocial shows (Mister Rogers' Neighborhood, a program in which there are many displays of cooperation, sympathy, sharing, understanding the feelings of others); or films with neutral content. Naturalistic observations were made in the classroom before, during and after

From *Roots of Caring, Sharing, and Helping* by Paul Mussen and Nancy Eisenberg-Berg. W. H. Freeman and Company. Copyright © 1977.

the period during which the programs were shown. Aggressive children (those initially above the median in aggression) became less able to tolerate delays and more disobedient to rules after exposure to the aggressive programs, but those who were initially nonaggressive (below the median) did not become more aggressive.

Exposure to prosocial television programs resulted in positive changes in behavior, such as greater persistence at tasks, more obedience to school rules, and greater ability to tolerate delays. Most important from our point of view were the gains in levels of cooperation, nurturance, and sympathy, as well as in verbalization of their own and others' feelings, among children of lower socioeconomic status. These effects were still discernible two weeks later. Unexpectedly, some children from higher socioeconomic levels showed *increased* prosocial behavior after exposure to the aggressive and neutral programs. Further investigation revealed that these children habitually watched fewer aggressive programs than their peers, and the investigators argue that the fast-moving, noisy, aggressive programs stimulated their social activity, which was reflected in increased prosocial behavior.

The positive effects of viewing prosocial behavior can be enlarged by training following the television viewing. This was demonstrated in a study in which kindergarten children were assigned to one of five treatments for four sessions: (1) prosocial television programs and verbal-labeling training; (2) prosocial television programs and training in role-playing; (3) prosocial television programs plus verbal labeling *and* training in role-playing; (4) prosocial television programs plus irrelevant training; (5) neutral television programs and irrelevant training. Verbal labeling consisted of group discussion of the events similar to those portrayed in the program and of the feelings and actions of the participants. In role-play training, the children manipulated puppets enacting events and dialogue similar to those in the program. The irrelevant activity assigned to the controls groups was playing with commercial games.

To evaluate the effects of the various training experiences, the investigators tested the children's learning of the content of the programs, generalization of the learning to other situations resembling those portrayed in the program, and actual helping behavior (assisting in repairing another child's collage that had been damaged).

As predicted, exposure to prosocial programs has positive effects. Furthermore, both kinds of additional training, verbal labeling and role-playing, enhanced learning and had broad generalization effects, resulting in increased helping in a situation that was far different from that modeled on television. The labeling training in itself was not effective in raising boys' helping behavior, but when added to role-playing, it further augmented the girls' tendencies to assist another.

The results are notable and have wide social implications, for they indicate that several forms of prosocial interactions can be stimulated by prosocial television programs, even with relatively short exposures. The investigators drew their conclusions carefully and were willing to extrapolate from the laboratory findings to naturalistic settings.

The clear effects of television and training in this relatively small-scale study suggest that this type of prosocial television can have a strong impact on children who watch it in naturalistic contexts where viewing can occur over a much longer period of time than 1 week. These results appear to be readily applicable to naturalistic settings because the children generalized both learning and behavior to situations quite different from those to which they were exposed in the television and training, and because this generalization occurred in measures administered 2 or 3 days after the television viewing.

Additional extensive effects of exposure to prosocial television have been noted in other recent studies. In one, nursery school children were observed during and after four days of exposure to either Sesame Street, a program in which the characters reinforce others positively and negatively, or Mister Rogers' Neighborhood in which there is a great deal of prosocial behavior and very few punishments. Viewing Mister Rogers' Neighborhood proved to be very effective in augmenting children's prosocial behavior; after viewing this program children initiated more social contacts and reinforced their peers more frequently, that is, they offered more praise and approval, sympathy, affectionate physical contact, and emotional support.

Watching Sesame Street produced more complicated results but, in general, led to intensification of behaviors that were initially of low frequency. Thus, children who originally gave little positive reinforcement to peers were likely to give more reinforcement after exposure to Sesame Street; those who were originally low in punitiveness became more punitive.

These impacts are not restricted to children of nursery school age. Some of the first graders in one study were shown an episode from the Lassie series in which a boy risked his life to save a dog, and others were shown either a Lassie episode without such altruism or a family situation comedy. Subsequently, each child had an opportunity to come to the aid of some distressed puppies, but only at some cost—helping the puppies meant giving up a game in which the child could win a valuable prize. The children who had seen the altruistic Lassie episode gave substantially more help to the puppies in distress than did the children exposed to either of the other programs.

The overwhelming weight of the evidence supports the hypothesis that exposure to television programs that model prosocial behavior enhances children's prosocial tendencies. These findings come from studies that made use of actual television programs and involved heroes that were generally known to the children, and further confirmation is found in studies using films especially created for research. Children who were exposed to generous models in these specially designed films donated more of the prizes they had won to needy children than did those who witnessed stingy models.

The uniformity in the findings from diverse studies leave no doubt that the impacts of television viewing are profound and pervasive. The effects can be positive, enhancing prosocial behavior, or negative, reducing prosocial behavior and increasing antisocial responses, depending on the people and events portrayed and the behavior modeled. It is inevitable that we draw a moral from these frequently replicated research findings, and we cannot ignore that moral. Given television's potential for promoting prosocial behavior, we must ask what keeps it from doing so. After an extensive review of virtually all the relevant literature on the topic, Lieberg, Neale, and Davidson argue that the answer to that question lies, to a considerable degree, in "the commercial structure of television and its influence on program content." They point out that as consumers, concerned citizens are in an excellent position to pressure advertisers to alter their programs by refusing to purchase the products of advertisers whose programs promote violence and by patronizing those who sponsor prosocial performances.

The reader may not agree with their analyses of why the positive, prosocial potential of television is unrealized, or with their recommendations for remedying the situation. But it is difficult to disagree with their final conclusion and advice:

It behooves us, in a world on the brink of disaster, to harness television's potential to contribute to our society in ways which we deem more desirable. All of us must bear the responsibility for what is being taught on television. Accepting it squarely can lead to programming which serves the highest values of society—a medium which is truly in the public interest. In the past, children have seen and learned violence on TV's window and today they continue to do so. In the future they might, instead, learn constructive solutions to the problems they will face. Which will it be? The choice is ours.

COURTESY OF THE NATIONAL GALLERY OF ART, WASHINGTON, D.C. ANDREW MELLON FUND.

The Copley Family, by John Singleton Copley.

12

The Young Child: Families and Their Impact

The family is one of the more fundamental units within our culture. This unit of interacting personalities has many functions, and its influence on children and adults is great.

FAMILY FORMS

In the United States the predominant family form is the *nuclear family*. The nuclear family is composed of two parents and their children. The U.S. Census Bureau defines a family as two or more people living together who are related by blood, marriage, or adoption. This broader definition covers more than just the nuclear family.

Most children in America are raised within nuclear families. There are other family forms, however, present in American culture as well as in other cultures. The *three-generation family* is composed of a nuclear family (parents and children), and the parent or parents of one or both of the adults in the nuclear family. The three generations represented are the grandparents, the parents, and the children. The three-generation family has been popular in the history of our society, but there are indications that this family form is decreasing in occurrence. The decrease is due to the mobility of families in our culture and the devaluation of the aged in our society. The economic environment of present-day society is usually not conducive to having many three-generation families.

Three-generation family: parents, children, and grandparents living in one household

Members of a three-generation family share a moment together.
BRUCE DAVIDSON, © MAGNUM PHOTOS, INC.

Extended family:
parents, children, and other relatives living in one household

The *extended family* is somewhat different in structure. In addition to the nuclear family, other family members are part of the household. Uncles, aunts, cousins, nephews, and nieces make up the membership of extended families. Small houses, urban living, and social mobility work against this system. These sorts of families have never been very common in the United States, and they remain relatively unpopular today.

The *single-parent family* is another common configuration in America today. Made up primarily of the mother and her dependent children, these families are not necessarily dysfunctional. As many as one child in six or seven may be in a single-parent family. One of the unfortunate aspects of many single-parent families, particularly those headed by the mother, is poverty.

THE FAMILY AS TRANSMITTER

The family is one institution within a larger society. The following diagram shows other institutions that function within our culture. There are at least five significant institutions within American society: the family, the economic structure, the educational system, the

The Young Child: Families and Their Impact

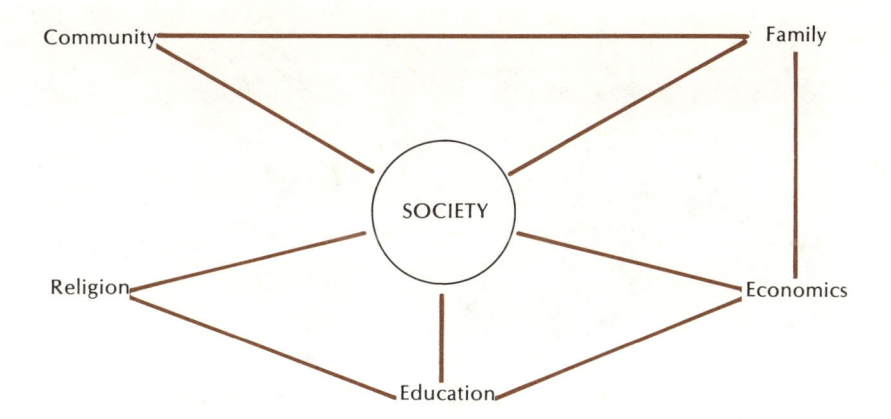

```
Community                               Family
         \                             /
          \                           /
           \                         /
            \        SOCIETY        /
            /                       \
           /                         \
          /                           \
   Religion                            Economics
            \                         /
             \                       /
              \     Education      /
```

religious system, and the community. These institutions are each part of the larger society. They are also related to each other; they affect each other, as much as they affect the larger social order.

Through history, the relative influence of any of these institutions has changed. The educational system is large and complex today; children spend a great deal of their time within the influence of the educational system. Two hundred years ago, the formal educational system was much less visible and significant in the life of children. The role of the religious system has also changed, depending upon the complex interaction with other institutions. For instance, today counties or states usually run orphanages and programs for the poor, services that were previously provided by religious groups.

Individual children seem to be at the bottom of a very complicated system of institutions and relationships. In a sense, they are the recipient of what society has to offer. *Each of these institutions is a transmitter*. They send messages to children, influencing them in behavior and attitude. While the family is probably the most important transmitter to children, particularly when they are young, other institutions also have their input. The school has its impact at certain times and in certain areas, as does the religious system, the community, and the other societal institutions.

Institution: a significant practice or organization in a society

THE FAMILY AS AN AGENT OF CHANGE

Change is implicit in families, because family members are continually aging. This developmental process (for both children and adults) lays a foundation of change for the family; the family is not a stagnant institution. Children, in their relations with the family, are *initiating* change as well as receiving its effects.

In the 1950's the station wagon became the principal means of travel for many American families with more than two children.
ROBERT V. ECKERT, JR., EKM-NEPENTHE.

The family also changes externally in relation to the changes going on within the community and society. Economics, for example, can dictate many changes and policies for the American family. Cultural values sometimes appear to change in movements; these sweeping changes affect the family.

As a result of the combination of these internal and external changes, the family form itself may change. For example, last year there were more than 1 million children involved in divorce proceedings of their parents. There are, as a result, many one-parent families, which are technically families and operate as families in the sense of relations, but are not really nuclear families as we have defined them. There are more single-parent families in the United States today than there ever have been.

INSTRUMENTAL-EXPRESSIVE DIMENSIONS OF THE FAMILY

Parsons and Bales (1955) have developed a model of family role function that is directly related to the child's role in the family. This is called the instrumental-expressive model.

The expressive functions are the communicative, empathetic ones. They are the roles concerned with emotional relationships, child care, expression of feeling, and the like. The instrumental function is largely a maintenance one. Gathering resources and performing operational tasks are "instrumental" activities. When these definitions are placed on a power dimension, specific roles begin to emerge. The low instrumental role is typically that of a male child; the low expressive role is typically that of a female child. These instrumental-expressive divisions are basic parts of the transmission the family sends to children. Children learn their position very quickly and their behavior is reflective of these orientations. This is particularly true during the middle years of childhood, when a great deal of behavior modeling is occurring.

Expressive role:
the more emotional functions in a family

Instrumental role:
the maintenance functions in a family

The following chart shows three fundamental dimensions of family interaction. The operation of the family is largely in terms of the interaction of the individual members with each other. The nature of these ongoing interactions determines the quality of the socialization and the ultimate behavior of the child.

THE FAMILY AS AN INTERACTIVE UNIT

Dimensions of Family Interaction*

Interaction Based on Family Theme	Interaction Based on Role-Power Dimension	Interaction Based on Reciprocity
1. Perfectionistic	1. Adult-centered	Parents ⟷ Children
2. Egocentric	2. Child-centered	1. Mother-father
3. Chaotic	3. Adult-directed	2. Sex of child
4. Devitalized		3. Social class

*Adapted from Gans, 1962.

Families develop themes of operation as they go on. For example, in one family, loud voices are okay. In another everything Mom wants comes before others' needs. These themes are unique to each family, but are a function of many things: the personalities of the participants, the situation of the family, etc. A perfectionistic theme, for example, places children in a position of doing everything according to the exact prescriptions of their parents. A chaotic family leaves children uncertain of their role in the family and their abilities to cope with the demands being placed upon them.

In adult-centered families the children are considered miniature adults (very high expectations); the family is basically for the adult members. The child-centered basis of role-power interaction is concerned with the development of the children; parents appear more interested in the welfare of their children than those in

Reciprocity:
the mutual effects that people have on each other

adult-centered families do. Adult-directed patterns have more sophisticated parents who are concerned with the psychodynamic development of their children. Concepts like self-concept and ego-strength are very important to these parents (Gans, 1962).

Reciprocity, or actors mutually affecting each other, is the essence of the interactive interpretation of the family. This reciprocity is affected by the age of the child, the sex of both the child and the parents, and perhaps even the social class of the family.

Birth Order

The effects of birth order on personalities of children is another illustration of the interactive relationship between the developing personality of the child and the family. There are many studies that indicate first-born children are higher achievers, both academically and interpersonally. First borns tend to be more aggressive, get better grades, and achieve higher positions in society than do later-born children (see for example, Belmont and Marolla, 1973). The figure opposite demonstrates some of these findings.

According to these data, first-born children score higher on the National Merit Scholarship tests. Each successive birth position indicated a slightly lower mean score on this exam. There are also consistent sex differences in the scores.

Last-born children, on the other hand, do less well on standardized tests of achievement. The "baby" of the family often assumes many characteristics similar to that of a baby: dependency, lower levels of assertiveness, and achievement. What of the middle-born children? Apparently, they possess none of the behavioral extremes of either the first born or the last born. The majority of the evidence indicates that middle-born children are easygoing and very normative in their attitudinal and behavioral patterns.

Why the difference due to birth order? The answer probably lies in the change in family interaction patterns that each birth brings. If the family is a system, the addition of a new member is going to change the way the system operates. The nature of the interaction, the way needs are being met, and even the way tasks around the house get done change with the arrival of each child.

There have been criticisms of the birth order studies. One criticism is that it is difficult to determine if the differences mentioned above are due to birth order or some other factor, or a combination of other factors. Sometimes it is very hard to control for the effects of other variables. In some studies nonrepresentative samples

The Young Child: Families and Their Impact

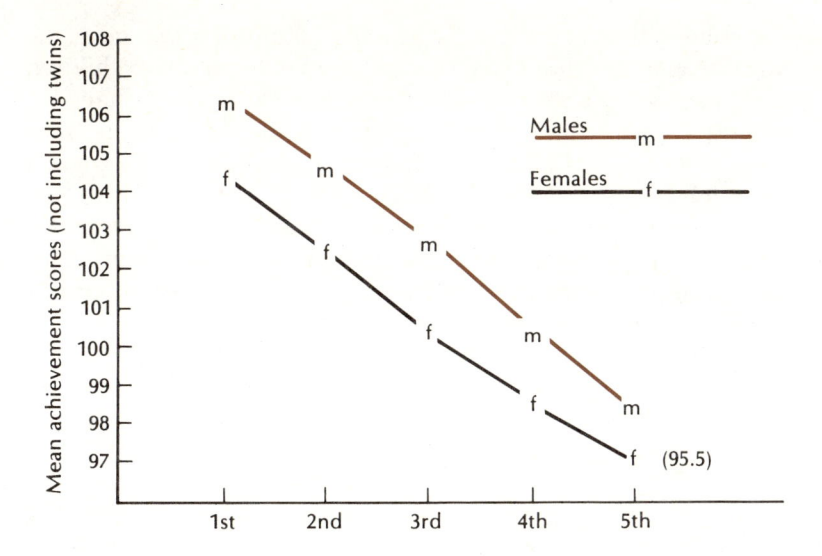

are used, making it difficult to generalize the findings to other populations.

Family Size

America has a bias against two family configurations: a family without children, and a family with only one child. These biases have deep historical and cultural origins, and are persistent even today in an age of overpopulation and ecological concern. Just as birth order creates different family interaction patterns, family size will also create differences within the family. As we said above, as families increase in size, their interaction patterns change. One suggested effect of all of this is known as the *confluence theory* (Zajonc and Markus, 1975). This theory states that with the addition of each family member, there is a unique and very specific contribution to the interaction within the family. The result is that as the family gets larger, the intelligence level of each successive child is lower than his or her predecessor. They report IQ differences that are illuminating:

In families with five children—IQ differences of over 7 points between first and last born

In families with four children—IQ differences of over 5 points

Two-child bias:
the belief that it is better to have more than one child

Confluence theory:
a theory about the effects of larger families upon the children

The child's duties and roles within the family also change as the family size changes. For example, in the small family (two children or less), each child's role may be more diffuse and comprehensive. The child may not have just one duty around the house, such as taking out the trash. In the larger family, the tasks may be assigned specifically to one child.

Authority patterns within the family may also be dependent upon the size of the family. For example, if there is only one child, it may be quite possible to use more explanation techniques in discipline. If there are *eight* children, there may not be the time nor the inclination to explain things to the children. The larger the family, therefore, the greater the likelihood that discipline patterns will assume stricter dimensions.

Parenting Styles

Parenting operates around two dimensions: Autonomy———Control, and Love ———Hostility (Schaefer, 1959). Parents need to strike a balance on each of these dimensions. Too much control placed on children can be stifling and inappropriate for the development of independence; too little control can produce chaos for children and very little direction. Too much hostility can affect children adversely. Is it possible to give a child too much love? If the love is smothering and stifling, then it is possible. A balance needs to be created.

Baumrind (1966, 1971) has created another way to look at parenting styles. In her work with parents and their approach to discipline, she came up with three basic patterns:

1. Authoritarian parents ". . . shape, control and evaluate the behavior of the child in accordance with a set standard of conduct, usually an absolute standard, theologically motivated and formulated by a higher authority" (1966, p. 890).

2. The authoritative parent ". . . directs the child's activities in a rational, issue-oriented manner . . . verbal give and take, shares with the child the reasoning behind the policy" (1966, p. 891).

3. The permissive parent is ". . . nonpunitive, acceptant in an affirmative manner toward the child's impulses, desires and actions" (1966, p. 889).

In the authoritative situation, consistency is a very important term; rules are enforced, and there is confrontation when rules are broken. The difference between this pattern and the authoritarian pattern, however, is that explanations are offered (an inductive technique). The authoritarian parent uses much less of this inductive approach, and considers a violation just that, a violation with

Induction:
disciplinary techniques using explanations rather than physical punishment

appropriate punishment necessary, and no need to explain it to the child.

The results of these different parenting styles in terms of children are not always clear. However, generally it appears that the authoritative style produces children who are more likely to be friendly and cooperative, more independent, and more goal directed (Baumrind, 1966, 1971). It is less easy to state what the children will be like under the other two parenting styles. Depending upon the characteristics of the child, extreme permissiveness can be very destructive to the child. On the other hand, if the child is more or less suited to this permissiveness, it may be just the right sort of parenting style. In final analysis, it appears that the authoritative parental style is the most effective and most appropriate approach to child rearing.

Single-Parent Families

Over 80 percent of the children in the United States live with both of their parents. Another 17–18 percent live with a single parent and the small remainder live in other situations (U. S. Census Bureau, 1975). Of those children that live with one parent, the vast majority live with their mother. The number of children in single-parent families appears to be increasing in the United States. No specific data of this nature are maintained, but for each year since 1974, over 1 million children per year have been involved in a divorce. This divorce situation produces one-parent families, with the mother having custody of the children most of the time.

A common assumption concerning single-parent families is that they are bad for the children, that two parents are a necessity for proper child development. The truthfulness of this assumption depends upon many factors. For example, crucial variables might include the age of the child at the time of the separation, the sex of the child, even social class. What interaction, if any, the child has with the parent that does not live at home may be a factor, too. In some situations, it may be better for the children if the marriage ends and a single-parent situation is created. Single-parent families are not inherently pathological.

The female single parent faces some problems that the male single parent may not face. In many cases, these mothers possess minimal job skills; as a result, there is often a money problem. Society offers little in the way of support for these mothers: day care services are often lacking, and there are few job training opportunities for them. The female single parent is faced with a three-part problem: (1) enacting the role of parent alone; (2) enact-

FAMILY CONSTELLATIONS AND THEIR IMPACT ON CHILDREN

A single-parent family has fun at the park.
JOHN R. MAHER, EKM-NEPENTHE.

ing the role of financial provider; and (3) enacting a social role, trying to put her life back together. Men face similar problems, but very often their economic pressures are somewhat less.

Direct effects of single-parent families on the children are very difficult to state. The single parentness does not cause anything specifically, but may contribute to many different situations. Our society is simply not set up to deal with these types of families.

Dual-Career Families

Dual-career family: both parents having careers

More and more families in the United States are finding it necessary to have two wage earners. This fact, combined with an increased interest in careers on the part of women, has produced a large proportion of women in the labor force and more women pursuing competitive, lucrative careers.

It has been assumed for a long time that mothers working outside of the home is bad for children. At least part of this feeling is

A formal portrait of three-generation family early in the Twentieth Century.
COURTESY OF THE SONOMA COUNTY HISTORICAL SOCIETY.

based upon an erroneous assumption: that women have never worked. Historically, women have always worked, providing for the needs of their families along with males and also many times when the males failed to do so. But it is not working that is producing the problem; it is *where* women are working. Now, more than every before, women are enacting this work role outside of the home. There is a fear that if the mother (as primary nurturing agent) is out of the home, her children will suffer from a lack of appropriate attention and caregiving.

Hoffman (1974), in reviewing the literature on maternal employment, has been able to make several distinct statements concerning the effects of maternal employment.

There is not much support for the contention that the children of working mothers are deprived children. They do not appear to be emotionally starved or lacking in security and trust. It is the quality rather than quantity of the time spent together that seems to make a difference. However, it is difficult to "prove" the quality in a relationship of this type.

Working parents tend to overcompensate. Because of their job commitments, there is a tendency on the part of many working

Another multi-generation American family portrait taken in the 1970's.
GARY ASH

parents to make the time they have with their children as favorable and productive as humanly possible. Sometimes working parents overdo their attentions.

Hoffman did not find significant differences in the child-rearing practices of working mothers versus nonworking mothers. Apparently, job status is not the primary determinant of parenting style.

Contrary to the belief of many, working mothers are not the primary cause of juvenile delinquency. They are not even a minor cause. Working mothers provide a different role model for their children, but there is very little evidence that the single fact that they work outside of the home is a *cause* of juvenile delinquency.

The emotional relationship of the mother to her job is a crucial variable. If she enjoys her work and receives positive support from that job, there will be little negative effect upon the child. If the mother resents her job, however, the potential for problems with the children is much greater.

Both the single-parent family and the dual-career family point to the need for effective, well supported day care programs in the United States.

ISSUE

The Depletion of Children's Family Resources

Human beings create networks of support. These networks, which are made up of other people occupying various roles, provide individuals with the feeling that they have aid when they need it, that they fit somewhere, and that basic needs will be met. Adults have very elaborate social support networks made up of relatives (near and distant family), friends, neighbors, and so on.

☐ Children do not have the social complexity present in their lives that adults do. Consequently, the social support network children will create to help meet their needs is more than likely a function of their family. In a very pragmatic sense, what has happened to children's social support systems?

☐ Within this chapter we have mentioned many variables, such as dual-career families and single-parent families. We stated that the bulk of the literature does not support the contention that these special circumstances hinder children's development. By taking another approach, we would like to explore the possibility that massive changes within the family may mean substantial and significant changes in children's social support systems.

☐ Depending upon the statistics you read, about one child of every six in the United States lives with only one parent. Many studies have shown that this is usually not harmful. The point we may be missing is that there probably are not short-term effects, at least any that will show up in the research studies. This fact probably owes to the resilience of children, more than anything else. What is fundamentally important, however, are the long-term consequences. How will these children go about selecting a mate for themselves? What sorts of expectations will they have for marriage? In what ways will their child-rearing techniques be different from those of their parents and their grandparents? Ultimately, what do these possible differences have to do with the salience and future of American society?

☐ Children's familial resources are also changing in terms of the number of siblings they have. The average family of today is considerably smaller than the family of past times. It is possible that the smaller family unit has less shock resistance than earlier families; crises have different meanings in these smaller, unprotected nuclear families. Parents have disappeared, grandparents have long since disappeared, and siblings are disappearing. The people resources in the children's social support systems are decreasing in number.

☐ The factor that may be most relevant is the rate of the social change in our society. This rapid mutability and secularism barely gives a generation of children a chance to develop traditions. Without basic cultural rites as solidifying agents, modern children have one less viable element in their social support system.

> Segal and Yahraes have said it succinctly: ". . . children today find considerably fewer resources of affection, guidance and support in the family than ever before. For the typical child, it is either from parents or from no one that he or she will receive psychological nurture" (1978, p. 168). There is a burning question that has not been answered: can only two parents rear a child alone? Are the numbers of children not having adequate social support systems reflected in rates of violence, drug abuse, and running away?

MORAL DEVELOPMENT OF THE CHILD

The socialization of children's moral systems has to do with the development of a conscience, a value system, and empathy. There are several important theoretical approaches.

Social Learning Approach

Conscience:
a sense of the moral goodness of one's behavior

Empathy:
the capacity to participate in another's feelings

Social learning theory states that cognitive maturation is important in moral development, but emphasizes rewards, life success, greater awareness, positive self-image, and greater ego strength as being vital to the development of moral principles. Morality can be trained; prosocial behavior can be taught to children through the use of role playing and the judicial use of rewards.

Crucial here is the need to stay relatively independent of rewards; autonomous prosocial behavior on the part of the child is what is desired. The advice to parents on how to teach their children prosocial behavior includes: warm, supportive parental behaviors, and powerful models who reward the children for appropriate behavior, set good examples for the children to model, and use reasoning in explaining appropriate behavior. All the time this is happening, parents need to be aware of age-related changes in behavior and modify their strategies accordingly.

A large part of what makes up moral behavior is dependent upon the culture. Using culture-specific material, moral behavior is socialized through induction (explanations), power assertion (use of force), and love withdrawal.

Cognitive Adaptation Theory of Moral Development

This theory is represented by two major theorists: Piaget and Kohlberg. In Piaget's way of looking at it, children's moral development moves from the *morality of constraint* to the *morality of cooperation* (Piaget, 1965). The morality of constraint is absolute in its perspective and the rules of behavior are inflexible. Assigning blame is very objective and there is a strong belief in arbitrary punishment. The morality of constraint is the product of two basic factors: cognitive immaturity and children's lack of power in comparison to adults.

The morality of cooperation is a much more open point of view. Rules become more flexible and intention on the part of the rule violator is taken into consideration. This movement into the morality of cooperation rests upon three consequences: (1) general intellectual growth; (2) the experience of social equality with peers; and (3) liberation from some of the parental constraints.

These two stages apparently overlap somewhat, with the more mature stage gradually overtaking the first stage. Piaget says that all children make this transition unless there are very stringent limits placed upon them by the environment (Piaget, 1965).

Kohlberg has developed a theory of moral reasoning also based upon the principle of cognitive maturation. He has suggested that there are six stages in the development of moral reasoning that are parts of three broad periods. These stages are sequential, and the sequence is invariant.

Level I Preconventional or premoral level
    Stage 1: punishment and obedience
    Stage 2: instrumental relativist

Level II The conventional level
    Stage 3: the good boy/nice girl orientation
    Stage 4: the law and order orientation

Level III Postconventional morality or the morality of self-accepted moral principles
    Stage 5: the social contract/legalistic orientation
    Stage 6: the universal-ethical principle orientation

(Adapted from Kohlberg, 1966).

This theory of moral reasoning came from a study of boys aged 10, 13, and 16. These boys were asked to respond to moral dilemmas that were violations of traditionally accepted ways of doing things. The subjects were asked to indicate their manner of resolution to the dilemma. One of the more famous dilemmas used was the so-called Heinz dilemma:

In Europe, a woman was near death from a special kind of cancer. There was one drug that the doctors thought might save her. It was a form of radium that a druggist in the same town had recently discovered. The drug was expensive to make, but the druggist was charging ten times what it cost him to make it. He paid $200 for the radium and charged $2,000 for a small dose of the drug. The sick woman's husband, Heinz, went to everyone he knew to borrow the money, but he could only get together about $1,000, which is half of what it cost. He told the druggist that his wife was dying, and asked him to sell it cheaper or let him pay later. But the druggist said, "No, I discovered the drug and I'm going to make money from it." So Heinz got desperate and broke into the man's store to steal the drug for his wife.

After reading the dilemma, the subjects are asked questions. Should Heinz steal the drug? Why? Which is worse: letting someone die or stealing? What does the value of life mean to you, anyway? Would it be as acceptable to steal it for a stranger as for his wife? Suppose he is stealing it for a pet he loved dearly; would this be all right?

Kohlberg was attempting to determine how the subjects were reasoning. Perhaps the way children reason is predictive of their behavior. Moral development is dependent upon the cognitive development of the child.

There is research evidence supporting the work of Kohlberg; some of the evidence is cross-cultural. There is still much controversy concerning the theory, however. Some people are very concerned about a social class emphasis that is in much of Kohlberg's work (there is a social class bias in the development of the upper portions of moral reasoning.) Other people feel there are real methodological problems in the research (see Kurtines and Grief, 1974).

The Holistic Theory

Holistic: describing all aspects of a person

Much less publicized, this theory rests upon two major requisites: (1) gratification of basic psychic needs; and (2) the cultivation of imagination. The use of these creative forces may foster the development of self-esteem and lay the groundwork for responsible moral behavior. Personality development is a whole entity; it is more than just cognition. The holistic approach to moral development states that the entire being (perceptual-emotional-cognitive-social) plays a role in the development of moral behavior.

The Young Child: Families and Their Impact

Summary

1. There are many types of families, like the three-generation or the single-parent family, but they all share the basic function of socialization of the children. The family is a basic transmitter of important information to the child. The family functions interdependently with other institutions.

2. The family is an interactive unit. Interaction is based on: family theme, role power, and reciprocity. Interactive phenomena like birth order and family size seem to affect the nature of child care and development.

3. Parenting styles come in many forms. One way to look at parenting is on two continua: autonomy-control and love-hostility. Another way to look at parenting is Baumrind's theory that permissive, authoritarian and authoritative styles of parenting exist.

4. Family constellations have specific impacts on children. For example, single-parent households have certain problems, while dual-career families have other unique problems to deal with. The long-term effects of either form are not yet known, but research indicates that neither necessarily is detrimental to children.

5. The moral development of children is usually explained in one of three ways: through the social learning perspective; through the cognitive development theory (Piaget and Kohlberg), and through the holistic perspective.

Thought Questions

1. In your estimation, which is better for the children: a nuclear family, a three-generation family, or an extended family? Cite advantages and disadvantages of each type of family.

2. How does the instrumental-expressive dichotomy affect early child development? Are things changing today? Are men still the instrumental members of the family?

3. Differentiate between first borns and last borns. Why the difference? Does your birth position in your family seem to have affected you?

4. Describe how each of the parenting styles as delineated by Baumrind could work in the child's benefit. How could each of them be detrimental?

5. Why are there so many single-parent families in the U.S. today? What happens to the children in them? Are dual-career families something just recently invented? What factors make or break a dual-career family?

6. Do all children reach the postconventional level of morality? Do all people need to reach the postconventional level in order for our society to function?

Suggested Readings

Felker, D. *Building Positive Self Concepts.* Minneapolis, Minn.: Burgess, 1974. *This is a how-to-do-it book focusing on children's self-concepts. It deals with parent and teacher roles in the development and maintenance of these self-concepts.*

Ginott, H. *Between Parent and Child.* New York: Avon, 1965. *Ginott has written a highly useful book dealing with the communication patterns between parent and child. This book is still being used for parent education classes and contains information and ideas still very relevant today.*

Gordon, T. *P.E.T.: Parent Effectiveness Training.* New York: New American Library, 1970. *Thomas Gordon's book is concerned with the issue of effective communication strategies. Gordon's philosophies have evolved into entire parent effectiveness classes enjoying considerable success throughout the country.*

Patterson, G. *Applications of Social Learning to Family Life.* Champaign, Ill.: Research Press, 1976. *Emphasizing the practical approach, Patterson describes the variety of child-rearing situations and problems. Applying social-learning principles, the author discusses child management and parent-child relations.*

READING

The family is the primary agent of socialization of American children. Much of what children learn is the result of the complex interaction of the personalities within the family, whether the family is nuclear, single parent, three generation, or extended.

Within the family, many factors affect the socialization processs: the nature of the familial interaction (warm and accepting, cold and rejecting, overly demanding, or many other variables); the place in the family occupied by the child (birth order); and the style of parenting in the family.

In the following article by Bruce Brown, social-class differences in parenting style are discussed. The paper also explores possible differences in parental behavior in a public place according to social class.

Parenting in our society is literally a no-win proposition. If certain forms of discipline are used in public, the parent will be the object of criticism. In society, parents are given the complete responsibility for their children but ironically are finding their authority for those children being eroded (by the school system, the peer group, and other societal situations). One of the most difficult things for parents to overcome is the manufactured belief that if a child is bad or is misbehaving, the parents are probably doing something wrong in their interaction with the child. The sooner we drop this idea and recognize parents as human beings, the sooner will appropriate expectations be given to parents in terms of their children's behavior.

Parents' Discipline of Children in Public Places
Bruce W. Brown

Numerous studies have investigated the relationship between social class and parents' discipline techniques. To the best of this author's knowledge, none of the previous studies have dealt specifically with discipline in public places. The purpose of the present exploratory research is to study discipline techniques used by parents in public places and to see if the relationship between social class and discipline techniques holds when dealing with discipline in public. It seems plausible that the presence of an "audience" in public places might have some effect on this relationship, for example, possibly decreasing the use of restrictive discipline techniques because "others are watching," or increasing the use of such techniques in order to "get the job done quickly."

Social Class and Discipline Techniques

Goals of Discipline

Several studies have supported the notion that the goals of child discipline differ among class lines. Duvall's analysis indicates that working-class parents' values are "traditional" as compared to the "developmental" values of the middle-class. In other words, working-class parents are more concerned with training their children to conform to external standards, while middle-class parents are more concerned with the child's control of his own behavior. Similarly, Kohn's and Kohn and Carroll's studies found that working-class parents stress obedience to parental commands more than middle-class parents. Mid-

Parenting involves the need for parents to discipline children appropriately.
ROBERT V. ECKERT, JR., EKM-NEPENTHE.

dle-class parents were found to be more concerned that the child be capable of making his own decisions, while working-class parents thought it was most important that the child not break "proper rules."

Kohn explains these social class differences as follows:

Members of different social classes, by virtue of enjoying (or suffering) different conditions of life, come to see the world differently to develop different conceptions of social reality, different aspirations and hopes and fears, different conceptions of the desirable.

Furthermore, these social class differences may be explained by the occupations of parents. Middle-class occupations require a greater degree of self-direction, whereas working-class occupations involve to a greater degree the following of explicit rules set down by those in authority. Therefore, parents from both social classes are preparing their children to survive in the world as they know it. Finally, as Kohn explains, these social class diferences may be explained in part by the differences in educational attainment.

Middle-class parents by virtue of their education may be better equipped to pay greater attention to the child's internal dynamics as facilitated by their learned ability to deal with the subjective and ideational.

Types of Discipline

Parents' perceptions of desirable child behavior are important because these perceptions influence their objectives in child-rearing as well as the discipline techniques they employ to attain these objectives. Bronfenbrenner, in his review article, concluded that middle-class parents are less likely to use physical punishment and more likely to rely on reasoning, isolation, appeals to guilt, and other methods involving the threat of loss of love. However, Erlanger points out that the social class differences may not be as large as Bronfenbrenner suggests.

Kohn found that working-class parents will resort to physical punishment when the immediate consequences of the child's disobedience are most extreme, and will refrain from punishing when this might lead to an even greater disturbance. Middle-class parents, on the other hand, will punish a loss of self-control, a characteristic which they value highly. Rosen found that working-class parents are more likely to use physical punishment and are less likely to rely on reason and appeals to guilt. In an historical analysis of child discipline techniques, Waters and Crandall found that from 1940 to 1960, the higher the family status the less dictatorial were mothers' attempts to influence their children's behavior and the less severe were their penalties for misbehavior. Straus found that "the use of physical punishment is linked to the parents' perception of the kind of world (social class position) that the child will live in as an adult." Finally, Steinmetz provides further evidence and clarification of the relationship between "occupational environment" of parents and the use of physical punishment, with those parents engaged in occupations allowing self-direction being least likely to resort to physical punishment.

In conclusion, the literature indicates that the goals of child-rearing and the discipline techniques employed differ along class lines with working-class parents being less likely to tolerate the "breaking of proper rules" and more likely to resort to physical punishment.

Method

Most previous studies of child discipline have involved obtrusive research designs such as questionnaires, interviews, or obtrusive observations. Such designs are open to behavioral distortion by subjects in the direction of social desirability. The present study provides an opportunity to observe discipline episodes in an unobtrusive manner. Covert observation was used to study parental discipline of children in public places. More specifically, the "complete observer" as described by Gold was the role taken by the author. This role involves observing others without their awareness and without participating in their "world" in any significant way. A question of ethics emerges here. Does the researcher have the right to observe other persons' behavior without their knowledge for the purpose of scientific study? Is this not an invasion of privacy? This question of ethics was resolved in the present study because it involved behavior in public places. As Rosenblatt explains, observation of behavior in public places invades privacy less because people are unlikely to display in public, behavior they would prefer to keep from others.

In this study public place "refers to any region in a community freely accessible to members of that community." Observation sessions were conducted in two phases: the first, a 9 week period during late 1976 and the second, a 7 week period during early 1978. Observation sessions of approximately one and a half hours were made weekly. An enclosed shopping mall was chosen as an observation site because all family members are potentially available since shopping is not an age or sex segregated activity.

The determination of social class was based on the author's subjective evaluation. Subjects were classified as either working-class or middle-class. The key factor involved in this determination was the condition of the subject's clothing. For example, were garments expensive or "cheap," new or old, in style or out of style? As Argyle points out, "in all societies, clothes are used to send information about the personality, status, and group membership of the wearer. . . ." There is empirical evidence to support the validity of such a measure of social class. Sisson found that a person's social class could be determined fairly accurately from still photographs of their clothing. Although, this may seem relatively "unscientific," it is the author's contention that we all make such judgments of other persons' social class in our everyday lives and that we are usually accurate within acceptable limits.

Results

Parents, in their efforts to discipline their children, employ numerous techniques. *Discipline* is defined as any attempt to alter or control a child's behavior. As such, discipline is not limited to such "all time favorites" as yelling and spanking, but also includes reasoning and requesting. A distinction is made here between *restrictive* and

Table 1
Taxonomy and Frequency of Discipline Techniques by Social Class

Discipline Techniques	Frequency Middle-Class	Working-Class
A. Restrictive Techniques		
Hitting or physical force	8	12
Yelling	31	37
Direct commands (without yelling)	26	40
Coming down to child's face level	6	2
Using child's full name	2	0
Threatening	6	14
Staring	6	0
B. Autonomy-Granting Techniques		
Reasoning	13	7
Requesting	14	13
Bribing	4	4
	N=116	N=129

autonomy-granting techniques. This distinction is based on whether the child is being forced, commanded, or threatened into altering their behavior (restrictive), as opposed to relying on their own volition to alter their behavior (autonomy-granting). Table 1 presents a taxonomy of discipline techniques and the frequency with which they were used.

Similar to previous research, a difference was found between social classes in the probability of using restrictive vs. autonomy-granting discipline techniques. Of the working-class parents, (N=129), 81% were found to use restrictive techniques such as hitting, yelling, and direct commands. Middle-class parents (N=116) used such restrictive techniques in 72% of the cases. These social class differences were not statistically significant. One explanation for this may be that, as Erlanger asserts, those social class differences which are operating may simply not be very large. However, it must be kept in mind that Erlanger was concerned with social class differences in the use of *physical* punishment, whereas the present analysis is concerned with restrictive discipline techniques in general, physical punishment being only one of them. A more plausible explanation of the present findings may be that parents view their children's misbehavior in public places as an "emergency situation" and respond with those techniques which are believed to produce the quickest results, i.e., restrictive techniques such as hitting, yelling.

One reason that parents may perceive their children's public misbehavior as an emergency situation is because of several "folk beliefs" about parenthood which are prevalent in American society. Folk beliefs are "widely held beliefs which are not supported by the facts." Those folk beliefs which apply are:

1. Children will turn out well if they have "good" parents.
2. Today's parents are not as good as those of yesterday.
3. There are no bad children—only bad parents.

Because of these folk beliefs, parents may feel that they are being judged as "good or bad" parents based on their children's behavior in public places.

Raina's study of parents' perceptions of the "ideal child" also helps to explain parents' responses to their children's misbehavior in public. Raina found that the following characteristics of an ideal child ranked within the top ten: considerate, courteous, and obedient. Among the ten least desired characteristics were the following: disturbs, stubborn, and critical. Overall, it appears that American parents want children who will be well behaved and do what they are told. Any demarcations from these notions of the "ideal child" may be seen as suggesting that not only does a parent not have an "ideal child," but also that "poor" parenting may be the cause.

As Goffman says, "The rule of behavior that seems to be common to all situations and exclusive to them is the rule obliging participants to 'fit in.'" In the present study, parents seemed to be disciplining their children precisely for not "fitting in." It is assumed that this lack of "fitting in" is perceived by parents as a threat to the "front" which they present to others in public. Swenson explains that embarrassment occurs, ". . . when the front a person is presenting to others is not what he wishes it were. . . ." Not only is embarrassment likely to occur, but as Lundgren found, discrepancies between the ways in which individuals view themselves and the ways they perceive others as responding to them may lead to stress. Many parents, particularly those who used restrictive discipline techniques, were observed to first "look around" to see if others had noticed their child's misbehavior. It was evident from the expression on their faces that embarrassment and stress were at least some of the emotions that many of these parents were experiencing. Therefore, in an effort to present the "good and adequate parent self," parents try to alter their children's misbehavior by disciplining them. However, it is a tricky business because if parents ignore their children's misbehavior they run the risk of being perceived as inadequate parents, but if they discipline too harshly they also run the risk of being perceived as inadequate parents. To complicate matters even further, it is exactly those discipline techniques which are the "harshest" which will usually get the quickest results. Is it any wonder that parents would often rather leave their children at home?

Conclusion

This exploratory study found that parents' discipline of children in public places did not differ significantly along social class lines. Overall, restrictive discipline techniques were used more frequently among both middle-class and working-class parents. A limitation of most previous research has been the dependence upon obtrusive forms of measurement which run a greater risk of subjects distorting their behavior in the direction of social desirability. One advantage of the present study is that discipline episodes were unobtrusively observed as they occurred in "real life."

Because of the exploratory nature of this study several limitations and suggestions for future research need to be mentioned. Certain discipline techniques, such as hitting and yelling, are more noticeable than other techniques, such as reasoning and requesting. The audio component of hitting and yelling operated to attract the author's attention during the observations. Therefore, some techniques had a greater likelihood of being observed and others may have been missed entirely. Also, a suggestion for future research would be to keep the observations unobtrusive, but then, if feasible, interview parents afterwards in order to obtain objective information on social class as well as other variables such as religion, age, occupation, and family life cycle stage. This would serve not only to improve the research methodologically, but would also add to its theoretical value.

In conclusion, a recurrent theme throughout the research was that children were being disciplined for not "fitting in" while in public. This not "fitting in" is seen as threatening parents' presentation of the "good and adequate parent self," thereby causing them embarrassment, and thus explaining, in part, the popularity of the restrictive discipline techniques with their hoped for quicker results. These findings have important implications for parent-effectiveness training programs. If we are to convince parents that there are effective alternatives to the use of restrictive discipline techniques, then we must work toward debunking the myth that "there are no bad children, only bad parents." In other words, until parents' self-esteem becomes less dependent on the behavior of their children, they will hesitate to use those autonomy-granting discipline techniques, which are integral to parent-effectiveness programs, because they take much longer to implement.

UNIT IV
THE MIDDLE YEARS

NATIONAL MUSEUM, STOCKHOLM. PHOTO BY PETER ADELBERG.

Boy Playing the Flute, by Judith Leyster.

13

Middle Childhood: Issues in Cognition

The period of middle childhood is dominated by the school experience. Class peer-group activities, student-teacher relationships, parental attitudes toward schooling, and the particular school curriculum itself deeply influence children's intellectual progress as well as social standing and self-concept. It is a period during which children absorb a tremendous amount of cultural information. It is also the period of basic educational learning: learning to read and to compute with numbers.

Because of the nature of our educational system, children's progress is evaluated and graded at every turn. This naturally affects children's social status since the grading occurs in a context in which competitive peer relations and peer pressure are increasingly important. Children who are developmentally young or disinterested in academics are often shuffled to a particular peer group because they are "slow" in terms of school learning. The school label may have nothing to do with their true intellectual potential, but it does affect friendships and social status.

To what extent the school system responds to the individual child's needs is the subject of unending study and controversy. Should the school run on absolute principles? Should children conform to these? Or should the school serve the child's needs? What is true learning? What is useless learning? Where should the school stand in terms of parental demands? There are many questions that concern the role of formal education in the lives of children. For despite the fact that children spend many hours in school, and the school experience overshadows children's lives at this time, other aspects of growth and involvement are also extremely significant. In this chapter we will explore in particular the child's intellectual development and its relationship to the school experience.

PIAGETIAN LOGIC: THE STAGE OF CONCRETE OPERATIONS

Piaget's three stages that use the word *operation* are: preoperational thought, concrete operational thought, and formal operational thought. The concrete stage lasts about four to six years, on the average. Its identifying characteristics appear in the fifth, sixth, or seventh year and dominate the child's thought processes until about the eleventh or twelfth year. In the ongoing process of intellectual development, it is not easy to make definite boundaries. Piaget saw the concrete stage as a necessary intermediate stage between unformed preoperational logic and the eventual internalized formal logic mastered in adolescence. The essential activity of this stage is physical manipulation of the world. Often this is obtained through play.

Concrete operational thought differs from the other two in that the child needs to have definite and solid or observable materials at hand with which to make a judgment. In preoperational thought, the child's thoughts are not yet integrated into a full and rational system. Despite what the child sees, the conclusions may be irrational. Formal operations, like formal logic, can be dealt with entirely inside the mind. During the period of concrete operations, the child is capable of devising a rational explanation for why the world works as it does, but only with the aid of materials in hand (or in sight). The child is incapable of constructing explanations from abstract evidence.

To illustrate how this works, let us consider the identifying features of concrete operational thought:

1. Conservation
2. Decentration
3. Ability to classify, grasp sequence, and master spatial relations
4. Reversibility
5. Egocentrism

Middle Childhood: Issues in Cognition

The maturation of these cognitive skills (conservation, decentration, classification, seriation, etc.) signals the transition to concrete operational thought. Egocentrism is found in both cognitive periods, although it may be different in appearance at each stage.

One of the problems younger children had toward conservation was that they focused on states. When children reach concrete operations they show "increased attention to transformations as well as states" (Flavell, 1963, p. 166). Instead of measuring the final height of the water poured into two differently shaped glasses, children will notice that all the water from one glass went into the other glass. Children now pay attention to the pouring of the water rather than just to the final appearance of the glasses. They will also remember that one glass is more full looking than the other one, and use this information in making later comparisons.

As long as children can watch the water being poured, they can make a judgment. However, they could not tell you whether a glass that is 4 mm in diameter filled to the 3 mm mark has more or less water than a glass 3 mm in diameter filled to the 4 mm mark even if they were told the formula for this problem ($\pi \times$ Diameter $\times$ Height $=$ Volume). This type of abstract figuring is beyond them. When children *can* do this type of figuring, we say that they have passed from concrete to formal operations in that area.

As we pointed out earlier in this book, conservation is a concept affecting several ideas: number, weight, volume. Children tend to arrive at and leave certain areas of conservation sooner than others. Conservation of number (quantities) usually comes before conservation of weight, which usually comes before conservation of volume. A child of six might already conserve numbers, but a child of eleven or twelve might still not understand conservation of volume (Ginsburg and Opper, 1969).

During these interesting years, a child might use concrete evidence to solve one problem and preoperational tactics to solve another problem. The child's mastery of one area does not transfer to another area, so results in problem solving are often inconsistent. Success in solving certain problems can depend on how the child sees the problem. For instance, suppose a child is shown two pieces of cake, and one is squashed. If asked if they have the same amount of cake in them, the child may or may not be able to answer correctly. If the child sees the problem as one that involves quantity (how much?—one piece here and one piece there), he or she might say "Yes." If the child is trying to judge volume, he or she might say "No" or "I don't know."

Decentration:
the ability to focus on several aspects of an object or event

Children's ability to notice transformations is part of *decentration*, an important feature of concrete thought. In the preoperational stage, children often fix on one aspect of something. As they grow older, they take more details into consideration at once. They integrate several aspects of an object or event, forming a more complete picture of it.

When preoperational children are asked to set sticks of different lengths in sequence, they center on top edges or separate sticks or set the sticks at random. Now, at the concrete stage, children decenter and can grasp the idea of *sequence*. They see the sticks as part of a larger pattern of small to large or big to little.

Decentering also opens children to patterns in *classification*. Rather than centering on a color, shape, personal preference, or one descriptive word, children begin to understand that small categories can be parts of a larger one. Big, blue triangles and little, yellow triangles are all triangles. A preoperational child centering on color, when asked how many triangles there were, might tell you the number of blue triangles and ignore any others. Concrete operational children will see that the idea "triangles" includes the blue triangles as a subcategory.

Lastly, decentration helps children master *spatial relations*. Preoperational children cannot envision a spatial arrangement from other positions (for instance, mirror images or aerial views). This is largely due to young children's ego-centered personality. Older children have a sense of distances, placement, and perspective. They have a backlog of experiential evidence on which to base judgments. This knowledge is demonstrated in their drawings and in making practical guesses. When comparing distances on a map, when determining the placement of players on a field, or when guessing the height of two trees, they rely on physical evidence and known clues.

Accuracy in judgments increases with age, but distortions of fact are also common in midchildhood. This can be attributed to a new form of *egocentric decision making*. Young children are egocentric because they cannot put themselves in another's place. They have difficulty accommodating variety in life. In middle childhood, children accept variety, but they are not always certain how to fit the parts into a whole. To organize their thoughts on a new subject, they will often grab at a few facts, make a hasty explanation (hypothesis), and then rationalize contrary information to fit their hypothesis. In one study, children and adolescents were shown pictures of Stonehenge and asked to guess if it were used as a fort or as a religious shrine (Peel, 1960). At intervals, they were given

Middle Childhood: Issues in Cognition

more and more facts about the site. Once the nine-year-old children had made their decision, they would work new facts into the original explanation. Material that could not possibly fit, they assumed was untrue or wrong. The adolescents would change their hypothesis when the facts refuted their original explanation.

Another aspect of the concrete stage is that children are able to understand what the reverse of an action would be. Reversibility seems to accompany an understanding of conservation. Understanding *reversibility* means understanding that $2 + 3 = 3 + 2$, or that if you cut a triangle into pieces you could put the pieces back together to form one big triangle again, etc. Piaget felt that reversibility was *"the* core property or cognition-in-a-system—the one from which all others derive" (Flavell, 1963, p. 189). In other words, if you knew something "forward and backward" you really understand it.

Reversibility: the ability to understand the reverse of an operation

ORGANIZATION OF THOUGHT

Children's systems for ordering information are another aspect of intellectual growth in these years. In general, school-aged children show increasing efficiency in their ability to organize ideas throughout the concrete stage. The study of memory is our main avenue for exploring this change. Newly learned material has lasting importance only when it can be retained.

Memory

People first demonstrate memory in infancy. They may recognize a face or a room. Later, we have evidence of it in deferred imitation, symbolic play, and the use of language. Memory seems to be essential for cognitive growth. Without it information cannot be recalled for use. How images come to be imprinted and stored in the first place is currently the subject of many studies and experiments.

Memory: the ability to recall previously learned information

In 1890, the psychologist William James proposed that there were two sorts of memory: primary and secondary. His theory was simply one of several for many years. Others proposed that memories crowded the mind like furniture stored in a warehouse, or that memories were ordered like cards in a file cabinet. These theories were usually the outgrowth of studies on other topics. The first theory to deal just with memory appeared in the mid-1960s (Kagan et al., 1973). It revived James's idea of two sorts of memory, and proposed that primary memory had limited storage space. If a memory could no longer be kept in primary memory, it had to move to secondary memory or be discarded (Waugh and Normal, 1965). Building from this idea, Atkinson and Shiffrin proposed in 1968 that memory worked like a computer with memory banks (structures) and intricate information-processing programs (controls). These theories have deeply influenced later studies. No doubt the "machine model" is popular now, in part, because it corresponds to studies made to improve artificial intelligence in computers.

Today we call primary memory a *short-term* memory system. After a few seconds or minutes the memory is lost unless it is consciously kept in mind. This is called *rehearsal*. Secondary memory is a *long-term* memory system. Long after the event the mind can retrieve information stored there. There has also been some study of what may be a third category, *sensory memory*. As it was studied in the 1960s, this storage system is shorter lived than short-term memory and works unconsciously, like a reflex. A sensory memory seems to remain completely intact immediately after an event, and then breaks down after a few seconds (Sperling, 1963).

Although intelligence tests have included tests of memory throughout this century, it is only in the last 15 years that psychologists have made tests specifically to explore the development of memory processes in children. They have found that at all ages people remember the items at the end of a series better than those given at the beginning. This is called the *recency effect*. Also, *recognition memory* is better at all ages than *recall memory*. Even four-year-olds can recognize (by pointing) 12 pictures shown to them before. If asked about the pictures, they are not likely to recall more than two or three (Kagan et al., 1973). Psychologists have found that older children perform better because they use strategies for remembering. Strategies improve memory. Pointing to where missing items used to stand (Flavell et al., 1970), labeling (naming) items (Kingsley and Hagen, 1969), grouping and classifying (Moely et al., 1969, and Liberty and Ornstein, 1973), practicing them (rehearsal), and forming a mental image or imaginary context (Brown, 1975) are strategies children were observed using in different experiments.

The younger children are when tested, the fewer strategies they employ. Four- and five-year-olds use grouping and labeling, but they do not usually classify items or rehearse them. Six- and seven-year-olds label items, group them in some way, and may even classify them into distinct categories, but they also do not usually

Sensory memory: an unconscious, short-lived, reflexive memory

Games like checkers involve various memory systems depending upon the age and skill of the player.
ROBERT V. ECKERT, JR., EKM-NEPENTHE.

rehearse. Mentally or physically reviewing information seems to make a significant difference in performance on memory tests, but most young children do not spontaneously think to use this "trick." Not until they are 10 or 11 do children spontaneously rehearse. In each age group some children use more advanced strategies if they are told what to do, but only on that test. On the next test they use their old tactics again (Keeney et al., 1967 and Moely et al., 1969). As children grow older, they begin to see the advantage of strategies. Not only do older children use more strategies, but they also know they are using them, and they use them more efficiently. For instance, older children tend to classify lists of words into fewer, more inclusive, more useful categories than younger children (Lange and Hultsch, 1970). They also will choose among various strategies to suit the task at hand.

It is well recognized that *affective* conditions influence performance on memory tests. Affective conditions include planned and unplanned distractions, personal attitudes in the testing room, and physical and emotional well-being at the time of the test. For instance, young children cannot usually recall long lists of words using their limited strategies. If children become discouraged while trying to memorize such a list, they may "give up" and score poorly. If they are preoccupied with other thoughts, or feel hot, hungry, or otherwise uncomfortable, they may remember fewer items than they could—even on a short list. After all, the test situation is an artificial one. Children are usually asked to remember groups or lists of pictures, words, or numbers. This requires more concentration than real-life situations in which children are engaged in an activity that is meaningful to them (Brown, 1975). It is reasonable to assume, however, that affective conditions influence children's memory skills and development in natural settings, too.

Piaget proposes that memory itself changes as we grow older. We encode our images with the understanding that we have at the time. When recalling the memory from the past, we *reconstruct* it. We literally rebuild the memory, using any new strategies or information we possess to give the memory meaning (Piaget and Inhelder, 1969). The preoperational boy who could not draw the intermediate stages of a tumbling tower of blocks did not understand transformations. Six months later he may be able to draw the stages correctly from memory. This theory implies that each child's memories are personal. Machine model theories tend to neglect this aspect.

Reconstruction: the way in which memory grows as children understand more

INTELLIGENCE PREDICTIONS

Older research indicates that there are moderately strong correlational relationships between IQ performance and factors like reading comprehension, English usage, and performance in other academic areas (Bond, 1940; Honzik et al., 1948). The *predictiveness* of intelligence tests, however, remains one of the controversies raging over their use. One of the problems with trying to make a prediction that a child will perform at a certain level based on the results of an IQ test is the variability of the test score. It needs to be administered more than just once or twice; it is inappropriate to make a large number of predictions about children's future performance on the basis of one or two tests (McCall, Applebaum and Hogarty, 1973).

There are many factors that affect the predictiveness of IQ tests. There are indications, for example, that tests may not be applicable to and consequently not predictive for minority children. In one study, performance on the Wechsler was a valid predictor for the school performance of Anglo children but not for the black and Mexican-American children in the study (Goldman and Hartig, 1976). On the other hand, IQ tests may be predictive very early. For example, one study used IQs between the ages of 3 and 18 to predict adult educational and occupational status after the age of 26 (McCall, 1977). McCall found that by the second grade IQ scores were as predictive of adult status as were adult IQs.

CULTURAL BIAS IN INTELLIGENCE TESTS

In 1972 Francine Patterson, a psychology student at Stanford University, acquired a 13-month-old gorilla from the San Francisco Zoo. Her object was to study Koko's ability to learn Ameslan (American Sign Language). Koko became a star pupil. Incidentally, Koko was given human intelligence tests. Although Koko's IQ scores compared well with an average child's of her age (85 to 95), Patterson found that Koko's scores suffered from the "human bias" in the tests.

> One quiz asked the child, "Point to the two things that are good to eat." The depicted objects were a block, an apple, a shoe, a flower, and an ice-cream sundae. Koko, reflecting her gorilla tastes, picked the apple and the flower. Another asked the child where he would run to shelter from the rain. The choices were a hat, a spoon, a tree, and a house. Koko naturally chose the tree. Rules for the scoring required that I record these responses as errors (*National Geographic* 154:4, 1978).

This example of cultural bias is not as outlandish as it seems. In exactly the same way, intelligence tests discriminate against any child reared in a subculture different from the technological, white, middle-class, American culture for which the test was made. As cultural minorities have struggled for fair treatment, one target of their protests has been the standardized intelligence test. IQ scores have frequently been used for school placement or student evaluation. Minority and poverty children, who often do not test as well as white middle-class American children, are sometimes labeled slow or even retarded. This labeling has damaging repercussions. Studies on teachers' attitudes toward students indicate that many teachers do not exert themselves for students they believe to have low intelligence. The children, too, often develop low self-esteem and lose motivation for learning when relegated to slow classes (Rosenthal and Jacobson, 1968). Thus the prophecy is self-fulfilling. Worst of all, this pattern is often set as early as kindergarten or first grade and carries through the school years.

Three components dominate intelligence test performance: verbal abilities, motivation, and cultural orientation and training. Since the tests rely heavily on reading, children with poor verbal skills in English will have difficulty understanding and responding to the test items, and so may appear to be of lower intelligence than they really are.

To score well, as many items as possible must be completed, often within a time limit. The motivation to do this is a highly variable factor. In an experiment by Katz, Hency, and Allen (1968) black boys between seven and ten performed significantly better when directed by a black rather than a white experimenter.

Culture-Free Tests

Culture-free test: an intelligence test without cultural biases

Is it possible to devise an intelligence test that is free of cultural bias? Several proposals have been made. One approach is to test children with items from their own culture. The Stanford-Binet test does this for white middle-class American children with good schooling in Western European and American cultural ideas. The sociologist Adrian Dove half-seriously devised a short 30-question test called the Counterbalance General Intelligence Test (known as the Chitling Test) to demonstrate the disadvantage minority groups (in this case black children) face when taking standardized tests. Here is a sampling of the items.

A "handkerchief head" is: (a) a cool cat
                                (b) a porter
                                (c) an Uncle Tom
                                (d) a hoddi
                                (e) a preacher

A "gas head" is a: (a) fast-moving car
                         (b) stable of "lace"
                         (c) "process"
                         (d) habit of stealing cars
                         (e) long jail record for arson

T-Bone Walker got famous for playing: (a) trombone
                                (b) piano
                                (c) T-flute
                                (d) guitar
                                (e) ham-bone

(*Newsweek*, 1968)*

*Answers: c, c, d

Another idea is to devise test items that are familiar to all ethnic groups, and state them in simple, concrete language. A question like, "Cub is to bear as gosling is to _____" might use the more familiar examples of puppy/dog—kitten/cat. Or instead of the abstract "A weighs less than B; B weighs less than C; therefore _____," the test might ask, "If Bob can hit harder than Jason, and Jason can hit harder than Glenn, then _____." This problem uses the same reasoning principles.

ENHANCING INTELLIGENCE

In the early part of this century, H. M. Skeels, a psychologist, found that when he moved orphans who had been raised in sterile institutional settings into loving and more stimulating environments, their IQs increased. These children, marked as retarded by earlier tests, scored anywhere from 7 to 58 points higher within a few years. Into adulthood, every aspect of their lives proved more normal and productive than those of the children left in the orphanage (Skeels and Dye, 1939).

We may have genetic limitations, but a more immediate concern for most people is developing the intellectual capacities we, and our children, have. The benefits of emotional stability and environmental stimulation demonstrated by Skeels's experiment have been substantiated by more recent studies. Lower-class preschoolers whose mothers or fathers show attentive nurturing behavior consistently show more intelligent behavior than peers without such attention (Radin, 1971, 1972). Also good nutrition seems to be important for mental development. This fact is the lasting contribution of the Head Start program of the 1960s and 1970s. Specifically training children to be intelligent does not seem to be possible, however. Early educational programs in nurseries, preschools and day care centers have shown immediate, temporary enhancement, but no long-lasting cognitive acceleration in children. Cultural and parental attitudes toward learning, some stimulation, and general physical and psychological well-being seem to be of greater importance.

LEARNING DISABILITIES

Some children do not progress evenly in academic learning. They may be children of any IQ level. They differ from handicapped children in that they have no obvious physical impediment. They are not blind or deaf, although they sometimes may act as if they were. They are not simply developmentally young, nor are they simply slow learners. On the contrary, they may learn quickly in one area, but will struggle endlessly in another. Their performance is notably erratic. These children are the *learning disabled*.

Learning disabilities are neurological in origin. There is some disruption to the perceptual processing systems within such children that makes it difficult or impossible for them to decode certain impressions—sights, sounds, spatial arrangements. These deficiencies then result in a specific learning problem. The labels for these problems reflect their nature. *Dyslexia* is difficulty with reading. *Dysgraphia* is difficulty with writing or redrawing shapes. Sometimes when the specific problem is too difficult to identify, or too general, children are said to have *"minimal brain damage."* They do not display the characteristics of serious brain damage, but obviously their brains are sending some scrambled messages. We have already (in Chapter 9) mentioned the behavior-related disability of *hyperactivity*, in which behaviors inhibit children's ability to take in information. All of these problems, of course, are beyond a child's control.

Dyslexia:
a reading disability

Minimal brain damage:
ambiguous term for nonspecified damage to the brain

It is important to point out that "this is basically a psychoeducational problem, not a medical problem" (Cruickshank, 1977, p. 55). Such difficulties are apparent and cause problems only in the setting of formal education, where these children cannot complete customary tasks. Outside the school environment, their disability is merely an idiosyncratic trait, not a major embarrassment. As these children grow older, they usually develop adequate coping techniques, so that eventually learning disabilities are "outgrown."

The issue of learning disabilities is a very broad and complex one. This section is short, and does not go into the detail needed for a complete understanding of this emotional issue. By introducing the topic, we encourage the student to go on to investigate this issue through coursework and independent study.

VITAL ISSUES IN EDUCATION

Schools are receiving a lot of criticism today. Since 1963, scores on the Scholastic Aptitude Test (SAT), the traditional college entrance test, have declined steadily (*Science News* 112, 1977). Public opinion faults schools for the lower achievement levels. Criticism of schools includes charges of permissiveness, too much time spent on nonacademic subjects, too many electives, too little instruction in the basics, and too little attention to covering necessary cultural information.

The question is, who is responsible for this situation? How did it come about? What should be done?

Education was once the sole responsibility of the family. In many primitive cultures this is still true. In ancient Athens citizenship was granted only to those with an education that covered reading, writing, counting, music, and gymnastics. How children came to master these subjects was left to the parents. They could instruct the children themselves, obtain a tutor, send the children to a school, or just let them absorb the necessary information without formal instruction. The state allowed the family complete control of this situation (Cubberly, 1920).

The history of education is a fascinating one and is too long to cover here. Through the centuries, the family eventually assigned the role of educator to an institutional system completely outside the home. Today in the United States, guidelines and requirements are set by a bureaucracy of federal and state governments, district committees, and local school boards. Supposedly, the taxpayers control educational standards, although the bureaucracy that sets the standards and the legal system that enforces school attendance are both established by the state. Public opinion constantly shifts and struggles with questions of authority and responsibility. On one hand, the public views teachers as professionals who are the best judge of educational priorities. They are also held responsible for children's achievements. On the other hand, some parents want to be able to control curriculum (for instance, what books their children should be allowed to read). They see this control as their right.

Parents and other taxpayers have the ultimate decisions, since they vote for district finances. Without adequate funds, teachers face losing their positions or find themselves teaching with inadequate materials. To avoid this, teachers try to keep abreast of public expectations. On the other hand, teachers themselves feel they should have more freedom to teach what they see as important for their students. They also want more control of their jobs in general. These reasons partly account for the growing strength of teachers' unions.

To return to the original question of who is responsible, we must look not only at the school-family dispute, but also at technological and social influences. Television has deeply influenced American life. Not only is it a major distraction to homework, reading, and chats with others (by which cultural information is passed along), it also seems to program children to being entertained constantly. Teachers simply cannot be expected to compare favorably with a

Some parents of today contend that the public schools in the United States should abandon permissiveness and return to the regimentation that they believe existed in the schools of an earlier era.
COURTESY SONOMA COUNTY HISTORICAL SOCIETY.

beautiful (or handsome) singer, a comedian, or a family full of laughs. Social attitudes affecting education also contribute to the current trend toward lower achievement. Absenteeism is condoned by parents and teachers far more than it was 20 years ago. Grades and competition have been devalued. And homework is no longer assigned in many schools (*Science News* 112, 1977). The current situation reflects a change of climate in public opinion.

Teachers

Teachers today are given considerable responsibility for raising children. Not only do they care for them during a large part of the day, they are also often expected to act as parent substitutes. They are sometimes expected to teach personal moral values and practical competency skills, instill obedient behavior patterns, or teach about sexual maturation. These are realms that formerly belonged to parents. Although it is not truly their job, many teachers find themselves giving this instruction and guidance by default.

One concern about this situation is that in the elementary grades the majority of teachers are female. This gives children an almost continuous female role model during their formative years. In fact, when asked to assign masculine or feminine labels to neutral objects, school children assigned a feminine character to school-related objects (Maccoby and Jacklin, 1974).

The Disadvantaged Child in the Schools

What happens to the disadvantaged child in the school system? The handicapped child? The child with learning disabilities? How does the public education system serve them?

First of all, there are usually counselors, psychologists, and special instructors associated with a school or district who can assist teachers to identify, integrate, or direct to help students who do not fit into the normal classroom. There are also many schools that accommodate children who require special attention—though not as many public ones as are needed. The teachers at these schools are trained to work with the children's problems. The student-teacher ratio is lower than in the average classroom. The children are in a setting where growth may more easily take place. The advantage of these facilities to disabled children is immeasurable.

The degree to which public schools can accommodate the handicapped depends on the nature of the handicap, how recently the school was built, and how wealthy or urban the school is. For instance, it is not easy for a school to obtain a Braille library of school texts. If the school can do so, however, blind children can sometimes integrate happily into a regular classroom. The deaf are less easily integrated. They cannot communicate with the class unless the teacher and some of the students can speak Ameslan (American Sign Language). For this reason, they often attend only special schools for the deaf, or deaf and blind. Children with physical handicaps will have some difficulties, depending on the nature of the handicap. If the child requires a wheel chair, the school must be built to accommodate it. Recently, it has become a requirement in some states to provide entrances and passageways for the handicapped in all public buildings. This does not mean that the neighborhood school will have one. Since every child has the right to demand a public education, no longer must a handicapped child's parents find and pay the high price of a private school. However, in reality the parents may prefer that to a long bus ride to the district's only school equipped to help special children.

ISSUE

Busing School Children to Achieve Racial Integration

One of the most significant issues surrounding education in the United States is the busing of children out of their neighborhoods and into other schools in order to achieve racial balance in all schools within a particular district. This movement appears to be based on a philosophical principle: particular schools may have a character that causes them to affect students in particular ways. Ghetto schools probably have a smaller tax base, and since schools are often funded through the property tax base, the dollars available for these schools may be limited. This lack of funds hampers the necessary upkeep on the physical plant, and may affect the materials used in the classroom, like books and expendable supplies.

☐ The busing movement has many unique characteristics to it. For example, most movements that attempt to bring about massive social change have a great deal of political support, as well as grassroots support from many people. There is little doubt that busing does have the support of many people and organizations. But in a new report, Gary Orfield states that busing is unique because seldom in history has a decision that is mainly a court decision been given so little support by elected officials (*Must We Bus: Segregated Schools and National Policy,* Washington: Brookings Institution, 1978). As we have witnessed in places like Boston, there is often violent reaction against busing by the people in the neighborhoods. Boston is only one of many places where there is little in the way of grassroots support.

☐ Another of the puzzling dimensions of the busing controversy is the fact that there has been little systematic study devoted to a social change of this magnitude. We really have very little data saying there are positive or negative effects of busing. For example, there is little direct evidence that busing will harm the education of white children—one of the many unsubstantiated charges made by the movement's opponents. This concern is raised often in the heated discussions surrounding busing. It appears that the *way busing is handled,* not busing itself, may have an effect on the performance of children, but there is also little evidence to support this argument.

☐ Some people criticize busing because of the increase in violence that it brings. Here again, there are few instances of violence, but generally, desegregation through the use of busing has been nonviolent and orderly in nature. As in many things, media coverage of particular situations heightens our sensitivity to the issue, and in some cases probably contributes to unruly behavior.

☐ The busing issue has had its share of casualties, other than the children who seem perpetually caught in the middle of this huge legal and social struggle. For example, the president of the Los Angeles Board of Education was recalled by a very potent coalition that was strongly opposed to "forced busing." Interestingly,

Middle Childhood: Issues in Cognition

ROBERT V. ECKERT, JR., EKM-NEPENTHE.

black voters were 90 percent against the recall, but turned out in too few numbers to make much of a difference in the election.

☐ The busing issue comes down to two basic questions: Is busing of school children the answer to the segregation problem? Does the busing problem actually go deeper—are Americans really ready and willing to desegregate? The future of American children is really very much dependent on finding out the answer to these crucial questions.

Summary

1. One of the developmental milestones of middle childhood is the entrance of the child into the American system of compulsory education. Compulsory education in the U.S. is age-graded (there are specific levels of accomplishment), and each student is evaluated in progress before being allowed into the next level.

2. The period of concrete operations is a significant development in children's middle years. Lasting four to six years, this period is characterized by the development of conservation and decentration, the acquisition of the ability to understand the reversibility of operations, and the ability to effectively classify environmental components.

3. While memory is manifested in all but the youngest of babies (and it may be present there as well), memory is an increasingly important aspect of children, particularly in their relationship with the school system. Memory appears to be made up of three parts: short-term memory, long-term memory, and something called sensory memory. Many factors affect the memory processes of children, one

of which is their affective state. Piaget conceptualizes memory as a process of reconstructing the existing memory on the basis of the new information the child is acquiring.

4. As was also mentioned in an earlier chapter, there may be a significant problem in bias in the construction of most intelligence tests. Culture-free tests, or those without bias, are very hard to construct, and are not used to a great extent. Some intelligence tests probably discriminate against any child reared in an environment qualitatively different than that from which the test came.

5. The education of our children is a vital issue. Public education is currently debating, among other things, busing children to achieve racial equality, serving handicapped children and those who apparently have learning disabilities, the demands placed on teachers, and the insidious decline of children's test scores since 1963.

Thought Questions

1. What is the significance of a compulsory school system? Should tax dollars be provided to support private education? What are the advantages and disadvantages, in your mind, of having specified grades in school?

2. What is different about the period of concrete operations in comparison with the preoperational and sensorimotor periods? How does the period of concrete operations prepare the child for formal education?

3. Should we eliminate all tests of intelligence? Why? What are the advantages and disadvantages of parents knowing their child's IQ?

4. What is the rationale for busing children to achieve racial equality? What do you see as problems in this procedure? What are the advantages?

Suggested Readings

Bloomberg, M., ed. *Creativity: Theory and Research.* New Haven, Conn.: College and University Press, 1973. *This anthology of readings on the creative process includes works of some of the big names in the field: Carl Rogers, Paul Torrance, and many others.*

Kaufman, B. *Son Rise.* New York: Harper & Row, 1976. *This is a father telling the story of his autistic child. It realistically and movingly tells the parental, medical, and family reaction to the child's problem.*

Sattler, J.M. *Assessment of Children's Intelligence.* Philadelphia: W.B. Saunders, 1974. *This is a basic assessment textbook. All kinds of tests are described, ranging from the WISC to the WPPSI. Psychological problems of children are also discussed.*

READING

Special education and related research have made very significant strides recently in terms of identification and treatment of children with a wide variety of learning disorders. In the previous chapter, we briefly mentioned learning disabilities and the very recent educational trend designed at keeping many handicapped children in the regular classroom, called mainstreaming.

In a very sensitive article by Erika Duncan, the plight of eight-year-old Athelantis Perry is examined. The author boldly explores the stereotypes that have been created about all handicapped persons and examines the taboo Americans seem to have about handicapped people, whether it is a physical handicap or a mental handicap. The hardships involved in this case, both for Athelantis and his parents, point to the bureaucratic insensitivity in regard to these children and to the very real challenge that mainstreaming presents to parents, teachers, and the entire school system.

A Sense of Hope
Erika Duncan

This year, eight-year-old Athelantis Perry is starting school for the first time. His mother had tried to register him when he was five, but the public school system seemed to have no place for a brain-injured child who was half-blind yet already reading well, studying French and writing script, although his fingers had no middle knuckles and had until recently been webbed. She also tried the private schools, where the boy's tuition would have been covered by the government under a bill that grants aid for education to all children unable to be appropriately placed publicly, but no one was willing to take him. One head mistress confessed that Athelantis, with his tearing, bulging eyes, his slightly pointed head and still-meshed toes, made her personally uncomfortable. Another said she was concerned that admitting such a child would adversely affect her funding sources.

We are so terribly frightened by deviation and abnormality that most children with severe physical handicaps are kept hidden by their parents and denied even the hope for life within the mainstream. Because of the stigma attached to their very existence, they learn to experience themselves as burdens, responsible for the inevitable shrinking and withdrawal that the lives of those closest to them must undergo in order to accommodate their weight and shelter them. Even if they are adequately cared for, it is very hard for them to find the strength to later go out in the world.

Throughout history there has been a taboo associated with severe disability. In most societies, those with apparent physical differences have been isolated from their more normal peers out of a terror of invisible contamination and contagion. Whereas in primitive cultures babies born greatly deviating from the norm were often openly destroyed (or less frequently became the objects of worship, still a form of isolation and protection from contact), in contemporary Western society the hostile reaction to the handicapped on the part of the healthy has been much more insidious. With our emphasis on concepts of survival of the fittest and bodily strength, we are far too inclined to view the handicapped person as a stereotype defined by the particular nature of the disability. Through the avoidance of identification with the individuals who bear marked manifestations of the physical weaknesses we find so frightening, we are able to keep away the consciousness of our own impermanence, our ultimate vulnerability to body breakage and decay and death. Yet more and more, the handicapped themselves are forcing us to acknowledge the power of their being in the world. They are demanding not only equality but those changes in our society that will make room for the meaningful contributions to the common life their special struggle has equipped them for. And like all oppressed peoples just learning to break free, they bring to this struggle new areas of energy and insight that will feed us all.

It is in this context that the story of eight-year-old Athelantis Perry becomes important. Because his parents happened to have a great deal of strength, he never developed the sense of hopelessness that most such children have. A victim of Apert's syndrome, one of a family of Crouzon diseases, he spent the greater portion of his early years in clinics and hospitals, undergoing first the operation necessary to separate the fused cranial sutures that threatened to compress his growing brain and permanently stunt his mental life, and later, the slow freeing of his fingers that were first surgically divided into pairs and then into the individual digits they were meant to be. Only one separation could be accomplished at a time, and operations on alternating hands were often many months apart, keeping mother and child in a constant state of anxiety and anticipation. (His thumbs were free from the beginning, giving him the same chance to learn to grasp and work forefinger and thumb in opposition that normal babies have, a crucial developmental advantage over many children with similar problems.) Although Athelantis feels sad that his "toes are stuck," his parents have decided to leave them meshed because his feet are growing normally and have full movement. He will never wear sandals like the other children whom he envies, but at least eight additional operations will be avoided. Eventually, after his growth rate has subsided somewhat, a breaking of his finger bones is planned, so that he will be given a slight curve where his middle knuckles ought to have been. Although that portion of his fingers will remain immobile, his hands will look more natural and will be better equipped to grasp. This procedure, however, will not take place for quite a while. Right now the family is taking a rest. Besides, with permanent teeth starting to come in, complicated orthodontics will soon have to begin, because his tiny lower jaw, which in Apert's grows much more slowly than the upper, is unable to house the complete set of permanent teeth he was endowed with, now crowding beneath his gum in double layering.

When Athelantis Perry was born looking just like a lost sea creature, his father, the family physician and a friend all fell upon one another's shoulders and cried. The parents were advised to leave the baby in the hospital until he died. Many children born looking like him are abandoned. But Ernie, the infant's father, a black man from the rural South, insisted that "if the baby is gonna die, he ought to die home." Ernie had grown up in an extended family where it was taken for granted that all people in trouble would be taken in and cared for, where even illegitimate babies could always find a place. Barbara, the child's mother, a white woman, is a person who refuses to give up easily, as the next few years of her life would testify. Her perseverance and fighting nature in this extremely trying situation were a continual source of amazement to all who knew her. From the time the couple received the phone call from the hospital where their baby had been detained for an accurate diagnosis, saying he would survive and could come home, their belief never wavered. Because the child seemed sent from an era long gone in human evolution, they named him Athelantis for the legendary sunken continent, adding an extra syllable for cadence. The vigilance over his life became their special mission.

The early years were difficult ones, especially for Barbara, because she was the one to undergo the endless days of waiting in poor clinics, wards and surgeons' offices. She was also the one to make most of the important medical decisions, which, because of the lack of respect so often shown the patient in our system, frequently had to be made on the spur of the moment in order to ensure the proper scheduling of the next operation, the next surgical process. Most mothers experience to some extent the weight and loneliness that the sole responsibility for those daily decisions affecting the destinies of their children brings about. For Barbara these feelings were greatly intensified, since in her case the decision that lay on her shoulders could determine life or death. An error in judgment could mean possible retardation as opposed to normal mental functioning. And any unwise hesitation or letting down of guard could have serious consequences, as in the case where a cranial operation was postponed for several weeks by careless physicians, causing a dangerous pressure on the optic nerve that had a permanent effect on the boy's vision.

Middle Childhood: Issues in Cognition

Those early years took quite a toll on Barbara and Ernie's marriage because of all the weight on Barbara; but the couple remained undefeated, finding new sources of strength through the experience. Perhaps, in certain ways, they were better equipped than most people to deal with what by any standards was a frightfully difficult situation. They were also more ready to help *any* child that they might have in the battle they knew that life would be. Long before "'Lantis" was born, they were aware that as the product of an interracial marriage he would have to struggle and be strong. Quite early in the pregnancy, they had had to come to terms with the problems that such a struggle would present to them. Thus, ironically, they were actually in a better position to deal with the many hardships the boy's multiple handicaps caused them than an "idyllic" couple anticipating a clear, unclouded future.

Too often in those other cases, the coming of a seriously disabled child is experienced as a terrible blow to the parents. In an effort to preserve an endangered self-image, parents frequently keep such a child hidden or isolated from the other areas of their lives. This reflects what we do as a culture when we refuse to mainstream those people whose handicaps and pains make us uncomfortable. But in the long run, the parents' failure to incorporate the damaged child into the overall meaning of their existence creates such splits of self-perception and such doubts in sense of purpose, that the entire structure of the family must start to shrivel from the artificiality of the premises upon which it has been erected. And finally even those so carefully protected areas of "safe" outside activity gradually begin to topple from the strain. This, too, probably happens on a broader scale to our whole society, which only hurts itself in its refusal to listen to the voices of its wounded.

Not surprisingly, the parents of Athelantis Perry are politically and artistically committed people who are interested in issues that go far beyond their personal problems. Ernie, who works with delinquent children through the New York State Division for Youth, is deeply committed to helping entire families in crisis. He and Barbara met when she was working with gangs and pursuing a particular interest in deviant behavior and delinquency. Barbara is also a writer and printmaker, with a long history of involvement in children's theater. Because they were already involved in the creation of change, they were less likely to be defeated either by a tragic-seeming individual situation or by a society that presented so many obstacles to their child's eventual acceptance by the mainstream.

Unlike so many others, they never tried to hide the child or separate his care from their important work. Instead, they gathered new directions for themselves from his existence. In turning those very obstacles that his difficulties presented into the positive material for their own political activity, their social work and art, they acquired the sense of mission that all artists and transformers need, one that endowed the hardships they underwent with deeper meaning and helped them endure.

Out of the years of days and weeks spent in the gloomy waiting rooms of welfare hospitals and on the clinic lines, seeking the medical help and the respect not freely offered to the downtrodden and bleak, Barbara was able to write her moving book, *Care Without Care*, a personal account and exposition of what too often happens in hospital treatment for the poor. Published by Avon, the book was used in training student MDs and makes a passionate plea for a more humanized kind of medical care. More recently she has been active in the mainstreaming of handicapped children into the public school system. And, always involved in children's theater projects, she has lately turned her efforts toward a "theater for hurt children," creating dramatic productions meant to provide handicapped children with the rich variety of visual, auditory and sensory stimuli that she believes will awaken their full learning potential. When funding sources for her theater projects disappeared (partly, she suspects, because her focus on the handicapped created some discomfort), she began working with the same ideas in books, printed herself by letterpress. These children's stories and puppet play scripts are her most recent undertaking, produced in a back room of her apartment under the imprint of "Ten Penny Players."

Somehow, over the past few years, she also managed to write a book on Mother Mandelbaum, the turn-of-the-century matriarchal leader of a ring of "pacifist pickpockets" that resulted in the rescue of women from the alternative horrors of starvation or prostitution, and child pickpockets from Fagin-type oppressors. Interestingly, inherent in the subject matter that she chose is the investigation of the creation of alternative survival systems for outlaws who are unable to fit in, a reflection of her internal awareness that she, too, would have to make the world in which her son could truly thrive. The Mother Mandelbaum manuscript remains unpublished.

Because Barbara never tried to separate her involvement with helping 'Lantis from her own professional development, because she was able to energize the concerns that first grew up around him and turn them into the subject of the work most vital to her, this child who might well have grown up experiencing himself as a burden has been given the opportunity to feel himself an active participant in the full life activity of his parents, a person in his own right, central also to his world. Through their commitment to the boy's potential in a total context, this child whom many others would have dismissed as hopeless has been offered real help, real hope.

Considering the obstacles, Athelantis's progress and functioning have been astounding, perhaps because astounding demands have been placed on him. Strong in his sense of self, he forces those other children most frightened by his physical abnormalities to deal with him. There was a little girl in his nursery school who was afraid to hold his paddle-shaped hand, so he would choose her as a partner when the group went on walks so that she might get used to him. And just last summer, although his fingers cannot bend as other children's fingers do, his mother told him that he could not go to daycamp unless he learned to tie his shoelaces. Of course, he did!

Barbara is someone who has never been able to take no for an answer. Dissatisfied with the rehabilitation program offered by the hospital, she discovered the Institute for the Achievement of Human Potential in Philadelphia. For 16 months, the family participated in the institute's controversial patterning program. During that period, literally every minute of the day was accounted for in a rigid series of very strenuous exercises. When Harry Kimmel, MD, the boy's pediatrician, was asked what he thought about the institute's approach, which is based on the relearning of the correct method of creeping upon which all later neurological balance is said to depend, he admitted that he had been skeptical about the program, and still was. (It was unbelievably time consuming, and the creeping exercise alone called for three people to assist, one on each side to manipulate the limbs and one to turn the head in rhythm.) Nonetheless, he encouraged Barbara to try it. "It organized her and gave her the force to believe in something. It created a new religion for her," he said. "And how could anyone quarrel with something which had worked so wonderfully?"

Talking to him reassured me, for I was having great difficulty reconciling my own reluctance to put into print any expression of approval for such a seemingly rigid method of child training and progress charting, which was in violent opposition to everything I felt was right, with my very real admiration for Athelantis and Barbara and for all that they had done. Kimmel, who had known the Perrys for many years, was also full of admiration for Barbara. "It is the mother! It is the mother!" he kept repeating and explained that he had another young patient with the same syndrome who was not doing nearly so well. He related how Barbara had always appeared at office visits with a stopwatch and a whistle, directing Athelantis. "Now do a head stand," "Now put on your mask," timing the child while he inhaled his own carbon dioxide in the waiting room to stimulate his brain cells to demand more oxygen.

Later I learned Barbara had helped Athelantis build his vocabulary by charting his progress day by day with him, and when she would spin him upside-down by his feet for several minutes (part of the institute's program), she would throw word cards on the floor (her own invention) so that no learning time was wasted. I was able to stifle my own negative reaction to such exaggerated pushing, and realize that for Barbara and the boy, this emphasis on progress and moment-to-moment mastery had given them the energy to surmount unbelievable obstacles. I was also able to realize that each afflicted family, however, must create their own method of handling their problems, based on their own needs and instincts, unimpeded by the judgment of the outer world. Far too often, we deprive people of the opportunity to create their own realities and solutions out of our emphasis on conformity and being right.

Fortunately, the Perrys were strong in their belief in what they had decided to do. It was with great pride that Ernie showed me Dr. Glenn Domon's inscription in his book about the Philadelphia institute's program. The inscription read, "For the Perry Family! Who have been found to be good enough—and wise enough—to be entrusted with that most precious of all things—a hurt child."

Barbara's sense of conviction about the program and the intensity with which she went about the healing of her child shows most vividly perhaps in the long open letter she sent to all her neighbors. In it she wrote: "The doctors and specialists don't really know whether or not Athelantis is brain damaged. He, however, definitely has problems that have to be corrected. His fingers are fused and don't bend; his right eye wanders and also has hardly any vision; he isn't speaking as well as other children his age. Whether it's brain damage or a result of overhospitalization and a lot of time in casts is irrelevant. The path to recovery for him is the same.

"They have set up a program of exercises (physical and mental) that we have to do to help give more input to his brain. Since we all have 100,000,000,000 neurons in our brain and use only about 10,000,000,000 there is a lot of room . . . for additional stimulation. What we have to do is reprogram his brain; give him so much stimulation of one sort or another that we bridge the sick or dead neurons and turn on those that are dormant. . . . We have to make him crawl because that is necessary for him, but we also are starting him on an intensified reading program. We have to do the things that infants are supposed to do, only more so, as well as things that children of his age do. And we have to do those things over and over again. The key to making Athelantis well is the frequency with which we do things, the intensity and the duration. . . .

"What we want from you is your help, 15 minutes of your time, a week, every other week, once a month, that's all if that is all you have, more if you have more than 15 minutes. . . . We do not want to be a drain on any one of you. . . . The things I'm going to tell you have to be done by us and Athelantis every day in the exact sequence (given us) for as often as the doctors and therapists tell us, because if we don't, Athelantis will not get well. And we are determined that he's going to get as well as every other little kid is."

And indeed he is now functioning well above his age level in many areas. During the period of his patterning, the house was teeming with people. Friends from the art and theater world would come to teach the child to creep or help him with extensive eye exercises, with voice training, with ballet lessons and French. Because of the diversity of those who came to work with him, the conversations that he overheard across the table, where he lay facedown while his limbs were being redirected, were stimulating. And unlike so many other physically abnormal children, he was never hidden. He was taken to the theater, to movies and to art openings of friends. He had a chance to experience a warm, accepting and exciting community. A neighbor, noting his interest in the musical instruments she collected, taught him to play the piano and the drums. Although his hands could never have the normal span required for true mastery of the piano, she was struck by how diligently he practiced and the length of his attention span. Later she gave him a scholarship so he could go to music school.

While I walked over to P.S. 41 in Greenwich Village to speak to Athelantis's teacher, I was most eager to find out how he was doing. It was his first experience in a school situation, and I was worried about how it would work out. I had watched him on registration day, sitting radiantly in his new starched white shirt and tie, waiting to be interviewed. I had watched Barbara sitting next to him, also expectant, hoping that after all the hard work she had gone through to have him accepted and appropriately placed, there would be no further obstacles. I hoped that they would not be disappointed.

I was worried about Athelantis and felt that he was entering school with still another handicap, one that surely he did not need. Deprived of the first three years of school in which the academic skills he learned so well in isolation generally form only one small part of a larger curriculum that concentrates initially on social skills and group experience, how would he adjust all at once to a standard of discipline and expectation of "good conduct" that in the other children had been developed over a period of years in rhythm with their own increasing readiness to cope with external demands?

There was no need to worry. Barbara had rigidly worked with him, first in the patterning program, and then later through the Calvert Correspondence Home Study Program. According to their next-door neighbor, Barbara and Athelantis would sit for many hours doing math and language drills together. School was extremely easy by comparison. Also, Athelantis had an overwhelming need to please. When the class had a contest to make the most words out of a given array of letters, it was very important for Athelantis to be the winner. And upon the few occasions when his work was wrong, he was loath to admit it. In fact, his desire for approval was so all pervasive that once when he forgot his homework, he took the notebook of another child and insisted that it was his, although he must have realized that the difference in the handwriting would give his trick away. Hopefully, as his confidence grows he will develop the courage to be wrong sometimes, a facility that the focus on achievement usually obscured while there were still so mamy obstacles to be transcended.

At a time when his classmates are barely learning how to print neatly, Athelantis completes all his school assignments in script. By and large, he is doing very well and appears to be quite comfortable in the classroom. Joan Ponzini, his teacher, is very warm and seems to accept him totally. The other children have never asked her any questions about 'Lantis and why he is the way he is. Their attitude seems to be a reflection of hers. Mostly they take him for granted, except "when he is pesty, which he often is," she explained. Although he is very eager for recess and lunch, asking over and over how soon they will be, he is often alone at these times. Sometimes, when he cannot think of another way to make contact, he will begin to tease the other children in order to get them to pay attention to him. Perhaps it is also a projection of his fear of being teased himself. But the other children do not tease him. They just stay away. Like Athelantis and like our whole culture, the children appear to be hiding from their own curiosity and fears.

Ponzini was not told about Athelantis before the first day when he appeared as "one of the children." Ethel Mates, the guidance counselor, said that they deliberately chose her as his teacher because they knew she would not be upset by having such a child, because "she would not go screaming through the halls, 'Look what they gave me!' as perhaps some other teacher would." They also chose her because "she runs a classroom where children feel safe. There are a lot of rules that are enforced but the atmosphere is flexible and warm." Because Ponzini does not see Athelantis differently from the other children, she is not overprotective in a destructive way. According to Mates, "If the teacher feels a child is very brittle, then the class follows."

Athelantis definitely is not brittle. The side he shows the world is one of slightly warlike confidence. Before Athelantis started school, his father taught him how to fight back in case the other children bothered him. When a child attacked him in the yard one day recently, he kicked back in such a way that "he will never be attacked again."

Athelantis is rough. He has had to be in order to buck a world in which too often his most essential rights have been subjected to challenge. But it is important for all those in contact with him to appreciate the origins of his veneer of toughness and to work creatively with him to foster the self-confidence that he will need in order to begin to shed it. It is important also to understand the extreme vulnerability that lies beneath the rough exterior of this clearly intelligent boy of eight whose spoken lamentations over his fate have never gone beyond a mild protestation over the fact that his "stuck toes" make the wearing of sandals impossible, whose creative writing assignments always stop at the word good (the day is "good"; flowers are "good"; leaves are "good"; and so is rain and every other subject that he tackles) as though if he were ever to let down his guard and utilize his descriptive abilities more fully something most dreadful might come from his pen. This is a child who in his enormous efforts to surmount his many obstacles and to succeed has never asked aloud the most vital question, "Why am I made this way?" And without the internal permission to articulate his largest question out of which all other questions come, how much mental meandering and wondering might have been lost?

This situation also comes into play at P.S. 41, where the child's unusual appearance is being totally ignored. Perhaps it is better this way. Certainly it is much easier for all involved. Still, I came away with the sense of something missed. Irene Neurath, director of Corlears School, a much smaller place with a focus on individuality in learning, described her reactions to the situation. "We have been taught to shut away what is terribly unpleasant to think about, yet in doing so we are depriving ourselves of the opportunity to learn to cope, so it becomes even more terrible than it needs to be." It was her feeling that all children need to cope with the fears of bodily injury aroused by difficulties like Athelantis's in the same way they must assimilate concepts of death.

She spoke of children's need of adult assistance in acquiring ways to articulate their questions, because the silence born of an inability to handle the feelings activated by abnormality reflects the same avoidance of important issues that once centered around the subject of skin color and indirectly perpetuated racial prejudice. "None of us has been trained to this kind of exposure that calls for an intellectual reconsideration of a human problem," she concludes, adding that the handling of that situation would be a new experience for all involved, a situation in which there are no easy answers.

But Corlears is a small homogeneous educational community with several teachers to a class. In a large public school, would it be possible to turn Athelantis's presence in the classroom into a learning experience that would help the other children come close to him in a whole new way, acknowledging his special strengths and weaknesses and encouraging him to break through the barrier of his fears? Or would such an approach only risk the further singling out of a child who had already suffered too much? It is hard to say.

As things stand now, Athelantis is too often ignored by the other children. If it is his physical difference that has caused this isolation, this is thoroughly concealed both from him and from the other children, because, at a surface glance, they appear to be reacting totally appropriately to his generally provocative behavior. Often, when we fear rejection of the deepest essences of who we are, we create the negative behavior that will cause the very rejection we are so afraid of, so that it will be our behavior that is seen as bad, not ourselves, thus leaving our vulnerable inner core intact. This I believe is what Athelantis has done in giving the other children real reasons to dislike what *can* be changed so he will never have to test whether his irreparable differences can be accepted, so he will not have to risk disappointment.

How logical then, in this context, is the request of the little girl who sits near him to have her seat changed because his habit of putting his belongings all over her desk makes her uncomfortable, an annoying habit that he has been reminded about often? How much easier for all involved than the embarrassing possibility that *he* might make her uncomfortable. Gradually, in obedience to our society's unspoken dictates, these children are learning to sublimate those feelings of discomfort that perhaps, if they were faced more openly, could bring about the changes in our basic attitudes that we so badly need.

Since there is nobody to help the children articulate their uneasiness and see Athelantis's problems in a more total context, they turn against him in a way that aggravates his own aggression. Thus we are left with a vicious cycle that prevents the true shifting of reactions toward abnormality that could break through the silence and the fear. Worse still, the negative stories brought home by the other children, accurate only in the most superficial sense, serve to rekindle the barely buried prejudices of their parents in ways that give them the "permission" to oppose mainstreaming on a larger scale wtihout having to feel guilty. Thus we are left with a self-fulfilling prophecy of partial failure.

Too long have we lived with self-fulfilling prophecies. Cruelly we have looked down on black people for having unstable family arrangements while forgetting that it was the ruthless breaking apart of all familial ties among the slaves that originally caused this, because only those who learned to make a life outside the family structure were ultimately able to survive. Athelantis, too, has had to make adaptations in order to survive outside a system that refused to let him in.

Whether this belated school experience that he has been so eager for will prove to be all that he dreamed it could, or whether the system will again emerge victorious in showing the disruptive influence of mainstreaming such a child, will depend a great deal on the understanding of his teachers. If they are able to see his difficulties in the context of the many problems of his past and utilize his presence in the class as part of a unique opportunity to extend the life experience of the other children, if they are able to appreciate his bravery and help the other children partake in his many areas of special knowledge, then a true growth will have occurred. Then more and more children like Athelantis can be admitted to public school, hopefully at the beginning when there will be fewer obstacles; and the whole structure, our whole attitude toward abnormality, can start to shift.

His teachers, however, will have to show the same willingness to overcome the age-old prejudices and fears that deviation from the norm evoke, to show the same courage and hope his parents have. This is the real challenge.

Snap the Whip, by Winslow Homer.

14

Middle Childhood: Games and Social Development

Childhood is a culture all by itself. Childhood has its own behavioral patterns, its own artifacts, and its own language (to a certain degree). A major part of this culture is the game behavior of children.

Games are specific expressions of childhood play. Earlier we discussed the various forms of play and the factors that affect the type of play children engage in. Early play was termed solitary play, followed by parallel play, and developing into group play, which takes forms called cooperative and associative play. It is in these last developmental stages of play that children begin to play organized, rule-oriented games.

Games are characterized by the presence of specific rules for specific objectives of the game. The rules are not always the same nor are they consistent for the same group of children from day to day. This phenomenon of variability in rules of the game can be attested to by anyone who has seen a group of children play sandlot baseball. Depending upon the experience of the children and the type of place they are playing, there is great variability in the rules used. Children's games are ". . . systemic culture patterns which are distinctive, ancient and widespread among the cultures

CHILDREN'S GAMES

Game: an activity engaged in for amusement

of the world; . . . [they are] recreational activities characterized by organized play, competition, two or more sides, criteria for determining the winner and agreed upon rules" (Robertson and Sutton-Smith, 1962, p. 166).

Play is a cultural universal among children. Children of cultures throughout the world engage in play activities of all types, using a tremendous variety of tools and equipment (if needed at all). Games, however, are somewhat culture specific in that some games are more popular in certain cultures and other games are not. Despite the cultural specificity, Phillips (1967) has summarized five major elements concerning children's participation in games.

First, there are a number of games that have been played by children for a very long period of time. Hide-and-seek, for example, has been played by children for hundreds of years. There is evidence that it was played by children during the Roman years. Hopscotch also has its roots in antiquity. Louis XIII of France played charades and hide-and-seek as a child over 350 years ago. Some of the games played by American children today were played by children in England three and four centuries ago. "Farmer in the Dell" and "London Bridge Is Falling Down" are two examples of these old games.

Secondly, from the evidence we have, it appears that some games are universal. Tag is seen in nearly all cultures, as are some forms of hide-and-seek. Children in industrialized nations play these games, as do children in preliterate societies. Perhaps it is not the children that differentiate these different types of societies.

Within specific cultures, there are age differentiations attached to particular games. At certain ages children play certain games. As they get older, the definition of appropriate games changes. The parents reinforce the change in game behavior, but there is also significant peer pressure to conform to the group's standards. Consequently, if the child prefers to play an age-inappropriate game, there may be much pressure from members of his peer group, possibly in the form of harassment and teasing.

In most naturally occurring children's games, the spectator role is virtually nonexistent. In games that children set up for themselves, without the "help" of adults, everyone has an active role; no one just watches (unless there is some specific reason for kicking the child out of the group). As we shall see later, many of the games children play today in the United States have built into them a spectator aspect.

Children are very creative in their game playing, whatever their cultural heritage. Depending upon the situation, location, and the

Appropriate games: games defined as proper for a certain age or sex

needs of the children, the games may be manufactured spontaneously, with rules being made up as they go along. Children may also take a game with predefined rules and adapt those rules to the situation they are in. This creativity is rich and a delight to observe.

As we have seen, some games children play are universal; some are very old. Some games are unique to a specific culture, others appear to be universal. The games children play reflect the heterogeneity and creativity of children. This uniqueness is one of the landmarks of child development.

Historical Changes in Children's Games

One specific study has looked at the historical changes in the games children play. Sutton-Smith and Rosenberg (1961) examined the period in America from 1896 to 1959. During this period of time, children's singing games, acting games, and cooperative parlor games lost a great deal of their popularity. Children in 1896 were much more likely to engage in these activities than were children in 1959.

Chasing games (tag) and imitative games were found to be as popular in 1959 as they were in 1896. Some leader-type games, some physical skill games, and a few selected organized sports were much more popular in 1959 than they were in 1896.

These researchers found some sex differences in the 63 years covered by the study. The game behavior of girls became more and more like the game behavior of boys during this time period. The range of behavior for both sexes in their game playing was more restricted in 1959 than in 1896. This was especially true for the boys; playing hopscotch, jacks, or house was much more inappropriate for boys in 1959 than it was for boys in 1896. In some cases, the range of behavior for girls widened somewhat.

There appears to be a relationship between some of these changes in game behavior and the changing sex role of the American male (young or old). Many more boys are involved in rough and aggressive games (football, basketball, and even baseball). We feel this trend toward aggressive game playing reflects our cultural uneasiness concerning masculinity. By channeling our boys into these types of games, we may be attempting to assure that they will grow up to be strong men, capable of supporting our society.

The types of games children play are supposed to be indicative of their underlying motives and future abilities. With our cultural emphasis on Pop Warner football, Little League baseball, and other

Organized, competitive athletics for children of nearly all ages are characteristic of many American communities today.
ROBERT V. ECKERT, JR., EKM-NEPENTHE.

cultural sports movements, we are demonstrating our collective concern for the development of these children. It is more than just ensuring these kids have a place to play; it is a desire to ensure the appropriate forms of stimulation and learning for our children. Unknown to most of us, these mass game movements are limiting the flexibility of children. It is possible that diminishing this flexibility hinders successful adaptation to a complex and secular society.

1959 to the Present: Two major developments have occurred since 1959. One that we have already mentioned is the tremendous increase in organized games for children. The other is the massive incorporation of television into American homes.

As mentioned earlier, television is present in over 95 percent of American homes. In one sense, TV has the capacity to do away with children's games. All children need to do is sit in front of the "glowing blue box" and be entertained for hours on end. We would suggest that this significant involvement with TV has produced a loss of spontaneity in children's games, a loss of creativity, and, most important, a loss of time to play games. Television has homogenized children's game playing and curtailed it. For exam-

Middle Childhood: Games and Social Development

ple, after a recent space adventure series was released, there was a rash of space-oriented games for young children. Unlike other childhood group play, the characters, the roles, and most of the action were rigidly defined by the plot. The usual inventiveness of group play was subdued by many rules.

There has also been a significant increase in outside organization of children's games. This intervention has produced several societal institutions of childhood sport, as mentioned earlier. Organized sports—baseball, football, soccer, swimming, gymnastics—have infiltrated the culture of childhood. This organization extends down to the youngest of children; some gymnastic programs start when the children are three and four years of age.

Organized games: games, especially sports, that are no longer spontaneous and are controlled by adults

There may be an unknown conspiracy between television and organized games. Sports coverage on TV accentuates the trend to organized sports; there are few shows featuring sandlot baseball games or children playing spontaneous, inventive sorts of games. In some instances the child performers are glorified, a trend that started in gymnastics with Olga Korbut and continued to other youthful gymnasts. Even movies and TV serials like "The Bad News Bears" have had a similar influence on Little League and other organized sports.

James Michener has written an interesting book called *Sports in America* (1976). The subject of children's involvement in sport is given an entire chapter, in which Michener makes some definitive comments:

1. Children are introduced to highly organized sports too young.
2. Adults conducting children's programs place too much emphasis on winning.

The adult intrusion into the games of children has brought with it adult values: competition and winning (at nearly any cost). Michener concludes by saying:

Winning: emerging the victor

> I believe that children require play and competition in order to develop. I believe that play is a major factor in civilizing infants. . . . Children should have the widest possible experience of play. . . . Heavily organized competition with end-of-the-season championships should not be initiated before the age of twelve, if then.
>
> A sense of competition is natural in children. . . . [It] provides healthy emotional outlets and must not be suppressed; but it should not be exaggerated either. Adults must not dominate the play of children (Michener, 1976, p. 153).

Theoretical Aspects of Game Playing

Games serve several interesting purposes for children. On one hand, games allow children to deal with any anxiety they may be feeling during the maturation process (normative anxiety). Specific life situations, like a parental relationship, may be dealt with through game playing. Playing and games may provide children with the means to work through their feelings. When the situation has been dealt with, the child will discontinue the particular play pattern (Robertson and Sutton-Smith, 1962; Phillips, 1967). Prolonged attention to this particular game activity after a crisis may indicate some difficulty on the part of the child in dealing with the problem.

Games give children pleasure and enjoyment. This very important dimension is sometimes forgotten or dismissed. Play and games are the language of childhood.

Games allow children to exercise power and control over their world. A basic way to learn how to handle power is to have power; games allow children this feeling of mastery. Through this experience, children learn to use power effectively.

Games allow children the luxury of being with other children by engaging in peer interaction. Cooperation is learned, and appropri-

Some types of play involve nothing more than a minimum of equipment and a maximum of imagination.
ROBERT V. ECKERT, JR., EKM-NEPENTHE.

ate goal-directed behavior results. Through the involvement with games, children enhance their own self-image. Games allow children a measure of self-affirmation by giving them a position in a group and allowing them the exercise of power.

Intervening Factors in Children's Games

Technology has been an intervening factor in children's games. As we have mentioned, television is one aspect of technology that plays a significant role. Urbanization, which is definitely related to the rise of technology, has changed the nature of neighborhoods and networks between children. These changes have meant that neighborhoods are quite often not available for impromptu game playing. Because communities are less stable, informal child groups have been slowly but surely replaced by formal, coached play groups.

Parents represent another intervening variable. Even though their intentions may be the very best, their intrusion on a mass scale removes the spontaneity and peer-support aspects of children's games. Parental intrusion turns an independent form of activity into a dependent activity—dependent for a ride to a field far away from home, dependent upon officials and coaches, and dependent upon many other adults. Parents in America intrude into the games of their children more than parents in any other culture in the world. Some of the things we say to children as they compete in these games are very revealing. For example, how will a child interpret: "Winning isn't everything, it's the *only* thing!" Or how will a young boy playing junior high school football react to a coach telling him, "Football is a lot like life; how you do out on the field today will be reflected in how you do in life!" The implication is that if you do not do your best on the field today, you will probably fail in life. We can only guess at the dubious motivational impact statements like these may have, and only future generations maturing into adulthood will tell us of the impact of this sort of intrusion into children's games.

CHILDREN'S HUMOR

The humorous side of children is also a part of the culture of childhood. The types of stories and jokes that children like to tell are reflective of several things: the intellectual level of the child, the influence of the peer group, and the level of egocentricity of the child. Early in their lives children will enjoy sharing "funny" incidents with their parents. These recountings are simple, with many details missing or forgotten. There is often so much silliness on the part of the child that it is difficult to get the whole story out; the anticipation of the punch line is too much to bear.

The uses of children's humor vary. Certainly children's humor can act as a tension releaser for the entire family. Some of the things a child may say or do may be so incredible that the entire family reacts. Humor is sometimes used to deal with situations that the child does not understand. A difficult parent-parent relationship may confuse the child; his reaction may be a humorous one. Humor aids in the development of relationships with other children. It also aids in basic social skill development, mastery of language (including some not-so-savory aspects of the language), and, if humorous writing gets the child to read, humor may aid in the development of reading skills.

Middle Childhood: Games and Social Development

ISSUE

The Hurried Child

At the age of 16, Tracy Austin had become one of the very best professional women tennis players in the world.
WIDE WORLD PHOTOS.

David Elkind (1979) has indicated that America seems to be producing a new type of child. This child is pushed hard, very early in life, to achieve and be successful. These children are called the hurried children.

☐ The motivation for this parental pushing lies in society. The style of parenting in vogue within America goes in cycles; the proper way of raising a child gets redefined every 15 or 20 years. The free school movement and the "do your own thing" ethic of the 1960s and early 1970s have clearly not worked, and, as is often the case, there has been backlash.

☐ Today there has been a revival of fundamentalism in areas ranging from education to religion. Expectations for achievement by children have grown stronger and stronger. We push children into competitive situations, hoping they will learn the ropes and be better people for it. We insist that they perform up to standards in school; if they do not, privileges are taken away.

☐ The clinical manifestations of this "do something" ethic are varied. Some children cannot cope with the pressure and drop out of mainstream life. Drugs become a way of life. A young girl who is told to do something, but finds difficulty in doing anything, winds up getting pregnant; she has accomplished something! Nowhere is the pushing so evident as it is in academic achievement. We train children in skills related to learning earlier than ever. Television commercials advertising programs to teach three-year-olds to read are seen every day, which state that it is to children's advantage to be able to read before the first grade.

☐ One of the problems with urging this precocity on the part of children is that the children often have to live up to live models. Young athletes like Nadia Comaneci or Tracy Austin become models for performance. These outstanding child performers are exceptions to the rule, but children all over the country try to live up to the skills and abilities of these people. Parents sometimes push their children to be like these "super kids" and when they cannot measure up, both parents and children are disappointed.

☐ Hurried children make for anxious adults. Childhood is a time for smooth, relaxed development. By adding these artificial pressures, we are denying a part of the child; considerable consolidation of information and experience needs to take place during childhood. If we rush children through with unwarranted expectations, we do not allow the distillation-maturation process to take hold. We feel this is unfortunate, and represents a distinctly contrived aspect of child development appearing on the scene.

PEERS AS SOCIALIZING AGENTS

Peer group:
a group of companions similar in age and/or sex

The middle years of childhood are a time of rapid increase in peer contact for children. The peer group is a transmitting agent for information, and as children mature, the peer group usually increases in importance. Friendship ties during the middle years provide a supportive network for children and provide answers to questions (questions that adults do not usually understand). These supportive networks are most often same-sex and similar-age in composition. Very often, during this time, boys want nothing to do with girls, and girls very often feel the same way about boys.

The size and complexity of the peer group increase markedly with age. Part of the reason for this is entrance into the school situation. This greatly broadens children's perspective, and the boundaries of their peer group usually expand.

Middle Childhood: Games and Social Development

The peer group varies in structure and function, depending upon the culture. The U.S. culture puts relatively few constraints on developing friendship patterns. Due to the nature of our human settlements (families, homes, and communities), children are freer than they have ever been in terms of responsibilities; peer networks proliferate.

Research on the Peer Group

Success in relating to the peer group appears to be related to the specific personality characteristics of the individual child. The shy and withdrawn child seems to be less popular in the peer culture in comparison with children who are friendly and able to relate socially. Certain social skills contribute to effective peer group relations. On the other hand, involvement in peer group functions undoubtedly contributes to the development of social skills. In one sense this appears to be a "Catch-22" situation for the child (Hartup, 1970; 1975).

In an interesting study on the relationship between popularity, cognition, and social development, Bardin and Moan (1971) found a similarity between the way cognitive skills and social skills progress from kindergarten through the third grade. A portion of children's cognitive development is affected by the quality of their peer relations. The peer group operates as a social support system, enhancing the enthusiasm and curiosity necessary for cognitive development.

Children structure their peer groups purposefully. Because of this, children with special needs or in special situations are excluded from peer group activities. These children suffer in terms of popularity and ultimately self-esteem. Bryan (1974) has indicated that learning-disabled children, particularly females, are perceived as being much less attractive, and end up being rejected much more often by their peers than comparison children who do not have a learning disability. Children may be so purposeful in the selection of their peer support group that children with *any* observable difference may be excluded. Sometimes it is overweight children who do not get much of a chance for peer activities.

Recently, Hartup has indicated that success in peer relations may be dependent upon the child's family environment (Hartup, 1979). If there is an environment that will produce secure attachments (consistency, warmth, security), it is likely that the child's social-communicative skills will be more developed and there will be a more positive engagement with peers. Children's relationship with their parents provides the base for peer interactions.

Functions of the Peer Group

The primary function of the peer group is education. Children learn a considerable portion of their frame of reference from their peers. Values, behavior patterns, and even language patterns may have their basis in the peer group.

Another major function of the peer group is social support and friendship. During these developmental years and even later, the peer group provides children with an ongoing sense of security and trust. In times of stress, having allies can be a vital source of strength for children.

The elaboration of children's developing autonomy and independence is partly in the hands of the peer group. These age-mates provide children with a relevant base of operations on their own. Beyond the normative confines of their parents, children can move

Pressure from the peer group can sometimes mean that individuals are aggressively excluded from the group for any number of reasons.
ROBERT V. ECKERT, JR., EKM-NEPENTHE.

Middle Childhood: Games and Social Development

ahead in a qualitatively different way in their quest for independence.

Within the peer group, children can try on different roles, such as leadership roles. Trying out these different positions may help make the actual enactment of similar roles in adulthood easier. If given a responsibility by the peer group, a child will gain in appreciation of what a responsibility means; this experience will be an aid when other situations call for the assumption of these roles.

Role experimentation: trying out different roles, usually within one's peer group

As children mature through the middle years, the influence of the peer group grows stronger. More and more support is provided by the peer group, and children begin to identify a clear self-image within the group. The nature of children's relationships with their parents begins to change. This is the beginning of a dilemma that will peak sometime during adolescence. The conflict between the influence of the parents and the influence of the peer group has its beginnings in middle childhood.

Friendships: Paradoxically, the middle years are also a time when very important singular friendships develop. In some instances these friendships exist apart from the peer group; in other situations they are a part of the peer group. The peer group meets certain needs; these friendships meet many of the same needs and probably more. These relationships tend to be closer, ones wherein deep sharing can take place.

These relationships are often very lasting, even without frequent contact between the participants. They tend to be with people of the same sex and very exclusive in nature.

Neighborhood: The structure of the neighborhood also affects children's relationships with each other. Children living in high-rise apartments with a common bus ride to school and a neighborhood playground share one sort of experience. It is quite different from that of children who live in the suburbs in single-family dwellings, walk to school, and play in their backyards. The structure of the environment can affect the behavior of children. The freedom afforded children in the suburbs fosters a different sort of appreciation of space and may even structure a different perspective for children's relationships with each other.

Human settlements: families, neighborhoods, and communities

Different neighborhoods affect the relations between parents and children. Some structures are facilitative to human interaction, others are not. It is very difficult to supervise children or have a meaningful relationship with children playing outside from the thirteenth floor of a high-rise apartment house. Even the internal arrangement of the housing (number of rooms, space available per child, and so on) can alter the relationship between parents and children. There is evidence linking crowding to ineffectual parent-child relations and higher levels of tension.

Children's behavior is a function of their space, the location surrounding that space, and the time and the people interacting with them. This environmental approach is one way to more clearly identify the forces acting upon children.

Summary

1. Children's games are the specific expressions of childhood. Games are characterized by the presence of rules and specific objectives; this differentiates them from random play. Games reflect the developmental situation of the child, the culture the child is in, and the degree of parental involvement. Some games are universal (they are found in all children) and many games played today are very old. In most naturally occurring children's games there is no spectator role.

2. It appears that children are introduced to highly organized sport too early. Adults who run these programs place far too much emphasis on winning. Games are for the pleasure and enjoyment of children; adults often seem to forget this basic axiom. The primary intervening factors in children's games are parents, and secondly, technology (particularly television).

3. The peer group is a very salient part of the child's world. The middle years of childhood are a time of rapid increase in peer contacts. The peer group, while a universal, varies considerably according to culture in structure and function. Among the major functions of the peer group are education, friendship, and social support.

Thought Questions

1. How are children's games a reflection of their culture?

2. What does the emphasis on winning do to the nature of children's games?

3. How are American children "hurried"? Does this have anything to do with children's games?

4. What factors will resolve the conflict of parents versus peers that children begin to have during the middle years? What can children learn from peers that they cannot learn from parents?

5. Of what importance is social support to a child?

Suggested Readings

Aldis, O. *Play Fighting*. Menlo Park, Calif.: Behavioral Science Research Fund, 1975. *One of the more unique books in the field, this book explores the phenomenon of roughhousing and play fighting in children. The author also attempts to explain the thrill-seeking behavior often seen in children of virtually all ages.*

Caplan, F., and T. Caplan. *The Power of Play*. New York: Anchor Press/Doubleday, 1974. *Play is a child's work; it is the medium for communication and the vehicle for learning. Caplan and Caplan give us a very readable description of children's play, emphasizing the nature and meaning of various play activities.*

Minuchin, P.P. *The Middle Years of Childhood*. Monterey, Calif.: Brooks/Cole, 1977. *Middle childhood is often the least discussed period in child development. This book is an excellent presentation of the period we call middle childhood.*

READING

The games that children play are as unique and exciting as the children who play them. Some games transcend cultural boundaries and appear universal; other games seem to be confined to a particular culture. To be sure, American children play some games that were played a thousand years ago in Europe. They also have more video and computer games than children in any other culture.

Ruth Bogdanoff and Elaine Dolch, writing in *Young Children*, introduce the relationship between children's play and Piaget's theory of cognitive development. Moving through key concepts of the theory, the authors relate games like hide-and-seek to the specific types of thought required to play the game, such as transformation, decentration, and reversibility.

The authors present a table near the end of the article that is particularly interesting for students and teachers. It relates children's level of cognition to the type of games they can play and makes suggestions for activities for children of different developmental levels. The positive aspects of play in groups and cooperation between children are highlighted in the article's conclusion.

Old Games for Young Children: A Link to Our Heritage
Ruth F. Bogdanoff
Elaine T. Dolch

Group games and gamelike activities are an integral part of human social interaction. Infants begin to explore their surroundings by devising gamelike activities. They grasp and release objects. Soon they learn to drop them on the floor. If the objects are picked up and handed back to babies, the game has begun. Very young children quickly learn to play "Peek-a-Boo" or "Where's the Baby?" These games become "Hide and Seek" when older children play them.

The traditional games upon which we will focus are those which have been played for hundreds of years. Affairs of honor and ownership were often decided on game fields; for example, certain Native American nations played lacrosse to resolve territorial hunting, fishing, and farming rights. Today, as in centuries past, athletes compete in games of skill and grace in a multitude of settings from city sidewalks and open fields to international arenas.

In our constant search for innovative and appropriate ways to help young children learn about themselves, others, and the world about them, we plan activities that have gamelike characteristics. Sometimes we instigate games that we remember from our own childhoods. Most of these have roots in our rich cultural heritages. We hope you will choose games that appeal to you and that seem right for the children with whom you work and play.

"Little Sally Walker," "Doggie, Doggie, Where's Your Bone?" Do you know how to play those games? Do you know in what way they are alike? Each has been played for generations in all parts of the United States. These games or their variations have been played for centuries from Scandinavia to Africa and from England to China. Although the origins of folk games are difficult to document, researchers have found references to "Ring Around the Rosie" in Great Britain, southern France, and Germany. "Oats, Peas, Beans" and "London Bridge" are other games that were played in diverse forms in ancient times in African countries and all through western Europe. In the United States these games are played by many ethnic groups with their own variations. The themes and actions tend to be universal while the variations reflect the lifestyles and cultural mores of the people who play them.

In the past, adults played similar games at various kinds of celebrations, festivals, and parties. Sometimes they were played at the end of the day's work as families gathered on the town square or village green. Other group games were part of religious rituals. Frequently political happenings, current events, or caricatures of famous people were the inspirations for these activities. Many evolved from traditions associated with various professions such as farming, food preparation, and soldiering. Other games were concerned with courtship and marriage. Chance, physical strength, and strategy became elements typical of more complex games to be played by adults and older children.

When families gathered, everyone from the youngest to the oldest member was there to participate or watch. Young children learned game rules, rituals, and traditions as they observed and played with adults. As work-play polarizations increased, adults played fewer and fewer folk games. Children then taught the games to other children. Because games today are taught by children, not parents, children learn to play the games of the neighborhood and adapt them according to their understanding and experience. Thus children in different locales may play games that have originated in other cultures, but in each locale the games have their own ethnic flavor.

Our culture currently emphasizes organization, strict age grouping, and often supervised, contrived togetherness. Many twentieth century children are catapulted from one adult-directed or supervised activity to another. The rich traditions of playing games could soon be lost unless adults provide opportunities for the young to learn to play them. The renewed interest in the preservation of our multiethnic origins is but one good reason for us to consider games that might serve some of our goals in early childhood education. Within the wide varieties of activities that might be classified as games, children can be offered experiences that are not only fun, but that also strengthen all aspects of growth and development.

Games from a Piagetian Viewpoint

Piaget and DeVries and Kamii underline the value of game-playing to support the development of thought processes and moral judgment that emerge during the concrete operational period. This stage, between the ages of seven and twelve, follows the sensorimotor period of infancy and the preoperational period of the preschool and kindergarten years during which children have integrated language with perceptions and actions into their thought processes. While children in the concrete operational stage are still bound in thinking to concrete experiences, they can now manipulate ideas and actions mentally without using physical materials.

For example, ten-year-old Sara can choose and buy an appropriate gift for mother, though she may need to plan several months in advance to earn the money. Unless an appropriate gift were suggested by an adult, Eric, a preschool child, would only be able to choose something for his mother from within his immediate field of choice at the time of selection. He could not take into account pertinent factors, such as money needed, whether the gift was too large to carry or too awkward to hide, and so forth.

Children who are thinking at the concrete operational level, as Sara is, have a different qualitative thought process than those at the preoperational level, as Eric is. They are developing characteristics of operational thought, i.e., transformation, decentration, and reversibility, while egocentrism is diminishing. These thought processes enable concrete operational level children to reason, use logic, and generalize from past experience. If we look at the nature of the games described by Piaget and then at the characteristics that differentiate the preoperational level from the concrete operational level, it will be apparent why games facilitate intellectual and moral development during that period and why those same games are not appropriate for the preoperational child.

Kinds of Games

The games to which Piaget refers require cooperation and coordination or collaboration on the part of the players while they are engaged in a contest of powers prescribed within a framework of rules. The rules limit the action and ensure a winner and a loser. In "Hide and Seek," for example, the players through cooperation organize themselves into hiders and a seeker, with a home-safe base. The hiders oppose the seeker by trying not to be seen until they can run home free. Rules that limit the how, when, and where one hides, and that determine when one may run home free and penalties for the losers are accepted by all the players.

Thought Processes Required

From a developmental point of view, games such as "Hide and Seek," which require the players to keep the overall movement of the game in mind while planning strategy for competition, are not likely to be successful for children at the nursery school and kindergarten level. Children who are functioning at the preoperational level lack the thought processes of transformation, decentration, and reversibility. Furthermore, they still retain a strong egocentric viewpoint. They understand the actions of games as a series with each situation unrelated to the other, except that the situations occur together in time.

Transformations

Players must be able to understand that the situation in which they find themselves may be caused by a preceding action. As when Sara planned not only the gift, but how she would get the necessary money, so eight-year-old Federico, as he plays "Hide and Seek," must realize that his *run* to home base related the hiding situation to his arrival home safely on base. At the concrete operational stage, he can play this transforming part of the situation. However, if Federico were younger and thus thinking preoperationally, he might see his role as one of hiding, then of touching base to be safe, overlooking the run to home as part of the process of the game. Then, if he should be caught as he runs to base, he might think it is unfair because in his mind he *is* at home base because he wants to be there. He does not see the necessary process of running home as part of the sequence of the game.

Decentration

Decentration, another thought process of the concrete operational stage, is essential to understanding the object of the game. Action taken in winning/losing games must be congruent with the goal of the game. Children at the preoperational level cannot decenter sufficiently to see the game as a whole and the relationship of all its actions to the goal. Therefore, they have no basis to select action appropriate to the outcome of the game. For example, if Kai hides at the preoperational level he may be thinking so hard about keeping hidden (he is centering on hiding) that he does not try to run home. Or, he may center on the whereabouts of "It" and leave his hiding spot to find "It." When children do not comprehend the overall goal of the game and their roles in relation to others, they have difficulty in keeping the game moving toward the goal.

Making Use of Past Experience Through Reversible Thought

Reversibility is the ability to think of an action and then reverse that action to the original situation. Children can learn to generalize from past mistakes and choose successful game actions as they gain experience. In the preoperational stage, Kai tends to hide in the same spot each time even though he is easily caught there. He uses the same strategy to run home unless a better way is demonstrated to him. The child, Rosa, in the concrete operational period can reason that because she used a particular hiding spot and was caught, she can cancel that thought and try another hiding space. She can generalize from one experience to another because reversible thinking is more flexible.

Diminished Egocentrism

The choice of successful game action also requires that the egocentrism of the young child must have waned sufficiently so that the players can see the opponent's point of view as well as their own. At the concrete operational level, children can usually manage this, some earlier than others. Sara was able to put herself into mother's position to consider what she could use as a gift. Federico (at the concrete operational level) avoids "It" because he can guess what "It" will do, where "It" will look, or how fast "It" can run before he acts or delays action accordingly. Furthermore, with egocentrism diminished, the player can accept the rules as objective limits and does not feel failure as a personal penalty affecting self-concept.

Egocentrism is still strong with preoperational children. They tend to think only of their own role in the game. Kai finds it hard to wait during games to get into the action. If he is hiding and feels the wait is too long, he may come out of his hiding spot and say, "Here I am!" If he is caught, he will not understand why and may feel it is an unexpected disappointment that he may attribute to the other players' hostility toward him or to his own incapability. He may even reject or ignore the idea that he is a loser and continue playing as though he were not caught. The preoperational child is still too egocentric to accept a winner or loser as the game's outcome.

Lack of development of thought processes in the preoperational child (i.e., transformations, decentration, ability to make use of past experience through the use of reversible thought), combined with the usual childhood egocentrism, is an obstacle to playing the kinds of games to which Piaget refers. The young child is incapable of choosing actions from several intangible alternatives that are appropriate to the game as a whole and that determine who wins or loses. Games such as "Hide and Seek" belong in the curriculum for children in the concrete operational period of the school years.

Should games be played in preschool? If so, what kind? We think playing carefully chosen and appropriately taught games offers advantages for young children. Table 1 outlines the progression of complexity, as children advance through preoperational to concrete operational periods.

Characteristics of Games Appropriate for Children at the Preoperational Level

Cooperation or Collaboration

Games of all types develop social awareness. All games require cooperation or collaboration to some extent. Chauncey and Kessen indicate that group singing and dancing games are taught to Russian and Chinese children two to six years of age. Some of these games are traditional, some are revised, but all are used to further group consciousness and consideration of peers. We may differ with the Russians and Chinese in our viewpoint of social and political values, but as world population grows, it may be well to enhance group awareness in our children. For many years early childhood educators have been primarily concerned with preserving the individuality of each child. The time may have arrived to balance this focus on individuality with concern for the group.

The games discussed here will emphasize cooperation. These games have been most widely played in this country. Teachers may wish to adapt these games or use adaptations of other games from the heritage of children in their programs.

Role Alternation or Role Reversal

The goal orientation of competitive action/counteraction can be replaced by role alternation or role reversal to give function to the players. For example, in the "Farmer in the Dell," the player assumes one role identity (one of the chorus) and then another (the farmer's spouse, etc.) in sequence. This is role alternation. In games like "Punchinello" where the player is a follower and then a leader (Punchinello) and then a follower again, the players reverse roles although they do not act against each other. Participating in more than one role requires children to modify their actions to fit those of others. This becomes a preliminary decentering opportunity for those approaching the concrete operational level where they are ready to make this change. According to Sutton-Smith, "In sum, there is abundant evidence, in these pastimes of the four- to seven-year-olds, of social actions and counteractions, paving the way for the true role reversibility of games proper."

Ritualized Sequence of Action

Some games use a ritualized sequence of play to structure the action, rather than rules to guide the action. Rather than ending when a winner is determined, the sequence game, sometimes called a pattern game, terminates after everyone has had a turn or after the sequence of movement or activity is complete, as in "Mulberry Bush." Preschool children easily remember the sequence of the action through which they move. The predetermined sequence minimizes the need for choices for children who are so young and egocentric that they are unable to make a viable choice that will keep the game moving toward its goal. Yet such a sequence allows room for choices based on children's ideas that do not affect the flow of the game to its outcome. For instance, "Sally Walker" chooses her own successor. "Punchinello" determines his own actions as well as his successor. Games that use role alternation or role reversal as a sequence of action are appropriate for the preoperational child although the youngest ones may need help from adults in making a choice.

Late Preoperational Stage Exceptions

In the late preoperational stage (between five and seven years), as children enter a phase transitioning into operational thought, the use of some games with a minor element of competition may be appropriate. Games in which a child who is caught may become "It" without losing the game work well if the adult is cognizant of the game-playing experience of the group and minimizes this competitive part of the game-playing situation for players who do not yet understand it (Level IV). Children are likely to become increasingly aware of other players' actions because of a singling out process which affords a chance to use intelligence adaptively. Some children are ready for this competitive experience earlier than others. With or without the element of competition, all of these games offer active use of thought processes essential to children's development as they must adapt to the moves of other players and make simple choices.

Further Advantages of Group Game Playing for Preschoolers

Sensory Discrimination

Games based predominantly on a sequence of action and role alternation offer many advantages for children throughout the preoperational period. Games also provide experiences in different kinds of sensory discrimination such as *visual* discrimination where the child must attend to visual cues as in "Find My Child" or in hiding games; *auditory* discrimination as in "Hide the Clock"; and *tactile* discrimination where the child must be alert to the cue to action as in "Duck, Duck, Goose." Alertness to sensory cues is required in many games.

Verbal Skills

Language and verbal skills are encouraged through the responses to challenges as in "Find My Child." As players describe definitive characteristics of the "child" who is "lost," each verbally expresses concepts. When actions are coordinated with words, i.e., "Mulberry Bush" or "Looby Loo," skill in clarifying word meaning through actions is the focus of the game. The difficulty of the game should be based on children's ability to comprehend verbal instructions, their ability to use language meaningfully, and their understanding of cues given as in pantomimes.

Motor Coordination and Self-Concept

Coordination of gross and fine motor movement to those of other players as they move in and out, under and over, and around and through, give experience in directionality. Such understandings of self in space can only develop through experience and are critical both for game skill later and the basic understanding of space and time. Games should be chosen which will use skills children have developed and extend their growth.

Concept Formation

Concepts of color and number are also included in games. "I see something yellow" facilitates color concepts, and games such as "Knock, Knock" encourage one-to-one correspondence. Of course, all singing and dance games encourage rhythm and timing as well as familiarity with simple melodies.

Teacher's Role

Many areas of function and understanding are introduced and reinforced as children acquire game skills from the simplest to the most sophisticated levels. Games should be chosen to match the children's abilities, interests, and cultural backgrounds as well as the program's curriculum goals. Traditional words and actions of games will often be adapted to fit particular needs and interests of the teacher and children. For example, "Little Sally Walker" may become "Little Barry Barlow" or the name of one of the children in the group. The "Farmer in the Dell" may choose a husband or a spouse instead of a wife. Children's everyday experiences and creative ideas will determine the action in games like "Paw Paw Patch" or "Mulberry Bush." "Duck, Duck, Goose" may become "Triangle, Triangle, Circle" to emphasize pertinent concepts. Opportunities for improvisations of folk games are endless.

Suggestions for Introducing and Playing Games

- Relate the game to a familiar activity, routine, characterization, or finger play.
- Demonstrate the details of playing the game.
- Avoid complicated verbal instructions—sing or chant words to help the children become familiar with music and rhyme.
- Coordinate words with actions—actions give meaning to words and make them easier to remember.

Teacher-supported innovations stimulate problem solving and creative thinking. Encouraging children to take initiatives of action within the framework of game sequences is valuable experience in preparing children to meet greater challenges where the choices are between alternative actions that evoke penalties.

The rich potential of stimulating growth and development through the playing of games is realized when young children participate and cooperate spontaneously, not because they have been coerced into being part of the group. It is essential, too, that the teacher become an enthusiastic, involved participant!

Table 1. Developmental Guidelines for Choosing Games

Level	Child's Thought Development	Game Requirements	Suggested Games
I	**Preoperational**	Pattern or sequence game Two-step sequence	Ring Around the Rosie Roll the Ball (small group)
	Very limited verbal understanding	No verbal instruction necessary to teach game	Hokey Pokey (modified) Humpty Dumpty and other nursery rhymes
	Strong egocentrism	Continuous participation by all No waiting necessary Two to four children	This is the way the ____ walks (tune of Mulberry Bush)
	Little group awareness, child involved primarily with adults	Game depends on adult action No role alternation required	
II	**Preoperational**	Basic pattern game Not more than three steps in sequence	Punchinello (circle style) Did You Ever See a Lassie?
	Verbal understanding not dependable	No verbal instruction required	Hide the Clock Little Sally Walker
	Egocentrism still strong	Continuous participation Five to eight children	Paw Paw Patch

Table 1 (*continued*)

Level	Child's Thought Development	Game Requirements	Suggested Games
II cont.	Awareness of other children's presence but most interest in adult's expectation of child's behavior	Role alternation with help of the leader only	Variation of Mulberry Bush (with child's choice of action)
III	**Preoperational**	Basic pattern game Four to five steps in sequence Limited choice of action within framework of game	Looby Loo Doggie, Doggie, Where's Your Bone? Musical Chairs (modified) Are You My Kitten? Duck, Duck, Goose (modified) Mulberry Bush
	Coordination of language with action nearly complete	Some verbal instruction supported by demonstration	
	Egocentrism less strong in game situation	Wait short periods for turn with group action interspersed	
	Good awareness of all players but limited understanding of their roles in game	Six to ten players One-to-one interaction possible	
	Primary interest in own role	Role alternation between players may now be part of game	
IV	**Late preoperational**		A Tisket-a-Tasket Squirrel in the Trees Charlie over the Water Find My Child London Bridge Knock, Knock
	More objective understanding of role in action of game	Players required to make some choices of action	
	Good verbal understanding	May use verbal cues as well as action	
	Egocentrism diminishing	Turn taking can be part of game	
	Enjoys coordination with group Will subject own interests to group effort	Understand and enjoy role alternation and some role reversal Eight to twelve children	

Table 1 (continued)

Level	Child's Thought Development	Game Requirements	Suggested Games
V	**Concrete operational**		Word games (G-H-O-S-T)
	Reversible thought and lessened egocentrism	Decisions of strategy determine outcome of game	Tag (modified)
			Hide and Seek
	Understand rules as objective framework for action		Kick the Can
			Competitive races and relays
	New interest in competition within coordinated effort	Competition may be used	Follow the Leader
		Team action may substitute for personal involvement	Darts
			Horseshoes
			Pease Porridge Hot
	Uses language easily for thought	Verbal element can be definitive part of game	Simon Says

UNIT V
ADOLESCENCE

REPRODUCED BY PERMISSION OF THE PHILADELPHIA MUSEUM OF ART. PURCHASED: JOHN H. McFADDEN, JR. FUND

Gloucester Farm (1884, '56–118–1) by Winslow Homer.

15

Adolescence: A Period of Transitions

The time in the life of the child marking the transition from childhood to adulthood is called *adolescence*. Adolescence is a period of change, of peaks and valleys of emotional and physical development, and of heterogeneity. Adolescence is a time of peer group solidarity, more disagreement with parents, and preparation for adult society in terms of vocational, educational, and personal maturity.

Years ago it was suggested that adolescence is a period of "storm and stress" (Hall, 1904). Many people feel the same way today; adolescence is a time of unrest and confusion. Other people feel adolescence is not inherently stressful, but admit it is a time of many significant changes.

The definition of adolescence is often made in terms of when it begins and when it ends in a biological sense. In this culture, it is common to assume that adolescence begins roughly at 13 years of age and ends roughly at age 18. These time definitions are highly variable. *Puberty*, or the beginning of the sexually mature body, is one of the early milestones of adolescence. There are other physical signs of adolescence, including the development of secondary sex characteristics. Among these secondary sex changes are the appearance of pubic hair, ancillary hair, voice changes in males, and breast development in females. The exact beginning of adolescence is difficult to determine and varies considerably among individuals. As we shall see later, the end of adolescence is also difficult to determine.

Puberty: the time at which a person becomes capable of reproduction

ADOLESCENCE AS A TRANSITION

Adolescence is a period of changeover from one developmental period to another. It is also a developmental period in its own right, but its transitional nature is very significant. Societies make use of transitions to move individuals into different statuses within the social order. In most societies, these transitions consist of a process and a ritual. One of the most frequently appearing transitions is that from child to adult, particularly in the case of males.

The Process: Most societal transitions consist of three parts: separation, the liminal phase, and aggregation (Van Gennep, 1960). When a boy appears to be ready to make the transition from childhood to manhood, for example, one of the first things that happens is that he is identified and isolated within that culture. People are made aware of his status.

Liminal phase: the transition between one status and another, such as child and adult

During the *liminal phase*, which varies in length of time depending upon the culture and the nature of the transition, the person is in a sort of limbo: he is neither his former status (child) nor is he the next status (adult). This very confusing period may be relatively uncomfortable for the individual, not having a clear idea of what his status is within the culture.

As the process nears its end, the individual is gradually drawn back into the mainstream of society, in his new status. This moving back into society, called *aggregation,* realigns the individual in society and typically informs the rest of the culture as to the results of the transition. If the boy makes it through all of the required tests, he becomes a man in the culture; if he fails, he is rejected and never attains the full respect and power of males in that culture.

The Ritual: The rituals involved in these transitions are often bizarre by our standards. In some cultures there are "rites of manhood" that must be performed by all participants if they expect to make the transition. There may be a task required, such as directing the males to live for three days on only what they can gather through hunting. They may be required to withstand painful and demanding *rites de passage*. The rituals also provide an acceptable outlet for emotional release and a necessary form of social support for the participants.

Rites-de-passage: ceremonies that accompany the transition from one status to another

One process in our society that appears to have a functional ritual attached to it is the transition from being a spouse to being a widow or widower. There are funeral services, people provide instrumental and emotional support, and the transition to being a widow is made easier. At the end of the process, the individual has attained a new status, complete with operational support net-

Adolescence: A Period of Transitions

In Judaism, each young boy is expected to study in the synagogue for his bar mitzvah. The bar mitzvah is a ceremony at the age of 13 which acknowledges the boy's passage to adulthood and his responsibility for his moral and religious duties.

JOHN R. MAHER, EKM-NEPENTHE.

works. Our culture, however, has no distinct ritual for passage into or out of adolescence.

The typical adolescent period in the United States corresponds closely to an overextended liminal period. There does not appear to be very much process, and ritual is virtually nonexistent. Some predominant characteristics of American adolescence are confusion and insecurity. Because of the extended nature of our educational system and the trend away from occupational apprenticeship, the aggregation of the adolescent into the mainstream of American society may be fuzzy or nonexistent.

This liminal character of adolescence is exemplified by discontinuities in role conditioning and expectations. At certain times we expect adolescents to "grow up" and to stop acting like children. On the other hand, we perpetuate dependence upon adults and insist that adolescents are really children. At times we consciously resist adolescents' desire to grow up. In some cases, this merely adds to the confusion of the adolescent period.

A SOCIO-INTERACTIONAL APPROACH

Developmental task: interactions between a person and society that mark a transition period

There is some sort of dynamic interaction between the individual adolescent and society. There is a dynamic combination of biological destiny, cultural heritage, and interaction between the two. One manifestation of the interaction between the individual and society is the existence of developmental tasks. Developmental tasks are specific examples of individual-societal interaction, present at each developmental level. Havighurst has defined a developmental task as something ". . . midway between an individual and a societal demand" (Havighurst, 1951, p. 4). In a later work, Havighurst suggested that there are specific developmental tasks of adolescence, which if accomplished will aid the adolescent in the transition to adulthood.

Developmental Tasks of Adolescence*

1. *Acceptance of one's body and a masculine or feminine role*
2. *Development of new relations with age-mates of both sexes*
3. *Emotional independence from parents and other adults*
4. *Attainment of confidence in terms of economic independence*
5. *Cultivation of new intellectual skills*
6. *Acquisition of culturally responsible behavior*
7. *Preparation for marriage and family*
8. *Integration of socially acceptable, appropriate values*

*Adapted from Havighurst, 1972.

Some of these developmental tasks are distinctly culture bound. Numbers 3, 6, and 8 are heavily dependent on the culture in which they exist. Aspects of intellectual development are probably intrinsic to the individual, but certainly a part is dependent upon the environment children find themselves in. The importance of Havighurst's work lies in two fundamental points: first, there are developmental milestones within the period of adolescence that appear predictive of normative behavior; secondly, there is an interaction between the social, biological, and psychological worlds of the adolescent.

PHYSICAL DEVELOPMENT

The basic physiological event occurring during adolescence is puberty and all of the developments associated with sexual maturation. The hormonal changes associated with sexual maturation have a wide variety of secondary effects.

There is actually a prepubertal period where a number of related changes occur prior to actual sexual maturation. Most of these changes are in terms of secondary sex characteristics, as discussed earlier. These characteristics include the budding of the breasts in females, voice changes and facial hair in males, and pubic/ancillary hair. In females these changes begin as early as 10 or 11 years of age, with menarche (the first menstrual period) usually occurring between the ages of 12 and 14. The time of earliest pregnancy in teenage girls is usually around the age of 14, when the ovarian cycle is consistent. There are many instances of younger girls having babies, however. In boys, the prepubertal period begins at 12 or 13 years of age (sometimes much younger), and puberty (marked by mature spermatazoa) anywhere between 14 and 16 years. Females mature anywhere from one to three years earlier than males.

Menarche: the beginning of menstruation

These physiological changes are the function of a complex series of hormonal changes that occur in the normally developing adolescent. A hormone is a substance that originates in an organ or gland; if this gland is ductless, the hormone is secreted directly into the bloodstream of the individual. Hormones typically have very specific properties and affect very specific areas. In terms of adolescent physical development, we are primarily interested in the endocrine glands, which include the pituitary, the thyroid, the parathyroids, the pancreas, and the gonads (either ovaries or testes).

Hormone: a substance transported by the bloodstream that stimulates the body by chemical action

A portion of the pituitary called the anterior pituitary secretes two very fundamental hormones that directly affect the adolescent: the *growth hormone* (GH) and the *gonadotropic hormones* (which are related to sexual maturation). The growth hormone, which is apparently produced throughout life in varying amounts, is directly related to the increases in body size and weight that occur during adolescence. It is also primarily responsible for the growth spurt, which we will discuss below. The gonadotropic hormones have direct implications for sexual development, because they stimulate the gonads, which in turn produce their own hormones.

In females, the ovaries produce a number of different estrogens, which directly influence the development and maintenance of primary and secondary sex differences. In males, androgens are produced primarily in the testes. One androgen, testosterone, is specifically responsible for development and maintenance of primary and secondary sex characteristics in the male. (Tanner, 1973; Root, 1973).

It is oversimplistic to view the hormonal relationships in the human body, particularly during adolescence, as simple cause-effect relationships, or even to view estrogens as being only in females and androgens only in males. There are traces of estrogens in males, as there are traces of testosterone in females. While the

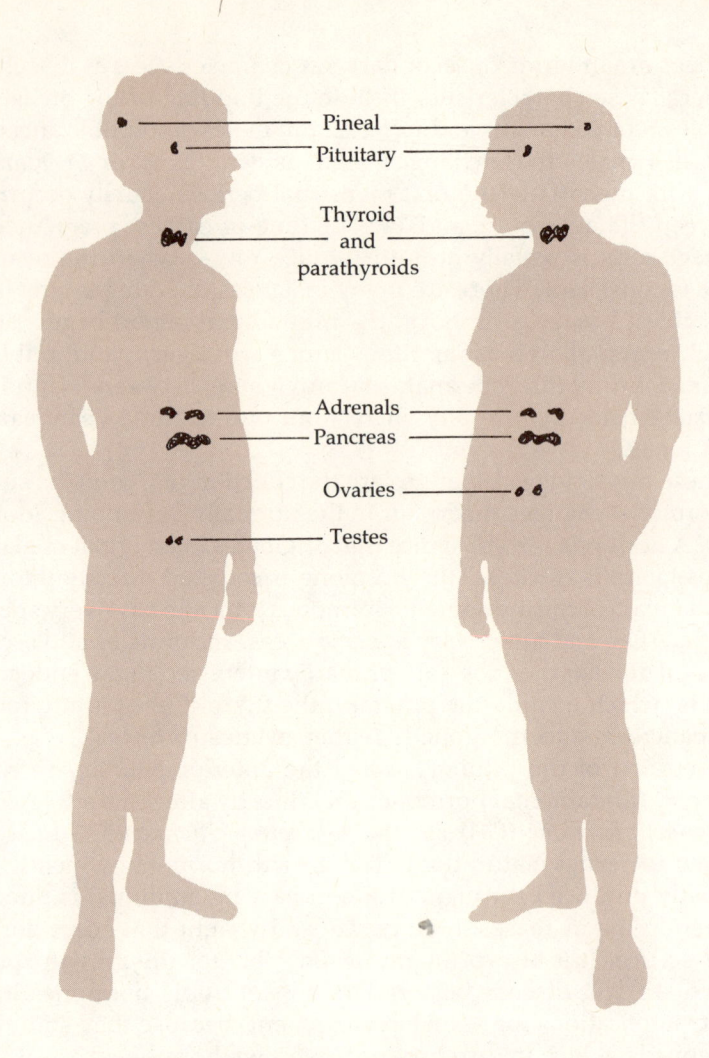

Locations of the endocrine glands in the male and female.

complexity of these hormonal relationships is considerable, the traits we observe as masculine and feminine are the result of the *balance* between the two groups of chemicals. When this balance is disturbed, there may be observable differences present.

The intense hormonal activity of adolescence is also related to other aspects of the body; the effects are not confined to sexual maturation. For example, the skin problems often associated with adolescents (acne) are related to the chemical balance within the body. Very often these problems subside as the body reacquires its normative biochemical patterns. Another example of a secondary effect is the voracious appetite we sometimes see in adolescents. This appetite is related to the tremendous nutritional demands

Adolescence: A Period of Transitions

placed on the body by the growth spurt, which of course is related to the amount of growth hormone present.

The adolescent "growth spurt" is a very rapid increase in height (sometimes weight also) that occurs early in the adolescent period. The growth spurt often precedes sexual maturation by a year or two, or even more. Tanner (1970) has indicated that the growth spurt in girls may begin as early as 7½ years and as late as 11 years and will last from 1½ to 2 years. In boys it begins as early as 10 and as late as 16 and usually slows down by the age of 15½ or 16.

The figure below shows the amount of growth per year for the ages from 1 to 18. The growth spurt occurs earlier for girls but does not develop as high a peak as does the growth curve for boys. The rapidity of the growth rate means that other components of the adolescent's body do not keep up. For example, weight gain usually does not create the same sort of pattern. Coordination is often

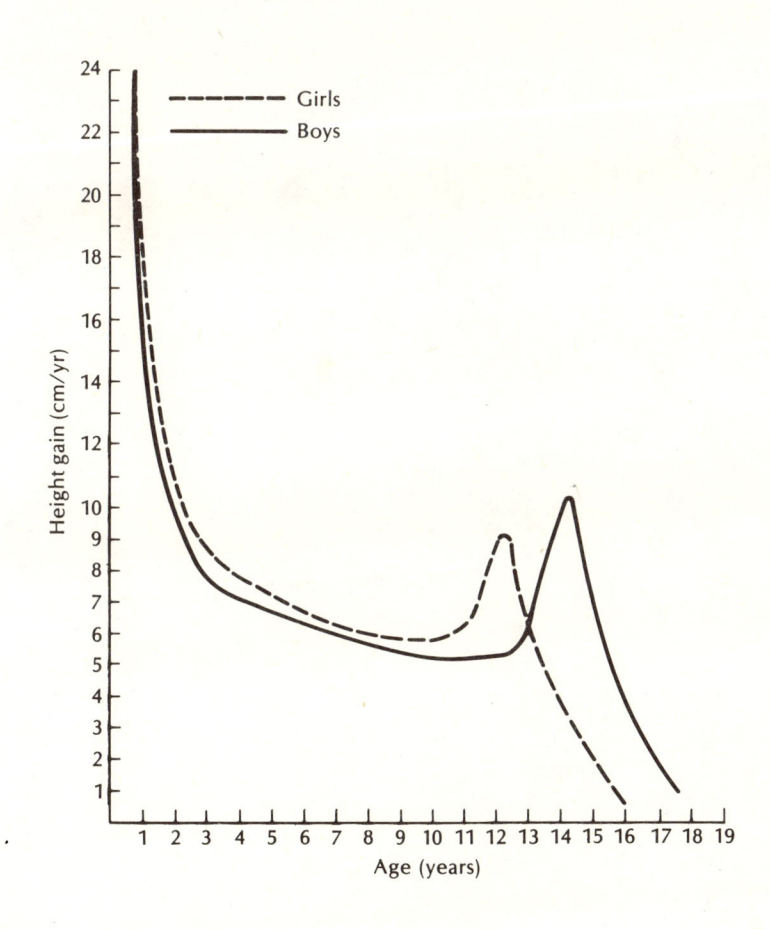

Adolescent growth spurt: a rapid increase in height that occurs early in adolescence

insufficient to cope with the longer body. The image of the adolescent male with very long legs that extend far below the end of his pants, tripping over nearly everything he comes across, reminds us all that the growth spurt period can be a very awkward period for the adolescent.

ISSUE:

The Secular Trend

From the title the reader may assume that this piece has to do with a religious dimension of adolescence. On the contrary, *secular* has to do with being wordly; another definition states that secular things are things that change. A sacred society is not conducive to change, for example.

☐ The secular trend is quite simply defined: it represents the tendency of adolescents of today to mature faster and to grow bigger and stronger than those of previous generations. What this means is that today's adolescents are taller, heavier, and stronger, and mature faster than their parents. In fact, it has been suggested that girls are reaching menarche ten months earlier than their own mothers (Muuss, 1970). That is a ten-month change in one generation. Tanner has indicated that the average age of menarche has declined four months per decade for the last century (Tanner, 1968). American youths are bigger today than they have ever been. It is not uncommon to see high school basketball teams with players 6'7" tall, or even taller. Football players are heavier and stronger than they have ever been, and even the size of the average person's shoe has grown considerably larger.

☐ Why the secular trend? Why these massive changes in the stature of the American adolescent? Two theories have been suggested. One states that the evolutionary destiny of the human being is only now being fulfilled. The trend toward earlier maturation is merely the result of a species-specific mechanism; eventually we will reach the evolutionary maximum in terms of early maturation, and the secular trend will stop.

☐ Another theory states that improved nutrition and generally more effective disease control has allowed improvements in physical condition, and hence an earlier maturation. Support for this argument comes from the fact that the secular trend is more noticeable in industrialized nations. The improved diet that industrialization sometimes offers allows for earlier development of society's children. Is there an optimal point at which nutrition is the best it can be and the secular trend will eventually level off? There is some evidence that in industrial nations this is already happening (Peterson, 1979).

☐ At some point in the future, we may reach the evolutionary limit in terms of early maturation and physical development (Muuss, 1970). What that point is and when it will be reached is not known. Future implications are also hard to predict, but as Peterson has stated:

> Our improved health has led to a lengthening of the reproductive years; puberty is coming earlier, and at the same time, the age when fertility ends is

> getting later and later. The longer period of reproduction has implications not only for biological processes, but also for social and psychological development. (Peterson, 1979, p. 47.)

ADOLESCENT NUTRITION

Given the incredible bodily changes occurring within adolescents, it is not surprising that they are in need of great amounts of energy just to keep up with the growth rate. The fast pace of the typical American adolescent only adds to this nutritional need. Adults are often amazed at the amount of food that a relatively skinny adolescent can eat. What is even more surprising is that many adolescents can eat voraciously and not gain a single extra pound of weight.

The quality of adolescents' diet is very important in assuring proper growth and development. The type of development that is occurring during adolescence is as important as the amount of growth. For example, research indicates that nutrition of adolescent females may be related to problems they may suffer years later when they become pregnant. Basic stores of nutrients and basic development of the reproductive system is occurring in adolescence; the diet of the adolescent female may play a significant role in the viability of later pregnancies. More importantly, the dietary practices established during adolescence by both sexes may be the dietary practices they retain throughout their life. Strange dietary patterns may be all right for the adolescent or young adult who may have the strength to overcome the problems they cause. But patterns like ingesting large amounts of fat invariably catch up to people during the middle years of life.

There is a significant difference in the number of calories needed for males and females. Boys start needing more of these energy units at about the age of 11. With increasing age, the caloric needs differentiate by sex. The sex difference in calories needed remains somewhat stable during adult life, as the activity patterns of men tend to be different from women's patterns.

There are three distinct nutritional patterns observable in adolescents. *Obesity* is a relatively common problem among American adolescents. Secondly, there is a significant amount of food faddism in adolescent eating patterns of today. Lastly, there is a rare but very severe psychological disorder called *anorexia nervosa*.

Calorie:
a unit of energy-producing value in food

Obesity:
a condition of excessive body fat

Caloric Needs by Sex and Age

	Age	Weight (lbs.)	Height (in.)	Energy (calories)
Males	7–10	66	54	2400
	11–14	97	63	2800
	15–18	134	69	3000
	19–22	147	69	3000
Females	11–14	97	62	2400
	15–18	119	65	2400
	19–22	128	65	2400

Source: National Academy of Sciences, National Research Council; Recommended Daily Dietary Allowances, Revised 1974.

Obesity results when the number of calories ingested exceeds the number needed for proper growth and development. Knittle (1972) has suggested that there are two periods in children's lives when the *number* of fat cells in the body increases: between the ages of 5 and 7, and between the ages of 9 and 12. Early adolescence is one of the times when there is the potential for a significant increase in the number of fat cells in the body. If this is true, adolescents may come with a built-in propensity for obesity. This does not appear to be possible, given the builds of many teenagers. In fact, researchers are questioning the idea that there are only two times in children's lives when the number of fat cells is significantly increased (see Fomon, 1974, for example). Whether there is an increase in the number of fat cells, or whether the fat cells that are present merely increase in size, there *is* a significant potential for being obese during this period. In fact, some observers suggest that American adolescents are fatter and in worse physical condition than adolescents anywhere.

Obesity presents very real problems for adolescents. As we shall see, adolescents are preoccupied with their image; how they appear to others is very important. An overweight adolescent may face the problem of social isolation, which ironically may be self-imposed. Fat adolescents may feel that they cannot do what other people are doing, and quite often there is a certain amount of ridicule from the peer group. This insensitive labeling can be damaging to the identity and self-concept of adolescents. The deflating effect of this sort of peer criticism may actually push overweight adolescents into eating more. It is something that they can enjoy, and it will never talk back to them!

Interestingly, adolescents often perceive themselves as overweight when they are not. In one study it was shown that while approximately 70 percent of the females studied wanted to lose weight, only 15 percent had any weight problem. Over half of the boys wished to gain weight, even though few of them (less than 20 percent) were below normal in the amount of fat in their bodies (Huenemann et al., 1966).

Food faddism is another adolescent nutritional pattern, and it appears to be increasing in severity. The current interest in "back-to-nature" eating may be one significant influence in the appearance of these food fads. Adolescence is a period of change, both physically and psychologically. Values are in the process of change, and as a result, eating habits may undergo significant changes during adolescence. The obese adolescent may try any diet available in order to lose weight. The adolescent athlete may ingest vast quantities of protein pills and eat strange concoctions of egg yolks and buttermilk in order to "develop properly."

There are many nontraditional diets floating around the youth subculture. These range from the Zen macrobiotic diet, to the water diet (which consists of drinking great quantities of water, eating nothing but protein, and going to the bathroom frequently), to the carbohydrate diet. Why do adolescents fall for these fad diets? They are different from the way their parents eat, for one thing, and therefore probably the right thing to do. Some of the devotion to certain diets borders on the fanatical; and if there is one developmental stage where idealism may run rampant, it is adolescence. The largest danger for the adolescent in food faddism is the possibility of nutritional neglect.

Among a few adolescents, there is a serious psychological disorder, anorexia nervosa, related to nutritional patterns. This problem is found more often in adolescent females than in adolescent males. "Clinically, this disorder may be characterized by progressive and/or significant weight loss, alternate binge eating and dieting with avoidance of any 'fattening' foods, amenorrhea, hyperactivity and compulsive exercising patterns, and preoccupation with food and nutrition" (Lucas, 1977, p. 139).

The incidence of this problem has been estimated to be about 1 out of every 150 teenage girls (Crisp, 1974). While the problem may begin due to a real overweight condition, it soon escalates into a severe psychological problem. Frequently these girls will eat a great deal, and then induce vomiting and swallow huge amounts of laxatives in order to clean out their bodies. Many times the problem is not even noticed until it is very severe.

The effects of anorexia nervosa include a general decline in nutritional status. This leads to the decline of other bodily systems, and disease often invades the body. The self-induced vomiting disrupts the fluid balance in the body, and in a few instances, death is the result.

PSYCHOLOGICAL ASPECTS OF PHYSICAL GROWTH

There is a close relationship between physical development and psychological development. These two broad forces are interdependent; given the human condition, they are inseparable. The timing of physical development, for example, may be a significant variable.

Early Maturation: Adolescents who mature before their peers find the world a different place, and they often feel alone, way out ahead of everyone else. For males, early maturation may be advantageous in some circumstances. Being more "mature" and possessing visible secondary sex characteristics like a beard may enhance males' status within their peer group. If they develop physical skills commensurate with their appearance, they may be able to succeed in athletics. Success in sports often means popularity with peers, particularly females, enhanced status with adults, and increased self-confidence. A problem for adolescent females who mature very early is the large amount of sexual attention that will be paid to them by older males. This is flattering, but there is seldom enough emotional maturity to go along with the advanced physical development.

Early maturation may cause problems for adolescents of both sexes. Because of these adolescents' advanced physical development, adults may create inappropriately high expectations for them. Their physical appearance is misleading; what appears to be more adult than child may not be because their emotional maturity has not kept pace with their physical growth. Thus, some early-maturing adolescents may not be able to live up to the expectations of their parents and teachers. This failure may be very disappointing to adolescents and lead to higher levels of insecurity and self-doubt.

Late Maturation: Late-maturing boys are often the targets of verbal and physical ridicule. The harassment and teasing of immature, smaller teenage boys is an institution in high school locker rooms. The resulting high levels of tension and animosity often directly impinge on these adolescents' developing self-concept. The negative messages these young people get are very believable to them, given the malleability of their self-concept. However, there is little

Young people often consider cigarette smoking a mark of their maturity and adulthood.
ROBERT V. ECKERT, JR., EKM-NEPENTHE.

evidence that late maturation produces any significant problems that are carried into adulthood. If these adolescents can put up with the peer pressure, they may even be at a slight advantage compared to early-maturing males in that they do not have to deal with the premature expectations that early maturers face.

Late-maturing females share some of the same problems. There is some indication that the peer pressure is not as great for girls; this may be due to more normative expectations for girls' sex-role development. (For more detailed discussions of this phenomenon, see Hamachek, 1976; Peskin, 1967; and Hurlock, 1973).

SEXUAL BEHAVIOR AND ATTITUDES

There are a number of studies available that indicate several distinct trends in the sexual behavior of adolescents (Robinson et al., 1972; Yankelovich, 1974; Vener and Stuart, 1974; Sorenson, 1973; and Zelnick and Kantner, 1972). First, there is a positive relationship between the age of adolescents and the amount of sexual behavior engaged in. As they get older, both males and females engage in more and more sexual behavior.

Adolescence is usually a time during which boys and girls both discover they enjoy doing things together.
ROBERT V. ECKERT, JR., EKM-NEPENTHE.

Boys have a higher level of sexual activity than do girls. Boys begin their sexual activities earlier, and get involved more often and at higher levels of intimacy. Girls appear to be more reluctant to get into very intimate relationships quickly. This sex difference reflects cultural attitudes and restrictions: boys need to "sow their wild oats" and girls need to save themselves for their husbands. These simplistic orientations still exist and undoubtedly create the kinds of sex differences we see in the data.

Sexual Revolution: Fact or Fantasy?

During the last 10 to 15 years, it has become increasingly popular to thunder from the speaking platforms of American life (from the churches to the U.S. Senate) about the immorality of modern American youth. The implication is that a massive sexual revolution has taken over among young adults.

First of all, sexual behaviors and attitudes have changed; there is little doubt about that. There is a much more liberal attitude about discussing sexuality, and there appear to have been similar changes behaviorally. It is naïve, however, to assume that people in the "good old days" (whenever that was) did not engage in sexual activities during adolescence. It is an unfortunate simplification and overgeneralization to assume that adolescents have gone sexually wild. We conclude that there have been changes, as most things have changed over time. There is insufficient evidence, however, to label the changes as a revolution.

One of the sad facts about adolescent sexuality is that there is a persistent trend among these young people to not use contraceptive devices when engaging in sexual behavior. Apparently using contraceptives takes away from the spontaneity and the romantic dimension of the act. Random sexual relations among adolescents are relatively rare. But there appears to be a counterrevolution, if you will, directed at perpetuating feeling and commitment in the relations of adolescents. Many young people are very idealistic about their interpersonal relations, as we shall see later.

Summary

1. Adolescent physical growth and development is dynamic, both in rate of growth (quantitative) and type of growth (qualitative). A common assumption made about adolescence is that it is a period of storm and stress. This is probably true in the United States.

2. Adolescence is a transition period; it is the change from being a child to being an adult. Transitions appear to have three components: separation, the liminal phase, and the aggregation of the individual back into the mainstream of society. American adolescence was characterized as being an overextended liminal phase of development.

3. Using a sociointeractional perspective, it is possible to state several key developmental tasks of the adolescent period. These tasks, which are midway between an individual need and a societal demand, have to do with the acceptance by adolescents of their new and different physical being, emotional independence from the world of their parents, and preparation for entrance into society as a competent adult.

4. The physical period of adolescence is marked by the appearance of the growth spurt, the beginning of the sexually mature body (puberty), and the appearance of secondary sex characteristics.

5. Nutrition plays a key role in adolescent physical development. Given the significant body changes that adolescents are going through, they need great amounts of energy. Adolescents are very concerned about their body im-

age; consequently faddish diets are common, as are dietary problems characteristic of adolescents, such as obesity and anorexia nervosa.

6. Physical growth and development have a significant psychological aspect. Early-maturing boys and girls are placed in situations where inappropriately high expectations are made of them. Early maturing boys are expected to be better athletes and more mature than their age-mates; likewise, early maturing girls are often sought out by older boys as appropriate sexual objects. Late maturation can be a problem for boys, especially in peer group relations, which may also be a problem for late-maturing females.

7. Sexuality is one physiological aspect that is very important to the adolescent. Male and female adolescents differ somewhat in sexual behavior and attitudes, and there is some evidence that there is an ongoing revolution in sexual behavior and attitudes among American adolescents.

Thought Questions

1. How are adolescents physically different from younger children? What are the psychological implications of these differences?

2. How is adolescence a transition period? In America is this transition efficient?

3. What do developmental tasks have to do with the adolescent acquiring a firm sense of self?

4. How might obesity affect the self-concept of an adolescent? What factors would drive an adolescent to anorexia nervosa?

5. For the typical adolescent, which is more advantageous: early maturation or late maturation? Cite sex differences and the factors that may affect the nature of the situation (family, peer group, teachers, etc.).

Suggested Readings

Bruck, H. *The Golden Cage: The Enigma of Anorexia Nervosa.* Cambridge, Mass.: Harvard University Press, 1978. *Anorexia nervosa is one of the most troubling psychiatric problems for the adolescent. Bruch presents a thoughtful and scholarly treatment of this most challenging situation.*

Erikson, E. "Identity and the Life Cycle," *Monographs of Psychological Issues,* I, 1959. *This is a primary source in child development. Erikson presents his theory of identity development and goes through the entire life span. An important work for the serious student in child development.*

Muuss, R. E. *Theories of Adolescence*. 3rd ed. New York: Random House, 1975. *A definitive work in the field of adolescence. Muuss offers a readable discussion of the theoretical dimensions of the adolescent period.*

READING

Adolescence brings with it increased sexual activity. Boys have more sexual contacts than girls, they have them earlier, and they talk more about their activities. In terms of a sexual revolution, there is certainly an attitudinal one in that there is much more talk of sex. Behaviorally there have also been significant changes that could also be called revolutionary in their extent.

As was indicated in this chapter, adolescents are more involved in sexuality, yet remain consistent in their nonuse of contraceptives. Of course one of the more unfortunate results of this is that there are a great many pregnancies occurring in this country among teenagers, some as young as 12 and 13 years.

John Kelly addresses this issue in a recent article from *Family Health.* Dr. Kelly shows the magnitude of the problem and the very difficult position many parents find themselves in: tell their teenagers about contraceptives and implicitly condone their activity, or not tell them and run the risk of having a pregnant teenager. It appears that only a consistent effort on the part of medical doctors, the educational system, and parents will help to make adolescents' transition into adult behavior patterns more productive and less traumatic. Helping with sexual education and awareness is one way to accomplish this task.

Epidemic: Teenage Pregnancy
John C. Kelly, M.D.

Julia is an intelligent, pretty teenager who seems to have everything a 16-year-old could want. Her parents lavish her with presents—a new car on her last birthday—and they give her the freedom of running her own life.

But Julia is a neglected and troubled child. When she came to see me recently, she was three months pregnant. To make matters worse, instead of giving her the support she needed, her parents had rejected her. They considered the pregnancy a personal affront, a threat to their social standing. Despite the great material display of affection, there was no communication between Julia and her parents.

I found it difficult in such a highly charged atmosphere to discuss the pregnancy with Julia and her family. The two options available to the girl—to have a therapeutic abortion or to have the child—were both loaded with such medical and emotional consequences that either choice would have a lasting effect on her life. The family could reach no decision, so they arranged to meet with me again in a week's time. But I saw Julia and her parents sooner than that.

I got a call one night at 2 A.M. from Julia's parents. Julia had locked herself in her room after an argument with her parents and had slashed her wrists. She survived this tragic act, but later ran away from home.

Julia's story isn't unusual. With changing circumstances, unintended pregnancies are a reality for millions of teenagers, regardless of social and economic class. Consider these statistics, compiled by Planned Parenthood: At least one million teenage girls, ages 15 to 19, become pregnant each year. While the overall birth rate has been declining in the United States, out-of-wedlock babies born to teenage mothers are rising. During the early 1970s, children born to unmarried 14- and 15-year-old girls increased by 75 percent.

Most of the blame for these teenage pregnancies rests on a relaxed attitude toward birth control. Young people just aren't using contraceptives in the initial stages of sexual experimentation; and since intimacy is beginning at a young age, it is not unusual for me to see a pregnant girl who is only 13 years old.

By the time these youngsters reach their mid-teens, we expect them to know about and be practicing birth control. But according to a 1976 study, about 37 percent of sexually active unmarried adolescents did not use a contraceptive the last time they had intercourse. They are either ignorant about contraceptive techniques, could not get the protection when they needed it, or for some reason chose not to use it.

These alarming statistics about teenage sexual activity are only part of the story—they don't tell us about the emotional hurt of an abortion, the early marriages that wreck educational and career plans and usually end in divorce, or the strain of motherhood for a girl barely out of childhood herself.

To further complicate the situation, teenage pregnancies are a major health problem. Why? Because out of fear or confusion, unmarried teenage girls are in their second trimester of pregnancy before they seek proper medical attention. Poor eating habits and stress are also major contributory factors. Children born to very young mothers tend to be underweight. Over all, poor prenatal care accounts for the high infant mortality rate for babies born to teenagers.

In addition, the young mother runs a much greater risk of serious illness or even death. Young mothers, ages 15 to 18, are twice as likely to die from a hemorrhage or miscarriage than those who are older. Toxemia—a problem interfering with kidney function during pregnancy—is also commoner in teenagers.

What can we as parents, educators and physicians do about these enormous problems? I have the feeling that we are all turning our backs while the sexual revolution claims new territory among the very young who are ill-prepared for it. Parents find themselves in a moral bind: To provide their children with contraceptives or birth-control information implies an open endorsement of active sex for the child, and thus most parents can't bring themselves to do it. So sex as a topic of discussion is assigned to a strange dark corner of the parent-child relationship.

Many parents find it easier to leave their children's sexual education to the school system, but classes in family hygiene or sex education are a big comforting myth. Even where school districts do offer sex education programs, only a few teach anything about birth control or contraceptive techniques. Most of these courses deal with the physical changes brought on by adolescence and the anatomy of human reproduction. The emphasis seems to be on the mechanics of sex—not the practical aspect of dealing with the reality of it.

I don't mean to fault our entire educational system. Many individual teachers and schools are prohibited by outmoded state and local laws from discussing birth control methods. Until this situation changes, parents must find out exactly what their children are taught and be prepared to fill in the gaps. Or, better still, they should help in the initial teaching process by explaining the facts openly and frankly.

If our schools are part of the problem, the medical profession is also at fault. Doctors should not be a last resort, but a source of information and advice to be used *before* a child becomes pregnant. I'm not suggesting that a girl just past puberty be automatically marched into the doctor's office and put on the pill or fitted with a diaphragm. Each case is different. What the physician can do is provide the child with information and guidance about birth control in a compassionate and nonjudgmental way.

Physicians have an obligation to raise the issue of sex education with parents of teenagers and the young people themselves. In my own family practice, I ask parents what they think their children should know about sex and contraception. Many admit that they are bewildered. They can't communicate with their kids, so they genuinely welcome an offer of help from a concerned third party. This ice-breaking discussion will usually lead to a second meeting between a teenage patient and myself, in which sex and birth control are discussed openly, without shame. I generally find that my young patients have very specific questions to ask about sex.

I am presently developing videotape cassettes on sex and contraception that can be played on a regular television set in a doctor's office. After a session with the doctor, the teenage patient can stay a little longer to watch the videotape. Then the patient is given printed material based on the program to take home. Eventually I hope to make these tapes and television systems available to all physicians.

It seems more sensible to spend money and time on contraception and sex education programs than to care for pregnant adolescents. However, a Health, Education and Welfare task force recently recommended that the Federal Government put more emphasis on care rather than on prevention of pregnancies among unwed teenagers. This advice in my opinion is misguided. The vast majority of teenage girls do not become pregnant by choice. We need realistic sex education programs and wider access to birth-control methods.

Teenage pregnancy has become an epidemic in this country, and there are no easy solutions to the problem. But as our society continues to peddle sex, the least we can do is to make sure our children can handle it.

Jeanne d'Arc. Fifteenth-century manuscript illustration of Joan of Arc in the Archives Nationales, Paris.

PHOTO BY GIRAUDON

16

Adolescence: Values and Egocentrism

As we stated in the previous chapter, adolescence is a distinct developmental period as well as preparation for the next period. There are developmental milestones and developmentally appropriate tasks that change the individual significantly. "The basic view is that adolescents are not just preadults, preparents or preworkers, but human beings at an important stage of development in their lives, with experience particular to it" (Konopka, 1976).

INTELLECTUAL DEVELOPMENT

Great strides are made in cognitive development early in children's lives. The amount of things learned early in life is amazing, and probably exceeds the "amount" of things we learn later in life. The learning of the basic language, for example, is an impressive feat, including as it does the symbols, the sounds of the symbols, word order, and all of the grammatical rules.

The period of adolescence also contains significant amounts of change in the area of intellect. There is a fundamental transition from thought patterns that are essentially concrete and grounded to thought patterns that are much more abstract and propositional. Adolescence is the time when most of the intellectual patterns to be used in adulthood are formed, practiced, and solidified.

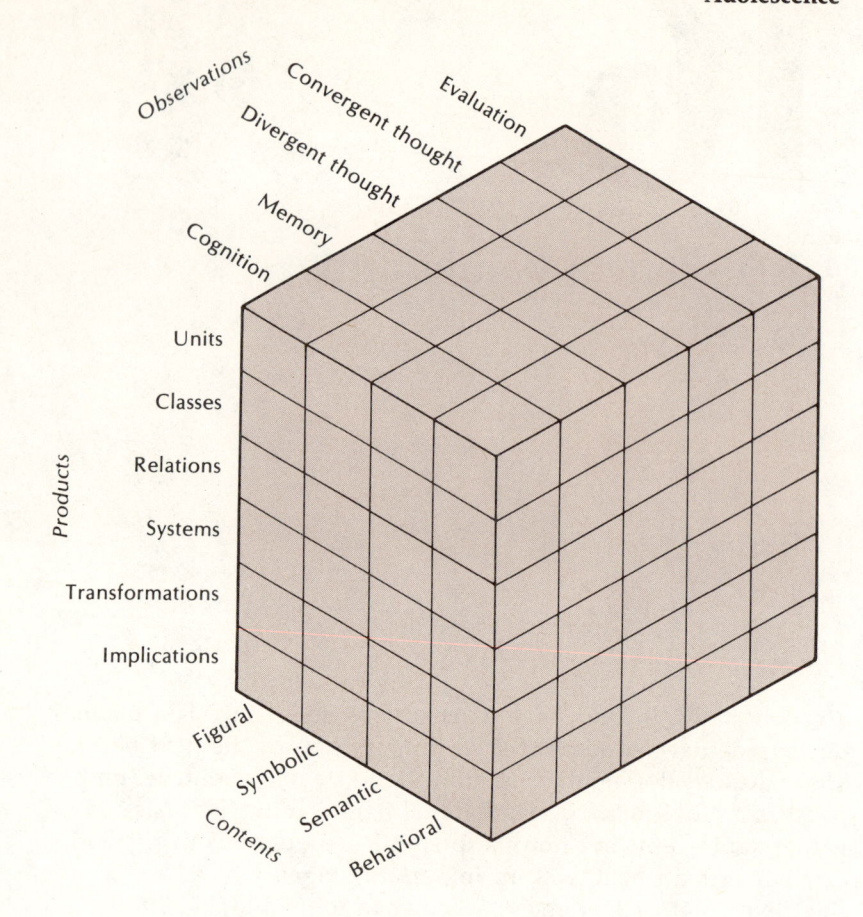

Formulations of Intellectual Growth

There are many ways to conceptualize intelligence, and many of them have already been mentioned. Intelligence tests can concoct a maturational age, which when plugged into a formula along with the chronological age, can give us a child's intelligence quotient.

We feel, however, that intellectual abilities are actually a group of heterogeneous factors or characteristics that provide individuals with the ability to perform intellectually. The heterogeneity of the factors ensures flexibility of intellectual thought. The model most closely representing this concept, and which most accurately describes the complexity of adolescent thought, is the model proposed by Guilford in 1959.

The figure above shows Guilford's model in terms of operations, products, and contents. In intellect, there are several operations in existence:

Heterogeneity: variety

Recognition—a pure cognitive-perceptive ability

Memory—invaluable in building cognitive structure

Creative thought processes—divergent processes, according to Guilford

Convergent thought processes—logical and orderly thought processes

Evaluation—the value dimension of thought

The contents of the intellect process symbols, words along with the behavior related to symbols. These are the tools employed by individuals to make intellectual sense out of an array of information. The application of a process through to a content results in what Guilford calls *products*, and they come in one of six forms:

Units—single words or numbers

Classes—groups of similar objects

Relations—the functional connections between objects in the environment

Systems—more complex relations tied together

Transformations—the revision and modification of information

Implications—the drawing of inferences from observed relations and making conclusions

The exact arrangement of the intellectual cube (see figure) varies with the individual, the culture, and probably the species. Certain social forces such as environmental deprivation can alter the contents and the products. Very few assessment techniques can adequately measure all of these factors. IQ tests probably measure knowledge already acquired, and don't come close to measuring the complex interactions indicated by the Guilford model.

The Guilford model is complex, and in that way is a good model to use in relating to adolescent intellectual growth. Both the model and adolescent intellectual growth are multifaceted and defy simplistic explanations. In order to understand adolescents, and in particular their intellectual growth and development, we must look at many different types of information and abilities. Only if we look at individuals as interactive beings can we hope to understand the complexity of intellectual growth.

Intellectual Growth and Development as Change

Adolescents are synergistic beings. They are more than just the sum of their previous experience. Childhood conditions and ex-

Synergism: a process that produces a total effect greater than the sum of the individual parts

periences may be contributing to adolescents' present situation, but we cannot be sure they are causal. For the sake of argument, let's assume that event A is a family status of poverty; event B is a parental divorce; and event C is a significant geographical move that occurs during the teenage years. Can we assume that $A + B + C = P$ (existing adolescent personality)? And will this scenario exist for all people who go through the same life events? Probably not, in both cases. P is the result of the interaction between life events, genetic makeup, and some unknown factor that remains very elusive.

We assume that adolescents, intellectually and formatively, are active participants in their environment. It is more than just their environment acting upon them; they initiate some of the interaction and greatly affect the tone of the interaction.

In adolescence, there is a distinct idiosyncratic developmental pattern and interactive component, and these forces come together to form the whole child.

PIAGET'S THEORY OF ADOLESCENT INTELLECTUAL GROWTH

The stage of concrete operations lasts from the ages of 7 to 11, and the stage of formal operations (that of the adolescent) runs from age 11 to age 15. Piaget has stated that in the stage of concrete operations, four basic accomplishments are noted:

Combinativity—the ability to form classes of objects

Reversibility—understanding that operations work both ways

Associativity—understanding that there may be alternate ways of solving problems

Identity—an understanding that an operation when combined with its opposite is nullified.

(Adapted from Muuss, 1975.)

These characteristics are all accurate and their development is very interesting to observe. The problem is that because the Piagetian theory is outlined in stages, we often assume that there are clear divisions between the stages. Are all of the abilities mentioned above always present by the age of 11? We feel that there is *no clear-cut transition point* between concrete operations and formal operations.

The timing of the change into formal operational thought is idiosyncratic; it *usually* begins by the age of 11, but not always. The move to formal operations is an important one: "The concrete operational system can be conceived of as analogous to a logical group in the sense that it involves a set of elements and operations and rules for their combination" (Elkind, 1968, p. 140). Concrete operations, however, probably do not supply children with the intellectual freedom they desire. Anything hypothetical or abstract may be beyond their grasp. If a child at the concrete level tries to incorporate a system containing two or more variables ". . . he flounders because he lacks an operational system appropriate to such a situation" (Elkind, 1968, p. 141). This may be the fundamental deficiency of concrete operational thought.

Thus, the transition to formal operations represents a new way of thinking. The adolescent in his new mode of thinking can still put things into appropriate classes and orders and into proper relationship with each other. The adolescent, however, can do something else:

Idiosyncratic:
unique to each individual

> a necessary something which is precisely what renders his thought formal rather than concrete. He takes the results of these concrete operations, casts them into the form of propositions and then proceeds to operate further on them, i.e., make various logical connections between them. . . . Formal operations, then, are really operations performed upon concrete operations (Flavell, 1963, p. 205).

As has been demonstrated in much of David Elkind's work, the logic employed in adolescence becomes much more complex (see, for example, Elkind, 1961, 1961b, 1967, 1968, and 1970). Elkind uses the phrase "propositional logic" in describing the thought patterns of the adolescent. It is a qualitative elaboration of earlier ways of thinking. It allows for the consideration of the hypothetical, the abstract, and the subtle.

For the first time, by using formal operations children can literally think about their own thoughts. The enhanced level of introspective skills, combined with new abstractness, gives adolescents a new philosophical approach to the world. They possess another advantage over their younger counterparts: a much greater range of thought. Ideas become important; idealism becomes a way of life and a new and exciting way of interacting with the world. Innovative and very creative thought patterns are the result. We are not saying, however, that there is a parallel increase in the levels of maturity in adolescents. Very often maturity does not keep up with the new-found cognitive skills. Consequently, some adolescents come off as arrogant, stubborn, and introverted. This developmental lag will dissipate with time.

UNIQUE FEATURES OF ADOLESCENT THOUGHT PATTERNS

One result of all of these intellectual changes is a very distinct change in children's relationships with their parents. Intergenerational communication has long been a topic of conversation and conjecture: Is there a generation gap? If so, what produces it and what can we do about it? What factors alienate adolescents from their parents? What alienates parents from their children?

Nowhere in the course of parent-child relationships is the power and ability of children as great as it is in the adolescent period. Very rarely will younger children be able to put up a logical and consistent argument against parental demands. In no previous time in their lives have children's challenges to parental authority been so persistent and salient. At least two major questions are being asked: (1) Are parents in complete control of their children? and (2) Where will this new-found boldness on the part of adolescents end? One interesting and potentially vital part of the answer to these and other questions is the fact that adolescents' developmental level touches on an important dimension for their parents: if their children have developed to this point, it is a sure sign that the parents are aging.

The changes brought about by adolescence require a redefinition of the parent-child relationship. The old ways of handling a disagreement with the child will not work any longer; parents are dealing with an individual who in some respects has the wisdom of an older person, but also has the maturity of a child. Ironically, because of these differences, communication is often interrupted, precisely at a time when the adolescent may need parental guidance more than ever.

In many families the rapidity of the change produces overt family conflicts. It is not unusual in America today to have the police called to break up a conflict between an adolescent child and the parents. In some cases these conflicts become deadly. Rigidity and inflexibility are characteristic of both adolescents and parents. There really is a gap in terms of understanding and empathy between adolescents and parents.

The speed of the intellectual change is a key factor. Young people are not prepared for the speed at which things change, nor are their parents. In both cases, there is a great deal of overreaction to the changes. Fortunately, the problems between adolescents and parents usually improve with age. "More than one individual has observed as he grew older (and out of adolescence) his parents grew smarter" (Dusek, 1977, p. 101).

ADOLESCENT EGOCENTRISM

Egocentrism in some form is characteristic of children at most developmental stages. The exact nature of this egocentrism is directly dependent upon the intellectual level of the child. The adolescent demonstrates a unique form of egocentrism that manifests itself in two basic patterns: (1) the imaginary audience, and (2) the personal fable (Elkind, 1967).

The Imaginary Audience: Imagine yourself on a stage, performing in a play or musical production. The audience is watching you, perhaps your every move. It is very important that you make the appropriate moves, the correct statements, and dress in a way so that the audience will appreciate you and you will play the role correctly.

Adolescents are doing exactly this; they are performing, acting out their roles to the fullest. There is a large amount of self-consciousness, along with a very strong need to fit into the peer group and be accepted. All of these factors contribute to adolescents feeling that they are constantly playing to an audience, and they must be dressed correctly and be able to say the right things and do all the things that will make for a good "performance." The ironic part of all of this is that the audience is largely imaginary; it is real only to the adolescent.

The behavior of adolescents is affected by this perception of playing before an audience. The imaginary audience is responsible for some of their finicky behavior and their preoccupation with looking just right. The imaginary audience is very personal to the individual adolescent; ". . . since the audience is of his own construction and privy to his own knowledge of himself, it knows just what to look for in the way of cosmetic and behavioral sensitivities. . . . The notion of the imaginary audience helps to explain the observation that the affect which most concerns adolescents is not guilt but rather shame; that is the reaction to an audience" (Elkind, 1967).

The imaginary audience seems developmentally appropriate because adolescents have an intense desire to learn about themselves. Their image is very important to them, and the feedback from the imaginary audience is usually safe. The imaginary audience can help them develop an image of how other people think of them. This is important in the development of an integrated self-concept.

The Personal Fable: Sometimes we feel that we are absolutely alone in the world; no one has ever gone through a situation like we are experiencing. Consequently no one understands the situation; help is unavailable. The adolescent is firmly convinced that "no one understands." As Elkind has said, ". . . perhaps because he is of importance to so many people . . . he comes to regard himself and particularly his feelings as something special and unique. Only he can suffer with such agonized intensity, or experience such exquisite rapture. How many parents have been confronted with the typically adolescent phrase 'but you don't know how it feels' . . ." (Elkind, 1967, p. 1031).

IDEALISM

Idealism:
the forming of standards of excellence or perfection

The egocentrism of adolescence combines with enhanced cognitive abilities and a touch of rebelliousness to produce very high levels of idealism. This idealism is beautifully open, honest, and naïve. The idealism of adolescence produces a strong desire in many adolescents to get involved in social reform movements of nearly all types.

The idealism of adolescents makes them prime candidates for movements of any form. The solidarity offered by a group, the "answers" provided by that group, and the honest feeling that they are "making a difference" are all very attractive elements to young people who are mystified by the complexity of the world. Consequently, it may feel good to belong to practically any group, as long as they belong.

In pre–World War II Germany, Hitler recognized the idealism of youth. Building on that idealism, the elite German youth corps came into being, composed of bright, energetic young people who felt they were doing the right thing—even if it meant turning their parents in to the Gestapo (secret police). Idealism is a great source of power for both adolescents and for the individual or group who can harness that idealism. As Inhelder and Piaget state, ". . . The adolescent goes through a phase in which he attributes unlimited power to his own thoughts so that the dream of a glorious future or transforming the world through ideas . . . seems to be not only fantasy but also an effective action which in itself modifies the empirical world. This is obviously a form of cognitive egocentrism" (Inhelder and Piaget, 1958, p. 345).

As adolescents mature, and their intellectual faculties expand, this form of egocentrism fades. The phaseout is a function of a significant increase in interpersonal contact, specifically with members of the opposite sex.

ADOLESCENT VALUE SYSTEMS

A value is a feeling or orientation that renders an idea useful. In human development, it is an indication of the relative worth of an idea and the role it plays within the individual. A value may be placed on an issue, a place, a person, a movement, and so on. The process of valuing is dependent upon the individual and the individual's situation. The decision concerning relative worth is a function of the interaction between the individual and the environment.

Value: the relative worth of an idea or object

One of the systems or environments that significantly affects the adolescent's value system is the family. The family is the primary unit of value transmission, and a number of factors related to the family are important to the learning of values:

1. The degree of parental warmth, acceptance and trust
2. The frequency and intensity of parent-teen interaction and communication
3. The type and degree of discipline used
4. The role-model parents offer the child
5. The independence opportunities the parents provide

(Adapted from Rice, 1978.)

There is a relatively high correlation between parental warmth and effective learning of values in children. Force-feeding is not a particularly effective way to teach values to children, particularly adolescents. A warm environment sets an effective stage for value learning and a positive parent-child relationship will contribute significantly to the child's development of appropriate values.

Parents are very important social models for their adolescents. A parent who is modeling negative, inappropriate behavior may be indirectly encouraging similar behavior in the child. Some modeling effects are not immediately apparent, but show up later. For example, it is likely that interpersonal skills and marital styles are learned from parents, and these style similarities may not show up for years. There is a relationship between the status of a child's parents' marriage when the child is 16 and the likelihood of that child being divorced in adult life. This so-called transmission effect reflects the transmission of attitudes, values, and styles from parent to child.

Adults need to provide adolescents with real independence and a measure of real power, not contrived and phony. Adolescents who are deprived of these types of experiences may miss very important learning opportunities. A familial environment laced with negativity and dependence encourages the development of an adolescent ill-prepared to meet the challenges of our complex society.

Thornburg (1973) reinforces this logic by stating that the family is the center of the child's initial social learning. Education in values begins very early within the family. The figure below is a representation of the Thornburg model of family socialization. This conceptual model of the nature of human socialization puts the learning of values into perspective.

In the area of operations, the transition is from acquisition to social learning confirmation, to social maturation (adolescence), to social integration, and so on up the developmental ladder.

Social maturation implies alternative social learning. The primary influence in the person's life has changed. Adolescents have strong affiliative needs. Peer affiliation helps to solidify self-concepts, integrate the individual into group relations, and facilitate the emancipation process (from the parents). Affiliation also spurs competitive feelings within adolescents, because there are always other peer groups, athletic teams, or social cliques that create feelings of competition.

Values influence behavior, but behavior also reflects values. In fact, there are times when it is difficult to tell if the situation creates the value or if the value creates the situation. In riots over People's Park at the University of California at Berkeley over ten years ago, it was often difficult to decide if some of the young people had values that produced the behavior, or whether the intensity of the setting carved out new values for the adolescents almost instantaneously. Many facets of the Free Speech Movement of the 1960s had this characteristic about them.

Social integration is the time when older adolescents are beginning to move into the mainstream of society. There is a gradual

Developmental Socialization: A Conceptual Model

Operation	Social-learning acquisition	Social-learning confirmation	Social maturation	Social integration	Social identity
Stage	Early and middle childhood	Preadolescence	Adolescence	Late adolescence and young adulthood	Adulthood
Age range	Birth–8	9–13	14–18	19–23	24 on
Task	Acquisition of social behaviors	Learned behaviors confirmed and solidified	Alternative social learning	Synthesis of self-social ideas	Finding one's social role
Primary influence	Parental	Parent/peer	Peers	Peer/society	Society
Peer influence	Minimal	Loosely defined	Strong	Strong	Loosely defined
Stage transfer	Facilitates →	Solidifies ←	Breaks away ↓ Facilitates ↑	Facilitates ↑	Interrelates ←

Busing of schoolchildren is one public issue in the United States that has brought out the idealistic qualities in many young people of all ages.
UNITED PRESS INTERNATIONAL.

devaluation of the peer group as the demands of a career and society begin to pull at adolescents' support systems. Many of the same values are carried into adulthood, but they are often modified, objectified, and stabilized. Levels of intrapersonal consistency begin to rise.

THE SCHOOL EXPERIENCE

Another dimension of adolescent cognitive development is the socially mandated involvement with schools. School is a significant event in the lives of children from the age of 5 to at least age 16, usually through graduation from high school. During adolescence, however, there is a big difference. After the age of 16 in most states, adolescents do not need to go to school if they do not want to. So while school may be very important for adolescents interpersonally, vocationally, and intellectually, they may choose to drop out.

The U.S. Census Bureau estimates that in 1975, 94 percent of youths aged 14 to 17 were enrolled in high school (Statistical Ab-

Adolescence: Values and Egocentrism

Attendance at school can sometimes be a significant problem to adolescents because most states require young persons to attend at least until they reach the age of 16.
ROBERT V. ECKERT, JR., EKM-NEPENTHE.

stract U.S., 1976). At any one time the dropout rate may be as high as 15 percent, depending upon the location and time. There appear to be several specific reasons for dropping out:

(1) Academic problems. It is not much fun to carry a burdensome label around with you. The labels of "dumb" or "slow" are particularly deflating. These bad feelings may drive the adolescent out of school.

(2) Socioeconomic factors. In some situations, an adolescent may have to leave school in order to help support his family financially. This may help the family for a while, but will eventually be disastrous for the adolescent.

(3) Pregnancy. This is a prominent reason for dropping out of female adolescents. The pregnant female may choose to drop out because of her appearance and/or social pressure. Some school officials would just as soon see these girls out of school because of the "example" they may be inadvertently setting for the other students. Most larger school districts now have continuation high schools for girls who have dropped out because of this reason.

(4) School is a "turn-off." This is a common excuse. School seems irrelevant and it would be better to get a job and make some

Dropping out: leaving school at a legally sanctioned age

Vocational education programs offer some young people meaningful training for a job while they are still in high school.
JOHN R. MAHER, EKM-NEPENTHE.

money. Some aspects of school may be boring and "irrelevant," and curriculum changes may help in these cases.

It is clear that dropping out has traumatic effects on potential wages earned and level of basic interpersonal and vocational skills. In a society that demands a college education in so many areas, to be without a high school education is a distinct disadvantage.

ISSUE

Adolescents and the Schools—A Crossroad

As we have already mentioned, the United States has an organized, efficient system of schools. This system was designed to provide all children, regardless of social position and heritage, with an education that would prepare them to enter society and be a productive member of that society. Education was to be the savior for the society—a means by which the nation could be extended and even improved. What was revolutionary about this educational system was its offer of equal opportunity and its support by taxes.

☐ There appear to be at least two very important dimensions of education in the United States that bear close scrutiny. First, given all of the noble intention mentioned above, just how well has our education fared? How have our children done, not only in the schools, but in the application of information? Has education meant an enhanced quality of life for all of the people of the United States or has some of education's promise been a pipe dream?

☐ Secondly, what direction has the education of our children taken? Has education provided American children with the sorts of skills necessary to accomplish its goals? Specifically, have we devalued mechanical and vocational education, valued academic preparation, and thereby deprived the nation of skilled workers?

☐ These two issues are very important for the adolescent in America. At no other point in childhood is the individual on the verge of entering society as an adult. In no other stage in the life-cycle of the child are there such significant expectations for production. Adolescence is the jumping-off point into adulthood. Education is the key to the efficacy of the first few bold steps into the demanding and exciting world of the adult.

☐ In chapter 13 it was pointed out that there has been a significant, consistent decline in national test scores over the last several years. From this perspective, then, formal education does not appear to be fulfilling its preordained destiny: preparation of children for adulthood. Intellectually, it appears that adolescents are entering the world of adulthood without basic educationally derived skills: reading, writing, and basic arithmetic. More and more of our young people are entering adulthood with poor levels of basic skill development. These deficits weigh heavily on the success of the transition; adolescents without these sorts of skills caught in our confusing and demanding society are placed immediately into a vulnerable position, from which they may not ever completely recover.

☐ The second issue is equally important. For many years the school systems have either purposely or carelessly devalued the importance and relevant nature of vocational education. There was a time in the history of our nation when vocational education was useful and highly valued. A craftsperson was an esteemed individual; in fact, most people eventually developed a skill. As industrialism and urbanization advanced, less and less influence was placed on vocational education, and more and more emphasis was placed on academic pursuits.

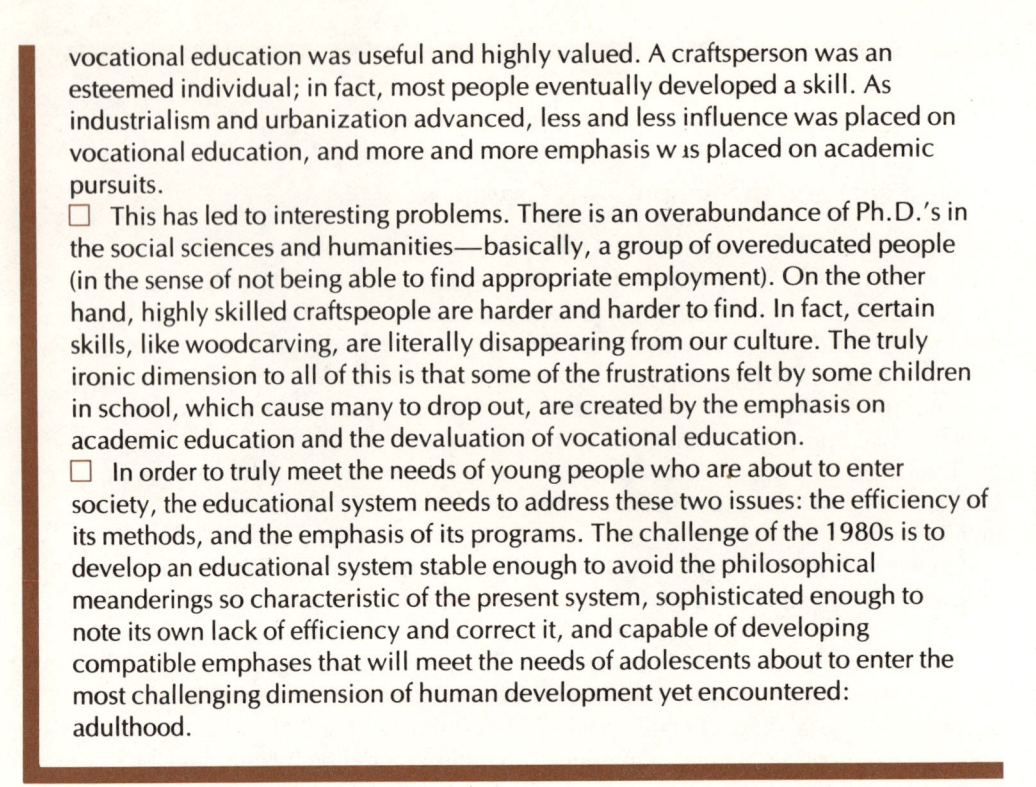

☐ This has led to interesting problems. There is an overabundance of Ph.D.'s in the social sciences and humanities—basically, a group of overeducated people (in the sense of not being able to find appropriate employment). On the other hand, highly skilled craftspeople are harder and harder to find. In fact, certain skills, like woodcarving, are literally disappearing from our culture. The truly ironic dimension to all of this is that some of the frustrations felt by some children in school, which cause many to drop out, are created by the emphasis on academic education and the devaluation of vocational education.

☐ In order to truly meet the needs of young people who are about to enter society, the educational system needs to address these two issues: the efficiency of its methods, and the emphasis of its programs. The challenge of the 1980s is to develop an educational system stable enough to avoid the philosophical meanderings so characteristic of the present system, sophisticated enough to note its own lack of efficiency and correct it, and capable of developing compatible emphases that will meet the needs of adolescents about to enter the most challenging dimension of human development yet encountered: adulthood.

Summary

1. The period of adolescence also reflects a great deal of individual change in cognitive abilities. The fundamental transition is from thought that is concrete and somewhat limited, to abstract, idealistic, and propositional ways of thinking.

2. In intellect there are several dimensions in simultaneous existence: operations, products, and contents. These interrelating dimensions highlight the multifaceted and complicated nature of adolescent thought. It is clear that intellectually, adolescents are synergistic beings. There are subtle, unknown dimensions to their interaction in the environment.

3. The transition to formal operations represents a new way of thinking for the child. Adolescents can efficiently classify and serialize the environment and their logic is much more sophisticated. For the first time, they can literally think about their own thoughts.

4. Adolescent egocentrism comes in two forms: the imaginary audience, where youths are convinced that everyone is watching them and that everything about themselves is very important; secondly, the personal fable, which is adolescents' conviction that no one has ever experienced the trauma they are going through.

5. Adolescent value systems are significantly affected by several factors. The family is the primary unit of value transmission. The degree of parental warmth and trust, as well as

the nature and intensity of adult-adolescent interaction, all affect the development of adolescent value systems. Values influence behavior, but behavior also reflects values. There are times when it is difficult to tell if the situation created the value or the value created the situation.

6. The school experience is an exceedingly important one in the determination of successful entry into adulthood. Many factors go into children not making it through school; these include academic problems, socioeconomic factors, pregnancy, and the turn-off nature of formal education.

Thought Questions

1. Do all people make the transition into and through formal operations? What happens if a person does not? What are the implications?

2. Differentiate between operations, contents, and products. Give examples of each dimension. Of what importance is each dimension to the attainment of skills necessary to make a successful transition into adulthood?

3. Differentiate between the imaginary audience and the personal fable. Are there any situations where the inability to leave these situations could be a problem for the individual? What if the adolescent stays egocentric?

4. How do different socioeconomic situations affect the family as a transmitter of values? How can the family transmission of values be used as an explanation of juvenile delinquency?

5. How can we make the school system more responsive to the needs of society, and, most important, how can we make the school system more responsive to the needs of adolescents?

Suggested Readings

Duska, R., and M. Whelan. *Moral Development: A Guide to Piaget and Kohlberg.* New York: Paulist Press, 1975. *Basically this is a guide for parents who wish to use moral education theory at home. A good attempt at putting two very involved theories into lay terminology.*

Erikson, E. *Identity, Youth and Crisis.* New York: Norton, 1968. *Identity and stage-dependent growth are the dominant themes of this work. In the ten years since this book was published, it has become a classic of sorts in the adolescent literature.*

Gordon, S. *The Sexual Adolescent.* Belmont, Calif.: Duxbury Press/Wadsworth, 1973. *This book is written by a nationally recognized authority on adolescent behavior. It approaches each of the issues (the school, the church, and the family) and contains a very useful resource section.*

READING

Children are given a rich physiological and psychological heritage. The biological component lays the fundamental developmental pattern and the subsequent psychological and physical maturation all contribute to creating a whole person.

The physiological base rapidly proliferates into more of a biosocial context. It is this biosocial reality that appears to be the fundamental component in life development. It would be nice if there were a simple formula that would produce the correct balance between each of the factors and automatically produce a normal, healthy child. It is not quite that simple. It would be nice if we could take all of the good things in life (if we could decide what they are) and put them into packages to send to every baby born. This would assure that the children would turn out to be normal. Using the same logic, if children did not receive the correct package of characteristics, they would probably turn out to be deviant or juvenile delinquents, or most likely criminals. The simplicity of this way of thinking is misleading. It is also inaccurate.

The following reading by Julius Segal and Herbert Yahraes shows that the biosocial context can have quite different effects on children. Deprivation greatly affects some children and hardly bothers others. Some children raised in the best homes turn out well and others turn out badly. Why do some children seem impervious to the effects of a debilitating environment? What characteristics do these invulnerables possess? "Children Who Will Not Break" is an intriguing look into a world where children challenge all of the aversive realities and not only survive, but excel.

Children Who Will Not Break
Julius Segal
Herbert Yahraes

Sandra is sixteen, born in poverty and raised in violence and deprivation. In her short lifetime, she has endured the death of two older sisters, the bitter separation and divorce of her parents, and a series of illnesses that seriously threatened her life. In one of the foster homes which sheltered Sandra, physical abuse and neglect were her daily portion.

By all known criteria, Sandra should be a psychological casualty, engulfed by symptoms or outright disabilities reflecting her young career of trauma and stress. In fact, the opposite is true. Sandra is an apparently well-adjusted adolescent, living now with a benevolent aunt newly arrived in this country, enjoying the rewards of close friends, and zestfully planning a college career.

How did Sandra get that way? How did she avoid the penalties we have learned to expect as sequels to deprivation and trauma? What is it that allowed her—and countless other children like her—not only to escape the ravages of pathology that so often follow prolonged and crushing stresses but to grow to maturity graced with a sense of optimism and an aura of well-being?

Answers to this enigma are only now beginning to emerge, primarily because psychologists focused much more heavily in the past on finding the roots of pathology rather than of mental health.

At the forefront of those working to reverse the trend is Norman Garmezy, professor of psychology at the University of Minnesota. Garmezy and his coworkers have been devoting their efforts to studies aimed at identifying not only factors which place children at risk for the development of mental illness and emotional disorders, but perhaps more important, those which seem to "innoculate" the child against the ravages of adversity.

Children from Poor and Pathological Homes

Children of the poor have long been regarded as especially vulnerable to mental health problems—and for good reason. Even as he searches out the invulnerables, Garmezy acknowledges that the stresses of the poor "layer their lives with burdens far in excess of those any responsible society should allow," among them social disorganization, unstable and broken families, poor prenatal care, and birth defects. The impact of such burdens is reflected in the relatively heavy incidence of mental illness among young members of the lowest social classes. In one study, for example, sociologist Leo Srole and his colleagues surveyed a large sample of New York City families and then divided them, according to the fathers' socioeconomic status, into six groups. Those in the lowest group had the poorest mental health. Only one-tenth of the people at this level were rated as well. In explanation, Srole suggested that poverty and the conditions associated with it, "create a 'sick' slum community that often carries its own pathogenic 'contagion,' in particular for the children in its midst." The life setting of the slum-level child, he pointed out, is "heavily weighted with deprivations of body, mind and spirit. . . ."

Earlier in this book studies are reported showing that children of the mentally ill also carry with them through life an increased probability of becoming ill themselves, and of succumbing to stresses throughout their development. To be born to a schizophrenic parent is to run a higher risk than other children either of developing a psychosis or, at least, of leading a troubled life.

Despite the increased risks to their mental health, however, the fact is that many children both from disadvantaged and from psychologically diseased families not only survive but even triumph over the hazards strewn before them. America's young population includes untold numbers destined to soar above their limiting environment and to develop into productive children and young adults. Somehow, such children manage to pick their way safely among the psychological land mines all about them and to grow into wholesome, competent, human beings.

Garmezy has forcefully challenged the inevitability of a poor mental outcome for all disadvantaged children. Instead of an image of despair, degradation, and deficit, he invites us to focus on children who, despite their membership in the lowest social and economic classes, not only remain unscarred but function at a remarkably high level.

The fate of "high-risk" children growing up among schizophrenic parents is also far from uniform. Given both a poor genetic track record and an environment that has aptly been described as "crazy-making," clearly not all such children break down. Some emerge relatively unscathed, while still others actually learn from their experience how to overcome obstacles and to cope with problems. For them, the environment becomes not an overwhelming threat but a challenge to be met and mastered.

Among those born into schizophrenic households, Washington University psychiatrist E. James Anthony estimates that 16 percent will develop to be "odd, queer, peculiar, strange or crazy children and adults," and 31 percent will grow to be shy, seclusive, oversensitive, or apathetic. Another 32 percent, however, will be only mildly maladjusted and neurotic, and 12 percent will become average, well-adjusted persons. Moreover, 9 percent will not only escape psychological blight but develop into outstanding, creative people. Anthony calls the last group the *superphrenics*. These are "supernormal" children who have developed remarkable capacities to adapt to the corrosive presence of mental illness among their parents.

As an example, Anthony tells of a woman, suffering from schizophrenia of the paranoid type, who insisted on eating at restaurants because she thought someone was poisoning the food at home. Her twelve-year-old daughter adopted the same phobic attitude. Another daughter, ten, would eat at home when the father was there; he was normal. Otherwise she would go along to a restaurant. But a seven-year-old son always ate at home, and when the psychiatrist asked how he could do so, the boy simply shrugged and said, "Well, I'm not dead yet."

The older girl eventually developed an illness like her mother's. The younger went to college and did reasonably well. The boy—the invulnerable—performed brilliantly all through school and afterward. His mother's illness apparently had given him both a tremendous need and a tremendous ability to overcome all sorts of problems.

To describe a central characteristic of children blessed with apparently unusual capacities for normal development, investigators in the "risk research" field with increasing frequency use *competence*. The invulnerables achieve success in their academic school tasks. They are able to sustain friendships, are valued by their peers, and assume responsibility for others. They model themselves after constructive figures, absorb constructive values, and live in the anticipation of success rather than failure. In the words of psychiatrist J. C. Whitehorn, as he defined people of good mental health, they "work well, play well, love well, and expect well."

To date, most researchers studying invulnerable children have focused on the first of these criteria—specifically, school achievement—as the major index for competence. In doing so, they have admittedly highlighted only one of the social roles society requires children to play—that of a student. Although Garmezy agrees that the ideal definition of competence is considerably broader, he does not dismiss the importance of school achievement as an earmark of invulnerability. School, after all, is the child's factory, his place of work, and it is a considerable feat, he believes, for a child to "work well" despite enormous stress. These children of defeated and sick families are clearly resisting hardship, and are adapting, sometimes miraculously, to a threatening and hostile world.

Portrait of the Invulnerables

Garmezy and his research colleague, Keith Nuechterlein, reviewed all existing studies bearing on disadvantaged children who somehow display a high degree of competence in spite of the stressful environments in which they are mired. Other investigators—among them Anthony—have focused their attention on the surprisingly resilient children among the offspring of psychotic parents. Out of their combined findings there begins to emerge a profile of the "invulnerables."

• To begin with, these children are socially skillful, bringing a tone of warmth and ease to their relationships with both peers and adults. They are open, easygoing youngsters, popular and well liked, standing in sharp contrast to more fragile children of comparable background, who are often lethargic, tense, sullen, restless —and considerably less well accepted by their peers.

• Competent children are well regarded not only by their peers but also, and perhaps more important, by *themselves*. Such children operate out of a sense of power rather than impotence and of self-regard rather than self-derogation; the emphasis is on their pluses rather than their minuses. They feel capable of exerting control over their environment—of influencing events, rather than becoming the passive victims of fate. Sociologist James Coleman's extensive 1966 study of 645,000 students drawn from the third, sixth, and twelfth grades of 4,000 American public schools provides strong evidence of the power of this attitude in the achievements of disadvantaged youth. It was a sense of "personal control" that was more closely related to achievement than a variety of other school or family characteristics measured in his survey. A 1969 survey by sociologist Edgar Epps describing 2,800 black and white children from inner-city schools in Atlanta and Detroit showed similarly that the best predictor of academic achievement was the child's sense of control over the environment.

• Competent children reveal also a reflective rather than an impulsive approach to life. They seem to operate with a sense of caution and self-regulation, keeping a sensible rein on their impulses. Rather than "shooting from the hip," such children will reflect a while when challenged—not only in their academic work but in their social relationships as well. They manage, in effect, to keep their "gut" reactions under control. For example, when confronted by children who want to fight, they can ignore them or simply walk away; there is no insistent need to "act out" every impulse that bubbles to the surface.

• The child who survives adversity is motivated from within to perform well. Contrary to the stereotype of disadvantaged children as lacking in drive, many emerge from studies as quite the opposite. Their reactions to school success and failure appear much like those shown by highly motivated, middle-class schoolchildren. Teachers rate these youngsters as goal-directed, eager to learn, doing more than is required of them, and participating fully in class discussion. Moreover, the children themselves express a preference for educational pursuits, and aspire to high vocational goals; they take responsibility for learning, accept blame for failure, and display a willingness to defer immediate gratification for the sake of long-range achievement.

• The families of disadvantaged but achieving youngsters show more concern for education—reflected in the parents' aspirations for their children's educational achievement and their willingness to assist actively with homework and to participate in school-related organizations. Even the physical aspects of the homes of achieving, lower-class children are different—less crowded, for example, and neater and cleaner; and there are more books.

• Parents of disadvantaged but competent children appear to permit them considerable self-direction in everyday tasks and to recognize the validity of their personal interests and goals, thus helping them in their struggle for growth and autonomy. In spite of omnipresent parental interest, support, and encouragement, the roles of parent and competent child remain well differentiated. Mothers of underachieving youngsters, in contrast, appear to behave more as siblings; they are more heavily involved in fulfilling their own needs, and expect their children to assume responsibilities far beyond their age and capabilities.

• A significant factor emerging from the life histories of competent children from disadvantaged families appears to be the presence in the environment of a charismatic, inspirational person. These children seem to be "turned on" by an identification with at least one figure among the adults who touch their lives. Often this is a parent. Consider a boy named James, born and raised on the Upper East Side among desperate living conditions. He was one of seven children, two of whom died in infancy. He was surrounded by trouble and illness. His father was an alcoholic. James early began working at odd jobs and had a regular one at fourteen. He and his brothers brought every cent home so that the family would have enough to eat; sometimes, even so, it did not. A number of his schoolmates and street companions wound up in the penitentiary; one died in the electric chair. What saved him and his brothers? Here are the words of James himself: "We had a mother to answer to. . . . We loved her profoundly, and our driving force was to do what she wanted because we knew how much it meant to her." The speaker? James Cagney.

The inspirational person is not necessarily a member of the family. He or she may be a playmate's parent, an older friend, a teacher, a member of the clergy, a physician—anyone who can help a child acquire self-assurance and a vision of what can be achieved.

• Resistance to the stress of living with a psychotic parent appears to require in a child a well-developed sense of personal identity. At the Washington University School of Medicine in St. Louis, Harriet S. Lander has found that such children are less submissive and less suggestible than others. They are able to maintain a safe psychological distance from the psychotic parent, and are thus not drawn into the preoccupations and delusions of the abnormal adult world about them. Anthony regards this loss of closeness in relationships as the price such children must pay for their invulnerability. Invulnerables seem to develop an objective, dispassionate, and remote relationship to people, thus allowing them to maintain their own integrity and to fend off disturbing influences.

• Finally, children who appear invulnerable in spite of a psychotic parent are able somehow to find the silver lining in the heavy emotional clouds hanging over them. Swiss psychiatrist Manfred Bleuler reminds us that some psychotics can be incredibly good parents, and that some children can see beyond a schizophrenic mother's pathology to her true parental qualities. They learn to distinguish what is strange or sick in a parent from what is good and lovable. Moreover, a nonschizophrenic parent can make up for the devastating impact of the one who is ill. "Sometimes," Bleuler observes, "gifted, warm-hearted marriage partners are able to nullify all the evil influences of the other, schizophrenic partner."

The foregoing portrait of invulnerable children is beginning to serve as a base for significant research explorations. It has sparked a number of investigators in their attempts to find, early in the lives of children, the signposts of competence and psychological strength. If they are successful, their results may enable us to build into the lives of all high-risk children the capacities to conquer the psychological Everests strewn in their developmental path.

REPRODUCED BY PERMISSION OF THE GEORGIA MUSEUM OF ART, THE UNIVERSITY OF GEORGIA.

Playground, by Paul Cadmus

17

Adolescence: Social Realities

The physical course of development in adolescence has many significant behavioral and psychological correlates. Some of these psychological developments are observable, or overt, while others remain in the background and concealed (covert). The intellectual changes within adolescents mean that the world is starting to look very different from the way it looked to them as a child. This different perspective implies input will be interpreted differently.

As we have indicated, adolescence has an integrative nature to it. Many divergent elements make up the adolescent. None of the processes operates independently, and understanding the interdependence of processes like self-concept, physical development, and intellectual growth is one key to understanding adolescents. The child, and now the adolescent, must be considered as a whole being.

The adolescent is also part of society—a society with an extremely rapid rate of social change. This change is confusing, particularly for individuals who are themselves right in the middle of a great deal of personal change. One aspect of social change is the disruption of the balance between primary relations and secondary relations. Primary relations are supportive, emotional, and consistent. These are relations between people who know each other.

SOCIETAL CHANGES AND ADOLESCENTS

Social change: altering of basic elements of society

The industrial and urban revolutions have brought about drastic and rapid social change. The basic fiber of our culture has changed significantly over the last 100 years (contrasted to many cultures in which there has been relatively little social change in the last 1,000 years). Because of the forces of industrialization, the number of secondary, or utilitarian, nonpersonal relationships has increased very rapidly. The subsequent isolation and alienation is frustrating to human beings. More and more is expected of the family in terms of meeting the basic needs of individuals.

Adolescents, who are just entering the mainstream of American society, are in the process of internal change. The societal changes they encounter, along with the consistent increase in isolation of individuals, mean that they are the recipient of inconsistent and perhaps nonsupportive messages from inside as well as outside. Part of understanding adolescence is understanding what is happening in society. As society changes, the behavioral by-products directly affect the "normalcy" of adolescence and the nature of the entry into adulthood.

Ambivalence: simultaneous opposing points of view

In America, the period of adolescence is an ambivalent one. On the one hand, adolescents are looked up to by much of society: "It would be great to be that age again!" There are so few problems —no bills, no taxes, and so on. Older adults try very hard to be like adolescents in many ways. They dress, talk, and often behave like adolescents. The slang, mannerisms, and even the way the hair is done begin to look suspiciously like that of teenagers. It is as if we dress like adolescents, we can recapture the fun and enjoyment of being young again.

On the other hand, adults react to some of the emerging abilities of adolescents with a certain amount of disdain. We have to make sure that these "kids" know their place, and stay there. Their youthfulness and their promise are in direct contradiction to the aging process. There are at least five factors that contribute to the ambivalent position of adolescents (from Rice, 1978):

1. Adolescents remind adults of things they would just as soon forget. Some of the things young people do are exactly the same things that their parents did. Many times we do not wish to relive painful and/or embarrassing situations through our children.

Adult expectations for the behavior of adolescents may also be a little out of line. The emerging personality of the adolescent is very dynamic. This high level of energy may not fit into the structure created by the parent. Conflict is a frequent result.

2. The status and security of adults may be threatened by adolescents. The sophistication of the adolescent (compared to the child)

Adolescence: Social Realities

may be threatening to an adult who is not equipped to handle being challenged. As we said above, the youthfulness of the adolescent may also be a threat to the parent.

3. Physically, adolescence represents a peak of energy and development. It is the perception of many adults that adolescence is the best time of life, physically. When adults perceive adolescents to be "wasting" some of this precious time, a great deal of frustration is produced.

4. Adults are fearful of losing control over their children. At no time in their children's development has there been so much direct confrontation between parents and children. The frustrating part is that many times the adolescent is the one who is right!

5. The social change that we have already mentioned has probably produced different sets of values for the different generations. For example, there is probably a qualitative difference between the attitudes of today's adolescents and their parents about cohabitation before marriage. Adolescents may honestly see cohabitation as a good preparation for marriage, which may prevent divorce. Adults, on the other hand, cannot picture cohabitation as a part of their value system. The fact that adolescents have different attitudes toward cohabitation is probably a function of a high divorce rate, poor marriages, and different attitudes toward premarital sexuality. There are value differences between the generations.

ADOLESCENT SELF-CONCEPT AND IDENTITY

Identity is that collective answer to the question "Who am I?" The self-concept, on the other hand, is the barometer or measuring dimension that reflects the level of supportive and positive feelings about the self. The self-concept is like a butterfly; a beautiful, unique, and fragile entity that soars when supported and falls quickly when abused. The younger the individual, the greater the mobility of the butterfly, and usually, the quicker its movements.

The adolescent self-concept is fragile and susceptible to outside influences. The instability of the period contributes significantly to this relatively low level of solidarity of the adolescent self-concept.

Identity

The work of Erik Erikson is fundamental to a discussion of adolescent identity. Erikson used the term *ego-identity* to describe the psychological development of this period. Two of the basic principles around which ego-identity revolves are: (1) the distinc-

Ego-identity: the psychological development of adolescence

tiveness/uniqueness of the individual, and (2) the internal psychological consistency and separateness. These two levels of ego-identity are crucial to the development and maintenance of the psychological integrity of the adolescent.

This fifth stage of Erikson's stage theory (see chapter 2) is a crisis whose resolution is either in the form of "identity" or in the form of "identity confusion" (or diffusion). Identity confusion represents the failure to achieve integration of and continuity within the self-image. The developmental task of identity formation has not been accomplished. Having a confused, nonfunctioning identity has significant implications. First, it leaves the individual frustrated at being unable to be appreciated as a whole being; the person is perceived as confused or strange. Secondly, this problem carries over into adulthood. If the identity crisis is not handled effectively during this early period, there is a potential for disabling personal confusion later in life. This confusion is often manifested in psychological problems, aggressive acting-out problems, and so on.

Erikson has said that identity confusion is ". . . a failure to achieve the integration and continuity of self-images" (Erikson, 1968, p. 212). Maintaining a clear perception of self over time with so much change happening may depend upon special skills. For example, "A well-defined sense of identity is at least partially dependent upon the capacity of the individual to conceptualize himself in abstract terms, at times, almost like a spectator" (Conger, 1973, pp. 84–85).

Erikson indicates that the quest for identity is actually made up of several subconflicts. If each of the following are dealt with effectively, a firm sense of identity will result.

1. A general sense of confusion versus a general sense of commitment
2. Conflict over who is in control
3. Sexuality
4. Role experimentation and future work roles
5. Confidence

Each of these divergent issues needs to be dealt with by adolescents. A positive, integrated, and consistent identity is the result of paying attention to each of these issues, working on them, and resolving them. A normative identity will be the result. Here *nor-*

mative refers to a basic congruence between adolescents' perception of their identity and society's expectation for them. The normative identities of adolescents share broad categories but are usually quite different from each other.

Deviant identity patterns differ significantly from the societal norms. Personality deviance is a culture-bound phenomenon; different societies have different definitions of a deviant identity. Deviant identities are not always pathological. Some people are different from the mainstream, and have very little trouble with that fact. Some differences are so severe, however, that the individual has difficulty living within society. Some of these severe personality differences have their roots in adolescence.

Normative identity: congruence between the adolescent's perception of identity and society's expectations

Self-concept

The barometer of identity is the self-concept. This internal entity is reflective of the inner balance of the individual. According to Monge (1973), the adolescent self-concept has separate components to it. He suggests that there are at least four factors: achievement-leadership, adjustment, congeniality-sociability, and sex-appropriateness or self-concept.

Each of these factors reciprocally interacts with the others to create the specific psychological-personal frame of reference for the individual adolescent. There are significant age and sex differences in these factors, as demonstrated in the figure on page 450. Boys score higher in the areas of achievement and leadership and in adjustment capabilities. Boys score lower in the congeniality dimension, and while starting lower in the sex-appropriateness of behavior category, end up rating higher than the girls near the end of adolescence.

The decline in the adjustment factor with advancing age is interesting. It appears in both sexes and reinforces many of the feelings people have about adolescents and their ability to fit into society. The sex difference in terms of congeniality is also a traditional sex stereotype. Essentially, these trends are reflective of society's attitudes toward adolescents and its expectations of them.

To what extent are these personality differences inborn, and to what extent are they the result of socialization? Maccoby and Jacklin (1974) have stated that the topic of differences between males and females is hopelessly tangled in emotion and feelings. As we have stated in earlier chapters, there is probably no specific gene for high achievement or congeniality. The debate goes on and on.

I. Achievement-leadership factor
—— Male
----- Female

II. Adjustment factor

III. Sex-appropriateness — self-concept

IV. Congeniality — sociability

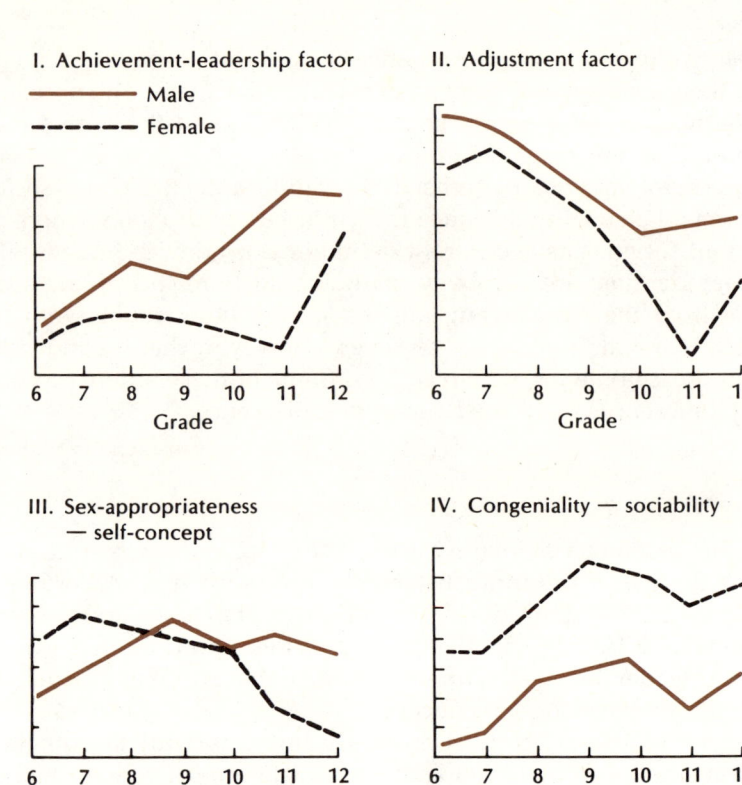

Factors Affecting Self-concept

Dusek (1977) has stated that there are three broad factors that directly affect adolescent self-concepts.

Parental Influences: Parent-adolescent relationships are crucial to the optimal development of the adolescent's self-concept. Parents' input into the psychosocial interior of the family has direct impact on their children. Parents may insist that their adolescents be perfect, a straight A student as well as a successful athlete. In other situations, the influence of the parents may be inconsistent. One time they may say that grades really do not matter, and the next week they may tell their children how much grades really do mean. Reasonable expectations, uniform enforcement, and consistent behavior patterns all contribute to the effective operation of the family and the normative psychological development of adolescents. Defined limits of behavior, however strict they may be, when consistently enforced are more comfortable for adolescents than no behavioral limits, or ones that are so far apart there do not appear to be any limits.

Structural factors may play a role in the impact of family relations on the adolescent self-concept. There is speculation that single-parent families, for example, operate quite differently than the two-parent family in terms of roles, expectations, and the like. Some people suggest that there is greater potential for deviant personality types coming out of single-parent families. There is no substantive evidence to support this statement. The structure of the family *may* have a significant impact on the adolescent's self-concept; however the causal nature of this impact is not clear.

Social Class Influences: Our culture is not a classless one. There are interaction patterns unique to specific social classes, and these class-bound interaction patterns have direct impact on the nature of parent-child relations.

There is some evidence, for example, that lower-class adolescents have less well integrated and poorer self-concepts (Dusek, 1977). The rationale for this finding is that there is less familial stability and more general insecurity in the lower social classes. These problems are more likely to produce adolescents who have

One social reality that both parents and adolescents usually have to confront is the desire among teenagers to get out of the house and be with their friends.
JEFFREY P. GROSSCUP.

greater problems with their self-concepts. The evidence most often cited to support these assertions includes greater participation in youth gangs, higher criminal rates, more adolescent pregnancies, and more teenage marriages.

On the other hand, there is some evidence that these social class differences may be overexaggerated. There are inadequate reporting techniques for many of the problems we mentioned. There may be greater visibility to lower-class individuals and it is quite possible that parents with greater resources may be able to hide any problems their children are having. For example, if a lower-class adolescent female becomes pregnant she may have to go to a neighborhood health clinic for prenatal care. There is a very distinct possibility that she will be counted in the official data on adolescent pregnancies. The female adolescent from a higher income bracket may have the advantage of being treated by a private family physician, who is less likely to make any sort of statistical report to the people who collect these kind of data.

Social class may also be important in other "dollar-related" aspects. Given adolescents' concern with their image, not having the money to dress just right and have the right kinds of accessories may be very frustrating to lower-class adolescents. Depending upon the individual adolescent's sensitivity, this sort of problem can mushroom into a great deal of resentment.

Maturational Influences: Self-concept is related to physical development, particularly in the cases of early and late maturation (discussed in detail earlier). The self-concept, as an abstract, whole entity, is made up of physiological, intellectual, social, and emotional dimensions. It would be nice if all of these forces matured at the same time and at the same rate, but there are significant differences in when and how these different aspects of children develop. Consequently, it is not possible to make assumptions about the "total" maturity of adolescents. Depending upon the strength of individuals and the nature of their support networks, differential maturation can present problems to adolescents.

Adolescents' self-concept may also be related to school performance. The type of experience they have in school with grades, peer relations, and the rest of the school atmosphere will affect their self-concept. If they get negative feedback from these sources, it will undoubtedly affect the way they feel about themselves, and it probably works the other way as well. If they have a good image of themselves and are confident of their abilities, school performance

Adolescence: Social Realities

Personal appearance is one aspect of an adolescent's self-concept that can greatly influence the young person's overall adjustment.
JOHN R. MAHER, EKM-NEPENTHE.

may be enhanced. There is a reciprocal relationship between self-concept and the school experience.

Self-concept relates to the overall adjustment of the adolescent. The type of information received from the environment along with basic personality reserves allows adolescents to get through the difficult maturational processes and to eventually assume a normative behavior pattern.

Popularity

An important aspect of adolescent social relationships is the *degree* to which the young people are involved in the activities of their peer group. This involvement is at least partially determined by the popularity of the individual. This attraction is noted in terms of individual qualities, social graces, and other tangible and intangible qualities. The following table demonstrates the factors that are contributory to adolescent popularity.

Popularity: the state of being liked by one's peers

Characteristics Affecting Popularity*

Characteristics that help with popularity	Characteristics that hinder popularity
liking other people	nervousness
tolerance	timidity
flexibility	over-assertiveness
good nature	self-centeredness
sense of humor	inconsiderateness
confidence	
enthusiasm	

*Adapted from Conger, 1973.

The helpful characteristics represent an integrated and effective self-concept that is appropriately strong and consistent, yet not overbearing. The hindering characteristics are those of individuals who have never experienced themselves as love objects. They have little awareness of their abilities and a poor self-concept.

ISSUE

Juvenile Delinquency

A normative identity is one that generally conforms to the expectations of society. A deviant identity is one that significantly differs from the expectations of society for individuals' behavior. Nonnormative or deviant behavior in adolescents has been traditionally lumped under the category of juvenile delinquency. This issue remains one of the hottest and least understood of all problems in society.

☐ The traditional explanations for delinquent behavior by adolescents fall into one of three possibilities: the child was just born bad, or he came from a bad family background, or he came from a deprived environment and neighborhood. All of these instances are *correlationally* related to deviant adolescent behavior. In the first case, deviant behavior might be related to an inborn personality pattern. In the second case, poor families seem to be related to delinquent behavior (several old studies have tried to demonstrate the relationship between broken homes and deviant behavior). In the third case, children who grow up in poor neighborhoods are predisposed to this type of behavior because of the conditions in which they live.

☐ These correlational relationships are purely descriptive in nature. What we need are specific *causal* relationships. It is not possible to say that a broken home causes delinquent behavior; they may be related, but only correlationally.

☐ We would like to consider another possibility. Is it possible that in the majority of delinquent children and adolescents, we are not dealing with a pathological mind or a poor family background or a bad environment? Is it possible that most of these children have essentially normal personalities, and that a disorganized environment or society with misplaced priorities has actually facilitated and *defined* the aberrant behavior?

☐ Delinquent behavior is defined as behavior that deviates from the societal norm. Does this mean that the societal norm is rational, logical, and just? A deviant personality is not necessarily a pathological one. Unfortunately we often associate difference with pathology, and we get idiosyncratic behavior patterns confused with a culture-bound moral conviction. Deviancy exists only in the definitional sense. A culture determines its own level of deviation potential in its population by setting specific behavioral expectations.

☐ We have always had deviant behavior by children as well as adults. We have *not* always had juvenile delinquency, in the punitive sense. There is something about our mass society, with all of its alienating aspects and preponderance of secondary relations, that contributes to the formation of gangs (for identity and peer support) and to acting-out behavior by children (more for attention than anything).

☐ The traditional "cures" for delinquency are varied. On the one hand, some suggest that these incorrigible youths be separated from society forever; if they are out of sight, they are out of mind. On the other hand, some say we should isolate the causal factors (if that is possible) and eliminate them, thereby eliminating delinquent behavior.

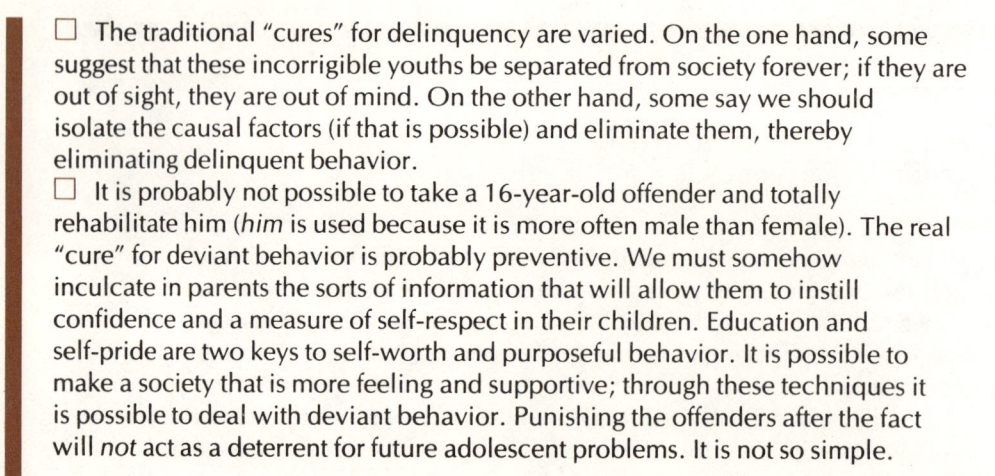

☐ It is probably not possible to take a 16-year-old offender and totally rehabilitate him (*him* is used because it is more often male than female). The real "cure" for deviant behavior is probably preventive. We must somehow inculcate in parents the sorts of information that will allow them to instill confidence and a measure of self-respect in their children. Education and self-pride are two keys to self-worth and purposeful behavior. It is possible to make a society that is more feeling and supportive; through these techniques it is possible to deal with deviant behavior. Punishing the offenders after the fact will *not* act as a deterrent for future adolescent problems. It is not so simple.

The pain of not fitting into the group, of being unpopular, is echoed in the words of Conger: "Few adolescents . . . are unaffected by social neglect or rejection. A few individualists, confident of their own goals and interests and possessed of a strong sense of ego identity, may neither need nor seek the approbation of peers. But most adolescents, still judging their own worth to a considerable extent in terms of others' reactions to them, are dependent upon the approval and acclaim of prestigeful peers" (Conger, 1973, p. 305).

RELIGION

As with idealism, there is a distinct cognitive dimension to religion. Because cognition is changing, there are often parallel changes in adolescents' conceptions of God, faith, and other components of religious belief. The transition from concrete operations to formal operations is a movement from the preoccupation with firm, observable elements of the environment, to abstract hypothetical and conjectural elements. The change relative to religion is similar. The abstraction that is the basis of most religion becomes operationalized in the adolescent. The term *belief* is probably not a part of a religious experience until there is sufficient cognitive maturation to allow such an abstraction, particularly with some very intangible concepts present.

The questioning of religious beliefs and the value of church attendance are a part of the cognitive maturation of some adolescents.
ROBERT V. ECKERT, JR., EKM-NEPENTHE.

Adolescents are not particularly avid church-goers. The adolescent population has suffered as dramatic a decline in church attendance in the last 10 to 15 years as any other portion of the population. Specifically, older adolescents, particularly those in college, have lower church attendance than younger adolescents. Adolescent males have a lower frequency of church attendance than females (Johnson et al., 1974).

Why don't adolescents go to church? One of the arguments has to do with the relevance of services: "Why go to church when I can believe and live a good life without spending time inside a building on Sunday mornings?" Much of the rhetoric centers around the fact that many adolescents consider the adults who do go to church to be hypocritical. "How can adults sit in church and be pious and yet go through the week doing many immoral things (like be unscrupulous businesspersons, and the like)?"

Church attendance is not necessarily a good indication of religiosity. Recently, within the last four to five years there has been a consistent and significant increase in adolescent involvement with religion; it has not been the typical sort of involvement, however. While there appears to have been a decline in stating religion as an important value (see the figure below), there have been some interesting developments. One has been the swing to fundamentalist Christianity by American young people. This movement is often associated with the participants' feeling that they have developed a personal relationship with Christ. These individuals do not necessarily worship in a traditional church, although they may do so. But they are very religious people; they are characterized by zealousness and excitement with their relationship, a very literal interpretation of the Bible, and an overwhelming persistence in the rightness of their beliefs.

This movement is very popular on college campuses, even among athletes, but there have also been strong attractions to Eastern religions like Hinduism and Buddhism. There are even indications of involvement in religious cults, such as the religious group headed by the Rev. Sun Myung Moon. All of these examples demonstrate the new and different approach adolescents are taking today.

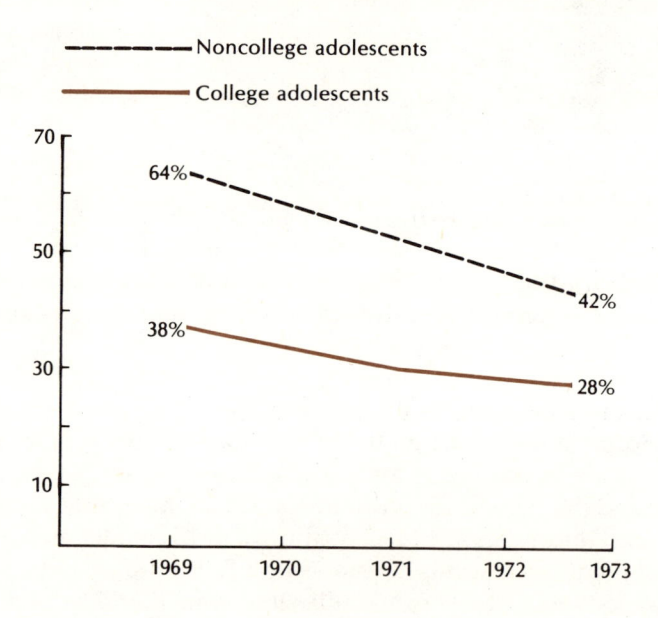

THE IMPORTANCE OF RELIGION TO COLLEGE AND NON-COLLEGE ADOLESCENTS

Summary

1. Adolescence has an integrative nature to it. Adolescents are part of society, a peer group, and a family. Each of these elements works in a reciprocal fashion to affect the nature of adolescence. In America the period of adolescense is an ambivalent one. Adults say it is the best time of life, yet at the same time are convinced that adolescents should stay in line; in fact, the youthfulness of the adolescent may be a threat to adults.

2. Identity is the collective answer to the "who am I" question. The adolescent self-concept, which is the barometer of identity, is fragile and susceptible to many outside influences. Erikson coined the phrase *ego-identity* to describe the salience and consistency of the adolescent.

3. The quest for identity is made up of several issues: a general sense of confusion versus a general sense of commitment, control, sexuality, role experimentation and future work roles, and confidence. Each of these divergent factors needs to be dealt with by the adolescent. The goal in most cases is the development of a normative identity.

4. There are three broad factors that affect adolescent self-concepts: parental influences, social class influences, and maturational influences. Each of these factors can play a significant role in the successful adaptation to adult roles.

5. Popularity is an important aspect of adolescent social development. There are specific characteristics that appear to help popularity and those that detract from popularity. Popularity is probably more important during adolescence than it is later.

6. Adolescent religion is another manifestation of cognitive development. The ability to operationalize abstract concepts enables young people to pursue a wide variety of religious experiences. Interestingly, even though formal church attendance is low, religion itself is experiencing a comeback of sorts in the form of fundamentalism and the Jesus movement.

Thought Questions

1. How is adolescence integrative? How is adolescence an ambivalent period? What factors make adults resent adolescents?

2. Why is identity fragile? What environmental factors affect the nature of the development of identity? What are the issues of the quest for identity?

3. Which is more important: parental influences, social class influences, or maturational influences in the determination and persistence of self-concept? Under what conditions are each of these factors *most* important to the adolescent?

4. How important is being popular? Why do adolescents spend so much energy trying to be popular? Or do they?

5. How is religious involvement a manifestation of cognitive growth? What is the importance of the back-to-fundamentals religion of many contemporary adolescents?

Suggested Readings

Combs, A. W. *Myths in Education.* Boston: Allyn & Bacon, 1979. *An absolutely fascinating book, it deals with the American culture, schools and their students and explodes many of the myths running around in education. A must reading for students and teachers.*

Gallatin, J. E. *Adolescence and Individuality.* New York: Harper & Row, 1975. *The primary dimensions of this valuable work are G. Stanley Hall and Erik Erikson. There is a good section on identity formation in families.*

Kenniston, K. *All Our Children.* New York: Harcourt, Brace, Jovanovich, 1977. *Kenneth Kenniston has written a scholarly and lucid book concerning the nature of present-day society and its relation to the developing child and the family.*

READING

One of the pressing issues facing our society has to do with insuring a viable future for all of our children. Up to this point, most of the readings have been directly applicable to the chapters that preceded them. In this chapter, an exception is made in order to consider our society's future. In order to appreciate the position children may find themselves in in the future, a glimpse into that future is in order.

Harold Shane provides us with a broad review of what the future might bring. Covering a wide range of topics, Shane shows how the world may be quite different for the next generation of children.

Some of the trends are alarming, some appear to be positive and functional. None of the trends appear to be unchangeable at this time; it is important, however, for students in the field of child development to begin to appreciate what the coming years may bring to the children, not only of this culture, but of the world.

Forecast for the 80's
Harold G. Shane

As the present decade draws to a close, it seems clear that history will preserve memories both of its distinctive traumas and of the turbulence it inherited from the 60's. This was the era that biophysicist John Platt summed up, with glittering insight, as "a crisis of crises."

Values collided during the 70's when our country's traditional Currier and Ives morality encountered the New Permissiveness. To add to the conflict, many U.S. Americans became uneasy about—and even began to mistrust—such hallowed institutions as their government, the schools, big business, the military, and law enforcement agencies. The Third World's demands for equity became increasingly insistent. At the same time, goods produced in the Third World for low wages—well designed, comparatively inexpensive clothing and electronic devices—threatened the incomes of U.S. production workers and all who depended on them.

The crisis in sources of energy became conspicuous when overseas oil producers temporarily cut off most of the 10 million barrels a day which the United States imports. The huge price increases which resulted aggravated the recession and further worsened unfavorable trade balances, thus greasing the downward skid of the dollar.

Depletion of our natural resources led to gloomy projections and to solemn talk of limits to growth. Most people, however, seemed to be too busy cashing in on the "good old bad old days" to ring in many good new changes. Currently, to our credit, many of us are endeavoring to reduce our per capita use of energy, which in 1974 was double that of the Federal Republic of Germany and triple that of Switzerland.

At least as portentous as these difficulties was the increasing balkanization of life in the United States, which fragmented old loyalties to home, church, school, and country. In addition, more workers became alienated from their jobs; consumers became more discontented with shoddy products; and because of inflation, people had increasing difficulty in maintaining their standards of living.

The schools continued to be hit by criticism from without and plagued by violence and vandalism from within. Enrollments tumbled by millions. In the instructional realm, however, alternative forms of schooling often sparkled with imagination. Bilingual education came into new prominence.

At best, all things considered, the 70's seem to have been a time of troubles. But what of the 80's? Specifically, what will the decade bring to education? Will the passage of time improve or restrict our educational options? Will the spirit of the times be a weariness of too much change in the schools? Or will it be a heightening of consciousness and sense of responsible service to our fellow humans sufficient to initiate an educational renaissance?

It is hazardous to skate on the thin ice of intuitive prediction. It is less dangerous, however, to present a forecast that is supported by the trends we are presently weaving into the fabric of our lives. Let us first look at selected trends which at present promise to make a difference in our lives, specifically in our schools. Then we will speculate about educational changes that are likely to occur if these trends continue.

Changes in the Family

High on the list of present trends I would place changes in the structure and soundness of the family. Teachers cannot assume that all their students share the background of a two-parent family in which the mother works at home.

A diminution of home guidance for the young is one result of social change in families. Many "families" today might better be labeled *affinity groups*, for they are held together by the mutual needs of their members rather than the traditional blood ties. Guidance for children in these groups may be anybody's responsibility—or nobody's.

Childless women, at one time one-fifth of the women of 24 to 29, now number more than 50 percent of that group. Because women will be older when they begin to bear children, their children will probably have fewer siblings.

Another change is the increase in the employment of mothers. In 1960, only 20 percent of the mothers of children of 17 or younger were employed. In 1978, more than 50 percent of our mothers were working and a third of this group had children less than six years of age.

As a natural outcome of women's new working status, the proportion of three- and four-year-olds who attend preschool has tripled since 1964, from 10 percent to approximately 32 percent. One is led to ask, What is the future role of mothers, and what are the added responsibilities of fathers, in two-career families?

Changing Parental Attitudes

A second probable phenomenon of the 80's is surfacing in the form of unprecedented parental attitudes. The results of a recent Yankelovich poll suggest that nearly half of the parents of children of 12 or younger are unwilling to make sacrifices for their children; that many consider bearing children an option rather than a social responsibility; and that many feel that children have no obligation to them in the future. The poll results further suggest that the new breed of parents are permissive, seek to avoid perpetuating traditional sex roles, and have little desire to push their children academically. If these results are accurate measures of attitudinal changes, and if such changes are increasing, the impact on schooling and teachers' roles could be enormous.

Developments in the Labor Force

The U.S. Department of Labor's Bureau of Labor Statistics (BLS) estimates that by 1990 the U.S. labor force will expand by 15 percent. This development may or may not be desirable, depending upon whether unemployment and underemployment are a problem at the time and whether there is an increase in *misemployment*—people's being hired to do work for which they lack interest or aptitude or both.

Four facts underscore the complexity of labor force problems:

• The number of persons with college degrees is increasing more rapidly than the professional-administrative positions to which half of them aspire.

• Blacks are twice as likely as whites to be unemployed.

• The rate of unemployment for teenagers is triple the national average (for black teens in our ghettos the rate is at least 40 percent).

• Several million immigrants (two-thirds Hispanic) and many women have successfully entered the world of work.

All of these facts affect the kind of education we should be planning for the 80's.

Mobility: America's Movable Roots and Ethnic Changes

In the 10 years since *Today's Education* published "Forecast for the 70's," a massive migration of U.S. Americans has begun, from Snowbelt to Sunbelt. The Northeast and North Central states are the big losers in the switch to the sun; Pennsylvania alone has lost 400,000 residents in a recent 10-year interval.

An intriguing aspect of our recent migrations is that a growing number of blacks have reversed the direction of their migration. Of several million blacks who moved between 1970 and 1978, an estimated 100,000 moved southward.

Another phenomenon is the changing ethnic profile of America. As noted above, most immigrants have Hispanic backgrounds, and Hispanics seem fated to become our largest ethnic group during the 80's and to outnumber the blacks appreciably during the 1990's.

The Aging of America

The graying of America has already been the object of much comment. The long-range impact of aging on our society and on our educational system, however, has been less understood and appreciated in the 70's than it will be during the decade ahead.

At present, between 4,000 and 5,000 citizens turn 65 every day, entering what is now called the *young old* age cohort. And the number in the *frail old* group—those of 75 or more—is increasing steadily, too. Probable developments of interest include—

• A 50 percent increase in the number of frail old in the next 20 years.

• By 1999, a leap from the present 22 million to well over 30 million persons in the population who are 65 or older.

• A median age in the United States which, from 27.9 in 1970, approaches 40 within the next two decades.

• Changes in advertising, merchandising, political strategies, entertainment—and education—to reach older target audiences.

• Increased employment of sitters for aged parents.

A Coming "Baby Boomlet"?

Aging is not the only population trend. At the other end of the age spectrum is the possibility of an echo of the baby boom of the 1950's. Despite the drop in the U.S. birthrate, the number of women of childbearing age will climb from 20 million in the 60's to 34 million by 1985. As a result, the trend in school enrollments could change from ebb to flood.

This increase may be largely offset, however, by a decline in the average number of children per woman. We will simply have to wait and see whether the pupil population swells and whether a scarcity of teachers once again occurs.

Inflation, Taxation, and Threatened Pensions

Trends which are difficult to assess, but which could be ominous for education in the 80's, depend on the course of inflation, taxation, and debt. If inflation is not sharply curbed, prices could increase by as much as 100 percent in the next 10 years. By the year 2000 the dollar could lose more than 90 percent of the purchasing power it had during the mid-60's.

Thus the parents of a child who is three years old today must save $1,660 annually at 5 percent interest to pay the cost of a four-year degree for the child at a state university. By the time the child reaches 18, the cost of tuition will have increased from $16,000 to more than $42,000 even if the inflation rate averages no more than a conservative 6 percent each year.

Taxation, or rather voters' resistance to it, also bodes ill for many U.S. social agencies, such as our schools.

Local, state, and federal taxes were 67.8 percent higher in 1977 than in 1972. During the same five-year period, consumer prices went up 47 percent. In last year's federal budget, the biggest single expenditure—$170 billion—went not for current defense expenditures or education or interest on the national debt, but for payments to U.S. Americans who are retired, ill, or poor. This expenditure cannot be cut.

In the 1980's, an added challenge to groups such as the NEA may well be that of coping with threats to the value of pension plans, on which an increasing number of teachers rely. Such plans are decreasing in real value as inflation erodes them. Despite adjustments for inflation in Social Security benefits, a retired teacher on a $300 pension lost $115.91 in buying power between January 1973 and September 1978.

The 1969 forecast in *Today's Education* anticipated seven major changes and a number of minor developments on the basis of ideas proposed by professional students of the future. Because of the protean developments in our society, more than a dozen educationally relevant forecasts merit our attention as we look ahead to the 80's.

For one thing, early childhood education, which elbowed its way to the footlights in the 70's, should continue to star. Especially if more babies actually make their debut, or if inflationary pressures continue, the number of mothers of children aged five or younger who work outside their homes could increase even further. Already more than tripled in 12 years, as noted earlier, nursery level enrollments could extend to include at least half of our three-to-five-year-olds.

Despite notable opposition from some sources, prenatal intervention and the pursuit of alternatives to the natural course of conception and gestation will increase. Social disapproval of pregnant women who expose the unborn to alcohol and narcotics will provide only a part of this story in the coming decade. Genetic histories, prenatal physical examinations, and occasional surgery performed on the fetus in the uterus should begin to be more widely accepted as part of society's responsibilities to its young.

Conception outside of the mother's body has already been accomplished. Troubling questions remain, however, about whether experiments involving test-tube babies are to be continued. In any event, the very early months of life promise to become the object of more intensified study than at present. Doctors and scientists will probably make greater efforts to provide whatever therapy a fetus needs as life begins.

Day care is likely to include a greater emphasis on helping children develop. Purely custodial care merely clogs early education's arteries without carrying much enrichment to young learners. In the 80's, therefore, programs for young children are likely to focus more clearly on guiding human development.

Prospects for the 80's look something less than cheerful for postsecondary education in the humanities and in the preparation of teachers. The U.S. Bureau of Labor Statistics foresees a "surplus" of 2.7 million graduates with the B.A. by 1985, and a Mellon Foundation inquiry concluded that by 1990 there would be a "surplus" of 60,000 Ph.D. recipients in the humanities.

Judging by an in-depth study by David Clark and Egon Guba—a study whose conclusions include projections into the 80's—we can expect a continued decline in teacher education enrollments and in funding. At least temporarily, these researchers conclude, support for quality programs will deteriorate.

Their views were reinforced late in 1978, when the *Occupational Outlook Handbook* published by the Department of Labor reported a six-year drop-off of nearly 9 percent in teacher education enrollments. Business and engineering schools are likely to continue to graduate more students for at least several years, while fewer students will major in history and English.

Because of the needs of a postindustrial society, postsecondary education as a whole will not languish. Unless they take advantage of the opportunity to serve a new clientele, however, schools may lose even more of their one-time monopoly to other educational agencies. These include instructional programs directly sponsored by the federal government, training ventures sponsored by business and industry, and training in vocational skills with "transfer value" provided by the armed services.

Secondary schools and universities can attract the growing crowd of potential students among the adult and elderly by cutting red tape and modifying admissions requirements for those who seek to bring their knowledge up to date or to broaden or deepen it.

The spread in the age ranges of children, youth, and mature learners at the same grade level or in similar areas of study is likely to increase during the coming decade, thus adding to a demand for more teachers. This seems inevitable for several reasons. The holding power of the schools has been increasing steadily: more and more young people stay in school after their sixteenth birthday. The decline in scores on mass standardized tests and the pressures for "competency-based" diplomas seem to reflect the presence of a large number of slower-learning students in the educational continuum. These young people will take longer than others to finish their schooling. Especially as opposition to "social promotions" builds up, more and more pupils may spend at least 13 or 14 years rather than 12 in school.

The schools will therefore need more teachers. Furthermore, educational theory will probably continue to support the designing of instruction to give students continuous progress in nongraded, personalized instructional blocks.

The Education for All Handicapped Children Act (PL 94-142) will encourage the schools to initiate long-overdue educational practices designed to prevent problems for all children. More liberal policies on the age of students at admission, more careful grouping, individual educational plans (including greater heed to the needs of bilingual students), and greater understanding of and consideration for human differences will, perforce, begin to permeate more classrooms.

At the same time, however, considerable turmoil can be anticipated as PL 94-142 has an impact. This turmoil, already evident, can be expected to carry over into the early years of the coming decade. The way in which the severely handicapped are brought into the school will continue to pose dilemmas in regard to locating, placing, and safeguarding them; paying for their education; recruiting teachers competent to help them; and designing the mandatory written, individualized educational plans for as many as 8 million students who may eventually be classified as handicapped under the present broad federal definition.

Concepts of what constitutes a basic education will move along two diverse but compatible tracks. A decline in mass standardized test scores beginning in the middle school years, the parental concern reflected each year in opinion polls, and legislated requirements will accelerate trends toward achieving the "educational excellence" which became a slogan in the early 60's and helped start the curriculum reform movement of that era.

In addition, however, the problems of a threatened biosphere will require the teaching of new basics: the knowledge that will help the next generation work to restore greater equilibrium between humans and their overexploited environment.

The quest for ways to motivate youth to learn will increase in both scope and tempo. A need to improve students' motivation has occurred because of two developments. First, provisions for human welfare have reduced the threat of want which goaded an older generation to work. At the same time, many youth have begun to recognize that there isn't enough affluence to go around as human aspirations and numbers make ever-greater demands on the earth's finite and dwindling resources.

An important task of education in the home and at school, it would seem, thus becomes the creation of a self-image in U.S. students that is focused on the future. If learners have hope that they can fulfill satisfying personal and vocational prospects, they will seek to build skills and talents that make them useful to themselves and to society. Giving them this motivation won't be easy, but the importance of the task will certainly be more widely acknowledged in the next decade.

Space limitations preclude a complete assessment of the forces and trends which will create issues and sharpen educational problems during the 80's. However, the following probabilities clearly merit a place in an inventory of education's tomorrows.

• Action (direct experience) learning and service (community improvement) activities, urged by persons such as James Coleman and Alvin Toffler in the 70's, may bring new vitality and validity to schooling.

• Despite the limitations on the amount of money schools can spend on hardware, technology should become increasingly significant to education in the 80's. Look for the use of tiny integrated circuit modules (already available) for programming hand-held computers, sophisticated educational materials that can be coupled to home or school TV screens, and the first practical use of holography—projection of three-dimensional images in the classroom by means of laser beams.

• It is highly likely that teacher militancy will increase if inflation continues to threaten the profession's economic security. Jeopardized pension plans, in particular, will become an increasingly hot issue if the cost of living doubles between 1979 and 1989—and it will, if present trends continue.

• A substantial increase in federal participation in funding local school districts can be expected. State legislators will attempt to mollify voters in a "Proposition 13" mood by supporting more conservative taxation policies. Patently, the federal government will be under greater pressure to pay more of the costs of quality education as local resources diminish.

A superficial examination of trends based on a quick reading of books, magazines, and reports dealing with the future may lead one to infer that the 1980's will not be a happy decade for schooling in the United States. Such a conclusion, I think, is dangerous nonsense.

There are excellent reasons for looking to the 80's with confidence. For one thing, our profession has enormous human resources in the form of highly educated professionals with a great deal of intellectual wattage. Enrollments at the elementary school level may or may not begin to increase by the mid- and late 80's and recreate the market for large numbers of teachers. In any event, there remains an enormous opportunity to increase the quality of U.S. education.

Among many other things, the teaching profession has learned a great deal as it coped with the educational problems of the 70's. Educators are constantly seeking ways to eliminate the decline in test scores while striving to retain the schools' proud record of continually increasing their holding power. The value of alternative forms of schooling has been recognized; generally these forms have not been left outside of public education but have become a part of it. The importance of early childhood education also has begun to be recognized, and programs for young children have become more widespread.

In short, despite possible shoal waters ahead for the schools, the 80's can bring better times for both learners and teachers. Because of the increasing scope of their clientele, educators have a number of new opportunities. These include, for example, making education more "special" and personalized for all children—not just for the handicapped; endeavoring to meet the needs of mature and senior learners; and strengthening the concepts of genuine multiethnic and multilingual education in our pluralistic society.

… UNIT VI

NEW DIRECTIONS

REPRODUCED BY PERMISSION OF THE PHILADELPHIA MUSEUM OF ART:
THE PRINT CLUB PERMANENT COLLECTION.

Gefallen (Killed in Action) 1921 Lithograph by Käthe Kollwitz.

18

Children and Stress: A Contemporary Analysis

This chapter is devoted to a discussion of a few very important and unique occurrences in the lives of some American children. These special circumstances are not necessarily positive nor negative; they have the potential for both. We will open with a brief discussion of psychological crises and their relationship to child development and finish with a discussion of the effects of divorce, death, and poverty upon children.

STRESS IN A CHILD'S LIFE

A crisis (or the presence of a *stressor*) is defined as an upset in a steady state (Caplan, 1964). There are certain developmentally appropriate crises; passing from one developmental stage to another is a normative sort of crisis. There are environmentally induced problems, however, which are far from being normative in a child's life.

The central factor in determining whether a crisis will be significant in a child's development is the balance between the difficulty of the stressor (the severity of the problem) and the adequacy of the child's support networks (both internal and external). According to Caplan, support for children comes in the form of three types of supplies:

Crisis:
an emotionally significant event in a person's life

1. Physical supplies: the satisfaction of basic physical needs; basic patterns of loving and support; emotional support
2. Social supplies: familial acceptance; peer group acceptance; the development of an adequate self-image; social acceptability
3. Psychological supplies: trust, nurturance; psychological warmth; congruent feedback, and so on.

Classification of Child-Centered Crises

Taxonomy: classification scheme

There is a taxonomy of various problems that occur in child development. The classification scheme puts the disorders, which have varying causes and effects, into categories by symptom and suggested origin.

Group 1—psychopathological syndromes: childhood psychiatric problems (autism, schizophrenia, depression, anorexia nervosa)

Group 2—Developmental crises: these arise out of apparently normal but perhaps sudden demands that occur routinely during childhood. A demand for toilet training may be developmentally appropriate, yet may produce significant problems for the child.

Group 3—Situational crises: a basically healthy child is placed in a disrupted social and/or familial situation. Parental illness, parental loss (death or divorce), or parental maladjustment are all examples of this situation.

Stress Models: In responding to stress, there are specific stages that children go through. One way to look at the place stress plays in children's lives is illustrated in the figure below.

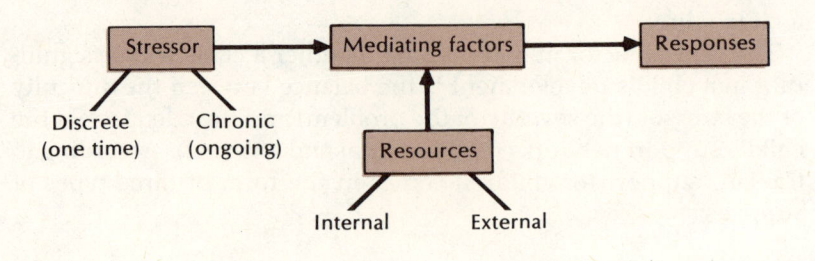

```
                  Stressor ─────▶ Mediating factors ─────▶ Responses
                  ╱      ╲                ▲
            Discrete   Chronic            │
           (one time) (ongoing)       Resources
                                      ╱      ╲
                                  Internal  External
```

Children and Stress: A Contemporary Analysis

A stressor can be a one-time thing (discrete), or it can be a continuing problem for the child (chronic). Some normative developmental crises are discrete; they happen only once. Puberty happens only one time in the life of the human. In many of the problems, however, there are at least possibilities for long-term effects. Some situations are life-long, like poverty.

The stressor interacts with mediating factors to determine children's response patterns to the crisis. The real situation is actually much more complicated than the drawing can indicate. The effect of the stressor is dependent upon the idiosyncratic coping strength of individual children, their temperament, and the utility of outside help. Not all stressors are perceived in the same way by all children. Even children within the same family respond to a crisis in different ways. The developmental level of the child is one factor that may make a great deal of difference.

One other way to look at the effect of a stressor is to look at the "roller-coaster" profile of adjustment, as proposed by Reuben Hill. In normal times, children operate on a more or less steady level. When a stressor is introduced, they react.

Discrete: noncontinuous, separate

Chronic: continuous, recurring

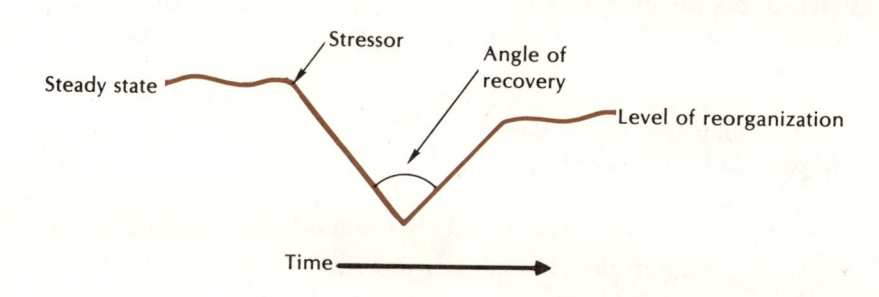

A period of disorganization invariably occurs. This disorganization varies considerably from child to child. Some children are completely overwhelmed by their parents splitting up, but other children seem to take it almost in stride. The angle of recovery depends upon the severity of the problem and the salience of the coping/supportive network of the child. The ultimate level of reorganization reflects the child's situation after the crisis.

There are four general reactions to stress. These reactions are based on the relationship between the perception of the stress and the actual number of stressors. The following table demonstrates these possibilities.

General Reactions to Stress*

| | Number of Stress Events | |
Perceived Stress	High	Low
High	overwhelmed	self-destructive
Low	challenged	lucky

*Adapted from Cheriboga, 1978.

An individual child in the position of high perceived stress along with a high level of actual stressors is overwhelmed by the experience. On the other hand, a child who does not perceive the stress to be high, for whatever reason, yet experiences a high number of stressor events, will respond in a very different way. The perception and the coping style of the child make a significant difference in the child's reaction to stress.

Some children do not have a large number of stressor events in their lives. Their perception of stress, however, is high. These children do not cope well with stressors, even minor ones. Coping style and strategy is at least partially learned. Some of the familial experiences likely have significant impact in the development of coping skills.

Generally, there are several distinct factors that make up children's ability to cope. Berman (1977) has identified at least six factors that aid in coping:

1. The individual characteristics of the child; often unidentifiable
2. The stage of development of the child
3. The previous experience the child may have had with the stressor
4. The nature of the crisis
5. The preparation the child may have had for the crisis
6. The events during the crisis

Coping style: one's method for dealing with problems

DIVORCE

Divorce just about doubled between 1965 and 1975. However, the yearly increase in the divorce rate, which has ranged anywhere from 4.5 percent per year to 11.5 percent, seems to be slowing. The national divorce rate for 1976 was 5.0 per 1,000 population. More recent data from 1977 and 1978 suggest that the national divorce rate has stayed at about 5.1 to 5.2/1,000 population.

The estimate of the number of children involved in divorce in 1976 was 1,117,000; this represented a decline of over 5,000 children from the 1975 estimate. This is the first decline in the total number of children affected by divorce since 1960. The average number of children per divorce decree has been declining for a number of years. The highest it ever got was 1.36 children per divorce in 1964. In 1975 it was 1.08, and in 1976 it was 1.03.

In 1976, of the couples in the divorce registration area (a statistical representation of the U.S.), 44 percent reported having no children under the age of 18. The remaining 56 percent of the couples reported one or more children, with the majority of them being small families with 1 or 2 children (1976 data). Only 11 percent of the couples reported three or more children. In 1964, only 37 percent of the couples reported no children under the age of 18. Twenty percent of the divorcing couples in 1964 reported three or more children. The number of divorcing couples with three or more children was cut nearly in half between 1964 and 1976.

Although couples divorcing in recent years appear to have had fewer children, children today have a greater likelihood of being affected by a divorce. The number of children involved in divorce per 1,000 total children in the population of the United States has gone from 8.7 in 1964, to 16.9 in 1975, to 17.1 in 1976. The likelihood of being involved in a divorce has increased for American children by a substantial margin.

The Developmental Impact

The literature on divorce is quick to affirm that divorce is a stressor in the lives of children. The predivorce tension of the couple may be transmitted to children and become part of their perception (Roberts and Roberts, 1974; Anthony, 1974). There are many direct and indirect effects, ranging from emotional disruption, aggressive behavior, poor school performance, heightened levels of anxiety, loyalty conflicts, violent and assaultive behavior, confusion, fear and guilt (Tooley, 1976; Roberts and Roberts, 1974; Kapit, 1972; McDermott, 1970).

Most of these are psychiatric studies, with clinical populations. Many of them suffer from a lack of generalizability. One of the more significant studies of the effects of divorce on children has been developed by Wallerstein and Kelly in Marin County, California. This study began in 1970 and included 60 families who had a total of 136 children. The 131 children who ended up participating in the study were approximately half boys and half girls. The sample was essentially white and middle class. The study was longitudinal in design, with follow-ups at 18 months after divorce and four years after divorce.

In the published reports of the study (1974, 1975, 1976), much information was provided concerning developmentally appropriate responses to divorce. The 34 preschool children in the project were divided into three groups on the basis of their reaction to a parental divorce.

Behavioral regressions: reversion to an earlier behavioral level

The Youngest Preschool Group (2½ to 3¼ years): "All of these children responded to the family disruption with observable and significant behavioral changes, with acute regressions in toilet training despite a history of stabilized control, increased irritability, whining, crying, general fearfulness, acute separation anxieties, various sleep problems, cognitive confusion, increased autoerotic activities, return to transitional objects, escalation in aggressive behavior, and tantrums" (Wallerstein and Kelly, 1975, p. 602). We can only wonder if there could be anything else that might go wrong!

The Middle Preschool Group (3½ to 4½ Years): In contrast to the previous group, these children did not favor regression as their coping mechanism. There was some irritable behavior, along with whiny, tearful, and aggressive behavior. The response was slightly more adaptive.

The Oldest Preschool Group (Aged 5 to 6): Like their younger counterparts, all of these children experienced heightened anxiety at the time of divorce. Restlessness, whininess, and moodiness also characterized these children. These kids were sad, to be sure, but at least one of the children in this group expressed relief that his parents were splitting up.

The sex differences among these preschoolers were minimal, at least at the time of parental separation. At the 18-month follow-up the researchers found the girls to be in worse psychological condition than the boys (this finding contradicts most of the available information).

Latency Age Children (Aged 7 to 8): There was a great deal of sadness on the part of these children, and perhaps even more difficulty coping with the parental divorce. Later latency children (aged 9 and 10) operated at widely discrepant levels. The children used denial, sought out the support of others, and displayed a more sophisticated understanding of what was happening.

Adolescents operated on the most sophisticated level in response to the divorce. They redeveloped their relationship with each of their parents, and there were signs that the parental divorce was affecting the adolescents' entry into adulthood. In some cases there was a pushing into adulthood; in other situations there was a delaying of the process.

At the four-year follow-up, most of the children did not see the divorced family as an improvement over what they had prior to the divorce. Only about 20 percent of the children, four years after the divorce, felt that there had been an improvement in their lives (Kelly, 1979).

The Interactional Effects

A project under the leadership of Hetherington, Cox and Cox has studied the effects of divorce a little differently from the one discussed above. This project had a total of 96 families involved, half of which were divorced families and half of which were control families (or those used for comparison). The families were essentially middle class, and custody had been granted to the mother in each of the divorced homes.

Using a measure of family disorganization, an estimate of the levels of confusion was made in both the intact families and the divorced families. Measurements were taken at two months, one year, and two years after the divorce. The table below shows the average score as reported by the men and women in the families. The higher the score, the greater the level of disorganization.

Disorganization: condition of confusion and lack of control

The households of divorced mothers and fathers are more disorganized than those of intact families. This disorganization is most apparent in the first year after the divorce and decreases by the second year after the divorce. Children of divorced parents ". . . are more likely to get pick-up meals at irregular times. Divorced mothers and their children were less likely to eat dinner together. Bedtimes were more erratic and the children were read to

Levels of Family Disorganization*

	Intact (Control) Homes		Divorced Homes	
	Father	Mother	Father	Mother
Two months after	15.73	13.17	23.83	20.31
One year after	15.15	12.96	22.60	22.85
Two years after	15.29	12.75	19.19	17.56

*Source: Hetherington et al., 1975.

less at bedtime and were more likely to arrive at nursery school late" (Hetherington, Cox and Cox, 1975, pp. 9–10).

Other significant findings of the Hetherington project are summarized below:

1. Divorced parents make fewer maturity demands of their children.
2. Divorced parents apparently communicate less effectively with their children.
3. There is a steady decline in the nurturance of divorced fathers with their children after the divorce.
4. Divorced parents appear to be less consistent than parents in intact families; the most significant problem with consistency occurs at about the end of the first year after the divorce.
5. The lack of consistency is noted in terms of the lack of control divorced parents have over their children.
6. Mothers and fathers behave differently after the divorce. A divorced mother is more restrictive during the first postdivorce year. The father (noncustodial) creates what Hetherington and her colleagues call the "everyday is Christmas" syndrome. These fathers wanted their children to be happy when they visited them so no expense nor favor was spared with the children.

Disorganization and disrupted family function appear to peak at one year. The restabilization process picks up momentum at the one-year mark and has had significant effects by the end of the second postdivorce year.

Divorce As It Relates to Play Patterns

Hetherington et al. also looked at the frequency and type of play children in divorced and intact families exhibited. At two months following the divorce, both boys and girls showed much shorter durations of play; in addition, the play was more functional and there was a great deal more onlooker behavior (Hetherington et al., 1979).

For girls, after two years most of the differences between them and the girls from the intact families disappeared. For boys, however, the effects remained more persistent. There were many more feminine play patterns and the boys had much greater difficulty in getting into imaginative play than the boys from the intact homes.

During the first postdivorce year, the boys became "incompetent bullies." They were anxious and became more aggressive in their interactional patterns with other children, but when they failed to dominate things the way they wished, they ran to adults for help. This problem was still evident two years after the divorce. Paradoxically, the incompetent bully tactic alienated the boys from adults as well as other children. Consequently, many of these boys found themselves playing with younger children; they were literally driven out of their peer group. The boys were also more likely to play with girls; this resulted in more feminine play patterns.

The effects of divorce appear more traumatic for boys. Boys apparently receive nonsupportive, sometimes negative feedback from significant adults. These adults may be assuming that little boys can handle the problem with less aid from them. In general, children get worse during the first year and improve during the second year. The improvement is not as great for boys as it is for girls.

The Quality of Parent-Child Relations

After a divorce, the quality of the relationship between parents and children is of great importance. For a sample of divorced families, the figure below indicates the quality of parent-child relationships in terms of three basic patterns: low-low, where the child has a poor relationship with both parents; low-high, where the child has a good relationship with one parent and a poor one with the other; and high-high, where the child has a good relationship with both parents (Hess and Camara, 1979).

School work effectiveness and social relations both improved as the quality of the parent-child relationship improved, and at the

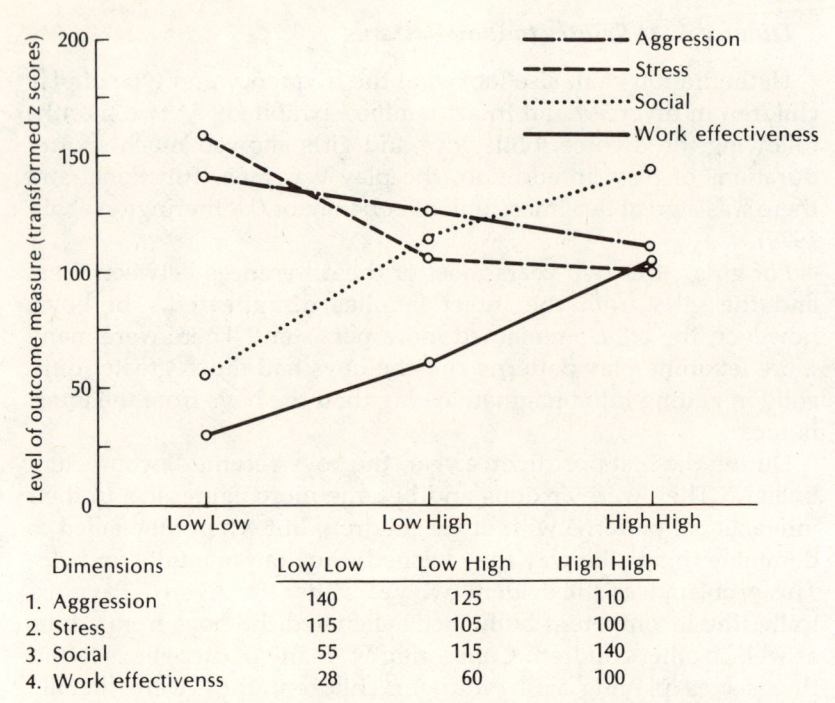

[Figure: Level of outcome measure (transformed z scores) plotted against Low Low, Low High, High High for Aggression, Stress, Social, and Work effectiveness.]

Dimensions	Low Low	Low High	High High
1. Aggression	140	125	110
2. Stress	115	105	100
3. Social	55	115	140
4. Work effectivenss	28	60	100

same time, levels of aggression and stress dropped. It may be that the stress dimension of divorce remains somewhat high despite the nature of the parent-child relations. But overall, the quality of the relationship makes a big difference in children's adjustment.

Custody

The assignment of children in terms of where they are to live after the divorce is called the *custody* arrangement. Custody of children is legally sanctioned by the courts. Over 90 percent of the custody awards in the United States today are to the mother; and most of these are not contested (no dispute is made between the parents as to where the children are to live). Centuries ago, the custody award was made to the father most of the time; a mother was not considered capable of supporting the child in the proper way.

The determination of custody rests upon the doctrine of "whatever is in the best interests of the child." There are four rules of thumb, based on old English law, that determine the best interests of the child:

1. Infants should be placed in the custody of the mother.
2. A girl should be in the custody of the mother and a boy

Custody:
awarding of responsibility for a child's upbringing

should be in the custody of the father if he no longer needs the attention of the mother.
3. If the children are mature enough, their wishes should be taken into consideration when awarding custody.
4. Rights of visitation should normally be granted to the noncustodial parent.

As a result of the application of these principles, four major types of child custody have evolved in this nation. The *traditional* custody decision is that one parent (usually the mother) is granted full legal custody of the child, while the noncustodial parent is granted visitation rights.

In *third-party* custody, the child is placed in the custody of someone other than the two parents. This relatively rare form occurs when the judge handling the case, for some reason, decides that neither of the original parents should have custody of the children. This might occur in the case of an abusing parent; the judge may feel that the atmosphere of the home is not right for the child.

Split custody is one of the rarest custody awards made. In situations of serious problems between the children or severely extenuating circumstances with the parents, the judge will elect to place one child in the custody of the mother and another child in the custody of the father. There is virtually no research available on the effects of split custody decisions, and it remains an extremely sensitive area of discussion.

Lastly, there is *joint* custody, a relatively new form. In this situation each parent has equal custody of the children. This plan works much better if the parents live near each other and are on good speaking terms.

Custody arrangements, the parents' ability to talk things over, and the developmental situation of children all come together to create the environment surrounding children's experience with divorce. If children become pawns in a parental fight over power, their adjustment will be less functional. If they are not given a developmentally appropriate explanation, their adjustment will suffer. Children are always the disadvantaged party in a divorce. More time needs to be spent meeting their needs.

DEATH

The relationship between children and the concept of death is a complicated one. There are four basic cognitive processes involved in a child's understanding of death:

1. Universality: all people, because they are human, die. To be human is to have this characteristic.
2. Irreversibility: death cannot be turned around; the dead are not sleeping, waiting to be awakened.
3. Causality: what causes death; what factors bring it about.
4. Fear: something that is not understandable may evoke fear in the child.

Because of these cognitive processes, there is probably some form of developmental sequence in the comprehension of death.

In one study, three-year-olds were compared to five-year-olds in terms of their understanding of death (Beauchamp, 1974). Five-year-olds differ significantly from three-year-olds on all four of the dimensions mentioned above. The two-year age difference makes a big difference in terms of comprehension of death. In the five-year-olds, there was an appreciation of the commonality of death to all living things. The older children had a firmer grip on the idea that dead means forever, were more realistic in their descriptions of how death comes about, and displayed lower levels of fear relative to death. There were no differences between males and females in this study, but there were some social class differences. Middle-class children seemed more realistic in their perceptions of universality, irreversibility, and causality, and appeared less fearful than did the lower-class children.

Another study more clearly demonstrated the developmental nature of a child's understanding of death. At Level 1 (the youngest children, aged 3½ to 4 and below), children indicate a relative ignorance in the understanding of death. There are few concepts of death, few death words, and a greater chance for some rather peculiar associations, e.g., hospitals equal death. Death is not a distinct and separate phase of life.

At Level 2, children view death as a temporary state. They are not sure about the permanence of death and are convinced that the person will return shortly. This is particularly true if they have been told that a dead person is really asleep. Ages are particularly difficult to attach to these and subsequent stages.

Level 3 is the "death is final" stage, with contingencies attached. An extension of level 2, this stage is characterized by a bit more cognitive sophistication and the beginning of clarity in the cognitive dimensions mentioned above. Somewhere around the age of seven (at the earliest) children will bring the cognitive dimensions together and appreciate the irreversibility, permanence, and universality of death (Melear, 1973).

Death of a loved one is often easier to bear when the grief is shared with others.
ROBERT V. ECKERT, JR., EKM-NEPENTHE.

Many of the problems children have with death result from a societal failure to appropriately integrate death within society and the family. We are talking of the cultural denial of death that exists in America. This denial does more to prevent children from coping with death than does an honest and realistic approach to death by adults. We do not have to be preoccupied with death to provide children support when they experience a death; our own adult problems in coping with death make the child's task that much more difficult.

Gaelin (1972) has indicated that there are several things teachers can do to help children cope with death. First of all, they can help develop an appropriate perspective toward death. This involves an appreciation of children's curiosity about death. Evading and ignoring questions children have about death probably does more harm than good. The old adage "If I ignore it, it will go away" probably is not the best practice in this case.

Teachers also need to appreciate children's comprehension of death. Cognitive and affective dimensions do not develop at the same time, and both are very important in children's learning of concepts that help understand death. As Bruner has indicated, "Any subject can be taught in some intellectually honest fashion to any child at any stage of development" (Bruner, 1961).

Teachers can also help children express their emotions concerning death. Play is one of the most illuminating and useful avenues of expression for children. Teachers can create supportive atmospheres for play that may have a slightly different theme. Then, teachers need to be very observant; if there are themes that do not get resolved or that persist over time, there may be a need for other kinds of help for the child.

POVERTY

The median income for American families in 1977 was approximately $16,000 (U.S. Census Bureau data, 1979). Of the approximately 57 million families in the United States, 18.4 percent had incomes between $10,000 and $15,000 per year, 18.1 percent had incomes between $5,000 and $10,000; and 9.3 percent had incomes below $5,000 per year. It is also interesting to note that the median income of whites is just about double that of blacks.

Income is one criterion in determining poverty in the United States. The current poverty line is about $6,191 per year, and approximately 11 percent of the nation's population lives below this level. The absence of other resources contributes to the cycle of poverty. These other resources include education, employment, and individual and community power.

Poverty may be a separate culture within the larger American culture. This culture of poverty may have a separate language and artifacts and may be passed down from generation to generation. We may be institutionalizing a second (lower) class of citizenship in this country, because the gap between the rich and poor does not seem to be narrowing.

In terms of children, poverty means high rates of stillbirth, greater incidence of low birth weight babies, and higher rates of father absence. The medical problems may be the result of poorer prenatal care, poorer environmental conditions, poorer diets, and generally poorer health.

Children are affected by the educational systems operating in their neighborhoods. There are more problems with school buildings and facilities in poor neighborhoods; the tax base has eroded and vandalism is at a higher level. Education has been the tradi-

Poverty may have many unexpected consequences for the growth and development of children in a family.
BRUCE DAVIDSON, © MAGNUM PHOTOS, INC.

tional, institutionalized hope for poor children. This "last hope" is in danger of going under, given the current financial problems of most school districts.

The types of housing in which children live are also very important to their development. High-density housing, poor ventilation, and decaying construction all are dysfunctional. Rats begin to infiltrate the neighborhood. There have even been a number of reports of "superrats" developing in poorer neighborhoods and attacking and killing children. Older, run-down houses may also have a problem with flaking paint, which is lead-based; children eating chips of this paint will suffer lead poisoning.

Is there a relationship between living in a impoverished environment and ability to learn? Clearly, children who come to school from an impoverished environment may have a different type of preparation. This may mean the children are looking at the classroom from a different perspective. The homogenization in our schools is not sufficiently flexible to deal with this problem.

There is a higher proportion of failure in school by children who come from impoverished environments. This has little or nothing to do with basic intelligence, and it is not necessarily due to big differences in the families. Lower-class homes are as full of child care-taking practices and attitudes as middle-class homes are (Selzer, 1974). What is lacking are the environmental (physical and psychological) supports necessary to adequately prepare for the school experience. There may not be the books, the preschool experience, or even the motivation to fit into the school situation.

Children and Stress: A Contemporary Analysis

ISSUE

Parents and Crises: A Help or Hindrance?

Crises, for both children and adults, have many similarities, whatever the particular event. Divorce, death, and poverty all share some of the same traumas, yet retain unique characteristics all their own. We have discussed what happens to children in each of these situations. The developmental and interactional occurrences specific to each crisis are apparent and found in the literature. One crucial variable, however, is the relationship of children to their parents and the relation of the parents to the crisis. Parents are a fundamental portion of children's supportive network. The nature of the parents' relationship to a crisis will determine the saliency of a child's supportive network.

☐ Children react to divorce in developmentally appropriate ways, as has been indicated in the chapter. The way the parents, both custodial and noncustodial, are dealing with the divorce is sure to help or hinder children's ability to deal with the problem. Parents can be a help to the child going through a parental divorce if they are aware of their emotions concerning the separation and have their feelings under control. If the parents have dealt with their own pain and have considered all of the contingencies attached to the problem, they can be of considerable aid to the child.

☐ If, on the other hand, parents have not been able to deal with their own divorce, are still very upset, and are still very set on getting back at their former mate, their children will be in an even more vulnerable position. Parents will sometimes use the children to get back at the former mate; this abuse greatly impedes children's progress in dealing with the divorce trauma. Parents will sometimes use children as scapegoats or as sounding boards, venting their hostilities at the expense of the children. In all of these situations the parents have actually gotten in the way of the children and their work; they have hindered the children.

☐ Death presents a similar situation, often much more difficult to deal with. Our society has avoided the discussion of death at every corner. Death as a topic in a school curriculum is frowned upon; our society, through sophisticated advertising and philosophical orientation, is disallowing the possibility of aging and ultimate death. It is no wonder that bereavement means a very difficult recovery period for most people, with little in the way of social support.

☐ Given this psychological taboo and people's inability to grasp the phenomenon of death, it is little wonder that death presents children with a confusing and potentially frightening visage. As we have indicated in the chapter, death is a profoundly cognitive occurrence; the concepts necessary for an understanding of death are advanced, and young children do not have a good hold on them. Children are quite vulnerable when it comes to death, and simplistic answers like "he has gone to Heaven" may not satisfy their intellectual needs for an answer.

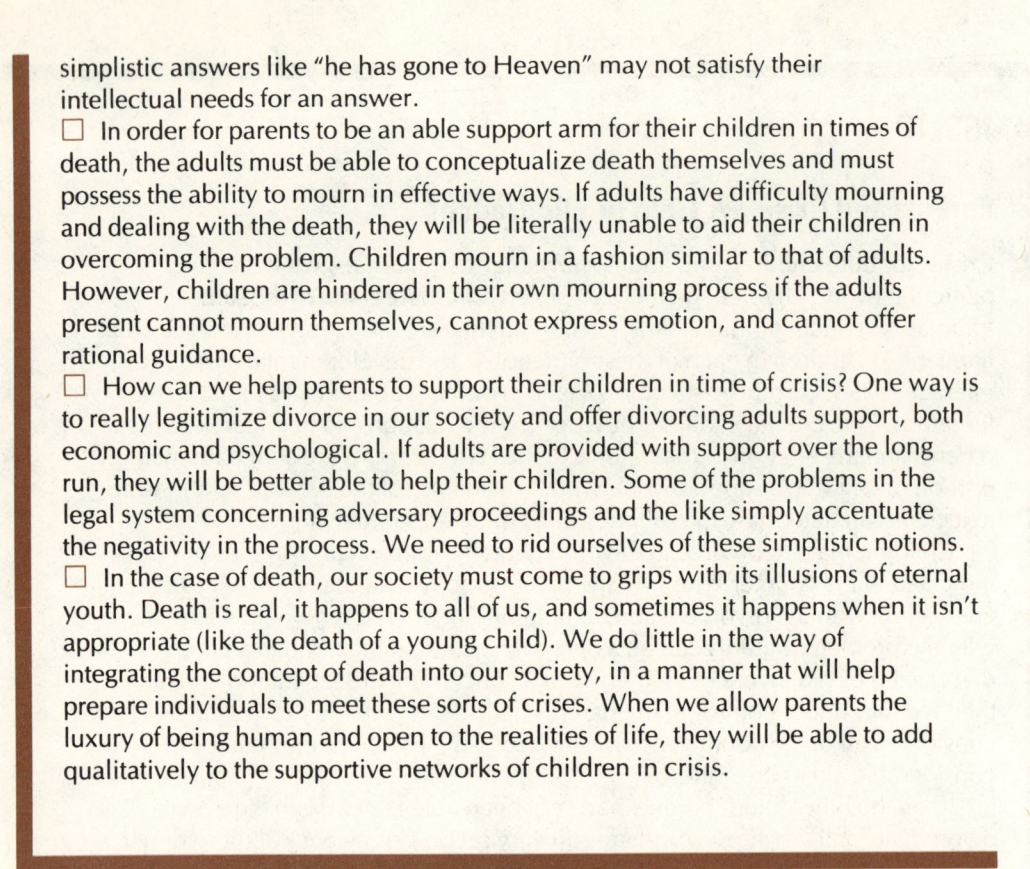

☐ In order for parents to be an able support arm for their children in times of death, the adults must be able to conceptualize death themselves and must possess the ability to mourn in effective ways. If adults have difficulty mourning and dealing with the death, they will be literally unable to aid their children in overcoming the problem. Children mourn in a fashion similar to that of adults. However, children are hindered in their own mourning process if the adults present cannot mourn themselves, cannot express emotion, and cannot offer rational guidance.

☐ How can we help parents to support their children in time of crisis? One way is to really legitimize divorce in our society and offer divorcing adults support, both economic and psychological. If adults are provided with support over the long run, they will be better able to help their children. Some of the problems in the legal system concerning adversary proceedings and the like simply accentuate the negativity in the process. We need to rid ourselves of these simplistic notions.

☐ In the case of death, our society must come to grips with its illusions of eternal youth. Death is real, it happens to all of us, and sometimes it happens when it isn't appropriate (like the death of a young child). We do little in the way of integrating the concept of death into our society, in a manner that will help prepare individuals to meet these sorts of crises. When we allow parents the luxury of being human and open to the realities of life, they will be able to add qualitatively to the supportive networks of children in crisis.

Summary

1. Crises have profound impacts on children. The central factor in determining how serious the impact of the crisis will be on the child is the balance between the difficulty of the stressor and the adequacy of the child's supportive networks.

2. The classification of child-centered crises reveals that they range from psychopathological problems to developmental crises to situational crises. Stressors can be discrete or chronic, and the angle of recovery is crucial in the reestablishment of a normative life-course.

3. The ability of the child to handle stress is dependent upon several factors: the characteristics of the child (often unidentifiable), the developmental level of the child, the previous experience of the child, the nature of the stressor, the preparation the child may have had for the stressor, and the course of events during the crisis.

4. The actual number of children involved in divorce is decreasing slowly. The chance of an American child being involved in a divorce sometime in his childhood, however, is twice

today what it was in 1964. The effects of divorce on children are both developmental (they depend on the age and development of the child) and interactional (divorce can alter the social milieu of the child).

5. The custody of children is determined by the courts and takes one of four forms: traditional, joint, split, and third party. The vast majority of custody decisions assign the children to the mother, in both contested and uncontested cases.

6. There are four cognitive processes involved in children's conceptions of death: universality, irreversibility, causality, and fear. Each of these dimensions is very important in determining the child's conceptual understanding of death. The youngest of children view death as temporary, if they have any understanding of it at all. Many of the problems children have with death are related to a societal failure to appropriately integrate death within society.

7. Poverty is a situation that significantly affects children. Poverty means higher rates of stillbirth and prematurity, higher rates of father absence, and greater incidence of environmental deprivation. Children are affected by poorer schooling, an eroded tax base (limited services), and vandalism and crime.

Thought Questions

1. What elements make up a child's support network?

2. Distinguish between discrete and chronic stressors. How are their effects on children different? Similar? How can we enhance a child's ability to handle stress?

3. Differentiate between the developmental and interactional effects of divorce on children.

4. Support and attack each of the four types of child custody on the basis of their merits. Is there a best way? What are the best interests of the child?

5. Describe the development of each of the four cognitive processes involved in a child's understanding of death. Should there be a "death course" in every school? What would such a course contain?

6. How do we ease the impact of poverty on children?

Suggested Readings

Cook, S.S. *Children and Dying*. New York: Health Sciences Publishing Corp., 1974. Cook discusses children's reaction to death. Perhaps the greatest strength of this book is the selective bibliographies. *Very handy book to own.*

Grollman, E.A., ed. *Explaining Divorce to Children.* Boston: Beacon Press, 1969. *Despite the publication date, this little book remains very handy in terms of explaining divorce to children. There are ten contributors who offer a sensitive treatment of this touchy area. Grollman has continued to write books dealing with children and crises like divorce and death.*

Roberta, A. *Childhood Deprivation.* Springfield, Ill.: C. Thomas, 1974. *In a variety of articles, Roberts discusses the special need situations of childhood: divorce, death, and child abuse, to name a few.*

Steinhauer, P.D., and Q. Rae-Grant. *Psychological Problems of the Child and His Family.* Toronto: Macmillan of Canada, 1977. *This work is very thorough in its treatment of the relation between stress and child development. Recommended strongly for students who are interested in social work and other applied areas of the discipline.*

READING

Death is something that occurs every day and ultimately affects every person; this fact makes little difference when it comes to the pain and difficulty associated with understanding death. This is especially true for children who may have limited cognitive awareness.

Erna Furman, writing recently in *Young Children*, indicates that death presents a formidable challenge to the understanding capabilities of most children. Offering thoughtful and time-tested suggestions, Furman explores the relationship between children and death and shows the nature of bereavement in both children and adults.

Helping Children Cope with Death
Erna Furman

Many of us go through life for long periods without thinking about death. When it suddenly strikes very close to us, it comes as a shock, not only because it always represents a loss but also because we get the horrible feeling that "this could be me; this could happen to me, to my family, to my children and friends." We have a tendency to deal with this fear by adopting one of two extreme attitudes. We may feel the impact as though the tragedy had really happened to us. We put ourselves in the shoes of the bereaved or of the dying and feel so overwhelmed and anxious that we are unable to extend ourselves appropriately to those who need our help. At the other extreme, we shield ourselves and behave as if "this is not real; this did not happen to me; I don't want to hear, read, or talk about it." This reaction too prevents us from extending a helping hand because it keeps us from coming to terms with our own feelings. Often we waver from one extreme to the other until, hopefully, we reach a kind of middle ground where we are able to feel, "There but for the grace of God go I; it is not me but it could be." When we arrive at this hard-to-reach point we begin to be able to think and feel with others and to help them as well as ourselves.

Many years ago at the Hanna Perkins (therapeutic) Nursery School, we were working without thinking about death. Then within one year, two mothers of young children died, leaving their families as well as therapists, teachers, peers, and friends stunned. We had to cope with the immediate reality and struggle to come to terms with what had happened. But this was only the beginning. In the course of the next few years, we found that, without having sought cases of bereavement, we had in intensive treatment 23 children of all ages who had lost a parent through death. Each analyst who treated a bereaved child and worked with the family found it so difficult and painful that we turned to each other to share and learn together. We hoped that in this way we would be better able to understand and help our patients and, perhaps, formulate some thoughts that might be of general interest and serve to assist others. I would like to share with you some of the things we learned, trying to pick out what might be particularly helpful to teachers of young children.

As you know, it does not take the death of a parent to bring children to an encounter with death. Many grandparents, siblings, relatives, and pets die. There are also many daily events which bring children face to face with death, be it a passing funeral procession or a dead worm in the backyard. The worst bereavement is the death of a parent. It is a unique experience distinct from all other losses, such as divorce or separation, and distinct from other experiences with death. Many nursery school teachers may be fortunate enough never to have a pupil whose parent dies, but they are surely called upon to help with some less tragic bereavements and the many daily encounters with death—the ants a child steps on or the dead mouse someone brings for show-and-tell.

Our bereaved children came to treatment with many different symptoms. Parental death is unique; it happens to unique people who respond in unique ways. Our patients most often responded in a disturbed, unhealthy fashion, sometimes at the time of the bereavements, sometimes not until many years later. But we were deeply impressed that some children only about two years of age, because of very optimal circumstances, could master their tragic loss. By contrast, we had much older patients who could not master it at all. I do not mean to imply that the two-year-olds master this stress more easily; on the contrary, it is harder. Nor is it short-lived for them; it lasts longer. I am not speaking of the degree of pain and anguish, but the ability to master ultimately. To me that means that these children were upset, struggled and suffered, but were able to mourn their parents and to progress in their development. The danger of parental bereavement does not lie in the formation of isolated symptoms or difficulties. The main danger is that it may arrest or distort a child's development toward becoming a fully functioning adult. Many of the factors involved touch upon the role of the teacher and offer an opportunity to develop in children those qualities which will enable them to master a future bereavement or to help them and their peers to cope with a current loss or minor encounter with death.

Helping Children Understand Death

The first crucial factor is children's ability to understand death in its concrete manifestations, i.e., to understand that death means no life, no eating, no sleeping, no pain, no movement. Those children who at the time of bereavement already had a rather good grasp of the concrete facts of death had a much easier time. We found that children from toddler age on show interest in dead things. They find dead insects or birds. When they can tell that a sibling is different from a teddy bear, that one is animate and the other not, they can also begin to understand what *dead* means. For example, when the toddler plays with a dead fly and notes that it does not move, it helps to confirm the child's observation by using the word *dead* and explaining that the fly will never move again because it is dead. Most young children have not yet been helped to acquire this kind of basic concrete understanding of what *dead* means, how things die, and what we do with the corpse. It is much easier to acquire concrete understanding of death from insects or small animals, since they do not have great emotional significance for the child; this knowledge paves the way for later understanding of death in people.

McDonald studied the responses of the peers of our two bereaved Hanna Perkins Nursery School pupils. She found that children's first interest focused on what death is. They could not direct themselves to the aspects of loss, empathy, or sympathy for a peer's loss until they could understand concretely what death means. McDonald also noted that each of the children's questions required a special effort of thoughtful awareness and listening by the teachers. Initially, and without knowing it, teachers closed their eyes and ears and implied, without words, that death was not a welcome topic. Once their attitude changed, the children's questions just poured out. It is very difficult for all of us to talk about death, even dead insects. Most of us were not helped in this respect when we were children so we tend not to help children or do not know how to help. With special effort and by struggling to come to terms with questions about death ourselves, it is possible to overcome our difficulty to some extent.

Support for Parents

Parents usually do not mind when teachers talk at school about death as it relates to insects, worms, or even animals. Some teachers have found it helpful to meet with parents to discuss how such incidents are handled. Parents, perhaps even more than teachers, find it very difficult to talk with children about death, fearing that sooner or later the child will say, "Will I die?" "Will you die?" We are frightened of the answers that we would rather not give. However, the eventual next step in children's understanding death is that of relating it to themselves and to those they love and need. A meeting with parents on this subject does sometimes help to bring such questions into the open and offers the teacher an opportunity to help the parents. Whether a teacher wishes to arrange such meetings depends on the teacher's relationship with the parent group and the extent to which both sides are ready to grapple with the subject of death.

When a child asks, "Can this happen to me or to my mommy?" the answer should take into account the child's sense of time. A parent is hesitant to say, "No, I won't die," because he or she eventually will die. Yet should the parent say, "Yes, I will die," the child understands this to mean tomorrow or next week. We find that a young child can best understand when the parent says, "No, I do not expect to die for a long, long time," stressing the *no*, and adding that he or she expects to enjoy the child as a grown-up and have many years of being a grandparent.

Parents usually also raise the question of spiritual answers to the question of death. Children before age five or six are incapable of abstract thinking and therefore unable to grasp religious or philosophical explanations. They usually distort them into concrete and often frightening concepts that have little to do with religion. I know some very religious parents who chose not to introduce religious explanations to their children under the age of five precisely because they knew these concepts would be distorted and might later interfere with the children's attitudes about religion. By contrast, doubting or unbelieving parents quite often use explanations that involve *heaven* and *God*. This happens because they have not thought matters through themselves and want to shield the child from something frightening. In shielding the child they only shield themselves and create confusion in the child. Something that is not really believed by the adult cannot come across as true or reassuring to the child.

In our experience the most understanding parents have given concrete explanations of death and burial. When, in response to what they had heard from others, the children asked, "What about heaven?" or "Does God take people away?" the parents replied, "Many people believe that. Many people believe other things too and as you get older you will learn about them and will understand them better. Right now it is important that you understand how we all know when someone is dead."

The concrete facts of death are usually much less frightening to children than to adults. An anecdote about one of Barnes' patients illustrates this point. A father had struggled very hard to help his young children understand what *dead* meant and what being in a coffin meant because their mother had died. Some months later their grandfather died. As the father tried to tell his little girl that they would choose a nice box with a soft blanket inside so that grandfather would be very comfortable, the little girl interrupted him and said, "But daddy, if he is really dead then it doesn't matter about his being comfortable in the coffin." For that moment the child certainly had a better grasp than the father.

Bearing Unpleasant Feelings

Another factor which facilitates a child's mastery of bereavement is the ability to bear unpleasant feelings, particularly sadness and anger. Obviously, there is no way to anticipate the kind of feelings that come with a bereavement. Separations are very different from a loss through death, but there are some similarities. Separations, to a small extent, involve the same feelings of longing, sadness, and anger that we find in much greater intensity at a time of bereavement. Young children are able to bear these feelings to an incredible extent if they have been given appropriate help in developing this strength.

How does one help a child achieve such mastery? Basically there are two ways. One is to expose children only to bearable separations. When separations are too long they become unbearable and therefore not conducive to experiencing feelings. A very few hours of separation are bearable for a baby, perhaps half a day for a toddler, and at most a couple of days for a nursery school child. But it takes more than adjusting the lengths of separation. The second important step is the adults' willingness to help children recognize their feelings, express them appropriately, and cope with them. Before and after the separation this is the parents' task; during the separation the caregiving person can help.

It is often thought that children who do not react, do not make a fuss, or even enjoy the parents' absence, are well-adjusted, good children. To me, these children have not built appropriate mental muscles to bear unpleasant feelings. They shut themselves off from such feelings and therefore have no control of them. For nursery school teachers an excellent time to practice with children in building up the mental muscles for knowing and bearing unpleasant feelings is, of course, during entry to nursery school. At that time one can help parents understand that children who have no feelings, who react as though nothing has happened, or who immediately "love" the school, are children who are shut off from their feelings and in danger of stunting their emotional growth. Many mothers who do not welcome the child's unhappy or angry response to separation at the start of school would be very concerned if the child did not react feelingly to the loss of a loved person or readily preferred someone else in that person's stead. Yet how could a child acknowledge very intense feelings without previous help to cope with them in less threatening situations?

Coping with Bereavement

So far we have considered how difficult it is to talk about death even in terms of animals and insects, and how hard to bear loneliness, sadness, and anger in terms of brief separations. We know, of course, how much greater the hardship is when we have to think about it and feel fully the total loss of a loved person. There is no easy way to cope with bereavement. There is no shortcut, either for the bereaved or for those who help them. The goal of assisting bereaved persons is not to foreshorten their or our own pain and anguish but to strive toward inner mastery. Even if we achieve it, it does not mean that we have come to terms with death once and for all. In order to be able to help we too have to empathize anew with each bereavement and struggle through it again.

I would like to turn now to what teachers can do, and often have done, when a child in the nursery school suffers the death of a parent, sibling, or close relative. I do not have any easy remedies to offer, and my suggestions are much more easily said than done because pain and anxiety are an essential part of the task.

The teacher's first question often is, "Should I mention the loss to the child?" I have heard time and again about the fear of causing a child hardship by referring to his or her loss. Some years ago I met a boy whose father had died. His teacher had reported that the boy had no feelings about, or reaction to, the death of the father. When I saw this boy, said "Hello" and expressed my natural sympathy, he broke into tears at once. He cried for an hour and I had to see him a second time before he could begin to talk. I asked him later why he had never shown his feelings at school. The boy replied, "You know, that teacher was so mean! He never even bothered to come to me and say 'I am sorry your father died.' I would never show my feelings to that kind of guy." I suspect that this was not a mean teacher but that his reaction of silence built a barrier between the child and himself.

This and similar experiences have convinced me that the teacher has to take the first step by mentioning the loss and expressing sympathy in a way that implies, "This will be with us a long time. I hope you will feel free to come to me, talk with me, or feel with me about it." In practice, some children will come to the teacher much more than others. However often they do or do not come, the teacher needs to empathize with each and every feeling that may arise and help children tolerate them. This means not to falsify feelings, not to hold them back, not even to pour them out in order to be rid of them, but to recognize and contain them.

At opportune times the teacher can also help by talking with the child about the factual aspects of the bereavement—how the loved one died, where he or she is buried, and changes in the family setting and routine. I think it is equally important for the teacher to report to the parent what the child shows, thinks, or feels about this experience so that the parent can further help the child and perhaps be alerted to some aspect which has not yet been expressed at home.

In addition to work with the child, a second area in which the teacher can be helpful is with the parents or surviving parent. Hopefully, before a loss occurs, the teacher will have built the kind of relationship with the parent which will make it possible for him or her to inform the teacher as a friend, a special professional friend who has the parent's and child's welfare at heart. The parent will welcome talking with this teacher and perhaps accept some suggestions—how to tell the child about the death, how to talk it over with the child, whether to take the child to the funeral, what plans to make for the immediate future.

Assisting Parents

Let me now share with you some of the things we have found helpful to parents at such a time. Adults with young children do not die uncomplicated deaths; the deaths are always untimely.

This is also true about the death of siblings. It is most important that the child understand not only that the parent or sibling is dead, but also what the cause of death was. When these two things are not understood, when they are distorted or denied, it is impossible for the child even to begin mourning. I do not mean overwhelming the child with frightening details. Hopefully a teacher can help a parent to tell the child enough and in such a manner that the child can achieve a considerable amount of understanding.

Parents always want to know whether they should take the child to the funeral, and what they should say about it. We can only give an answer after we learn more about the specific situation. The child's attendance at the funeral will depend on the type of service, how the parent feels about it, how comfortable the parent is with the rites the family observes, and how able the parent is to extend himself or herself emotionally to the child during the funeral.

Many families are willing to adapt the services to the needs of all the family. Children often find an open casket difficult. They find long services difficult. If the funeral rites are not suitable for a young child or if the parent is unable to care effectively for the child during the services, it is better that the child remain at home with a familiar person and with the full verbal knowledge of what is happening during that time. I had a patient who was sent to the zoo on the day of her father's funeral in the hope that she would not have to be sad. This hope was not fulfilled, and the arrangement produced an almost insurmountable barrier within the child and between child and surviving parent. Mourning has to happen together. Pain and anguish have to be shared. It is not fair to shut out the child.

When it comes to immediate plans for the future, the teacher can sometimes impress upon parents how very important it is for the child to keep the home and remaining family together. Adults often find it much easier to leave the place of distress, to throw away the things that remind them of the deceased. For children the opposite holds true. They need the concrete continuation and help of their surroundings in order to come to terms with what is missing. Sometimes people have asked how parents and children can ever be of support to one another when they have such different needs. When parents understand that their children's greatest need is continued physical and emotional care by the surviving parent, they usually compromise for the sake of the child and find that they benefit as well. Being a good parent brings a measure of self-esteem that cannot be gained in any other way and is especially helpful at a time of bereavement when so many other things seem not worthwhile.

Helping Others in the Group

Along with assisting the bereaved child and parent, the teacher has to extend help to the other children in the nursery school. This usually starts by discussing with the bereaved parent what to tell the other children and their families. Hopefully the bereaved parent is able to share the truth in simple realistic terms with his or her own child and is willing to have this information passed on. Then the teacher needs to take a few painful hours to call every parent in the nursery group. Each call is long and difficult and should, if possible, include several items: a brief account of what happened to their child's peer, which terms or phrases will be used in the nursery school to discuss the sad event, how the parents can tell their own child and how helpful it would be if the child learned the news first from them, and how to cope with some of the child's questions.

If a bereaved parent is initially unable to allow discussion of the cause of death, the teacher may have to say, for example, "Chris's father died. It is still too hard for Chris's mommy to talk about it, but she will tell us what happened later and I will share it with you." Hopefully, the teacher's relationship with the parent will help to make this delay brief.

The next morning all children will have been told of the death, even if not its cause, by their parents, and the teacher can sit down with them and initiate the first discussion of facts and feelings. The most important point to cover is, "This talk is only a beginning. We will talk about it and feel about it often and for a long time. It will be with us because it is a sad and scary thing."

There are usually three main questions that arise sooner or later: "What is dead?" "Can it happen to me?" and "Can it happen to you?" Until these questions are accepted and coped with, it is generally not possible for the peers or or their parents to extend genuine sympathy to the bereaved. When we are able to assist children in gaining gradual mastery, many months of painful struggle seem indeed worthwhile.

The Mourning Process

If the death is understood, if its cause is understood and the disposal of the body is understood, and if the bereaved child is reasonably sure of his or her own survival and of having bodily and emotional needs met to a sufficient extent, mourning will start of itself. It is a process that is not always visible from the outside because, contrary to what many people think, mourning does not consist of wailing, rages, crying, or complaining. Sometimes there are no overt signs of upset and yet the feelings may be there.

I worked with a mother and child. The little boy lost his father two years previously and experienced some difficulty in the aftermath. The mother told me that she had never cried in front of the child, since she only cries when she is alone in bed. The boy, who supposedly had not reacted at all to his father's death and had certainly never cried or raged, told me in his separate interview that he was not a person who ever cried in front of people. He only cried when he was alone in bed and nobody knew that he cried. He cried night after night but his mother never cried. Although mother and child expressed feelings in the same form, they did not know that the other even had feelings. It was sad to see how hard they had made it for themselves and for each other. However, even if they had not cried at all they might have been able to mourn because mourning is a mental process that consists primarily of two parts: on one hand, a very gradual and painful detachment from the memories of the deceased, and on the other hand almost the opposite, a taking into oneself some traits or qualities of the deceased. How much there is of each part and whether the proportion leads to a healthy adaptive outcome depend on many factors, including the age of the bereaved person, the nature of the bereavement, the preceding relationship, the personality of the deceased. With young children it is particularly important that they take into themselves the healthy rather than the sick attributes of the dead parent and that they detach themselves sufficiently, so that, in time, they will be free to form a parental bond with a new person.

Sometimes parents intuitively understand the ways in which their child's long inner mourning proceeds and sense when the child encounters difficulties. Sometimes it is much harder. It certainly is not a mark of failure to seek professional assistance at such a time. That is yet another area where the teacher can support the surviving parent. The sooner help is given, the better the chances of preventing possible damage to the child's growing personality.

Young America (1950) by Andrew Wyeth.

Epilogue:
Children in the Future

Learning about children is an exciting and demanding activity. There are several important dimensions to childhood that need to be kept in mind. One of them is that a significant portion of child development is normative. Most children develop in broadly similar ways at about the same time and end up essentially the same. This aspect of the study of child development has led to the discovery of norms for the development of children. Everyone from parents to teachers to physicians uses norms to assess the progress of children.

On the other hand, a great deal of child development is idiosyncratic. Children, while having broadly similar directions and rates of growth and development, also mature at their own rate and in their own time. It is inaccurate to assume that just because a child is nine years old that certain behaviors and abilities must be present for the child to be normal. In a sense it is normal to be just a little bit different in development.

Another very important dimension is the idea that children do not develop on islands separate from all other people. They develop in a contextual fashion. This means that all of the individuals, groups, and other things around them affect their development. Some of the environments that significantly affect American children include the family, the school system, the social class, the nutritional ecosystem, the peer group, and the neighborhood. The exact effect of these different agents is unknown. A significant amount of research and study has gone into predicting just what sort of context produces the best type of child. So far that research is very inconclusive and at times misleading. One of the most fascinating things about child development is that there is no "cookbook" to optimal development. It is the result of a synergistic combination of all the factors that make up children, including their genetic background.

As we enter the 1980s, one thing is certain about our society: it is continuing in a pattern that has been part of our society ever since its inception. Change is fundamental to the American way of life. Parenting, education, family life, and many other things have all undergone significant change during the years, and some of these items, like education and child rearing, seem to change nearly every year. As one new theory of educating children comes along, schools change to be in line with that way of thinking, only to change again ten years later.

There are also some consistent patterns in family life and child development. Physically, children develop essentially the same. Some of the patterns in parent–child relations present today were also present 100 and 200 years ago. So, as we enter the decade of the 1980s, we carry with us a legacy of significant change on the one hand and significant similarity on the other hand. Perhaps one significant force, like the economic system and the resultant technological advances, will determine the exact nature of the next decade; perhaps not.

Children have come a long way since the colonial years. Their status in society has been elevated greatly, compared to the way children were treated during those early years. To be sure, there will be more advances in neonatology and fetology so that the early days and months of a child's life will carry with them less risk than in the past.

Children will spend more and more time out of the home in the coming decade. Due to the necessity for working women and the significant increase in the desire of women to work, alternate child care facilities will need to be developed. This means a significant realignment of the nation's priorities in relation to the child care needs of the country. At the present time too little time and money is spent in these activities to meet people's needs.

Understanding children is fundamental to understanding ourselves. We see greater interest in understanding children and families in the next decade, an interest that is motivated partly because we have the time to be more involved in parenting, and also because of the strong need to look at ourselves that will undoubtedly become more visible in the next ten years.

Epilogue: Children in the Future

Whether children will ever obtain an equitable place in society in terms of legal protection and services is not known. We can only hope that the educational-political-industrial complex that makes policy for the country will see the future of our nation lies in our children. They are indeed the greatest resource a society has. We need to enhance this potential.

Glossary

Acuity the accurateness of the behavior; for example, visual acuity refers to the accurateness of the infant's vision

Adolescent growth spurt a period of very rapid increase in height starting roughly two years earlier for girls (as early as 7½) and lasting 1½ to 2 years

Aggression forceful, sometimes violent behavior intended to gain mastery over a situation or person

Ambivalence opposing points of view coexisting at the same time; adolescents are often the subject of ambivalence, i.e., they are caught between opposing points of view concerning how they are to behave

Amniocentesis the process of drawing out and analyzing a small amount of amniotic fluid. This test can detect many problems and disorders in the fetus.

Anxiety an apprehensive uneasiness about some contingency

Appropriate games games that are defined, usually by adults, as being the type of game to be played by the child. Appropriateness is most often determined by the age and sex of the child.

Attention the ability of the child to direct sensory equipment to a particular task or situation

Attention disruption the technique of measuring infants' perception in which the observer looks for a change in the activity of the child in response to the stimulus

Autonomy a sense of independence vital for appropriate development of the child

Basic trust   a feeling of security and comfort usually experienced by infants reared in consistent and warm environments

Behavioral regressions   one possible behavioral manifestation in young children after a severe crisis, like divorce, implying the reappearance of behaviors that had disappeared, such as wetting their pants

Biological primacy   the prominent role women play in the birth of children, due to their physiology. In most cultures, this is also followed by social primacy for women.

Calorie   the energy-producing value in food when oxidized in the body

Capitalistic orientation   an influence in child development that maintains a continuous developmental model. Growth and development are quantitative, measured against standards (norms) for development. This orientation is an Anglo-American one.

Centration   the tendency of young children to focus on one aspect of a situation or object, and to ignore the other aspects; demonstrated through the use of conservation experiments

Cesarean section   the surgical removal of the fetus

Chronic   continuous and ongoing

Classical   the pairing of stimuli in a learning situation

Classification   the cognitive ability that allows the child to categorize objects on the basis of similar characteristics

Cognition   thought-related processes; thinking and making comparisons among environmental components

Compensatory education   an educational program designed to make up for deficits in the child's development. Head Start is a compensatory education program.

Conception   the penetration of the egg cell by one sperm cell, resulting in the formation of a unique zygote

Confluence theory   the theory that as families increase in size, the nature of the interaction within the family also changes, ultimately resulting in lower intelligence levels of successive children

Conscience   a sense about the moral goodness of one's behavior; often determines the behavior of the individual

Glossary

Context understanding looking at a child in its environment, and looking at all of the child, not just selected aspects. Being aware of the context in which children develop is very important in understanding their behavior and motivations.

Coping style each individual's unique method for dealing with a particular problem

Crisis an upset in a steady state

Cross-sex identification the identification of a child with the parent of the opposite sex, believed to be a vital aspect of child development

Culture-free test one that is devoid of specific and/or subtle cultural biases that might affect the child's performance

Custody the legal definition of who the child will live with and who will have legal responsibility for the child; very important in divorce cases

Decentration the growing ability of the child to appreciate each dimension of a given perception, demonstrated through the use of conservation experiments

Demand feeding feeding a baby when the baby wishes to be fed. This idea is in direct opposition to scheduled feeding. Most children develop their own schedules of feeding.

Developmental task a contingency placed on the child that is halfway between a need on the child's part and a demand by society

Dilatation the process of opening the cervix. This is one result of the muscular contractions of labor.

Discrete occurring only once

Disorganization the sense of irregularity that follows a crisis

Dominance the situation in which one allele in a pair has a greater impact in determining a characteristic than the other allele

Dropping out the legal ability for adolescents to stop going to school. This usually means a poorer outlook for the individual's life, but not always.

Dual-career family a family configuration in which both mother and father have careers that offer them psychic reward and a chance for advancement

Dyslexia generally a disturbance in the ability to read, commonly affecting the perception of individual letters, like *b* and *d*

Ecosystem a network of simultaneously occurring components surrounding an event (like childbirth) that have the potential to significantly alter the outcome of the event

Effacement the process of thinning the cervix in anticipation of delivery. This is another result of the muscular contractions of labor.

Egocentrism the belief on the part of the child that the world revolves around him, the sun comes up for him, and his parents exist for his benefit

Ego-identity the internal consistency and distinctiveness of an individual

Elasticity the flexibility of the bones of young children due to incomplete ossification

Empathy the ability to participate in the feelings of another person

Endocrine system the series of glands (and subsequent hormones) responsible for the regulation of body chemistry. The main gland in this system is the pituitary.

Endometrium the lining of the uterus where the zygote typically implants

Equilibration the very strong desire in the developing child to produce and maintain balance of the cognitive structures

Ethnocentrism the belief that the way your culture does something is the only and best way to do it, a very common attitude among Americans

Expressive role the emotional, communicative, and interpersonal role, most commonly socialized more strongly in women

Extended family a family structure encompassing the nuclear family and other relatives

Fear an unpleasant emotion caused by the anticipation of danger. This emotion may be produced by a wide variety of real and imagined people, places, or things.

Fetal monitoring the process of electronically monitoring the status and progress of the fetus *in utero*. There are two types: an external monitor placed around the mother's abdomen, and an internal monitor in which electrodes are placed on the scalp of the fetus.

Forceps double-bladed instruments placed around the head of the fetus designed to aid the delivery of the baby, used in cases of difficult delivery

Game an activity engaged in for amusement and/or diversity

Gametes the broad group of cells that carry on the reproductive function in the human. The sperm cell and egg cell are gametes.

Gene the smallest unit of genetic transmission, located on the chromosome

Gentle birth a technique pioneered by Dr. Frederic LeBoyer that prescribes a warm delivery room, soft lights, and a soothing postdelivery bath for the baby. This technique is designed to ease the baby's entrance into the world.

Hemispheres the large outer portions of the human brain. These hemispheres are responsible for voluntary movement.

Heterogeneity as used in this book, the variety of characteristics that provide the individual with the ability to think. In the Guilford model, heterogeneity is exemplified by operations, contents, and products.

Holistic encompassing the entire being. The holistic theory of moral development rests on the assumption that the basic psychic needs of the individual must be met along with the cultivation of imagination.

Hormone a substance originating in an organ or gland, transported by the bloodstream, that stimulates another part of the body by chemical action. Hormones are active in small quantities and do not supply energy.

Human settlements families, neighborhoods, and communities. The nature of the settlement is crucial in the normative course of child development.

Idealism the tendency in adolescents to overlook certain details for the sake of a belief or a goal. Idealism can go so far as to make people ignore the means and concentrate on the end.

Idiosyncratic used in this book as applied to timing of children's developmental stages. For example, adolescents enter the period of formal operations when they are ready, at a time unique to each individual.

In utero means literally "inside of the uterus." A fetus *in utero* is still in its mother's uterus.

Induction a technique of dealing with people, especially children, that employs nonaversive methods, a great deal of conversation, and explanations as to why a certain behavior is not allowed

Infanticide practice of killing newborn infants or very young children. This technique was somewhat common in some cultures. It was used for population control and to make the culture consistent with certain traditional beliefs.

Institution an entity in society that serves to organize society and provide continuity for its members

Instrumental role the maintenance/support role, which is usually nonemotional; this role is typically assigned to the male.

Intelligence the ability to learn

Intensity of emotions as used in this book, the degree of emotional involvement on the part of the child—how angry, how happy

Intuitive phase a stage of development in which the child can functionally use symbols to represent objects; a more complex level of reasoning

Labor the process of uterine muscular contractions that literally push the baby out of the uterus

Learning relatively permanent changes in behavior that occur as the result of experience

Liminal phase the period in the transition of adolescence where the child is caught between the status of a child and the status of an adult. Some people suggest that adolescence in America is a prolonged liminal phase.

Locomotion the ability of the young child to move around; includes crawling, walking, etc.

Marasmus the deterioration noted in children who have been deprived of appropriate, minimal care (as in some institutions of the nineteenth century)

Meiosis the cell reduction process whereby gametes are produced in the gonadal tissue

Memory the ability to recall information that has been learned

Menarche the beginning of menstruation in the female; commonly occurring between the ages of 12 and 14

Mercantilistic-socialistic orientation an influence in child development that emphasizes qualitative growth and development, and devalues the use of single standards against which everyone is compared

Midwife a person who assists with the birth of a baby. This person is not a physician, but may be a nurse.

Minimal brain damage an ambiguous term defining possible damage to the brain, but not specifying the degree of damage or the specific area affected

Motivation the desire to do something. In order for a child to learn, the child must have the desire to learn, however unsophisticated it may be.

Motor development the maturation of physical skills, both large muscle (walking) and prehension skills (grasping with the fingers)

Myelin a fatty substance that coats (sheaths) the nerve fibers, indicative of mature nerve cells. This coating is an ongoing process that probably lasts through adolescence.

Natural childbirth the form of birthing in which there is no episiotomy and no drugs are used for pain

Nature-nurture the argument concerning biological versus environmental determinants of child development. The nature side says most of development is biologically determined; the nurture side says most of what children are is a result of learning and other experience.

Neonate means literally "new life," or "new person"; used to describe the newborn baby

Neuron nerve cell; fundamental functional unit of nervous tissue

Nonexistent average a term employed by Helms and Turner to indicate that for many developmental occurrences in children, there is no average age because each child is slightly different.

Norm a standard of behavior and development. A norm is usually determined through systematic and controlled observation.

Normative identity a personality pattern in the adolescent that is in harmony with the basic principles of society

Obesity a condition characterized by an abnormal amount of fat on the body

Object permanence the understanding that an object exists even though it may be out of sight

Operant conditioning learning that makes use of reinforcing agents

Organized games games for children in America that are controlled and dominated by adults, especially parents

Ossification the process of mineralization of the bones. The bones change from a soft cartilagelike substance to hard bone material.

Overgeneralization grammatical errors made by children who have been exposed to rules of language. A common example is use of the past tense of verbs, such as "I hurted my foot."

Parallel play a form of play in which children play beside each other but do not interact with each other

Peer group the relevant aggregate of age-mates with whom children grow. The peer group exerts a considerable influence on the development of children.

Pivotal grammar a type of grammar characteristic of the two-word stage in language development; all connectives are missing

Placenta the flat, disc-shaped membrane that serves as the support agent for the developing fetus. It is linked to the fetus by the umbilicus.

Play for children, the basic method of learning about their world

Popularity the state of being commonly liked or approved, very important to children of the middle and adolescent years

Preconceptual phase a nonsymbolic stage of development in which the child relies on objects to represent other objects

Prehension the act of grabbing an object, also letting the object go

Prematurity a condition of the newborn if delivery occurs earlier than 37 weeks of gestation and/or less than 2,500 grams (5 pounds) in birth weight

Prepared childbirth a birth in which both the husband and wife are trained in the psychology of pregnancy and delivery and in the psychology of birthing in a rational and controlled manner. Birthing becomes a cooperative process between the husband (or coach) and the mother.

Puberty the period of life at which the child becomes functionally capable of reproduction

Reciprocity actors in a social setting mutually affecting each other

Reconstruction the Piagetian phrase for the way children rebuild their memories as they experience more things and their understanding changes

Reflective smiling infant smiling of short duration, which is not essentially social; the first type of smiling to appear in the infant

Reflex an automatic and often inborn response to a stimulus. This response is automatic and never reaches the level of consciousness.

REM sleep the type of sleep associated with rapid movements of the eye and probably related to dreaming; found in children as well as adults

Research control the ability of the researcher to eliminate biases in the study of children, such as controlling for the influence of social class

Reversibility the ability of the child to understand what the reverse of an operation is. This ability apparently accompanies conservation.

Rites de passage ceremonies that accompany the transition from one status to another, found in many cultures. The U.S. appears to have few viable *rites de passage* in the transition from child to adult (adolescence).

Role experimentation trying on of different roles, usually quite possible within the confines of the peer group

Sacred society a culture that is stable and in which the religious order dictates social change. Its opposite, a secular society, is one in which the church reflects the social change that has already occurred.

Sensory memory an unconscious form of memory that appears to work like a reflexive response. Shortly after the event, this form of memory breaks down.

Sex linkage the fact that some traits are related directly to the sex of the individual, usually carried by the female and demonstrated in the male

Sex role the belief about the gender appropriateness of a particular behavior, attitude, or feeling

Sissy label attached to a boy who behaves like a girl, usually considered a serious problem

Social change the dynamic aspect of society in which basic elements are altered, depending upon the dominant social/psychological/economic themes of the time

Social smiling smiling by the infant in response to appropriate social stimuli

Socialization the process of transmitting culturally relevant material to children

Symbolism using an image to represent the actual object; a developing cognitive ability of children

Synergism the characteristic of producing more together than could be produced separately. For example, adolescents are more than just the sum of their previous experience.

Tabula rasa literally "clean slate." An idea proposed by John Locke that children are essentially blank slates at birth and are "filled in" by experience.

Taxonomy a classification

Temperament a unique balance of elements making up a child's basic outlook toward the world; personality

Teratogen an agent (compound, substance, or situation) that produces deformities in the fetus. Thalidomide is an example.

Theory the underlying principles of a given phenomenon

Three-generation family includes the nuclear family plus one or more grandparents

Tomboy the label attached to a girl who behaves like a boy; not considered particularly serious early in life

Transductive reasoning the tendency of young children to jump from particular to particular in creating a relationship between two separate items, reaching conclusions based on past experience and immediacy of their desires

Trisomy three chromosomes paired instead of the normal two at some location in the cell; produces severe problems, often fetal death

Two-child bias the belief, common in America, that it is better to have more than one child

Underestimation phenomenon the tendency of adults to not fully appreciate children's abilities. It occurs in all domains of child development (cognitive, social, interpersonal).

Glossary

Value the feeling that makes an idea useful and/or worthy of pursuit

Viability the ability of the fetus to survive extrauterinely, reached in the later stages of pregnancy

Visual cliff an experimental technique that simulated the existence of a sharp drop-off, used to test infants' perception of depth

Winning the desire to emerge the victor at game playing, an attitude reflective of adult intrusion into children's games

References

Ainsworth, M.; Salter, D.; and Bell, S. M. 1973. "Some Contemporary Patterns of Mother-Infant Interaction in the Feeding Situation" in *Readings in Child Psychology*, edited by Brian Sutton-Smith. New York: Appleton Century Crofts (Meredith Corp.), pp. 93–111.

Aitken, F. C., and Hytten, F. E. 1960. "Infant Feeding: Comparison of Breast and Artificial Feeding." *Nutrition Abstracts and Review* 30:341–71.

Ambrose, J. A. 1961. "The Development of Smiling in Early Infancy" in *Determinants of Infant Behavior*, edited by B. M. Foss. Vol. I. London: Methuen.

Anastasi, A. 1968. *Psychological Testing*, 2nd ed. New York: MacMillan.

Anthony, E. J. 1974. "Children at Risk from Divorce: A Review" in *The Child in his Family: Children at Psychiatric Risk: III*, edited by E. J. Anthony and C. Koupernik. New York: Wiley.

Apgar, V. 1953. "A Proposal for a New Method of Evaluation of the Newborn Infant." *Current Researches in Anesthesia and Analgesia* 32:260–67.

Aries, P. 1962. *Centuries of Childhood*. New York: Knopf.

Arms, S. 1975. *Immaculate Deception*. Boston: Houghton Mifflin.

Atkinson, R. C., and Shiffrin, R. M. 1968. "Human Memory: A Proposed System and its Control Processes" in *The Psychology of Learning and Motivation*, edited by K. W. Spence and J. T. Spence. Vol. 2. New York: Academic Press.

Avery, G. 1975. *Neonatology*. Philadelphia: Lippincott.

Azrin, N. H., and Foxx, R. M. 1974. *Toilet Training in Less Than a Day.* New York: Simon & Schuster.

Baldwin, A. L. 1967. *Theories of Child Development.* New York: Wiley.

Bandura, A. 1977. *Social Learning Theory.* Englewood Cliffs, N.J.: Prentice-Hall.

Bandura, A., and Walters, R. H. 1963. *Social Learning and Personality Development.* New York: Holt, Rinehart and Winston.

Bardin, D. R., and Moan, C. E. 1971. "Peer Interaction and Cognitive Development." *Child Development* 42:685–99.

Barnet, A. B.; Lodge, A.; and Arrington, J. C. 1965. "Electrocetonogram in Newborn Human Infants." *Science* 148:651–54.

Bauer, D. H. 1976. "An Exploratory Study of Development Changes in Children's Fears." *Journal of Child Psychology and Psychiatry* 17:69–74.

Baumrind, D. 1966. "Effects of Authoritative Parental Control on Child Behavior." *Child Development* 37:887–907.

———. 1971. "Current Patterns of Parental Authority." *Developmental Psychology Monographs* 4:99–103.

———. 1972. "Socialization and Instrumental Competence in Children" in *The Young Child: Reviews of Research,* edited by W. W. Hartup. Vol. 2. Washington: National Association for Education of Young Children.

Bayley, N. 1969a. *Bayley Scales of Infant Development: Birth to Two Years.* New York: Psychological Corp.

———. 1969b. *Manual for the Bayley Scales of Infant Development.* New York: Psychological Corp.

Beauchamp, N. F. 1974. "Young Children's Perception of Death." Ph.D. dissertation, Purdue University.

Bee, H. 1978. "The Effects of Poverty: An Overview" in *Social Issues in Developmental Psychology,* edited by H. Bee. New York: Harper & Row.

Behrman, R., ed. 1973. *Neonatology.* St. Louis, Mo.: Mosby.

Bell, S. M., and Ainsworth, M. 1972. "Infant Crying and Maternal Responsiveness." *Child Development* 43:1171–90.

Belmont, L., and Marolla, F. A. 1973. "Birth Order, Family Size and Intelligence." *Science* 182:1096–1101.

Bem, S. 1974. "The Measurement of Psychological Androgyny." *Journal of Consulting and Clinical Psychology* 42:155–62.

Bereiter, C. 1972. "An Academic Preschool for Disadvantaged Children: Conclusions from Evaluation Studies" in *Preschool Programs for the Disadvantaged,* edited by J. C. Stanley. Baltimore: John Hopkins.

Bereiter, C., and Engleman, S. 1966. *Teaching Disadvantaged Children in the Preschool.* Englewood Cliffs, N.J.: Prentice-Hall.

Berges, M., et al. 1972. 1973. "The Syndrome of the Postmature Child: A

Study of its Significance." *Early Child Development and Care* 1: 239–84 (pt. 1) and 2:61–94 (pt. 2).

Berman, G. 1977. "Family Disruption and its Effects" in *Psychological Problems of the Child and His Family*, edited by P. D. Steinhauer and Q. Rae-Grant. Toronto: Macmillan, pp. 371–82.

Biller, H., and Meredith, D. 1976. *Father Power.* New York: McKay.

Bliss, E. L., and Branch, C. 1960. *Anorexia Nervosa.* Vancouver, B.C.: Hoffer.

Block, J. H. 1973. "Conceptions of Sex Role: Some Cross-cultural and Longitudinal Perspectives." *American Psychologist* 28:512–26.

Bloom, L. 1970. *Language Development: Form and Function in Emerging Grammars.* Cambridge: M.I.T. Press.

———. 1973. *One Word at a Time: The Use of a Single Word Utterance Before Syntax.* Janua Linguarum Series Minor.

———. 1975. "Language Development" in *Review of Child Development Research*, edited by F. D. Horowitz. Vol. 4. Chicago: University of Chicago Press, pp. 245–305.

Bloom, L.; Lightbown, P.; and Hood, L. 1975. "Structure and Variation in Child Language." *Monographs for the Society for Research in Child Development* 40:2.

Bond, E. A. 1940. *Tenth Grade Abilities and Achievement.* New York: Columbia University Press.

Bornstein, M. H. 1975. "Qualities of Color Vision in Infancy." *Journal of Experimental Child Psychology* 19:401–19.

Boué, H.; Boué, A.; and Lazar, P. 1975. "Retrospective and Prospective Epidimeological Studies of 1500 Karyotyped Spontaneous Abortions." *Teratology* 12:11.

Bower, T. G. R. 1974a. "Repetition in Human Development." *Merrill Palmer Quarterly* 20:303–20.

———. 1974b. *Development in Infancy.* San Francisco: W. H. Freeman Press.

———. 1976. "Repetitive Processes in Child Development." *Scientific American* 235:38–47.

———. 1977. *A Primer on Infant Development.* San Francisco: W. H. Freeman.

Bowlby, J. 1969. 1973. *Attachment and Loss. Vol. I: Attachment; Vol. II: Separation.* New York: Basic Books.

Brackbill, Y. 1978. "Obstetrical Medication and Infant Development" in *Handbook of Infant Development*, edited by J. D. Osofsky. New York: Wiley.

———. March 1979. "Long-term Effects of Obstetric Medication." Paper presented at the Society for Research in Child Development, San Francisco.

Braine, M. 1963a. "On Learning the Grammatical Order of Words."

Psychological Review 70: 323–48.

———. 1963b. "The Ontogeny of English Phrase Structure: The First Phase." *Language* 39:1–13.

Bremner, R. H. 1970–1974. *Children and Youth in America: A Documentary History.* Vol. I–IV. Cambridge: Harvard U. Press.

Broad, William J. Nov. 25, 1978. "Lost in Thought." *Science News* 114(22):360–61.

Bronfenbrenner, U. 1974. "Developmental Research, Public Policy and the Ecology of Childhood." *Child Development* 45:1–5.

———. 1976. Appendix: Research on the Effects of Day Care on Child Development. In Advisory Committee on Child Development, *Toward a National Policy for Children and Families.* Washington: National Academy of Sciences.

Brown, Ann L. 1975. "The Development of Memory: Knowing, Knowing about Knowing, and Knowing How to Know" in *Advances in Child Development and Behavior*, edited by H. W. Reese. New York: Academic Press.

Brown, R. 1973a. *A First Language.* Cambridge: Harvard U. Press.

———. 1973b. "Development of the First Language in the Human Species." *American Psychologist* 28:97–106.

Brown, Roger W. 1965. *Social Psychology.* New York: Free Press, p. 171.

Bruner, J. 1961. *The Process of Education.* Cambridge: Harvard U. Press.

Bryan, T. H. 1974. "Peer Popularity of Learning Disabled Children." *Journal of Learning Disabilities* 7:621–26.

Butterfield, E. C., and Siperstein, G. N. 1972. "Influence of Contingent Auditory Stimulation upon Nonnutritional Suckle" in *Third Symposium on Oral Sensation and Perception: The Mouth of the Infant*, edited by J. F. Bosma. Springfield, Ill.: Thomas.

Campbell, D. T., and Stanley, J. C. 1963. *Experimental and Quasi-Experimental Designs for Research.* Chicago: Rand McNally.

Caplan, Frank, ed. 1973. For the Princeton Center for Infancy and Early Childhood, *The First Twelve Months of Life.* New York: Grosset and Dunlap.

Caplan, G. 1964. *Principles of Preventive Psychiatry.* New York: Basic Books.

Cartwright, C., and Cartwright, P. 1974. *Developing Observational Skills.* Hightstown, N.J.: McGraw-Hill.

Cheriboga, D. April 1978. Professor of Human Development, University of California, San Francisco. Personal communication.

Chertok, L. 1975. *Psychosomatic Methods in Painless Childbirth.* Elmsford, N.Y.: Pergamon Press.

Chess, S., and Thomas, A. 1973. "Temperament in the Normal Infant" in *Individual Differences in Children*, edited by J. C. Westman. New York: Wiley, pp. 83–104.

References

Chomsky, N. 1968. *Language and the Mind.* New York: Harcourt, Brace, World.

Cohen, L. B., and Salapatek, P. 1975. *Infant Perception: From Sensation to Cognition.* New York: Academic Press.

Collins, M. C. 1978. *Child Abuser: A Study of Child Abusers in Self Help Group Therapy.* Littleton, Mass.: Pub. Sciences Group.

Conger, J. J. 1973. *Adolescence and Youth: Psychological Development in a Changing World.* New York: Harper & Row.

Cratty, B. J. 1970. *Perceptual Motor Development in Infants and Children.* New York: Macmillan.

Crisp, A. H. 1974. "Primary Anorexia Nervosa or Adolescent Weight Phobia." *Practitioner* 212:525.

Crook, K. C., and Lippsitt, L. P. 1976. "Neonatal Nutritive Sucking: Effects of Taste Stimulation upon Sucking Rhythm and Heart Rate." *Child Development,* 47:518–22.

Cruickshank, William. 1977. "Myths and Realities in Learning Disabilities." *Journal of Learning Disabilities* 10:51–58.

Cubberly, E. P. 1920. *The History of Education.* Boston: Houghton Mifflin.

Davis, Glenn. 1976. *Childhood and History in America.* New York: Psychohistory Press.

DeMause, L. 1974. *The History of Childhood.* New York: Psychohistory Press.

Dennis, W. 1940. *The Hopi Child.* New York: Appleton Century.

De Tocqueville, A. 1900. *Democracy in America.* New York: Collier.

Deutsch, M. et al., eds. 1968. *Social Class, Race and Psychological Development.* New York: Holt, Rinehart and Winston.

Donnison, J. 1977. *Midwives and Medical Men.* New York: Schocken Books.

Dorfman, A., ed. 1972. *Antenatal Diagnosis.* Chicago: U. of Chicago Press.

Douglas J. W. B. 1956. "The Age at Which Premature Children Walk." *Med. Off.* 95:33–35.

Dusek, J. B. 1977. *Adolescent Development and Behavior.* Palo Alto: Science Research Associates.

Eiman, P. D., et al. 1971. "Speech Perception in Infants." *Science* 171:303–6.

Elkind, D. 1961a. "Children's Discovery of the Conservation of Mass, Weight and Volume." *Journal of Genetic Psychology* 98:219–77.

———. 1961b. "Quantity Conception in Junior and Senior High School Students." *Child Development* 32:551–60.

———. 1966. "Conceptual Orientation Shifts in Children and Adolescents." *Child Development* 37:493–98.

———. 1967. "Egocentrism in Adolescence." *Child Development* 38:1025–34.

———. 1968. "Cognitive Development in Adolescence" in *Understanding Adolescence*, edited by J. F. Adams. Boston: Allyn & Bacon.

———. 1970a. *Children and Adolescents: Interpretative Essays on Jean Piaget*. New York: Oxford U. Press.

———. 1970b. "Erik Erikson's Eight Stages of Man." *New York Times Magazine*, April 5.

———. 1976. *Child Development and Education*. New York: Oxford U. Press.

———. 1979. "Growing Up Faster." *Psychology Today* 12(9):38–42.

Elkind, D., and Weiner, I. B. 1978. *Development of the Child*. New York: John Wiley.

Erikson, E. 1963. *Childhood and Society*. New York: Norton.

———. 1968. *Identity, Youth and Crisis*. New York: Norton.

———. 1977. *Toys and Reasons*. New York: Norton.

Escalona, S. 1954. "The Use of Infant Tests for Predictive Purposes" in *Readings in Child Development*, edited by W. E. Martin and C. B. Stendler. New York: Harcourt, Brace, Jovanovich, pp. 95–103 and p. 314.

Espenschade, A. S., and Eckert, H. M. 1967. *Motor Development*. Columbus, Ohio: C. E. Merrill Books.

Fagan, J. F. 1972. "Infants' Recognition Memory for Faces." *Journal of Experimental Child Psychology* 14:453–76.

Fantz, R. 1961. "The Origin of Form Perception." *Scientific American* 204:66–72.

———, et al. 1962. "Maturation of Pattern Vision in Infants during the First Six Months." *Journal of Comparative and Physiological Psychology* 55:907–17.

———. 1965. "Visual Perception from Birth as Shown by Pattern Selectivity." *Annals of the New York Academy of Sciences* 118:793–814.

Fantz, R. L., and Fagan, J. F. 1975. "Visual Attention to the Size and Number of Pattern Details by Term and Preterm Infants during the First Six Months." *Child Development* 46:3–18.

Fantz, R. L., and Miranda, S. B. 1975. "Newborn Infant Attention to Form of Contour." *Child Development* 46:224–28.

Farson, R. E. 1974. *Birthrights*. New York: Macmillan.

Fielding, W. L. and Benjamin, L. 1962. *The Childbirth Challenge*. New York: Viking Press.

Fisher, S., and Greenberg, R. P. 1977. *The Scientific Credibility of Freud's Theories and Therapy*, New York: Basic Books.

Fitzgerald, H. E., and Porges, S. W. 1971. "A Decade of Infant Conditioning and Learning Research." *Merrill Palmer Quarterly* 17:79–117.

Flavell, J. H. 1963. *The Developmental Psychology of Jean Piaget*. New York: Van Nostrand.

References

———. 1977. *Cognitive Development*. Englewood Cliffs, N.J.: Prentice-Hall.

Flavell, J. H.; Friedrichs, A. G.; and Hoyt, J. D. 1970. "Developmental Changes in Memorization Processes." *Cognitive Psychology* 1:324–40.

Flerx, V. C.; Fiddler, D. S.; and Rogers, R. W. 1976. "Sex Role Stereotypes: Developmental Aspects and Early Intervention." *Child Development* 47:998–1007.

Fomon, S. J. 1974. *Infant Nutrition*. Philadelphia: Saunders.

Fox, D. J. 1969. *The Research Process in Education*. New York: Holt, Rinehart, Winston.

Freud, S. 1953. "Three Essays on the Theory of Sexuality." *The Complete Works of Sigmund Freud*, Standard Edition, vol. 5. New York: Hogarth Press.

———. 1959. *Collected Papers*, vol. 3. New York: Basic Books.

———. 1969. *An Outline of Psychoanalysis*. New York: Strachey, James, Norton.

Furth, H. G. 1966. *Thinking Without Language*. New York: Free Press.

———. 1970. "On Language and Knowing in Piaget's Developmental Theory." *Human Development* 13:241–57.

Gaelin, D. 1972. "Guidelines for Teachers in Handling the Subject of Death with Children." *Young Children* 8:35.

Gans, H. J. 1962. *The Urban Villages: Group and Class in the Life of Italian Americans*. New York: The Free Press.

Garcia, J. 1972. "I.Q.: The Conspiracy." *Psychology Today*, 6(4), 27–30.

Gardner, E. J. 1972. *Principles of Genetics*. 4th ed. New York: Wiley.

Gardner, H. 1978. *Developmental Psychology*. Boston: Little, Brown.

Gesell, A., and Thompson, H. 1938. *The Psychology of Early Growth*. New York: Macmillan.

Gesell, A., et al. 1940. *The First Five Years of Life*. Yale University: Clinic of Child Development, New York: Harper & Row.

Gesell, A.; Ilg, Frances L.; and Ames, Loise Bates. 1946. *The Child from Five to Ten*. New York: Harpers.

Gesell, A.; Ilg, Frances L.; and Ames, Louise Bates, with Bullis Glenna. 1970. *The Child from Five to Ten*. rev. ed. New York: Harper & Row.

Gesell, A. et al. 1974. *Infant and Child in the Culture of Today*. rev. ed. New York: Harper & Row.

Gewirtz, J. L. 1965. "The Course of Infant Smiling in Four Child Rearing Environments in Israel" in *Determinants of Infant Behavior*, edited by B. M. Foss. vol. 3, London: Methuen.

Gibson, E. J. 1969. *Principles of Perceptual Learning and Development*. Englewood Cliffs, N.J.: Appleton-Century-Crofts.

Gibson, E. J., and Walk, R. D. 1960. "The Visual Cliff." *Scientific American* 202:64–71.

Ginsburg, Herbert, and Opper, Sylvia. 1969. *Piaget's Theory of Intellectual Development*. Englewood Cliffs, N.J.: Prentice-Hall.

Glaser, P., and Strauss, M. 1967. *The Discovery of Grounded Theory*. Chicago: Abeline.

Goldman, R. D., and Hartig, L. K. 1976. "The WISC May Not Be a Valid Predictor of School Performance for Primary-Grade Minority Children." *American Journal of Mental Deficiency* 80:583–87.

Goode, W. J. 1971. *Social Systems and the Family*. Indianapolis: Bobbs-Merrill.

Goodman, M. E. 1970. *The Culture of Childhood*. New York: Columbia U. Press.

Goodnow, J. 1977. *Children Drawing*. Cambridge: Harvard U. Press.

Gray, S. W., and Klauss, R. A. 1965. "An Experimental Preschool Program for Culturally Deprived Children." *Child Development* 36:887–98.

Greenberg, M., and Morris, N. 1974. "Engrossment: Newborn's Impact upon the Father." *American Journal of Orthopsychiatry* 44(4):520–31.

Greenburg, J. Nov. 11, 1978. "Blind Drawings: A New Perspective." *Science News* 114.

Greenburg, D. J., et al. 1973. "First Mothers Rooming In with their Newborns: Its Impact upon the Mother." *American Journal of Orthopsychiatry* 43:783–88.

Grollman, Sigmund. 1964. *The Human Body, Its Structure and Physiology*. New York: Macmillan.

Guilford, J. P. 1959. "The Three Faces of Intellect." *American Psychologist* 14:469.

Guthrie, R. D., et al. 1977. "The Newborn" in *Introduction to Clinical Pediatrics*, edited by D. W. Smith. 2nd ed. Philadelphia: W. B. Saunders.

Hagan, J. W.; Jongeward, R. H.; and Kail, Robert V., Jr., 1975. "Cognitive Perspectives on the Development of Memory," in *Advances in Child Development and Behavior*, edited by H. W. Reese. vol 10. New York: Academic Press.

Haire, D. 1975. *The Cultural Warping of Childbirth*. Seattle: International Childbirth Education Supplies Center.

Hall, G. S. 1904. *Adolescence: Its Psychology and Its Relations to Physiology, Anthropology, Sociology, Sex, Crime, Religion and Education*. 2 vols. New York: Appleton.

Hall, J. G. 1977. "The Genetic Approach to Childhood Disorders" in *Introduction to Clinical Pediatrics*, edited by D. W. Smith. 2nd ed. Philadelphia: W. B. Saunders.

Hamacheck, D. E. 1976. "Development and Dynamics of the Self" in *Understanding Adolescence*, edited by J. F. Adams. 3rd ed. Boston: Allyn and Bacon.

References

Handel, G. 1972. *The Psychosocial Interior of the Family*. New York: Aldine.

Hanson, R. A. 1974. "Attitude Change with Kindergarten Children." M.A. thesis, North Dakota State University, p. 12.

Harlow, H. 1958. "The Nature of Love." *American Psychologist* 13:673–85.

Hartup, W. W. 1970. "Peer Interaction and Social Organization" in *Carmichael's Manual of Child Psychology*, edited by P. Mussen. vol. 2. New York: John Wiley.

———. 1975. "The Origins of Friendship" in *Friendship and Peer Relations*, edited by M. Lewis and L. A. Rosenblum. New York: Wiley.

———. March 1979. "Current Issues in Social Development." Presented at the meeting of the Society for Research in Child Development, San Francisco.

Haslam, R. H. 1977. "Neurological Disorders" in *Introduction to Clinical Pediatrics*, edited by D. W. Smith. 2nd ed. Philadelphia: W. B. Saunders.

Havighurst, R. J. 1951. *Developmental Tasks and Education*. New York: Longmans, Green.

———. 1972. *Developmental Tasks in Education*. 3rd ed. New York: McKay.

Havighurst, R. J., and Taba, H. 1949. *Adolescent Characters and Personality*. New York: John Wiley.

Heinstein, M. 1966. "Childrearing in California." Berkeley: Bureau of Maternal and Child Health, California State Department of Public Health.

Hellman, L. M., and Pritchard, J. A. 1971. *Williams Obstetrics*. 14th ed. Englewood Cliffs, N.J.: Appleton-Century-Crofts.

Helms, D. B., and Turner, J. S. 1975. *Exploring Child Behavior*. Philadelphia: W. B. Saunders.

Hertig, A. T., et al. 1959. "34 Fertilized Human Ova, Good, Bad and Indifferent, Recovered from 210 Women of Known Fertility. A Study of Biologic Wastage in Early Human Pregnancy." *Pediatrics* 23:202.

Hess, R. D., and Camara, K. A. March 1979. "Family Relationships after Divorce and Children's School Performance and Social Behavior." Paper presented at the Society for Research in Child Development, San Francisco.

Hess, R. D., and Shipman, V. C. 1968. "Maternal Influences upon Early Learning: The Cognitive Environments of Urban Preschool Children" in *Early Education*, edited by R. D. Hess and R. M. Bear. New York: Aldine.

Hetherington, E. M.; Cox, M.; and Cox, R. March 1975. "Beyond Father Absence: Conceptualization of the Effects of Divorce." Paper presented at the Society for Research in Child Development, Denver.

———. March 1979. "Family Interaction and the Social, Emotional and Cognitive Development of Preschool Children following Divorce." Paper presented at the Society for Research in Child Development, San Francisco.

Hill, R. 1958. "Social Stresses on the Family." *Social Casework* 39:139–50.

Hobbs, Nicholas. 1975. *The Future of Children*. San Francisco: Jossey-Bass.

Hoffman, L. W. 1974. "Effects of Maternal Employment on the Child: A Review of the Research." *Developmental Psychology* 10:204–28.

Hoffman, M. L. 1970. "Moral Development" in *Carmichael's Manual of Child Psychology*, edited by P. Mussen. vol. 1. New York: Wiley.

Honzik, M. P.; MacFarlane, J. W.; and Allen, L. 1948. "The Stability of Mental Test Performance between 2–18 Years." *Journal of Experimental Education*.

Horowitz, F. D., ed. 1975. "Visual Attention, Auditory Stimulation and Language Discrimination in Young Infants." *Monographs of the Society for Research in Child Development* 39(158).

Huenemann, R. L., et al. 1966. "Views of Teenage Subjects on Body Conformation, Food and Activity." *American Journal of Clinical Nutrition* 18:325.

Hurlock, E. 1973. *Adolescent Development*. 4th ed. Hightstown, N.J.: McGraw-Hill.

Huttel, F.; Mitchell, I.; Fisher, W.; and Meyer, A. 1972. "A Quantitative Evaluation of Psychoprophylaxis in Childbirth." *Journal of Psychosomatic Research* 15:81.

Hyde, J. S.; Rosenberg, B. G.; and Behrman, J. 1977. "Tomboyism." *Psychology of Women Quarterly* 2:73–75.

Inhelder, B., and Piaget, J. 1958. *The Growth of Logical Thinking From Childhood to Adolescence*. New York: Basic Books.

Johnson, A. L., et al. 1974. "Age Differences and Dimensions of Religious Behavior." *Journal of Social Issues* 30:43–67.

Kagan, J. 1964. "Acquisition and Significance of Sex Typing and Sex Role Identity" in *Review of Child Development Research*, edited by M. Hoffman and L. Hoffman. vol. 1. Beverly Hills, Calif.: Sage.

———. 1971. *Change and Continuity in Infancy*. New York: Wiley.

———. 1979. *The Growth of the Child*. New York: Norton.

Kagan, J.; Klein, R. E.; Haith, M. M.; and Morrison, F. J. 1973. "Memory and Meaning in Two Cultures." *Child Development* 44:221–23.

Kapit, H. E. 1972. "Help for Children of Divorce and Separation" in *Children of Separation and Divorce*, edited by I. R. Stuart, New York: Grossman.

Kaplan, F., and Kaplan, T. 1973. *The Power of Play*. New York: Anchor Press.

Katz, I. 1967. "The Socialization of Academic Motivation in Minority Group Children." *Nebraska Symposium on Motivation* 15:133–91.

Katz, I.; Henchy, T.; and Allen, H. 1968. "Effects of Race of Tester,

Approval-Disapproval and Need on Children's Learning." *Journal of Personality and Social Psychology* 8:38–42.

Katz, L. G. May 1973. "Perspectives on Early Childhood Education." *Educational Forum*.

Keeney, T. J.; Cannizzo, S. R.; and Flavell, J. H. 1967. "Spontaneous and Induced Verbal Rehearsal in a Recall Task." *Child Development* 38:953–66.

Kellogg, Rhoda. 1970a. *Analyzing Children's Art*. Palo Alto: National Press Books.

———. 1970b. "Understanding Children's Art" in *Readings in Educational Psychology Today*, edited by J. P. Dececco. Del Mar, Calif.: CRM.

Kellogg, R., and O'Dell, S. 1967. *The Psychology of Children's Art*. New York: CRM-Random House.

Kelly, J. B. March 1979. "Four Years Later: Children and Adolescents Reflect on their Parents Who Are Divorced." Paper presented at the Society for Research in Child Development, San Francisco.

Kelly, J., and Wallerstein, J. 1976. "Effects of Parental Divorce: Experiences of the Child in Early Latency." *American Journal of Orthopsychiatry* 16:172–79.

Kennel, J. H., et al. 1974. "Maternal Behavior One Year after Early and Extended Post-partum Contact." *Developmental Medicine and Child Neurology* 16:172–79.

Kessen, W., et al. 1970. "Human Infancy: A Bibliography and Guide" in *Carmichael's Manual of Child Psychology*, edited by P. Mussen. 3rd ed. New York: John Wiley.

Kingsley, P. R., and Hagen, J. W. 1969. "Induced versus Spontaneous Rehearsal in Short-term Memory in Nursery School Children." *Developmental Psychology* 1:40–46.

Klaus, M. H., and Kennel, J. H. 1970. "Mothers Separated from their Newborn Infants." *Pediatric Clinics of North America* 17:1015–37.

Kluckhohn, C., and Kelly, W. 1945. "The Concept of Culture" in *The Science of Man in the World Crisis*, edited by R. Linton. New York: Columbia U. Press.

Knittle, J. L. 1972. "Obesity in Childhood: A Problem in Adipose Tissue Cellular Development." *Journal of Pediatrics* 81:1048.

Kohlberg, L. 1963. "The Development of Children's Orientations toward a Moral Order: I. Sequence in the Development of Moral Thought." *Vita Humana* 6:11–33.

———. 1966. "A Cognitive-Developmental Analysis of Children's Sex-Role Concepts and Attitudes" in *The Development of Sex Differences*, edited by E. E. Maccoby. Stanford: Stanford U. Press.

Kohn, M. L. 1963. "Social Class and Parent Child Relationships: An Interpretation." *American Sociological Review* 68:471–80.

———. 1977. *Class and Conformity: A Study in Values*. Chicago: U. of Chicago Press.

Konopka, G. March 1976. "The Needs, Rights and Responsibilities of Youth." *Child Welfare.*

Kotelchuck, M. 1976. "The Infant's Relationship to the Father: Experimental Evidence" in *The Role of the Father in Child Development*, edited by M. E. Lamb. New York: Wiley.

Kurtines, W., and Grief, E. B. 1974. "The Development of Moral Thought: Review and Evaluation of Kohlberg's Approach." *Psychological Bulletin* 81:453–70.

Labov, W. 1969. "Contraction, Deletion and Inherent Variability of the English Copula." *Language* 45:715–62.

———. 1972a. *Language in the Inner City: Studies in the Black English Vernacular*. Philadelphia: U. of Pennsylvania Press.

———. 1972b. "Academic Ignorance and Black Intelligence." *Atlantic Monthly* 229:59–67.

Labov, W., and Cohen, P. 1967. "Systematic Relations of Standard and Nonstandard Rules in the Grammars of Negro Speakers." *Project Literacy Report #8*, Ithaca: Cornell University Press.

LaMaze, F. 1958. *Painless Childbirth*. London: Burke.

Lange, G. W., and Hultsch, D. F. 1970. "The Development of Free Classification and Free Recall in Children." *Developmental Psychology* 3:408.

Langenbach, M., and Neskora, T. W. 1977. *Day Care: Curriculum Considerations*. Columbus, Ohio: Merrill.

Laslett, P. 1972. *Household and Family in Past Time*. New York: Cambridge U. Press.

LeBoyer, F. 1975. *Birth Without Violence*. New York: Knopf.

Lenneberg, E. H. 1967. *Biological Foundations of Language*. New York: Wiley.

Lenneberg, E. H., and Lenneberg, E. eds. 1975. *Foundations of Language Development: A Multidisciplinary Approach*. vol. 1. New York: Academic Press.

Lesser, G. S. 1965. "Mental Abilities of Children from Different Social Clan and Cultural Groups." *Monographs of the Society for Research in Child Development* 30(4):1–115.

Levine, M. I., and Seligman, J. H. 1973. *The Parents' Encyclopedia of Infancy, Childhood and Adolescence*. New York: Crowell.

Lewis, M., and Rosenblum, L. eds. 1975. *The Origins of Fear*. New York: Wiley.

Liberty, C., and Ornstein, P. A. 1973. "Age Differences in Organization and Recall: The Effects of Training in Categorization." *Journal of Experimental Child Psychology* 15:169–86.

Lipsett, L. P., et al. 1966. "Enhancement of Neonatal Sucking through Reinforcement." *Journal of Experimental Child Psychology* 4:163–68.

References

Locke, J. 1964. *Some Thoughts Concerning Education.* Woodbury, N.Y.: Barron's Educational Series.

Lucas, B. 1977. "Nutrition and the Adolescent" in *Nutrition in Infancy and Childhood*, edited by P. L. Pipes. St. Louis: Mosby, pp. 132–44.

Lynn, D. 1974. *The Father: His Role in Child Development.* Monterey: Brooks/Cole.

Maccoby, Eleanor, and Jacklin, Carol. 1974. *The Psychology of Sex Differences.* Stanford: Stanford U. Press.

Macfarlane, A. 1977. *The Psychology of Childbirth.* Cambridge: Harvard U. Press.

Maller, O., and Dessor, J. A. 1974. "Effect of Taste on Ingestion by Human Newborns" in *Fourth Symposium on Oral Sensation and Perception: Development in the Fetus and Infant*, edited by J. Bosma. Washington, D.C.: Government Printing Office.

Martel, J. G., ed. 1974. *Smashed Potatoes.* Boston: Houghton Mifflin.

Marx, J. 1973. "Drugs during Infancy: Do They Affect the Newborn Child?" *Science* 180:174–75.

McCall, R. B. 1977. "Childhood's IQ's as Predictors of Adult Educational and Occupational Status." *Science* 197:482–83.

McCall, R. B.; Appelbaum, M. I.; and Hogarty, P. S. 1973. "Developmental Changes in Mental Performance." *Monographs of the Society for Research in Child Development* 38(150).

McDermott, J. F. 1970. "Divorce and its Psychiatric Sequelae in Children." *Archives of General Psychiatry* 23(5):421–27.

McFee, J. K., and Degee, R. M. 1977. *Art, Culture and Environment.* Belmont, Calif.: Wadsworth.

McKinney, J. P. 1964. "Hand Schema in Children." *Psychonomic Science* 15:99–100.

McLearn, G. E. 1968. "Behavioral Genetics: An Overview." *Merrill Palmer Quarterly* 14:9–24.

McLennan, C. E., and Sandberg, E. C. 1974. *Synopsis of Obstetrics.* 9th ed. St. Louis: Mosby.

McNall, S. G., ed. 1968. *The Sociological Perspective.* Boston: Little, Brown.

Mead, Margaret, and Wolfenstein, Martha, eds. 1955. *Childhood in Contemporary Cultures.* Chicago: U. of Chicago Press.

Mead, M., and Newton, N. 1967. "Cultural Patterning of Perinatal Behavior" in *Childbearing: Its Social and Psychological Aspects*, edited by S. A. Richardson and A. F. Guttmacher. Baltimore: Williams and Wilkins, pp. 142–244.

Meares, R., et al. 1976. "Possible Relationship between Anxiety in Pregnancy and Puerperal Depression." *Journal of Psychosomatic Research* 20(6):605–10.

Melear, J. D. 1973. "Children's Conceptions of Death." *Journal of Genetic Psychology* 123(2):359–60.

Michener, J. 1976. *Sports in America*. New York: Random House.

Miller, L. B., and Dyer, J. L. 1975. "Four Preschool Programs: Their Dimensions and Effects." *Monograph of the Society for Research on Child Development* 40(162).

Mischel, W. 1970. "Sex Typing and Socialization" in *Carmichael's Manual of Child Psychology*, edited by P. Mussen. New York: Wiley.

Moely, B. E.; Olson, F. A.; Halwes, T. G.; and Flavell, J. H. 1969. "Production Deficiency in Young Children's Clustered Recall." *Developmental Psychology* 1:26–34.

Moerk, E. L. 1975. "Verbal Interaction between Children and Their Mothers during Preschool Years." *Developmental Psychology* 11:788–94.

Moffitt, A. 1971. "Consonant Cue Perception by 20 to 24 Week Old Infants." *Child Development* 42:717–31.

Money, J., and Erhardt, A. 1972. *Man and Woman, Boy and Girl*. Baltimore: The Johns Hopkins Press.

Monge, R. H. 1973. "Developmental Trends and Factors in Adolescents' Self Concept." *Developmental Psychology* 8:382–93.

Montague, Ashley. 1971. *Touching*. New York: Columbia U. Press.

Montessori, M. 1964. *The Montessori Method*. New York: Schocken.

Moore, S. G., and Kilmer, S. 1973. *Contemporary Preschool Education: A Program for Young Children*. New York: Wiley.

Mussen, P., and Eisenberg-Berg, N. 1977. *Roots of Caring, Sharing and Helping*. San Francisco: W. H. Freeman.

Muus, R. E. 1970. "Adolescent Development and the Secular Trend." *Adolescence* 5:267–84.

———. 1975. *Theories of Adolescence*. 3rd ed. New York: Random House.

Newton, N. 1977. "The Effect of Fear and Disturbances on Labor" in *21st Century Obstetrics Now*, edited by L. Stewart and D. Stewart. vol. 1. Seattle: NAPSAC, Inc.

Nye, F. I. 1976 *Role Structure and Analysis of the Family*. Beverly Hills, Calif.: Sage.

Owen, F. W.; Adams, P. A.; Forrest, T.; Stolz, L. M.; and Fisher, S. 1971. "Learning Disorders in Children: Sibling Studies." *Monographs of the Society for Research in Child Development*, Ser. 144, 36(4).

Palardy, J. M. 1969. "What Teachers Believe, What Children Achieve." *Elementary School Journal* 69:370–74.

Papousek, H. 1967. "Conditioning during Early Postnatal Development" in *Behavior in Infancy and Early Childhood: A Book of Readings*, edited by Y. Brackbill and G. G. Thompson. New York: Free Press.

Parsons, T., and Bales, R. F. 1955. *Family, Socialization and Interaction Process*. New York: Free Press.

Patterson, Francine. 1978. "Conversations with a Gorilla." *National Geographic* 154(4):438–65.

Peel, A. E. 1960. *The Pupils' Thinking*. London: Oldbourne.

Peskin, H. 1967. "Pubertal Onset and Ego Functioning." *Journal of Abnormal Functioning* 72:1–15.

Peterson, A. C. 1979. "Can Puberty Come any Earlier?" *Psychology Today* 12(9):45–47.

Phillips, J. L. 1975. *The Origins of Intellect: Piaget's Theory*. San Francisco: W. H. Freeman.

Phillips, R. H. 1967. "Children's Games" in *Motivations in Play, Games and Sports*, edited by R. Swolenko and J. A. Knight. Springfield, Ill.: Thomas.

Piaget, J. 1926. *The Language and Thought of the Child*. New York: Harcourt.

———. 1951. *Plays, Dreams and Imitation in Childhood*. Translated by C. Cattegno and F. M. Hodgson. New York: Norton.

———. 1965. *The Moral Judgment of the Child*. New York: Free Press.

Piaget, J., and Inhelder, B. 1969. *The Psychology of the Child*. London: Routledge and Kegan Paul.

Pines, Maya. 1973. *The Brain Changers*. New York: Harcourt, Brace Jovanovich.

Porges, S. W. 1974. "Heart Rate Indices of Newborn Attitudinal Responsivity." *Merrill Palmer Quarterly* 20:231–54.

Poznanski, E. O. 1973. "Children with Excessive Fears." *American Journal of Orthopsychiatry* 43:428–38.

Radin, N. 1971. "Maternal Warmth, Achievement Motivation and Cognitive Functioning in Lower Class Preschool Children." *Child Development* 92:1560–65.

———. 1972. "Father-Child Interaction and the Intellectual Development of Four-year-old boys." *Developmental Psychology* 6:353–61.

Rattner, H. 1977. "History of the Dehumanization of American Obstetrical Practice" in *21st Century Obstetrics Now*, edited by D. Stewart and L. Stewart. vol. 1. Seattle: NAPSAC, Inc.

Reichle, J. E.; Longhurst, T. M.; and Stepanich, L. 1976. "Verbal Interaction in Mother-Child Dyads." *Developmental Psychology* 12:273–77.

Rice, F. P. 1978. *The Adolescent: Development, Relationships and Culture*. 2nd ed. Boston: Allyn and Bacon.

Riegel, K. 1972. "Influence of the Economic and Political Ideologies on the Development of Developmental Psychology." *Psychological Bulletin* 78:129–41.

Roberts, A. R., and Roberts, B. J. 1974. "Divorce and the Child: a Pyrrhic Victory?" in *Childhood Deprivation*, edited by A. R. Roberts. Springfield: Thomas.

Robertson, J. M., and Sutton-Smith, B. "Child Training and Game Involvement." *Ethnology* 1:166–85.

Robinson, I. E., et al. 1972. "The Premarital Sexual Revolution among College Females." *Family Coordinator* 21:189–94.

Root, A. W. 1973a. "Endocrinology of Puberty: 1. Normal Sexual Maturation." *Journal of Pediatrics* 83:1.

———. 1973b. "Endocrinology of Puberty: 2. Aberrations of Sexual Maturation." *Journal of Pediatrics* 83:187.

Rosenfeld, A. Sept. 7, 1974. "If Oedipus' Parents Had Only Known." *Saturday Review*, pp. 49–50.

Rosenthal, R., and Jacobson, L. 1968. *Pygmalion in the Classroom*. New York: Harcourt, Brace, Jovanovich.

Ross, D. M., and Ross, S. A. 1976. *Hyperactivity: Research Theory and Action*. New York: Wiley.

Rotter, J. B. 1954. *Social Learning and Clinical Psychology*. Englewood Cliffs, N.J.: Prentice-Hall.

Rousseau, J. 1911. *Emile*, trans. by B. Foxley. New York: E. P. Dutton & Co.

Rubin, R., et al. 1973. "Psychological and Educational Sequelae of Prematurity." *Pediatrics* 52:352–63.

Rugh, R., and Shettles, L. B. 1971. *From Conception to Birth*. New York: Harper & Row.

Rutter, M. 1971. "Parent-Child Separation: Psychological Effects on the Children." *Journal of Child Psychology and Psychiatry and Allied Disciplines* 12:233–60.

———. 1974a. "The Development of Infantile Autism." *Psychological Medicine* 4:147–63.

———. 1974b. *The Qualities of Mothering: Maternal Deprivation Reassessed*. New York: Aronson.

Sage, Wayne. July 1975. "Violence in the Children's Room," *Human Behavior*.

Sameroff, A. J. 1975. "Early Influences on Development: Fact or Fancy?" *Merrill Palmer Quarterly* 21:267–94.

Sameroff, A. J., and Chandler, M. J. 1975. "Reproductive Risk and the Continuum of Caretaking Causality." in *Review of Developmental Research*, edited by F. D. Horowitz. Chicago: U. of Chicago Press, pp. 187–244.

Scarr, S., and Salapatek, P. 1970. "Patterns of Fear Development during Infancy." *Merrill Palmer Quarterly* 16:53–90.

Schaefer, E. S. 1959. "A Circumplex Model for Maternal Behavior." *Journal of Abnormal and Social Psychology*. vol. 59. 226–335.

References

Schell, R. E., and Hall, E. 1979. *Developmental Psychology Today.* 3rd ed. New York: Random House.

Science News, "On Further Examination: The SAT Score Decline." Sept. 3, 1977, 148–49.

Sears, R. R.; Maccoby, E.; and Levin, H. 1957. *Patterns of Child Rearing.* New York: Row, Peterson.

Segal, J., and Yahraes, H. 1978. *A Child's Journey.* New York: McGraw-Hill.

Selzer, N. 1974. "Disadvantaged Children and Cognitive Development." *Merrill Palmer Quarterly* 19:4.

Senn, M. J. E. 1975. "Insights on the Child Development Movement in the United States." *Monographs of the Society for Research in Child Development* 166.

Shepard, T. H. 1976. *A Catalog of Teratogenic Agents.* 2nd ed. Baltimore: Johns Hopkins Press.

Shepard, T. H., and Smith, D. W. 1977. "Prenatal Life" in *Introduction to Clinical Pediatrics,* edited by D. W. Smith. 2nd ed. Philadelphia: W. B. Saunders.

Shirley, M. M. 1931. *The First Two Years, Vol. II: Intellectual Development.* Minneapolis: U. of Minnesota Press.

Shu, C., 1973. "Husband-Father in Delivery Room?" *Hospitals* 41:90–94.

Simner, M. L., 1971. "Newborn's Response to the Cry of Another Infant." *Developmental Psychology* 7:349–78.

Siqueland, E. R. 1968. "Reinforcement Patterns and Extinction in Human Newborns." *Journal of Experimental Child Psychology* 6:431–42.

Skeels, H. M., and Dye, H. 1939. "A Study of the Effect of Differential Stimulation on Mentally Retarded Children." *Proceedings of the American Association on Mental Deficiency* 44:114–36.

Skinner, B. F. 1974. *About Behaviorism.* New York: Knopf.

———. 1979. "My Experience with the Baby Tender." *Psychology Today* 12(10):28+.

Skolnik, Arlene. 1978. *Intimate Environment.* Boston: Little, Brown.

Slaby, R. G., and Frey, K. S. 1975. "Development of Gender Constancy and Selective Attention to Same-Sex Models." *Child Development* 46:849–56.

Smirnov, A. A., Zinchenko, P. I. 1969. "Problems in the Psychology of Memory" in *A Handbook of Contemporary Soviet Psychology,* edited by M. Cole and I. Maltzman. New York: Basic Books.

Smith, D. W. 1977. *Introduction to Clinical Pediatrics.* 2nd ed. Philadelphia: W. B. Saunders.

Smith, N. J. 1977. "Nutrition in Infancy and Childhood, Including Obesity." in *Introduction to Clinical Pediatrics,* edited by D. W. Smith. 2nd ed. Philadelphia: W. B. Saunders.

Sorenson, R. C. 1973. *Adolescent Sexuality in Contemporary America.* New York: World.

Spears, W. C., and Hohle, R. H. 1967. "Sensory and Perceptual Processes in Infants" in *Infancy and Early Childhood,* edited by Y. Brackbill. New York: Free Press.

Sperling, G. A. 1963. "A Model for Visual Memory Tasks." *Human Factors* 5:19–31.

Spock, B. 1968. *Baby and Child Care.* New York: Meredith, pp. 242–48.

Stanfield, J. P. 1977. "The Mother-Child Dyad: Nutritional Aspects." *Journal of Food and Nutrition* 4(4).

Stern, G. 1973. *Principles of Human Genetics.* 3rd ed. San Francisco: W. H. Freeman.

Sternglanz, S. H., and Serbin, L. A. 1974. "Sex Role Stereotyping in Children's Television Programs." *Developmental Psychology* 10:710–15.

Stone, L. J., and Church, J. 1979. *Childhood and Adolescence.* 4th ed. New York: Macmillan.

Sumner, W. G. 1960. *Folkways.* New York: Dover Publications.

Sutton-Smith, B. 1971. "A Syntax for Play and Games" in *Child's Play,* edited by B. Herron and B. Sutton-Smith. New York: Wiley, pp. 298–310.

Sutton-Smith, B., and Rosenberg, B. G. 1961. "Sixty Years of Historical Change in the Games of American Children." *Journal of American Folklore* 74:17–46.

Swanson, H. D. 1974. *Human Reproduction.* New York: Oxford U. Press.

Tanner, J. M. 1968. "Earlier Maturation in Man." *Scientific American* 218: 21–27.

———. 1970. "Physical Growth" in *Carmichael's Manual of Child Psychology,* edited by P. Mussen. vol. 1. New York: Wiley.

———. 1973. "Growing Up." *Scientific American* 229(3):34.

Taub, H. B., et al. 1977. "Indices of Neonatal Prematurity as Discriminators of Development in Middle Childhood." *Child Development* 48: 797–805.

Tavris, C., and Offir, C. 1977. *The Longest War: Sex Differences in Perspective.* New York: Harcourt, Brace, and Jovanovich.

Terman, L. 1921. "In Symposium: Intelligence and its Measurement." *Journal of Educational Psychology* 12:127–33.

Thomas, A., et al. 1963. *Behavioral Individuality in Early Childhood.* New York: New York U. Press.

Thomas, A., and Chess, S. 1977. *Temperament and Development.* New York: Brunner/Mazel.

Thomas, A.; Chess, S.; and Birch, H. 1968. *Temperament and Behavior Disorders in Children.* New York: New York U. Press.

Thompson, F. K. 1975. "Gender Labels and Early Sex Role Development." *Child Development* 46:339–47.

Thornburg, H. D. 1973. "Behavior and Values: Consistency or Inconsis-

References

tency?" *Adolescence* 8:513.

Todd, V. E., and Heffernan, H. 1977. *The Years Before School: Guiding Preschool Children.* New York: Macmillan.

Tooley, K. 1976. "Antisocial Behavior and Social Alienation Post Divorce: The Man of the House and His Mother." *American Journal of Orthopsychiatry* 46:33–42.

Tulkin, S. R., and Kagan, J. 1972. "Mother-Child Interaction in the First Year of Life." *Child Development* 43:31–41.

VanGennep, A. 1960. *The Rites of Passage.* Chicago: U. of Chicago Press.

Vener, A. M., and Stuart, C. S. 1974. "Adolescent Sexual Behavior in Middle America Revisited: Generational and British-American Comparisons." *Journal of Marriage and the Family* 36:728–35.

Wagner, I. F. 1939. "Curves of Sleep Depth in Newborn Infants." *Journal of Genetic Psychology* 55:121–35.

Wallerstein, J., and Kelly, J. 1974. "The Effects of Parental Divorce: The Adolescent Experience" in *The Child in his Family: Children at Psychiatric Risk: III,* edited by E. J. Anthony and C. Koupernik. New York: Wiley.

———.1975. "The Effects of Parental Divorce: Experiences of the Preschool Child." *Journal of the American Academy of Child Psychiatry* 14(4):600–16.

———. 1976. "The Effects of Parental Divorce: Experiences of the Child in Later Latency." *American Journal of Orthopsychiatry* 46(2):256–69.

Waugh, N. C., and Norman, D. A. 1965. "Primary Memory." *Psychological Review* 72:89–104.

Wechsler, D. 1944. *The Measurement of Adult Intelligence.* 3rd ed. Baltimore: Williams and Wilkins.

Weitz, S. 1977. *Sex Roles: Biological, Psychological and Social Foundation.* New York: Oxford U. Press.

Wente, A. S., and Crockenberg, S. 1976. "Transition to Fatherhood: Lamaze Preparation, Adjustment Difficulty and the Husband-Wife Relationship." *Family Coordinator* 25(4):351–57.

Werner, E. E. 1979. *Cross Cultural Child Development.* Monterey: Brooks-Cole, p. 1.

Westman, J. C. 1970. *Individual Differences in Children.* New York: Wiley.

White, B. L. 1975a. "Critical Influences in the Origins of Competence." *Merrill Palmer Quarterly* 21.

———. 1975b. *The First Three Years of Life.* Englewood Cliffs, N.J.: Prentice-Hall.

White, B., and Held, R. 1966. "Plasticity of Sensory-Motor Development" in *The Causes of Behavior,* edited by J. Rosenblith and W. Allinsmith. Boston: Allyn and Bacon.

White, B. L., and Watts, J. C. 1973. *Experience and Environment: Major Influences on the Development of the Young Child.* Englewood Cliffs, N.J.: Prentice-Hall.

Williams, P. 1974. *Behavior Problems in School: A Source Book of Readings.* London: U. of London Press.

Wishy, B. 1968. *The Child and the Republic.* Philadelphia: U. of Pennsylvania Press.

Wolff, P. H. 1963. "Observations on the Early Development of Smiling" in *Determinants of Infant Behavior, vol. II,* edited by B. M. Foss. London: Methuen.

Wright, H. F. 1960. *Recording and Analyzing Child Behavior.* New York: Harper & Row.

———. 1972. "A Controlled Follow-up Study of Small Prematures Born from 1952 to 1956." *American Journal of Diseases of Children* 124:506–21.

Yakovlev, P. I., and Lecours, A. R. 1967. "The Myelogenetic Cycles of Regional Maturation of the Brain" in *Regional Development of the Brain in Early Life,* edited by A. Minkowski. Oxford: Blackwell.

Yankelovich, D. 1974. *The New Morality.* Hightstown, N.J.: McGraw-Hill.

Young, L. 1964. *Wednesday's Children: A Study of Child Neglect and Abuse.* New York: McGraw-Hill.

Zac, M.; Sameroff, A.; and Farnum, J. 1975. "Childbirth Education, Maternal Attitudes and Delivery." *American Journal of Obstetrics and Gynecology* 123:185.

Zajonc, R. B. 1976. "Family Configuration and Intelligence." *Science* 197(4236):227–36.

Zajonc, R. B., and Markus, G. B. 1975. "Birth Order and Intellectual Development." *Psychological Bulletin* 82:74–88.

Zelnick, M., and Kantner, J. F. 1972. "The Probability of Premarital Intercourse." *Social Science Research* I, 9:335–41.

Index

Abortion, 7
Accidents, of young children, 255–56
Ackerley, George, 16
Adolescence
    and adults, 446–47
    cognitive development in, 51, 423–28
    development of self-concept in, 430, 447–54
    developmental tasks of, 404
    early maturation in, 413
    egocentrism in, 429–30
    idealism in, 430–31
    late maturation in, 413–14
    nutrition in, 410–13
    physical development in, 404–10
    popularity in, 453–54
    pregnancy in, 419–21, 435
    psychological development in, 413–14
    religion in, 456–58
    and schools, 434–38, 452–53
    sexual behavior and attitudes in, 414–16, 419–21
    and social change, 445–46
    as transition, 402–3
    value systems in, 431–34
Aggression, 41, 299–300
    biological determinants of, 299–300
Ainsworth, M., 162
Aitken, F. C., 160
Alleles, 62–63
Allen, H., 358
Almy, Millie, 55

Ambrose, J. A., 209
Amniocentesis, 73, 84, 85, 86, 96, 115, 119
Amniography, 85–86
Anal stage, 38, 249. *See also* Freudian theory
Anastasi, A., 280
Androgens, 405–6. *See also* Hormones
Anger, and independence, 211–12
Anorexia nervosa, 412–13
Anoxia, 99
Anthony, E. J., 473
Anxiety, 211, 224
Apgar score, 101–2, 264
Applebaum, M. I., 356
Aries, Phillipe, 8, 145, 255
Art, children's, 245–47
Atkinson, R. C., 354
Attachment. *See also* Bonding
    father-infant, 214–215, 222–24
    mother-infant, 200–201, 220–22, 229
Attention, 186
Attention-disruption technique, 175–76
Autism, 252
Autonomy, 211–12
    vs. shame and doubt, 212, 225
Aversive contingency, 42
Azrin, N. H., 251

Baby-tender, 44–46
Balance, 240–41

Baldwin, A. L., 189
Bales, R. F., 326
Bandura, A., 40, 41, 42, 43, 245
Bardin, D. R., 385
Barnet, A. B., 177
Baumrind, D., 330, 331
Bayley, N., 157, 280
Behavioral generalization, 41
Behaviorism, 44–46
Bell, S. M., 162
Belmont, L., 328
Benjamin, L., 127
Bereiter-Engleman preschool, 314
Berges, M., 98
Berman, G., 472
Birch, H., 217–19
Birth, complications of, 95–100, 112–16
Birthing. *See* Childbirth
Birth order, 328–29, 341
Birthrate, 25, 28, 463
Bloom, L., 285, 286
Bogdanoff, Ruth F., 390
Bond, E. A., 356
Bonding, 215, 221–22. *See also* Attachment
Bornstein, M. H., 177
Boué, A., 70
Boué, H., 70
Bower, T. G. R., 5, 150, 154, 165, 210, 217
Bowlby, John, 220
Brackbill, Yvonne, 72
Brain, development of, 150–52
Braine, M., 285
Bremner, R. H., 8, 9, 10, 11, 16, 17
Bromwich, Rose, 195
Bronfenbrenner, U., 315
Brown, Ann L., 354, 356
Brown, Bruce, 341
Brown, Roger, 244, 284, 286
Bruner, J., 482
Bryan T. H., 385
Busing, 364–65
Butterfield, E. C., 188

Camara, K. A., 477
Capitalistic orientation, 22
Caplan, G., 469
Carcinogens, 73
Centration, 271

Cesarean delivery, 93, 98–99, 107–9, 119
Chandler, M. J., 132
Chess, S., 217–19
Child abuse, 256–59
Childbirth. *See also* Delivery; Labor; Natural Childbirth; Prepared childbirth
  in birth centers, 138
  in birthing rooms, 139–41
  fear of, 125–27, 128–29
  at home, 137–38
  techniques of, 124–30, 136–41
Child development
  practical aspects of, 33
  research in, 32–33, 183–85
  study of, 20–23
  theories of, 31–51
Childhood
  in colonial America, 9–10
  in early cultures, 7–8
  evolution of, 19–20
  history of, 7–20
  in Industrial Revolution, 11
  in mid-1800s, 15–17
  psychogenic theory of, 18
Child labor, 11–15
Children
  negative attitudes toward, 25–28
  rights of, 12, 17–18
Chomsky, N., 283–84
Chromosomes, 61–62, 63–64
Church, J., 177
Circular behaviors, 191, 192
Classification skills, 275–77, 352
Cobb, Lyman, 16
Cognitive development
  in adolescence, 423–28
  concrete stage of, 50, 350–53, 426–27
  and culture, 277–78, 359
  formal operations stage of, 51, 426–28
  and language, 288–89
  in middle childhood, 350–56
  Piaget's theory of, 46–51, 55–57, 188–89, 267–79, 288, 350–53, 426–28
  preoperational stage of, 267–77
  sensorimotor period of, 49, 188–91, 201–2
  variations in, 277–78

Index

in young children, 267–81
Collins, M. C., 257
Competency, of children, 7, 229–30, 442–43
Conception, 60–61
Concrete operations stage, 50, 350–53, 426–27
    classification in, 352
    conservation in, 351
    decentration in, 352
    egocentrism in, 352–53
    game-playing in, 391, 397
    reversibility in, 353
    seriation in, 352
    transformations in, 351
Conditioning
    classical, 187
    operant, 187
Conger, J. J., 448, 456
Conservation, development of concept of, 274–75, 351
Contractions, 90–91
Coping mechanisms, 37, 39, 472, 492–93
Cox, M., 475–76
Cox, R., 475–76
Cratty, B. J., 241
Crisis. *See* Stress
Crisp, A. H., 412
Crockenburg, S., 128
Crook, K. C., 182
Cross-sex identification, 300–301
Cruickshank, W., 360
Crying, by infants, 197–98, 200
Cubberly, E. P., 361
Culture
    of childhood, 6
    definition of, 6
    influence of, on cognitive development, 277–78, 359
    influence of, on moral behavior, 336
    and personality deviance, 449
    transmission of, 6
Custody, 478–79

Day care, 28, 171, 228–33, 311, 312, 334, 464
    characteristics of competent personnel in, 232–33
Death, 479–82, 485–86, 489–94

children's understanding of, 480, 490–92
role of teachers in coping with, 481–82, 489–94
Decentration, 351, 352, 391, 392
Deductive reasoning, 272
Deferred imitation, 268
Degee, R. M., 247
Delivery, 94–95. *See also* Childbirth; Labor
DeMause, Lloyd, 18–20
Dennis, W., 165
Depth perception, 177–78
Dessor, J. A., 182
de Tocqueville, Alexis, 15–16
Developmental norms, 34–35, 170, 497
    in behavior, 34–35
    in physical development, 157–58
Dewey, John, 21
Dick-Read, Grantley, 125
Dilatation, 91
Discipline. *See* Punishment
Diseases
    influence of, on growth rates, 154
    prevention of, 255, 263
    of young children, 254–55, 262–65
Disorganization, 471, 475–76
Divorce, 171, 326, 331, 472–79, 485, 486
    custody arrangements after, 478–79
    developmental impact of, 473–74
    effects of, on parent-child relationship, 476, 477–78, 485
    effects of, on play patterns, 477
    interactional impact of, 474–75
Dolch, Elaine T., 390
Dominance, 62–63
Donnison, J., 123
Dove, Adrian, 282, 358
Down's syndrome, 66
Doyle, Mary C., 136
Duncan, Erika, 367
Dusek, J. B., 429, 450, 451
Dye, H., 359
Dyer, J. L., 315

Early childhood education, 195, 310–15
   evaluation of, 315, 359
   future of, 464, 466
   philosophies of, 314
   types of, 312–14
Early intervention. *See* Early childhood education
Eckert, H. M., 241
Education. *See* Early childhood education; Schools
Effacement, 91
Egocentrism, 270–71, 391, 392–93
   in adolescence, 429–30
   in infancy, 191
   in middle childhood, 352–53
Eiman, P. D., 180
Eisenberg-Berg, Nancy, 318
Elkind, David, 169, 208, 277, 383, 427, 429–30
Embryo, 69
Endocrine system, 152, 405–7. *See also* Hormones
Environment, effects of. *See also* Poverty; Social class
   on children's mental health, 440–43, 482–84
   on fetus, 73–75
   on learning, 5
   on personality, 217
Environmentalism, 10
Episiotomy, 95
Equilibration, 48, 57, 277
Erhardt, A., 66
Erikson, Erik, 38–39, 447
   stage theory of, 38–39, 225, 447–48
Escalona, S., 281
Espenschade, A. A., 241
Estrogens, 405–6. *See also* Hormones
Ethnocentrism, 120
Experimental research. *See* Research

Fallopian tubes, 60, 78
Family. *See also* Parents
   as change agent, 325–26, 335–36
   disorganization of, 471, 475–76
   forms of, 323–24, 462
   influence of, on peer group success, 385–86
   interaction in, 327–31
   loss of resources of, 335–36
   roles in, 326–27
   as socializing agent, 324–25, 341, 432–33
   as transmitter of values, 431–32
Family size, 329–30
   effect of, on intelligence scores, 329
   effect of, on roles, 330
Fantz, R. L., 177, 210
Farson, Richard, 18
Father
   authority of, 9, 10, 15–16
   role of, in childbirth, 108, 121, 122–23, 137
   role of, in infant development, 214–15, 222–24
Fear
   of childbirth, 125–27, 128–29
   developmental aspects of, 210–11
   idiosyncratic nature of, 211
   by infants, 210
   of strangers, 224
Feeding
   breast vs. bottle, 160–62
   in infancy, 158–63, 215–16
   schedule vs. demand, 162–63
Feingold, Ben, 253
Fetal alcohol syndrome, 74–75
Fetology, 82–86
Fetoscopy, 85
Fetus, 69–70
   assessment of, 72–73
   development of, 69–70, 89
   effects of medicine on, 72
   environmental impact on, 72, 73–75
   monitoring of, 73, 82–86, 108, 119
   movement of, 73
   nutrition of, 70–71
Fielding, W. L., 127
Fisher, S., 37–38
Fitzgerald, H. E., 187
Flavell, J. H., 189, 351, 353, 354, 427

Index

Flerx, V. C., 305
Fomon, S. J., 411
Food faddism, 412
Forceps, 98
Formal operations period, 51, 426–228
    egocentrism in, 429–30
Foxx, R. M., 251
Frank, Lawrence, 21
Freud, Sigmund, 35–38, 249
Freudian theory, 35–38, 249
    stages in, 35–37
    critiques of, 37–38
Friendships, in middle childhood, 387
Furman, Erna, 489
Furth, H. G., 288

Gaelin, D., 48
Galactosemia, 85
Games, children's, 375–81, 390–97. *See also* Play
    age differences in, 376
    cultural influences on, 376
    influence of parents on, 381
    and levels of cognitive development, 390–97
    organization of, 379
    purposes of, 380–81
    sex differences in, 377
    universality of, 376, 390–91
Gametes, 59–60
Gans, H. J., 328
Gardner, H., 105, 210
Genes, 62
    effect of, on personality, 217
Genetic counseling, 67–68
Genetic disorders, 66–67
Genetics, 59–68
Genotype, 62
Gentle birth, 129–30
Gesell, Arnold, 5, 34–35, 241–42, 243
Gewirtz, J. L., 209
Gibson, E. J., 178, 248
Gifted children, 291–94
    characteristics of, 292
    education of, 292–94
Ginsburg, H., 269, 275, 277, 351

Glaser, P., 32
Goldman, R. D., 356
Gonadotropic hormone, 405
Goodman, M. E., 6, 7
Grammar. *See also* Language
    Chomsky's theory of, 283–84
    errors in, 287
    pivotal, 285
    semantic, 286
    use, of, in early childhood, 283–84, 285–86, 287
Greenberg, R. P., 37–38
Greenburg, J., 248
Grief, E. B., 338
Grossmann, John, 112
Growth. *See also* Physical development
    in adolescence, 405, 407–8
    in infants, 146
    in young children, 237–39
Growth hormone, 152, 153, 405, 407
Growth rates, effects on, 153–54
Guilford, J. P., 424–25

Hagen, J. W., 354
Hall, E., 188
Hall, G. Stanley, 21, 401
Hall, J. G., 66, 67–68, 72
Hamachek, D. E., 414
Handel, G., 5
Handicapped children, 363, 367–73, 464
Harlow, H., 161
Hartig, L. K., 356
Hartup, W. W., 385
Haslam, R. H., 106
Havighurst, R. J., 404
Head Start, 28, 195, 312, 314, 359
Hearing
    in infants, 178–80
    loss of, 249
    in neonates, 106
Heffernan, H., 312
Held, R., 165
Hellman, L. M., 96, 97, 98
Helms, D. B., 4
Hency, T., 358
Heredity. *See* Genetics
Hertig, A. T., 70

Hess, R. D., 477
Hetherington, E. M., 214, 475–76, 477
Hill, Reuben, 471
Hoffman, L. W., 333, 334
Hogarty, P. S., 356
Hohle, R. H., 177
Holistic development, 3–4
Honzik, M. P., 356
Hormones
    in adolescence, 405–7
    in aggression, 299
    gonadotropic, 405
    growth, 152, 153, 405, 407
Horowitz, F. D., 179–80
Huenemann, R. L., 412
Hultsch, D. F., 355
Humor, children's, 381–82
Hurlock, E., 414
Hurried children, 383–84
Huttel, F., 128
Hyaline membrane disease, 100, 263
Hyde, J. S., 306
Hyperactivity, 252–54
Hytten, F. E., 160

Idealism, in adolescence, 430–31
Identification, and sex-role development, 300–3
Identity. *See* Self-concept
Idiosyncratic development, 4–5, 497
    of adolescents, 425–26
Imaginary audience, 429–30
Imitation, 5, 41
    in learning sex role, 300–3
Independence, 190
Inductive reasoning, 272
Industrial Revolution, 11, 446
Infant mortality, 75–77
Infanticide, 7–8
Infants. *See also* Neonates
    crying by, 197–98, 200
    emotions in, 207–13
    endocrine system of, 152
    feeding of, 158–63, 215–16
    hearing of, 178–80
    learning by, 186–88
    measuring perception of, 175–76
    motor development of, 163–66
    muscular development of, 148–49
    neurological development of, 149–52, 197–98
    physical development of, 145–55
    reflexive behaviors of, 187
    skeletal growth of, 146–48
    sleep patterns of, 155, 216
    smell by, 185–86
    stimulation of, 195–204
    taste discrimination by, 181–82
    touching by, 180–81
    touching of, 180
    vision of, 176–78
    warmth and safety of, 155–56
Inhelder, B., 356, 430–31
Intellect, Guilford model of, 424–25
Intellectual development. *See* Cognitive development
Intelligence
    enhancement of, 359
    testing of, 279–83
Intelligence tests, 279–83
    cultural bias in, 282–83, 357–59
    predictiveness of, 356–57
In vitro conception, 78–79
Irreversibility, 271–72

Jacklin, Carol, 154, 244, 298, 363, 449
Jacobson, Arminta Lee, 228
Jacobson, L., 357
Jensen, Arthur, 282
Johnson, A. L., 457
Juvenile delinquency, 455–56

Kagan, J., 145, 244, 287, 353, 354
Kantner, J. F., 414
Kapit, H. E., 473
Kaplan, F., 309
Kaplan, T., 309
Katz, I., 358

Index

Katz, L. G., 315
Keeney, T. J., 355
Kellogg, Rhoda, 245, 247
Kelley, J., 474, 475
Kelly, John C., 419
Kelly, W., 6
Keniston, Kenneth, 27
Kennel, John, 221
Kessen, W., 163, 216
Kiester, Edwin, Jr., 82
Kilmer, S., 311
Kingsley, P. R., 354
Klaus, Marshall, 221, 222
Klinefelter's syndrome, 66
Kluckhohn, C., 6
Knittle, J. L., 411
Kohlberg, L., 336–38
Konopka, G., 423
Kotelchuck, M., 214, 215
Kurtines, W., 338

Labor, 90–95. *See also* Childbirth; Delivery
    medication during, 72, 100, 120, 137
    stages of, 91–92, 95
Labov, W., 288
LaMaze, Ferdinand, 125
LaMaze technique, 122, 125–28
Lange, G. W., 355
Langenbach, M., 245, 251
Language
    and cognition, 288–89
    development of, 50, 283–87
    use of grammar in, 284, 285, 286, 287
    effect of social class on, 287–88
Lazar, P., 70
Learning
    generalization of, 41
    by infants, 186–88, 191
Learning disabilities, 134, 186, 359–60, 385
    types of, 360
Learning theory, 40–43
LeBoyer, Frederic, 129–30, 208
Lenneberg, E. H., 145, 284, 286
Levin, H., 251
Liberty, C., 354

Lipsett, L. P., 182, 186, 188
Locomotion, 165, 241
Longhurst, T. M., 288
Lucas, B., 412

McCall, R. B., 356, 357
Maccoby, Eleanor, 154, 244, 251, 298, 363, 449
McDermott, J. F., 473
Macfarlane, A., 186
McFee, J. K., 247
McKinney, J. P., 249
McLennan, C. E., 96, 100
McNall, S. G., 8
Maeroff, Gene, 291
Maller, O., 182
Markus, G. B., 329
Marolla, F. A., 328
Maternal bleeding, 95–96
Mead, M., 121, 123, 251
Meares, R., 128
Medication. *See* Labor, medication during
Meiosis, 60
Melear, J. D., 480
Memory, 353–56
    categories of, 354
    tests of, 354–56
Menarche, 154, 405
Mental illness, effects of, on children, 441–43
Mercantilistic-socialistic orientation, 22
Methylmalonic acidemia, 84–85
Michener, James, 379
Middle childhood
    cognitive development of, 350–56
    friendships in, 387
    peer group in, 384–87
    social development of, 384–88
Midwives, 119, 123–24, 137
Miller, L. B., 315
Mitosis, 60
Moan, C. E., 385
Modeling. *See* Imitation
Moely, B. E., 354, 355
Moffitt, A., 180
Money, J., 66

Monge, R. H., 449
Montague, Ashley, 161, 162
Montessori preschool, 314
Moore, S. G., 311
Moral development, 336–38
    cognitive adaptation theory of, 336–38
    holistic theory of, 338
    social learning theory of, 336
    stages of, 337
Mother. *See* Attachment; Family; Parents
Motor development
    of infants, 163–66
    influenced by personality, 251–52
    sex differences, 243–45
    of young children, 240–45
Muscular growth
    in infants, 148–49
    in young children, 238
Mussen, Paul, 318
Muus, R. E., 409, 426
Myelinization, 149–50, 163

Natural childbirth, 124–28. *See also* Prepared childbirth
Neighborhood, effect of, on children, 387–88, 482–83
Neonatal assessment, 101–2
Neonates, 100–106. *See also* Infants
    behaviors of, 105–6
    circulation of, 103–4
    digestion of, 104
    immunity of, 105
    respiration of, 102–3
    temperature regulation of, 104–5
Nerve development, in infants, 149–52, 163
Neskora, T. W., 245, 251
Newton, N., 121, 123
Normal, D. A., 354
Norms
    in behavior development, 34–35
    in physical development, 157–58

Nursery schools. *See* Early childhood education
Nutrition
    in adolescents, 410–13
    deprivation of, 132–33, 153
    of mothers during pregnancy, 132–33

Obesity, 410–12
Object permanence, 189
Observation, 51–52
O'Dell, S., 247
Offir, C., 300, 301
Operant conditioning. *See* Conditioning
Opper, S., 269, 275, 277, 351
Oral stage, 37. *See also* Freudian theory
Orfield, Gary, 364
Ornstein, P. A., 354
Ossification. *See* Skeletal growth
Ovulation, 59–60

Papousek, H., 188
Parenting, styles of, 330–31, 341
    effect of social class on, 341–45
Parents. *See also* Family; Father
    changing attitudes of, 462
    influence of, on development of self-concept, 450–51
    as models for adolescents, 431–32
    relationships of, with adolescents, 428–29, 446–47, 450–51
    role of, in children's games, 381
    as support in crisis, 485–86
Parsons, T., 326
Patterson, Francine, 357
Pavlov, Ivan, 125, 187
Peel, A. E., 352
Peer group, 384–87
    and adolescence, 453–54, 456
    and cognitive skills, 385

Index

and family environment, 385–86
functions of, 386
influence of, 387
and personality of child, 385
Perception, 247–49. *See also* Hearing; Touch; Vision
accuracy of, 278
affected by cognition, 248
in infants, 175–86
in young children, 247–49
Personal fable, 430
Personality, 217, 453. *See also* Self-concept; Temperament
determinants of, 217
environmental effects on, 217
Peskin, H., 414
Peterson, A. C., 409–10
Phenotype, 62
Phillips, J. L., 50
Phillips, R. H., 376, 380
Physical development. *See also* Growth
in adolescence, 404–10
in infancy, 145–55
psychological aspects of, 413–14, 452–53
in young children, 237–39
Piaget, Jean, 46–48, 188–89, 268–72, 274–75, 277, 279, 336–37, 356, 430–31
cognitive theory of, 46–51, 55–57, 188–89, 267–79, 288, 350–53, 426–28
Pines, Maya, 152
Pituitary gland, 152, 405
Placenta, 70–72
Play. *See also* Games
effects of divorce on, 477
functions, of, 202–3, 309
group, 310
by infants, 309–10
parallel, 310
solitary, 310
use of symbols in, 268–69
Popularity, 453–54
Porges, S. W., 176, 187
Poverty, effects of, on children, 440–43, 482–84. *See also* Social class

Pregnancy
in adolescence, 419–21, 435
length of, 89
nutrition during, 132–33
weight gain during, 132–33
Prehension, 180–81, 241–42
Prematurity, 96–98
causes of, 96–97
effects of, 97–98, 163
Prenatal care, 89–90. *See also* Pregnancy
Prenatal development. *See* Fetus
Preoperational thought stage, 50, 267–79
centration in, 271
conceptualization in, 273, 277
egocentrism in, 270–71
game-playing in, 393–96
irreversibility in, 271–72
perceptions in, 278
preconceptual and intuitive phases of, 270
static thought in, 272
transductive reasoning in, 272
use of symbols in, 268–70
Prepared childbirth, 125–29. *See also* LaMaze technique; Natural childbirth
Preschools. *See* Early childhood education
Presentation, breech, 93, 107
Pritchard, J. A., 96, 97, 98
Psychoanalytic theory. *See* Freudian theory
Psychobiological development, 5–6, 169–72
Puberty, 401, 404–6. *See also* Adolescence
Punishment
as behavior modifier, 42
in colonial era, 9, 10
in mid-1800s, 15–17
and social class, 341–45

Quantity, children's concepts of, 274–75, 351. *See also* Conservation
Quickening. *See* Fetus, movement of

Radiation, effects of, on fetus, 74
Radin, N., 359
Rattner, H., 120
Reflexive behaviors, 49, 105–6, 150–51, 187
Reichle, J. E., 288
Reinforcement, 40, 41–42
Religion
    in adolescence, 456–58
    as influence on colonial society, 10
Research
    in child development, 32, 33, 51–52, 183–85, 239
    with children, 183–85
    purposes of, 183
    risk-benefit ratio of, 185
    types of, 183
Reversibility, 353, 391, 392
Rh factor, 75, 83–84
Rice, F. P., 431, 446
Roberts, A. R., 473
Roberts, B. J., 473
Robertson, J. M., 376, 380
Robinson, I. E., 414
Root, A. W., 405
Rosenberg, B. G., 377
Rosenfeld, A., 64
Rosenthal, R., 357
Ross, D. M., 252
Ross, S. A., 252
Rotter, J. B., 40
Rubella, 74, 254, 263
Rubin, R., 97
Rutter, M., 252

Sage, W., 256
Salapatek, P., 178
Sameroff, A. J., 132
Sandberg, E. C., 96, 100
Scarr, S., 178
Schaefer, E. S., 330
Schell, R. E., 188
Schools
    and adolescents, 434–38, 452–53
    busing to, 364–65
    criticism of, 360–62, 461
    dropping out of, 434–35
    future of, 461–66, 498
    handicapped children in, 363, 465
    importance of, in middle childhood, 349–50
    poor children in, 483
    role of, vs. family's, 361, 462
Sears, R. R., 251
Secular trend, 154, 409–10
Segal, Julius, 220, 282, 336, 440
Self-concept
    development of, in adolescence, 430, 447–54
    development of, by infants, 189
    effect of obesity on, 411
    factors affecting, 450–53
    sex differences in, 449–50
Selzer, N., 484
Senn, M. J. E., 21, 22
Sensorimotor period, 49, 188–91, 201–2
    developmental stages of, 191–92
Sentences. *See also* Language
    length of, 285, 287
    structure of, 284, 285–86
Serbin, L. A., 308
Seriation, 275, 352
"Sesame Street," 186, 319
Sex determination, 63–64
Sex differences. *See also* Sex-role development
    in adolescent sexual behavior, 415
    biological determinants of, 298–300
    in caloric needs, 410
    in developing self-concept, 449–50
    at different ages, 305
    in games, 377
    in identity formation, 172
    as influence on growth rates, 153
    learned aspects of, 300–303
    in motor development, 243–245
Sex education, 420–21
Sex linkage, 64–66
Sex role, development of, 244–45, 297

Index

behavioral limits determined by, 303–6
biological determinants of, 298–99
influenced by television, 307–8
learned aspects of, 300–303
role of teachers in, 363
timing of, 303–6
Sexual behavior and attitudes in adolescence, 414–16, 419–21
age level of, 414
sex differences in, 415
Shane, Harold G., 461
Shepard, T. H., 68, 69, 71, 73, 74, 105
Shettles, Landrum, 64
Shiffrin, R. M., 354
Shirley, M. M., 157
Simner, M. L., 180
Single-parent families, 27, 171, 324, 326, 331–32, 451
Siperstein, G. N., 188
Siqueland, E. R., 188
Skeels, H. M., 359
Skeletal growth
in infants, 146–48
in young children, 238–39
Skinner, B. F., 44–46
Sleeping
of infants, 155, 197–98, 216
of neonates, 105, 155
Smell, by infants, 185–86
Smiling, 208–10
reflective, 208
selective social, 209
unselective social, 208–9
Smith, D. W., 68, 71, 74, 105
Smith, N. J., 159, 215
Smoking, effect of, on fetus, 75
Social class, effect of. *See also* Poverty
on children's temperament, 131–32
on development, 195–96
on development of self-concept, 451–52
on discipline, 341–45
on family disorganization, 131
on growth, 153–54
on language, 287–88
on mental health, 130–31
on prematurity, 97

Socialization, 5, 6
of adolescents, 432–33
by family, 324–25, 341, 432–33
in middle childhood, 384–88
of young children, 297–310
Social learning, 39–43, 336
Social-psychological development, 5
Sorenson, R. C., 414
Space, children's concepts of, 273–74, 352
Spears, W. C., 177
Sperling, G. A., 354
Spina bifida, 112–16
Stanford-Binet test, 279, 280, 358
Static thought, 272
Stepanich, L., 288
Stern, G., 59, 60, 62, 65, 66, 72
Sternglanz, S. H., 308
Stoler, Peter, 262
Stone, L. J., 177
Straus, M., 32
Stress, 469–72
categories of, 470
coping with, 472
definition of, 469
effects of, on children, 470–72
parental support in, 485–86
Stuart, C. S., 414
Sumner, W. G., 7
Sutton-Smith, B., 376, 377, 380
Swanson, H. D., 66, 72
Symbols, use of, in preoperational stage, 50, 268–70
Syphilis, 74

Tanner, J. M., 150, 153–54, 239, 250, 405, 407, 409
Taste
in infants, 181–82
in neonates, 106
Taub, H. B., 97
Tavris, C., 300, 301
Teachers. *See* Schools
Television, 28, 132, 186, 211, 361–62
influence of, on children's games, 378–79
role of, in developing prosocial behavior, 318–20

Television *(cont.)*
　role of, in sex-role
　　development, 302, 303, 307–8
Temperament
　definition of, 199, 218
　difficult, 199, 218–19
　easy, 218–19
　genetic determinants of, 217, 219
　interactional nature of, 219–20
　and motor development, 251–52
　slow-to-warm-up, 199, 218–19
Teratogens, 73–74
Test tube babies, 78–79, 464
Thomas, A., 217–19
Thompson, F. K., 305
Thompson, H., 34–35
Thornburg, H. D., 432–33
Time, children's concepts of, 273
Todd, V. E., 312
Toilet training, 36, 249–51
Tooley, K., 473
Touching. *See also* Prehension
　by infants, 180–81
　of infants, 180
Transductive reasoning, 272
Transformation, 351, 391, 392
Trust vs. mistrust, 38–39, 225
Tulkin, S. R., 287
Turner, J. S., 4
Turner's syndrome, 66

Ultrasonography, 86, 96, 115
Umbilical cord, 70, 93
Underestimation, 6, 188

Value system, in adolescence, 431–34
Van Gennep, A., 402
Vener, A. M., 414
Vision
　of infants, 176–78
　loss of, 248–49
Visual acuity, 177
Visual cliff experiment, 177–78

Vocabulary. *See* Language
von Hartz, John, 25

Wagner, I. F., 216
Walk, R. D., 178
Wallerstein, J., 474
Walters, R. H., 40, 41, 245
Watson, John, 21–22
Waugh, N. C., 354
Wechsler Intelligence Scale for Children (WISC), 279, 280
Winer, I. B., 208
Weitz, S., 299–300
Wente, A. S., 128
Werner, E. E., 154
White, B. L., 105, 165, 180, 191
Williams, P., 134
Wolff, P. H., 209
Woodworth, Robert, 21
Working mothers, 27, 71, 332–34, 498
Wright, H. F., 52, 97

Yahres, Herbert, 220, 282, 336, 440
Yankelovich, D., 414
Young children
　abuse of, 256–59
　accidents of, 255–56
　art of, 245–47
　cognitive development of, 267–81
　diseases of, 255
　motor skills of, 240–45
　perception of, 247–49
　physical development of, 237–39
　socialization of, 297–310
　toilet training of, 249–51
Young, L., 257

Zac, M., 128
Zajonc, R. B., 329
Zelnick, M., 414
Zygote, 68, 78